The Business Environment

Pearson

At Pearson, we have a simple mission: to help people make more of their lives through learning.

We combine innovative learning technology with trusted content and educational expertise to provide engaging and effective learning experiences that serve people wherever and whenever they are learning.

From classroom to boardroom, our curriculum materials, digital learning tools and testing programmes help to educate millions of people worldwide – more than any other private enterprise.

Every day our work helps learning flourish, and wherever learning flourishes, so do people.

To learn more, please visit us at **www.pearson.com/uk**

The Business Environment:
A Global Perspective

Eighth edition

Ian Worthington, Chris Britton and Ed Thompson

Leicester Business School, De Montfort University, Leicester

 **Pearson**

Harlow, England • London • New York • Boston • San Francisco • Toronto • Sydney • Dubai • Singapore • Hong Kong
Tokyo • Seoul • Taipei • New Delhi • Cape Town • São Paulo • Mexico City • Madrid • Amsterdam • Munich • Paris • Milan

PEARSON EDUCATION LIMITED
KAO Two
KAO Park
Harlow CM17 9NA
United Kingdom
Tel: +44 (0)1279 623623
Web: www.pearson.com/uk

───────────────

First published in Great Britain in 1994 (print)
Second edition published 1997 (print)
Third edition published 2000 (print)
Fourth edition published 2003 (print)
Fifth edition published 2006 (print and electronic)
Sixth edition published 2009 (print and electronic)
Seventh edition published 2015 (print and electronic)
Eighth edition published 2018 (print and electronic)

ISBN: 978-1-292-17435-8 (print)
            978-1-292-17437-2 (PDF)
            978-1-292-17436-5 (ePub)

British Library Cataloguing-in-Publication Data
A catalogue record for the print edition is available from the British Library

Library of Congress Cataloging-in-Publication Data
A catalog record for the print edition is available from the Library of Congress

10 9 8 7 6 5 4 3 2 1
22 21 20 19 18

Print edition typeset in 9.5/13 pt Stone Serif ITCPro by 75
Printed in Slovakia by Neografia

NOTE THAT ANY PAGE CROSS REFERENCES REFER TO THE PRINT EDITION

For Lindsey, Tom and Georgina, for Rachael, Philip, Nick and Megan, and for Ramanjeet, Darshan, Sandra and David – with our love

Brief contents

Contents

Part One INTRODUCTION

Part Two CONTEXTS

5 The macroeconomic environment 99

Ian Worthington

6 The demographic, social and cultural context of business 135

Ian Worthington

Part Three FIRMS

10 Legal structures   229

Ian Worthington

11 Size structure of firms   259

Chris Britton

Part Four MARKETS

Part Five CONCLUSION

Contributors

Authors

Ian Worthington, BA (Hons), PhD (Lancaster), is Emeritus Professor of Corporate Sustainability at De Montfort University, Leicester, UK. He has published in, and reviewed for, a variety of academic journals in both the UK and United States and is also author of a recent book entitled *Greening Business: Research, Theory and Practice*.

Chris Britton, BA (Hons), MSc, was formerly a Principal at De Montfort University where her teaching and research interests included industrial economics, labour markets and executive recruitment. With Ian Worthington and Andy Rees she is also co-author of a book on business economics.

Ed Thompson, BA (Hons), MSc, PhD, PGCertHE, FHEA, is Associate Professor at the Department of Strategic Management and Marketing at De Montfort University. His research is focused on organisational behaviour, crisis management and governance.

Contributors

Diane Belfitt, BA (Hons), Diploma in Welfare Law, has taught law at a number of institutions, including Leicester Polytechnic, Leicester University and Charles Keene College in Leicester. She has examined for a number of examination boards.

Martin Morgan-Taylor, LLB, LLM, FRAS I, LTM, is a Principal Lecturer in the School of Law at De Montfort University, Leicester, where he teaches business and commercial law on a range of undergraduate and postgraduate courses. His research interests include online trading, consumer protection, and light pollution and nuisance. He is a legal adviser on the latter to the Campaign for Dark Skies and the British Astronomical Association.

David Orton, BA (Hons), is a Lecturer at Coventry University. His teaching and research interests lie in the fields of strategic management and crisis and business continuity management.

Preface to the eighth edition

Why study the business environment?

The business environment is our environment, it is the world we live in and all aspects of the business environment should be viewed in terms of people. Business ethics is about fairness in how a business operates; a business environmental policy is about how we pollute or preserve our own world; employment and unemployment are about people's ability to house and feed themselves. This is a book about all of us and the world we live in, and the world businesses live in as well, because businesses are just organisations of people and material things.

In reading about the business environment you are reading about your world. You are reading about why the prices of the things you buy might go up or down, or why at any given time it might be harder or easier for you to get a job. By understanding the things in this book that make up your world you will better understand how this world works, what changes mean and the implications they might have on your organisations (whether they are organisations that we work for, or the organisations that we have at home). In my own life, understanding the business environment has helped me make decisions about when and where and how to buy a home, and what and what not to invest in. Understanding the world allows us to make informed decisions.

Many of my students aspire to work for firms in the financial sector trading internationally. Depending on the outcomes of Brexit, some firms are better to work for than others, some firms are more exposed to risk and some are more or less likely to pull out of the UK. It will be sensible for somebody going for an interview to carry out some research on the potential employer. You have to understand the business environment in order to make sense of what you are reading.

The first aim of this book is to set out the way things are in the world today. It will do this by breaking down everything outside of a business (and cover a little bit inside as well) into chapters organised in a logical way. In effect, what we mean by external and internal environments in a global context in which business operates today. The second part will cover aspects of the business environment as you might find them in a PESTLE analysis (Political, Economic, Social, Technological, Legal, Ethical/Ecological). The third part will cover firms and industries, as well as how government regulates business. The fourth part will consider the importance of markets as a concept, nationally and internationally. Finally, we will consider how the business environment feeds into strategy making for organisations.

The second aim of the book is to offer you examples and opportunities to apply what you have learned. This edition has doubled the number of case studies from the previous edition to present applied knowledge. The business environment is not always simple, and some of these case studies illustrate how counter-intuitive some interactions between parts of it can be.

My authorship

This book is now in its eighth edition, the previous seven having been written by Ian Worthington and Chris Britton. Ian approached me to author this edition in a more stable world (2015), a time of majority government and before Brexit, a time when writing a book on the business environment seemed like a less troublesome undertaking!

I have quite a broad background in terms of my experience with the business environment, having worked for large and small private and public sector organisations. My first degree in business studies equipped me with most of my foundational business environment knowledge. Subsequently I gained a master's degree in project management, and a doctorate in organisational behaviour. In most of my organisational work I have applied an actor–network theory perspective to how the world works. Actor–network theory considers all things related, nothing existing in isolation. This has proven a logical approach writing this book too; the environment is a world of many connections, some obvious and others less so. I hope through reading this book that you will come to understand the world in a similar way.

New to this edition

With this edition I have attempted to increase the number of case studies, sometimes updating, sometimes replacing and sometimes supplementing what was in the seventh edition. I have tried to incorporate a greater range of industries in case studies (from the service and hospitality sectors in particular), as well as a wider international perspective. International content has been increased where possible too, but the level of detail in terms of British legislation and companies was worth maintaining as well.

I feel I have to preface this edition with two caveats. The first is that, as I finish the manuscript, we are about six months into Brexit negotiations between the UK and EU. This means that there are lots of uncertainties on what is going to happen in terms of law, trade and immigration in particular. This is not so much a problem as one might think, as this book sets out concepts which are applied to contexts; the context will change over the next two to five years but the concepts will persist. The second is on data. I have updated data wherever possible – but in some circumstances there are simply no more updates. Sometimes data are reported in a different way, so continuity could not be maintained if the datasets were any more up to date, and in a few cases data had been collected by agencies which have been disbanded as a result of austerity. As a result, some of the datasets are not as up to date as I would have preferred, but they are sufficient to illustrate the points made in the book.

Thanks on behalf of Ian, Chris and myself to Vicky Tubb and Donna Goddard from Pearson for their work on this edition. And for the first time in a preface for this title I get to thank Ian and Chris for their overwhelming scholarly contribution on which I have developed. I feel as if I have moved into their house: redecorated, modernised and in places extended, but they built it. I hope that I have done it justice. This time, errors are *my* own.

Take it from someone with a British PhD in Organizational Behavior: organization is spelled with a Z in *English* English (it's in the *OED*).

Ed Thompson

Acknowledgements

We are grateful to the following for permission to reproduce copyright material:

Figures

Figure 7.7 adapted from *The UK R&D Landscape*, Centre for Business Research and UK~IRC (Huges, A. and Mina, A., March 2012) p. 13 (www.cbr.cam.ac.uk/pdf/RDlandscapeReport.pdf); Figure 12.4 adapted from STAN Database for Structural Analysis from OECD.StatExtracts http://stats.oecd.org/ (20 May 2014); Figure 14.13 adapted from Halifax Price Index, www.lloydsbankinggroup.com; Figure 15.3 adapted from Still, Sparkling and Fortified Wine – UK – September 2013, http://oxygen.mintel.com/display/638252/; Figure 16.9 adapted from Bank of England, www.bankofengland.co.uk/; Figure 18.2 adapted from *The right game: use game theory to shape strategy*, Harvard Business Review, 73(4), pp. 57–71 (Brandenburger, A. and Nalebuff, B. 1995).

Tables

Table 3.1 adapted from The World Bank, *World Development Indicators*, 2013 and *The Little Data Book*, 2013, © World Bank. https://openknowledge.worldbank.org/handle/10986/13191 and https://openknowledge.worldbank.org/handle/10986/13205. Creative Commons Attribution license (CC BY 3.0 IGO). This is an adaptation of an original work by The World Bank. Responsibility for the views and opinions expressed in the adaptation rests solely with the author or authors of the adaptation and are not endorsed by The World Bank; Table 3.3 adapted from OECD (2013), "Foreign affiliates", in OECD Science, Technology and Industry Scoreboard 2013: Innovation for Growth, OECD Publishing. http://dx.doi.org/10.1787/sti_scoreboard-2013-64-en; Table 4.4 adapted from MEPs by Member State and political group: www.europarl.europa.eu, © European Union; Table 7.2 Adpated from Labour market statistics, 2011 edition, p 24. © European Union, http://ec.europa.eu/eurostat/documents/3930297/5967006/KS-32-11-798-EN.PDF/7c804143-b30e-4c3a-be32-8041e3c3ab8f?version=1.0; Table 7.3 From Labour market statistics, 2011 edition, p35. © European Union, http://ec.europa.eu/eurostat/documents/3930297/5967006/KS-32-11-798-EN.PDF/7c804143-b30e-4c3a-be32-8041e3c3ab8f?version=1.0; Table 7.11 adapted from Electricity production by fuel (ENER 027), http://www.eea.europa.eu/data-and-maps/indicators/electricity-production-by-fuel-1/electricity-production-by-fuel-assessment-3, European Environment Agency (EAA), © European Union, 1995–2014; Table 11.1 after FTSE All-Share Ranking (unofficial guide) June 2014, www.stockchallenge.co.uk/ftse.php; Table 11.4 adapted from Figures D.10.1. and D.10.2. from OECD (2010), *Measuring Globalisation: OECD Economic Globalisation*

Indicators 2010, OECD Publishing. http://dx.doi.org/10.1787/9789264084360-en; Table 15.8 adapted from Adbrands.net, 2012. All rights reserved © Mind Advertising Ltd 1998–2018; Table 16.12 adapted from Financial Indicators – Stocks: Private sector debt, http://stats.oecd.org/index.aspx?queryid=34814. OECD. StatExtracts http://stats.oecd.org/.

Text

Case study on page 360 adapted from Halifax Price Index, www.lloydsbankinggroup.com.

Part One

INTRODUCTION

1 Business organisations: the external environment

Ian Worthington

Business organisations differ in many ways, but they also have a common feature: the transformation of inputs into outputs; it is through this process that the value is created. This transformation process takes place against a background of external influences which affect the firm and its activities. This external environment is complex, volatile and interactive, but it cannot be ignored in any meaningful analysis of business activity.

Learning outcomes

Having read this chapter you should be able to:

- indicate the basic features of business activity
- portray the business organisation as a system interacting with its environment
- demonstrate the range and complexity of the external influences on business activity
- identify the central themes inherent in the study of the business environment

Key terms

Environmental change
External environment
General (or contextual) environment

Immediate (or operational) environment
Inputs
Open system

Outputs
PEST analysis
PESTLE analysis
Transformation system

Introduction

Business activity is a fundamental and universal feature of human existence and yet the concept of 'business' is difficult to define with any degree of precision. Dictionary definitions tend to describe it as being concerned with buying and selling, or with trade and commerce, or the concern of profit-making organisations, and clearly all of these would come within the accepted view of business. Such a restricted view, however, would exclude large parts of the work of government and its agencies and the activities of non-profit-making organisations – a perspective it would be hard to sustain in a climate in which business methods, skills, attitudes and objectives have been vigorously adopted by these organisations. It is this broader view of business and its activities that is adopted below and that forms the focus of an investigation into the business environment.

The business organisation and its environment

A model of business activity

Most business activity takes place within an organisational context and even a cursory investigation of the business world reveals the wide variety of organisations involved, ranging from the small local supplier of a single good or service to the multi-billion-dollar international or multinational corporation producing and trading on a global scale. Given this rich organisational diversity, most observers of the business scene tend to differentiate between organisations in terms of their size, type of product and/or market, methods of finance, scale of operations, legal status, and so on. Nissan, for example, would be characterised as a major multinational car producer and distributor trading on world markets, while a local builder is likely to be seen as a small business operating at a local level with a limited market and relatively restricted turnover.

> **web link**
>
> Further information on Nissan is available at *www.nissan-global.com*
> The Nissan UK website address is *www.nissan.co.uk*

While such distinctions are both legitimate and informative, they can conceal the fact that all business organisations are ultimately involved in the same basic activity, namely the transformation of **inputs** (resources) into **outputs** (goods or services). This process is illustrated in Figure 1.1.

In essence, all organisations acquire resources – including labour, premises, technology, finance, materials – and transform these resources into the goods or services required by their customers. While the type, amount and combination of resources will vary according to the needs of each organisation and may also vary over time, the simple process described above is common to all types of business organisation and provides a useful starting point for investigating business activity and the environment in which it takes place.

A more detailed analysis of business resources and those internal aspects of organisations which help to transform inputs into output can be found in Chapters 2 and 7 below. The need, here, is simply to appreciate the idea of the firm as a **transformation system** and to recognise that in producing and selling output, most organisations hope

Figure 1.1   The business organisation as a transformation system

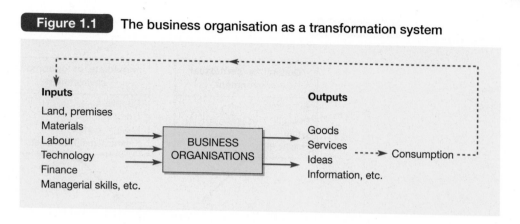

to earn sufficient revenue to allow them to maintain and replenish their resources, thus permitting them to produce further output which in turn produces further inputs. In short, inputs help to create output and output creates inputs. Moreover, the output of one organisation may represent an input for another, as in the case of the firm producing machinery, basic materials, information or ideas. This interrelationship between business organisations is just one example of the complex and integrated nature of business activity and it helps to highlight the fact that the fortunes of any single business organisation are invariably linked with those of another or others – a point clearly illustrated in many of the examples cited in the text.

The firm in its environment

The simple model of business activity described above is based on the systems approach to management (see Chapter 2). One of the benefits of this approach is that it stresses that organisations are entities made up of interrelated parts which are intertwined with the outside world – the **external environment** in systems language. This environment comprises a wide range of influences – economic, demographic, social, political, legal, technological, etc. – which affects business activity in a variety of ways and which can impinge not only on the transformation process itself, but also on the process of resource acquisition and on the creation and consumption of output. This idea of the firm in its environment is illustrated in Figure 1.2.

Figure 1.2   The firm in its environment

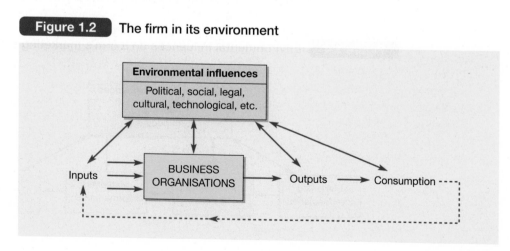

Figure 1.3   Two levels of environment

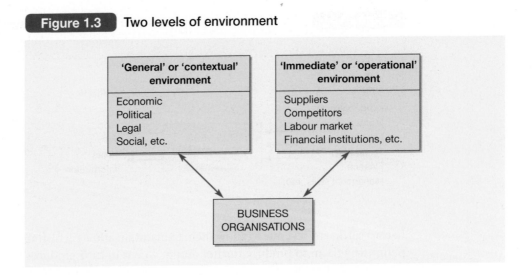

In examining the business environment, a useful distinction can be made between those external factors that tend to have a more immediate effect on the day-to-day operations of a firm and those that tend to have a more general influence. Figure 1.3 makes this distinction.

The **immediate** (or **operational**) **environment** for most firms includes suppliers, competitors, labour markets, financial institutions and customers, and may also include trade associations, trade unions and possibly a parent company. In contrast, the **general** (or **contextual**) **environment** comprises those macroenvironmental factors such as economic, political, socio-cultural, technological, legal and ethical influences on business which affect a wide variety of businesses and which can emanate not only from local and national sources, but also from international and supranational developments. Macroenvironmental factors might be thought of as factors so large that the business cannot change them.

This type of analysis can also be extended to the different functional areas of an organisation's activities such as marketing or personnel or production or finance, as illustrated in Figure 1.4. Such an analysis can be seen to be useful in at least two ways. First, it emphasises the influence of external factors on specific activities within the firm and in doing so underlines the importance of the interface between the internal and external

Figure 1.4   Environmental influences on a firm's marketing system

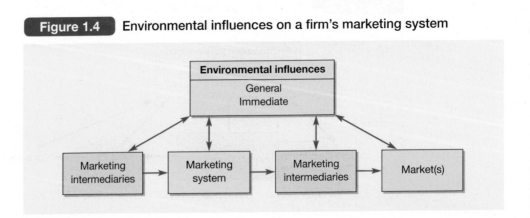

environments. Second, by drawing attention to this interface, it highlights
while business organisations are often able to exercise some degree of con
internal activities and processes, it is often very difficult, if not impossible, to control the
external environment in which they operate.

The general or contextual environment

While the external factors referred to above form the subject matter of the rest of the
book, it is useful at this point to gain an overview of the business environment by highlighting some of the key environmental influences on business activity. In keeping with
the distinction made between general and more immediate influences, these are
discussed separately below. In this section we examine what are frequently referred to as
the 'PESTLE' factors (i.e. Political, Economic, Socio-cultural, Technological, Legal and
Ethical influences). A **PESTLE analysis** (or **PEST analysis**) can be used to analyse a firm's
current and future environment as part of the strategic management process (see
Chapter 18). PESTLE examines factors external to the firm; these might represent
opportunities or threats and later can be used in a SWOT analysis (whereas strengths and
weaknesses are internal factors).

The political environment

A number of aspects of the political environment clearly impinge on business activity.
These range from general questions concerning the nature of the political system and its
institutions and processes (Chapter 4) to the more specific questions relating to government involvement in the working of the economy (Chapter 5) and its attempts to influence market structure and behaviour (Chapters 11, 15, 17). Government activities, both
directly and indirectly, influence business activity, and government can be seen as the
biggest business enterprise at national or local level (Chapter 13). Given the trend towards
the globalisation of markets (Chapters 3 and 16) and the existence of international trading organisations and blocs, international politico-economic influences on business
activity represent one key feature of the business environment (Chapters 4, 7 and 16).
Another is the influence of public, as well as political, opinion in areas such as environmental policy and corporate responsibility (Chapter 9).

The economic environment

The distinction made between the political and economic environment – and, for that
matter, the legal environment – is somewhat arbitrary. Government, as indicated above,
plays a major role in the economy at both national and local level (Chapters 5 and 13)
and its activities help to influence both the demand and supply side (e.g. see Chapter 14).
Nevertheless there are a number of other economic aspects related to business activity
which are worthy of consideration. These include various structural aspects of both firms
and markets (Chapters 10, 11, 12 and 15) and a comparison of economic theory and
practice (e.g. Chapters 14, 15 and 16).

mini case | The impact of regional economic conditions

For a company that trades in different markets across the world, macroeconomic conditions (see Chapter 5) in a particular part of its overall market can play a key role in determining its corporate sales and profitability. French carmaker PSA Peugeot Citroën, for instance, experienced a significant decline in sales in 2012 as demand fell in Southern Europe on the back of the recession in the eurozone. In response to the problem, the company announced significant job cuts aimed at reducing costs and looked to the French government for a series of multi-billion-euro loans to keep it afloat until trading conditions improved.

As the global economy slowed, steel industries have been heavily affected. After a period of rapid expansion (driven mostly by the growth of Chinese infrastructure and social development), China's economy has now started to slow as demand from more developed countries who consume Chinese-made products has fallen. This has led to a dramatic drop in the price of steel as it is no longer needed for building more factories and infrastructure. To support its own steel industry China has been selling steel at less than the cost European steelmakers can produce it. This is an example of the slowdown in European and American economies causing Chinese businesses to act more aggressively, which has eventually led to the collapse of large parts of the British steel industry such as the (Indian-owned) Tata steel works at Port Talbot near Cardiff in 2016.

Since market conditions can vary substantially in different locations, some businesses can experience significant variations in performance in different parts of their operations. US car giant Ford, for example, announced significant losses in Europe in 2012 alongside 'spectacular' results in its North American division. Like Chrysler and other competitors including GM, Ford was able to offset its European losses with stronger sales in the United States. It also posted pre-tax profits in its South American and Asian markets.

web link Further information on the organisations mentioned in this mini case is available at *www.groupe-psa.com/fr*; *www.tatasteel.com*; *www.ford.com*; *www.chrysler.com*; *www.gm.com*

The social, cultural and demographic environment

Both demand and supply are influenced by social, cultural and demographic factors. Cultural factors, for example, may affect the type of products being produced or sold, the markets they are sold in, the price at which they are sold and a range of other variables. People are a key organisational resource and a fundamental part of the market for goods and services. Accordingly, socio-cultural influences and developments have an important effect on business operations, as do demographic changes (Chapters 6 and 7).

The technological environment

Technology is both an input and an output of business organisations as well as being an environmental influence on them. Investment in technology and innovation is frequently seen as a key to the success of an enterprise and has been used to explain differences in the relative competitiveness of different countries (Chapter 7). It has also been responsible for significant developments in the internal organisation of businesses in the markets for economic resources.

The legal environment

Businesses operate within a framework of law, which has a significant impact on various aspects of their existence. Laws usually govern, among other things, the status of the organisation (Chapter 10), its relationship with its customers and suppliers and certain internal procedures and activities (Chapter 8). They may also influence market structures and behaviour (e.g. Chapters 15 and 17). Since laws emanate from government (including supranational governments) and from the judgments of the courts, some understanding of the relevant institutions and processes is desirable (e.g. Chapters 4 and 8).

The ethical and ecological environment

Ethical considerations have become an increasingly important influence on business behaviour, particularly among the larger, more high-profile companies. One area where this has been manifest is in the demand for firms to act in a more socially responsible way and to consider the impact they might have on people, their communities and the natural environment (Chapter 9).

The immediate or operational environment

Resources and resource markets

An organisation's need for resources makes it dependent to a large degree on the suppliers of those resources, some of which operate in markets that are structured to a considerable extent (e.g. Chapter 7). Some aspects of the operation of resource markets or indeed the activities of an individual supplier can have a fundamental impact on an organisation's success and on the way in which it structures its internal procedures and processes. By the same token, the success of suppliers is often intimately connected with the decisions and/or fortunes of their customers. While some organisations may seek to gain an advantage in price, quality or delivery by purchasing resources from overseas, such a decision can engender a degree of uncertainty, particularly where exchange rates are free rather than fixed (Chapter 16). Equally, organisations may face uncertainty and change in the domestic markets for resources as a result of factors as varied as technological change, government intervention or public opinion (e.g. conservation issues).

Customers

Customers are vital to all organisations and the ability both to identify and to meet consumer needs is seen as one of the keys to organisational survival and prosperity – point not overlooked by politicians, who are increasingly using business technique attract the support of the electorate. This idea of consumer sovereignty – where res are allocated to produce output to satisfy customer demands – is a central ten market economy (Chapter 5) and is part of a capitalist ideology whose infl become all-pervasive in recent years, the idea being that companies com most efficient way to organise society. Understanding the many factors affecting both individual and market demand, and the ways in which firms organise themselves to satisfy that demand, is a vital component of a business environment that is increasingly market led.

Competitors

Competition – both direct and indirect – is an important part of the context in which many firms operate and is a factor equally applicable to the input as well as the output side of business. The effects of competition, whether from domestic organisations or from overseas firms (see Chapter 16, for example), are significant at the macro as well as the micro level and its influence can be seen in the changing structures of many advanced industrial economies (Chapter 12). How firms respond to these competitive challenges (e.g. Chapter 11) and the attitudes of governments to anti-competitive practices (Chapter 17) is a legitimate area of concern for students of business.

Analysing the business environment

In a subject as all-encompassing as the business environment it is possible to identify numerous approaches to the organisation of the material. One obvious solution would be to examine the various factors mentioned above, devoting separate chapters to each of the environmental influences and discussing their impact on business organisations. While this solution has much to recommend it – not least of which is its simplicity – the approach adopted below is based on the grouping of environmental influences into three main areas, in the belief that this helps to focus attention on key aspects of the business world, notably contexts, firms and their markets.

mini case   Fresh but not so easy

A recurring theme in this and previous editions of the book is the need for businesses to monitor and, where necessary, respond to changes in the business environment. Equally important is the requirement for a firm to understand the needs of the customers in the markets in which it currently operates or in which it wishes to expand its operations as a means of growing the organisation. Even some of the world's largest and most sophisticated companies can sometimes get this wrong.

Take the case of Tesco PLC's foray into the US grocery retailing market with the launch of its Fresh & Easy stores in 2007–8. Initially established in a number of states on the US west coast, the experiment was aimed at providing a low-risk method of entry into a large and lucrative market, with the focus on providing fresh produce at low prices in competition with existing retailers such as Trader Joe's and Walmart. As a preliminary step, the company sent some of its senior executives to the United States to live with American families for several months in order to understand their shopping habits and product preferences. It also ran a high-profile promotional campaign to support its plans to open up 1000 stores in California and neighbouring states before launching the brand on the east coast.

Tesco's hope that it would be able to break even in two years quickly evaporated and the company was forced to pump hundreds of millions of pounds into the venture to keep it afloat. Apart from the rather unfortunate coincidence of the launch of its brand with the sub-prime crisis and subsequent recession in the United States, retail analysts have pointed to some fundamental errors in understanding the preferences of US consumers. Mistakes are said to have included an unclear image; cold and antiseptic stores; the introduction of self-pay checkouts; using cling film on fresh products; an over-emphasis on ready meals; an unwillingness to embrace the 'coupon culture' that is an important part of the US shopping experience; and problems in ensuring high-quality produce. Some consumers also apparently complained that the name Fresh & Easy reminded them of a deodorant or a sanitary product.

By the time of its withdrawal from the US market in September 2013, Tesco had reputedly lost more than £1.8 billion. On the positive side, Tesco has made ventures into other markets. Trent Hypermarket, owned jointly by Tesco and Tata, plans for 200 stores in the Indian cities of Mumbai, Pune, Hyderabad and Bengaluru.

web link Tesco's website address is: *www.tesco.com*

Following a basic introduction to the idea of the 'business environment', in Part Two consideration is given to the political, economic, social, cultural, demographic, legal, ethical and ecological contexts within which businesses function. In addition to examining the influence of political and economic systems, institutions and processes on the conduct of business, this section focuses on the macroeconomic environment and on those broad social influences that affect both consumers and organisations alike. The legal system and the influence of law in a number of critical areas of business activity are also a primary concern and one which has links with Part Three.

In Part Three, attention is focused on three central structural aspects: legal structure, size structure and industrial structure. The chapter on legal structure examines the impact of different legal definitions on a firm's operations and considers possible variations in organisational goals based on legal and other influences. The focus then shifts to how differences in size can affect the organisation (e.g. access to capital, economies of scale) and to an examination of how changes in scale and/or direction can occur, including the role of government in assisting small business development and growth. One of the consequences of changes in the component elements of the economy is the effect on the overall structure of industry and commerce – a subject which helps to highlight the impact of international competition on the economic structure of many advanced industrial economies. Since government is a key actor in the economy, the section concludes with an analysis of government involvement in business and in particular its influence on the supply as well as the demand side of the economy at both national and local levels.

In Part Four, the aim is to compare theory with practice by examining issues such as pricing, market structure and foreign trade. The analysis of price theory illustrates the degree to which the theoretical models of economists shed light on the operation of business in the 'real' world. Similarly, by analysing basic models of market structure, it is possible to gain an understanding of the effects of competition on a firm's behaviour and to appreciate the significance of both price and non-price decisions in the operation of markets.

The analysis continues with an examination of external markets and the role of government in influencing both the structure and the operation of the marketplace. The chapter on international markets looks at the theoretical basis of trade and the development of overseas markets in practice, particularly in the context of recent institutional, economic and financial developments (e.g. the Single Market, globalisation, the euro). The section concludes with an investigation of the rationale for government intervention in markets and a review of government action in three areas, namely privatisation and deregulation, competition policy and the operation of the labour market.

To emphasise the international dimension of the study of the business environment, each of the four main parts of the book concludes with a section entitled 'International business in action', which draws together some of the key themes discussed in the previous chapters. By examining specific issues and/or organisations, the aim is to highlight linkages between the material discussed in the text and to provide an appreciation of some of the ways in which business activity reaches well beyond national boundaries.

The concluding chapter in the book stresses the continuing need for organisations to monitor change in the business environment and examines a number of frameworks through which such an analysis can take place. In seeking to make sense of their environment, businesses need access to a wide range of information, much of which is available from published material, including government sources. Some of the major types of information available to students of business and to business organisations – including statistical and other forms of information – are considered in the final part of this chapter.

Central themes

A number of themes run through the text and it is useful to draw attention to these at this point.

Interaction with the environment

Viewed as an **open system**, the business organisation is in constant interaction with its environment. Changes in the environment can cause changes in inputs, in the transformation process and in outputs, and these in turn may engender further changes in the organisation's environment. The internal and external environments should be seen as interrelated and interdependent, not as separate entities.

Interaction between environmental variables

In addition to the interaction between the internal and external environments, the various external influences affecting business organisations are frequently interrelated. Changes in interest rates, for example, may affect consumer confidence and this can have an important bearing on business activity. Subsequent attempts by government to influence the level of demand could exacerbate the situation and this may lead to changes in general economic conditions, causing further problems for firms. The combined effect of these factors could be to create a turbulent environment which could result in uncertainty in the minds of managers. Failure to respond to the challenges (or opportunities) presented by such changes could signal the demise of the organisation or at best a significant decline in its potential performance.

The complexity of the environment

The environmental factors identified above are only some of the potential variables faced by all organisations. These external influences are almost infinite in number and variety and no study could hope to consider them all. For students of business and for managers alike, the requirement is to recognise the complexity of the external environment and to pay greater attention to those influences which appear to be the most pertinent and pressing for the organisation in question, rather than to attempt to consider all possible contingencies.

Environmental volatility and change

The organisation's external environment is further complicated by the tendency towards **environmental change**. This volatility may be particularly prevalent in some areas (e.g. technology) or in some markets or in some types of industry or organisation. As indicated above, a highly volatile environment causes uncertainty for the organisation (or for its sub-units) and this makes decision-making more difficult.

Environmental uniqueness

Implicit in the remarks above is the notion that each organisation has to some degree a unique environment in which it operates and which will affect it in a unique way. Thus, while it is possible to make generalisations about the impact of the external environment on the firm, it is necessary to recognise the existence of this uniqueness and where appropriate to take into account exceptions to the general rule.

Different spatial levels of analysis

External influences operate at different spatial levels – local, regional, national, supranational, international/global – exemplified by the concept of LoNGPEST/LoNGPESTLE (see Chapter 18). There are few businesses, if any, today that could justifiably claim to be unaffected by influences outside their immediate market(s).

Two-way flow of influence

As a final point, it is important to recognise that the flow of influence between the organisation and its environment operates in both directions. The external environment influences firms, but by the same token firms can influence their environment, and this is an acceptable feature of business in a democratic society which is operating through a market-based economic system. This idea of democracy and its relationship with the market economy is considered in Chapters 4 and 5.

Synopsis

In the process of transforming inputs into output, business organisations operate in a multifaceted environment which affects and is affected by their activities. This environment tends to be complex and volatile and comprises influences which are of both a general and an immediate kind and which operate at different spatial levels. Understanding this environment and its effects on business operations is vital to the study and practice of business.

Summary of key points

- Business activity is essentially concerned with transforming inputs into outputs for consumption purposes.

- All businesses operate within an external environment that shapes their operations and decisions.

- This environment comprises influences that are both operational and general.

- The operational environment of business is concerned with such factors as customers, suppliers, creditors and competitors.

- The general environment focuses on what are known as the PESTLE factors.

- In analysing a firm's external environment attention needs to be paid to the interaction between the different environmental variables, environmental complexity, volatility and change, and to the spatial influences.

- While all firms are affected by the environment in which they exist and operate, at times they help to shape that environment by their activities and behaviour.

case study   Facing the unexpected

In previous editions of the book we have stressed how the business environment can sometimes change dramatically and unexpectedly for the worse, using the 11 September 2001 attack on the World Trade Center in the United States as an example of what is known as an exogenous shock to the economic system. Mercifully, events of this kind tend to be relatively rare, but when they occur they present a considerable challenge to the businesses and industries affected.

The same is true when natural disasters occur, as the following examples illustrate.

2010 – the eruption of an Icelandic volcano sent a cloud of volcanic ash over large parts of Europe, resulting in the grounding of aircraft and weeks of disruption of air travel. Airlines in particular were badly affected and faced additional costs because of stranded passengers and cancelled flights. Beneficiaries included hoteliers who had to accommodate people unable to travel and alternative transport businesses (e.g. ferry operators).

2013 – sudden and devastating storms in the Burgundy and Bordeaux regions of France destroyed swathes of the French wine industry, resulting in a loss of jobs and income in the affected local communities, with a knock-on impact on local businesses. In China, a heatwave across the central and eastern parts of the country badly affected the farming industry and tempted the government to spend millions on artificial steps to trigger rain. In some areas power failures occurred as the demand for electricity soared as individuals and organisations turned on the air-conditioning. Much warmer conditions were also experienced in parts of Northern Europe, including the UK, resulting in increased sales of certain items (e.g. barbecues, sunscreen) and tempting many people to holiday at home. Other adverse natural events in 2013–14 included a super typhoon in the Philippines, extensive fires in parts of Australia, a major drought in California and severe storms and flooding in southern England, all of which had major effects on businesses and communities in the affected areas.

2015–16 – in 2015 terrorists armed with assault rifles and hand grenades attacked a beach resort in Tunisia. The British Foreign Office issued travel advice to avoid all but essential travel to the country, as have many other governments. The result has been a 37% fall in foreign spending in Tunisia, whose economy is 8% dependent on tourism. In 2016 attacks on Brussels and Paris had an impact on tourism across Europe, with hotel occupancy in London down as a result.

While there is little a business can do to protect itself totally against events of this kind, many larger firms, especially multinationals, tend to put in place contingency plans to manage unexpected crises, whether they are caused by human or natural events. A business continuity plan (BCP) can help an organisation to respond quickly and effectively to a negative situation and hopefully to survive the experience and learn from it. Smaller firms on the whole tend to lack the financial and human resources needed to adopt such resilience measures and some may not survive an adverse change in the external environment. For other organisations such a change may bring with it business opportunities, an unexpected though possibly welcome gain from an event that has a negative impact on other firms.

Case study questions

1 Can you think of any other examples of major unanticipated events in your own country (or areas of your own country) that have had a serious adverse effect on its firms and/or industries?

2 Can you think of any businesses that may have benefited commercially from this event or these events?

Review and discussion questions

1 In what senses could a college or university be described as a business organisation? How would you characterise its 'inputs' and 'outputs'?

2 Taking examples from a range of quality newspapers, illustrate ways in which business organisations are affected by their external environment.

3 Give examples of the ways in which business organisations can affect the external environment in which they operate.

Assignments

1 Assume you are a trainee in a firm of management consultants. As part of your induction process you have been asked to collect a file of information on an organisation of your choice. This file should contain information not only on the structure of the organisation and its products but also on the key external influences that have affected its operations in recent years.

2 For a firm or industry of your choice, undertake a PESTLE analysis indicating the likely major environmental influences to be faced by the firm/industry in the next five to ten years.

Further reading

Daniels, J. D., Radebough, L. H. and Sullivan, D. P., *International Business: Environments and Operations,* 14th edition, Prentice Hall, 2012.

Fernando, A. C., *Business Environment,* Dorling Kindersley/Pearson Education India, 2011.

Hamilton, L. and Webster, P., *The International Business Environment,* 3rd edition, Oxford University Press, 2015.

Steiner, G. A. and Steiner, J. F., *Business, Government and Society: A Managerial Perspective,* 13th edition, McGraw-Hill/Irwin, 2011.

Wetherly, P. and Otter, D. (eds) *The Business Environment: Themes and Issues,* 3rd edition, Oxford University Press, 2014.

Worthington, I., Britton, C. and Rees, A., *Economics for Business: Blending Theory and Practice,* 2nd edition, Financial Times/Prentice Hall, 2004, Chapter 1.

web link

Web links and further questions are available on the website at:
www.pearsoned.co.uk/worthington

2 Business organisations: the internal environment

Ian Worthington

The systems approach to the study of business organisations stresses the interaction between a firm's internal and external environments. Key aspects of the internal context of business include the organisation's structure and functions and the way they are configured in pursuit of specified organisational objectives. If the enterprise is to remain successful, constant attention needs to be paid to balancing the different influences on the organisation and to the requirement to adapt to new external circumstances. This responsibility lies essentially with the organisation's management, which has the task of blending people, technologies, structures and environments.

Learning outcomes

Having read this chapter you should be able to:

- outline the broad approaches to organisation and management, paying particular attention to the systems approach
- identify alternative organisational structures used by business organisations
- discuss major aspects of the functional management of firms
- illustrate the interaction between a firm's internal and external environments

Key terms

Bureaucracy	Human relations approach	Project team
Classical theories of organisation	Human resource management	Public sector
		Re-engineering
Contingency approach	Management	Scientific management
Divisional structure	Marketing	Sub-systems
Downsizing	Marketing concept	Systems approach
Formal structures	Marketing mix	Theory X and Theory Y
Functional organisation	Matrix structure	Theory Z
Functional specialisation	Organisation chart	Virtual organisation
Hierarchy of needs	Private sector	Voluntary (or third) sector
Holding company	Profit centre	

Introduction

Under the systems approach to understanding business activity presented in Chapter 1, the organisation lies at the heart of the transformation process and tends to be seen as a kind of 'black box' which contains a multitude of elements – including structures, processes, people, resources and technologies – that brings about the transformation of inputs into outputs (see below). While the study of the business environment rightly focuses on the external context of business organisations, it is important to recognise that firms also have an internal environment that both shapes and is shaped by the external context in which they operate and make decisions. This notion of the interplay between an organisation's internal and external environments is a theme that runs through many of the chapters in this book.

As students of business and management will be aware, the internal features of business organisations have received considerable attention from scholars researching these fields, and a large number of texts have been devoted to this aspect of business studies. In the discussion below, the aim is to focus on three areas of the internal organisation that relate directly to a study of the business environment: approaches to understanding organisations, organisational structures, and key functions within the enterprise. Further insight into these aspects and into management and organisational behaviour generally can be gained by consulting the many specialist books in this field, a number of which are mentioned at the end of this chapter. Issues relating to a firm's legal structure are examined in detail in Chapter 10.

A central theme running through any analysis of the internal environment is the idea of **management**, which has been subjected to a wide variety of definitions. As used in this context, management is seen both as a system of roles fulfilled by individuals who manage the organisation (e.g. entrepreneur, resource manager, coordinator, leader, motivator, organiser) and as a process that enables an organisation to achieve its objectives. The essential point is that management should be seen as a function of organisations, rather than as a controlling element, and its task is to enable the organisation to identify and achieve its objectives and to adapt to change. Managers need to integrate the various influences on the organisation – including people, technology, systems and the environment – in a manner best designed to meet the needs of the enterprise at the time in question and be prepared to institute change as and when circumstances dictate.

The concept of the organisation: an initial comment

According to Stoner and Freeman (1992: 4), an organisation can be defined as two or more people who work together in a structured way to achieve a specific goal or set of goals. Defined in this way, the term covers a vast array of structures in the:

- **private sector** – that part of the economy where ownership and control of the organisation is in the hands of private individuals or groups and where profit-seeking is a central goal;
- **public sector** – that part of the economy under the control of government and its agencies and where the state establishes and runs the different types of organisation on behalf of its citizens and for their general well-being;

- **voluntary (or third) sector** – comprising those organisations, including charities, voluntary bodies and community businesses, that are not-for-profit enterprises and non-governmental.

Leaving aside the blurring of definitions of these three generic sectors that has occurred over recent years (e.g. where third-sector organisations are commissioned to deliver public services), the concept of the 'business organisation' as used in this text covers enterprises of all types and in all sectors. In this book the concept also encapsulates those organisations where the objectives are set by one individual who both owns and controls the business and has no other employees (i.e. sole traders with zero staff).

Despite coming in a wide variety of shapes, forms and sizes, business organisations share a number of common features. Mullins (2013) identifies four such features:

- people (i.e. employees);
- objectives (i.e. what the organisation is set up to achieve);
- structure (i.e. the organisational framework through which the objectives are pursued and efforts are coordinated);
- management (i.e. the directing and controlling aspect of the enterprise).

To these we could add the idea of resources (including finance) and technologies. We also need to recognise the existence of an external environment that faces all types of enterprise. This is, after all, a fundamental feature of the systems approach to understanding business organisations and how they operate.

Understanding the nature of organisations: theories of organisation and management

To gain an insight into the principles that are felt to underlie the process of management, it is useful to undertake a brief examination of organisational theories. These theories or approaches – some of which date back to the late nineteenth century – represent the views of both practising managers and academics as to the factors that determine organisational effectiveness and the influences on individuals and groups within the work environment. Broadly speaking, these approaches can be broken down into three main categories: the classical approach, the human relations approach and the systems approach. Since the last of these encompasses the model presented in Chapter 1, particular attention is paid to this perspective.

The classical approach

Classical theories of organisation and management mostly date from the first half of the twentieth century and are associated with the work of writers such as Taylor, Fayol, Urwick and Brech. In essence, the classicists viewed organisations as **formal structures** established to achieve a particular number of objectives under the direction of management, the emphasis being on purpose, structure, hierarchy and common principles. By identifying a set of guidelines to assist managers in the design of the organisational structure, the proponents of the classical view believed that organisations would be able to achieve their objectives more effectively. Fayol, for example, identified 14 principles which included the division of work, the scalar chain, centralisation and the unity of command – features which also found expression in Weber's notion of 'bureaucracy'. Urwick's rules or principles similarly emphasised aspects of organisation structure and operations – such as specialisation, coordination, authority, responsibility and the span of control – and were presented essentially as a code of good management practice.

Within the classical approach special attention is often given to two important sub-groupings, known as **scientific management** and **bureaucracy**. The former is associated with the pioneering work of F. W. Taylor (1856–1915), who believed that scientific methods could be attached to the design of work so that productivity could be increased. For Taylor, the systematic analysis of jobs (e.g. using some form of work study technique) was seen as the key to finding the best way to perform a particular task and thereby achieving significant productivity gains from individuals, which would earn them increased financial rewards. In Taylor's view, the responsibility for the institution of a scientific approach lay with management, under whose control and direction the workers would operate to the mutual benefit of all concerned.

The second sub-group, bureaucracy, draws heavily on the work of Max Weber (1864–1920), whose studies of authority structures highlighted the importance of 'office' and 'rules' in the operation of organisations. According to Weber, bureaucracy – with its system of rules and procedures, specified spheres of competence, hierarchical organisation of offices, appointment based on merit, high level of specialisation and impersonality – possessed a degree of technical superiority over other forms of organisation, and this explained why an increasing number of enterprises were becoming bureaucratic in structure. Despite Weber's analysis appearing somewhat dated nowadays, bureaucratic organisation remains a key feature of many enterprises throughout the world and is clearly linked to increasing organisational size and complexity. Bureaucracy is often seen as something which restricts organisations from making internal changes or taking advantage of opportunities, leading to ineffectiveness. Modern defenders of bureaucracy (du Gay, 2000) argue that bureaucratic systems are fair, treating situations and individuals rationally and equally. Notwithstanding the many valid criticisms of Weber's work, it is difficult to imagine how it could be otherwise.

The human relations approach

Whereas the classical approach focuses largely on structure and on the formal organisation, the **human relations approach** to management emphasises the importance of people in the work situation and the influence of social and psychological factors in shaping organisational behaviour. Human relations theorists have primarily been concerned with issues such as individual motivation, leadership, communications and group dynamics, and have stressed the significance of the informal pattern of relationships that exists within the formal structure. The factors influencing human behaviour have accordingly been portrayed as a key to achieving greater organisational effectiveness, thus elevating the 'management of people' to a prime position in the determination of managerial strategies.

The early work in this field is associated with Elton Mayo (1880–1949) and with the famous Hawthorne Experiments, conducted in the United States at the Western Electric Company between 1924 and 1932. These experiments showed that individuals at work were members of informal (i.e. unofficial) as well as formal groups and that group

Figure 2.1   A hierarchy of needs

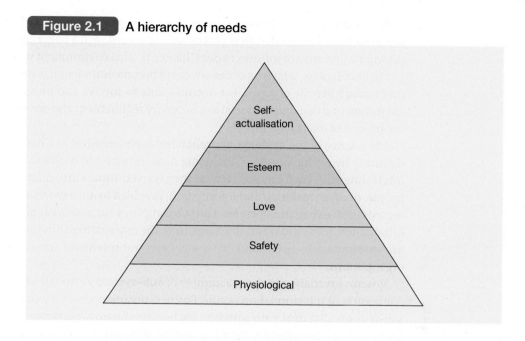

influences were fundamental to explaining individual behaviour. Later work by writers such as Maslow, McGregor, Argyris, Likert and Herzberg continued to stress the importance of the human factor in determining organisational effectiveness, but tended to adopt a more psychological orientation, as exemplified by Maslow's '**hierarchy of needs**' and McGregor's '**Theory X and Theory Y**'. Maslow's central proposition was that individuals seek to satisfy specific groups of needs, ranging from basic physiological requirements (e.g. food, sleep, sex), through safety, love and esteem, to self-actualisation (i.e. self-fulfilment), progressing systematically up the hierarchy as each lower-level need is satisfied (see Figure 2.1). To McGregor, individuals at work were seen by management as either inherently lazy (Theory X) or committed to the organisation's objectives and often actively seeking responsibility (Theory Y). These perceptions consequently provided the basis for different styles of management, which ranged from the coercive to the supportive.

McGregor's concern with management styles is reflected in later studies, including Ouichi's notion of **Theory Z**. According to Ouichi, one of the key factors in the success of Japanese manufacturing industries was their approach to the management of people. Theory Z organisations were those that offered workers long-term (often lifetime) employment, a share in decision-making, opportunities for training, development and promotion, and a number of other advantages which gave them a positive orientation towards the organisation. For Ouichi, the key to organisational effectiveness lay in the development of a Japanese-style Theory Z environment, adapted to western requirements.

The systems approach

More recent approaches to organisation and management have helped to integrate previous work on structures, people and technology, by portraying organisations as socio-technical systems interacting with their environment. Under this approach – which became popular in the 1960s – organisations were seen as complex systems of people, tasks and technologies that were part of and interacted with a larger environment, comprising a wide range of influences (see Chapter 1). This environment was frequently subject to fluctuations, which on occasions could become turbulent (i.e. involving rapid and often unpredictable change). For organisations to survive and prosper, adaptation to environmental demands was seen as a necessary requirement and one that was central to the process of management.

The essence of the **systems approach** has been described in Chapter 1 but is worth repeating here. Organisations, including those involved in business, are open systems, interacting with their environment as they convert inputs into output. Inputs include people, finance, materials and information, provided by the environment in which the organisation exists and operates. Output comprises such items as goods and services, information, ideas and waste, discharged into the environment for consumption by 'end' or 'intermediate' users and in some cases representing inputs used by other organisations.

Systems invariably comprise a number of **sub-systems** through which the process of conversion or transformation occurs. Business organisations, for example, usually have sub-systems that deal with activities such as production, marketing, accounting and human resource management, and each of these in turn may involve smaller sub-systems (e.g. sales, quality control, training) which collectively constitute the whole. Just as the organisation as a system interacts with its environment, so do the sub-systems and their component elements, which also interact with each other. In the case of the latter, the boundary between sub-systems is usually known as an 'interface'.

While the obvious complexities of the systems approach need not be discussed, it is important to emphasise that most modern views of organisations draw heavily on the work in this area, paying particular attention to the interactions between people, technology, structure and environment and to the key role of management in directing the organisation's activities towards the achievement of its goals. Broadly speaking, management is seen as a critical sub-system within the total organisation, responsible for the coordination of the other sub-systems and for ensuring that internal and external relationships are managed effectively. As changes occur in one part of the system, these will induce changes elsewhere and this will require a management response that will have implications for the organisation and for its sub-systems. Such changes may be either the cause or effect of changes in the relationship between the organisation and its environment, and the requirement for managers is to adapt to the new conditions without reducing the organisation's effectiveness.

Given the complex nature of organisations and the environments in which they operate, a number of writers have suggested a **contingency approach** to organisational design and management (e.g. Lawrence and Lorsch, Woodward, Perrow, Burns and Stalker). In essence, this approach argues that there is no single form of organisation best suited to all situations and that the most appropriate organisational structure and system of management is dependent upon the contingencies of the situation (e.g. size, technology, environment) for each organisation. In some cases a bureaucratic structure might be the best way to operate, while in others much looser and more organic methods of organisation might be more effective. In short, issues of organisational design and management depend on choosing the best combination in the light of the relevant situational variables; this might mean different structures and styles coexisting within different parts of an organisation.

Other theoretical approaches

To complement these traditional approaches to understanding the nature of organisations, Mullins (2013) highlights the contribution of theories of decision-making and social action. Decision-making theory, he suggests, can be seen as a sub-division of the systems approach in which the focus of attention is on the process of managerial decision-making and how information is gathered, processed and used in deciding how to act. The organisation in effect is seen as an information-processing network and successful management is concerned with making choices and resolving conflicts, often against a background of a changing internal and external environment.

Social action approaches emphasise the need to view the organisation from the standpoint of the individual employees or actors, each of whom has their own goals and interpretation of their work situation and whose behaviour is guided by their view of what work means to them and the satisfaction they are seeking. Organisations are portrayed as arenas in which individuals with different views and expectations interact. Conflicts of interest are regarded as a normal feature of human behaviour and an inevitable part of organisational life.

Organisational structures

Apart from the very simplest form of enterprise in which one individual carries out all tasks and responsibilities, business organisations are characterised by a division of labour which allows employees to specialise in particular roles and to occupy designated positions in pursuit of the organisation's objectives. The resulting pattern of relationships between individuals and roles constitutes what is known as the organisation's structure and represents the means by which the purpose and work of the enterprise are carried out. It also provides a framework through which communications can occur and within which the processes of management can be applied.

Responsibility for establishing the formal structure of the organisation lies with management and a variety of options is available. Whatever form is chosen, the basic need is to identify a structure that will best sustain the success of the enterprise and will permit the achievement of a number of important objectives. Through its structure an organisation should be able to:

- achieve efficiency in the utilisation of resources;
- provide opportunities for monitoring organisational performance;
- ensure the accountability of individuals;
- guarantee coordination between the different parts of the enterprise;
- provide an efficient and effective means of organisational communication;
- create job satisfaction, including opportunities for progression;
- adapt to changing circumstances brought about by internal or external developments.

In short, structure is not an end in itself but a means to an end and should ideally reflect the needs of the organisation within its existing context and taking into account its future requirements.

mini case · 'Into the Dragon's Den'

As the chapter illustrates, the structure of an organisation is a means by which an enterprise can achieve its objectives. As the environment in which a business operates changes, a firm should be willing to adapt the structure to meet the new circumstances. This might mean moving beyond the traditional models discussed below, in an effort to improve performance.

The global pharmaceutical giant GlaxoSmithKline (GSK) illustrates this idea of an evolving organisational structure. In July 2008, GSK announced that in future its scientists would have to pitch their ideas for new drugs to a development board, based essentially on the lines of *Dragons' Den,* a popular UK television programme where would-be entrepreneurs seek to gain backing for their ideas from a group of financiers. The board would include two venture capitalists and would be a mixture of executives from inside the company and GSK outsiders, the plan being to stimulate innovation by requiring smaller teams of scientists to pitch three-year business plans to the new drug discovery investment board in an effort to secure funding for new drug treatments.

 web link   You can access the website for GSK at *www.gsk.com*

The essence of structure is the division of work between individuals and the formal organisational relationships that are created between them. These relationships will be reflected not only in individual job descriptions but also in the overall **organisation chart**, which designates the formal pattern of role relationships, and the interactions between roles and the individuals occupying those roles. Individual authority relationships can be classified as line, staff, functional and lateral and arise from the defined pattern of responsibilities, as follows:

- *Line relationships* occur when authority flows vertically downwards through the structure from superior to subordinate (e.g. managers–section leader–staff).
- *Staff relationships* are created when senior personnel appoint assistants who normally have no authority over other staff but act as an extension of their superior.
- *Functional relationships* are those between specialists (or advisers) and line managers and their subordinates (e.g. when a specialist provides a common service throughout the organisation but has no authority over the users of the service). The personnel or computing function may be one such service that creates a functional relationship. (Note that specialists have line relationships with their own subordinates.)
- *Lateral relationships* exist across the organisation, particularly between individuals occupying equivalent positions within different departments or sections (e.g. committees, heads of departments, section leaders).

With regard to the division of work and the grouping of organisational activities, this can occur in a variety of ways. These include:

- *by function or major purpose,* associated particularly with departmental structures;
- *by product or service,* where individuals responsible for a particular product or service are grouped together;

- *by location,* based on geographical criteria;
- *by common processes* (e.g. particular skills or methods of operation);
- *by client group* (e.g. children, the disabled, the elderly).

In some organisations a particular method of grouping will predominate, in others there will tend to be a variety of types, and each has its own particular advantages and disadvantages. In the next sections, we examine five popular methods of grouping activities in business organisations. Students should attempt to discover what types of structure exist within their own educational institution and the logic (if any) that underlies the choices made.

Functional organisation

The functional approach to organisation is depicted in Figure 2.2. As its name indicates, in this type of structure activities are clustered together by common purpose or function. All marketing activities, for example, are grouped together as a common function, typically within a marketing department. Similarly, other areas of activity, such as production, finance, personnel and research and development, have their own specialised sections or departments, responsible for all the tasks required of that function.

Apart from its obvious simplicity, the functional organisation structure allows individuals to be grouped together on the basis of their specialisms and technical expertise, and this can facilitate the development of the function they offer as well as providing a recognised path for promotion and career development. On the downside, functional specialisation, particularly through departments, is likely to create sectional interests which may operate to the disadvantage of the organisation as a whole, particularly where inequalities in resource allocation between functions become a cause for inter-function rivalry. It could also be argued that this form of structure is most suited to single-product firms and that it becomes less appropriate as organisations diversify their products and/ or markets. In such circumstances, the tendency will be for businesses to look for the benefits that can arise from specialisation by product or from the divisionalisation of the enterprise.

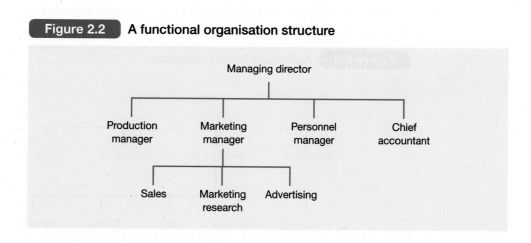

Figure 2.2　A functional organisation structure

Organisation by product or service

In this case the division of work and the grouping of activities are dictated by the product or service provided (see Figure 2.3), such that each group responsible for a particular part of the output of the organisation may have its own specialist in the different functional areas (e.g. marketing, finance, personnel). One advantage of this type of structure is that it allows an organisation to offer a diversified range of products, as exemplified by the different services available in National Health Service hospitals (e.g. maternity, ortho-paedic, geriatric, and so forth). Its main disadvantage is the danger that the separate units or divisions within the enterprise may attempt to become too autonomous, even at the expense of other parts of the organisation, and this can present management with prob-lems of coordination and control.

The divisional structure

As firms diversify their products and/or markets – often as a result of merger or takeover – a structure is needed to coordinate and control the different parts of the organisation. This structure is likely to be the divisional (or multi-divisional) company.

A **divisional structure** is formed when an organisation is split up into a number of self-contained business units, each of which operates as a profit centre. This may occur on the basis of product or market or a combination of the two, with each unit tending to operate along functional or product lines, but with certain key functions (e.g. finance, personnel, corporate planning) provided centrally, usually at company headquarters (see Figure 2.4).

The main benefit of the multi-divisional company is that it allows each part of what can be a very diverse organisation to operate semi-independently in producing and mar-keting its products, thus permitting each division to design its offering to suit local mar-ket conditions – a factor of prime importance where the firm operates on a multinational basis. The dual existence of divisional **profit centres** and a central unit responsible for establishing strategy at a global level can, however, be a source of considerable tension, particularly where the needs and aims of the centre appear to conflict with operations at the local level or to impose burdens seen to be unreasonable by divisional managers (e.g. the allocation of central overhead costs).

Much the same kind of arguments apply to the **holding company**, though this tends to be a much looser structure for managing diverse organisations, favoured by both UK

Figure 2.3   A product-based structure

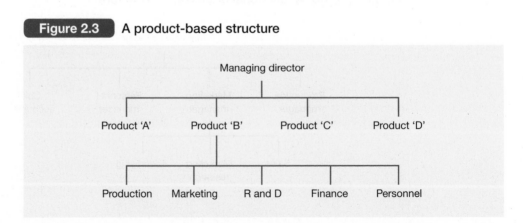

Figure 2.4   A divisional structure

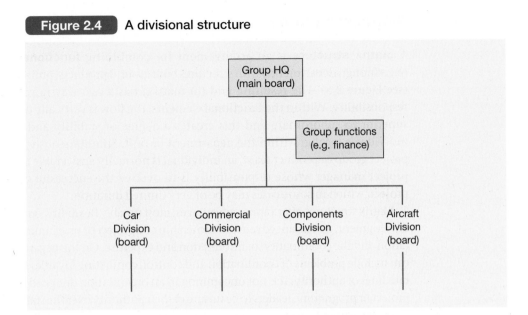

and Japanese companies. Under this arrangement, the different elements of the organisation (usually companies) are coordinated and controlled by a parent body, which may be just a financial entity established to maintain or gain control of other trading companies. Holding companies are associated with the growth of firms by acquisition, which gives rise to a high degree of product or market diversification. They are also a popular means of operating a multinational organisation.

mini case   Mergers and competition

In 2016 a £10.25 billion proposed acquisition was halted by the European Commission: Hutchinson-owned Three had planned to buy Telefónica-owned network provider O2, both one of four mobile network operators in the UK (the others being EE and Vodaphone). O2 and Three argued that combining their businesses to form one large company would mean that they were better able to compete with larger providers such as Sky and BT.

The European Commission argued that an O2–Three merger would change the structure of the market to leave only three competing businesses operating all of the networks in the UK (other smaller companies, such as Giffgaff, Sky Mobile and Tesco Mobile, only use the network run by the four network operators). The Commission argued that this would result in less competition and higher prices for customers across the sector.

O2 was originally formed between BT and Securicor, before being sold in 2005 to Telefónica, a Spanish company that also owns companies in Germany, Spain, France, Brazil, Columbia, the United States, and elsewhere. Mobile phone companies change hands quite frequently with relatively little difficulty. This is because business models and cultures are relatively similar. Consider which parts of the mobile phone company you encounter on a daily basis, and how long it would take to notice if your provider was sold to an international holding company.

web link   For information on the proposed merger see, for example, *www.ft.com*

Matrix structures

A **matrix structure** is an arrangement for combining **functional specialisation** (e.g. through departments) with structures built around products, projects or programmes (see Figure 2.5). The resulting grid (or matrix) has a two-way flow of authority and responsibility. Within the functional elements, the flow is vertically down the line from superior to subordinate and this creates a degree of stability and certainty for the individuals located within the department or unit. Simultaneously, as a member of a project group or product team, an individual is normally answerable horizontally to the project manager whose responsibility is to oversee the successful completion of the project, which in some cases may be of very limited duration.

Matrix structures offer various advantages, most notably flexibility, opportunities for staff development, an enhanced sense of ownership of a project or programme, customer orientation and the coordination of information and expertise. On the negative side, difficulties can include problems of coordination and control, conflicting loyalties for staff and uncertain lines of authority. It is not uncommon in an organisation designed on matrix lines for project or programme leaders to be unsure of their authority over the staff from the contributing departments. Nor is it unknown for functional managers to withdraw their cooperation and/or support for projects located outside their immediate sphere of influence.

Project teams

Despite its flexibility, the matrix often has a degree of permanence; in contrast, the **project team** is essentially a temporary structure established as a means of carrying out a particular task, often in a highly unstable environment. Once the task is complete, the

---

Figure 2.5   A matrix structure in a business school

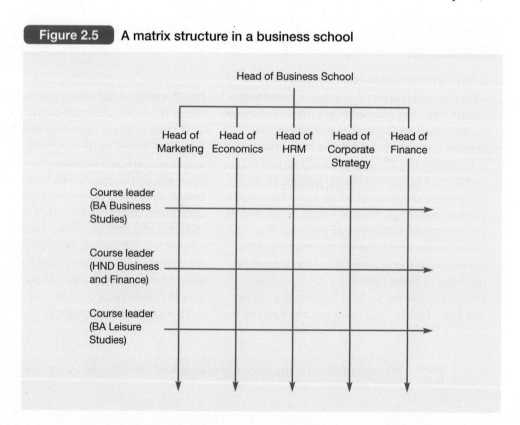

team is disbanded and individuals return to their usual departments or are assigned to a new project.

Fashioned around technical expertise rather than managerial rank, and often operating closely with clients, project teams are increasingly common in high-technology firms, construction companies and some types of service industry, especially management consultancies and advertising. Rather than being a replacement for the existing structure, they operate alongside it and utilise in-house staff (and, in some cases, outside specialists) on a project-by-project basis. While this can present logistical and scheduling problems and may involve some duplication of resources, it can assist an organisation in adapting to change and uncertainty and in providing products to the customer's specifications. Project teams tend to be at their most effective when objectives and tasks are well defined, when the client is clear as to the desired outcome and when the team is chosen with care.

The virtual organisation

As indicated above, traditional organisations have structures that are designed to facilitate the transformation of inputs into output. Increasingly, as the business environment changes, relationships both within and between organisations have needed to become more flexible and this has given rise to such developments as the growth in teleworking and the establishment of dynamic broker/agent networks involving considerable outsourcing of sub-tasks to 'agents' (e.g. manufacturing, distribution) by the core organisation (the 'broker'). It is fair to say that this demand for greater flexibility has been driven partly by the market and partly by cost considerations, and the process of change has been facilitated by relatively rapid developments in information technology. One area currently exciting the interest of writers on management and organisation is the concept of the virtual organisation, arguably the ultimate form of organisational flexibility (see Chapter 11 for a further discussion of the concept in the context of networking).

The term virtual organisation or firm signifies an extremely loose web of essentially freelance businesses or individuals who organise themselves to produce a specific customer product (e.g. an individual holiday package with particular features unique to the customer). Without any permanent structure or hierarchy this so-called firm can constantly change its shape and, despite existing across space and time, tends to appear edgeless, with its inputs, outputs and employees increasingly dispersed across the linked world of information systems. Given modern forms of communication, opportunities exist for the creation of totally electronic-based organisations trading in expertise and information with no real-world physical identity. This stands in stark contrast to the traditional view of the firm as an arrangement which adds value by transforming basic economic inputs (e.g. land, labour, capital) into physical outputs or services.

Structural change

Internal change is an important feature of the modern business organisation. In order to remain competitive and meet stakeholder needs, a firm may have to find ways to restructure its organisation as the environment in which it operates changes. Solutions can range from a partial or wholesale shift in the organisation's structural form to strategies for reducing the overall size and shape of the company (e.g. **downsizing**) or a radical redesign of business processes (e.g. **re-engineering**).

Whereas business re-engineering normally connotes a root-and-branch reform of the way in which the business operates, downsizing essentially involves shrinking the organisation to make it leaner and fitter and hopefully more flexible in its response to the marketplace. For some companies this means little more than reducing the size of the workforce through natural wastage and/or redundancies, as and when opportunities arise; for others it involves delayering the organisation by removing a tier, or tiers, of management, thus effectively flattening the organisation's hierarchy and helping it to reduce its unit costs of production.

In its most systematic and long-term form, downsizing can be used as a vehicle for cultural change through which an organisation's employees are encouraged to embrace notions of continuous improvement and innovation, and to accept that structural reform is a permanent and natural state of affairs. Under this approach, retraining and reskilling become vital tools in implementing the chosen strategy and in shaping the organisation to meet the demands of its changing environment. The danger is, however, that a firm may become too concerned with restructuring as a cure for all its problems, when the real cause of its difficulties lies in its marketplace. Cutting the number of employees, in such a situation, is unlikely to make unattractive products attractive, nor is it likely to boost morale within the organisation.

Aspects of functional management

Most organisational structures reflect a degree of functional specialisation, with individuals occupying roles in departments, units or sections which have titles such as Production, Finance, Marketing, Personnel, and Research and Development. These functional areas of the internal organisation, and the individuals who are allocated to them, are central to the process of transforming organisational inputs into output. The management of these functions and of the relationships between them will be a key factor in the success of the enterprise and in its ability to respond to external demands for change.

The interdependence of the internal functions can be demonstrated by a simple example. Providing goods and services to meet the market's needs often involves research and development, which necessitates a financial input, usually from the capital market or the organisation's own resources. It also requires, as do all the other functions, the recruitment of staff of the right quality, a task which is more often than not the responsibility of the personnel or human resources department. If research and development activities lead to a good idea which the marketing department is able to sell, then the production department is required to produce it in the right quantities, to the right specifications and at the time the market needs it. This depends not only on internal scheduling procedures within the production department, but also on having the right kinds of materials supplied on time by the purchasing department, an appropriate system of quality control and work monitoring, machinery that is working and regularly serviced, the finished items packed, despatched and delivered, and a multitude of other activities, all operating towards the same end.

The extent to which all of these requirements can be met simultaneously depends on internal factors, many of which are controllable, and also on a host of external influences, the majority of which tend to be beyond the organisation's control. To demonstrate this interface between the internal and external environments, two key areas of functional management are discussed briefly below – marketing and human resource management. An examination of the other functions within the organisation would yield similar findings.

Human resource management (HRM)

People are the key organisational resource; without them organisations would not exist or function. All businesses need to plan for and manage the people they employ if they are to use this resource effectively and efficiently in pursuit of their objectives. In modern and forward-looking organisations this implies a proactive approach to the management of people that goes beyond the bounds of traditional personnel management and involves the establishment of systems for planning, monitoring, appraisal and evaluation, training and development, and integrating the internal needs of the organisation with the external demands of the marketplace. Such an approach is associated with the idea of **human resource management**.

As in other areas of management, HRM involves a wide variety of activities related to the formulation and implementation of appropriate organisational policies, the provision of opportunities for monitoring, evaluation and change, and the application of resources to the fulfilment of organisational ends. Key aspects of 'people management' include:

- recruitment and selection;
- working conditions;
- training and career development;
- job evaluation;
- employee relations;
- human resource planning;
- legal aspects of employment.

In most, if not all, cases these will be affected by both internal and external influences (e.g. size of the firm, management style, competition, economic and political developments), some of which will vary over time as well as between organisations.

The provision of these activities within an organisation can occur in a variety of ways and to different degrees of sophistication. Some very small firms may have little in the way of a recognisable HRM function, being concerned primarily with questions of hiring and firing, pay and other working conditions, but not with notions of career development, staff appraisal or job enrichment. In contrast, very large companies may have a specialist HRM or personnel department, often organised on functional lines and responsible for the formulation and implementation of personnel policies throughout the organisation. Such centralisation provides not only some economies of scale, but also a degree of standardisation and consistency across departments. To allow for flexibility, centralised systems are often combined with an element of decentralisation which permits individual departments or sections to exercise some influence in matters such as the recruitment and selection of staff, working conditions, training and career development.

To illustrate how the different aspects of HRM are influenced by external factors, one part of this function – recruitment and selection of staff – has been chosen. This is the activity within the organisation that seeks to ensure that it has the right quantity and quality of labour in the right place and at the right time to meet its requirements at all levels. To achieve this aim, the organisation initially needs to consider a large number of factors, including possible changes in the demand for labour, the need for new skills and likely labour turnover, before the processes of recruitment and selection can begin. These aspects in turn will be conditioned by a variety of factors such as changes in the demand for the product, the introduction of new technology, and social, economic and demographic changes, some of which may not be anticipated or expected by strategic planners.

Once recruitment and selection are ready to begin, a further raft of influences will impinge upon the process, some of which emanate from external sources. In drawing up a job specification, for example, attention will normally need to be paid to the state of the local labour market, including skill availability, competition from other employers, wage rates in comparable jobs and/or organisations, and socio-demographic trends. If the quality of labour required is in short supply, an organisation may find itself having to offer improved pay and working conditions simply to attract a sufficient number of applicants to fill the vacancies on offer. Equally, in fashioning its job advertisements and drawing up the material it sends out to potential applicants, a firm will need to pay due attention to the needs of current legislation in areas such as equal opportunities, race discrimination and employment protection, if it is not to infringe the law.

Among the other external factors that the enterprise may need to take into consideration in recruiting and selecting staff will be:

- the relative cost and effectiveness of the different advertising media at reaching people with the desired skills;
- existing relationships with external sources of recruitment (e.g. job centres, schools, colleges, universities);
- commitments to the local community;
- relationships with employee organisations (e.g. trade unions, staff associations);
- opportunities for staff training and development in training and educational institutions.

Ideally, it should also pay some attention to possible future changes in the technology of the workplace, in order to recruit individuals either with appropriate skills or who can be retrained relatively easily with a minimum amount of disruption and expense to the organisation.

The marketing function

The processes of HRM are a good illustration of the interactions between a firm's internal and external environments. An even better example is provided by an examination of its marketing activities, which are directed primarily, though not exclusively, towards what is happening outside the organisation.

Like 'management', the term **marketing** has been defined in a wide variety of ways, ranging from Kotler's essentially economic notion of an activity directed at satisfying human needs and wants through exchange processes, to the more managerial definitions associated with bodies such as the Chartered Institute of Marketing. A common thread running through many of these definitions is the idea that marketing is concerned with meeting the needs of the consumer in a way that is profitable to the enterprise. Hence, strategic marketing management is normally characterised as the process of ensuring a good fit between the opportunities afforded by the marketplace and the abilities and resources of an organisation operating in it.

> **web link**
>
> Information about the Chartered Institute of Marketing is available at *www.cim.co.uk*

This notion of marketing as an integrative function within the organisation – linking the needs of the consumer with the various functional areas of the firm – is central to modern definitions of the term and lies at the heart of what is known as the **marketing concept**. This is the idea that the customer is of prime importance to the organisation and that the most significant managerial task in any enterprise is first to identify the needs and wants of the consumer and then to ensure that its operations are geared to meeting those requirements profitably. Though it would be true to say that not all organisations subscribe to this view, it is generally accepted that the successful businesses are predominantly those with a customer rather than a production or sales orientation. Equally, the evidence suggests that the need to adopt such a customer-centred approach applies not only to private sector trading organisations, but also increasingly to public sector enterprises and to bodies not established for the pursuit of profits but for other purposes (e.g. charities, political parties, trade unions).

When viewed from a customer perspective, marketing can be seen to comprise a range of activities that goes beyond the simple production of an item for sale. These activities include:

- identifying the needs of consumers (e.g. through market research);
- designing different 'offerings' to meet the needs of different types of customers (e.g. through market segmentation and positioning);
- choosing products, prices, promotional techniques and distribution channels that are appropriate to a particular market (i.e. designing a 'marketing mix' strategy);
- undertaking market and product planning;
- deciding on brand names, types of packages and methods of communicating the product to the customer;
- creating a marketing information system.

As already indicated, in carrying out these activities the firm is brought into contact with a range of external influences of both an immediate and an indirect kind. This external marketing environment can have a fundamental impact on the degree to which the firm is able to develop and maintain successful transactions with its customers and hence on its profitability and chances of survival.

To illustrate how a firm's marketing effort can be influenced by external factors, the following brief discussion focuses on 'pricing', which is one of the key elements of the **marketing mix**: that is, the set of controllable variables that a business can use to influence the buyer's response, namely product, price, promotion and place – the 4Ps. Of all the mix elements, price is the only one that generates revenue, while the others result in expenditure. It is therefore a prime determinant of a firm's turnover and profitability and can have a considerable influence on the demand for its products and frequently for those of its competitors (see Chapter 14).

> **web link**
>
> There are lots of useful websites discussing the idea of the 'marketing mix'. Try typing the term into Google.

Leaving aside the broader question of a firm's pricing goals and the fact that prices will tend to vary according to the stage a product has reached in its life cycle, price determination can be said to be influenced by a number of factors. Of these, the costs of production, the prices charged by one's competitors and the price sensitivity of consumers tend to be the most significant.

In the case of cost-based pricing, this occurs when a firm determines its price based on the cost of buying or producing the product and adding a profit margin or 'mark-up' to arrive at the final selling price. Such an approach tends to be common among smaller enterprises and retailers (e.g. builders, corner shops) where costs are often easier to estimate and where likely consumer reactions are given less attention than the need to make an adequate return on the effort involved. The essential point about this form of price determination is that many of the firm's costs are influenced by external organisations – including the suppliers of materials, components and energy – and hence pricing will often vary according to changes in the prices of inputs. Only larger organisations, or a group of small businesses operating together, will generally be able to exercise some influence over input prices and even then not all costs will be controllable by the enterprise.

Organisations that take an essentially cost-based approach to pricing will sometimes be influenced by the prices charged by competitors – particularly in markets where considerable competition exists and where the products are largely homogeneous and a buyer's market is evident (e.g. builders during a recession). The competitive approach to pricing, however, is also found in markets where only a few large firms operate and where the need to increase or maintain market share can give rise to virtually identical prices and to fierce non-price competition between the market leaders (see Chapter 15). In the UK, for instance, a big cross-Channel ferry operator will normally provide the service to customers at the same price as its rivals, differentiating its offering in terms of additional benefits (e.g. on-board entertainment) rather than price. Where this is the case, the external demands of the market rather than costs constitute the primary influence on a firm's decisions, and changes in market conditions (e.g. the actual or potential entry of new firms; changes in a competitor's prices; economic recession) will tend to be reflected in price changes.

This idea of market factors influencing pricing decisions also applies to situations where firms fix their prices according to the actual or anticipated reactions of consumers to the price charged for a product – known in economics as the price elasticity of demand (see Chapter 14). In this case, the customer rather than a firm's competitors is the chief influence on price determination, although the two are often interrelated in that consumers are usually more price sensitive in markets where some choice exists. Differential levels of price sensitivity between consumers of a product normally arise when a market has distinct segments based on factors such as differences in income or age or location. In such cases a firm will often fix its prices according to the segment of the market it is serving, a process known as 'price discrimination' and one that is familiar to students and older people claiming concessionary fares on public transport.

While the above discussion has been oversimplified and does not take into account factors such as the price of other products in an organisation's product portfolio (e.g. different models of car), it illustrates quite clearly how even one of the so-called controllable variables in a firm's marketing mix is subject to a range of external influences that is often beyond its ability to control. The same argument applies to the other elements of the marketing function, and students could usefully add to their understanding of the internal/external interface by examining how the external environment impinges upon such marketing activities as promotion, distribution or market research.

Synopsis

The internal dimension of business organisations constitutes an extensive field of study and one to which students of business devote a considerable amount of time. In seeking to illustrate how a firm's internal organisation is influenced by its external environment, emphasis has been placed on a selected number of aspects of a firm's internal operations. Of these, its structure and functions were seen to provide a good illustration of the interface between the internal and external environments. Appreciating the existence of this interface is facilitated by adopting a systems approach to organisational analysis.

Summary of key points

- Management is a key aspect of the internal environment of the business organisation.

- Theories of organisation and management fall broadly into three categories: classical theories, human relations approaches, systems approaches.

- The systems view of organisations depicts businesses as open systems interacting with their external environment as they convert inputs into outputs.

- The external environment of the organisation affects all aspects of the business, including its structures, functions and processes.

- To carry out their tasks, businesses can structure themselves in a variety of ways, including functionally, by product/service, by divisions, in a matrix format or via project teams. Each has its advantages and disadvantages.

- Structural change tends to be a feature of large modern organisations.

- Within the organisation, the different business functions such as marketing, production, HRM, purchasing, and so on are influenced by external factors of both a general and operational kind.

- An examination of the marketing and HRM functions reveals the importance of the wide range of external influences that can impinge upon these day-to-day areas of organisational work.

- Investigations of other functional areas within the organisation would produce a similar picture.

case study   Reshuffle at Microsoft

When an organisation's fortunes appear to change for the worse, there is always a temptation to seek a remedy through a change in senior personnel and/or in the overall structure of the enterprise (e.g. leading professional football teams in Europe seem to change managers fairly regularly when results go badly). Whether this is invariably a good idea is open to question. Supporters see it as a way of revitalising the business by bringing in new faces with new ideas, of challenging existing ways of thinking and working; critics frequently portray it as 'rearranging the deckchairs on the *Titanic*', a failure to address the fundamental problem(s) facing the organisation. Time will tell which of these two viewpoints applies to the global business examined in this case study.

Microsoft announced two reorganisations in 2017, first of its cloud, enterprise and artificial intelligence sections, and most recently of its sales divisions. Much of the change is driven by slower than expected sales of hardware such as tablets and PCs, and greater than expected sales of cloud computing services based at its own data centres, such as Azure. This is just the latest reorganisation in Microsoft's long history.

In 2013, faced with a demonstrable shift in consumer demand away from PCs and towards tablets, smartphones and touch devices – where it was struggling to compete with companies such as Apple and Google – Microsoft Chief Executive Steve Ballmer announced a major reorganisation of the business. Aimed at promoting faster innovation and a much sharper focus on meeting consumer needs, Ballmer heralded the demise of the divisional approach favoured by his predecessor (Bill Gates), which was evidently seen as creating a hierarchical structure of competing businesses, each with its own strategy and with separate finance and marketing teams.

The centrepiece of the 2013 arrangements was the organisation of the business on the basis of function. Instead of divisions, Microsoft operated via a number of functional groupings, including engineering, marketing, finance, advanced strategy and research, and business development and evangelism. In what is likely to prove an important change, the engineering division will be split into four major areas or groupings: operating systems, devices and studios, applications and services, cloud and enterprise. Responsibility for running the main functions within the new organisation will be vested in a reshuffled senior executive team. Commenting in 2013, The *Guardian* (12 July: 24) suggested that they were reminiscent of the reorganisation undertaken by its rival Apple the previous year. This, it suggested, had been designed to encourage even greater collaboration between various aspects of the business: the world-class hardware, its software and its services teams.

Put another way, structure can sometimes be an aid and sometimes an obstacle to a firm achieving its strategic objectives. Where the latter is the case, a partial or even radical restructuring of the organisation may be a necessary condition for putting the business on the right track. As this series of reorganisations have shown, arrangements need constant review to make sure that businesses are able to suit the needs and demands of the market.

Case study questions

1 What are thought to be the main advantages of restructuring an organisation that is facing problems?

2 Why is a decision to restructure an organisation unlikely to prove a 'sufficient condition' for its future success?

case study

Thomas Cook expansion

The travel agent Thomas Cook announced a deal with the Chinese company Fosun in 2015. In return for 5 per cent of its company, Thomas Cook would take control of Club Méditerranée (Club Med) from the Fosun Group, operating its hotels directly rather than just profiting from selling bookings at the destination. The new partnership has also enabled Thomas Cook to draw on the knowledge of its new partners to develop opportunities in the Chinese market, as well as access to the other company's assets.

Thomas Cook plans to develop further partnerships to gain access to more resorts, destinations and markets with other regional operators. It may also be able to get further funding from new investing partners. By bringing together companies in these sorts of deals Thomas Cook can profit as both a seller and a provider of services.

Case study questions

1 What factors might Thomas Cook look for in new potential partners, and can you identify any likely collaborators in this market?

2 How might a large company's structure have to adapt to incorporate an acquired chain, as happened with Thomas Cook and Club Med?

Review and discussion questions

1 In the systems approach to organisations, reference is made to 'feedback'. What is meant by this term and how can feedback influence the process of transforming 'inputs' into 'output'?

2 Should a firm's internal structure be influenced by considerations of management or by the market it serves? Are the two incompatible?

3 Examine ways in which a firm's external environment can influence one of the following functional areas: finance or production or research and development.

4 Describe the structure of an organisation with which you are familiar (e.g. through employment or work experience), indicating why the organisation is structured in the way it is. Are there any alternative forms of structure the organisation could adopt?

Assignments

1 As a student on a business-related course, you have decided to get some practical experience of the business world by running a small venture with a number of colleagues which you hope will also earn you enough income to support you during your time at college or university. Your idea involves printing and selling customised T-shirts throughout the institution and possibly to a wider market. Design an appropriate organisational structure which you feel will help you achieve your objectives, indicating your rationale for choosing such a structure and the formal pattern of relationships between individuals.

2 In self-selecting groups of three or four, identify an organisation that you feel has a bureaucratic structure. Produce a report indicating:

(a) those features of the organisation's structure, management and operations that best fit the idea of bureaucracy;

(b) the practical consequences of these features for the working of the organisation.

Give examples to support your comments.

Further reading

Cole, G. A. and Kelly, P., *Management: Theory and Practice,* 7th edition, International Thomson Business Press, 2011.

Daft, R. L., *Organizational Theory and Design,* 11th edition, South-Western Cengage Learning, 2012.

Du Gay, P., *In Praise of Bureaucracy: Weber, Organization, Ethics,* Sage, 2000.

Handy, C., *The Age of Unreason,* 2nd edition, Arrow Books, 1995.

Mullins, L. J., *Essentials of Organizational Behaviour,* 3rd edition, FT/Prentice Hall, 2011.

Mullins, L. J., *Management and Organizational Behaviour,* 10th edition, Financial Times/Prentice Hall, 2013.

Pugh, D. S. and Hickson, D. J., *Great Writers on Organizations,* 3rd omnibus edition, Ashgate, 2007.

Stoner, J. and Freeman, R., *Management,* 5th edition, Prentice Hall, 1992.

web link

Web links and further questions are available on the website at:
www.pearsoned.co.uk/worthington

3 The global context of business

Chris Britton

Businesses of all sizes operate in international markets: products are sold across borders; the resources used in production can come from anywhere in the world; communication is instantaneous; and financial markets are inextricably linked, as the events surrounding Brexit demonstrate. Individual businesses operate across borders in a variety of ways – they can do this directly, through the formation of strategic alliances, or through merger and takeover. It is clear then that businesses need to be aware of the global context of their markets.

Learning outcomes

Having read this chapter you should be able to:

- understand the difference between globalisation and internationalisation
- outline the main elements of globalisation
- illustrate the role of the multinational enterprise
- introduce the implications of globalisation for business

Key terms

Capital market flows
Consortium
Cross-subsidisation
Customs union
Emerging economies
Foreign direct investment (FDI)
Franchising

Free trade area
Globalisation
Hyperglobalisation
International trade
Internationalisation
Joint venture
Licensing

Multinational Corporations (MNCs)
Regional trade agreements (RTAs)
Regionalism
Strategic alliance
Transfer pricing
Transformationalism

Introduction

Businesses operate in a global context: even if they do not trade directly with other countries, they might be affected by a domestic shortage of skilled labour or may be subject to developments on the global financial markets. There is a difference between globalisation and internationalisation in the business literature, but both result in increased exposure to global forces. This means that businesses need an understanding of the process of globalisation. The nature of globalisation is changing; it used to mean the westernisation of the developing world, but developing economies such as Brazil, China and India are redefining processes and institutions. In 1980 the share of the developing countries in world exports was 34 per cent; by 2011 it was 47 per cent and the share of world imports had gone up from 29 to 42 per cent in the same period. Globalisation is here to stay and the World Bank forecasts that the share of global gross domestic product (GDP) for developing countries will rise from 29 (2010) to 39 per cent (2030).

Globalisation versus internationalisation

These terms are often used interchangeably but they refer to different processes. Although there is not a single accepted definition of **globalisation**, it is a term used to describe the process of integration on a worldwide scale of markets and production, and the free movement of capital across the globe. The world is moving away from a system of national markets isolated from each other by trade barriers, distance or culture. Advances in technology and mass communications have made it possible for people in one part of the world to watch happenings in far-off places on television or via the Internet. So, for globalisation, national boundaries are not important economically; free trade and movement of labour and other resources result in the breakdown of these boundaries and one big global marketplace. **Internationalisation**, meanwhile, refers to the increased links between nation states with respect to trade and the movement of resources. The relevant thing here is that the nation state is still important; it is participating and cooperating with other nation states to a common end.

Regionalism and regional trade agreements are also important in this process, the EU being an example. The main difference is that with internationalisation the nation state remains important, whereas the process of globalisation breaks down the barriers between nation states. An extreme view of this process is called **hyperglobalisation**, where the world market is seen as a borderless global marketplace consisting of powerless nation states and powerful multinational corporations. The more generally accepted view is called **transformationalism**, which sees the process of globalisation as bringing about changes both in the power of countries and companies and in national characteristics and culture. Any differences do not disappear but are maintained, albeit in changed forms. The population in India might drink Coca-Cola and listen to western music, but this does not mean that the people hold the same views and values as the west. Similarly, even within the EU national differences remain important (especially in times of crisis).

Although these definitions are important theoretically, they are difficult to apply in practice, so here the term globalisation is used to mean the process of integration of markets, however that happens. Until recently globalisation meant the westernisation (or Americanisation) of markets, but the world has started to change. Companies from **emerging economies** have started to compete with the older **multinational corporations (MNCs)** and the nature of the MNC is being redefined. Globalisation has taken place because of closer economic ties between countries and because of developments in mass communications, transportation, electronics and the greater mobility of labour. A heated debate has taken place over the past decade between the pro- and the anti-globalisation lobbies.

The arguments put forward by the proponents of globalisation stem from the benefits brought about by increased **international trade** and specialisation (see Chapter 16 for a discussion). These proponents argue that all countries open to international trade have benefited – only those that are closed to international trade (some African countries, for example) have become poorer. In the case of China, the opening up to world trade in 1978 has led to increases in GDP per capita, up from $1,988 per head in 1978 to $10,757 per head in 2014. Since the 2014 peak it has dropped a little to $9,996 in 2015 because of the slowdown in net importing economies around the world (buying less of what China exports). The pro-globalisation arguments can be summarised as follows:

- Increased globalisation leads to greater specialisation so that all countries involved benefit from the increased international trade.
- Countries that are open to international trade have experienced much faster growth than countries that are not.
- Barriers to trade encourage industries to be inefficient and uncompetitive.
- It is not just the large multinationals that benefit from globalisation – small and medium-sized companies are also engaged in global production and marketing.

The arguments against globalisation are just as strong. It is claimed that the benefits of higher world output and growth brought about through globalisation have not been shared equally by all countries. The main beneficiaries have been the large multinationals (and those that can afford to buy a share of them) rather than individual countries or people. It is suggested that the international organisations that promote free trade should pay more attention to the issues of equity, human rights and the natural environment rather than focusing simply on trade. It is also argued that increased globalisation leads to economic instability. The anti-globalisation arguments can be summarised thus:

- The benefits of globalisation have not been shared equitably throughout the world.
- Globalisation undermines the power of nation states – it empowers the large multinationals at the expense of governments, many multinationals being financially bigger than nation states.
- The large organisations that promote free trade (such as the World Trade Organization and the International Monetary Fund) are not democratically elected and their decisions are not made in the public eye.
- The policies of these organisations are aimed at trade only – human rights and environmental concerns are often ignored.

The main international organisations concerned with globalisation are discussed in more detail in Chapter 5. They are the World Trade Organization (WTO), the International Monetary Fund (IMF), the World Bank and the Organization for Economic Cooperation and Development (OECD). In addition to these there is the United Nations Conference on Trade and Development (UNCTAD), which is a permanent intergovernmental body of the United Nations that aims to maximise investment to the developing nations and to help them in their integration into the world economy.

There are several key elements of economic globalisation: international trade, **foreign direct investment (FDI)** and **capital market flows**. The OECD categorises members into three bands – high-income countries, which includes the EU, North America and Australasia; middle-income countries, which includes East Asia and the Pacific Rim; and low-income countries, which includes South Asia and Africa.

International trade

The share of international trade in goods as a percentage of GDP increased between 1990 and 2011 for all income groups and particularly for the low-income group (see Table 3.1). The same is true for services. Thus there is evidence of increased globalisation. Note that there are differences within each group – in the low-income group, for example, although the share has increased overall, there are countries that have experienced negative growth (Botswana and Togo for instance, both of which are open to international trade). Although the share of developing countries has increased over time, world markets are still dominated by the developed world, especially in high-value, high-tech products. It is also true that increased trade does not automatically lead to increased development, as in parts of sub-Saharan Africa where the products sold are basic primary products.

Table 3.1 Elements of economic globalisation

	Trade in goods as a % of GDP		Gross private capital flows as a % of GDP*		Gross FDI as a % of GDP	
	1990	2011	1990	2005	1990	2011
Low income	23.6	58.1	2.4	6.7	0.4	3.8
Middle income	32.5	53.0	6.6	13.3	0.9	2.7
High income	32.3	53.0	11.0	37.2	1.0	2.7

*Not available after 2005.
Source: Adapted from Table 6.1, *World Development Indicators*, 2013, and the Little Data Book 2013, both World Bank.

Capital market flows

This refers to the flows of money from private savers wishing to include foreign assets in their portfolios. This also increased in all income bands between 1990 and 2005 (Table 3.1) – later figures are not available. The overall figures hide a greater volatility than in international trade or FDI and the fact that the flows have been largely restricted to emerging economies in East Asia. Capital market flows occur because investors want to diversify their portfolios to include foreign assets; it is therefore aimed at bringing about short-term capital gains. Unlike FDI, there is no long-term involvement on the part of the investor.

Foreign direct investment

This refers to the establishment of production facilities in overseas countries and therefore represents a more direct involvement in the local economy (than capital market flows) and a longer-term relationship. Between 1990 and 2000, the value of FDI worldwide more than doubled; since then FDI has moved in line with world economic conditions (see case study on FDI at the end of the chapter). FDI represents the largest form of private capital inflow into the developing countries. Each of the three elements of economic globalisation has a different effect and carries different consequences for countries. Capital market flows are much more volatile and therefore carry higher risk – these flows introduce the possibility of 'boom and bust' for countries where capital market flows are important. The financial crisis in the emerging countries in 2013–14 had a lot to do with these capital flows. Openness to trade and FDI are less volatile and it is these that are favoured by the international organisations such as the World Bank and the WTO. It is also true that the benefits of globalisation have not been shared equally between those taking part – the developed nations have reaped more benefit than the poorer nations.

The role of multinational enterprises

Substantial amounts of foreign trade and hence movements of currency result from the activities of very large multinational companies or enterprises. Multinational enterprises/companies (MNEs/MNCs), strictly defined, are enterprises operating in a number of countries and having production or service facilities outside the country of their origin. These multinationals usually have their headquarters in a developed country, but this is beginning to change. At one time globalisation meant that businesses were expanding from developed to developing economies. The world is a different place now – business flows in the opposite direction and often between developing countries. One indication of this is the number of companies from the emerging nations that appear in the Global 500 list of the world's biggest companies. In 1980, 23 (5 per cent) came from emerging countries; in 2010, the number had gone up to 85 (17 per cent) and of these 54 were Chinese, including Lenovo, a Chinese computer manufacturer which bought IBM's personal computer business in 2005.

Multinationals can diversify their operations across different countries and many are well-known household names (see Table 3.2). The footloose nature of such companies brings with it certain benefits.

Table 3.2 The world's 10 largest non-financial MNCs, ranked by foreign assets, 2012

Rank	Company	Home economy	Transnationality index %[*]
1	General Electric	United States	23
2	Royal Dutch Shell plc	UK/Netherlands	77
3	BP	United Kingdom	84
4	Toyota Motor Corporation	Japan	55
5	Total SA	France	79
6	Exxon Mobil Corporation	United States	65
7	Vodafone Group plc	United Kingdom	90
8	GDF Suez	France	59
9	Chevron Corporation	United States	60
10	Volkswagen Group	Germany	58

[*]Measured as the average of three ratios: foreign assets to total assets, foreign sales to total sales, and foreign employment to total employment.
Source: Adapted from Annex Table 28, *World Investment Report,* UNCTAD, 2013.

1   MNCs can locate their activities in the countries that are best suited for them. For example, production planning can be carried out in the parent country, the production itself can be carried out in one of the newly industrialised countries where labour is relatively cheap and marketing can be done in the parent country where such activities are well developed. The relocation of production may go some way to explaining the decline in the manufacturing sector in the developed nations.

2   An MNC can cross-subsidise its operations. Profits from one market can be used to support operations in another one. The **cross-subsidisation** could take the form of price cutting, increasing productive capacity or heavy advertising.

3   The risk involved in production is spread not just over different markets but also over different countries.

4   MNCs can avoid tax by negotiating special tax arrangements in one of their host countries (tax holidays) or through careful use of **transfer pricing**. Transfer prices are the prices at which internal transactions take place. These can be altered so that high profits can be shown in countries where the tax rate is lower. The principle in place is that the transfer price should represent what an 'arm's length' customer would pay or an 'arm's length' supplier would charge (see mini case study on transfer pricing).

5   MNCs can take advantage of subsidies and tax exemptions offered by governments to encourage start-ups in their country.

The very size of MNCs gives rise to concern as their operations can have a substantial impact upon the economy. For example, the activities of MNCs will affect the labour markets of host countries and the balance of payments. If a subsidiary is started in one country there will be an inflow of capital to that country. Once it is up and running, however, there will be outflows of dividends and profits that will affect the invisible balance. Also, there will be flows of goods within the company, and therefore between countries, in the form of semi-finished goods and raw materials. These movements will affect the exchange rate as well as the balance of payments and it is likely that the effects will be greater for developing countries than for developed countries.

mini case Transfer pricing

Although transfer pricing has always been a feature of the operation of multinationals, it became a huge public issue in 2013 and very unpopular. A survey by the Institute of Business Ethics in the UK found that tax avoidance had replaced remuneration as the issue that most concerned them about corporate behaviour. In times of austerity, cutbacks in government spending and falls in real wages, anything that reduces the tax liability of large companies is seen as bad. There were many reports of the small amount of tax paid by multinationals such as Google, Starbucks and Amazon in countries where they do large amounts of business. In 2011, in the UK Amazon had sales of £3.35 billion but reported a tax expense of £1.8 million, while Google paid the UK government £6 million on a turnover of £395 million. Neither of these is illegal, both companies were operating within the law – it is tax avoidance, not tax evasion (see e.g. Chapter 9). This is an issue that affects all countries, rich and poor alike – according to Christian Aid, poor countries lose an estimated $160 billion per year from tax avoidance by multinational companies.

The problem with multinationals is that they can use tax loopholes such as transfer pricing to pay tax in the country where the tax rate is lower, and as tax rates are largely under the control of individual countries, there is little that one country can do alone. There are international controls over transfer pricing which have been in place for some time. The European Commission, for instance, has had a Joint Transfer Pricing Forum since 2002, and the OECD issued guidelines in 1979 which were updated in 2010.

The greater public awareness and the outcry the issue has created have increased the calls for more controls, both nationally and internationally. In 2013 the Global Alliance for Tax Justice was formed, made up of tax campaigners from many different countries, with the aim of increasing the pressure on international organisations. There is agreement in the OECD and the EU that multinational companies must reveal more information about their activities on a country-by-country basis, which would make action possible. Also, there are moves towards greater transparency; some tax havens (countries where tax rates are low) have agreed to start sharing information about bank accounts.

As well as government action on tax laws and increased transparency at national and international levels, there has been 'naming and shaming' of the companies avoiding tax. This may have several effects on a company. First, the information could encourage customers to boycott the company – there have been such campaigns against Amazon and Google. Second, there will be reputational effects on the companies involved, and this could damage their claims to act with corporate responsibility. Third, as in the case of Starbucks in the UK, it could result in the payment of tax to the government. There has been direct action against these companies around the world, including sit-down protests and occupations which have sometimes caused stores to close. Social media have increased the velocity of these protests. It is difficult to assess the impact of naming and shaming – information on the extent of any boycott or its financial impact is impossible to come by. What is true is that with continued austerity there will be continued public pressure on governments and international organisations and that the campaign will continue.

There is also the possibility of exploitation of less developed countries, and it is debatable whether such footloose industries form a viable basis for economic development. Added to this, MNCs take their decisions in terms of their overall operations rather than with any consideration of their effects on the host economy. There is therefore a loss of economic sovereignty for national governments.

The main problem with multinationals is the lack of control that can be exerted by national governments. As the mini case study shows, there are increased calls from around the world for more transparency, monitoring and control of their activities. In 2011 the OECD updated its *Guidelines for Multinational Enterprises,* which are not legally binding but are promoted by OECD member governments. These seek to provide a balanced framework for international investment that clarifies both the rights and responsibilities of the business community. The publication contains guidelines on business ethics, employment relations, information disclosure and taxation, among other things. Against all this is the fact that without the presence of MNCs, output in host countries would be lower, and there is evidence that on labour market issues the multinationals do not perform badly.

Transnationality

The transnationality index gives a measure of an MNC's involvement abroad by looking at three ratios – foreign assets/total assets, foreign sales/total sales, and foreign employment/total employment. As such it captures the importance of foreign activities in its overall activities. In Table 3.2 Vodafone Group plc has the highest index – this is because in all three ratios it has a high proportion of foreign involvement. Since 1990 the average index of transnationality for the top 100 MNCs has increased from 51 to 54.4 per cent.

These multinationals are huge organisations and their market values often exceed the gross national product (GNP) of many of the countries in which they operate. There are more than 60,000 MNCs around the world and they are estimated to account for a quarter of the world's output. The growth in MNCs is due to relaxation of exchange controls, making it easier to move money between countries, and the improvements in communication, which make it possible to run a worldwide business from one country. The importance of multinationals varies from country to country, as Table 3.3 shows.

Table 3.3 Share of foreign affiliates in manufacturing production and employment, 2010

Country	% share of foreign affiliates in manufacturing production	% share of foreign affiliates in manufacturing employment
Ireland	83	48
Hungary	63	46
Czech Republic	59	41
Great Britain	40	31
Netherlands	41	30
Luxembourg	34	25
Germany	27	16
Finland	24	19
Italy	18	11

Source: Adapted from OECD (2013), Foreign affiliates, in OECD Science, Technology and Industry Scoreboard 2013: Innovation for Growth, OECD Publishing. http://dx.doi.org/10.1787/sti_scoreboard-2013-64-en.

As we can see, foreign affiliates are very important for some countries and not so important for others; in the case of Italy the level of foreign presence is low. For all of the countries, foreign affiliates have a bigger impact on production than employment.

Globalisation and business

Businesses of all sizes need to have an awareness of their international context. As noted above, even if they are not directly involved in international trade, firms will be affected by international forces that lie largely outside their control. Globalisation has meant that the financial crisis of 2008, for instance, affected virtually the whole world. Some of the issues facing businesses are discussed below in brief; many of them are discussed later in the book in more detail.

Markets

Globalisation means that firms are faced with bigger markets for their products. Many of these markets are covered by **regional trade agreements (RTAs)**, which are groupings of countries set up to facilitate world trade. All such agreements have to be notified to the WTO and they can take a variety of forms. The most basic relationship and the most common is a **free trade area (FTA)**, where trade barriers between members are abolished but where each member maintains its own national barriers with non-members. An example of this is the North American Free Trade Agreement (NAFTA). Agreements can also take the form of a **customs union** or common market, where members abolish trade barriers among themselves and adopt a common external tariff which is applied to non-members, as in the EU. All of these agreements increase the size of the marketplace for producers in the member countries and the enlargement of these agreements (the EU, for example) means that markets are increasing all the time.

In addition to these trade agreements, the opening up of the emerging economies (e.g. China and India) to international trade, their high growth rates and the corresponding increase in per capita income mean that there has been a huge increase in the demand for goods and services. The population in India is 1237 million, income per head has doubled since 2000 and GDP growth rate was 7.3 per cent in 2014. The Chinese population stood at 1357 million in 2013, income per head has doubled since 2000 and the growth rate in 2014 was 7.3 per cent. Many believe that China's high growth rate has been fuelled by exports, but recent research shows that demand is more consumption driven than previously thought. It also shows that consumer demand has changed in favour of products that have a higher imported content. This is good news for the rest of the world.

Labour markets

It has been estimated that the global integration of emerging markets has doubled the supply of labour for the global production of goods. The OECD estimates that the percentage of the world population living outside their country of birth doubled between 1985 and 2010. About half of this is between the developed countries, the other half from developing to developed countries. The impact of migration is considered in more detail in the international case study at the end of Part Two ('Contexts').

International labour mobility can be used by businesses for hard-to-fill vacancies. Typically these are at the low-skill, high-risk and low-paid end of the spectrum and at the high-skill, high-paid end. Legal labour migration can be permanent (where migrants settle permanently) or temporary (where migrants eventually return home). The regulations pertaining to these will differ. In addition to international labour migration there are three other alternatives: outsourcing (e.g. the location of US call centres in India involves the movement of jobs rather than people); cross-border commuting (e.g. the commuting of Poles into Western Europe); or the use of Internet trade (where the work could take place anywhere).

For businesses wishing to recruit internationally, there are practical problems including locating the necessary people, language differences and dealing with the rules and regulations involved in employing migrants, such as work permits and visas. These requirements will vary from one country to another.

Other resources

As well as labour, businesses have to source and purchase other resources such as raw materials and energy. Natural resources are differentially distributed around the world and therefore they require international trade to take place if firms are to acquire these inputs. The market for energy, for example, is a global market, with attendant concerns about the environmental impact of the methods used for its generation. The issue of resources is further discussed in Chapter 7.

mini case   Currency crisis in emerging markets

Since the start of the global financial crisis in 2008, the emerging economies have done well out of international capital flows. Low interest rates in the developed nations (designed to stimulate the economies) made international capital look for higher rates of return and the emerging economies with their high growth rates were the recipients. It is estimated that $4 trillion has flowed into the emerging economies since 2008. This is speculative money looking for high rates of return. The tapering of quantitative easing (QE) in the United States in 2014 has made it a more attractive place to invest, and there are worries that the emerging economies may face a sudden stop to these capital flows (see the case study on QE at the end of Chapter 5).

How did this happen? Since 2008 there have been four rounds of QE in the United States where the Federal Reserve Bank pledged to buy up bank debt, Treasury bonds and longer-term bonds. This has the effect of increasing liquidity in the economy – like 'printing money' – in the hope that this will stimulate economic growth. It also has the effect of reducing the rate of interest, which is good for borrowers and business but bad for savers and investors. Speculators want to maximise their rate of return and if the rate of interest in the United States (and other developed nations) is too low, they look to other places to put their money. The emerging nations, including India, Turkey and South Africa, had high growth rates and were the recipients of these speculative flows.

With improvements in the state of the US economy, a tapering of QE was signalled by the Federal Reserve Bank in May 2013 and announced formally in December. This announcement had a significant effect on the emerging countries – there were dramatic falls in their exchange rates (the Turkish lira lost 10 per cent of its value between December 2013 and January 2014 and smaller

falls have occurred in South Africa, Argentina, Brazil, India and Chile). Five countries have been identified as 'fragile' because they have large balance-of-payments deficits that need financing – these are Turkey, India, South Africa, Brazil and Indonesia. Hours before the December announcement, the Turkish central bank increased the benchmark interest rate from 4.5 to 10 per cent. In South Africa the rate of interest went up to 5.5 per cent and in India it was 8 per cent. These interest rate rises attempt to stop the flow of international capital away from the country and to prop up their currencies, but of course have undesirable effects on other economic variables. It reduces the level of demand in the economy; it causes inflation through the higher price of imports; it means that the countries cannot service their external debts, so there may be political repercussions; and it affects their ability to finance their large balance-of-payments deficits. In 2001, in similar circumstances, Argentina defaulted on its external debts and the repercussions of that are still being felt.

It is not clear where this will end; the measures introduced in Turkey to support its currency have not worked and the pressure is still on all of these countries. Of course, this crisis is not only about US monetary policy, there are factors specific to each country, such as political unrest in Turkey and the annexation of the Ukraine by Russia. But many argue that the Federal Reserve is, in effect, the banker to the whole world and should consider other economies and not just the American one when deciding on policy.

This mini case shows how interrelated global markets are and how quickly measures announced in one part of the world can affect others. By the same argument, the repercussions of tapering of QE in the United States will find its way back to the United States. Globalisation is contagious.

Financial markets

Businesses need to raise capital to be able to produce, trade and invest. Although much of this takes place domestically, banks operate internationally and so businesses are exposed to global forces. Never has this been seen more vividly than in the events of recent years.

Globalisation and the small and medium-sized firm

With global shipping and commerce becoming increasingly simple across international platforms (such as eBay, Amazon, White Rabbit Express – Japan; Alibaba/Ali-Express – China) and distribution networks, many small and medium-sized enterprises (SMEs) are able to trade quite easily in the global marketplace, growing international operations is more difficult. They will not have the same access to resources, finance or markets as the large multinationals or even the large national companies which could either trade directly or expand internationally through mergers and takeovers. SMEs, however, have a number of options for international growth, which are outlined briefly below as they are discussed more fully in later chapters of the book.

- A **strategic alliance** is a collaborative agreement between firms to achieve a common aim, in this context a presence in other markets. These agreements can take many forms.
- **Franchising** is an arrangement where one party (the franchiser) sells the rights to another party (the franchisee) to market its product or service. There are different types of franchise relationship (see Chapter 10) and this is a possibility for international expansion. It is an attractive option for companies seeking international expansion without having to undertake substantial direct investments.
- **Licensing** is where a company (the licensor) authorises a company in another country (the licensee) to use its intellectual property in return for certain considerations, usually royalties. Licensors are usually multinationals located in developed countries (see Chapter 10).
- A **joint venture** is usually a jointly owned and independently incorporated business venture involving two or more organisations. This is a popular method of expanding abroad as each party can diversify, with the benefit of the experience of the others involved in the venture and a reduction in the level of risk. Where a large number of members are involved in such an arrangement, this is called a **consortium**.

Synopsis

This chapter has looked at the global context of business. No business is immune from international forces, no matter what it is producing or how small its markets are. The whole concept of globalisation has been discussed, along with the claimed costs and benefits. The elements of globalisation have been outlined together with the impact of globalisation on businesses.

Summary of key points

- There is a difference between globalisation and internationalisation that centres on the role of national boundaries.

- There are costs and benefits associated with the process of globalisation.

- There are three main business-related elements of globalisation – international trade, capital market flows and foreign direct investment.

- Multinational enterprises are very important in the process of globalisation.

- With the arrival of the emerging economies in the global marketplace, some changes in the nature and the process of globalisation are evident.

- Globalisation affects all firms in one way or another – through markets, access to resources or finance.

- There are several different possibilities for small and medium-sized businesses wishing to expand internationally.

case study — Global financial markets – too big to fail

The financial crisis which hit banks across the world in 2008 seems like a long time ago now, although we are still living with its consequences. It took this event to demonstrate the interconnected nature of economies, banks and businesses across the world, and it showed us how vulnerable we in the EU were to changes in the US economy.

The origins of the financial crisis can be boiled down to US banks lending mortgage money to people who would have difficulty repaying. Mortgages are secured on houses, so as long as house prices were going up banks did not lose money. If a house price increased by 3 per cent a year and somebody's home was repossessed by a bank after two years (because the borrower could not meet the mortgage repayments), the bank would have made 6 per cent in the increase in value of the home which they could then resell.

During this time property prices were increasing, and properties were becoming valuable for their investment potential as well as for their function as a home.

It was only when house prices stopped growing, and ultimately began to decline, that this became a problem for banks lending on sub-prime mortgages. This also became a problem for other banks when these loans were mixed up with lots of other loans and bundled together in investment packages called 'mortgage-backed securities', which were then traded with other banks.

These bundles of loans were put together for investors in the form of mortgage-backed securities to minimise risk: loans on a house in the US South East were combined with an apartment in the North West and condo in the South West, and so on. The idea was that it was unlikely for all of these property prices to decline, and all of these debtors to default. Once the true risk of these products was known, property prices fell because their value was defined partly by their investment potential. As banks encountered difficulty they stopped lending, some organisations went out of business if they could not get loans from banks, people lost their jobs and they could not repay their mortgages.

At the start of 2008 these financial investment products were still seen as generating good returns; banks still wanted to invest in them and they were traded internationally. Financial institutions from all over the world had money invested in the US (and other) property markets. But these investments were complicated. By the time investors understood that these products were worth much less than they had thought, it was not clear which properties they had money tied up in. Banks which had lots of money invested in this type of product started to go bust. American banks such as Lehman Brothers went bankrupt, or came very close to doing so. In the UK the bank Northern Rock collapsed and others (Royal Bank Of Scotland, Lloyds Bank) had to be rescued by the government investing in them as other investors rushed to take their money out (a government bailout of private sector debt). All across Europe the effects of the financial crisis were felt: in Cyprus, for instance, rather than the government bailing out the banks, citizens were told that they had to 'bail in', with banks taking some of their savings in order to survive.

It was only as this crisis unfolded that the level of interconnection between banks in different countries really became clear. And although these banks traded internationally, responses to the crisis in the banking sector were being handled by national governments who could not individually deal with these international problems.

Case study questions

1 In hindsight what might have prevented the financial crash?

2 What benefits are there in allowing companies to make international investments?

---

case study   ## FDI flows

FDI is an important element in the process of globalisation and economic integration as it creates long-term links between economies. Unlike capital market flows, it carries a long-term interest in an economy and it is a source of investment funds; it promotes sharing of ideas between countries and can be an important tool in development. Inward flows are all direct investment in a country by non-residents; outflows represent direct investment by residents in other countries. FDI can take the form of the opening of new factories or subsidiaries, or mergers and acquisitions, and as would be expected MNEs are very active in the process. FDI flows have always been mixed and volatile. There have been record flows of FDI and great variability in the performance of countries and groupings of countries. Tables 3.4 and 3.5 show inflows and outflows between 1970 and 2016 for selected groupings of countries.

These tables show great variability between the groupings and within each grouping there is even greater variability.

Table 3.4 FDI inflows for selected groupings of countries 1970–2016 (% of world total)

	1970	1980	1990	2000	2010	2016
Developing	28.4	13.6	16.9	17.2	46.4	37
Transition	–	–	0.04	0.4	4.6	3.9
Developed	71.6	86.4	83.1	82.4	49	59.1
BRICs[*]	5.8	3.7	2.3	5.9	18.9	15.8
EU27	38.9	39.9	46.6	49.9	26.1	32.3
G8	50.4	68.7	55.7	54.9	29.2	45.5

[*]Brazil, Russia, India and China.
Source: Adapted from *unctadstat.unctad.org*

Table 3.5 FDI outflows for selected groupings of countries 1970–2016 (% of world total)

	1970	1980	1990	2000	2010	2016
Developing	0.3	5.2	5.4	7.7	27.0	26.4
Transition	–	–	–	0.3	3.6	1.7
Developed	99.7	94.8	94.6	92.0	69.4	71.9
EU27	–	43.9	54.2	67.9	33.0	32.4
G8	85.6	81.0	71.8	58.4	47.9	44.1

Source: Adapted from *unctadstat.unctad.org*

What is most interesting about Table 3.4 are the differences in performance between the groupings. Since the year 2000, FDI inflows fell for the EU relative to the rest of the world, while there was growth for developing countries. The main reasons for this were the continuing effects of the recession and the expansion of the EU that occurred in 2004. Between 2000 and 2010 the financial crash slowed both inward and outward investment from developed counties, while developing and BRICS nations continued to see inward and outward investment. Things change very quickly in such an interrelated world.

Case study questions

1 Why are FDI flows cyclical in nature?

2 How might a country make itself more attractive to inward FDI?

Review and discussion questions

1 What role does the advancement of ICT have in the process of globalisation?

2 What are the arguments for and against foreign ownership of strategic industries such as energy?

3 How are multinationals changing?

4 For a business considering expansion into another country, what methods of expansion are available? What are the advantages and disadvantages of each?

5 What has been the impact of the financial crisis in 2008 on the process of globalisation?

Assignments

1 You work in a local office of a multinational enterprise and your line manager has been invited to take part in a discussion arranged by the local newspaper on the pros and cons of globalisation. Prepare a briefing paper outlining the arguments for your line manager.

2 You have been asked to give a presentation on regional trade agreements to students of business at a local college. Research which regional trade agreements your country is a member of and what effects membership has on labour mobility. Prepare PowerPoint slides together with notes to accompany each slide.

Further reading

Daniels, J. D., Radebaugh, L. and Sullivan, D., *International Business: Environments and Operations,* 15th edition, Prentice Hall, 2014.

Griffiths, A. and Wall, S., *Applied Economics,* 12th edition, Financial Times/Prentice Hall, 2011.

Worthington, I., Britton, C. and Rees, A., *Business Economics: Blending Theory and Practice,* 2nd edition, Financial Times/Prentice Hall, 2005.

web link

Web links and further questions are available on the website at:
www.pearsoned.co.uk/worthington

The global car industry and the changing business environment

All businesses are affected by external factors, many of which lie outside their direct control. While some of these influences concern developments within an organisation's operational environment (e.g. loss of a supplier), others relate to changes of a more general or contextual kind, which can affect a wide variety of businesses, sometimes in different ways (e.g. fluctuations in the exchange rate). As the opening chapter of this book has illustrated, these general/contextual variables include political, economic, socio-cultural, technological, legal and ethical influences that can occur at all spatial levels from the local to the global. For organisations operating in the international/global marketplace, developments at both the micro- and macroenvironmental levels can represent a significant challenge (or opportunity) and can have a substantial influence on the strategic decision-making process.

To illustrate how organisations can be affected by some of the broader contextual changes discussed in Part Two, we examine the car industry, which comprises many well-known international brands, including Ford, Toyota, General Motors, Chrysler, Honda, Renault, Groupe PSA, Fiat, Nissan, BMW and Volkswagen. As the mini case in Chapter 1 demonstrates, even some of the world's largest and most powerful businesses in this industry have faced variable trading conditions over recent years because of developments in their external environment, and many have been forced to respond in a variety of ways.

What have been some of the major challenges and how have they affected the key players?

Rises in oil and other commodity prices

A combination of increased demand (e.g. because of growth in China and India) and tight, limited supply has meant that oil and other commodity prices (e.g. steel) have fluctuated dramatically and this has affected production costs in the industry. As these price changes also affect consumers, sales of vehicles in some countries have tended to decline and many customers are switching to more economical/fuel-efficient models when petrol prices increase.

Economic fluctuations

The falling sales of vehicles being experienced in some parts of the world have not been helped by a general downturn in many economies as a result of the impact of the global financial crisis. While some countries were in recession, governments announced 'scrape' schemes where the government would subsidise some of the price of a new car if customers traded in their old ones. This meant that customers were encouraged to buy cars, funding jobs in car sales and manufacture. From the government's perspective, older, dirtier cars were taken out of use and replaced with more efficient cars. This was to avoid a trend where consumers have tended to defer spending on larger, more expensive items such as cars in times of economic uncertainty or downturn. Schemes like this have affected both the market for new vehicles and the second-hand market in many parts of the world.

Emerging markets

While many economies are facing difficult circumstances, growth in some countries (e.g. China, India, Brazil, Russia) has created an opportunity for car producers to exploit new and expanding markets. By the same token, this growth is encouraging newer companies to come into the marketplace and to increase the possibility of future competition in the traditional areas of the international car market (e.g. Europe and the United States).

Environmental issues

The growing threat of climate change has led to the environmental impact of cars and other vehicles becoming a prime concern for both governments (see below) and consumers. As far as the latter are concerned, there has been a slight shift in consumer taste away from high-polluting, gas-guzzling models (e.g. SUVs, 4x4s, pick-ups) towards more fuel-efficient vehicles that have a smaller environmental impact. Rising oil prices have reinforced this trend towards smaller cars. There has also been increased investment in electric vehicles and hybrids.

Changes in the market

There has also been a dramatic change in how people own and use cars. Ten years ago most people bought cars and paid for them by taking out a loan, sometimes with the car retailer. After the end of that loan repayment they owned the car and could use it for years to come, or sold it in part-exchange for money off a new one. Now the majority of people lease cars, where they pay an initial deposit and an amount every month for use of the car. At the end of the lease period they have the option of purchasing the car at its used value or returning it and starting a new lease. This has meant that car manufactures can sell more new cars, and used car retailers have a shrinking market.

Legislative/policy developments

Concerns over cars' contribution to climate change have resulted in governmental and intergovernmental negotiations over future legislation and/or targets regarding vehicle CO_2 emissions. In the EU, for example, member states have set obligatory targets for vehicle emissions for the period up to 2020. Some governments have set goals to prevent new petrol and diesel cars being registered after a set dates; in the UK this is 2030. (See Chapter 17 on how governments can affect markets.)

Currency fluctuations

For firms involved in international trade, exchange rate fluctuations/volatility can sometimes be problematical (see Chapter 16). Such fluctuations in the values of the dollar, yen and euro in recent years have had a direct impact on the major car producers in the United States, Japan and Europe, making prices sometimes more and sometimes less competitive. As oil is also priced in dollars, a fluctuation in the dollar exchange rate has also impacted on the industry. Brexit has had a dramatic affect of reducing the value of the pound between 2016 and the end of 2017, making cars seem more expensive in the UK.

Brexit

One of the key factors in negotiations over trade after Brexit has been the need for Europe to export goods to the UK and the default standards for import and export set out by the World Trade Organization (WTO); if the UK does not negotiate a deal with Europe around trade, import and export between the two would revert to WTO standards. The WTO tariffs for trade on goods such as cars are likely to increase the price of a car imported to the UK from, say, Germany by 2 to 3%. The UK economy is based on services, particularly in the financial sector. There is no framework under the WTO for trading services, meaning a separate deal will have to be reached. This is one of the factors affecting the value of the pound in a time of uncertainty.

How should the major players respond/ how have the major players responded?

As the analysis above illustrates, the international car industry has faced significant changes in the external environment over recent years. While some of these changes have generated opportunities for the major players, many have been particularly challenging and have caused vehicle manufacturers to look at both the supply side (e.g. costs) and the demand side (e.g. market development) of their businesses. Some of the key questions being faced by the major brands are:

- How can costs be reduced (e.g. should the workforce be reduced)?
- What product mix should be offered to consumers (e.g. should some of the less fuel-efficient models be phased out)?
- What markets should be targeted (e.g. should the focus shift towards the emerging markets)?
- How should the new markets be accessed (e.g. are cross-national collaborations a better solution than direct manufacturing)? (See the mini case on joint ventures in Chapter 10).
- Where should production take place (e.g. can costs be reduced and/or new markets be exploited more effectively by manufacturing cars in the emerging countries)?
- How can the new, emerging competitors be challenged (e.g. should new models be developed)?

- How can legislative requirements be met (e.g. how and where should the industry lobby against tougher emission standards)?

- Where should future investment take place (e.g. as the UK withdraws from the EU, should production facilities be relocated to mainland Europe)?

For the major international players in the car industry, these are some of the important strategic issues they are facing and a number of key trends have emerged. For example, many car producers are looking towards Asia as a suitable place for manufacture and/or joint venture, with India and China potentially becoming global hubs for small-car production, thanks to lower costs and the skills of the workforce. Added to this, the big players are being forced towards global product development (with future models likely to be based on a common platform and sold on a global basis) and/or some form of integration (e.g. Chrysler's merger with Fiat and the decision by Daimler, Renault and Nissan to work together in certain areas, particularly technology sharing). Political uncertainties (e.g. the UK's relationship with the EU) are also likely to delay future investment decisions.

Part Two

CONTEXTS

As is becoming apparent, the business environment is very complex. It is made up of many different factors which combine in expected and unexpected ways to alter the way that companies do business. In attempting to unpick some factors that influence organisations there are two commonly used acronyms: PEST (Political, Economic, Social and Technological) and PESTLE (as before, but including Legal and Environmental). In Chapters 4–9 we will examine PESTLE factors and explore what events, changes and phenomena might be considered within each element of the business environment. This form of analysis is the most common type of environmental scanning (sometimes known as 'horizon scanning') where an organisation tries to identify what factors will affect it and make changes to ensure it remains successful. In practice it does not necessarily matter whether some factors are identified under one heading or another, so long as they are identified. In this book we have tried to identify clear differences between them, but the real business environment might not be so clear cut.

4

The political environment

Ian Worthington

Politics is a universal activity which affects the business world in a variety of ways. Understanding political systems, institutions and processes provides a greater insight into business decisions and into the complexities of the business environment. Given the increasing globalisation of markets, this environment has an international as well as a domestic element and the two are closely interrelated. Appreciating some of the key aspects of this environment and its impact on business organisations is vital for students of business and managers alike.

Learning outcomes

Having read this chapter you should be able to:

- explain the political context within which business operates
- demonstrate the relevance of political values to the organisation of business activity
- identify and discuss key political institutions and processes at a variety of spatial levels
- illustrate how business organisations can influence, as well as be influenced by, the political environment

Key terms

Authoritarian
Backbench MPs
Bureaucrats
Cabinet
Checks and balances
Civil servants
Coalition government
Constitution
Council of Ministers
Decisions
Democracy
Direct (or pure) democracy
Directives
Directorates-General
Electoral system
European Commission
European Council
European Court of Justice
European Parliament
Federal system of government

First-past-the-post system
Government
Government departments
House of Commons
House of Lords
Judiciary
Legislature
Lobbies
Manifesto
MEPs
Ministers
MPs
Parliament
Parliamentary system of government
Plebiscites
Political accountability
Political executive
Political parties
Politics

Presidential system of government
Pressure groups
Prime Minister
Professional lobbyist
Proportional representation
Qualified majority vote (qmv)
Recommendations and opinions
Referendums
Regulations
Representative system of government
Secretary of State
Separation of powers
Sovereignty
Supreme Court
The Council of the European Union
Unitary system of government

Introduction

The European Union is a group of nations in Western Europe. Originally Belgium, France, Italy, Luxembourg, the Netherlands and West Germany agreed the Treaty of Rome in 1957 to allow the free movement of people, goods and money between their countries (the European Economic Community, or EEC) as a way of encouraging economic growth and prosperity within a 'common market'. Since that time the EU has grown to include 28 states of varying economic development with different industries, economic polices and labour markets. Some member states agreed to share a common currency, the euro, coming into effect in 1999 for financial purposes, with the hard currency (coins and notes) available in 2002. Members of the EU pay some fees to the EU and allow for some multinational laws to be made by groups of international politicians (elected from member states); this allows alignment of things like measurements and standards so that a tonne of steel from a German company is the same as a tonne of steel purchased from a Polish company. Some states such as Norway are not a part of the EU, but they pay for access to the common market and allow the free movement of people and goods to and from the EU.

The history of Europe has (almost) always been one of expansion, with more and more countries joining. Individual nations see this as advantageous where businesses in their country can then export and import at lower cost, and people can move to and from their country to find work, partially solving problems of unemployment and skills shortages. In the UK there has been a large number of people moving to the country to find work because it is comparatively higher paid than the same work in some Eastern European countries; some workers are then able to send money home. In addition some of the fees paid from the UK to Europe are repaid, while some are distributed to other less well-off member states which are in need of more development. These issues of jobs, law making and economics have led to some people arguing that we should leave the EU. In 2016 there was a referendum (a vote by all the eligible citizens of a nation) which determined that we should leave, though the details have yet to be worked out and are likely to take years before the UK eventually exits. This may involve the unravelling of many pieces of European legislation which are intertwined with our own national laws; some laws will need to be adopted into UK law, while others may need replacing completely.

What this simple example reminds us is that business activity takes place not only within but also across state boundaries and frequently involves governments, whether directly or indirectly, in shaping the business environment. Consequently the political and economic arrangements within the state in which a business is located and/or with which it is trading can have a fundamental impact on its operations – even to the extent of determining whether it is willing or, in some cases, able to trade at all. It is this politico-economic context within which businesses function and the philosophical foundations on which it is based that are the focus of this and the following chapter.

As a prelude to a detailed analysis of the political environment, it is necessary to make a number of general observations regarding political change and uncertainty and the impact on business activity. First, the nature of a country's political system – including its governmental institutions – tends to reflect certain underlying social values and philosophies which help to determine how decisions are made, including decisions about the allocation of resources. Thus, while governments may come and go, the values on which their decisions are based tend to be more enduring and as a result disputes normally centre around 'means' (e.g. sources of revenue) rather than 'ends' (e.g. controlling inflation). While this gives a certain degree of stability to the business environment, this stability cannot be taken for granted, as events in Eastern Europe and the Middle East have readily demonstrated. In short, the political environment of business is a dynamic environment, containing elements of both continuity and change, and students and practitioners of business alike need to be constantly aware of developments in this area if they are to gain a greater insight into the background of business decision-making.

Second, changes in the political environment also emanate from a country's institutional arrangements. The tendency in democratic states, for example, to have regular elections, competing political parties offering alternative policies and a system of pressure groups helps to generate a degree of discontinuity, which renders predictions about the future more uncertain. For a business, such uncertainty can create not only opportunities but also a degree of risk which will often be an important influence on its decisions. Moreover, given that perceptions of such risks (or opportunities) are also normally reflected in the attitudes and behaviour of a country's financial and other markets, this represents a further variable that at times can be critical for an organisation's future prospects. For many businesses, taking steps to maximise opportunities (or to minimise risk) may ultimately make the difference between short-term failure and long-term survival.

Third, it is important to emphasise that political influences are not restricted to national boundaries – a point emphasised by the opening paragraphs in this chapter and by the increasing importance of international and supranational groupings such as the G8 nations, the EU and the World Trade Organization, all of which are discussed below. These external politico-economic influences form part of the environment in which a country's governmental institutions take decisions, and their impact on domestic policy and on business activity can often be fundamental. No discussion of the business environment would be complete without an analysis of their role and impact, particularly in shaping international political and economic relationships.

Fourth, the precise impact of political factors on a business tends to vary to some degree according to the type of organisation involved. Multinational corporations – operating on a global scale – will be more concerned with questions such as the stability of overseas political regimes than will the small local firm operating in a localised market, where the primary concern will be with local market conditions. That said, there will undoubtedly be occasions when even locally based enterprises will be affected either directly or indirectly by political developments in other parts of the globe – as in the case of an interruption in supplies or the cancellation of a foreign order in which a small business is involved as a subcontractor. In short, while some broad generalisations can be made about the impact of global (or domestic) political developments on an individual organisation, each case is to some extent unique in both space and time, and observers of the business scene need to be cautious and open-minded in their analysis if they are to avoid the twin dangers of oversimplification and empiricism.

Finally, it needs to be recognised that businesses are not merely reactive to changes in the political environment, but can also help to shape the political context in which they operate and can influence government decision-makers, often in a way that is beneficial to their own perceived needs. One of the hallmarks of **democracy** is the right of individuals and groups to seek to influence government, and businesses – both individually and collectively – have been active in this sphere for centuries. It would be a mistake to underestimate their impact on government policy or on the shaping of values in the established capitalist nations of Western Europe and elsewhere.

Political systems

The nature of political activity

All social situations at certain times require decisions to be made between alternative courses of action. Parents may disagree with their offspring about the kind of clothes they wear or how late they stay out at night or how long they grow their hair. Students may challenge lecturers about a particular perspective on an issue or when they should submit a piece of work. The members of the board of directors of a company may have different views about future investment or diversification or the location of a new factory. In all these cases, some solution needs to be found, even if the eventual decision is to do nothing. It is the processes involved in arriving at a solution to a problem, where a conflict of opinion occurs, that are the very essence of political activity.

Politics, in short, is concerned with those processes that help to determine how conflicts are contained, modified, postponed or settled, and as such can be seen as a universal social activity. Hence, individuals often talk of 'office politics', the 'politics of the boardroom' or the 'mediating role' played by a parent in the event of a family dispute (also sometimes known as 'small-p politics'). For most individuals, however, the term 'politics' tends to be associated with activities at state level, where the resolution of conflict often involves large numbers of people and may even involve individuals in other states (sometimes 'big-P Politics'). Political activity at this level is clearly qualitatively different from the other social situations mentioned, and given the scale and complexity of the modern state, the problems requiring solutions can often be acute and chronic. Solving those problems tends to be seen, at least in part, as the function of government.

Government as a process is concerned with the pursuit and exercise of power – the power to make decisions which affect the lives of substantial numbers of people, be it at local, regional, national or even international level. Government may also refer to the institutions through which power tends to be formally and legitimately exercised, whether they be cabinets, parliaments, councils, committees or congresses. Whereas the pursuit and exercise of power tends to be an enduring feature of any society, governments are normally transitory, comprising those individuals and/or groups who, at a particular time, have the responsibility for controlling the state, including making laws for 'the good of society'. How governments exercise their power and the ideological foundations on which this is based helps to indicate the nature of the political system and its likely approaches to the resolution of conflicts.

Authoritarian political systems

Broadly speaking, political systems can be seen to range across two extremes, on the one hand authoritarian and on the other democratic. In an **authoritarian** political system the disposition is to settle conflicts through the enforcement of rules, regulations and orders by an established authority. This authority may be an individual (e.g. a monarch or other powerful individual) or a group of individuals (e.g. a political party or military junta) which may have assumed political power in a variety of ways (e.g. by birth, election or coup). Once in power, the individual or group will tend to act so as to limit the degree of participation by others in the process of decision-making, even to the extent of monopolising the process altogether and permitting no opposition to occur. Where this is the case, a society is often described as being 'totalitarian' and is perhaps best historically

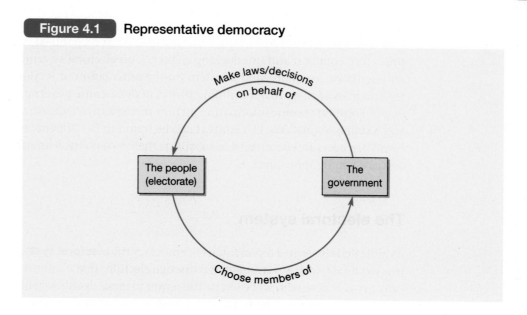

Figure 4.1   Representative democracy

exemplified by Nazi Germany and Stalinist Russia; in these cases forces such as the police and military are crucial in maintaining control.

Democratic political systems

In contrast, in a democratic political system, the assumption is that as far as possible conflicts should be resolved by rational discussions between the various parties concerned, with the final solution being accepted voluntarily by all participants, even if they disagree. At one extreme, such consultation may involve all individuals, who have – in theory at least – equal influence over the final outcome (e.g. as in referendums or plebiscites).

Given the scale and complexity of modern states, however, such examples of direct (or pure) democracy tend to be rare and it is invariably the case that the democratic solution to conflict resolution is achieved 'indirectly' through a system of political representation and responsibility. Under such a system, the wishes and views of individuals are said to be represented in an established authority (e.g. a government) that has normally been chosen by the people and is accountable (responsible) to them at regular intervals through a variety of mechanisms, including regular and free elections (see Figure 4.1). Implicit in this, of course, is the requirement that individuals are able to change this authority and select another individual or group to represent them. Monopolisation of political power by any one individual or group can only occur, therefore, with the expressed consent of the people.

Government in democratic states

Democratic institutions and processes

Democracy means far more than just popular government or a system of regular elections; the democratic approach to government implies the existence of a complex array of institutions and processes through which the wishes of the people are articulated and carried out. While the specific institutional arrangements tend to vary between states, countries that are held to be democratic invariably have a political system which comprises four common and interlocking elements: an electoral system; a party system; a representative assembly; and a system for the articulation of sectional interests. The generic roles of these major building blocks of democratic government are discussed below. Location-specific information on how the system operates in a national (i.e. UK) and a supranational (i.e. EU) context can be found in the appendices to this chapter. Non-UK readers are encouraged to substitute their own political arrangements for those described in the appendices.

The electoral system

As indicated above, in a representative democracy the **electoral system** links the people (the electorate) with government; it is through elections that a country's citizens periodically get to choose who will exercise the power to make decisions which will ultimately shape the lives of individuals. Elections, in short, are a vital ingredient of a **representative system of government**. That said, the fact that elections exist in a particular country is not a sufficient guarantee that it is democratic in the accepted sense of the word.

In order to operate in a way that is normally regarded as democratic, a country's electoral system would need to exhibit a number of features which suggest that the wishes of individual citizens – as expressed through the ballot box – are reasonably reflected in the choice of government. Such features would include:

- a system of regular elections (e.g. every four to five years) based on universal adult suffrage (all adults have equal rights to vote);
- basic freedoms of speech, movement, assembly, etc.;
- freedom from coercion and the absence of illegal electoral practices;
- a secret ballot;
- free media.

Where conditions such as these are absent or are not fully operational, there will always be a suspicion that the electoral outcome may not be a true reflection of the wishes of the people. The act of voting, in other words, needs to be accompanied by a set of legal prescriptions that provides some kind of guarantee that an election to choose part, if not all, of the government is both free and fair.

To be democratic the electoral system must not only be transparent, but also ensure that the wishes of the majority – as expressed through the number of votes cast – are reflected in the final result. In a **first-past-the-post system** (e.g. in most current UK elections) a simple majority is sufficient to ensure victory; as a consequence some winning candidates may be elected with fewer than half of the votes cast. Where a system of **proportional representation** operates (e.g. in many other European countries) a redistribution of votes occurs when there is no outright winner, resulting in a final decision that can be said to represent more closely the wishes of the whole electorate. While the intricacies of different electoral systems are beyond the scope of this book, it is worth observing that the voting system a country uses can have important ramifications for the government elected to office. On the whole, a plurality or first-past-the-post system of voting usually – though not inevitably (e.g. the 2010 election in the UK) – results in majority government, with a single party dominating the organs of decision-making and able to pursue its legislative programme relatively free from constraint by the losing side(s). In contrast, where a proportional representation system is used, the result is often a **coalition government** made up of different parties, some of which may hold significantly or even radically different views from the largest party within the coalition. In effect, coalition government is predominantly a matter of negotiation, accommodation and compromise, an exercise in consensus building and persuasion, as commonly found in most types of organisational setting, including the business world.

The party system

While it is possible to have democratic government in a one-party state, democracy is normally taken to imply that citizens get to choose between alternative candidates when casting their vote at an election. Invariably such candidates tend to represent different **political parties** and to this extent a vote for a specific candidate can be said to equate to a vote for the party that he or she represents and which is ultimately hoping to form the government.

The existence of political parties, which compete for office at election time, is clearly a convenient – if sometimes questionable – means of organising a system of representative democracy; hence the universality of party systems in democratic states and the relative lack of candidates standing with no party tag at governmental elections at all spatial levels. Parties not only choose most of the candidates who compete in these elections, but usually also support and sustain them (e.g. financially) before, during and after the election campaign and help to organise a system of (largely unpaid) volunteers to work to get them elected, as well as providing candidates with a platform of policies on which to stand for office. Whereas some of these activities tend to be the responsibility of the party at national level, others are undertaken at a regional and/or local level, often in the constituency (i.e. geographical area) that a candidate hopes to represent once elected. Since questions of organisation, policy-making and finance are central to the operation and success of a political party in modern democratic states, party structures have tended to become complex, bureaucratic, multi-layered and increasingly professionalised. As in other types of organisational framework, they also provide an arena in which a substantial degree of in-fighting occurs between individuals of different temperaments, views and ambitions who are seeking to push the party in a particular direction.

From the electors' point of view, one of the primary benefits of the party system is that it provides a means of selecting political leaders and the kind of policies they are likely to pursue if the party achieves political office. Describing candidates by a party label (e.g. Democratic, Republican, Socialist, Conservative, Liberal, etc.) allows voters to choose those candidates whose views most closely represent their own, given that parties normally have an identifiable policy stance and produce some form of statement (or **manifesto**) outlining their policy preferences during an election campaign. Thus, while an individual elector is unlikely to agree with every single policy or proposed piece of legislation that a party puts forward in its attempts to gain office, he or she is at least able to express a preference between alternative approaches to government at the ballot box. To that extent it can be argued that there is likely to be a degree of congruence between the legislative programme of the party democratically elected to form the government and the wishes of the people who elected it, albeit that in some cases the government may have received less than 50 per cent of the popular vote.

It is worth remembering that party labels are not always a good guide to the policy or legislative preferences of individual candidates, since someone described as a 'Democrat' or 'Liberal' in one part of a country may hold radically different views on a range of issues from others of the same title elected to constituencies in other areas ('Social Democratic' parties across Europe tend to have increasingly liberal ideals). If anything, identifying election candidates in party political terms gives voters a broad indication of the underlying values and beliefs to which an individual subscribes: parties in practice are always destined to be (sometimes fragile) coalitions of groups and individuals representing a range of opinions and preferences under a party banner.

A representative assembly

As previously indicated, one of the key features of democratic government is the existence of a representative decision-making body, a group of individuals chosen by a country's citizens to help make important decisions on their behalf. In the same way that shareholders in a public company elect directors to guide the organisation and to represent their interest, voters at election time choose individuals they wish to represent them in government in the various organs of decision-making and policy implementation (see below). While not everyone chosen by the electorate becomes part of the small group of key decision-makers (the government or **political executive**), all normally have some kind of role to play in the decision-making process and usually get an opportunity to scrutinise policy and legislative proposals put forward by the governing element and to vote upon them. The fact that the electorate periodically has the opportunity to express its opinion on the performance of the incumbent decision-makers – and where necessary to replace them – provides for a degree of **political accountability**, a central tenet of a democratic system of government.

As more than two centuries of political theory have demonstrated, the concept of representation can have at least two meanings: decision-makers may represent the views of their constituents in the literal sense that they articulate them in or to government; or they may simply represent them in so far as they have been elected by a majority (simple or otherwise) of voters to be the representative of a geographical area. In practice, both these interpretations of representation can be seen to operate at different times, according to the predispositions of individual decision-makers and the influences emanating from the prevailing political culture in a country, region or area. For example, in a system of government where national political parties are relatively weak and where an individual's success in elections depends very much on supporting policies that are consistent with those of significant elements in one's electorate (e.g. in the United States), representation tends to be seen in the more literal sense of supporting local views and preferences. In contrast, where there is a strong party system and where individuals are held to be elected on the basis of party affiliation (e.g. the UK), elected representatives are generally expected to be loyal to the party in a policy sense, even if on occasion this results in a conflict with the views of the majority of one's constituents.

In modern democratic states the model of representative decision-making usually operates at all spatial levels. In Europe, for example, voters not only elect their own national governments (usually members of parliament) but also choose decision-makers at a local and/or regional level (mayors and councillors) and many European citizens are also able to vote in elections for pan-European institutions (i.e. for the European Parliament – see

Appendix 4.3). One of the consequences of this arrangement is that sometimes the party (or parties) elected to office at national level may be different from that (or those) in power locally, regionally and/or supranationally. Where this occurs, clashes between decision-makers representing different geographical areas tend to be inevitable and can give rise to problems of decision-making and policy implementation, thus potentially disrupting the programme on which a government has been elected to office.

In this context a useful distinction can be drawn between a **federal** and a **unitary system of government**. In the former, **sovereignty** (i.e. the legitimate power to make decisions) is divided between two or more levels of government (e.g. supranational, national and local/regional), each with independent powers that are usually laid down in a written constitution which is interpreted by the courts. Thus, in the United States, education is in the hands of the elected government at state (i.e. subnational) level, while defence and foreign affairs are federal (i.e. national) governmental responsibilities. In Germany, the federal government similarly has exclusive jurisdiction over foreign and defence policy and environmental protection, while the Länder (states) control such areas as education and the police.

In contrast, under a unitary system ultimate authority rests with the national government and any powers granted to subnational levels by the central sovereign authority can ultimately be rescinded, including the right of government at subnational level to exist. Under such an arrangement – particularly where it is written down in the form of a **constitution** – government at national level clearly holds the whip hand and would normally expect its view to prevail where a dispute over an issue or policy occurs between it and a subnational authority. That said, decision-makers in democratic states at all levels and under different governmental systems have, on the whole, a tendency to settle such conflicts through negotiation, bargaining and compromise rather than by exerting their power and authority, although this might be used on occasions. This predisposition goes some way to explaining why, in democratic systems of government, the policies and legislative programmes of elected governments are much more likely to be incremental than they are to be radical.

mini case Brought to book

Politicians can have a significant impact on business activity at both the macro and micro levels. In addition to making decisions on how the economy should be managed overall, elected representatives can make or propose changes to regulations and legislation which affect how businesses operate, what they can and cannot do, and how they treat their employees, customers, suppliers, and so on.

An illustration of how the political environment can potentially shape a firm's operations can be seen in the decision made by French MPs in October 2013 to support a bill to curb the discounting power of the globally influential company Amazon. Concerned that small, independent bookstores were facing unfair competition from the US giant, MPs from across all parties voted for a measure aimed at preventing Amazon from combining free delivery with 5 per cent discounts on books. Since 1981, France has had a law that establishes fixed book prices so that customers effectively pay the same for a book however or from wherever it is purchased, with extensive discounting banned. French legislators believe that small bookstores should be treated as a 'cultural exception' and should, if necessary, be protected from the kind of experiences suffered by UK independent book retailers when fixed prices were abandoned back in the 1990s.

A system for articulating sectional interests

Elections and a party system provide one way in which the views of an individual can be represented in government; an alternative is via the activity of **pressure groups**. Like competing political parties, the existence of pressure groups is usually regarded as an important indicator of a democratic system of government. For many citizens in democratic countries, joining such a group is seen as a much more effective way of influencing government than through the party system.

Whereas political parties seek influence by formally contesting political office, pressure groups seek to influence government in other ways, although this distinction is increasingly becoming blurred. In essence, pressure groups (or **lobbying groups**) are collections of like-minded people who have voluntarily joined together to try to influence government thinking and behaviour and to represent the interests of their members. Nowadays, many of these groups are highly organised and are powerful bodies, supported by substantial funding and formidable research facilities. Such groups (frequently referred to as non-governmental or civic society organisations) provide a vehicle through which a collective and non-party political view can be articulated in decision-making circles; as such they can be said to operate as a kind of safety valve within a democratic system of government.

Traditionally in pressure group literature, a distinction tends to be drawn between groups which represent 'somebody' and those that represent 'something'. The former are usually referred to as 'interest groups' or 'protective groups' and would include groups representing a particular section of the community, such as trade unions or professional associations. The latter tend to be known as 'cause groups' or 'issue groups', as exemplified by Greenpeace, Amnesty International, Second Amendment groups (those that campaign for the right to bear arms in the United States) and various animal rights groups. In practice, of course, it is often difficult to make such a clear-cut distinction, given that some interest groups such as trade unions often associate themselves with particular causes and may campaign vigorously alongside other groups in support of or against the issue concerned.

> **web link** Most large pressure groups have websites offering useful information. Greenpeace, for example, can be accessed at *www.greenpeace.org*

From a governmental point of view the existence of structures for articulating sectional interests is seen as an aid to efficient and representative decision-making. Pressure groups not only provide government with detailed information on specific areas of everyday activity without which rational decision-making would be difficult, but also fulfil a number of other important functions in a democratic system. These would include:

● helping to defend minority interests;
● assisting in the implementation of government policy and legislation;
● providing for continuity in communication and consultation between the governors and the governed between elections.

The successful introduction of reforms in a country's health service, for example, is dependent upon support from the various arms of the medical profession and from organisations representing the different interests of health service workers and patients.

Similarly, the effectiveness of government economic policies, and their subsequent impact on the business community, will be conditioned at least in part by the reactions of groups representing large employers, small and medium enterprises, workers, financial interests, etc., as well as by individual entrepreneurs and consumers.

This relative interdependence between government and pressure groups under a democratic system is exemplified by the practice of prior consultation; this is the arrangement whereby the elected government actively seeks the views of interested parties during the policy and/or legislative process. Such consultation may be 'formal' (e.g. where a group has representation on an advisory or executive body or where it is invited to offer its views on a proposal) or 'informal' (e.g. off-the-record meetings between representatives of the group and the government) or a mixture of the two; it may also involve a group in hiring the services of a **professional lobbyist** – often a former politician or bureaucrat familiar with the structure of decision-making in government and with access to key decision-makers (see the case study at the end of this chapter). Groups that are regularly consulted and whose opinion is readily sought by government may acquire 'insider status' and may even be incorporated into the formal decision-making process – prizes that are highly valued since they imply that the group has a legitimate right to be consulted by government prior to deciding on a particular course of action or inaction. In comparison, 'outsider groups' often find it difficult to make their voice heard in decision-making circles and for this reason may be forced to resort to different forms of direct action in order to publicise their views in the wider community in the hope of gaining influence through public sympathy and support.

As this discussion of 'insider' and 'outsider' groups illustrates, pressure groups can use a variety of methods to attract support for their cause or to protect and promote the interests of their members. These range from direct lobbying of government to marches, strikes, disruption and other forms of demonstrative action designed to attract media and hence public attention – although frequently such action can have an adverse effect. In addition, some of the larger and better resourced groups may employ experts to advise on policy issues and/or establish their own research facilities to provide information to strengthen their case (e.g. Greenpeace).

What method(s) a group employs and where it seeks to bring its influence to bear tends to vary from issue to issue and group to group, and generally reflects not only differences in group status and resources but also the structure of decision-making within the policy community concerned. In the United States, for instance, direct lobbying of Congressmen/women is a common tactic used by pressure groups, given the relative weakness of the party system and the tendency for an individual's electoral fortunes to be tied up with the views of key groups in the constituency. In the UK, the pressures of party discipline, the domination of the executive branch of government and the influence of senior civil servants tend to make direct appeals to key actors in government a more effective method of achieving political influence than operating at constituency level.

As a final comment it is worth recalling that decisions in a democracy may be made locally, nationally, supranationally or internationally and often require cooperation between different levels of government and/or between different agencies and arms of government at both the formulation and the implementation stages. Accordingly, pressure groups are increasingly to be found operating at the interface between the institutions of government and across the whole range of spatial levels from the local to the global. Given the large number of pressure points where vested interests can bring their influence to bear, it tends to be easier for a group to prevent or limit government action than to persuade decision-makers to change the direction of policy. To this extent policy formulation and implementation in democratic states is perhaps best portrayed as the 'art of the possible' rather than the 'science of the desirable'.

The three branches or functions of government

In a broad sense the process of governing involves three major activities: making decisions; putting them into effect; and adjudicating over them in the event of dispute or non-compliance. Each of these functions or branches of government, as they operate at a national level, is discussed in turn below. A similar form of analysis could, if necessary, be applied at other spatial levels.

The legislative function

Governing, as we have seen, is about making decisions which affect the lives of large numbers of people. Some of these decisions require new laws or changes to existing laws to bring them into effect so that the individuals and/or groups to whom they apply become aware of the government's wishes and requirements. In a democratic system of government this formal power to make the law (i.e. to legislate) is vested in a legislative body (the **legislature**) which is elected either wholly or partly by the people. As indicated above, this process of choosing a representative decision-making body by popular election is a central feature of the democratic approach to government.

Leaving aside for one moment the relative power of the legislative and executive branches of government, it is possible to identify a number of common features that apply to legislatures and the legislative function in most, if not all, democratic states. These include the following:

A *bicameral legislature*: that is, a legislature with two chambers, an upper house and a lower house, each with specific powers and roles in the legislative process. In most countries each chamber comprises representatives chosen by a separate electoral process and hence may be dominated by the same party or different parties or by no single party, depending on the electoral outcome. For a legislative proposal to be accepted, the consent of both chambers is normally required. This is one of the many **checks and balances** normally found in democratic systems of government (see below).

A *multi-stage legislative process,* involving the drafting of a legislative proposal, its discussion and consideration, and where necessary amendment, further debate and consideration and ultimate acceptance or rejection by either or both legislative chambers. Debates on the general principles of a proposed piece of legislation would normally involve all members of each chamber, whereas detailed discussion tends to take place in smaller groups or committees.

An *executive-led process*: that is, one in which most major legislative proposals emanate from the executive branch of government. In a **presidential system of government** (e.g. the United States), the chief executive (the president) is normally elected separately by the people and is not part of the legislature (in other words, there is a **separation of powers**). In a **parliamentary system of government** (e.g. the UK), members of the executive may also be members of the legislative body and hence may be in a position to control the legislative process.

Opportunities for legislative initiatives by ordinary representatives: that is, arrangements that permit ordinary members of the legislative assembly to propose new laws or changes to existing laws. In practice such opportunities tend to be limited and dependent to a large degree for their success on a positive response from the political executive.

Opportunities to criticise and censure the government and, in some cases, remove it from office (e.g. through impeachment): this is a vital function within a democratic system of government in that it forces decision-makers to defend their proposals, explain the logic of their actions and account for any mistakes they may have made. Opposition parties play an important role in this context within the legislative body and through media coverage can attack the government and articulate alternative views to the wider public. Specialist and standing committees for scrutinising legislation and the day-to-day work of the executive branch of government also usually exist in democratic regimes.

Control of the purse strings: that is, the power to grant or deny government the money required to carry out its policies and legislative programme. In theory this is a formidable power, given that no government can operate without funds. In practice the power of the legislature to deny funding to a democratically elected government may be more apparent than real and, where necessary, compromise tends to occur between the executive and legislative branches of government.

mini case   The power of the purse

In 2013 the Republican-led US House of Representatives used its constitutional power to impose an annual borrowing limit on the US Treasury aimed at reducing the size of the country's budget deficit. In what was widely seen as an attempt to derail President Obama's healthcare reforms, the House set a debt ceiling limit that would be insufficient to cover the President's budgetary requirements, including the interest on public borrowings that were becoming due for repayment. The threat that the United States would become technically bankrupt during October of that year – with potentially serious consequences for the recovery of the global economy – set alarm bells ringing in financial markets and led to calls from international bodies including the IMF for urgent action to find a way around the impasse that had developed between the White House and Congress.

Pending a solution to the crisis, the US government laid off hundreds of thousands of federal employees, a decision which affected not only the provision of public services but also many of the businesses dependent on the spending of the state and its employees. In Washington, for example, a wide range of smaller businesses – including hairdressers, taxi firms, cafés and restaurants – experienced a sudden loss of trade as their pool of regular customers declined substantially. For these business owners, the threat of a prolonged period of declining revenues was far more important than esoteric discussions about the appropriate level at which to set the country's debt ceiling.

Since a great deal of media coverage of the issue at the time understandably focused on the partisan roots of the problem and on possible compromises, it is easy to forget that both action and inaction by political decision-makers almost invariably has consequences for a country's citizens and its businesses. As the next chapter demonstrates, decisions on taxing and spending by government have a major impact on the economy at both the macro and micro levels; spending and income are after all opposite sides of the same coin.

As will be evident from the comments above, legislating is a complex and time-consuming process, offering numerous opportunities for individuals and groups both within and outside the legislative body (e.g. pressure groups) to delay and disrupt the passage of legislation. While no government can guarantee to achieve all its legislative aims, there is a cultural expectation in a democracy that, as far as possible, promises made before an election will be put into effect at the earliest opportunity by the democratically elected government. Such an expectation usually provides the incumbent administration with a powerful argument for legislative support on the occasions when it is confronted with intransigence within the legislative assembly or with hostility from outside sectional interests.

The executive function

Governing is not only about making decisions, it is also about ensuring that these decisions are put into effect in order to achieve the government's objectives. Implementing governmental decisions is the responsibility of the executive branch of government.

In modern states the term 'the executive' refers to that relatively small group of individuals chosen to decide on policy and to oversee its implementation; some of these individuals will hold political office, others will be career administrators and advisers, although some of the latter may also be political appointees. Together they are part of a complex political and administrative structure designed to carry out the essential work of government and to ensure that those responsible for policy-making and implementation are ultimately accountable for their actions.

The policy-making aspect of the executive function is normally the responsibility of a small political executive chosen (wholly or in part) by popular election. Under a presidential system of government, the chief executive or president is usually chosen by separate election for a given period of office and becomes both the nominal and political head of state. He or she subsequently appoints individuals to head the various government departments/ministries/bureaux which are responsible for shaping and implementing government policy. Neither the president nor the heads of departments normally sit in the legislative assembly, although there are sometimes exceptions to this rule (e.g. the Vice-President in the United States).

In contrast, in a parliamentary system the roles of head of state and head of government are separated, with the former usually largely ceremonial and carried out by either a president (e.g. Germany, India) or a monarch (e.g. UK, Japan). The head of government (e.g. prime minister), while officially appointed by the head of state, is an elected politician, invariably the head of the party victorious in a general election or at least seen to be capable of forming a government, possibly in coalition with other parties. Once appointed, the head of government chooses other individuals to head the different government departments/ministries and to be part of a collective decision-making body (e.g. a **Cabinet**) which meets to sanction policy proposals put forward through a system of executive committees and subcommittees (e.g. Cabinet committees). These individuals, along with the head of government, are not only part of the executive machinery of the state but also usually members of the legislative assembly and both 'individually' and 'collectively' responsible to the legislature for the work of government.

The day-to-day administration of government policy is largely carried out by non-elected government officials (sometimes referred to as **civil servants** or **bureaucrats**), who work for the most part in complex, bureaucratic organisations within the state bureaucracy. Apart from their role in implementing public policy, government officials help to advise **ministers** on the different policy options and on the political and administrative aspects of particular courses of action. Needless to say, this gives them a potentially critical role in shaping government policy, a role which has been substantially enhanced over the years by the practice of granting officials a significant degree of discretion in deciding on the details of particular policies and/or on how they should be administered.

Whereas politicians in the executive branch of government tend to be transitory figures – who come and go at the whim of the head of government or of the electorate – most, if not all, officials are permanent, professional appointees who may serve a variety of governments of different political complexions and preferences during a long career in public administration. Whatever government is in power, officials are generally expected to operate in a non-partisan (i.e. neutral) way when advising their political masters and when overseeing the implementation of government policy. Their loyalty in short is to the current administration in office, a principle which helps to ensure a smooth transition of government and to guarantee that the upheaval caused by a general election does not prevent the business of the state from being carried out as usual.

The judicial function

Governing is not just about making and implementing laws, it is also about ensuring that they are applied and enforced. The latter is essentially the role of the third arm of government, namely the **judiciary** and the system of courts. Like political institutions, legal structures and processes tend to a degree to be country specific and vary according to a number of influences, including history, culture and politics. For example, while some states have a relatively unified legal system, others organised on a federal basis usually have a system of parallel courts adjudicating on federal and state/provincial law, with a **Supreme Court** arbitrating in the event of a dispute. In some countries a proportion of the judges may be directly or indirectly elected by the public, in others they may be appointed by government and/or co-opted by fellow judges. Business students should make themselves familiar with the legal arrangements within their own country (see e.g. Chapter 8, which contains information on the legal system in England and Wales). In this section we look briefly at the judicial function as related to the concept of democracy.

Whereas in totalitarian systems of government the judiciary is essentially the servant of the ruling elite (e.g. the 'party'), in a democracy it is an accepted principle that there should be a separation between the judicial function and the other two branches of government in order to protect the citizen from a too-powerful state. This notion of an impartial and independent judiciary, free to challenge the government and to review its decisions, is regarded as one of the hallmarks of a democratic system of government, a further manifestation of the doctrine of the separation of powers.

In practice, of course, notions of judicial independence and role within the democratic political process tend to be the subject of a certain amount of debate, particularly in countries where senior appointments to the judiciary appear to be in the gift of politicians (e.g. Supreme Court judges in the United States are nominated by the President with the consent of the Senate) or where individuals with judicial powers also have an executive and/or legislative role (e.g. the Home Secretary in the UK). Equally there are questions over the degree to which the courts should have the power to review the constitutionality of decisions made by a democratically elected government. In the United States, for example, the Supreme Court has a long-established right to declare a law void if it conflicts with its own interpretation of the US Constitution. In the UK, the legal sovereignty of Parliament and the absence of a codified written constitution push the judiciary towards trying to interpret the intentions of the framers of government legislation, and any legal decision unwelcome by the government can be reversed by further legislation. That said, it is interesting to note that in recent years there has been an increased willingness on the part of the British judiciary to review administrative decisions, particularly those made by ministers.

Other aspects, too, call into question how far in modern democratic states there is a total separation between the different arms of government (e.g. increasing use of administrative courts/tribunals) and whether it makes sense to distinguish rigidly between rule making and rule adjudication. Certainly some of the past judgments by the United States Supreme Court (e.g. in the area of civil rights) demonstrate that the courts can be influential in shaping decisions on major issues of policy and suggest that the judiciary is susceptible to influences from its own values or to general societal pressures. In short, it seems fair to suggest that under current legal arrangements, legal adjudication is not far removed from the world of politics; arguably we may like to perpetuate the myth of an entirely separate and independent judiciary since this is a necessary aspect of the stability of many existing political systems.

Checks and balances in democracies

As will be evident from the analysis above, democracy implies the existence of a system of checks and balances, arrangements which serve to curb government action and restrict its influence on the day-to-day lives of its citizens. These restraints on the actions of the state at national level can be divided into two main types: political and social/economic.

Political checks and balances emanate primarily from three main sources:

- the separation of powers – particularly the notion that the three arms of government are in separate hands and that decisions require the concurrence of all branches of government;
- a bicameral legislature – with legislation having to be accepted by both houses and subject to scrutiny and amendment by opposition parties;
- the territorial division of powers – whether under a federal arrangement or through the devolution of power to regional bodies and/or local authorities. Supranationalism is a further development.

The point is not that these arrangements necessarily exist in their most complete form in democratic states but that – however imperfect in practice – their existence helps to provide time for reflection and delay in the decision-making process and to encourage consultation, negotiation and consensus building, the essence of the democratic approach to conflict resolution.

The notion of social and economic checks and balances refers to those countervailing pressures on the activities of the state and its agencies that derive from the existence of non-state structures and processes which affect the lives of individuals and which ultimately restrict the scope of government influence. These include private business organisations, professional associations, promotional bodies, churches and other groups which help to shape our economic, social and moral environment. As subsequent chapters will demonstrate, the bulk of economic decisions in democratic states is not taken by the government but by private individuals and organisations (i.e. firms) interacting through a market system. This acts as a kind of check and balance on the free activity of the public sector and is a fundamental characteristic of democratic government.

A model of the policy process

It is appropriate to conclude this examination of the political environment with a brief discussion of the process of governmental decision-making in democratic systems. Here, the basic model of the organisation in its environment introduced in Chapter 1 serves as a useful analytical tool (see Figure 4.2). Governments, like firms, are organisations which transform inputs into output and they do so in an environment largely the same as that which confronts other types of enterprise. Like other organisations, governments are a user of resources, especially land, labour, capital, finance and expertise, but in addition all governments face political demands and supports when considering their policy options.

As indicated above, political demands – including those directly or indirectly impinging on business activity – become translated into action through a variety of mechanisms, including the electoral system, party activity, pressure group influence and political communication; hence a government is always keen to point out that electoral victory implies that it has a mandate for its policies. The supports of the political system are those customs, conventions, rules, assumptions and sentiments that provide a basis for the existence of the political community and its constituent parts and thus give legitimacy to the actions and existence of the incumbent government. In democratic systems,

Figure 4.2   Government and its environment

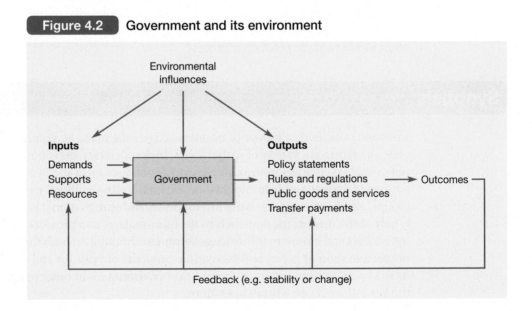

the belief in democratic principles, and the doctrines and practices emanating from that belief, are seen as central to the activities of government and its agencies.

The outputs of the political system vary considerably and range from public goods and services (e.g. healthcare) – provided predominantly from money raised through taxation – to rules and regulations (e.g. legislation, administrative procedures, directives) and transfer payments (i.e. where the government acts as a reallocator of resources, as in the case of the provision of state benefits). Taken together, the nature, range and extent of government output not only tend to make government the single biggest organisation in a state, but also influence the environment in which other businesses operate and increasingly in which other governments make decisions.

As far as governmental decision-making is concerned, this is clearly a highly complex process which in practice does not replicate the simple sequence of events suggested by the model. Certainly governments require 'means' (inputs) to achieve 'ends' (outputs), but the outputs of the political system normally emerge only after a complex, varied and ongoing process involving a wide range of individuals, groups and agencies. To add further confusion, those involved in the process tend to vary according to the decision under discussion as well as over time, making analysis fraught with difficulties. One possible solution may be to distinguish between the early development of a policy proposal ('initiation') and its subsequent 'formulation' and 'implementation', in the hope that a discernible 'policy community' can be identified at each stage. But even this approach involves a degree of guesswork and arbitrary decision-making, not least because of the difficulty of distinguishing precisely between the different stages of policy-making and of discerning the influence of individuals and groups at each phase of the process.

Notwithstanding these difficulties, it is important for students of business and for businesses themselves to have some understanding of the structure of decision-making, and of the underlying values and beliefs that tend to shape governmental action, if they are to appreciate (and possibly influence) the political environment in which they exist. Studies of political systems, institutions and processes help to provide insight into how and why government decisions are made, who is important in shaping those decisions and how influence can be brought to bear on the decision-making process. As an increasing number of individuals and groups recognise, knowledge of this kind can prove a valuable organisational resource that on occasions is of no less significance than the other inputs into the productive process.

Synopsis

Laws and policies that influence business activity are made by politicians and bureaucrats, operating at a variety of spatial levels. In democracies, decisions by governmental policy-makers emanate from a complex process of discussion and negotiation involving a range of formal and informal institutions, including political parties and pressure groups, and frequently involving international and supranational bodies. This process is part of the democratic approach to decision-making and provides opportunities for individuals and groups to influence government thinking on both the formulation and implementation of policy and legislation. Students of business and managers need to have a broad understanding of this political environment in order to appreciate one of the key influences on a firm's operations.

Summary of key points

- Politics is a universal activity that affects businesses of all types and sizes.
- It occurs at a variety of spatial levels from the local to the global.
- Political systems, structures and processes reflect underlying social values and philosophies and these influence the ways in which major decisions are taken.
- In any democratic system of government the key political institutions are likely to include an electoral system, a party system, a representative decision-making assembly and a system for articulating sectional interests.
- The three key functions of government are legislative, executive and judicial.
- While political institutions, practices and processes tend to vary between countries, democratic government is typified by a system of representative democracy and by political, social and economic checks and balances which act as a constraint on the actions of government.
- Such checks and balances in the system include the activities of pressure groups, which seek to influence government through a variety of means, and which often play a key role in policy formulation and implementation.
- Business organisations and the bodies that represent them are key pressure groups in democratic societies and an important part of the external environment in which government and its agencies operate.

Appendix 4.1 A democratic political system in action: UK national government

As far as the UK is concerned, the four interrelated elements of a democratic system of government are as illustrated in Figure 4.3.

Figure 4.3   The elected government at Westminster

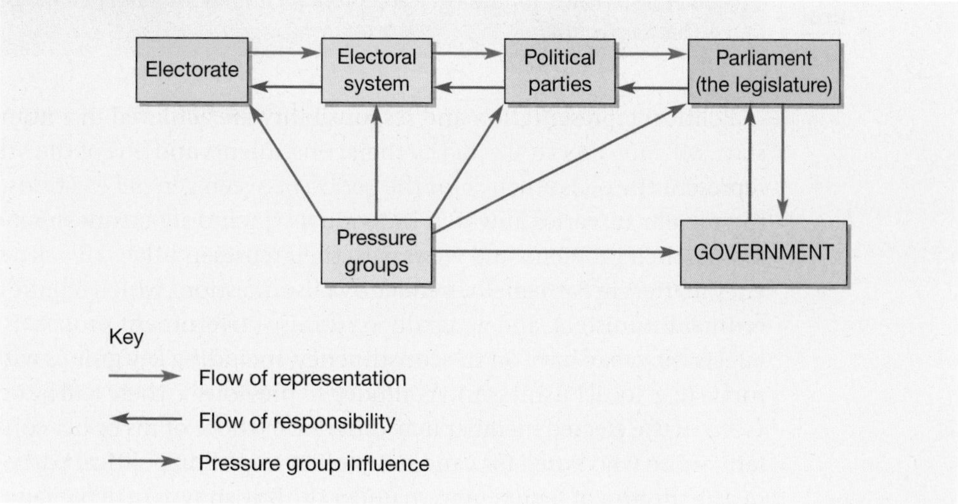

Key

→ Flow of representation

← Flow of responsibility

→ Pressure group influence

Through a system of regular elections, British citizens (the electorate) vote for candidates of competing political parties who are seeking to form the national government (or to be members of the devolved assemblies in Northern Ireland, Scotland or Wales). Successful candidates at the national elections become Members of Parliament (**MPs**) and the party with the largest number of MPs is invited by the monarch to form a government, with individuals within the government being allocated specific responsibilities for particular areas of work. The work of government is scrutinised by Parliament (see below), which acts as the people's representative between elections, thereby providing for a measure of public accountability. Equally, between (or during) elections individuals are free to seek to influence government by joining pressure groups or other types of organisation (e.g. political parties) and by making their views known to their elected representatives. The media are free and therefore able to scrutinise the government's performance and to inform the public about political developments.

> **web link**
> For information on the political arrangements in Northern Ireland, Scotland and Wales, see, for example, *www.nidirect.gov.uk*; *www.niassembly.gov.uk*; *www.parliament.scot*; *www.scot.uk*; *www.assembly.wales*; *gov.wales*

The legislative branch of government at national level

As indicated above, a directly elected legislature – representative of the people and responsible for making laws – is an important component of a democratic system of government. In the UK as a whole this function is carried out by **Parliament**, which comprises a non-elected upper chamber (the **House of Lords**) and an elected lower chamber (the **House of Commons**) whose members (currently 650 MPs) are elected by universal suffrage by the majority of citizens aged 18 and over. While it is true to say that the Lords retains some important powers, including the power to delay and scrutinise government legislation, the House of Commons remains the most important part of the UK legislature, particularly since it contains key members of the political executive, including the Prime Minister and most of the Cabinet. For this reason the discussion below focuses on the role of the House of Commons.

> **web link**
> Website addresses for the UK Parliament include *www.publications.parliament.uk* and *www.parliament.uk*

Political representation and responsibility are achieved in a number of ways. For a start, MPs are directly elected by their constituents and one of the MPs' main roles is to represent the constituency for the period between general elections. Apart from holding regular surgeries at which individuals (including businessmen and women) can discuss their problems and views with their representative, MPs also speak on constituency matters in Parliament, frequently raise questions which require answers from government ministers, and generally scrutinise government proposals for any potential effects they may have on the constituency, including key groups within the local electorate (e.g. local businesses). As alluded to previously, there will be occasions when the views of the elected member may differ from those of his or her constituents, particularly those who voted for candidates of an opposing political party, but this does not negate the idea of representation under the British system of parliamentary democracy.

MPs represent their constituents first and foremost by having been elected *by them* and hence they provide a direct link between the electorate and the government of the day, which is essentially drawn from the senior members of the majority party in Parliament. In the event of a coalition government (e.g. the UK after the 2010 election), the government will contain representatives of those parties making up the coalition.

Parliament also provides opportunities for the people's representatives to scrutinise and, where necessary, to criticise and challenge the decisions of government. In addition to such parliamentary mechanisms as question time and the adjournment debate, Parliament provides for a system of select committees of **backbench MPs** whose primary role is to scrutinise the work of government departments and other state agencies. Such committees – chaired by both government and opposition backbenchers – are able to question ministers and civil servants, call for departmental papers, cross-examine experts from outside government, and generally investigate the work of the executive, prior to reporting to Parliament on their findings. In bringing their views before Parliament and the public generally (especially through the media), select committees provide a check on government activity and hence form one of the strands by which governments remain answerable to the electorate in the period between elections.

Another significant strand is provided by the opposition, which represents not only an alternative choice of government but also a means of scrutinising and criticising the work of the incumbent administration. Fundamental to this role is the ability of opposition MPs to publicise the decisions of government and to present alternative views to the public via party political broadcasts or promotional literature or debates in Parliament, or by general media coverage. Such free and open discussion of issues and policies is a necessary condition for democracy and is an important element in the political education of the nation. Even where governments have large majorities, the role of opposition parties remains a vital component of democracy and helps to provide a curb on unlimited government action.

Turning to its role as a legislative body, there is little doubt that the UK Parliament is largely a legitimising institution, giving formal authority to the wishes of the majority party or coalition. Through its control of the process of legislation, the parliamentary timetable, the flow of information and the votes of its members, the government is able to ensure that its legislative proposals not only come before Parliament, but also are almost invariably accepted, even if some delay occurs from time to time in enacting the government's programme, particularly in the event of coalition government where a degree of compromise is often necessary. Opportunities for individual MPs to sponsor legislation (e.g. through private members' bills) are few and far between and the outcome of such proposals depends ultimately on government support (or reluctant acquiescence) if the legislation is to get through its various stages in Parliament. Not surprisingly, this effective stranglehold by the government on the legislative process has led some commentators to talk of an 'elective dictatorship' and to question the true extent of democratic decision-making, particularly when modern governments are invariably elected by less than 50 per cent of the electorate.

The executive branch of government

Putting laws and policies into effect is formally the work of the executive. In the UK this role is carried out by a wide variety of institutions and agencies that is part of the machinery of government. These include the Cabinet, government departments, local authorities, nationalised industries and a large number of other non-departmental public bodies or quasi-autonomous national government agencies, often referred to as 'quangos'. In the discussion below we focus initially on the key institutions at central level since these are fundamental to the process of decision-making in the UK. Discussion of some of the other agencies can be found in subsequent sections of this chapter.

web link

For information on how government departments are run, including non-political departments such as quangos, visit the government website at *www.gov.uk/ government/how-government-works*

Under the British system of government, the core of the executive is the Cabinet, headed by the **Prime Minister**, an office of crucial importance given the absence of an elected head of state with effective political powers. British Prime Ministers not only have a number of significant political roles – including leader of the governing party, head of the government and head of the Cabinet – but also have traditionally held a formidable array of political powers, including the power to:

- choose members of the Cabinet;
- choose other non-Cabinet ministers;
- promote, demote or dismiss ministers;
- appoint individuals to chair Cabinet committees;
- appoint top civil servants and oversee the operation of the Civil Service;
- confer certain appointments and titles; and
- determine the date of the general election within the five-year term of office.

This latter power no longer exists following the decision (in 2011) to institute a system of five-year fixed-term parliaments.

While the existence of such rights and responsibilities does not infer that Prime Ministers will inevitably be all-powerful, it is clear that holders of the office have a key role to play in the decision-making process and much will depend upon how an individual interprets that role, upon his or her personality and on the constraints he or she faces (both 'real' and 'imagined') in carrying it out. As the Conservative Prime Minister Mrs Thatcher (1979–90) found to her cost, retaining the office of Prime Minister is dependent not only on the electorate but also on maintaining the support and confidence of parliamentary colleagues in the period between elections. In the event of a coalition government, the Prime Minister also has to take account of the wishes of the other party leaders in the coalition and may involve them in some of the decisions outlined below.

As head of the Cabinet the Prime Minister chairs the committee of senior ministers that is the overall directing force – or board of management – within British central government. Comprising about 20 to 25 ministers who have been appointed by the Prime Minister to head the various government departments (or to fulfil some other important functions), the Cabinet is responsible for directing and coordinating the work of the whole executive machine. Its functions include:

- making decisions on the nature and direction of government policy, including public expenditure, economic policy, defence, foreign relations, industrial policy, and so on;
- overseeing and coordinating the administration of government;

- arbitrating in the event of disputes between ministers or departments;
- discussing, deciding and generally directing the government's legislative programme, including laws relating to business.

A large part of this work, of course, is carried out using a system of committees and subcommittees, comprising individuals chosen by the Prime Minister (including the chairperson) and supported by a small but powerful secretariat, headed by the Cabinet secretary (a civil servant). Apart from providing an opportunity for more detailed discussions of issues and policies prior to full consideration by the Cabinet, the committee system has the advantage of allowing non-members of the Cabinet (including non-Cabinet ministers and civil servants) to participate in discussions in which they may have an interest. In this way, the system helps to provide a mechanism for communication and coordination between government departments and serves as a training ground for junior ministers, many of whom will subsequently achieve full Cabinet responsibilities. An illustrative list of selected Cabinet committees in 2015 is shown in Table 4.1.

Table 4.1 Elected Cabinet committees, 2015

Constitutional Reform Committee
Economic Affairs Committee
Reducing Regulation Sub-Committee
Europe Committee
European Affairs Committee
Home Affairs Committee
Armed Forces Covenant Sub-Committee
National Security Council
Nuclear Deterrence and Security Sub-Committee
Threats, Hazards, Resilience and Contingencies Sub-Committee
Parliamentary Business and Legislation Committee
Public Expenditure Committee
Efficiency and Reform Sub-Committee
Social Justice Committee
Housing Implementation Taskforce
Health and Social Care Implementation Taskforce
Earn or Learn Implementation Taskforce
Immigration Implementation Taskforce
Childcare Implementation Taskforce
Tackling Extremism in Communities Implementation Taskforce
Troubled Families Implementation Taskforce
Exports Implementation Taskforce
Digital Infrastructure and Inclusion Implementation Taskforce
Syrian Returners Implementation Taskforce

Source: The Cabinet Office.

Much of the day-to-day work of central government is carried out in vast and complex administrative structures called government departments – a selected list of which is shown in Table 4.2. Working together with a substantial number of executive agencies and other public bodies, **government departments** are usually headed by a Cabinet minister (normally called a **Secretary of State**) and include other ministers outside the Cabinet (e.g. Ministers of State, Parliamentary Under Secretaries of State) who have been appointed by the Prime Minister and who may include individuals drawn from the world of business. Together these ministers constitute the political executive.

Table 4.2 Government departments, August 2016

Attorney General's Office
Cabinet Office
Department for Business, Energy and Industrial Strategy
Department for Communities and Local Government
Department for Culture, Media and Sport
Department for Education
Department for Environment, Food and Rural Affairs
Department for Exiting the European Union
Department for International Development
Department for International Trade
Department for Transport
Department for Work and Pensions
Department of Health
Foreign and Commonwealth Office
Her Majesty's Treasury
Home Office
Ministry of Defence
Ministry of Justice
Northern Ireland Office
Office of the Advocate General for Scotland
Office of the Leader of the House of Commons
Office of the Leader of the House of Lords
Scotland Office
UK Export Finance
Wales Office

As the head of a department, the Secretary of State has ultimate responsibility for its work and is answerable to Parliament through the various mechanisms referred to above. In addition, he or she is expected to give overall direction to the work of the department – within the policy of the government as a whole – and to represent its interest in the Cabinet (e.g. over the size and use of its budget), in Parliament (e.g. in steering through legislation) and in the outside world (e.g. in the media). Large areas of this work are delegated to the Ministers of State who assume responsibility for specific areas of departmental work and they in turn will tend to delegate some duties to the department's junior ministers. Such an arrangement not only ensures coverage of the different aspects of a department's responsibilities, but also provides invaluable experience and training for ambitious young MPs appointed to a ministerial post.

web link

Each government department has its own website with lots of useful material. Examples of current addresses include: *www.gov.uk/government/organisations/ department-for-work-pensions, www.defra.gov.uk, www.gov.uk/government/ organisations/department-for-international-trade*

Ministers are assisted in their work by permanent officials, known as civil servants, many of whom have spent a large part of their working lives in the government machine and hence are familiar with how it works and how to manipulate it in order to achieve particular objectives. Whereas ministers are politicians, civil servants are administrators vested formally with the task of carrying out the policies of the incumbent government, irrespective of their own political views and preferences. Perhaps not surprisingly, as key advisers to ministers on policy formulation and implementation, senior civil servants can exercise considerable influence over the nature and shape of government policy and legislation. For this reason, individuals or groups seeking to shape government thinking on an issue or piece of legislation frequently 'target' senior departmental officials in the hope of gaining influence in the policy process.

This potential for influence by senior civil servants is, of course, enhanced by the scope and complexities of modern government and by the fact that government ministers have a wide range of non-departmental as well as departmental responsibilities (e.g. as constituency MPs). Ministers consequently rely heavily on their officials for information and advice and civil servants are normally entrusted, under ministers, with the conduct of the whole gamut of government activities, including filling in the details of some legislation. Added to this, the need for policy coordination between departments requires regular meetings between senior officials, in groups that mirror the meetings of Cabinet subcommittees. Since these meetings of officials help to provide the groundwork and briefing papers for future discussions by ministers, they permit civil servants to influence the course of events, especially when a particular line or policy option is agreed by the senior officials in a number of departments.

It is perhaps worth noting at this point that, however pervasive its influence, the Civil Service is not the only source of policy advice for governments. Apart from traditional bureaucratic channels, ministers often turn to specially appointed bodies for help and guidance in making policy choices. Some of these sources are permanent (or relatively permanent) and include the various executive and advisory bodies set up by past and present governments to assist in the policy process in specific functional areas (e.g. Natural Environment Research Council). Others are temporary, having been specially constituted by government to consider a particular problem and to report on their findings prior to going out of existence (e.g. public inquiries, Royal Commissions). While the appointment of these advisory sources does not oblige the government to follow their advice, they can be regarded as useful sources of information, ideas and advice from outside the formal bureaucratic machine. Moreover, the fact that they tend to have a membership representing a wide cross-section of interests (including representatives of particular pressure groups, industrialists, trade unionists, MPs, academics and others drawn from the list of 'the great and the good') helps to widen the scope of consultation and thus to enhance the democratic process.

The last generation has also seen governments turning increasingly to special advisers and policy planning units for help with policy development. Whereas advisers are individuals appointed by ministers (including the Prime Minister), usually from outside the Civil Service, policy planning units and/or research units are groups of individuals generally recruited from and located within the government machine, with the aim of providing a range of policy and programme advice to both policy-makers and administrators. Often comprising young and highly qualified individuals seconded to a unit from a wide range of occupational categories and disciplines (including statisticians, social scientists, economists and general administrators), policy units are a valuable source of information and advice, and their operation at both central and local government level provides policy-makers with detailed research and analysis with which to support their policy judgements.

A further important development has been the increased use of 'focus groups', collections of individual citizens consulted by government on policy proposals prior to legislation and/or implementation. In canvassing the views of individuals affected by government policy, the government hopes to improve the policy process in a wide range of areas, including the delivery of public services where there has been a programme to provide round-the-clock availability and (ultimately) complete electronic access. While some see citizens' panels or focus groups as nothing more than a gimmick, others regard their use as a move towards a more modern and democratic form of government with increased levels of public accountability and access to information.

The judicial branch of government

The third arm of government, the judiciary – comprising the judges and the courts – is formally separate from and independent of Parliament and the government, despite the fact that until recently the head of the judiciary, the Lord Chancellor, was both a member of the government and a member of the House of Lords, where he or she presided as Speaker. In essence the role of the judiciary is to put into effect the laws enacted by Parliament and to keep the government within the limits of its powers as laid down in statutes and in common law, as interpreted by the judiciary. Since 1973, it has also been responsible for interpreting EU law. Given the complexities of the legal system and its relevance to the world of business, it is important to examine this aspect of government in more detail. This is undertaken in Chapter 8.

Appendix 4.2   Subnational government: UK local authorities

Democratic government occurs at subnational as well as national level and takes a wide variety of forms. In addition to the local branches of central government departments and public utilities, many states have local agencies for the administration of justice, local special-purpose authorities (e.g. in the health service) and a system of regional and/or local government, whether under a federal or a unitary arrangement. Such decentralisation and deconcentration of political authority are generally seen as beneficial, since they bring the formulation and administration of policy 'nearer to the people' and are said to provide for decisions that are more sensitive to local needs and aspirations. They can, however, raise the question as to the degree of autonomy of local agencies within a centralised system of government, a controversial and perennial source of debate and dispute in many parts of the world, as recent history has demonstrated.

Within the UK as a whole, political power is devolved at two main levels: regionally and locally. Scotland, Wales and Northern Ireland have their own directly elected regional assemblies (the Scottish Parliament; the National Assembly for Wales; the Northern Ireland Assembly) and systems of executive government (the Scottish Executive; the Welsh Assembly Government; the Northern Ireland Executive), each with differing levels of devolved authority. In England (outside of London), regional government does not currently exist, although voluntary regional chambers or assemblies were set up in the English regions to perform a number of core functions relating to regional issues such as housing development, planning, transport and strategic development. These have now been abolished.

Local government – the focus of this section – has a considerable historical pedigree and remains a key element of the country's system of institutionalised democracy and a major actor in the national as well as the local economy. Given its impact in the business environment, it deserves special attention.

As one form of local administration, local government has a number of distinctive features. For a start it involves self-government by the people of the locality as well as for them, with local authorities exercising considerable discretion in the ways they apply national laws within their areas. In addition, local decision-makers (councillors) are elected to oversee multi-purpose authorities, financed by revenue raised predominantly from local sources – although the proportion from central government has risen in recent years. In short, each local authority constitutes a miniature political and administrative system: each has the institutions and processes of government – including an electoral system, a legislative body (the council), appointed officials (local government officers), party activity, and conflict between individuals and groups within the local community over the allocation of resources and the enforcement of values.

Figure 4.4 illustrates this parallel between the basic operation of government at central and local level. The electorate in each local constituency (district, county, unitary, metropolitan district) periodically chooses between candidates who are mostly representing the same parties as those found at national level, and the successful candidates in the election are elected to represent their constituency in the deliberating body (the council). Senior members of this body are chosen to serve on the various committees and subcommittees, with the leading party on the council having an in-built majority in the committee system, where most decisions have traditionally been made prior to being sanctioned (or not) by the full council. Since the passage of the Local Government Act (2000), councils have been allowed to adopt one of three broad categories of constitution which provide for a separate executive. These three categories are (1) a directly elected mayor with a Cabinet selected by the mayor, (2) a Cabinet either elected by the council or appointed by its leader, and (3) a directly elected mayor and council manager.

For the most part, senior councillors are the political heads of the various local authority departments and agencies (e.g. housing, social services, education, and so on) that are responsible for providing those services within the local community which national laws require or, in some cases (e.g. sports centres), do not forbid. Much of this work is carried out by local officials who are appointed by the local authority to

Figure 4.4   **The local government system**

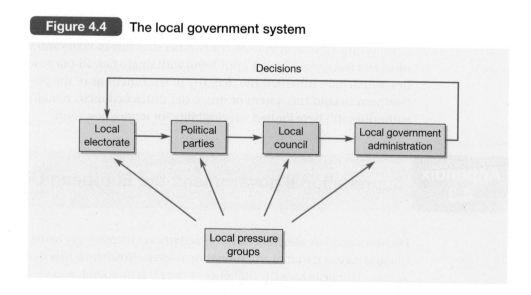

administer local services and to advise councillors on policy matters. As the local equivalent of civil servants, local government officers exercise considerable influence over the formulation as well as the implementation of local decisions. For this reason, they too tend to be targeted by local pressure groups which operate at all levels and stages of the political process in their attempts to influence local decision-making.

The current structure of local government in the UK is illustrated in Table 4.3. In England, outside the metropolitan areas, most 'shire' counties have a two-tier structure of county councils and district, borough or city councils, with the former providing the larger services (e.g. education and social services) while the latter have responsibility for a range of other services (such as highways, housing, leisure, refuse collection and local planning). Elsewhere (e.g. Cleveland, Humberside, Isle of Wight) 'unitary authorities' have either taken over the functions of the former county and district councils or operate alongside them as all-purpose authorities (e.g. Leicester, York). In the metropolitan areas (including London) the single tier of district councils (or London borough councils) remains unchanged from previous years.

Table 4.3 The structure of UK local government, 2013

Types of local authority		
England	**Wales and Scotland**	**N. Ireland**
Non-metropolitan areas County councils District councils Unitary councils (plus joint arrangements)	*All mainland areas* Unitary councils (plus three island councils in Orkney, Shetland and the Western Isles)	For the purpose of local government, Northern Ireland has 26 district councils with limited powers (e.g. collecting rubbish and providing leisure facilities)
Metropolitan areas Metropolitan district councils (plus joint boards)		
London London Borough Councils (plus Corporation of the City of London and joint boards)		

Following legislation in 1994, the two-tier structure in Wales and Scotland was abolished and was replaced (on 1 April 1996) with single-tier, all-purpose, unitary authorities, which have inherited the majority of the functions of the previous councils. In Northern Ireland the system of single-tier district councils remains, although these authorities still have limited responsibility for service provision.

Appendix 4.3   Supranational government: the European Union

Decisions and law affecting business activity are increasingly being made at supranational as well as national and subnational levels. Nowhere is this more evident than in Western Europe, where the influence of the EU is profound. As a significant part of the political environment of the major world economies, the EU deserves special consideration, particularly since its decisions often have global as well as regional consequences – affecting not only firms within its member states but also businesses and governments trading with these states, both directly and indirectly. The following analysis concentrates on the political institutions of the EU and their relative importance in the process of decision-making. The economic significance of the EU within the international marketplace is discussed in Chapter 16.

The EU's official website, called 'Europa', can be accessed at *europa.eu*. This provides links to lots of other useful sites.

The European Parliament

The **European Parliament** is a directly elected body, at the time of writing constituting 766 members (**MEPs**), with each member state's representation being roughly equivalent to the size of its population. The UK, for example, has 73 MEPs, elected at five-yearly intervals by UK citizens using a regional list system of proportional representation introduced for the June 1999 European elections. Since voting under a proportional system enhances the prospects of representation by smaller political parties, the European Parliament contains members representing a diversity of political parties which sit in political groups with similar affiliations. Table 4.4 shows, for example, the number of MEPs by broad affiliation as they stood following the 2018 elections.

Table 4.4 EPs by broad affiliation, 2018

Political group	Seats
E	217
S&D	189
ALDE	68
GREENS/EFA	51
ECR	74
GUE/NGL	52
EFD	45
NI	18
Total	751

Key

EPP: Group of the European People's Party (Christian Democrats)
S&D: Group of the Progressive Alliance of Socialists and Democrats in the European Parliament
ALDE: Group of the Alliance of Liberals and Democrats for Europe
GREENS/EFA: Group of the Greens/European Free Alliance
ECR: European Conservatives and Reformists Group
GUE/NGL: Confederal Group of the European United Left/Nordic Green Left
EFD: Europe of Freedom and Democracy group
NI: Non-attached Members
Source: *www.europarl.europa.eu*

For information on the European Parliament see *www.europarl.europa.eu*

The importance of party affiliation is emphasised by the fact that the European Parliament's organisation is deliberately biased in favour of multinational groupings, with recognition of a political grouping entitling the group to offices, funding, representation on committees and influence in debates and legislation. In order to decide its attitude to an issue or policy proposal coming before the Parliament or one of its committees, a group would normally meet for several days in the week before each session and the issue would be discussed and an agreed line would be decided. As in the case of national parliaments, the attitudes of the political groups have a significant impact on the discussions and decisions within the European Parliament, both in committee and when the House is in full session. Given the number of party groups, however, and the fact that no single group tends to have an absolute majority – unlike in some national parliaments – there is often a need for a group to try to build a coalition of support if it is to achieve its objectives in the European Parliament. Understandably – and perhaps inevitably – decisions by the European Parliament thus tend to involve compromise between individuals and groups, with the final outcome frequently being a course of action that is acceptable to a majority.

In terms of its role and methods of operation, the European Parliament essentially mirrors national parliaments. Under an elected president who is responsible for directing its activities and representing it externally and with other EU institutions, much of its detailed work is handled by specialist committees, meeting mostly in Brussels, which report on and offer recommendations to full sessions of the House, which take place in Strasbourg. Membership of each committee is broadly representative of the strengths of the party groupings and the chairpersons of the permanent committees tend to be influential figures in their own right. In addition to drawing up legislative proposals and carrying out detailed examination and amendment of draft laws, the committees discuss issues (e.g. women's rights, consumer protection, employment), question officials, hold public hearings at which experts and representatives of specialist organisations give evidence, and generally offer their opinion and advice on issues of concern to the EU. As in the case of national parliaments, detailed discussion in committee prior to debate and decision by the full house provides the European Parliament with an effective means of carrying out its duties and serves as a mechanism for scrutinising the work of both the Council and the Commission.

With regard to its functions, these predominantly fall into five main areas:

Legislation. The Parliament's formal approval is required on most proposals before they can be adopted by the Council of Ministers (see below); that is, the vast majority of European laws are adopted jointly by the European Parliament and the Council. Under the Lisbon Treaty (2009), the range of issues covered by the co-decision procedure has increased.

The budget. Along with the Council of Ministers, the Parliament acts as the Community's 'budgetary authority' and can reject the Council's draft budget and may modify expenditure proposals on 'non-compulsory' items. It can question the Commission's management of the budget and call in the Court of Auditors.

Supervision. The Parliament supervises the Commission, which it has the power to dismiss by a vote of censure and whose work it scrutinises using a variety of mechanisms. Under the Maastricht Treaty (1992) it has the right to be consulted on the appointment of a new Commission and can veto its appointment. The power of democratic supervision has been extended to other EU institutions, including the Council of Ministers.

Initiative. This includes debates on important regional and international issues and demands for changes to existing policies and/or legislation. Parliament must also approve applications from countries wishing to join the EU.

Relations with national parliaments. The European Parliament holds regular meetings with member states' national parliaments.

In the legislative field, authority traditionally rested with the Council of Ministers and the Commission, and Parliament's role was largely to sanction proposals put before it. Changes under the Single European Act (1986), the Maastricht Treaty (1992), the Amsterdam Treaty (1997), the Nice Treaty (2001) and the Lisbon Treaty (2009) have, however, helped to strengthen Parliament's position by establishing and subsequently extending new procedures for 'assent', 'cooperating' and 'co-decision', now known as the 'Ordinary legislative procedure'. Thus:

- In certain fields an absolute majority of the European Parliament must vote to approve laws before they are passed (e.g. foreign treaties, accession treaties, the Common Agricultural Policy).
- In specified areas Parliament now has a second reading of proposals and its rejection of such proposals can be overturned only by a unanimous decision of the Council of Ministers (e.g. Single Market laws, trans-European networks).
- Parliament can also reject certain legislation by an absolute majority vote if, after the second reading of a proposal and subsequent conciliation, the Council and Parliament are unable to agree (e.g. education and training, health, consumer protection).

The Lisbon Treaty also gave Parliament the power to appoint the President of the European Commission.

The Council of the European Union (the Council of Ministers)

The Council of the European Union (the **Council of Ministers**) – the EU's ultimate decision-making body – comprises one minister from each of the member states, with participants on the Council varying according to the issue under discussion (e.g. agricultural issues are discussed by Ministers of Agriculture from each state). Meetings of the Council, which are mainly held in Brussels, are chaired predominantly by the minister from the country holding the presidency, which currently rotates on a six-monthly basis (e.g. Greece and Italy held the presidency in 2014). Along with the meetings of ministers are regular meetings of officials (Council Working Groups), together with the work of the Committee of Permanent Representatives of the Member States (COREPER), whose task is to coordinate the groundwork for EU decisions undertaken by the numerous meetings of senior officials. In addition, the Council is serviced by a general secretariat, also based in Brussels.

web link

> The Council of Ministers' website is at *www.consilium.europa.eu*
> Information is also available through the EU's main website at *europa.eu*

The role of the Council of Ministers is to make major policy decisions and to respond to legislative proposals put forward mainly by the Commission. Its key roles are to pass EU laws, coordinate EU economic policy, approve the EU budget, sign international agreements and develop EU foreign and defence policies. Major EU decisions require unanimity in the Council, but, increasingly, many decisions (especially after the Amsterdam and Nice Treaties) are now being taken by **qualified majority vote (qmv)**.

Member states have weighted votes in the Council that are roughly proportional to their relative population sizes, with the total number of votes being 352 at the time of writing. A qualified majority is reached if two conditions are met: (1) 55 per cent of member states approve (in some cases a two-thirds majority is needed); (2) 65 per cent of the EU population is represented by those who voted in favour. If not, the decision will not be adopted.

While the 'right of initiative' under the Treaties rests with the Commission, the power of decision essentially lies with the Council, which may adopt Commission proposals as drafted, amend them, reject them, or simply take no decision, having consulted the European Parliament and normally a number of other bodies. If adopted, Council of Ministers' decisions have the force of law and are described as regulations, directives, decisions, or recommendations and opinions. **Regulations** apply directly to all member states and do not have to be confirmed by national parliaments to have binding legal effect. **Directives** lay down compulsory objectives, but leave it to member states to translate them into national legislation. **Decisions** are binding on those states, companies or individuals to which they are addressed, while **Recommendations and Opinions** have no binding force but merely state the view of the institution that issues them.

The Council's power to pass a law – even if the European Parliament disagrees with it – was reduced under the Maastricht Treaty. In specified policy areas, joint approval is now necessary and MEPs have an effective veto if the two sides cannot reach agreement following conciliation. Moreover, following Maastricht a Committee of the Regions has been established to advise the Commission and the Council on issues concerning the European regions – a development which should help to ensure a stronger regional voice at European level. That said, it is still the case that the Council remains responsible for setting general policy within the EU and relies on the Commission to take decisions on the detailed application of legislation or to adapt legislative details to meet changing circumstances. To this extent – and given the Commission's other responsibilities – the ultimate influence over EU decisions is, to say the very least, open to question, as is often the case at national level.

The European Council

The work of the 'specialist' councils within the Council of Ministers (e.g. Agriculture, Economics and Finance, Employment and Social Affairs) is coordinated by the General Affairs Council, comprising the Foreign Ministers of the member states. This Council is also responsible for preparing for the meetings of the **European Council**, which occur around four times each year. The European Council is attended by the heads of government/state of each member state, the EU's representative for foreign affairs, the President of the Commission and the European Council President, and its work invariably attracts substantial media coverage. Under the chair of its permanent President, the European Council's role is to discuss important policy issues affecting the EU and to set the EU's general political direction and priorities. These so-called 'summits' of heads of governments can have a profound effect on the development of the EU and its institutions.

web link   Information on the European Council is available via the Council of Ministers' website. See above.

The European Commission

The **European Commission**, which has its headquarters in Brussels and Luxembourg, is the EU's bureaucratic arm, currently comprising 28 Commissioners (one from each member state), nominated by their respective governments, and a staff of about 23 000 permanent civil servants drawn from all member states. Headed by a President, and organised into **Directorates-General**, each with a Commissioner responsible for its work, the European Commission's role is essentially that of initiator, supervisor and executive. More specifically its tasks are:

- to act as guardian of the Treaties so as to ensure that EU rules and principles are respected and implemented;
- to propose policies and legislation for the European Parliament and Council of Ministers to discuss and, if appropriate, adopt or amend;
- to implement EU policies and supervise the day-to-day running of these policies, including managing the funds that account for most of the EU budget (e.g. EAGGF, ERDF, ECSC);
- to represent the EU internationally (e.g. in the WTO).

 You can find further information on the Commission at *ec.europa.eu*

In carrying out these duties, the Commissioners are required to act in the interests of the EU as a whole and may not receive instructions from any national government or from any other body (Article 157 of the Treaty of Rome). Moreover, while each Commissioner is responsible for formulating proposals within his or her area of responsibility, the final decision is taken on a collegiate basis and the work is subject to the supervision of the European Parliament. As mentioned above, Parliament is the only body that can force the Commission to resign collectively; interestingly, it has no authority over individual Commissioners, although its endorsement is needed when the President of the Commission and the other Commissioners are appointed.

Much of the undoubted power and influence of the Commission stems from its central involvement in the legislative process. Proposals for consideration by the Council and the Parliament are initially drafted by the Commission, usually following consultation with the Economic and Social Committee (representing the interests of employers, trade unions, farmers, consumers, etc.) and other advisory bodies as appropriate. Moreover, EU Treaties specifically give the Commission the power to make regulations, issue directives, take decisions, make recommendations and deliver opinions, as well as to implement policies based on either Council decisions or Treaty provisions. Thus, while legislative power in the EU in general rests with the Council of Ministers and the EU Parliament, the Commission is also able to legislate in order to implement earlier Council regulations, particularly where technical or routine matters are concerned – a situation that has parallels in the operation of government at national level.

Further powers with regard to specific sectors (e.g. coal and steel) or particular aspects of EU work (e.g. the budget, international agreements) serve to enhance the Commission's influence and to confirm its position as the 'driving force' of the EU. Perhaps understandably, pressure groups seeking to influence the policy process within the EU regard the Commission as an important institution to target, together with Parliament and the Council of Ministers. Future changes in the relationship between these three institutions will undoubtedly have an effect not only on the legislative process but also on the practice of lobbying within the EU context.

The European Court of Justice

The **European Court of Justice**, which sits in Luxembourg, comprises 28 judges, who are appointed for a six-year period by consent of the member states, and 8 advocates-general. The Court's role is:

- to pass judgment, at the request of a national court, on the interpretation or validity of points of EU law;
- to quash, at the request of an EU institution, government or individual, any measures adopted by the Commission, the Council or national governments which are judged to be incompatible with the existing Treaties;
- to consider actions brought by individuals, companies or organisations against EU decisions or actions.

The Court can also be invited to offer an opinion, which then becomes binding, on agreements the EU proposes to undertake with third countries.

Three aspects of its work are particularly worthy of note:

- Individuals as well as member states can bring cases to the Court, and its judgments and interpretations apply to all (i.e. EU institutions, member states, national courts and private citizens) and are backed by a system of penalties for non-compliance.
- Its rulings on matters of European law, which has primacy over national law, are final and its decisions are binding on member countries.
- The Court has tended to follow the principle that EU Treaties should be interpreted with a degree of flexibility so as to take account of changing conditions and circumstances. This has permitted the Community to legislate in areas where there are no specific Treaty provisions, such as the fight against pollution.

web link The Court of Justice website can be accessed at *curia.europa.eu*. See also *europa.eu* for general information.

case study The business of lobbying

A key characteristic of a democratic political system is the right of individuals, groups and organisations to seek to influence government thinking and behaviour. For a business wishing to have its voice heard in official circles, a variety of approaches is possible, ranging from direct appeals to decision-makers to joint action with other firms via an industry body, trade association or a business representative organisation (see Chapter 13). A firm may even consider hiring the services of a professional lobby organisation to act on its behalf.

Professional lobby organisations are essentially businesses that have been specifically set up to influence others on behalf of their clients. Where government decisions are concerned, the complexities of modern political and administrative structures provide numerous opportunities and points of access for professional lobbyists, who often have extensive knowledge of the decision-making process and of the individuals to approach on a given issue. In order to bring influence to bear in the places and institutions where important decisions are made, many lobbying firms have established a presence in major centres of power, including Washington, Brussels and London, often employing hundreds of permanent staff whose job is to lobby for or against a particular policy or piece of legislation according to the needs of their client.

Cigarette packets in the UK are now very heavily regulated, but this was not always the case. One example of how businesses can use the services of professional lobbyists is the case of the EU's Tobacco Products Directive. Concerned over the health implications of smoking for EU citizens, EU member state governments agreed in June 2012 to a proposal that would require mandatory text and picture health warnings covering 75 per cent of the front and back of cigarette packets and to ban the sale of flavoured cigarettes that particularly appeal to younger smokers. A draft directive setting out these requirements was then sent to the European Parliament for a decision on whether to move forward on the issue or to allow time for further amendments.

To protect their interests, the major tobacco companies responded by launching an intense lobbying campaign aimed at potentially sympathetic MEPs whom they hoped would help to persuade others to oppose the suggested measures. Some estimates suggest that Philip Morris International – the makers of the brand Marlboro – alone spent more than €1 million wooing elected representatives to water down the proposals, reputedly employing over 150 staff and consultants during the process prior to the vote in the European Parliament. According to the Corporate Europe Observatory, which monitors the use of corporate lobbying in the EU, the tobacco industry has about 100 full-time lobbyists based in

Brussels, with an annual budget of more than €5 million. Given this resource, it is not surprising to learn that a report in *Reuters* on 4 October 2013 claimed that EU officials were concerned that lobbying activity by the industry was threatening to derail the proposed anti-smoking legislation.

When the issue was finally discussed in the Parliament after some delay, the original proposals regarding both the sale and promotion of cigarettes within the EU were considerably scaled back. MEPs rejected the plan to ban 'slim' cigarettes and opted for menthol-flavoured products to be phased out over eight rather than three years as had been proposed. They also agreed to reduce health warnings from 75 per cent to 65 per cent of the packet, the latter evidently having been put forward as a compromise by the industry. Following subsequent negotiations between the Council of the EU and the European Parliament, a revised directive was put forward which included the provision that member states retain the right to introduce more stringent measures, including plain packaging. In 2014 the directive on tobacco products had to be revised, becoming applicable in EU member states in May 2016. Since then branding on cigarette and tobacco packaging has had to become very minimal.

Case study questions

1 Why do governments frequently express concern over the activities of professional lobby organisations?

2 Why do some businesses and industries choose to use such organisations?

<table>
<tr><td>**case study**</td><td># Political campaign funding</td></tr>
</table>

In the UK political campaign funding is very tightly regulated. The idea behind these rules is that keeping money out of politics reduces the opportunity for special interests (from private organisations or others) to try to gain favour from people who eventually end up in power. This is not the case in other parts of the world. In the United States a great deal of political activity revolves

around the raising and spending of political campaign donations.

In the 2015–16 presidential race the total amount of funds raised by republican and democratic candidates reached $1,465,000,000. This is more than the entire GDP of the Seychelles. The largest individual donor for the Democratic Party, a hedge fund manager, raised $91,150,000 (his company

▶

donated another $90,000,000). The largest individual donor for the Republican Party, a casino owner, raised $82,562,000 (his company donated another $44,000,000). It is easy to see how these kinds of resources can lead to accusations of politicians being indebted to business and sectors.

Before the UK general election in 2017 the largest political donation to the Conservative Party was £1,500,000 from the company JCB; the Labour Party received £1,300,000 from the Unite trade union.

Case study question

1 What interests might these large donors like their political parties to represent?

Review and discussion questions

1 To what extent do you think a change of government in your country would affect the business community?

2 Many top civil servants take directorships in large companies on retirement from government. Why should companies be keen to recruit retired bureaucrats?

3 How far is the enlargement of the EU likely to benefit UK businesses?

4 In what ways could a business organisation seek to influence central government decision-makers on issues in which it has an interest (e.g. taxes on company profits or the level of interest rates)?

Assignments

1 You are employed as a research assistant by a group representing the interests of small and medium-sized enterprises (e.g. a Chamber of Commerce). Using contemporary source material (e.g. the Internet, manifestos, etc.), produce a draft report highlighting current government policy for the SME sector.

2 Imagine you are employed as a political lobbyist, with a special interest in conservation issues. You have been approached by a local conservation group which is concerned about government plans to build a bypass around a village in its area. The government's proposals for the road would cause significant damage to a Site of Special Scientific Interest (SSSI) and the group is determined to oppose the plans. Your brief is to draft an 'action plan' for the group, indicating what forms of pressure group activity you would recommend, in what sequence and using which channels of potential influence.

Further reading

Cocker, P. and Jones, A., *Contemporary British Politics and Government,* 4th edition, Liverpool Academic Press/Cambridge Media Group, 2015.

Coen, D. and Richardson, J., *Lobbying the European Union: Institutions, Actors and Issues,* Oxford University Press, 2009.

Hix, S., *The Political System of the European Union,* 3rd edition, Palgrave Macmillan, 2011.

Hodson, D. and Peterson, J. (eds), *Institutions of the European Union,* 4th edition, Oxford University Press, 2017.

Kavanagh, D. and Moran, M., *Politics UK,* Pearson Education, 2007.

Leach, R., Coxall, W. and Robins, L., *British Politics,* Palgrave Macmillan, 2011.

Moran, M., *Politics and Governance in the UK,* 2nd edition, Palgrave Macmillan, 2011.

Wilson, D. and Game, C., *Local Government in the United Kingdom,* 5th edition, Palgrave Macmillan, 2011.

Web links and further questions are available on the website at:
www.pearsoned.co.uk/worthington

5 The macroeconomic environment

Ian Worthington

Business organisations operate in an economic environment which shapes, and is shaped by, their activities. In market-based economies this environment comprises variables that are dynamic, interactive and mobile and which, in part, are affected by government in pursuit of its various roles in the economy. As a vital component in the macroeconomy, government exercises a significant degree of influence over the flow of income and hence over the level and pattern of output by the public and private sectors. Other key influences include a country's financial institutions and the international economic organisations and groupings to which it belongs or subscribes.

Learning outcomes

Having read this chapter you should be able to:

- compare alternative economic systems and their underlying principles and discuss the problems of transition from a centrally planned to a market-based economy

- illustrate flows of income, output and expenditure in a market economy and account for changes in the level and pattern of economic activity

- analyse the role of government in the macroeconomy, including government macroeconomic policies and the objectives on which they are based

- explain the role of financial institutions

- identify the key international economic institutions and organisations that influence the business environment in open, market economies

Key terms

Accelerator effect
Aggregate monetary demand
Balance of payments
Capital market
Capitalist economy
Central bank
Centrally planned economy
Circular flow of income
Consumer Price Index (CPI)
Consumer sovereignty
Credit rating agency
Crowding out
Cyclical unemployment
Deindustrialisation
Direct controls
Direct taxation
Economic growth
Economic scarcity
Economics
European Central Bank (ECB)
Exchange rate

Factory gate prices
Financial intermediaries
Fiscal policy
Free-market economy
Full employment
G7 nations
Government spending
Gross domestic product
Headline inflation
Income flows
Indirect taxation
Inflation
Injections
Interest rates
Leakages
Macroeconomic analysis
Macroeconomic environment
Microeconomic analysis
Monetary aggregates
Monetary policies
Money market

Money stock
Multiplier effect
National debt
Opportunity cost
Public sector net
  borrowing
Quantitative easing (QE)
Real cost
Real flows
Real interest rates
Real national income
Recession
Retail Price Index (RPI)
State bank
Stock exchange
Structural unemployment
Technological unemployment
Underlying rate of inflation
Wages/prices inflationary
  spiral
Withdrawals

Introduction

In April 2013, Japan's central bank announced its intention to embark on a huge programme of quantitative easing (see the case study at the end of this chapter) aimed at boosting the Japanese economy and ridding it of the deflation that had haunted the country for more than a decade. The plan was for the Bank of Japan to create new money and use it to buy trillions of yen worth of government bonds each month in the hope of increasing the overall level of demand, thereby pushing up both prices and wages. Part of a set of new macroeconomic policies known as 'Abenomics' – after Japan's new Prime Minister, Shinzo Abe – the scheme to effectively double the country's money supply had the support of the Bank of Japan, the Ministry of Finance and the private sector, which saw it as a means of persuading individuals to spend rather than hoard cash. Similar schemes in other countries, including the United States and the UK, represent one form of interventionary approach by governmental policy-makers aimed at steering the economy along a particular path thought to be beneficial for consumers and businesses alike.

What this simple example is designed to demonstrate is the intimate relationship between business activity and the wider economic context in which it takes place, and a glance at any quality newspaper will provide a range of similar illustrations of this interface between business and **economics**. What is important at this point is not to understand the complexities of global economic forces or their effect on businesses, but to appreciate in broad terms the importance of the **macroeconomic environment** for business organisations and, in particular, the degree of compatibility between the preoccupations of the entrepreneur and those of the economist. To the economist, for example, a recession is generally marked by falling demand, rising unemployment, a slowing down in economic growth and a fall in investment. To the firm, it usually implies a loss of orders, a likely reduction in the workforce, a decline in output (or a growth in stocks) and a general reluctance to invest in capital equipment and/or new projects.

Much of the detailed discussion of the economic aspects of business can be found in Parts Three and Four. In this chapter we concentrate on the broader question of the economic structure and processes of a market-based economy and on the macroeconomic influences affecting and being affected by business activity in this type of economic system. As suggested in the previous chapter, an understanding of the overall economic context within which businesses operate – including its core values and principles – is central to any meaningful analysis of the business environment.

Three further points are worth highlighting at this juncture. First, business activity not only is shaped by the economic context in which it takes place but helps to shape that context; consequently the success or otherwise of government economic policy depends to some degree on the reactions of both the firms and the markets (e.g. the stock market) that are affected by government decisions. Second, economic influences operate at a variety of spatial levels, as illustrated by the opening paragraph, and governments can sometimes find that circumstances largely or totally beyond their control can affect businesses, either favourably or adversely. Third, the economic (and, for that matter, political) influence of industry and commerce can be considerable and this ensures that business organisations – both individually and collectively – usually constitute one of the chief pressure groups in democratic states. This political and economic relationship between government and business is discussed more fully in Chapter 13.

Economic systems

The concept of economic scarcity

Like politics, the term 'economic' tends to be used in a variety of ways and contexts to describe certain aspects of human behaviour, ranging from activities such as producing, distributing and consuming, to the idea of frugality in the use of a resource (e.g. being 'economical' with the truth). Modern definitions stress how such behaviour, and the institutions in which it takes place (e.g. households, firms, governments, banks), are concerned with the satisfaction of human needs and wants through the transformation of resources into goods and services which are consumed by society. These processes are said to take place under conditions of **economic scarcity**.

The economist's idea of 'scarcity' centres on the relationship between a society's needs and wants and the resources available to satisfy them, the argument being that whereas needs and wants tend to be unlimited, the resources that can be used to meet those needs and wants are finite such that no society at any time has the capacity to provide for all its actual or potential requirements. The assumption here is that both individual and collective needs and wants consistently outstrip the means available to satisfy them, as exemplified, for instance, by the inability of governments to provide instant healthcare, the best roads, education, defence, railways, and so on at a time and place and of a quality convenient to the user. This being the case, 'choices' have to be made by both individuals and society concerning priorities in the use of resources, and every choice inevitably involves a 'sacrifice' (i.e. forgoing an alternative). Economists describe this sacrifice as the **opportunity cost** or **real cost** of the decision that is taken (e.g. every pound spent on the health service is a pound not spent on some other public service) and it is one faced by individuals, organisations (including firms), governments and society alike.

From a societal point of view the existence of economic scarcity poses three serious problems concerning the use of resources:

1 What to use the available resources for. That is, what goods and services should be produced (or not produced) with the resources (sometimes described as the 'guns v. butter' argument)?
2 How best to use those resources. For example, in what combinations, using what techniques and what methods?
3 How best to distribute the goods and services produced with them. That is, who gets what, how much and on what basis?

In practice, of course, these problems tend to be solved in a variety of ways, including barter (voluntary, bilateral exchange), price signals and the market, queuing and rationing, government instruction and corruption (e.g. resources allocated in exchange for personal favours), and examples of each of these solutions can be found in most, if not all, societies, at all times. Normally, however, one or other main approach to resource allocation tends to predominate and this allows analytical distinctions to be made between different types of economic system, one important distinction being between those economies that are centrally planned and those that operate predominantly through market forces where prices form the integrating mechanism. Understanding this distinction is fundamental to an examination of the way in which business is conducted and represents the foundation on which much of the subsequent analysis is built.

The centrally planned economy

In this type of economic system – associated with the post-Second-World-War socialist economies of Eastern Europe, China, Cuba and elsewhere – most of the key decisions on production are taken by a central planning authority, normally the state and its agencies. Under this arrangement, the state typically:

- owns and/or controls the main economic resources, including the means of production;
- establishes priorities in the use of those resources;
- sets output targets for businesses which are largely under state ownership and/or control;
- directs resources in an effort to achieve these predetermined targets; and
- seeks to coordinate production in such a way as to ensure consistency between output and input demands.

The fact that an economy is centrally planned does not necessarily imply that all economic decisions are taken at central level; in many cases decision-making may be devolved to subordinate agencies, including local committees and enterprises. Ultimately, however, these agencies are responsible to the centre and it is the latter which retains overall control of the economy and directs the use of scarce productive resources.

The problem of coordinating inputs and output in a modern planned economy is, of course, a daunting task and one which invariably involves an array of state planners and a central plan or blueprint normally covering a number of years (e.g. a five-year plan). Under such a plan, the state planners establish annual output targets for each sector of the economy and for each enterprise within the sector, identify the inputs of materials, labour and capital needed to achieve the set targets and allocate resources accordingly. Given that the outputs of some industries (e.g. agricultural machinery) are the inputs of others (e.g. collective farms), it is not difficult to see how the overall effectiveness of the plan would depend in part on a high degree of cooperation and coordination between sectors and enterprises, as well as on good judgement, good decisions and a considerable element of good luck. The available evidence from planned economies suggests that none of these can be taken for granted and each is often in short supply.

Even in the most centralised of economies, state planning does not normally extend to telling individuals what they must buy in shops or how to use their labour, although an element of state direction at times may exist (e.g. conscription in the armed forces). Instead, it tends to condition *what* is available for purchase and the *prices* at which exchange takes place, and both of these are essentially the outcome of political choices, rather than a reflection of consumer demands. All too often consumers tend to be faced by queues and 'black markets' for some consumer products and overproduction of others, as state enterprises strive to meet targets frequently unrelated to the needs and wants of consumers. By the same token, businesses that make losses do not have to close down, as the state would normally make additional funds available to cover any difference between sales revenue and costs. This being the case, the emphasis at firm level tends to be more on meeting targets than on achieving efficiency in the use of resources and hence a considerable degree of duplication and wastage tends to occur.

Given such an environment, the traditional entrepreneurial skills of efficient resource management, price setting and risk taking have little, if any, scope for development and managers behave essentially as technicians and bureaucrats, administering decisions largely made elsewhere. Firms, in effect, are mainly servants of the state and their activities are conditioned by social and political considerations, rather than by the needs of the market – although some market activity normally occurs in planned economies (especially in agriculture and a number of private services). Accordingly, businesses and their employees are not fully sensitised to the needs of the consumer and as a result quality and choice (where they exist) may suffer, particularly where incentives to improved efficiency and performance are negligible. Equally, the system tends to encourage bribery and corruption and the development of a substantial black market, with differences in income, status and political influence being important determinants of individual consumption and of living standards.

The free-market economy

The **free-market economy** (or **capitalist economy**) stands in direct contrast to the centrally planned system. Whereas in the latter the state controls most economic decisions, in the former the key economic agencies are private individuals (sometimes called 'households') and firms, and these interact in free markets, through a system of prices, to determine the allocation of resources.

The key features of this type of economic system are as follows:

- Resources are in private ownership and the individuals owning them are free to use them as they wish.
- Firms, also in private ownership, are equally able to make decisions on production, free from state interference.
- No blueprint (or master plan) exists to direct production and consumption.
- Decisions on resource allocation are the result of a decentralised system of markets and prices, in which the decisions of millions of consumers and hundreds of thousands of firms are automatically coordinated.
- The consumer is deemed to be sovereign, dictating the pattern of supply and hence the pattern of resource allocation.

In short, the three problems of what to produce, how to produce and how to distribute are solved by market forces.

Figure 5.1 illustrates the basic operation of a market economy. Individuals are owners of resources (e.g. labour) and consumers of products; firms are users of resources and producers of products. What products are produced – and hence how resources are used – depends on consumers, who indicate their demands by purchasing (i.e. paying the price) or not purchasing, and this acts as a signal to producers to acquire the resources necessary (i.e. pay the price) to meet the preferences of consumers. If consumer demands change, for whatever reason, this will cause an automatic reallocation of resources, as firms respond to the new market conditions. Equally, competition between producers seeking to gain or retain customers is said to guarantee that resources are used efficiently and to ensure that the most appropriate production methods (i.e. how to produce) are employed in the pursuit of profits.

Figure 5.1 The market economy

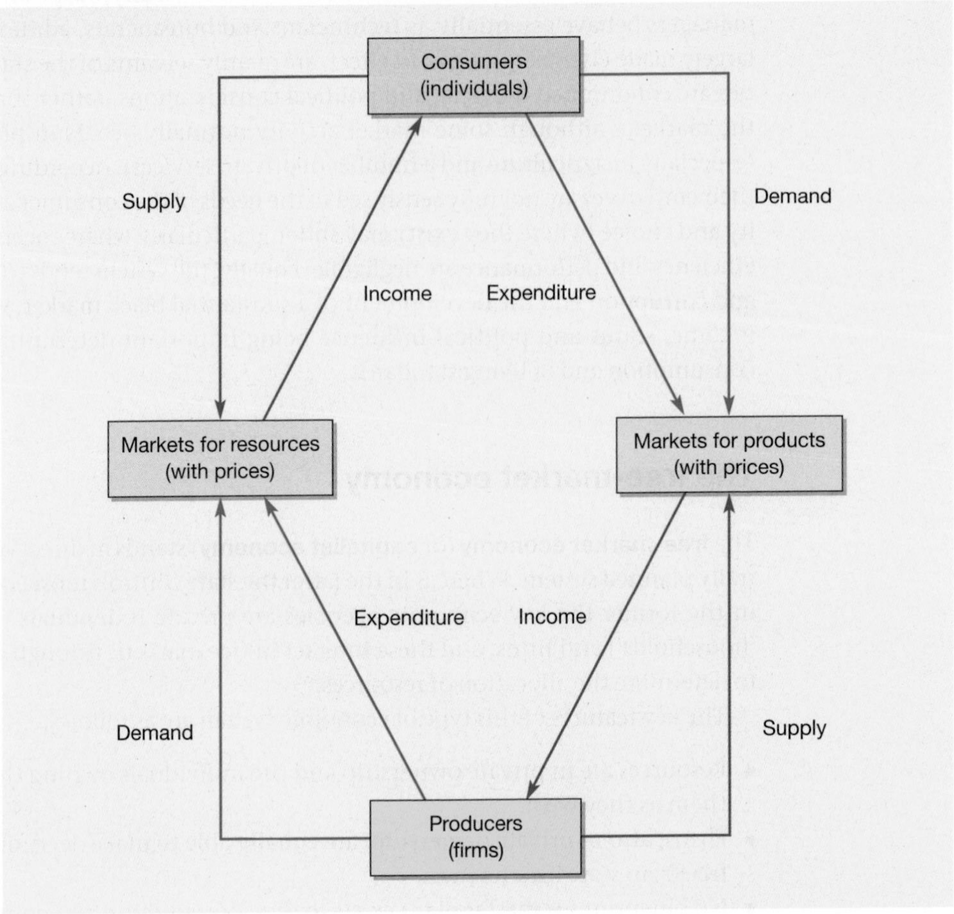

The distribution of output is also determined by market forces, in this case operating in the markets for productive services. Individuals supplying a resource (e.g. their own labour) receive an income (i.e. a price) from the firms using that resource and this allows them to purchase goods and services in the markets for products, which in turn provides an income for firms that can be spent on the purchase of further resources (see below). Should the demand for a particular type of productive resource increase – say, as a result of an increase in the demand for the product produced by that resource – the price paid to the provider of the resource will tend to rise and hence, other things being equal, allow more output to be purchased. Concomitantly, it is also likely to result in a shift of resources from uses which are relatively less lucrative to those which are relatively more rewarding.

This matching of supply and demand through prices in markets is described in detail in Chapter 14 and the analysis can also be applied to the market for foreign currencies (see Chapter 16). In practice, of course, no economy operates entirely in the manner suggested above; after all, firms are influenced by costs and supply decisions as well as by demand and generally seek to shape that demand, as well as simply responding to it. Nor for that matter is a market-based economy devoid of government involvement in the process of resource allocation, as evidenced by the existence of a public sector responsible for substantial levels of consumption and output and for helping to shape the conditions under which the private sector operates. In lots of economies the public sector owns a part or all of some industries, such as energy producers and rail organisations in many Central European countries. In short, any study of the market economy needs to incorporate the role of government and to examine, in particular, its influence on the activities of both firms and households. Such an analysis can be found in the later sections of this chapter.

Economies in transition

Most of the world's economies operate under a predominantly market-based system and the **centrally planned economy** in its original form is now largely a rare phenomenon. Three decades of reform have seen the old planned systems in Eastern Europe and elsewhere gradually giving way to the march of free enterprise, with some former communist states (e.g. Czech Republic) now members of the EU (see Chapter 16), while others – including Russia, China and Cuba – have gradually been experimenting with schemes aimed at developing an entrepreneurial culture and introducing capitalist market principles. Allowing business start-ups and expansion, deregulating some markets, partial privatisation of industries and sectors, and encouraging foreign investment are just some of the ways in which this economic transition has been taking place.

For states anxious to move from an entrenched system of state planning to a market-based economic system, the obstacles can be formidable and can help to slow down the progress of economic (and political) reform. For example, among the problems faced by Eastern European countries in the transitionary phase were:

- the need to create a legal and commercial framework to support the change to a market economy (e.g. company laws, laws on property rights, competition, external trade, the development of an appropriate accounting system);
- the need to establish different forms of free enterprise and to develop financial institutions capable of providing risk and venture capital, at commercial rates of return;
- the need to develop truly competitive markets, free from state control and protection;
- the need to liberalise labour markets and to develop entrepreneurial skills in a workforce traditionally demotivated by the old bureaucratic system;
- the need to allow prices to move to levels determined by market forces, rather than by political decision;
- the need to achieve macroeconomic stability as markets become more open, both internally and externally;
- the need to reduce the burden of international debt;
- the need to attract substantial overseas investment to assist in the rebuilding of the collapsed old socialist economies.

Meeting these requirements was not made any easier by economic collapse and the perceived need on the part of some reformers to bring about rapid economic change whatever the consequences. In Russia, in particular, widespread bribery, corruption and criminal activity have continued to undermine an economy struggling with economic and political instability that appears endemic and on occasions this has had a negative impact on foreign investment. We should not be surprised if the moves to restructure state economies prove a long and painful process for some countries in the coming years.

Politico-economic synthesis

The economic problem of resource allocation, described above, clearly has a political dimension, given its focus on the ownership, control and use of wealth-producing assets within society. This allows links to be made between a country's chosen economic system and its political regime. A useful way of representing possible relationships is illustrated in Figure 5.2. As suggested in Chapter 4, political systems can be characterised as ranging from democratic to authoritarian, depending on the degree of public involvement in decision-making processes. Similarly, economic systems can be seen to range from free-market to planned, according to the level of state intervention in the process of resource allocation. This two-dimensional model thus provides for four major combinations of politico-economic systems, ranging from democratic–free-market on the one hand (quadrant 1) to authoritarian–planned on the other (quadrant 3).

In applying this model to specific cases, it is clear that free-market approaches to resource allocation have predominantly been associated with democratic states. Such a link is not surprising. Democracy, after all, includes the notion of individuals being able to express their preferences through the ballot box and having the opportunity to replace one government with another at periodic intervals. In free markets, similar processes are at work, with individuals effectively 'voting' for goods and services through the price system and their expressed preferences being reflected in the pattern of resource allocation.

A link between authoritarian regimes and planned economic systems can equally be rationalised, in that government control over the political system is considerably facilitated if it also directs the economy through the ownership and/or control of the means of production, distribution and exchange. In effect, the relative absence of democratic mechanisms, such as free elections and choice between alternative forms of government,

Figure 5.2   Politico-economic systems

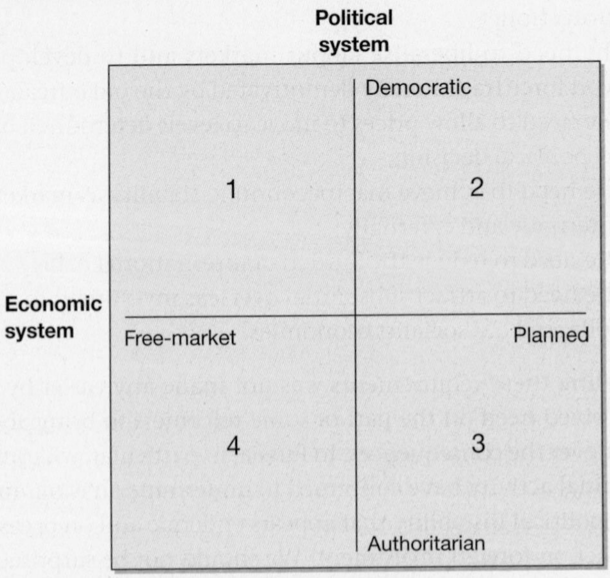

is echoed in the economic sphere by the inability of individuals to exercise any real influence over resource allocation. At the extreme, this could involve a government ban on any forms of free enterprise and total government control of the pattern of output and consumption in an economy which is devoid of effective **consumer sovereignty**.

Naturally the true picture is much more complicated than suggested by this simple dichotomy. Some authoritarian states, for instance, have predominantly capitalist economic systems (quadrant 4), while some democratic countries have a substantial degree of government intervention (i.e. moving them towards quadrant 2), either by choice or from necessity (e.g. wartime). Added to this, even in states where the political or economic system appears to be the same, considerable differences can occur at an operational and/or institutional level and this gives each country a degree of uniqueness not adequately portrayed by the model. That said, it is still the case that the basic congruity between democracy and free-market systems represents a powerful and pervasive influence in the business environment of the world's principal democratic states. The process of economic reform – as in Eastern Europe – accordingly tends to be accompanied by corresponding pressures for political change and these are often resisted by regimes not prepared to give up their political and economic powers and their elite status.

The macroeconomy

Levels of analysis

As indicated above, economics is concerned with the study of how society deals with the problem of scarcity and the resultant problems of what to produce, how to produce and how to distribute. Within this broad framework the economist typically distinguishes between two types of analysis:

1 **Microeconomic analysis**, which is concerned with the study of economic decision-taking by both individuals and firms.
2 **Macroeconomic analysis**, which is concerned with interactions in the economy as a whole (i.e. with economic aggregates).

The microeconomic approach is exemplified by the analysis of markets and prices undertaken in Chapter 14, which shows how individual consumers in a market might be affected by a price change. This analysis could be extended to an investigation of how the total market might respond to a movement in the price, or how a firm's (or market's) decisions on supply are affected by changes in wage rates or production techniques or some other factor. Note that, in these examples, the focus of attention is on decision-taking by individuals and firms in a single industry, while interactions between this industry and the rest of the economy are ignored; this is what economists call a 'partial analysis'.

In the real world all sectors of the economy are interrelated to some degree. A pay award, for example, in a particular industry (or in a single firm) may set a new pay norm that workers in other industries take up and these pay increases may subsequently influence employment, production and consumer demand in the economy as a whole, which could also have repercussions on the demand for a given product. Sometimes such repercussions may be relatively minor and so effectively can be ignored. In such situations the basic microeconomic approach remains valid.

The macroeconomics perspective recognises the interdependent nature of markets and therefore studies interactions in the economy as a whole, dealing with such questions as the overall level of employment, the rate of inflation, the percentage growth of output in the economy and many other economy-wide aggregates – exemplified by the analysis of international trade in Chapter 16 and by the macroeconomic model discussed below. It is worth noting that while the distinction between the micro and macro approaches remains useful for analytical purposes, in many instances the two become intertwined. For example, the reference at the start of this chapter to Japan's manipulation of the monetary base to overcome deflation in the economy is clearly a macroeconomic proposition. The idea that this approach will encourage households to spend rather than hoard cash leans heavily on microeconomic analysis, including notions of consumer preferences and anticipated price rises. Given that macroeconomic phenomena are the result of aggregating the behaviour of individual firms and consumers, this is obviously a common situation and one that is useful to bear in mind in any study of either the firm or the economy as a whole.

The 'flows' of economic activity

Economic activity can be portrayed as a flow of economic resources into firms (i.e. productive organisations) which are used to produce output for consumption, and a corresponding flow of payments from firms to the providers of those resources who use them primarily to purchase the goods and services produced. These flows of resources, production, income and expenditure accordingly represent the fundamental activities of an economy at work. Figure 5.3 illustrates the flow of resources and of goods and services in the economy – what economists describe as **real flows**.

In effect, firms use economic resources to produce goods and services, which are consumed by private individuals (private domestic consumption) or government

Figure 5.3   'Real flows' in the economy

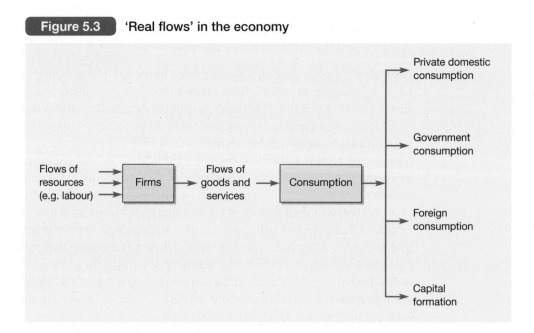

(government consumption) or by overseas purchasers (foreign consumption) or by other firms (capital formation). This consumption gives rise to a flow of expenditures that represents an income for firms, which they use to purchase further resources in order to produce further output for consumption. This flow of income and expenditures is shown in Figure 5.4.

The interrelationship between **income flows** and real flows can be seen by combining the two figures into one, which for the sake of simplification assumes only two groups operate in the economy: firms as producers and users of resources; and private individuals as consumers and providers of those resources (see Figure 5.5). Real flows are shown by the arrows moving in an anti-clockwise direction, income flows by the arrows flowing in a clockwise direction.

Despite a degree of oversimplification, the model of the economy illustrated in Figure 5.5 is a useful analytical tool, which highlights some vital aspects of economic activity of direct relevance to the study of business. The model shows the following:

1   Income flows around the economy, passing from households to firms and back to households and on to firms, and so on, with these income flows having corresponding real flows of resources, goods and services.
2   What constitutes an income to one group (e.g. firms) represents an expenditure to another (e.g. households), indicating that income generation in the economy is related to spending on consumption of goods and services and on resources (e.g. the use of labour).
3   The output of firms must be related to expenditure by households on goods and services, which in turn is related to the income the latter receive from supplying resources.
4   The use of resources (including the number of jobs created in the economy) must also be related to expenditure by households on consumption, given that resources are used to produce output for sale to households.
5   Levels of income, output, expenditure and employment in the economy are, in effect, interrelated.

Figure 5.4   Income flows in the economy

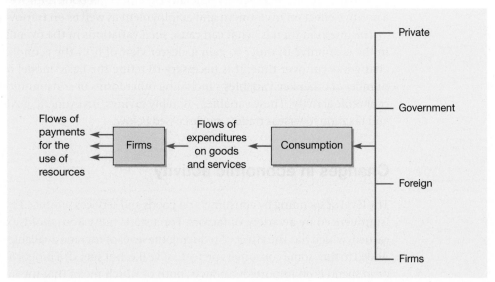

Figure 5.5 A simplified model of real flows and income flows

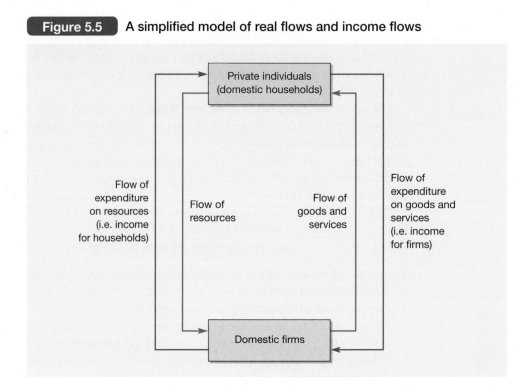

From the point of view of firms, it is clear from the model that their fortunes are intimately connected with the spending decisions of households and any changes in the level of spending can have repercussions for business activity at the micro as well as at the macro level. In a recession, an overall fall in demand can cause some businesses to close down while others experience a reduction in turnover and may be forced to make some staff redundant and/or delay investment decisions. As unemployment grows and investment is postponed or cancelled, demand may fall further and this will have a negative impact on many businesses. Once the economy gradually recovers and business confidence returns, many firms generally find the order book improves and this can have a positive effect on investment and employment as well as on turnover and profits.

The question then is: what can cause such variations in the overall level of spending in the economy? In order to gain a clearer view of how the economy works and why changes occur over time, it is necessary to refine the basic model by incorporating a number of other key variables – including other forms of consumption – that influence economic activity. These variables – notably savings, investment, government spending and taxation, overseas trade – are discussed below.

Changes in economic activity

The level of spending by consumers on goods and services produced by indigenous firms is influenced by a variety of factors. For a start, most households pay tax on income earned, which has the effect of reducing the level of income available for consumption. Added to this, some consumers prefer to save (i.e. not spend) a proportion of their income or to spend it on imported products, both of which mean that the income of domestic

Figure 5.6   The circular flow of income with 'leakages'

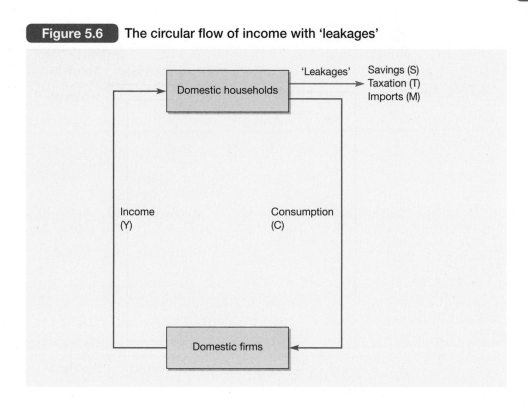

firms is less than it would have been had the income been spent with them. Circumstances such as these represent what economists call a **leakage** (or **withdrawal**) from the **circular flow of income** and help to explain why the revenue of businesses can fluctuate over time (see Figure 5.6).

At the same time as such 'leakages' are occurring, additional forms of spending in the economy are helping to boost the potential income of domestic firms. Savings by some consumers may be borrowed by firms to spend on investment in capital equipment or plant or premises (known as investment spending) and this generates income for firms producing capital goods. Similarly, governments use taxation to spend on the provision of public goods and services (public or government expenditure) and overseas buyers purchase products produced by indigenous firms (export spending). Together, these additional forms of spending represent an **injection** of income into the circular flow (see Figure 5.7).

While the revised model of the economy illustrated in Figure 5.7 is still highly simplified (e.g. consumers also borrow savings to spend on consumption or imports; firms also save and buy imports; governments also invest in capital projects), it demonstrates quite clearly that fluctuations in the level of economic activity are the result of changes in a number of variables, many of which are outside the control of firms or governments. Some of these changes are autonomous (i.e. spontaneous), as in the case of an increased demand for imports, while others may be deliberate or overt, as when the government decides to increase its own spending or to reduce taxation in order to stimulate demand. Equally, from time to time an economy may be subject to 'external shocks', such as the onset of recession among its principal trading partners or a significant price rise in a key commodity (e.g. oil price rises in 2007–8), which can have an important effect on internal income flows. Taken together, these and other changes help to explain why demand for goods and services constantly fluctuates and why

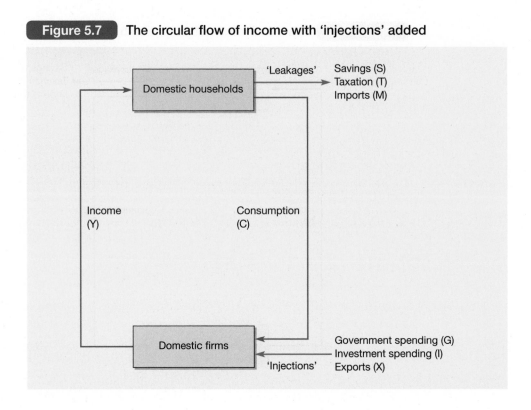

Figure 5.7   The circular flow of income with 'injections' added

changes occur not only in an economy's capacity to produce output, but also in its structure and performance over time.

It is important to recognise that where changes in spending do occur, these invariably have consequences for the economy that go beyond the initial 'injection' or 'withdrawal' of income. For example, a decision by government to increase spending on infrastructure would benefit the firms involved in the various projects and some of the additional income they receive would undoubtedly be spent on hiring labour. The additional workers employed would have more income to spend on consumption and this would boost the income for firms producing consumer goods, which in turn might hire more staff, generating further consumption, and so on. In short, the initial increase in spending by government will have additional effects on income and spending in the economy, as the extra spending circulates from households to firms and back again. Economists refer to this as the **multiplier effect** to emphasise the reverberative consequences of any increase or decrease in spending by consumers, firms, governments or overseas buyers.

Multiple increases in income and consumption can also give rise to an **accelerator effect,** which is the term used to describe a change in investment spending by firms as a result of a change in consumer spending. In the example above it is possible that the increase in consumption caused by the increase in government spending might persuade some firms to invest in more stock and capital equipment for extra production to meet increased consumer demand. Demand for capital goods would therefore rise, and this could cause further increases in the demand for industrial products (e.g. components, machinery) and also for consumer goods, as firms seek to increase their output to meet the changing market conditions. Should consumer spending fall, a reverse accelerator may occur and the same would apply to the multiplier as the reduction in consumption reverberates through the economy and causes further cuts in both consumption and investment. As the late Peter Donaldson has suggested, everything in the economy affects everything else; the economy is dynamic, interactive and mobile and is far more complex than implied by the model used in the analysis above (Donaldson and Farquhar, 1988: 84).

Government and the macroeconomy: objectives

Notwithstanding the complexities of the real economy, the link between business activity and spending is clear to see. This spending, as indicated above, comes from consumers, firms, governments and external sources and collectively can be said to represent total demand in the economy for goods and services. Economists frequently indicate this with the following notation:

Aggregate monetary demand = Consumer spending + Investment spending
+ Government spending + Export spending
– Import spending

or $$AMD = C + I + G + X - M$$

Within this equation, consumer spending (C) is regarded as by far the most important factor in determining the level of total demand.

While economists might disagree about what are the most significant influences on the component elements of AMD, it is widely accepted that governments have a crucial role to play in shaping demand, not only in their own sector but also on the market side of the economy. Government policies on spending and taxation, or on interest rates, clearly have both a direct and indirect influence on the behaviour of individuals and firms, which can affect both the demand and supply sides of the economy in a variety of ways. Underlying these policies is a number of key objectives pursued by government as a prerequisite to a healthy economy and which help to guide the choice of policy options. Understanding the broad choice of policies available to government, and the objectives associated with them, is of prime importance to students of the business environment.

Most governments appear to have a number of key economic objectives, the most important of which are normally the control of inflation, the pursuit of economic growth, a reduction in unemployment, the achievement of an acceptable balance-of-payments situation, controlling public (i.e. government) borrowing, and a relatively stable exchange rate.

Controlling inflation

Inflation is usually defined as an upward and persistent movement in the general level of prices over a given period of time; it can also be characterised as a fall in the value of money. For governments of all political complexions, reducing such movements to a minimum is seen as a primary economic objective (e.g. under the **Consumer Price Index** the UK government's declared inflation target is 2 per cent).

Monitoring trends in periodic price movements tends to take a number of forms. In the UK these have included:

1 The use of a **Retail Price Index (RPI)**, which measures how an average family's spending on goods and services is affected by price changes. The RPI has traditionally been the measure used for **headline inflation** in the UK and includes mortgage interest payments.

2 An examination of the **underlying rate of inflation**, which excludes the effects of mortgage payments (known as RPIX in the UK).

3 Measuring **factory gate prices**, to indicate likely future changes in consumer prices.

4 Comparing domestic inflation rates with those of the UK's chief overseas competitors, as an indication of the international competitiveness of UK firms.

With regard to the latter, the UK now uses a new measure of inflation known as the Consumer Price Index (CPI) to allow for a more direct comparison of the inflation rate in the UK with that of the rest of Europe. The CPI excludes a number of items that have historically been part of the RPIX, especially items relating to housing costs (e.g. mortgage interest payments and council tax).

In addition, changes in **monetary aggregates**, which measure the amount of money (and therefore potential spending power) in circulation in the economy, and movements of exchange rates (especially a depreciating currency – see Chapter 16) are also seen as a guide to possible future price increases, as their effects work through the economy.

Explanations as to why prices tend to rise over time vary considerably, but broadly speaking fall into two main categories. Supply-siders tend to focus on rising production costs – particularly wages, energy and imported materials – as a major reason for inflation, with firms passing on increased costs to the consumer in the form of higher wholesale and/or retail prices. Demand-siders, in contrast, tend to emphasise the importance of excessive demand in the economy, brought about, for example, by tax cuts, cheaper borrowing or excessive government spending, which encourages firms to take advantage of the consumer's willingness to spend money by increasing their prices. Where indigenous firms are unable to satisfy all the additional demand, the tendency is for imports to increase. This may not only cause further price rises, particularly if imported goods are more expensive or if exchange rate movements become unfavourable, but also can herald a deteriorating balance-of-payments situation and difficult trading conditions for domestic businesses.

Government concern with inflation – which crosses both party and state boundaries – reflects the fact that rising price levels can have serious consequences for the economy in general and for businesses in particular, especially if a country's domestic inflation rates are significantly higher than those of its main competitors. In markets where price is an important determinant of demand, rising prices may result in some businesses losing sales, and this can affect turnover and may ultimately affect employment if firms reduce their labour force in order to reduce their costs. Added to this, the uncertainty caused by a difficult trading environment may make some businesses unwilling to invest in new plant and equipment, particularly if interest rates are high and if inflation looks unlikely to fall for some time. Such a response, while understandable, is unlikely to improve a firm's future competitiveness or its ability to exploit any possible increases in demand as market conditions change.

Rising prices may also affect businesses by encouraging employees to seek higher wages in order to maintain or increase their living standards. Where firms agree to such wage increases, the temptation, of course, is to pass this on to the consumer in the form of a price rise, especially if demand looks unlikely to be affected to any great extent. Should this process occur generally in the economy, the result may be a **wages/prices inflationary spiral**, in which wage increases push up prices which push up wage increases which further push up prices, and so on. From an international competitive point of view, such an occurrence, if allowed to continue unchecked, could be disastrous for both firms and the economy. Thankfully, such a situation tends to be relatively uncommon in most economies, but, as recent problems in Zimbabwe have illustrated, hyperinflation can have disastrous consequences for a country's economy and its population (in mid-2008, for example, annual inflation in Zimbabwe was estimated at around 40 million per cent!).

Economic growth

Growth is an objective shared by governments and organisations alike. For governments, the aim is usually to achieve steady and sustained levels of non-inflationary growth, preferably led by exports (i.e. export-led growth), with growth being indicated by annual increases in **real national income** or **gross domestic product** (where 'real' = allowing for inflation and 'gross domestic product (GDP)' = the economy's annual output of goods and services measured in monetary terms). See also the concept of gross value added (GVA), which is an important measure in the estimation of GDP. (National Statistics Online www.ons.gov.uk has a good explanation of GVA.) To compensate for changes in the size of the population, growth rates tend to be expressed in terms of real national income per capita (i.e. real GDP divided by population).

Exactly what constitutes desirable levels of growth is difficult to say, except in very broad terms. If given a choice, governments would basically prefer:

- steady levels of real growth (e.g. 3–4 per cent p.a.), rather than annual increases in output which vary widely over the business cycle;
- growth rates higher than those of one's chief competitors; and
- growth based on investment in technology and on increased export sales, rather than on excessive government spending or current consumption.

It is worth remembering that, when measured on a monthly or quarterly basis, increases in output can occur at a declining rate and GDP growth can become negative. In the UK, a **recession** is said to exist following two consecutive quarters of negative GDP.

From a business point of view, the fact that increases in output are related to increases in consumption suggests that **economic growth** is good for business prospects and hence for investment and employment, and by and large this is the case. The rising living standards normally associated with such growth may, however, encourage increased consumption of imported goods and services at the expense of indigenous producers, to a point where some domestic firms are forced out of business and the economy's manufacturing base becomes significantly reduced (often called **deindustrialisation**). Equally, if increased consumption is based largely on excessive state spending, the potential gains for businesses may be offset by the need to increase interest rates to fund that spending (where government borrowing is involved) and by the tendency of government demands for funding **crowding out** the private sector's search for investment capital. In such cases, the short-term benefits from government-induced consumption may be more than offset by the medium- and long-term problems for the economy that are likely to arise.

Where growth prospects for the economy look good, business confidence tends to increase and, as indicated above, this is often reflected in increased levels of investment and stock holding and ultimately in levels of employment. In the UK, for example, the monthly and quarterly surveys by the Confederation of British Industry (CBI) provide evidence of how output, investment and stock levels change at different points of the business cycle and these are generally seen as a good indication of future business trends, as interpreted by entrepreneurs. Other indicators – including the state of the housing market and construction generally – help to provide a guide to the current and future state of the economy, including its prospects for growth in the short and medium term.

---

web link   The CBI's website address is *www.cbi.org.uk*

Reducing unemployment

In most democratic states the goal of **full employment** is no longer part of the political agenda; instead government pronouncements on employment tend to focus on job creation and maintenance and on developing the skills appropriate to future demands. The consensus seems to be that in technologically advanced market-based economies, some unemployment is inevitable and the basic aim should be to reduce unemployment to a level that is both politically and socially acceptable.

As with growth and inflation, unemployment levels tend to be measured at regular intervals (e.g. monthly, quarterly, annually), with the figures being adjusted to take into account seasonal influences (e.g. school-leavers entering the job market). Official statistics usually provide information on trends in long-term unemployment, areas of skill shortage and international comparisons, as well as sectoral changes within the economy. All of these indicators provide clues to the current state of the economy and to the prospects for businesses in the coming months and years, but need to be used with care. Unemployment, for example, tends to continue rising for a time even when a recession is over; equally, it is not uncommon for government definitions of unemployment to change or for international unemployment data to be based on different criteria.

The broader social and economic consequences of high levels of unemployment are well documented: it is a waste of resources; it puts pressure on the public services and on the Exchequer (e.g. by reducing tax yields and increasing public expenditure on welfare provision); it is frequently linked with growing social and health problems. Its implication for businesses, however, tends to be less clear cut. On the one hand, a high level of unemployment implies a pool of labour available for firms seeking workers (though not necessarily with the right skills), generally at wage levels lower than when a shortage of labour occurs. On the other hand, it can also give rise to a fall in overall demand for goods and services, which could exacerbate any existing deflationary forces in the economy, causing further unemployment and with it further reductions in demand. Where this occurs, economists tend to describe it as **cyclical unemployment** (i.e. caused by a general deficiency in demand) in order to differentiate it from unemployment caused by a deficiency in demand for the goods produced by a particular industry (**structural unemployment**) or by the introduction of new technology which replaces labour (**technological unemployment**).

A favourable balance of payments

A country's **balance of payments** is essentially the net balance of credits (earnings) and debits (payments) arising from its international trade over a given period of time (see Chapter 16). Where credits exceed debits, a balance-of-payments surplus exists, the opposite being described as a deficit. Understandably, governments tend to prefer either equilibrium in the balance of payments, or surpluses rather than deficits. For a government facing persistent balance-of-payments deficits, a sustained reduction in the size of the deficit may also be regarded as signifying a 'favourable' balance-of-payments situation.

Like other economic indicators, the balance-of-payments statistics come in a variety of forms and at different levels of disaggregation, allowing useful comparisons to be made not only on a country's comparative trading performance, but also on the international competitiveness of particular industries and commodity groups or on the development or decline of specific external markets. Particular emphasis tends to be given to the balance of payments on current account, which measures imports and exports of goods and services and is thus seen as an indicator of the competitiveness of an economy's firms and industries. Sustained current account surpluses tend to suggest favourable trading conditions, which can help to boost growth, increase employment and investment, and create a general feeling of confidence among the business community. They may also give rise to surpluses which domestic firms can use to finance overseas lending and investment, thus helping to generate higher levels of corporate foreign earnings in future years.

While it does not follow that a sustained current account deficit is inevitably bad for the country concerned, it often implies structural problems in particular sectors of its economy or possibly an exchange rate which favours importers rather than exporters. Many observers believe that the progressive decline of the UK's visible trading position after 1983 was an indication of the declining competitiveness of its firms, particularly those producing finished manufactured goods for consumer markets at home and abroad. By the same token, Japan's current account trade surplus of around $120 billion in late 1995 was portrayed as a sign of the cut-throat competition of Japanese firms, particularly those involved in producing cars, electrical and electronic products, and photographic equipment.

Controlling public borrowing

Governments raise large amounts of revenue annually, mainly through taxation, and use this income to spend on a wide variety of public goods and services (see below). Where annual revenue exceeds government spending, a budget surplus occurs and the excess is often used to repay past debt (formerly known in the UK as the 'public sector debt repayment' or PSDR). The accumulated debt of past and present governments represents a country's **national debt**. In the UK this stood at around £1.6 trillion in 2016, which was more than 80 per cent of GDP.

Where governments face annual budget deficits rather than budget surpluses, they are said to have a 'public sector borrowing requirement' or PSBR (now known in the UK as **public sector net borrowing** or PSNB). While such deficits are not inevitably a problem, in the same way that a small personal overdraft is not necessarily critical for an individual, large-scale and persistent deficits are generally seen as a sign of an economy facing current and future difficulties which require urgent government action. The overriding concern over high levels of public borrowing tends to be focused on the following:

1   Its impact on interest rates, given that higher interest rates tend to be needed to attract funds from private sector uses to public sector uses.
2   The impact of high interest rates on consumption and investment and hence on the prospects of businesses.
3   The danger of the public sector 'crowding out' the private sector's search for funds for investment.
4   The opportunity cost of debt interest, especially in terms of other forms of public spending.
5   The general lack of confidence in the markets about the government's ability to control the economy and the likely effect this might have on inflation, growth and the balance of payments.
6   The need to meet the 'convergence criteria' laid down at Maastricht for entry to the single currency (e.g. central government debt no higher than 3 per cent of GDP).

The consensus seems to be that controlling public borrowing is best tackled by restraining the rate of growth of public spending rather than by increasing revenue through changes in taxation, since the latter could depress demand.

A stable exchange rate

A country's currency has two values: an internal value and an external value. Internally, its value is expressed in terms of the goods and services it can buy and hence it is affected by changes in domestic prices. Externally, its value is expressed as an **exchange rate**, which governs how much of another country's currency it can purchase (e.g. £1 = $2 or £1 = €1.20). Since foreign trade normally involves an exchange of currencies, fluctuations in the external value of a currency will influence the price of imports and exports and hence can affect the trading prospects for business, as well as a country's balance of payments and its rate of inflation (see Chapter 16).

On the whole, governments and businesses involved in international trade tend to prefer exchange rates to remain relatively stable, because of the greater degree of certainty this brings to the trading environment; it also tends to make overseas investors more confident that their funds are likely to hold their value. To this extent, schemes that seek to fix exchange rates within predetermined levels (e.g. the European Exchange Rate Mechanism (ERM)), or that encourage the use of a common currency (e.g. the euro), tend to have the support of the business community, which prefers predictability to uncertainty where trading conditions are concerned.

mini case   Digging in for the long term

For firms engaged in international trade, the strength of the currency (i.e. the exchange rate) is an important consideration (see e.g. Chapter 16). As the value of one currency changes against other currencies, this usually alters the price of imported/exported products and this can make them more/less attractive to potential customers. To mitigate the impact of exchange rate changes, some firms engage in a process known as hedging, which basically involves trying to reduce or eliminate exchange rate risks, for example by buying a proportion of a currency forward (i.e. before it is needed) at an agreed price. An alternative strategy is to consider producing the product in different locations (e.g. setting up manufacturing facilities in other countries), which can offset some of the impact of currency fluctuations, as well as providing other potential benefits to a business.

A good example of the latter approach is provided by JCB, the UK-owned private company famous for its yellow construction equipment (e.g. diggers). In the 1990s, the company's business was mainly based in the UK and parts of Western Europe, but faced with a limited market and a strengthening pound, which made exporting difficult, the firm decided to seek a global presence by investing in manufacturing abroad. Focusing first on the United States, JCB built a plant in Georgia in the late 1990s to exploit the US market; this was followed by further plants in São Paulo in Brazil and new plants in India near Mumbai. It also acquired a German construction firm in 2005 and opened a further factory near Shanghai in 2006, thereby adding to its global reach.

Despite having to shed some jobs in the global recession, by 2013 the company's global workforce numbered around 10 000 based on four continents and it was selling its product in 150 countries via a network of dealerships. In September of that year the firm opened the world's biggest JCB dealer depot in Ekaterinberg, Russia, following a multi-million-pound investment.

In addition to the potential currency benefits of operating in different countries, JCB has gained a number of other advantages, including establishing a global brand name, access to low-cost suppliers and to developing markets, and reducing freight costs and tariff barriers. Globalisation, in short, can offer businesses many 'opportunities', but we must not forget that it can also give rise to substantial 'threats' at the corporate level, not least the danger of low-cost competitors invading one's own markets.

Government and the macroeconomy: policies

Governments throughout the world play various key roles in their respective economies. These include the following functions:

- consumer of resources (e.g. employer, landowner);
- supplier of resources (e.g. infrastructure, information);
- consumer of goods and services (e.g. government spending);
- supplier of goods and services (e.g. nationalised industries);
- regulator of business activity (e.g. employment laws, consumer laws);
- regulator of the economy (e.g. fiscal and monetary policies); and
- redistributor of income and wealth (e.g. taxation system).

The extent of these roles, and their impact on the economy in general and on business in particular, vary from country to country as well as over time.

Despite the economic significance of these roles, in most market-based economies democratically elected governments prefer levels and patterns of production and consumption to be determined largely by market forces, with a minimum of government interference. At the same time, the recognition that market forces alone are unable to guarantee that an economy will automatically achieve the objectives established by governments has meant that state intervention – to curb inflation, encourage growth, reduce unemployment, correct a balance-of-payments or budgetary problem or restore currency stability – invariably occurs to some degree in all countries. In broad terms, this intervention usually takes three main forms, described as fiscal policy, monetary policy and direct controls. These policy instruments – or 'instrumental variables' – and their effects on the business community are discussed below.

Fiscal policy

As indicated above, each year governments raise and spend huge amounts of money. The UK government's estimates for 2016, for example, suggested that **government spending** would be about £762 billion and was to be allocated in the manner illustrated in Figure 5.8. This spending was to be funded mainly from **direct taxation, indirect taxation** and national insurance contributions (see Figure 5.9). The PSNB was estimated to be nearly £80 billion.

Fiscal policy involves the use of changes in government spending and taxation to influence the level and composition of aggregate demand in the economy and, given the amounts involved, this clearly has important implications for business. Elementary circular flow analysis suggests, for instance, that reductions in taxation and/or increases in government spending will inject additional income into the economy and will, via the multiplier effect, increase the demand for goods and services, with favourable consequences for business. Reductions in government spending and/or increases in taxation will have the opposite effect, depressing business prospects and probably discouraging investment and causing a rise in unemployment.

Apart from their overall impact on aggregate demand, fiscal changes can be used to achieve specific objectives, some of which will be of direct or indirect benefit to the business community. Reductions in taxes on company profits and/or increases in tax allowances for investment in capital equipment can be used to encourage business to increase investment spending, hence boosting the income of firms producing industrial products and causing some additional spending on consumption. Similarly, increased government spending targeted at firms involved in exporting, or at the creation of new business, will encourage increased business activity and additionally may lead to more output and employment in the economy.

In considering the use of fiscal policy to achieve their objectives, governments tend to be faced with a large number of practical problems that generally limit their room for manoeuvre. Boosting the economy through increases in spending or reductions in taxation could cause inflationary pressures, as well as encouraging an inflow of imports and increasing the public sector deficit, none of which would be particularly welcomed by entrepreneurs or by the financial markets. By the same token, fiscal attempts to restrain demand in order to reduce inflation will generally depress the economy, causing a fall in output and employment and encouraging firms to abandon or defer investment projects until business prospects improve.

Figure 5.8 The allocation of UK government spending, 2013 budget

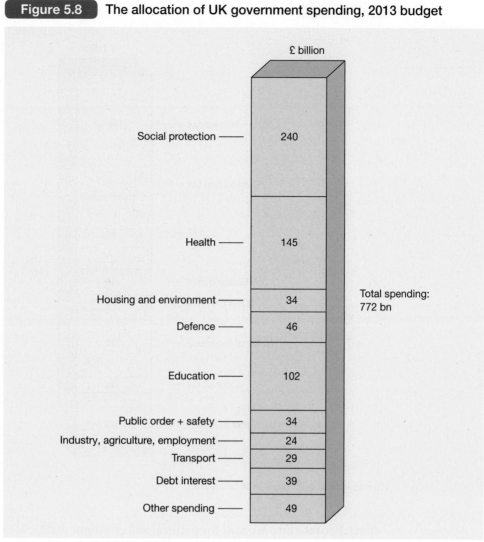

£ billion

Social protection —— 240

Health —— 145

Housing and environment —— 34

Defence —— 46

Education —— 102

Public order + safety —— 34

Industry, agriculture, employment —— 24

Transport —— 29

Debt interest —— 39

Other spending —— 49

Total spending: 772 bn

Source: Adapted from Budget Statement, 2013.

Added to this, it should not be forgotten that government decision-makers are politicians who need to consider the political as well as the economic implications of their chosen courses of action. Thus, while cuts in taxation may receive public approval, increases may not, and, if implemented, the latter may encourage higher wage demands. Similarly, the redistribution of government spending from one programme area to another is likely to give rise to widespread protests from those on the receiving end of any cuts, so much so that governments tend to be restricted for the most part to changes at the margin, rather than undertaking a radical reallocation of resources, and may be tempted to fix budgetary allocations for a number of years ahead (e.g. the introduction of the Comprehensive Spending Review in the UK).

Other factors too – including changes in economic thinking, self-imposed fiscal rules, external constraints on borrowing and international agreements – can play their part in restraining the use of fiscal policy as an instrument of demand management, whatever a government's preferred course of action may be. Simple prescriptions to boost the economy through large-scale cuts in taxation or increases in government spending

| Figure 5.9 | Sources of government revenue, 2013 budget |

£ billion

Income tax —— 182

Corporation tax —— 43

VAT —— 138

Total income: 716

Excise duties —— 48

Business rates —— 28

National Insurance —— 126

Council tax —— 30

Other revenues —— 120

Source: Adapted from Budget Statement, 2013.

often fail to take into account the political and economic realities of the situation faced by most governments.

Monetary policy

Monetary policies seek to influence monetary variables such as the money supply or rates of interest in order to regulate the economy. While the supply of money and interest rates (i.e. the cost of borrowing) are interrelated, it is convenient to consider them separately.

As far as changes in **interest rates** are concerned, these clearly have implications for business activity, as circular flow analysis demonstrates. Lower interest rates not only encourage firms to invest as the cost of borrowing falls, but also encourage consumption as disposable incomes rise (predominantly through the mortgage effect) and as the cost of loans and overdrafts decreases. Such increased consumption tends to be an added spur to investment, particularly if inflation rates (and therefore **real interest rates**) are low, and this can help to boost the economy in the short term, as well as improving the supply side in the longer term. Real interest rates allow for inflation.

Raising interest rates tends to have the opposite effect – causing a fall in consumption as mortgages and other prices rise, and deferring investment because of the additional cost of borrowing and the decline in business confidence as consumer spending falls. If interest rates remain persistently high, the encouragement given to savers and the discouragement given to borrowers and spenders may help to generate a recession, characterised by falling output, income, spending and employment and by increasing business failure.

Changes in the **money stock** (especially credit) affect the capacity of individuals and firms to borrow and, therefore, to spend. Increases in money supply are generally related to increases in spending and this tends to be good for business prospects, particularly if interest rates are falling as the money supply rises (see the case study at this end of this chapter). Restrictions on monetary growth normally work in the opposite direction, especially if such restrictions help to generate increases in interest rates which feed through to both consumption and investment, both of which will tend to decline.

As in the case of fiscal policy, the government is usually able to manipulate monetary variables in a variety of ways, including taking action in the money markets to influence interest rates and controlling its own spending to influence monetary growth. Once again, however, circumstances tend to dictate how far and in what way the government is free to operate. Attempting to boost the economy by allowing the money supply to grow substantially, for instance, threatens to cause inflationary pressures and to increase spending on imports, both of which run counter to government objectives and do little to assist domestic firms. Similarly, policies to boost consumption and investment through lower interest rates, while welcomed generally by industry, offer no guarantee that any additional spending will be on domestically produced goods and services, and also tend to make the financial markets nervous about government commitments to control inflation in the longer term (see section below, 'The role of the central bank').

This nervousness among market dealers reflects the fact that in modern market economies a government's policies on interest rates and monetary growth cannot be taken in isolation from those of its major trading partners and this operates as an important constraint on government action. The fact is that a reduction in interest rates to boost output and growth in an economy also tends to be reflected in the exchange rate; this usually falls as foreign exchange dealers move funds into those currencies that yield a better return and that also appear a safer investment if the market believes a government is abandoning its counter-inflationary policy. As the UK government found in the early 1990s, persistently high rates of interest in Germany severely restricted its room for manoeuvre on interest rates for fear of the consequences for sterling if relative interest rates got too far out of line.

Direct controls

Fiscal and monetary policies currently represent the chief policy instruments used in modern market economies and hence they have been discussed in some detail. Governments, however, also use a number of other weapons from time to time in their attempts to achieve their macroeconomic objectives. Such weapons, which are designed essentially to achieve a specific objective – such as limiting imports or controlling wage increases – tend to be known as **direct controls**. Examples of such policies include:

- *incomes policies,* which seek to control inflationary pressures by influencing the rate at which wages and salaries rise;
- *import controls,* which attempt to improve a country's balance-of-payments situation, by reducing either the supply of, or the demand for, imported goods and services (see Chapter 16);
- *regional and urban policies,* which are aimed at alleviating urban and regional problems, particularly differences in income, output, employment, and local and regional decline (see Chapter 13).

A brief discussion of some of these policy instruments is found at various points in the text below. Students wishing to study these in more detail are recommended to consult the books referred to at the end of this chapter.

The role of financial institutions

Interactions in the macroeconomy between governments, businesses and consumers take place within an institutional environment that includes a large number of financial intermediaries. These range from banks and building societies to pension funds, insurance companies, investment trusts and issuing houses, all of which provide a number of services of both direct and indirect benefit to businesses. As part of the financial system within a market-based economy, these institutions fulfil a vital role in channelling funds from those able and willing to lend, to those individuals and organisations wishing to borrow in order to consume or invest. It is appropriate to consider briefly this role of financial intermediation and the supervision exercised over the financial system by the central bank, before concluding the chapter with a review of important international economic institutions.

Elements of the financial system

A financial system basically comprises three main elements:

1 *Lenders and borrowers,* which may be individuals, organisations or governments.
2 *Financial institutions,* of various kinds, which act as intermediaries between lenders and borrowers and which manage their own asset portfolios in the interest of their shareholders and/or depositors.
3 *Financial markets,* in which lending and borrowing take place through the transfer of money and/or other types of asset, including paper assets such as shares and stock.

Financial institutions, as indicated above, comprise a wide variety of organisations, many of which are public companies with shareholders. Markets include the markets for short-term funds of various types (usually termed **money markets**) and those for long-term finance for both the private and public sectors (usually called the **capital market**).

Stock exchanges normally lie at the centre of the latter and constitute an important market for existing securities issued by both companies and government.

The vital role played by **financial intermediaries** in the operation of the financial system is illustrated in Figure 5.10 and reflects the various benefits that derive from using an intermediary rather than lending direct to a borrower (e.g. creating a large pool of savings, spreading risk, transferring short-term lending into longer-term borrowing, providing various types of funds transfer services). Lenders on the whole prefer low risk, high returns, flexibility and liquidity, while borrowers prefer to minimise the cost of borrowing and to use the funds in a way that is best suited to their needs. Companies, for example, may borrow to finance stock or work-in-progress or to meet short-term debts and such borrowing may need to be as flexible as possible. Alternatively, they may wish to borrow in order to replace plant and equipment or to buy new premises – borrowing which needs to be over a much longer term and which hopefully will yield a rate of return that makes the use of the funds and the cost of borrowing worthwhile.

The process of channelling funds from lenders to borrowers often gives rise to paper claims, which are generated either by the financial intermediary issuing a claim to the lender (e.g. when a bank borrows by issuing a certificate of deposit) or by the borrower issuing a claim to the financial intermediary (e.g. when the government sells stock to a financial institution). These paper claims represent a liability to the issuer and an asset to the holder and can be traded on a secondary market (i.e. a market for existing securities), according to the needs of the individual or organisation holding the paper claim. At any point, financial intermediaries tend to hold a wide range of such assets (claims on borrowers), which they buy or sell ('manage') in order to yield a profit and/or improve their liquidity position. Decisions of this kind, taken on a daily basis, invariably affect the position of investors (e.g. shareholders) and customers (e.g. depositors) and can,

Figure 5.10 **The role of financial intermediaries**

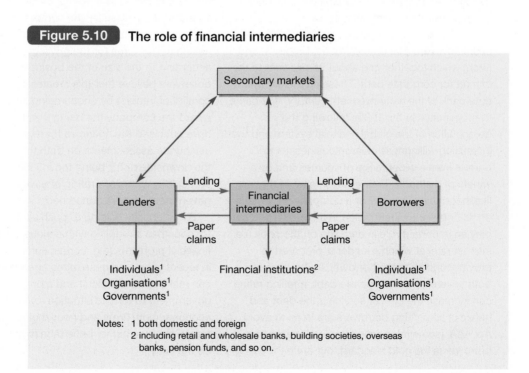

Notes: 1 both domestic and foreign
2 including retail and wholesale banks, building societies, overseas banks, pension funds, and so on.

under certain circumstances, have serious consequences for the financial intermediary and its stakeholders (e.g. the bad debts faced by financial institutions in the wake of the sub-prime mortgage crisis in the United States from 2007–8 onwards, the effects of which are still being felt today).

Given the element of risk, it is perhaps not surprising that some financial institutions have historically been conservative in their attitude towards lending on funds deposited with them, especially in view of their responsibilities to their various stakeholders. In general, UK retail banks have a long-standing preference for financing industry's working capital rather than investment spending, and hence the latter has tended to be financed largely by internally generated funds (e.g. retained profits) or by share issues. In comparison, banks in Germany, France, the United States and Japan tend to be more ready to meet industry's medium- and longer-term needs and are often directly involved in regular discussions with their clients concerning corporate strategy, in contrast to the arm's length approach favoured by many of their UK counterparts (see e.g. Neale and Haslam 1991: 141). As the global financial crisis has illustrated, however, the increasing complexity of financial instruments and the willingness of some traders to take risks in pursuit of higher corporate (and personal) rewards suggest that the past deregulation of the financial system may have come at a significant price.

---

mini case A new kid on the block: the rise of the credit rating agency

Credit rating agencies have become powerful and influential organisations in world finance, rating the 'creditworthiness' of both companies and countries and thereby often helping to influence lending and investment decisions.

Of more than 150 agencies worldwide, the three best known are Standard & Poor's, Moody's, and Fitch, which together rate about 95 per cent of the market for corporate debt. These agencies, which date back to the early twentieth century, first came to prominence in the 1980s following the deregulation of the global financial system and the increasing willingness of large businesses to borrow from a wider range of sources and by a variety of methods. Their assessments of the likelihood that a country or a company will default on its debts are widely trailed in the media and can play an important role in deciding on the price (i.e. interest rate) at which a lender is prepared to provide funding to the borrower. In the case of both sovereign and corporate debt, a falling rating can increase the cost of servicing the debt and hence is something borrowers are keen to avoid. An 'AAA' (sometimes called 'triple A') rating of a borrower is the gold standard, but once the rating falls below a certain level this is known as 'junk status', indicating that a default is more likely and invariably pushing up interest rates significantly.

It is interesting to note that credit rating agencies are funded by the companies they rate, with organisations wishing to acquire a rating having to pay a fee for the privilege, which varies according to the size of the business. Some observers believe that this creates a potential conflict of interest by encouraging an agency to award the company the rating it would like. Others have criticised the agencies for regularly inaccurate assessments on both the upside and the downside or for being too influential, particularly where the rating of sovereign (i.e. government) debt is concerned.

By potentially helping to push up interest rates for countries struggling with serious economic and financial problems (e.g. certain eurozone countries in recent years), adverse rating agency judgements can make it more difficult and more costly for a government to turn its situation round. In the real economy, both firms and households may be forced to pay a higher price than might otherwise be the case.

The role of the central bank

A critical element in a country's financial system is its **central bank** or **state bank**; in the UK this is the Bank of England. Like most of its overseas counterparts, the Bank of England exercises overall supervision over the banking sector, with the aim of maintaining a stable and efficient financial framework as part of its contribution to a healthy economy. Its activities have a significant influence in the financial markets (especially the foreign exchange market, the gilts market and the sterling money market). These activities include the following roles:

- banker to the government;
- banker to the clearing banks;
- manager of the country's foreign reserves;
- manager of the national debt;
- manager of the issue of notes and coins;
- supervisor of the monetary sector; and
- implementer of the government's monetary policy.

Since 1997 the Bank has also been granted 'operational independence' to set interest rates and to conduct other aspects of monetary policy free from Treasury interference as part of its core purpose of ensuring monetary stability (e.g. controlling inflation and protecting the currency). Interest rates are set at the monthly meetings of the Bank's Monetary Policy Committee (MPC), which is chaired by the Bank's governor. In order to facilitate forward planning by businesses and financial institutions and to promote market stability, the MPC also now provides forward guidance on aspects of monetary policy, particularly interest rates.

In response to the problems resulting from the global financial crisis, the Bank has recently acquired an enhanced role in promoting and developing greater financial stability. Under the Financial Services Act 2012, a Financial Policy Committee has been established with responsibility for taking action to remove or reduce systemic risks in the financial system and generally supporting government economic policy (i.e. a macro-level role). Alongside this new body is a Prudential Regulation Authority that has been set up to supervise the key financial institutions (e.g. banks, building societies, insurers) so as to protect policy holders and investors and promote sound practices within the financial system (i.e. a micro-level role).

For further information on the Bank of England, consult
www.bankofengland.co.uk

While central banks are nationally based institutions, the EU also has its own central bank, the **European Central Bank (ECB)**, which is based in Frankfurt. The main task of the ECB is to maintain the purchasing power of the euro and hence to promote price stability within the eurozone. Among its key roles are defining and implementing monetary policy for the eurozone, including foreign exchange operations and issuing euro banknotes. It has also been heavily involved in bond purchasing in struggling EU economies to support the value of the euro.

The ECB's website is *www.ecb.europa.eu*

International economic institutions and organisations

Given that external factors constrain the ability of governments to regulate their economy, it is appropriate to conclude this analysis of the macroeconomic context of business with a brief review of a number of important international economic institutions and organisations that affect the trading environment. Foremost among these is the EU, which is examined at length in Chapters 4 and 16. In the discussions below we look at the International Monetary Fund (IMF), the Organization for Economic Cooperation and Development (OECD), the European Bank for Reconstruction and Development (EBRD), the World Trade Organization (WTO) and the World Bank (IBRD).

The International Monetary Fund

The IMF is an international organisation currently of 184 member countries. It came into being in 1946 following discussions at Bretton Woods in the United States which sought to agree a world financial order for the post-war period that would avoid the problems associated with the worldwide depression in the inter-war years. Its original role was to provide a pool of foreign currencies from its member states that would be used to smooth out trade imbalances between countries, thereby promoting a structured growth in world trade and encouraging exchange rate stability. In this way, the architects of the IMF believed that the danger of international protectionism would be reduced and that all countries would consequently benefit from the boost given to world trade and the greater stability of the international trading environment.

web link The IMF's website is *www.imf.org*

While this role as international 'lender of last resort' still exists, the IMF's focus in recent years has tended to switch towards international surveillance and to helping the developing economies with their mounting debt problems and assisting Eastern Europe with reconstruction, following the break-up of the Soviet bloc. The role of assisting reconstruction in Eastern Europe is also undertaken by the European Bank for Reconstruction and Development (EBRD). See text below. More recently it has played a major role in lending to countries caught up in the global financial crisis in order to boost the global economy. To some extent its position as an international decision-making body has been diminished by the tendency of the world's leading economic countries to deal with global economic problems outside the IMF's institutional framework. The United States, Japan, Germany, France, Italy, Canada, the UK and Russia now meet regularly as the Group of Eight (G8) leading industrial economies to discuss issues of mutual interest (e.g. the environment, Eastern Europe). These world economic summits, as they are frequently called, have tended to supersede discussions in the IMF and as a result normally attract greater media attention. Key global and economic issues are also discussed at meetings of the **G20**, which includes the G8 countries and a number of other key players, including China, India and Brazil.

The Organization for Economic Cooperation and Development

The OECD came into being in 1961, but its roots go back to 1948 when the Organization for European Economic Cooperation (OEEC) was established to coordinate the distribution of Marshall Aid to the war-torn economies of Western Europe. Today it comprises 34 members, drawn from the rich industrial countries and including the **G7 nations**, Australia, New Zealand and most other European states. Collectively, these countries account for less than 20 per cent of the world's population but produce around two-thirds of its output – hence the tendency of commentators to refer to the OECD as the 'rich man's club'.

web link   You can access the OECD's website at *www.oecd.org*

The OECD is the main forum in which the governments of the world's leading industrial economies meet to discuss economic matters, particularly questions concerned with promoting stable growth and freer trade and with supporting development in poorer non-member countries. Through its council and committees, and backed by an independent secretariat, the OECD is able to take decisions which set out an agreed view and/or course of action on important social and economic issues of common concern. While it does not have the authority to impose ideas, its influence lies in its capacity for intellectual persuasion, particularly its ability through discussion to promote convergent thinking on international economic problems. To assist in the task, the OECD provides a wide variety of economic data on member countries, using standardised measures for national accounting, unemployment and purchasing-power parities. It is for these data – and especially its economic forecasts and surveys – that the OECD is perhaps best known.

The European Bank for Reconstruction and Development

The aims of the EBRD, which was inaugurated in April 1991, are to facilitate the transformation of the states of Central and Eastern Europe and beyond from centrally planned to free-market economies and to promote political and economic democracy, respect for human rights and respect for the environment. It is particularly involved with the privatisation process, project financing, technical assistance, training and investment in upgrading of the infrastructure and in facilitating economic, legal and financial restructuring. It works in cooperation with its members, private companies and organisations such as the IMF, OECD, the World Bank and the United Nations.

web link   Information on the EBRD can be obtained at *www.ebrd.com*

The World Trade Organization

The WTO, which came into being on 1 January 1995, superseded the General Agreement on Tariffs and Trade (the GATT), which dated back to 1947. Like the IMF and the International Bank for Reconstruction and Development (see below), which were established at the same time, the GATT was part of an attempt to reconstruct the international politico-economic environment in the period after the end of the Second World War. Its replacement by the WTO can be said to mark an attempt to put the question of liberalising world trade higher up on the international political agenda.

> **web link** The WTO can be accessed at *www.wto.org*

With a membership of more than 150 states (plus other observers), the WTO is a permanent international organisation charged with the task of liberalising world trade within an agreed legal and institutional framework. In addition it administers and implements a number of multilateral agreements in fields such as agriculture, textiles and services and is responsible for dealing with disputes arising from the Uruguay Round Final Act. It also provides a forum for the debate, negotiation and adjudication of trade problems and in the latter context is said to have a much stronger and quicker trade compliance and enforcement mechanism than existed under the GATT. See also Chapter 16.

The World Bank

Established in 1945, the World Bank (more formally known as the International Bank for Reconstruction and Development, or IBRD) is a specialised agency of the United Nations, set up to encourage economic growth in developing countries through the provision of loans and technical assistance. The IBRD currently has over 180 members.

> **web link** The IBRD can be accessed at *www.worldbank.org*

The European Investment Bank

The EIB was created in 1958 under the Treaty of Rome and is the financing institution of the EU. Its main task is to contribute to the integration, balanced development, and the economic and social cohesion of EU member states. Using funds raised on the markets, it finances capital projects which support EU objectives within the EU and elsewhere. Its interests include environmental schemes, projects relating to transport and energy, and support for small and medium-sized enterprises.

> **web link** For further information on the EIB see *www.eib.org*

Synopsis

Business and economics are inextricably linked. Economics is concerned with the problem of allocating scarce productive resources to alternative uses – a fundamental aspect of business activity. In market-based economies, this problem of resource allocation is largely solved through the operation of free markets, in which price is a vital ingredient. The existence of such markets tends to be associated primarily, though not exclusively, with democratic political regimes.

In all democratic states, the government is a key component of the market economy and exercises considerable influence over the level and pattern of business activity – a point illustrated by the use of elementary circular flow analysis. A government's aims for the economy help to shape the policies it uses and these policies have both direct and indirect consequences for business organisations of all kinds.

In examining the economic context in which firms exist, due attention needs to be paid to the influence of a wide range of institutions and organisations, some of which operate at the international level. Equally, as markets become more open and business becomes more global, the fortunes of firms in trading economies become increasingly connected and hence subject to fluctuations that go beyond the boundaries of any individual state.

Summary of key points

- Business activity exists in and is affected by the broader macroeconomic environment; it also helps to shape that environment.

- Economics is concerned with how societies allocate scarce economic resources to alternative uses and the 'real costs' of the choices that are made.

- Broadly speaking, two main approaches to the problem of resource allocation exist: state planning and the market.

- Most economies in the world are market-based economies which operate through a price mechanism. Within such economies the state also plays a key role in some allocative decisions.

- In market economies, economic activity essentially involves 'real flows' and corresponding flows of income and expenditure between producers and consumers.

- Combining these flows into a simple model of the macroeconomy illustrates that income basically flows round the economy in a circular motion.

- Levels of income in the economy are related to levels of output, expenditure and employment.

- Changes in the level of economic activity can be explained by examining changes in one or more of the key economic variables such as consumer spending, saving, government decisions on state spending/taxation and external trade.

- Within the macroeconomy, governments often play a key role in influencing both the levels and patterns of demand in pursuit of their macroeconomic objectives.

- Key government objectives usually include controlling inflation, promoting economic growth, reducing unemployment and creating a stable macroeconomic environment.

- To pursue these objectives governments use a range of policies, most notably fiscal and monetary policies.

- Government policy decisions take place within a broader economic and financial framework, which includes the influence of financial institutions and markets and the requirements that accrue from membership of different supranational and international organisations.

case study   Austerity

As the UK economy contracted in 2008 and took a long time to recover, people lost jobs and bought fewer goods, so corporate, income and sales tax (VAT) revenue fell. The government was getting less money in as demands on social support systems, such as unemployment benefits, increased. As a result the UK was getting further in debt.

Between 2010 and 2017 Coalition and Conservative governments implemented policies designed to cut government spending across most areas. Central government administration (Whitehall) and local governments were asked to find some of the highest proportions of the cuts. Some of the most visible cuts were to social welfare or 'benefit' systems

and local services such as youth centres, libraries and smaller hospitals. In this time the amount of extra money that the government is borrowing each year has reduced from around £150 billion to around £60 billion, but the total is still going up. Since 2010 the UK debt has risen from around 71% of UK GDP to 86%. One of the reasons for this is slower than expected growth.

Case study questions

1   What is the fiscal effect of austerity policies?

2   When might a government usually choose to borrow more money to spend in an economy?

case study   Quantitative easing (QE)

As indicated by the analysis presented in this chapter, governments have a variety of options available when tackling a problem such as recession in the economy. Where monetary policy is concerned, a traditional approach has been to lower interest rates in the hope of boosting demand by making money cheap to borrow. This option has become increasingly difficult in recent years as interest rates in many countries have fallen to historically low levels in the wake of the global financial crisis that occurred after 2008.

An alternative approach that has become widely used in recent years (e.g. in Japan, the UK, the United

States) is the policy known as **quantitative easing (QE)** or credit easing. In simple terms this involves a country's central bank 'creating' money electronically by crediting the accounts of financial institutions (e.g. banks, pension funds, insurance companies) in return for the purchase of assets, particularly government bonds held by these investors. In Japan the supply of money has almost been doubled by this method. By buying bonds, the central bank reduces their supply in the market, resulting in an increase in the price of these assets. Since bond prices move inversely to the yield they generate (i.e. the rate of interest on the asset), an increase in prices reduces long-term interest rates, thus making borrowing cheaper for businesses and mortgage holders. This, it is hoped, will help to stimulate demand, boost the housing and stock markets, and generally increase confidence among both firms and consumers.

The additional cash held by the financial institutions as a result of QE can also be used to purchase other assets, including equities and corporate bonds, and this could encourage firms to issue new stock to fund investment. In the case of the banks, this additional money can be lent on directly to consumers and businesses, thereby cascading through the economy and generally increasing economic activity. Coupled with low interest rates and a rising stock market, the conditions for a return to growth appear to be an inevitable consequence of this form of monetary stimulus to the economy.

Critics of QE tend to be less sanguine about its ability to achieve its objectives of boosting economic growth and reducing unemployment associated with a recession. One criticism is that there is no guarantee that the banks will pass on the additional cash to consumers and businesses. Instead, they may use it to speculate in, say, commodities (e.g. oil), thus pushing up commodity prices and making conditions even tougher for consumers, some of whom (e.g. pensioners about to invest in an annuity and savers generally) are already being adversely affected by low interest rates. In the UK, as QE was being implemented banks were being told to maintain higher levels of cash reserves, acting as a strong incentive to hold onto the funds that the Bank of England was readily handing over. Others have suggested that QE might be being used by a country surreptitiously to depress the value of its currency in the hope of making its exports more attractive on international markets. Given the tough global trading conditions that are affecting many countries at the moment, this development could prove highly controversial and could spark off an exchange rate and trading war.

There was a further concern that some of the global tidal wave of cheap money has found its way into emerging markets, such as India, and has helped to mask some underlying economic problems. With the Federal Reserve's announcement that it intends to taper off QE in the future – eventually reversing the huge investment flows – there are fears that any phasing out of QE, if handled badly, could have adverse consequences for global bond markets and interest rates.

In Japan QE policy has continued long past the financial crisis. Even before the global recession Japan had been facing a downturn: since 1997 interest rates and wages had been declining and the Japanese government had been increasing taxes to pay for public services. By 2013 Japan's economy had shrunk back to the size it was in 1991. In 2013 Japan's Prime Minister, Shinzō Abe, implemented 'three arrows' of negative interest rates, QE and structural reforms (austerity); the QE component was to be ongoing. Since 2013 the Bank of Japan has been buying ¥70–80 trillion (around £500 billion) worth of bonds per year, putting the same amount of money into the economy. This will continue each year for the foreseeable future.

While it is probably too early to judge the true impact of QE, its adoption by central banks in different countries does at least underline the belief among policy-makers that it is sometimes necessary to intervene in the economy in order to tackle or fend off economic problems. As with most things in economics, what the best approach is tends to be a matter of opinion; matching ends and means is rarely free of controversy.

Case study questions

1 QE is seen as one way in which a government can stimulate the economy. What other approaches could it use?

2 What might happen when central banks start to reverse QE, and when might be the right time to do it?

Review and discussion questions

1 To what extent do you agree with the proposition that the market economy is the 'best' form of economic system? Do you have any reservations?

2 Explain how interest rates could be used to boost the economy. Why, then, do governments frequently hesitate to take such steps?

3 Using circular flow analysis, suggest why a large programme of capital expenditure by government (e.g. on new motorways, roads, railways) will benefit businesses. How could such a programme be financed?

4 Which businesses are likely to benefit from a recovery in a country's housing market?

Assignments

1 Imagine you work in the economic development unit of a local authority (council). Produce a draft report outlining the benefits to the local economy of encouraging direct inward investment. Indicate any disadvantages.

2 You are a contributor to a new news website. As part of your first big assignment, you have been asked to provide information on the 'privatisation' of Eastern European economies. Using journals and newspapers, blog post about the different ways in which western companies have sought to exploit business opportunities in Eastern Europe.

Further reading

Begg, D. and Ward, D., *Economics for Business,* 5th edition, McGraw-Hill, 2016.

Donaldson, P. and Farquhar, J., *Understanding the British Economy,* Penguin, 1988.

Griffiths, A. and Wall, S. (eds), *Applied Economics,* 12th edition, Financial Times/Prentice Hall, 2011.

Griffiths, A. and Wall, S., *Economics for Business and Management,* 3rd edition, Financial Times/ Prentice Hall, 2011.

Mulhearn, C., Vane, H. R. and Eden, J., *Economics for Business,* 2nd edition, Palgrave Macmillan, 2011.

Neale, A. and Haslam, C., *Economics in a Business Context,* Chapman & Hall, 1991.

Neale, A., Haslam, C. and Johal, S., *Economics in a Business Context,* 3rd edition, Thomson Learning, 2010.

Worthington, I., Britton, C. and Rees, A., *Economics for Business: Blending Theory and Practice,* 2nd edition, Financial Times/Prentice Hall, 2005.

web link

Web links and further questions are available on the website at: **www.pearsoned.co.uk/worthington**

6 The demographic, social and cultural context of business

Ian Worthington

As an integral part of society, businesses are subject to a variety of social influences. These influences, which include demography, social class and culture, can change over time and affect both the demand and supply sides of the economy. Marketing organisations recognise and make use of these factors when segmenting markets for consumer goods and services.

Learning outcomes

Having read this chapter you should be able to:

- explain the notions of demography, social class, lifestyles, reference groups, culture and sub-culture

- identify key demographic and social trends that can affect organisations in the private, public and voluntary sectors

- provide examples of how demographic, social and cultural factors can influence both the demand and supply sides of the economy

- outline the concept of market segmentation and demonstrate how marketing organisations can use demographic and socio-cultural variables to segment consumer markets

Key terms

ACORN	Family life cycle	Psychographic
Ageing population	Geo-demographic	segmentation
Birth rate	segmentation	Reference groups
Cultural diversity	Lifestyle	Secondary reference
Culture	Market segmentation	group
Death rate	MOSAIC	Social class
Demographic time bomb	Natural population change	Social mobility
Demography	Net migration	Sub-culture
Dependent population	Primary reference group	VALS

Introduction

Previous chapters have demonstrated that human beings are a critical element of business activity, both in their role as producers (e.g. workers, managers, entrepreneurs) and as consumers of outputs provided by the private, public and voluntary sectors. Put simply, business activity ultimately takes place because of and for people, a point well illustrated by the concept of the circular flow of income (CFI) (Chapter 5) and by the systems model introduced in Chapter 1. In order to understand more fully the environment in which business organisations exist and operate, it is important to consider how broader 'social' influences affect business organisations by examining how they can impact upon both the demand and supply sides of the economy.

In this chapter we look at three such influences – demography, social aspects and the idea of culture – illustrating how these can affect both the amount and types of goods and services consumed within an economy and the different aspects of the production process. In the next chapter, on the resource context, we examine people as a key factor of production and look at a number of areas associated with the concept of the workforce.

As the CFI model clearly shows, the demand and supply sides of the economy are interrelated (e.g. consider the notion of 'derived demand'); the same is often true for demographic, social and cultural influences. In some countries, for example, changing attitudes to female participation in the workforce (a socio-cultural factor) have helped to influence family sizes (a demographic factor) and this in turn has had implications for the markets for goods and services and for human resources. To simplify the analysis, however, we have chosen to examine the different social influences and their impact on the economy separately, but would encourage you to think of the various ways in which the different factors can be interconnected, both in themselves and with other macroenvironmental variables (e.g. the political environment).

The examples provided below are by no means exhaustive and you might like to think of others based on your own interest and/or experience (e.g. public administration students should consider the impact of a changing demographic and socio-cultural environment on the supply of and demand for public sector services such as education, pensions and healthcare). Moreover, the analysis can also be applied across different countries and cultures and ideally should seek to demonstrate the impact of socio-cultural and demographic change on business activity in different national and cultural settings.

The demographic environment of business

Demography is the study of populations in terms of both their overall size and their structural characteristics. From a business point of view the key areas of interest include the age structure of a given population, its gender balance, its geographical distribution and the tendency for both the size and structure of the population to change over time. As noted above, demographic change can have important implications for both sides of the economy and hence for organisations of all types.

The size of the population

A country's population normally increases over time and will vary according to such factors as changes in the birth and death rates and in the rate of net migration. Take the UK population, which in 1971 was just under 56 million; by 2008 this had risen to 60 million. The most recent (2016) estimates suggest that over the next 23 years it will rise again, to 72.9 million, partly because of immigration and partly through natural change (see below). In comparison, Russia's current population of around 143 million is projected to fall by at least 25 million by 2050 as a result of a declining birth rate and a rising death rate in the wake of the country's economic collapse. If this occurs, the world's biggest country will have fewer people than countries such as Uganda and Egypt. It is worth remembering, however, that future population changes are only projections and that these can vary considerably over time as new data become available. For example, in late 2007 the UK's Office for National Statistics (ONS) provided three projections for the UK population by 2081: 63 million (lowest estimate), 108.7 million (highest estimate), 85 million (most likely estimate); in 2015 the actual UK population was estimated to be 65 110 000 by the ONS. These estimates show considerable variation and indicate how future population changes are relatively unpredictable, which can make forward planning in areas such as education, housing and healthcare provision very difficult.

Table 6.1 indicates the wide variations that can occur in the size of national populations by examining a range of countries across the globe. Within the EU we can see that major member countries such as France, Germany, Italy and the UK all had populations over 50 million in 2012, while the majority of the new member states had populations below 10 million. These figures are dwarfed, however, by India and China, which had populations of around 1.24 billion and 1.35 billion respectively. Such differences in overall population size have important economic implications in areas such as potential market size, workforce availability, public expenditure, economic growth and international trade.

Table 6.1 Population size in selected countries, 2016

Country	Population (millions)
Germany	82.3
France	65.2
UK	66.6
Italy	59.3
The Netherlands	17.1
Greece	11.1
Poland	38.1
Hungary	9.7
Slovakia	5.5
Malta	0.4
United States	326.8
India	1354.1
China	1415.0

Source: Worldometers.info.

The age and sex distribution of the population

In addition to examining the overall size of a country's population, demographers are interested in its structural characteristics, including the balance between males and females and the numbers of people in different age categories. Table 6.2 gives illustrative data for the UK population by age and gender for selected age groups and intervals over the period 1971–2021. As we can see from the figures in the right-hand column, women outnumber men in the UK population, despite the fact that the annual number of male births slightly exceeds that of female births. Moreover, the data clearly point to an **ageing population**, with an increasing percentage of the population in the over-65 group and a decreasing percentage in the under-16 category. Projections suggest that by 2061 the number of over-65s in the UK population will significantly exceed the number who are under 16, a trend which is sometimes described as the **demographic time bomb**. This clearly has important implications for both the private and public sectors, not least in terms of the overall demand for goods and services, including 'public goods' such as education, healthcare, social services, state pensions and social security arrangements.

Table 6.2 Distribution of UK population by age and gender, 1971–2021, at selected intervals

	Under 16 (%)	35–44 (%)	55–64 (%)	Over 65 (%)	All ages (millions)
Males					
1971	27	12	11	10	27.2
2001	21	15	11	14	28.8
2021*	18	13	13	18	31.4
Females					
1971	24	11	12	16	28.8
2001	19	15	11	18	30.2
2021*	17	12	13	22	32.4

*Projections.

Source: Adapted from *Social Trends.* Available via *www.ons.gov.uk.*

The UK's ageing population is a characteristic shared by many other countries, including those in the EU. Data produced by Eurostat indicate similar trends in both the original EU15 and in the new accession countries (Table 6.3). In comparison, both India and China have a much smaller percentage of the population in the over-65 category, the figures being around 5 per cent and 9 per cent respectively for 2012.

Table 6.3 Percentage of EU populations aged 65 and over for selected EU countries, 1970–2011

Country	1970	1991	2003	2011
Germany	13	15	17	21
Belgium	13	15	17	17
Spain	9	14	17	17
Finland	9	13	15	18
Denmark	12	16	15	17
Estonia	12	12	16	17
Lithuania	10	11	15	18
Czech Republic	12	13	14	16
Slovakia	9	10	12	13
EU-27 average	12	14	16	18

Source: Adapted from Eurostat available via epp.eurostat.ec.europa.eu/ © European Union, 1995–2014. Figures are rounded.

Other structural characteristics

Populations can also be examined in a number of other ways, including their ethnicity and geographical distribution. For instance, in the 2001 population census in the UK, around 8 per cent of people surveyed described themselves as belonging to a minority ethnic group; a Leeds University study in 2010 predicts this will rise to 20 per cent by 2051. The census data show that, in general, minority ethnic groups in the UK have a younger age structure than those in the 'White Group' and tend to be highly concentrated in large urban centres, particularly London. For the UK population as a whole, the majority of people live in England, with significant concentrations in regions such as the south-east, the Midlands, the north-west and the north-east, a fact that has important economic, political and social ramifications. Moreover, interregional movements of population, together with other factors such as international migration and differential birth and death rates, can result in significant local and regional variations in population over time, with a knock-on effect for both the public and private sectors (e.g. demand for housing and school places).

Population change

As the previous analysis indicates, populations can change in either size and/or structure, with important consequences for economic activity both within and between countries. The size and structure of a country's population depend on a number of variables, the most important of which are the birth rate, the death rate and the net migration rate.

The birth rate

The **birth rate** tends to be expressed as the number of live births per thousand of the population in a given year. In many countries this figure has been falling steadily over a long period of time for a number of reasons. These include:

- a trend towards smaller families as people become better off and health improves and death rates fall;
- the increased availability of contraception;
- the trend towards later marriages and later childbearing for social and/or economic reasons;
- declining fertility rates;
- changing attitudes towards women and work.

In some countries, governments have offered financial and other incentives to married couples to try to reduce the birth rate (e.g. China) as a means of controlling population growth. In others, incentives have been offered to try to reverse the actual or potential decline in the birth rate because of its economic consequences (e.g. France, Singapore). Changing birth rates are, of course, an important contributor to an ageing population, but they can also have other effects. For instance, a recent increase in the birth rate in the UK has led to a call by the Optimum Population Trust for British couples to restrict themselves to two children in order to reduce the impact of population growth on the natural environment.

The death rate

Like the birth rates, the **death rate** is usually measured per thousand of the population in a given year. For developed economies such as the UK this figure has tended to fall over time before reaching a plateau. Among the main contributors to this trend have been:

- rising living standards, including better housing, sanitation and nutrition;
- developments in medical technology and practice;
- better education;
- improved working conditions.

The difference between the birth rate and the death rate represents the **natural population change** (i.e. increase or decrease).

Net migration

Apart from the movement of population within a country (internal migration), people may move from one country to another for a variety of reasons. The balance between those leaving (emigrants) and those entering (immigrants) a country over a given period of time represents the rate of **net migration**. Along with changes in the birth and/or death rate, this can be a significant factor in population change and can have important consequences for the economy (e.g. the gain or loss of certain skills) and for the political system. In the UK, estimates by the Migration Observatory at Oxford University have suggested that around 50 per cent of the country's increase in population between 1991 and 2010 was due to the direct contribution of net migration, much of which was related to EU enlargement. Politically migration has been a significant issue, particularly in influencing the UK referendum in 2016 to leave the EU. Economically the impact of migration is broadly positive for the country receiving an increase in the working age population and tax revenue – although the impact is marginal. For countries such as Germany, to maintain a working age population they would have to have net migration of 4 million people each year.

Influences on the rate of net migration include:

- legal barriers (e.g. immigration laws);
- economic migrancy;
- the numbers fleeing persecution;
- government policy;
- political developments.

Demographic change and business

Changes in the size and/or structure of a country's population can affect enterprises in all sectors, in both the short and the long term. Given increased globalisation and international trade, the impact of demographic change has an international as well as a national dimension for a growing number of trading organisations.

The following examples provide illustrations of how a changing demography can influence both the level and pattern of demand within an economy and in turn help to explain why changes can occur in a country's economic and industrial structure (see Chapter 12) and why some countries engage in international trade (see Chapter 16).

Demographic change can also have important effects on the supply side of the economy. You should try to think of other examples.

- As populations grow in size, the demand for many types of goods and services also tends to grow (e.g. energy, consumer durables, food). A growing population also provides a larger workforce, other things being equal.
- An 'ageing population' increases the demand for a range of public, private and voluntary sector goods and services (e.g. healthcare, pensions, specialist holidays, sheltered housing). It also creates an increasingly **dependent population**. The Office for Budget Responsibility (OBR) in the UK has calculated that by 2018 the country's ageing population will be costing the Exchequer an additional £19 billion.
- A declining birth rate influences the demand for education, children's products, childcare, certain TV programmes, comics, toys, etc. It can also reduce the numbers of young people available to enter the workforce to replace those who retire.
- Changes in the ethnic make-up of the population can affect the demand for particular food products, clothing and media services and can place increased demands on public authorities (e.g. documents printed in different languages). Some researchers also argue that a more diverse workforce can improve an organisation's performance, while some sociologists have recognised that increased diversity can increase friction in teams.
- The regional redistribution of the population will affect the consumption of a range of goods and services, including housing, education, healthcare, transport, energy and many day-to-day products. It can also affect prices (e.g. in the housing market) and the make-up of the local labour market.

On a more general level, it is also worth remembering that demographic change can impact on a country's social as well as its economic structure and that this can result in increased (or reduced) demands on a range of organisations, particularly those in the public sector. For example, the growing imbalance being experienced in many countries between an increasing and dependent elderly population and a diminishing population of working age touches on many areas of public policy, from healthcare and social provision on the one hand to pensions and fiscal policy on the other. Governmental responses to the consequences of demographic change can have both direct and indirect consequences for a wide variety of organisations across the economy.

The social context

Being part of society, organisations are subject to a variety of societal influences that operate at both a general and a specific level. In this section we consider some of the key factors within an organisation's social environment, starting with the concept of social class. The notion that organisations also have responsibilities to society is examined in Chapter 9.

Social class

Throughout history, all societies have normally exhibited a certain degree of social and economic inequality that has given rise to the tendency to classify individuals into different social categories. For example, in India the 'caste system' has been an important source of social differentiation and one that has exerted a key influence over the life and opportunities available to members of the different castes. In other countries, including the UK, the categorisation of individuals has often been based around notions of **social class**, the idea of grouping together people who share a similar social status which is related to certain common features such as educational background, income and occupation. Whereas in some types of social system, movement between groups is either very difficult or impossible (e.g. the caste system), in others **social mobility** is frequently observed, with some individuals able to move relatively quickly between the different social strata (e.g. upper class, middle class, working class) as their personal circumstances change.

The process of allocating individuals to a particular class category has generally been based on socio-economic criteria such as income, wealth and occupational status. Advertisers and market researchers – including the Institute of Practitioners in Advertising – have tended to favour a scheme known as 'ABC1' (see Table 6.4), which uses an individual's occupation as a basis for allocation, the assumption being that a person's job is closely linked to key aspects of their attitudes and behaviour, including their choice of car, clothes, home furnishings, holidays, reading material, and so on. There is even evidence to suggest that class might be influential in an individual's choice of retail outlets (e.g. different UK supermarket chains appear to attract customers from different socio-economic groups).

Table 6.4 The ABC1 system of social grading

Social grading	Social status	Occupation
A	Upper middle class	Higher managerial, administrative and professional
B	Middle class	Intermediate managerial, administrative and professional
C1	Lower middle class	Supervisory or clerical, junior managerial, administrative and professional
C2	Skilled working class	Skilled manual workers
D	Working class	Semi- and unskilled manual workers
E	Lowest subsistence level	State pensioners or widows, casual workers, lowest-grade workers

mini case   A new class structure?

According to the Great British Class Survey (2013) – a collaboration between the BBC and academics from six universities – the traditional three-class model (working, middle and upper) may no longer be sufficient to describe the British class structure. Using economic, social and cultural indicators to define a person's social class, the researchers suggested that the following seven categories of class now seemed more appropriate to modern Britain. These are presented in descending (*sic*) order:

1 *Elite* – individuals educated at top universities, with average savings of more than £140,000 and possessing extensive social contacts. Members of this class constitute about 6 per cent of the population.

2 *Established middle class* – comprising around 25 per cent of the population, this group scores highly on economic, social and cultural capital, has a household income of £47,000 and some 'highbrow' tastes.

3 *Technical middle class* – a small new group of prosperous individuals, but who score lowly on social and cultural capital.

4 *New affluent worker* – people with middling levels of economic capital and who are young and socially and culturally aware.

5 *Traditional working class* – making up around 14 per cent of the population, this group tends to be property owners, largely middle-aged and with low scores on all forms of capital.

6 *Emergent social worker* – with a mean age of 34 and a high proportion of ethnic minority members, this group is relatively poor but has high social and cultural capital.

7 *Precariat* – or precarious proletariat, this group comprises about 15 per cent of the total population. Members have average savings of £800, an after-tax income of £8,000 and are unlikely to be university graduates.

As with any new system of classification of this kind, there are inevitably going to be criticisms. In a letter to *The Guardian* (6 April 2013), two leading UK academics pointed out that the current NS-SEC scheme used by the ONS, public organisations and researchers alike identifies eight social classes based on a wide range of socio-economic indicators. They also suggested that the authors seemed to have started by choosing a set of outcomes and then allocating individuals to different groups on this basis. In short, outcomes seemed to have been used to determine social class, rather than class determining outcomes, the latter being the approach normally used by social researchers.

Similar systems of classification have also been/are used for official purposes (e.g. the UK 10-year census of population). In the 1990s in the UK, government statistics used what was called the Registrar General's Social Scale – subsequently renamed 'Social Class based on Occupation' – to group the UK population into seven different categories according to their occupation (e.g. Group I was professional; Group II was managerial and technical; Group V was unskilled occupations). This system has now been replaced by NS-SEC (the National Statistics Socio-Economic Classification), which again focuses on occupation as the key criterion for class allocation. An example of NS-SEC is shown in Table 6.5. The figures in the right-hand column represent the socio-economic classification of the UK population of working age in autumn 2005. Current figures are difficult to obtain as some revision to the approach has taken place in recent years.

While it would be unwise to assume that a factor such as a person's social class will invariably affect their choice of goods and services, empirical evidence reveals some interesting variations in the levels of expenditure on particular products among different groups in the UK population, a fact not lost on marketing organisations, which often use socio-economic criteria as one way to segment a market (see below). According to data produced by the ONS (see Table 6.6), total expenditure was highest among the large employer and higher managerial group and was more than three times that of people in the never worked/long-term unemployed category. Within this overall pattern of expenditure some interesting data emerge, particularly with regards to priorities, as indicated by expenditure on different items by the different social groupings. For instance, expenditure on restaurants and hotels and on recreation and culture was significantly higher among the large employer/higher managerial group than other groups, while spending on housing, fuel and power was similar across most categories. Note that spending by people in the never worked/long-term unemployed group shows clear evidence of the impact of the prolonged recession in the UK economy after 2008.

Table 6.5 National Statistics Socio-Economic Classification (NS-SEC) – data from 2011 census

Category	Occupation	Estimated % of working population in 2011
1	Higher managerial and professional occupations	11.4
1.1	Employers and managers in larger organisations (e.g. company directors, senior managers, senior civil servants, senior police and armed forces officers)	
1.2	Higher professionals such as doctors, lawyers, teachers, social workers, clergy	
2	Lower managerial/professional occupations, including nurses, midwives, journalists, actors, musicians, prison officers, etc.	23.0
3	Intermediate occupations, for example clerks, secretaries, driving instructors	14.1
4	Small employers and own-account workers such as publicans, farmers, taxi drivers, window cleaners, painters and decorators	10.4
5	Lower supervisory, craft and related occupations, including plumbers, printers, train drivers and butchers	7.6
6	Semi-routine occupations, for example shop assistants, hairdressers, bus drivers, cooks	15.4
7	Routine occupations such as labourers, couriers, waiters, refuse collectors	12.1
8	People who have never had paid work or are long-term unemployed	6.2

Source: Office for National Statistics.

Table 6.6 Household expenditure (£/week) by socio-economic classification of household reference person, by selected categories, 2011

	Large employers and higher managerial	Intermediate occupations	Routine occupations	Never worked and long-term unemployed[*]
Transport	137.30	67.90	48.10	15.10
Recreation and culture	115.30	62.30	46.80	25.90
Food and non-alcoholic drink	69.90	56.30	53.50	42.60
Housing, fuel and power	74.50	67.60	73.00	44.70
Restaurant and hotels	83.20	43.20	32.00	18.30
Clothing and footwear	40.80	23.80	20.80	9.80
Alcohol, tobacco and narcotics	17.80	10.60	16.60	8.00
Communication	15.90	14.50	13.00	7.40
Education	14.80	4.70	[0.70]	[3.00]
Health	12.50	8.00	5.00	0.60
All expenditure groups	703.90	426.20	365.90	196.80

[*]This category excludes students. Figures in brackets are based on very small samples.
Source: Adapted from ONS, Family Spending, 2011.

Lifestyles

Another factor that can clearly affect people's attitudes and behaviour is the **lifestyle** that they choose to adopt. Lifestyles are basically concerned with the way in which people live and how they spend their money, decisions which are not necessarily always linked to their socio-economic position. Two individuals with the same occupation – and nominally in the same social class – may have entirely different lifestyles, a point well illustrated by examining two university lecturers. My own lifestyle is highly sophisticated, environmentally sensitive, artistic and cosmopolitan; that of a colleague – who happens to teach marketing – is narrow, parochial, philistine and consumption-driven. Then, what would one expect?!

Joking apart, lifestyle analysis provides another way of seeking to categorise and explain human behaviour, based on factors such as an individual's interests, activities and opinions as well as on their demographic characteristics. The proposition is that by examining distinctive patterns of consumer response, a marketing organisation can build up a clearer picture of an individual's habits, preferences and behaviour and by doing so can design more effective and appealing products, marketing programmes and/or communications that can be aimed at specific lifestyle groups. Data collected from a person's use of social networking sites and from their expenditure choices (e.g. their supermarket bills) are particularly useful in this regard.

While we should be cautious of over-generalising, the evidence suggests that in many countries the way in which people spend their time and money has changed considerably in recent decades as a result of changes in demography, working patterns, technology, income and a range of other factors. Once again we can illustrate this by looking at longitudinal data collected through the annual survey of social trends in the UK. These data show, for example, the following between 1971 and 2009:

- Household spending on communication (including mobile phones) increased more than 11-fold. Within this period, ownership of mobile phone equipment and services rose from 27 per cent in the late 1990s to 79 per cent in 2008, Internet access by households rising from 10 per cent to 66 per cent during the same period.
- There was an eight times increase in spending on recreation and culture and a fivefold rise in spending on overseas holidays. Alcoholic drinks and tobacco was the only category of expenditure that fell during the period.

Other social trends data indicate that:

- by 2009–10, 40 per cent of household waste per person was being recycled, composted or reused compared with less than 1 per cent in 1983–4;
- domestic energy consumption in the UK increased by 18 per cent between 1970 and 2009;
- there were 1.8 billion transactions by cheque in 1985 compared with only 0.6 billion in 2009 as a result of a rapid growth in the use of electronic payment methods;
- almost all (98 per cent) single music tracks were purchased digitally in 2009, with digital sales increasing more than 90 per cent between 2007 and 2009;
- in 2009–10, UK adults (16 and over) spent an average of 3.5 hours watching TV, 2.5 hours using a computer and 1 hour listening to the radio per day;
- sales of books by UK publishers fell by almost 6 per cent between 2007 and 2009.

If we take changing expenditure patterns in the UK as an indication of changes in lifestyles, then there has been a discernible shift in emphasis from essential products such as food, housing, water and fuel to the less essential items such as communications, and recreation and culture. This can be seen in Table 6.7, which highlights the changing volumes of household spending in particular categories of goods and services over a 38-year period.

Table 6.7 Volume of household expenditure on selected items, 1971–2009, expressed as index numbers (base year 1971)

Category of spending	1971	1991	2001	2009
Food and non-alcoholic drink	100	117	137	151
Alcohol and tobacco	100	92	88	90
Housing, water, fuel	100	139	152	160
Health	100	182	188	229
Communication	100	306	790	1126
Recreation and culture	100	279	545	869
Transport	100	181	246	273

Source: Adapted from ONS.

In light of the discussion on inflation in Chapter 5, it is worth noting that such changes in spending patterns over time are reflected in changes in the official 'basket of goods and services' used to calculate the RPI (and the CPI) in the UK. The 1980s saw CDs, CD players and condoms added to the basket, with computers, camcorders and mobile phone charges added in the next decade. By 2004–5 dishwater tablets had replaced dishwasher powder, wooden garden furniture sets had replaced plastic sets, and leather sofas had replaced ordinary ones. More bizarrely, hamsters and popcorn bought in cinemas had been added to the index, while baguettes, corned beef and writing paper were dropped (see e.g. *The Guardian,* 22 March 2005, p. 20). By 2007–8, the RPI contained fruit smoothies, USB sticks, peppers, muffins and small oranges and had discarded microwaves, TV repairs, washable carpets and 35mm camera films. In 2015 it included e-cigarette refills, online games subscriptions, music streaming subscriptions, headphones and sweet potatoes. What does this tell us about the changing lifestyles and spending habits of UK citizens? Are people in the UK increasingly subscribing to online content and getting healthier? Judging by the current statistics on obesity and alcohol consumption, we should be cautious about drawing this conclusion.

Many of the trends referred to above are, of course, mirrored in consumer aspirations and behaviour in other countries, particularly in respect of issues such as healthier lifestyles, increased foreign travel, greater access to communications technology and more environmentally-friendly products (though not necessarily rodent purchases!). Thus, while some firms have benefited from the changing trends (e.g. Facebook, Twitter, Apple, Google), others have experienced a decline in business as a result of factors such as changes in habits, in the law or in competition (e.g. France has experienced a substantial fall in the number of bistros and cafés over the last decade). Where change occurs, there will always be winners and losers.

Other social influences

While it is important to consider the influence of broad social factors such as class and lifestyles, it is also worth remembering that consumers are individuals and that they are subject to influences that operate at a personal level. Such influences include the wide variety of individuals and groups with whom we come into contact during our lifetime and who may influence our attitudes, values, opinions and/or behaviour. Primary among these are our interactions within the family, with friends or work colleagues, and through our involvement with sports and social clubs, religious organisations, trade unions, and so on. Such groups are sometimes referred to as **reference groups**.

Groups that have a regular or direct (i.e. face-to-face) influence on us are known as **primary reference groups**, while those whose influence tends to be more indirect and formal are known as **secondary reference groups**. The former, in particular, can be very influential in shaping our attitudes and behaviour, including our decisions on consumption.

The importance of reference groups – especially family and friends – is recognised by both economists and marketers, with the former using the notion of 'households' (see Chapter 5) to indicate that the consumption of goods and services often takes place within a collective family framework, as in the case of groceries, holidays, vehicles and many other everyday products. Marketers use concepts such as the **family life cycle** to show changing patterns of consumption as the individual moves from being a child in a family to being a parent with different needs and responsibilities.

While it is difficult to be precise about when and how far an individual's demand is shaped by the family and other reference groups, it is not difficult to think of particular examples when this is likely to be the case. For many services such as builders, restaurants, hotels, hairdressers and car repairs, consumers often rely on the advice of a trusted friend or colleague and firms can gain new business through such word-of-mouth recommendations. Equally, through membership and/or support of a particular group or club, individuals may be tempted to purchase particular goods and/or services (e.g. football kit, trainers, a CD, tickets), especially those with a desirable 'brand name' and endorsed by a well-known personality (e.g. sportsperson, musician, singer, film star). In such cases, the demand for the product is often less price sensitive (see Chapter 14) since it is a 'must-have' product.

The cultural environment

Culture

The term **culture** generally refers to a complex set of values, norms, beliefs, attitudes, customs, systems and artefacts, handed down from generation to generation through the process of socialisation, and which influences how individuals see the world and how they behave in it. Defined in this way, culture can be seen to have at least three important features:

- it comprises both material (e.g. human artefacts such as buildings, literature, art, music) and abstract elements (e.g. rituals, symbols, values);
- it is socially learned and transmitted over time; and
- it influences human behaviour.

As a concept, 'culture' is often applied in a variety of circumstances at both the macro and the micro level: terms such as 'western culture', 'Asian culture', 'European culture', 'New York City culture', 'youth culture', 'pop culture', 'entrepreneurial culture' and 'research culture' are just some of the examples of its usage in the modern world. What they have in common is that they imply certain shared aspects of human belief, understanding and behaviour that link individuals into some form of definable group and/or range of activities.

In a business context, it can be easy to underestimate the degree to which a person's perceptions, attitudes and behaviour can be shaped by cultural influences, some of which may be relatively enduring (e.g. certain 'core' values and beliefs) while others may be more open to change (i.e. secondary beliefs and values). In the United States, for example, American citizens believe in the right of individuals to bear arms and this is enshrined in the US Constitution. The buying and selling of handguns and rifles is thus acceptable within American society, despite the fact that they are frequently used in violent crimes, including robbery and murder. In other countries, trade in such weapons tends to be seen as highly questionable by most people and is usually heavily regulated by the government to certain types of weapons for use in acceptable pursuits such as hunting or rifle shooting. Cultural differences such as this can, of course, apply not only to the kinds of goods and services that are consumed (e.g. eating horsemeat in France is acceptable but not in the UK – as seen in the 2013 horsemeat scandal), but also to other aspects of both the production and consumption process and this can have important implications for an organisation's behaviour.

Examples include:

- who decides what is bought, how it is bought or where it is bought (e.g. in some cultures women have predominantly been the purchasers of household products);
- what colours are acceptable (e.g. the colour associated with bereavement varies across cultures);
- how far harmonisation of products and marketing activities is feasible (e.g. the EU's perennial debates over what constitutes an acceptable definition of certain products such as sausages, feta cheese, chocolate);
- what factors can enhance the prospect of a sale (e.g. bribes are acceptable in some cultures);
- how business is conducted (e.g. the length of negotiations, the meaning of a handshake);
- the method of communicating with the target audience (e.g. in the UK a single shared language allows organisations to use national media);
- how customer enquiries/complaints are dealt with (e.g. UK businesses using call centres in India often give their operators British names and train them to talk about everyday British preoccupations such as the weather and sport).

Culture not only influences an individual's response to products and the nature of the buying and selling process, but also exercises a significant influence on the structure of consumption within a given society. For companies that can gain acceptability on a global scale, despite cultural differences between countries, the potential benefits are huge (e.g. global brands such as Coca-Cola, McDonald's, Nike).

While the so-called 'Americanisation' of consumption is not to everyone's taste, other forms of cultural exportation are often more acceptable and can prove highly lucrative for the country concerned, exemplified by the UK's overseas earnings from culture and arts-related tourism (see Chapter 16). Many other countries benefit in similar ways.

mini case National cultures

Recognising and responding to cultural differences between countries can have an important impact on how successful organisations are in international trade. But is it possible to generalise about a country's culture?

One academic who has made a significant contribution in this area is Professor Geert Hofstede, who has developed a theory of culture that allows comparisons to be made between the main cultural characteristics in different countries. Hofstede's research is based on data collected from IBM employees across the world while he was working at the company as a psychologist. On the basis of his research Hofstede identified four cultural dimensions; later he added a fifth. These dimensions can be used to compare value systems at different levels, from the family through to the state.

The five cultural dimensions are as follows:

1 *Power distance* – this is concerned with the degree to which the members of a society accept an unequal or hierarchical power structure. In societies where the power distance is large, there is a perception that inequality exists and subordinates tend to be more dependent on their superiors. This can result in an autocratic or paternalistic style of management or governance (e.g. in some African countries), which can evoke either positive or negative reactions. Where the power distance is small, individuals tend to see themselves more as equals and management/governance styles tend to be more consultative and less hierarchical (e.g. in Northern European countries).

2 *Uncertainty avoidance* – this focuses on how members of society cope with uncertainty in their lives. Where levels of anxiety are generally high, this results in high uncertainty avoidance and people in these cultures are deemed to be more expressive and emotional (e.g. Latin American countries) than in low uncertainty avoidance countries (e.g. many Asian countries).

3 *Individualism* – this refers to the extent to which individuals in society see themselves as independent and autonomous human beings or as part of a collectivity. High individualist countries tend to be those such as the United States, the UK, Canada and Australia; low individualism is said to be prevalent in Asian and Latin American countries.

4 *Masculinity* – this is concerned with how far a society is predisposed to aggressive and materialistic behaviour and is linked to gender role. Hofstede associates masculinity with toughness, assertiveness and materialism and with a predisposition to conflict and competition. Femininity, in contrast, is characterised as caring, sensitive and concerned with the quality of life; the result is a more accommodating style based on negotiation and compromise. Hofstede's analysis suggests the more masculine countries include Austria and Japan, while Scandinavian countries tend to be the most feminine.

5 *Long-term orientation* – this relates to the degree to which a society embraces a long-term view and respect for tradition. In societies with a short-term orientation, people tend to stress the 'here and now', typified by western countries. Eastern cultures, by comparison, are generally held to have a longer-term orientation that emphasises concern for the future and for tradition as well as for the present.

One of the benefits of Hofstede's research is that it reminds us that cultural differences can and do occur between states and, as a result, there is no 'one-size-fits-all' style of management or governance that would be suitable across all countries. For companies that are multinational organisations, management styles and approaches in the country of origin may not necessarily be suitable in other parts of the organisation for cultural reasons. *Vive la différence*!

Sub-culture

A society is rarely, if ever, culturally homogeneous. Within every culture a **sub-culture** usually exists, comprising groups of individuals with shared value systems based on common experiences, origins and/or situations. These identifiable sub-groups may be distinguished by nationality, race, ethnicity, religion, age, class, geographical location or some other factor, and their attitudes, behaviour, customs, language and artefacts often reflect sub-cultural differences. At times such differences can be relatively easily accommodated and ultimately may become institutionalised through the legal and/or political process (e.g. the Scottish and Welsh Assemblies – see Chapter 4). At other times sub-cultural differences can be the source of a considerable degree of conflict between various sub-groups, resulting in serious divisions within a society and even in civil war and genocide.

The UK provides a good example of the notion of **cultural diversity** and can be used to illustrate how this can influence the demand for goods and services. In addition to nationality groups such as the Irish, Scots and Welsh, the country has provided a home for successive generations of immigrants from around the globe and this has created a rich mix of ethnic and other sub-groups, often concentrated in particular parts of the country and having their own language, traditions and lifestyles. In Leicester, for instance, where a significant proportion of the population is of Asian origin, there is a substantial Asian business community, part of which has developed to cater specifically for the local ethnic population (e.g. halal butchers, saree shops), as well as attracting custom from the wider community (e.g. Indian restaurants). Many Asian businesses in Leicester are small, family-owned enterprises, employing members of the extended family in keeping with cultural traditions. Aspects such as the organisation and financing of the business, its network of relationships and the working conditions for staff are also frequently influenced by cultural values, traditions and norms, although changes in these areas are becoming more apparent, especially among second- and third-generation Asian-owned enterprises.

Application: market segmentation

Marketers have long recognised the importance of demographic, social and cultural factors in shaping people's demand for goods and services. This is exemplified by the concept of **market segmentation**.

Market segmentation refers to the practice of dividing a market into distinct groups of buyers who share the same or similar attitudes and patterns of behaviour and who might require separate products or marketing to meet their particular needs. By segmenting a market into its broad component parts, businesses should be able to focus their marketing efforts more effectively and efficiently by developing product offerings and marketing programmes which meet the requirements of the different market segments.

Markets can be segmented in a variety of ways and this tends to differ between consumer markets and those which involve business-to-business transactions. Table 6.8 outlines some of the major variables used in segmenting consumer markets. As the table indicates, demographic, social and cultural factors provide a basis for identifying distinct market segments within the markets for consumer goods and services. In practice, of course, marketers may use either one (e.g. demography) or a combination (e.g. age, location and social class) of different variables to segment a market they are seeking to target.

Table 6.8 Methods of segmenting consumer markets

Type of segmentation	Key segmentation variables	Examples
Demographic	Age, gender, religion, ethnic group, family size, family life cycle stage	Children's products, ethnic foods, 18–30 holidays, retirement homes, cars
Socio-economic	Social class, income, occupation	Luxury products, convenience services, discount goods
Geographic	Country, region, urban/suburban/rural, town/city, climate	Country clothing, air-conditioning, regional specialities
Geo-demographic	House type and location	Conservatories, lawnmowers
Psychographic	Lifestyles, values, personality	Health/healthier products, cosmetics, cigarettes
Mediagraphic	Media habits (e.g. papers read)	Specialist magazines, eco-friendly holidays
Behavioural	Behavioural characteristics including time/occasion of purchase, loyalty, user status, benefits sought, attitude to product, etc.	Mother's Day products, disposable cameras, toothpaste

A good example of combining the different variables is provided by the notion of **geo-demographic segmentation**, which focuses on the relationship between a person's geographical location and their demographic characteristics, given that close links frequently exist between a person's place and type of residence and factors such as income, family size and attitudes. One well-known scheme of this type is **ACORN** (A Classification of Residential Neighbourhoods), which uses 40 variables from population census data to differentiate residential areas. Another is **MOSAIC**, developed by Experian, which draws on a variety of data sources (e.g. census data, financial data, property characteristics, demographic information) and uses a range of sophisticated analytical techniques to produce household profiles at full postcode level. Under the MOSAIC scheme, UK households are divided into 11 groups with names such as 'Symbols of Success', 'Suburban Comfort' and 'Grey Perspectives' and these are then further sub-divided into 61 types, again with interesting and evocative names, including 'Golden Empty Nesters', 'Sprawling Subtopia' and 'Childfree Serenity'. For a fuller description of MOSAIC and Experian's other products (e.g. commercial MOSAIC) and methodology you should access the company's website at *www.experian.co.uk* and follow the links.

With regard to factors such as social class and lifestyles, these tend to be grouped under the notion of **psychographic segmentation**, an approach that has attracted considerable attention in recent years given the reciprocal link between lifestyles and consumption indicated above. Lifestyle segments can be developed either as 'off-the-shelf' products by marketing agencies/management consultancies or can be customised for/by individual companies, although the latter often tend to be both complex and expensive to design. One established and popular example of the former is **VALS** (Values and Lifestyles) developed by SRI International. Under this model, individuals are allocated to different categories on the basis of a combination of demographic and lifestyle factors such as age, education, income and levels of self-confidence, and then these categories are grouped into a number of broader segments, which reflect a category's predominant orientations. Thus, under VALS 2, the three broad groups identified were: (1) people who were *principle-orientated* (i.e. guided by their views of how the world should be); (2) people who were *status-orientated* (i.e. guided by the opinions and actions of others); (3) people who were *action-orientated* (i.e. guided by the desire for social and physical activity, variety in life and risk taking). Again you can gain further information on this scheme by visiting the SRI website at ***www.sri.com***

Synopsis

All organisations are an integral part of the society in which they exist and carry out their activities and as a result are affected by a range of influences emanating from the demographic, social and cultural environment. These influences can change over time and help to shape both the demand and supply sides of business activity. Businesses and other organisations need to be aware of and respond to the process of societal change and to the opportunities and threats that such change can engender.

Summary of key points

- Organisations exist and operate within society and are subject to a variety of demographic and socio-cultural influences.

- Demography is concerned with population variables, including population size, structure and distribution.

- Changes in demography are primarily related to changes in birth and/or death and/or net migration rates.

- Demographic change can affect both the demand and supply sides of the economy.

- The social context of business includes factors such as social class, lifestyles and reference group influences. The consumption of goods and services in an economy can be linked to such factors.

- The cultural environment of business comprises those institutions and other forces that help to shape society's basic attitudes, values, perceptions, preferences and behaviour.

- Societies usually also contain sub-cultures, which can influence a person's beliefs, attitudes and actions.

- Like demography and social factors, cultural influences can change over time and can affect organisations. Businesses need to be sensitive to such change.

- The importance of demographic, social and cultural factors in business can be illustrated by the concept of market segmentation.

An invitation to 'tweet'

The last decade has seen a remarkable explosion in the use of social media/social networking sites by individuals, groups and organisations. Facebook, Twitter, Snapchat, Instagram, YouTube and others now attract billions of users across the globe on a daily basis, a growing number of whom use smartphones and tablets to access these media services. Interacting with others and creating and sharing content through Internet-based communities has become relatively commonplace, as has shopping for products on the Internet and accessing online music, videos and sports content.

Where businesses are concerned, social networking sites appear to provide substantial marketing opportunities for firms of all sizes. Media can be used to build stronger relationships with existing customers, attract new consumers, inform users about current and future goods and services, generally promote the business and the firm's brand name(s), and find out what customers think about the organisation and its performance, including the issue of customer satisfaction. Most major firms now have a Facebook site and/or use Twitter to communicate with existing and potential consumers who are encouraged to 'follow' the business via the different media and to receive regular updates on its products and activities.

As a tool for marketing communication, social media sites have a number of important advantages. They are often free to businesses; they have a broad (often global) reach; they are fast and easy to access; they can be used to target specific groups of individuals; they allow an organisation to communicate with particular customers or groups on a personal basis at any point in time and wherever they may be. Far from replacing other forms of marketing communication and promotion, social media usage has become an additional weapon in the armoury of participating businesses; many firms have been quick to recognise that for a rapidly growing number of individuals, accessing the different networking sites is an essential part of their daily lives and hence a potentially lucrative marketing opportunity that can be exploited by suppliers of goods and services.

For organisations that choose to use social media to market their businesses, there can be risks involved, a point illustrated by the following example. In October 2013, the UK's largest energy company, British Gas, announced its intention of increasing energy prices by 10 per cent, which was around three times the level of inflation. Faced with a consumer and political backlash over its decision, the company decided to use Twitter[1] to try to head off criticism of its price hike by inviting questions from concerned customers. In the event, the organisation's attempts to pacify angry consumers proved to be a PR disaster,[2] with almost 16 000 Twitter comments – most of which were vitriolic – raining down on the company within a few hours of the invitation. To compound the problem, British Gas evidently failed to answer customers' tweets, choosing instead to use the networking site to explain to customers the reason for the decision to raise energy prices substantially, despite an earlier promise by the parent group, Centrica, to use windfall profits from the previous winter to keep prices down.

As this example illustrates, communicating with customers through social media needs to be undertaken with care and forethought; bad news can spread as rapidly as good news, even if only 140 characters are available. It does not take much to get things wrong, however genuine the intention.

Notes

1 Twitter – which was established in 2006 – is a 'micro-blogging' service which allows individuals and organisations to send and receive short messages about all kinds of issues and topics, including world events (e.g. the 'Arab Spring'). Popular with ordinary individuals, celebrities and companies alike, it currently attracts more than 300 million active users a month worldwide, who send around 1 billion tweets every two and a half days. Like Facebook, Twitter derives most of its revenue from advertising. In 2016 the company's advertising revenue was $717 million.

2 British Gas's experience is reminiscent of the wrath engendered by Starbucks' invitation to 'spread the cheer' via Twitter at Christmas time 2012. ▶

This prompted a plethora of angry tweets over the company's failure to pay UK corporation tax, which had received widespread media coverage. In 2016 Coca-Cola sent a tweet showing a map of Russia which left off a significant part of the country. Some Russians replied with photographs of people pouring drinks down the toilet with the tag #BanCocaCola.

Case study questions

1 What are the key advantages for firms of using social networking sites to market themselves and/or their products?

2 Is the use of social media by businesses size dependent; that is, predominantly limited to larger firms?

case study

Supply and demands – a changing workforce

One of the biggest changes in people's working lives over the last few decades has been the end of them or, rather, when that age is expected to be. Since the end of the Second World War, around the time the welfare state (NHS, social housing, etc.) was created, the state pension age was set at 60 for women and 65 for men. Those born in 1950 would get their pension in 2010 (women) or 2015 (men) so long as they had sufficient national insurance contributions, presently 30 years' worth. After 2018, 35 years of NI contributions will be required, and the state pension age is in the process of rising to 66 for women by 2020, to match that of men. By 2028 the state pension age will be 67, and by 2044 it will be 68. This is largely because people can expect to live much longer than they used to. Many occupational pension schemes are based on the state pension age, but some vary.

In 2012 the Firefighters Pension Scheme changed for members who were below the age of 45 at that time. Previously firefighters retired at the age of 55, because after this time they were judged to be unlikely to be fit enough to undertake the physical demands of the job. The Williams' Review (2013) found that 85 per cent of firefighters were unable to meet the fitness standard adopted by the fire service by the time they are 55, and 92 per cent would be unable to meet the standard at 60. If they cannot meet the standard they may be forced to retire with a significant pension reduction. Added to this is the risk of 60-year-old men and women running into hazardous situations such as burning buildings.

Case study questions

1 What sort of work do we expect people to be doing as they get older?

2 How do we expect either older people to support themselves, or society to support a growing number of them?

3 What plans are you considering for retirement, and how might you have to prepare for them?

Review and discussion questions

1 What is meant by an 'ageing' population? Examine some of the key ways in which an ageing population can affect the supply side of the economy.

2 In a country of your choice, identify some of the major social trends over the last decade. How are these trends reflected in changing patterns of consumption?

3 What is meant by the term 'culture'? To what extent do you agree with the proposition that globalisation could destroy local cultural diversity?

4 Why do marketers segment markets? Give examples of particular markets where demographic segmentation might be appropriate.

Assignments

1 Assume you work in the HR department of a large retail organisation that is seeking to replace staff who are about to retire. Because of demographic and other trends you anticipate problems in recruiting school-leavers in sufficient numbers. Produce a report outlining the problem to senior executives and suggest possible solutions. Provide justifications for your recommendations.

2 Choose three countries from different continents. Produce data to show the age distribution of the population in each of the countries in a given year. Account for any differences in the age profile of the three countries and suggest ways in which these differences might affect their respective economies in both the short and the long term.

Further reading

Hofstede, G., *Culture's Consequences: Comparing Values, Behaviors, Institutions, and Organizations Across Nations,* 2nd edition, Sage, 2003.

Hofstede, G., Hofstede, G. J. and Minkov, M., *Cultures and Organizations: Software of the Mind,* 3rd edition (Google eBook), McGraw-Hill Professional, 2010.

Kotler, P. and Armstrong, G., *Principles of Marketing,* 17th edition, Pearson Education, 2017.

Masterson, R., Phillips, N. and Pickton, D., *Marketing: An Introduction,* 4th edition, Sage, 2017.

Morrison, J., *The Global Business Environment: Meeting the Challenges,* 3rd edition, Palgrave Macmillan, 2011, Chapter 6.

Office for National Statistics, available free online (*www.statistics.gov.uk*).

Williams, A. N., Wilkinson, D. M., Richmond, V. L. and Rayson, M. P., *Normal Pension Age for Firefighters: A Review for the Firefighter's Pensions Committee,* Department of Communities and Local Government, London, 2013.

Worthington, I., 'The social and economic context', in Rose, A. and Lawton, A., *Public Services Management,* Financial Times/Prentice Hall, 1999, pp. 26–43.

web link

Web links and further questions are available on the website at:
www.pearsoned.co.uk/worthington

7 The resource context: people, technology and natural resources

Chris Britton

Businesses carry out a variety of activities, but their main activity is to produce goods and services to be sold on the market. In the production process, inputs are turned into outputs. Key inputs into the production process are people, technology and natural resources.

Learning outcomes

Having read this chapter you should be able to:

- illustrate the importance of people, technology and natural resources to business
- explain what determines the quality of labour in the economy
- demonstrate the effect of technological change on business
- outline the main issues affecting natural resources

Key terms

Capital
Computer-aided design (CAD)
Derived demand
Educated workforce
Factor of production
Fixed capital
Fracking
Geographical immobility
Gross investment
Immobility of labour
Information technology
Infrastructure
Innovation
Investment

Land
Minimum wage
Natural resources
Negademand
Non-renewable resources
NVQs
Occupational immobility
Occupational structure
Participation rate
People
Process innovation
Product innovation
Renewable resources
Replacement investment

Research and development (R&D)
Resources
Social capital
Stock
Technological change
Technological unemployment
Technology
Trade union
Wage rate
Wages
Workforce
Working capital
Working week

Introduction

The main aim of business is to produce goods and services that people want. This production cannot take place without people, technology and natural resources. In economics, these three are called the factors of production and are categorised under the headings of labour, capital and land. This chapter will consider each of these in turn. **Resources** can be renewable or non-renewable. **Renewable resources** would include labour, water, fishing stocks, soil, air and solar power, even though many of these might not be renewable for a long period of time. **Non-renewable resources** would be most minerals, including oil, iron ore and coal, agricultural land, forests and electricity (in so far as most electricity is derived from minerals).

People

As indicated in Chapter 6, **people** are important in the economy as both producers and consumers of goods and services. For most products that are produced, people are the most important input into the production process. Therefore the quantity and quality of the people available in an economy will have a considerable impact upon the economy's ability to produce.

The quantity of people available for work depends upon a variety of factors:

- the size of the total population;
- the age structure of the population;
- the working population;
- the length of the working week;
- the wage level.

As well as the quantity of labour, productivity will be affected by its quality. This in turn depends upon:

- education and training;
- working conditions;
- welfare services (e.g. national insurance schemes, which cover sickness pay; the NHS, which maintains the health of workers; also many firms provide their own welfare services such as private pension plans, and so on);
- motivation;
- the quality of the other factors of production.

Some of the quantitative factors have already been discussed in the previous chapter. In this section we concentrate on the idea of the 'workforce' and associated issues, before considering the question of labour quality.

The workforce

The **workforce** is the number of people who are eligible and available to work and offer themselves up as such. The size of the workforce will be determined by the age at which people can enter regular full-time employment, which in the UK is 18 years, and the age at which they leave employment. In the UK the retirement age for men is 65 years and for women will be 66 by 2020. Those included in the definition of the workforce are:

- those working in paid employment, even if they are over retirement age;
- part-time workers;
- the claimant unemployed;
- members of the armed forces;
- the self-employed.

The workforce in 2013 was 32.3 million, which is about 51 per cent of the total population. The importance of the workforce is two-fold: it produces the goods and services needed in the economy, and through the payment of taxes it supports the dependent population (i.e. the very old and the very young).

An important determinant of the size of the workforce is the **participation rate** (i.e. the proportion of the population who actually work). Table 7.1 shows that the participation rate for men and women at three points in time: 1971, for some of the earliest dates for the employment of women to be measured; 2010, for just after the financial crisis and the lowest point since the 1980s; and 2017, for the most up-to-date figure at the time of writing. There has been a rise in participation rates for women at the same time as a fall in participation rates for men.

Table 7.1 UK employment rates (% in the range 16–64, seasonally adjusted)

	Men 1971 Jan–Mar	Men 2010 Jan–Mar	Men 2017 Sept–Nov	Women 1971 Jan–Mar	Women 2010 Jan–Mar	Women 2017 Sept–Nov
In employment	91.9	74.9	79.9	52.8	65.6	70.8

Source: Adapted from Table A03 Statistical bulletin: UK labour market, January 2018 www.ons.gov.uk

The trend has been for increased participation rates for women over time as families have become smaller and because of the changing role of women in society as a whole, labour-saving devices in the home, government legislation to promote equal pay and treatment, and the increase in the pension age of women. Also important in this process are the changes in industrial structure which have led to more part-time service jobs (see Chapter 12).

There has been an increase in participation rates of married or cohabiting women with dependent children, from 67 per cent in 1996 to 70 per cent by 2013. There has been a similar increase in participation rates of lone mothers – from 43 per cent to 60 per cent over the same time period.

Table 7.2 gives some comparisons with other EU countries. The UK has the third-highest activity rates for men and women after Denmark and Germany. There are marked differences in the activity rates for women across the EU, but in every country they are lower than the male activity rate.

For more information on labour markets:
in the UK see *www.statistics.gov.uk/hub/labour-market/* (now archived);
in Europe see *http://ec.europa.eu/eurostat*
and in the world *www.oecd.org*

Table 7.2 Economic activity rates* by sex for selected EU countries (%), 2010

	Males	Females	All
UK	74.5	64.8	69.5
France	68.3	59.9	64.0
Germany	76.0	66.1	71.1
Belgium	67.4	56.5	62.0
Italy	67.7	46.2	56.9
Denmark	75.8	71.1	73.4
EU-27 average	70.1	58.6	64.2

*As a percentage of the working age population.
Source: Adapted from Table 2.2, *http://epp.eurostat.ec.europa.eu/cache/ITY_OFFPUB/1*
(no longer active), © European Union, 1995–2014.

The length of the working week

The average length of time for which people work is also a significant determinant of the quantity of labour that is available in an economy. Generally, the shorter the **working week**, the less labour there is available. There has been, over the last 100 years, a gradual reduction in the length of the working week; 40 hours is now roughly the norm, with a gradual increase in the number of holidays that people take. More recently, this trend has been reversed: the average working week in the UK was 42.8 hours in 2010. Table 7.3 shows the length of the average working week in selected EU countries.

Table 7.3 Average hours worked per week* for selected EU countries, 2010

	All
UK	42.8
France	41.1
Germany	41.8
Belgium	41.2
Italy	40.7
Denmark	41.8
Netherlands	41.0
EU15 average	41.5
EU25 average	41.6

*Full-time employees.
Source: Table 2.8, *http://epp.eurostat.ec.europa.eu/cache/ITY_OFFPUB/1*
(no longer active), © European Union, 1995–2014.

Both men and women in the UK work a longer week than men and women in all other EU countries. A relatively new phenomenon in the UK is the use of zero-hours contracts – see mini case study.

---

mini case Zero-hours contracts

A growing trend in the UK is the use of the zero-hours contract (ZHC), where employees are not guaranteed any hours' work per week but are expected to be 'on call'. They can be called in as and when they are required (see Figure 7.1). They often typically work much more than zero hours,

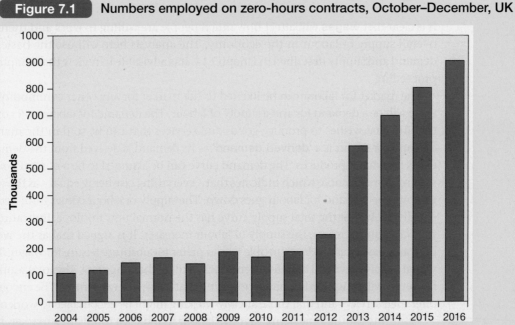

Figure 7.1   Numbers employed on zero-hours contracts, October–December, UK

Source: Adapted from People in employment on a zero-hours contract: Mar 2017

but nothing is guaranteed. They are only paid for the work they do and up until recently they often had to ask their employer's permission to take up other employment (this practice has now been outlawed). These sorts of contracts are not new – there are some jobs which by their very nature require ZHCs: for example, examination invigilation. Schools, colleges and universities have a big demand for invigilators at certain times of the year. It would be uneconomic for them to use permanent full- or even part-time employees for this job. In this case ZHCs benefit the employees as well, many invigilators being retired teachers who are happy with this working arrangement.

The Labour Force Survey (LFS) estimated that in quarter 4 of 2016, around 3 per cent of the UK workforce (905 000) were on ZHCs. The same survey estimated that approximately 1.7 million ZHCs existed in the UK (where some people had more than one, or one in addition to another job).

ZHCs are more commonly used in large companies (23 per cent of companies with more than 100 employees compared with 11 per cent of those companies with 50–99 employees). There are differences between sectors: they are most common in hotels and restaurants (19 per cent in 2011), health

(13 per cent in 2011) and education (10 per cent in 2011), as well as in gig economy sectors (see Chapter 10). It is estimated that some retailers and hospitality companies have more than 80 per cent of their workers on ZHCs.

There are arguments for and against ZHCs:

1 ZHCs give flexibility to both employer and employee.
2 There is less security for employees.
3 Employees are open to possible exploitation by employers.
4 There are problems with arranging childcare at short notice.

Although there is much bad press about ZHCs, it is not all negative. The CIPD found that the levels of job satisfaction of those on ZHCs were just as high as those of other employees. More than half of the employees surveyed by the CIPD said that they would not want to work longer hours (but they may be working more hours anyway). The debate continues in the press and has reached the level of government debate, with increased legislation on ZHCs in 2015–16.

Wages

It is clear that **wages** will affect how much people are willing to work and therefore the overall supply of labour in the economy. The analysis here will use the basic tools of demand and supply described in Chapter 14. It is advisable to review that chapter before proceeding.

The market for labour can be likened to the market for any other commodity, in that there will be a demand for and a supply of labour. The demand for labour will come from the firm that wishes to produce goods and services that can be sold in the market. The demand for labour is a '**derived demand**' as its demand is derived from the demand that exists for what it produces. The demand curve can be assumed to be a normal downward-sloping demand curve which indicates that – everything else being equal – as the wage rate goes up, the demand for labour goes down. The supply of labour comes from people. It is equally likely that the total supply curve has the normal upward slope, indicating that as the wage rate increases, the supply of labour increases. It is argued that as the **wage rate** increases past a certain level, people would prefer to substitute leisure for wages. The individual supply curve will therefore bend backwards at that wage rate. The total supply curve, however, will be upward sloping, indicating that those not working will be encouraged to offer their services and that those already working might be encouraged to work overtime.

Assuming for the time being that the labour market is a totally free market, the wage rate and the amount of labour being used will be determined by the forces of demand and supply, as in Figure 7.2. The equilibrium wage rate is £W and the equilibrium quantity of labour is L. If there is a change in the level of demand or supply, there will be a corresponding change in the wages and quantity of labour.

Trade unions and wages

In the UK there are four different types of **trade union**:

1 *Craft unions.* They represent one particular craft or skill, like the Boilermakers Union, which was formed in 1834 and was the longest-lived craft union in the TUC when it merged with the GMB in 1982. These were the earliest types of union.

Figure 7.2 The market for labour

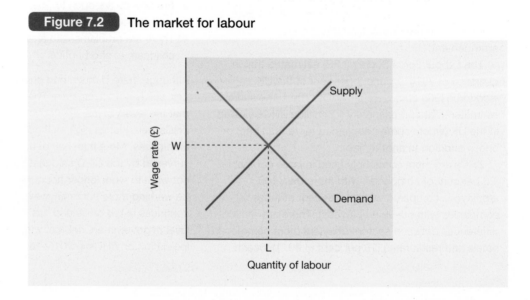

2 *Industrial unions.* They have members doing different jobs but in the same industry. Industrial unions are more common in other countries, but some UK unions come close to this type, for example the National Union of Mineworkers.

3 *General unions.* They contain members doing different jobs in different industries, such as the Transport and General Workers Union.

4 *White-collar unions.* They represent the non-manual workers like teachers, social workers, and so forth. Examples are UNISON, the University and College Union (UCU) or the British Medical Association (BMA).

web link For information on trade unions in the UK see *www.tuc.org.uk*

One of the main aims for all types of union has been to counteract and protect their members from the power of the employer. As far as wages are concerned, this has been achieved through collective bargaining. Over the years a situation has been reached where hardly any wage contracts are negotiated individually. Rather, they are collectively negotiated by trade unions and employers. Although there does seem to be a trend away from collective bargaining, coinciding with the anti-trade-union legislation of the 1980s and decline in the membership and power of the trade unions, the majority of wage increases are still negotiated by trade unions.

It is argued that the activities of trade unions through collective bargaining have served to increase the wage rate above its equilibrium level and thus cause unemployment. Figure 7.3 demonstrates this effect. Assume that the market-clearing wage rate is £W and the quantity of labour being used is L. Assume now that a trade union enters the market and has the power to enforce a wage increase to £W_1. At this wage rate the market does not clear; the demand for labour is L_1 while the supply of labour is L_2. There is therefore excess supply of labour, or unemployment. In this way trade unions are blamed for keeping wages at too high a level so that the market cannot clear.

Figure 7.3 can be used to illustrate the argument of those who oppose the setting of a **minimum wage**. Although this argument seems plausible enough, it is not quite as simple

Figure 7.3 The effect of trade unions on the labour market

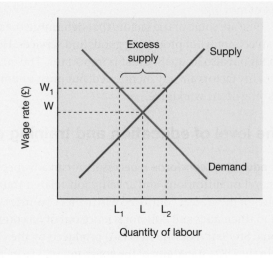

as it seems. There are other market imperfections which prevent the market from operating as smoothly as suggested and which contribute towards creating unemployment. There are some industries that have only one or two employers who can exercise a great deal of power over the market. The arguments over the minimum wage are also more complicated and centre on much wider economic and social issues. There are additional factors that may prevent people moving easily and smoothly between jobs. For example, people may not easily be able to change jobs if they are geographically or occupationally immobile.

Immobility of labour

People are **geographically immobile (immobility of labour)** for a variety of reasons:

- The cost of moving – it is an expensive business to move to another part of the country, particularly to areas where housing costs are high, such as London.
- There may be shortages of housing in certain areas, or it may be difficult or even impossible to sell a house in other areas.
- There will be many social ties in the form of family and friends that people may be reluctant to leave.
- For people with children, schooling will be important. For example, parents are reluctant to relocate when their children are working for important examinations.

People may also experience **occupational immobility** for the following reasons:

- Some jobs require some natural ability that an individual may not possess (e.g. entertainers, footballers, and so on).
- Training is required by many occupations (e.g. doctors, engineers). Without this training an individual could not do the job and the length of training might be a deterrent.
- To enter some occupations (like starting up your own business), a certain amount of capital is required. In some cases the amount of capital needed will be very high (dry cleaning, for example, where the machines are expensive to purchase), and for many this might prove to be a barrier to mobility.

In order to help people to be more mobile so that the labour market works more smoothly, the government over the years has evolved a variety of policies. Job centres and similar places attempt to overcome the lack of knowledge of available jobs. Training schemes are offered so that people can retrain, and relocation allowances can be paid to alleviate the cost of moving.

These are some of the factors that determine the number of people who are available in an economy for producing goods and services. However, it is not just the quantity of labour but also its quality that is important. The quality of the workforce is determined by many factors already mentioned, but most importantly by the level of education and training of the workforce.

The level of education and training of the workforce

An **educated workforce** is necessary for an advanced industrial nation, in terms of both general qualifications and specific job-related training. The UK does not fare well in either of these areas compared with other countries, being ranked 23rd for reading, 26th for mathematics and 20th for science out of 65 countries in the Programme for International Student Assessment (PISA) produced by the OECD.

In the UK, a stated aim of the government is to increase the proportion of young people staying on at school after the statutory minimum leaving age. Between September 2013 and 2015 the school leaving age was raised to 18 years old (but it remains at 16 for people starting apprentices or traineeships).

The UK government also has put in place policies aimed towards vocational courses for the over-16s. Table 7.4 gives some examples of these over the last three decades.

National Vocational Qualifications (**NVQs**) are qualifications that cover a specific skill, such as plumbing or carpentry, while General National Vocational Qualifications

Table 7.4 Examples of vocational courses for over-16s

Year	Scheme	Description
1983	Youth Training Scheme	Provided work-related training for 16- and 17-year-olds, both on and off the job. Largely introduced to fill the gap left by the demise of traditional apprenticeships
1985	Certificate of Pre-vocational Education	Full-time vocational courses for over-16s containing an element of work experience
1992	National Vocational Qualifications (NVQs), General National Vocational Qualifications (GNVQs)	A comprehensive system of vocational qualifications at four levels of achievement
1998	Work-based Training for Young People	This replaced the Youth Training Scheme with the aim of ensuring that young people have access to post-compulsory education or training
2004	National Qualifications Framework	This brings together general and vocational qualifications into one framework
2010	Qualifications and Credit Framework	National credit transfer system
2015	Registered Qualification Framework	International credit transfer system. Several countries have agreed to align their national systems in terms of size and levels. This replaces the NQF and QCF, though the QCF remains the main reference for UK qualifications

(GNVQs) are more general and indicate a broad knowledge of an area, such as the built environment. NVQ level 2 equates to GNVQ intermediate level and is equivalent to five GCSE grades A* to C. NVQ level 3 equates to GNVQ advanced level and is equivalent to two GCE A-levels, and level 4 equates to a degree or higher vocational qualification.

The Qualifications and Credit Framework (QCF) replaced the National Qualifications Framework in 2010. Under the QCF each qualification carries a credit value. There are three sizes of qualification: award, which equals 1–12 credits; certificate, which equals 13–36 credits; and diploma, which equals 37+ credits. The new system corresponds with the EU system so that the credits are internationally comparable. Part of the framework is shown in Table 7.5.

Table 7.5 National Qualifications Framework, up to level 3

Level	General	Vocational	Occupational
3 National Diploma, National Certificate	A-level	BTEC national award	NVQ level 3
2 First Diploma	GCSE (grade A*–C)	BTEC first diploma	NVQ level 2
1 Foundation	GCSE (grade D–G)	BTEC introductory certificate	NVQ level 1

Source: Qualifications and Credit Framework, *qca.org.uk*, 2005.

The UK government has used a variety of policies in an attempt to increase educational attainment and training. These include:

- the National Literacy and Numeracy Strategy, launched in 1998, which provides for a dedicated literacy hour and one mathematics lesson every day for primary school children;
- the use of Education Action Zones in areas of educational disadvantage;
- the introduction of the Education Maintenance Allowance, which offers financial incentives to young people from low-income homes to remain in education;
- an increased number of Modern Advanced Apprenticeships;
- e2e (entry to employment), which is an entry to a level 1 programme that uses work-based learning;
- in 2001 43 Learning and Skills Councils were set up with responsibility for all post-16 education up to university level;
- in 2002 Sector Skills Councils were set up;
- in 2010 the Learning and Skills Council was replaced by the Skills Funding Agency.
- in 2017 the Skills Funding Agency was replaced by the Education and Skills Funding Agency.

As well as school and higher education, job-related training is important in improving the quality of the workforce. Training at work can be of two types: on-the-job training and off-the-job training. There has been the development of a competence-based approach to training, which partly stems from the introduction of NVQs. The system is designed to be easily understood and to provide workers with the skills that are needed by industry. It is designed to unify what is a very diverse system of qualifications existing in the UK at present. Recent developments include:

- the Commission for Employment and Skills was set up in 2008 to bring industry into the heart of decision-making;
- in 2011 the Work Programme was set up to help long-term unemployed people back into work through work experience and training;
- in 2013 the Help to Work scheme was introduced to offer training for those who had been unemployed for more than three years.

The government also sponsors training for young people. This includes Apprenticeships and Advanced Apprenticeships. These schemes are designed for the 16–25-year age group and aim to provide training leading to recognised vocational qualifications – Apprenticeships at NVQ level 2 and Advanced Apprenticeships at NVQ level 3.

The Investors in People initiative has had an impact on training as it is based on four principles:

- top-level commitment to develop all employees;
- regular reviews of training and development of all employees;
- action to train and develop employees throughout their employment; and
- evaluation of the outcome of training as a basis for continuous improvement.

By October 2013, more than 37 000 UK organisations had achieved recognition under the standard, representing 38 per cent of the UK workforce.

The number of women receiving job-related training has increased over the last 20 years relative to men, and there has been a gradual increase for both sexes over the time period. There are significant differences between industries, with, for example, the service sector having a much higher level of training than agriculture, forestry and fishing, and between occupations.

Training is an important issue not just for school-leavers and the unemployed but for all employees. The *UK Employers' Skills Survey,* carried out in the UK in 2013, found that 31 per cent of vacancies were skill shortage vacancies. In 2013, only 38 per cent of establishments had a training plan, down from 48 per cent in 2007, although 60 per cent of establishments do provide training.

> **web link**
>
> For information on training schemes see
> *www.gov.uk* (Department for Business, Innovation & Skills)
> *www2.warwick.ac.uk/fac/soc/ier* (Warwick Institute for Employment Research)
> *www.nfer.ac.uk* (National Foundation for Educational Research)
> *www.gov.uk/government/publications/qualification-and-component-levels*
> *www.gov.uk/government/organisations/education-and-skills-funding-agency*
> *www.ssda.org.uk*

Occupational structure of the population

There will be changes in the **occupational structure** of the population over time. These will be caused by changes in industrial structure and technological change. There has been an increase in the number of non-manufacturing jobs at the same time as a fall in the number of manufacturing jobs. There are more women in the workforce now, partly because there has been an increase in demand for the types of goods that have been produced by women. There has also been an increase in the availability and quality of labour-saving devices in the home, which has released women into the workforce. There has been a decrease in the average family size so that if women leave the workforce to look after their children, they now do so for a shorter period of time. There has also been a change in attitude towards women working.

Figure 7.4 shows the structure of occupations in the UK by gender. There is a higher percentage of men than women in the professional/managerial occupations and there are more men working in skilled trades than women. Women are clearly concentrated in clerical/selling-type occupations.

Figure 7.4 The structure of occupations in the UK by gender

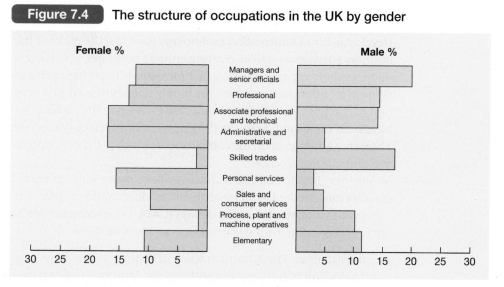

Source: Adapted from EMP08: All in employment by occupation, *www.ons.gov.uk*

There was a fundamental change in the nature of working life throughout the 1980s and on into the 1990s, continuing long into this century; this has to do with the notion of 'flexibility'. There has been an increase in the incidence of part-time working for both men and women, and an increased use of temporary contract and flexible working patterns. This was initially represented by firms having a 'core' permanent workforce that could deal with important business, combined with a more flexible 'peripheral' workforce that could be hired and fired on short-term contracts in response to increased or decreased demand. In 2013, 8 million people worked part-time in the UK; this represents about a fifth of the workforce. Approximately 3.8 million people were self-employed in 2008, rising to 4.6 million in 2015 (see mini case study on zero-hours contracts). Some businesses now operate entirely (or very nearly entirely) with people who are self-employed, or on zero-hour contracts in order to cut costs.

Technology

Technology is defined as 'the sum of knowledge of the means and methods of producing goods and services' (*Penguin Dictionary of Economics*). Technology is increasingly science based, encompassing subjects such as chemistry, physics and electronics, and refers to the organisation of production as well as the actual techniques of production itself. **Technological change** leads to the introduction of new products, changes in the methods and organisation of production, changes in the quality of resources and products, new ways of distributing the product and new ways of storing and disseminating information. Technology has a very big impact upon the world of business in all of these areas and has an important effect on the level and type of investment that takes place in an economy and therefore the rate of economic growth.

Technological change

There have been massive changes in technology in the past 10 years. This section will consider a few of these and assess their impact upon business and the economy.

Information technology

Developments in **information technology** have had the effect of transforming existing business activities as well as creating entirely new ones, involving the collection, handling, analysis and transmission of information. There has been a huge increase in the demand for information and, on the supply side, continued advances in the miniaturisation of components. These will continue even when the capabilities of the silicon chip have been exhausted, with the development of superconductors and optoelectronics. There are also advances in the computing area such as the development of new languages and artificial intelligence.

Advances in information technology have many impacts upon business. They are creating new products and making old products more profitable to produce through things such as **computer-aided design (CAD)**. The effects they are having on the different functions carried out by businesses can easily be seen:

● *Administration.* The administration of businesses has been revolutionised by the introduction of information technology. Most businesses have computer systems, records have been computerised and analogue/paper-based filing has become unnecessary.

- *Communication.* This has been eased by the introduction of email. Video conferencing has contributed to the change in working practices by making it possible for people to work anywhere. *Production.* The use of CAD will shorten the design and planning phase of the product and shorten the life cycle of the product. Japan applied this very early on in the field of consumer electronics and many of the products are withdrawn from sale and redesigned within a very short period of time.

- *Storage and distribution.* The computerisation of stock control has had implications for the storage requirements of firms. It has made implementation of the just-in-time method of stock control possible. This is easily seen in the case of supermarkets where the use of bar-codes on products makes it possible to carry out a stock check of a whole supermarket in a matter of hours. The shelves can then be loaded up as the stock check continues. Similarly, the use of bar-codes with Electronic Point of Sale (EPOS) makes stock control simpler.

- *Electronic Funds Transfer at Point of Sale (EFTPOS).* This system has also had a revolutionary effect in the area of retailing. Most retailers have stopped accepting cheques, but will now accept forms of contactless payment, including Apple Pay and bPay.

- *The Internet.* In 2012 there were an estimated 1.5 billion people wired to the Internet, in 2015 this figure was 3 billion. The highest percentage population penetration was in the United States (78.6 per cent), the lowest in Africa (15.6 per cent). There are three projects operating that will provide a cable system under the Indian Ocean linking African countries. Developments in cloud computing are enabling storage and processing power to become on-demand products, and platforms like Mechanical Turk (owned by Amazon) are changing the way people are (self-)employed to do simple tasks.

- *Artificial intelligence.* As the mini case study shows, the developments in this area have been huge and the growth is exponential. The use of robotisation and artificial intelligence has implications for many areas of business and law.

One aspect of business where information technology has become particularly important is in providing opportunities for firms to interact immediately with their customers and suppliers (including suppliers of labour), whoever and wherever they might be. Concepts such as e-commerce, e-business and e-markets are now part of the business lexicon and are an important area of study for undergraduate and postgraduate students alike.

mini case   The robots are coming

The pace of technological change over the past 50 years has been incredible and there is no sign of a slowdown. A few of these technological developments are discussed in this mini case study, together with their implications for the business world.

Robotisation

The increased use of robotisation can be seen in many areas of life: self-service checkouts at the supermarket; online education courses; hotels without reception staff; driverless cars. All of these replace people with machines, so they have implications for the labour force: will the main occupation be designing and maintaining machines? What many argue will happen is the loss of jobs in the middle of the market (admin and logistics, for example) but an increase in jobs that are IT related at the top of the market and a continuing demand at the bottom end of the market

▶

for jobs that cannot be carried out by machines, for example care for the elderly and children.

Some of these developments will have legal implications and often the law is slow to keep pace with technological change. A good example is the case of driverless cars – who will hold the insurance? The CEO of Amazon announced in November 2012 that within five years Amazon would be delivering parcels to customers using GPS-operated 'octocopters' – parcels could be delivered within 30 minutes of placing the order. This project is now called 'Amazon Prime Air' and was first tested in December 2016. This is another example that has huge implications for the labour force (loss of jobs) and the law – there are no rules in place for the use of commercial drones in the United States and there is much resistance from the general public. Several US states have banned the police from using drones.

Virtual wallets

In 2014 Apple launched 'Apple Pay', a service that uses 'Consumer Device Cardholder Verification Method' (CDCVM) technology to allow Apple devices to store customer payment information

such as account and card details and communicate with point of sale terminals. This has meant that people with iPhones, iPads and iWatches can use their devices to make payments without having to carry their cards. Each transaction can then be authorised using the customer's fingerprint on enabled devices. In return for the use of this service Apple receives up to 0.15% of the transaction as a fee from the banks involved (the fee varies by country); this is less than traditional bank fees for card payments.

There are many other examples of technological developments, such as the 3D printer (see mini case in Chapter 12), and all of them will have a dramatic impact on business. It is clear that these developments will continue apace. Apple has been investing millions in developing supply chain robotisation and acquired Prime Sense, the company that developed 3D sensing technology. Amazon acquired Kiva Systems in 2012 – a company that developed warehouse automation. And in December 2013 Google bought Boston Dynamics, a military robot company, only the latest in a succession of similar purchases. Watch this space!

Other technological developments

- *New materials.* The new material being heralded as the 'miracle material' of the twenty-first century is graphene. It consists of a single layer of carbon atoms bonded together in hexagons and is the strongest material ever measured. It is a replacement for silicon and will revolutionise computers.
- *Biotechnology.* This is expected to have wide-ranging effects on many fields. The development of new products like computers that can imitate the activity of the brain can shorten the development process for certain products by speeding up existing processes.
- *Energy.* The kind of developments that can take place in this field are the use of superconductors to transport electricity and research that might make renewable energy a viable source of energy. In 2016 Portugal ran all of the country on renewable energy for a whole week, the first time something of this scale had ever been attempted.

Technology and investment

The second input into the production process after people is **capital**. In economics, capital has a special meaning: it refers to all human-made resources that are used in production. Capital is usually divided into **working capital** and **fixed capital**. Working capital consists of the stocks of raw materials and components used in producing things. Fixed capital consists of buildings, plant and machinery. The main difference between the two is that fixed capital gives a flow of services over a long period of time, while working capital needs to be replaced on a regular basis. Because of its nature, working capital is much more mobile than fixed capital (i.e. it can be used for other purposes much more easily). Capital is a '**stock**' of goods used in the production process, a stock which is continually being used and therefore needing to be replaced. This stock provides a flow of services for the production process.

Capital includes a wide diversity of items, including factory premises, machinery, raw materials in stock, transport vehicles and partly finished goods. As well as these, there is what is often called '**social capital**', which refers to capital that is owned by the community, such as schools and hospitals. There is also spending on the **infrastructure**, which is important to all businesses rather than being linked to one particular business. The main components of this are transport, energy, water and information. The transportation system is obviously very important to a developed economy. Road, rail, air and water are used to transport goods, services and raw materials. The same is true for energy and water; both are used by industry in great quantities, and a good infrastructure in these is essential. The information distribution system is also part of the infrastructure and would include telephone systems and the post.

Table 7.6 Gross capital stock in 1997 and 2012 in the UK (£ billion)

		1997		2012			
		Net capital stocks £bn	Share of assets held %	Net capital stocks £bn	Share of assets held %	Year on year change £bn	Year on year % change
ABDE	Other production	160	6	279	8	119.2	2.1
C	Manufacturing	199	7	200	6	0.8	−1.5
F	Construction	252	9	248	7	−4.8	−2.1
G to T	Services	2128	78	2769	79	641.4	1.6
TOTAL		2739	100	3496	100	756.6	0.1

Source: Adapted from *www.ons.gov.uk*

The increase in the stock of capital over time is called **investment**. Investment will serve to increase the productive potential of the firm and the economy. Investment usually refers to the purchase of new assets, as the purchase of second-hand assets merely represents a change in ownership and therefore does not represent a change in productive potential. Investment is important for the firm as it is a mechanism for growth; it is an integral part of the **innovation** process and can have disastrous results for a firm if an investment goes wrong. Generally, the higher the level of investment in a country, the higher the level of economic growth will be (see Table 7.6 for a history of investment in the UK).

Total or **gross investment** can be broken down into **replacement investment**, which is investment to replace obsolete or worn-out machines, and new investment, which is any investment over and above this. This includes investment by firms, individuals (in dwellings mainly) and governments. As might be expected, the level of investment is affected by the state of the economy.

There is an important relationship between investment and technological change which runs in both directions. Investment can form the basis for improvements in technology, while improved technology, which brings about new ways of producing goods, will lead to greater investment. For private firms, the main determinants of the level of investment will be the rate of technological change and the scope for extra profit as a result of these changes.

Innovation and technology

There are two types of innovation that can occur as a result of technological change: **product innovation** and **process innovation**. Product innovation is the development of new products, such as the microprocessor, which will have far-reaching effects on business. New products impact upon the industrial structure of a country, as new industries grow and old industries disappear. This in turn will lead to changes in the occupational structure of the workforce, as we have seen. It has even had the effect of reducing the benefits large firms derive from economies of scale in cases where the technological change can be exploited by small firms as well as it can by large firms. Another example of product innovation which has affected the level of competition in the market is the development of quartz watches, which allowed Japan to enter the market and compete with Switzerland.

Process innovation, meanwhile, refers to changes that take place in the production process, such as the introduction of assembly-line production in the manufacture of cars. The two types of innovation are related, as the above examples show. The microprocessor (product innovation), which is a new product, has led to massive changes in the way that production and offices operate (process innovation).

Not all innovation is technological in nature; for example, changes in fashion in clothing are not technological. Innovative activity is important for all industry, whether manufacturing or non-manufacturing. In some industries (e.g. pharmaceuticals, computers), innovation is essential if firms wish to remain competitive.

 For information on innovation see the Department for Business, Energy & Industrial Strategy website at *www.gov.uk/government/organisations/department-for-business-energy-and-industrial-strategy*

Research and development

Most, but not all, technological changes have occurred through the process of **research and development (R&D)**. 'Research' can be theoretical or applied, and 'development' refers to the using of the research in the production process. Most research and development carried out by private companies is directed towards applied research and development. It is designed to develop new products and production processes that will render production more profitable. It is also aimed at improving existing products and processes. Most basic theoretical research carried out in the UK is financed from public sources and is undertaken in places like the universities.

Table 7.7 shows that the level of research and development expenditure in manufacturing industries in the UK in 2015 was £19,400 million, which represents around 1.2 per cent of GDP. Although total spending in real terms has risen over the past 20 years, the percentage share of R&D in GDP fell from 1.4 per cent in 1995 to 1.0 per cent in 2015. This is a long way short of OECD countries and the UK government's long-term target of around 3 per cent.

Table 7.7 Spending on R&D (£ million) in 2015 (2015 prices)

Product group	£ million	% of total
All product groups	19 400	100
All products of		
Scientific	4928	25.4
Manufacture of motor vehicles	2192	11.3
Computer programming	1610	8.3
Architecture and engineering	1513	7.8
Manufacture of other transport	1494	7.7
Manufacture of computer electronics	912	4.7
Other	6751	34.8

Source: Adapted from Table 15, Business Enterprise and Development, 2011, *www.ons.gov.uk*

It can be seen that there are wide differences in expenditure between industries, with manufacturing involved in a great deal more R&D spending than non-manufacturing. Even within the broad category of manufacturing there are wide differences, with chemicals accounting for more than a quarter of the expenditure. Table 7.8 shows the sources from which R&D is financed. As we can see, the majority of R&D is financed by companies themselves. If R&D is split into civil and defence spending, the government finances the majority of defence R&D, as would be expected.

Table 7.8 Sources of funds for R&D within industry in the UK for selected years (£bn)

	Private non-profit organisations	Higher education	Overseas	Government and research councils	Business	Total
2000	0.8	1.4	2.8	4.1	8.6	17.70
2005	1	2.2	4.2	5.2	9.6	22.20
2010	1.3	2.6	4.8	6	11.4	26.10
2011	1.3	2.6	5.2	6	12.4	27.50
2012	1.3	2.5	5.2	5.6	12.6	27.20
2013	1.4	2.7	5.3	6.3	13.6	29.30
2014	1.5	2.7	5.4	6.3	14.7	30.60

web link

For information on R&D see *www.oecd.org* or *https://royalsociety.org/topics-policy/projects/investing-in-uk-research-development/*

Figure 7.5 shows that the UK tends to fare badly in international comparisons of R&D spending.

Limits to technological change

Technological change has many effects on the economy and the environment and if uncontrolled can lead to problems, including high levels of unemployment or the exhaustion of natural resources. One area of concern is energy. The world's stock of energy is finite and we are still heavily dependent upon fuel that was formed millions of years ago. The development of nuclear power again represents a finite source of energy,

Figure 7.5   Gross domestic spending on R&D (% of GDP)

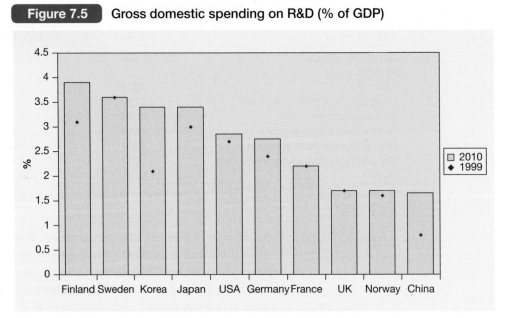

Source: Adapted from Figure 14, 'The UK R&D Landscape', CIHE and UK-irc

and also carries with it other problems, such as the disposal of nuclear waste and the possibility of accidents. For these and other reasons the scale of technological change needs to be controlled.

It is also the case that technological change can lead to high levels of unemployment in industries that are in decline. This type of unemployment often takes on a regional bias as the older traditional industries tend to be located in particular parts of the country. **Technological unemployment** is in some respects inevitable because in a changing world it would be expected that new industries would emerge and old industries die. The problem can be tackled by the government and industry through retraining, but what is also needed is a new and more flexible view of work where less time is spent working and more on leisure. Technological change can also give rise to the opposite problem of skill shortage in new industries, where particular skills are required. Technological change has not led to the massive increase in unemployment predicted by many in the 1970s and 1980s, but what might happen in the future is unknown.

Natural resources

In economics, **natural resources** are put under the heading of **land** as a **factor of production**. It would include all natural resources like the soil, minerals, oil, forests, fish, water, the sun, and so on. The uneven distribution of natural resources throughout the world means that they can be used as economic and political weapons.

Although the area of land in a country is fixed, land as a factor of production is not completely fixed in supply as more land can be made available through land reclamation schemes and better irrigation. The productivity of agricultural land can be increased by the use of fertilisers. It is true, however, that our natural resources are in finite supply. And often their true extent is not known with certainty.

It is in the area of natural resources that the distinction between renewable and non-renewable resources is most important. Natural resources can be either. Land can often be used for more than one purpose – for example, agricultural land can be used to grow one crop one year and another the next – but oil, once it is used up, cannot be used again. Technological developments such as **fracking** (see case study at the end of the chapter) will impact upon the level of natural resources. Fracking has enabled the extraction of natural gas and oil that was bound up in the shale rock, therefore increasing the quantities of these resources. However, they remain non-renewable. And even though land can sometimes be used for more than one purpose, it is immobile geographically and frequently occupationally. For example, land can be used for agriculture or industry, but using it for one of these makes it more difficult to use it for the other. If a factory is built on a piece of land, it would be both expensive and time consuming to clear the land for farming.

Table 7.9 shows the changing usage of agricultural land in the UK between 1971 and 2011. There are slight differences between the years, most notably the inclusion of 'set-aside' land in the 1993–2007 columns. This was part of EU Common Agricultural Policy where farmers were paid not to use land in an attempt to reduce the overproduction of agricultural goods.

Table 7.9 The use of agricultural land in selected years in the UK (thousand hectares)

	1971	1993	1997	2000	2003	2007	2011
Crops	4838	4519	4990	4709	4478	4350	4694
Bare fallow	74	47	29	33	29	165	–
Grasses	7240	6770	6687	6767	6884	7141	7343
Rough grazing*	6678	5840	5878	5803	5565	5552	5402
Set-aside	–	677	306	572	689	440	–
Woodland and other land on agricultural holdings	285	678	763	789	792	954	1297
Total	19 115	18 531	18 653	18 579	18 438	18 602	18 736

*Includes sole-right rough grazing and common rough grazing.
Source: Adapted from Table 21.3, *Annual Abstract of Statistics 2011*, www.ons.gov.uk

Protection of the environment

Increased knowledge of the effects of depletion of natural resources has led to increased environmental awareness among the population. There has been an increased interest in conservation and recycling and the search for alternative forms of energy. A survey by the Department of the Environment found that 90 per cent of the adult population in the UK was either 'fairly concerned' or 'very concerned' about the environment. The issues that have caused this concern include traffic congestion, global warming, air and water pollution and depletion of the ozone layer. This change in public opinion has already had a major impact on the way in which business operates and is likely to have even bigger effects.

Governments in the UK and elsewhere have a variety of targets for environmental protection relating to issues such as greenhouse gas emissions, biodiversity, renewable energy, recycling, packaging, and so on. Some of these targets are set through negotiations with other countries at both international (e.g. Kyoto Protocol) and supranational (e.g. EU) levels and hence are influenced by political, economic, social and technological considerations and by a variety of state and non-state actors (see Chapter 4). Given the growing importance of environmental issues in business, a separate chapter on ethics and the natural environment has been added (see Chapter 9).

One important resource in business whose exploitation and use have a significant impact on the natural environment is energy. The UK is not well endowed with high-grade minerals; the main natural resource is energy. There is a good deposit of coal and the discovery of North Sea oil and gas made the UK self-sufficient in energy supplies, and now fracking might do the same again. The usage of energy has doubled since 1970, but as Table 7.10 shows, there has been a change in the relative importance of the different sources of energy.

Table 7.10 Electricity supplied by fuel type, UK, 1980 to 2015 (TWh)

Year	Coal	Oil[2]	Gas	Nuclear	Renewables
1980	220.8	7.9	0	32.3	3.9
1990	213.4	19.2	0.4	58.7	5.8
2000	114.7	9.2	144.9	78.3	10.1
2010	102.3	5.6	172.5	56.4	24.7
2015[1]	72.4	4.3	97.8	63.9	79.4

1. 2015 data is provisional.
2. Includes pumped storage and other fuels.

Source: Table 23 UK Energy in Brief 2014 and Energy Trends March 2016,
http://visual.ons.gov.uk/uk-perspectives-2016-energy-and-emissions-in-the-uk/

Coal has lost its place to oil and gas as the most important sources of energy. The increase in the usage of both oil and gas is due to the discovery of North Sea oil and gas. The biggest single user of energy in the UK is the transport sector (38 per cent of energy produced), followed by domestic (27 per cent) and industry (17 per cent). A small but growing source of energy in the UK is renewables, with the government's target by 2020 being 15 per cent.

There is great variation in the fuels used for the generation of electricity across Europe, as Table 7.11 shows.

Table 7.11 Primary production of energy by source, 1000 tonnes of oil equivalent, 2016

	Nuclear	Solid fuels	Oil	Gas	Renewable
France	112 836	0	850	19	21 417
Belgium	6733	0	0	0	2959
Sweden	14 535	110	0	0	18 374
Spain	14 782	1246	233	54	16 874
Germany	23 677	43 003	2383	6335	38 886
UK	18 146	5115	43 813	35 659	11 835
Netherlands	1052	0	1409	39 003	4810
EU-28	221 202	144 874	69 144	107 588	205 043

Source: Adapted from *http://ec.europa.eu/eurostat/tgm/refreshTableAction.do?tab=table&plugin=1&pcode=ten00076 &language=en*

There has been a fall in the amount of electricity generated by nuclear power since 2004, although some EU countries use it as their primary generator of electricity. While its use produces lower emissions of greenhouse gases, there is an increased risk of accidental leakage of radioactivity as well as the problem of the disposal of radioactive waste. Many nations reconsidered investment in nuclear energy production after the Fukushima nuclear reactor meltdown in Japan following the earthquake and tsunami in 2011. The plant will take 30–40 years and an estimated $180bn to clean up. Electricity generation from oil and gas has tended to fall and an EU directive now requires 20 per cent of electricity (for the EU27 countries) to come from renewable sources by 2020. Countries are approaching this target, but as Table 7.11 shows, there are huge differences between them in how their energy is produced. Portugal managed to run on nothing but these sources of power for 107 hours between 7 and 10 May 2016. There is clearly a growing demand for alternative sources of energy. The alternatives of hydroelectric, wind and solar energy sources will also grow in importance. In the UK, the government has tried to promote the search for renewable energy sources through projects like the Renewables Obligation, which requires licensed electricity producers to obtain an increasing percentage of their electricity from clean sources (the UK average was 23.4 per cent in 2014–15). It also funds experimental work in the search for new sources of energy. One such source is 'biogas', which generates gas from household waste. The Committee on Climate Change claims that 1 in 20 of UK homes could be supplied with gas from this source. Biogas could also lead to fewer carbon emissions.

As well as recycling and searching for new sources of energy there is the concept of '**negademand**', where the use of less produces negative demand for those commodities. This concept can be applied to energy and water saving, driving and shopping. It is possible that technological change (like the 3D printer) could reduce the demand for energy (see the case study in Chapter 12).

> **web link**
>
> For information on the natural environment in the UK see *www.environment-agency. gov.uk* or *www.theccc.org.uk* (the Committee on Climate Change)
> In the EU see *www.eea.europa.eu* (the European Environment Agency)
> In the world see *www.oecd.org*

Synopsis

This chapter looked at the three main inputs into the production process: people, technology and natural resources. It considered each in turn and examined their importance to business and the main factors that determine both the quality and the quantity of these factors of production.

People are important in two ways: they are the producers of goods and services, and also the consumers of goods and services. The quantity of human resources available in an economy depends upon things like total population size, participation rates, length of working week and wages. The quality depends upon such things as the level of healthcare, education and training. There have been significant changes in the labour market over recent years.

One of the main features of the last 50 years has been the immense changes in technology that have had an enormous impact upon business, resulting in new products and markets and new methods of production and distribution.

As far as natural resources are concerned, the traditional view was that they were fixed in supply and therefore did not receive much consideration. However, with increased environmental awareness there is growing concern that this is not the case and that many of our natural resources are non-renewable and therefore need to be conserved.

Each of the three inputs into the production process has been considered separately, but they are interlinked and difficult to separate in reality. It has already been said that the productivity of people will be affected by the technology at their disposal, and this is also true of natural resources. All of the three inputs are 'stocks', from which streams of resources flow to firms. These flows are crucial to business, as without them production could not take place. Both the quantities and qualities of our stocks of these resources are important, as too is the replacement of the stocks that are being used.

Summary of key points

- Three main resources are used in the production of goods and services – labour, capital and land.

- The quantity of labour available depends upon population size, regulations in the labour market, the length of the working week and wage levels.

- The level of education and training determines the quality of available labour.

- The quantity and quality of capital depends on the level and type of investment taking place, the extent of research and development and the level of innovation.

- The quantity and quality of land are important elements in the production process and will depend on many things, including environmental controls.

case study   Agricultural work and Brexit

The agricultural sector in the UK has been supported by important European facilities in recent decades. The first is money, supplied through the Common Agricultural Policy (CAP) whereby European states are subsidised for maintaining production to ensure European food security despite its being uneconomic to do so. The second facility is a ready supply of cheap migrant labour.

In 2004 the EU enlarged to include 10 new countries, mostly from Eastern Europe. These included Poland, Hungary, Latvia, Lithuania, the Czech Republic and others. These countries had relatively underdeveloped economies by the standards of existing European member states. Where the gross domestic product (GDP) per capita was on average $20,000 of existing EU countries, the GDP per capita average of the new EU countries was around $9,000. One of the main principles of the EU is that of the free movement of labour and capital within the bloc. Since the inclusion of 10 new economies in 2004 many European (often skilled) workers have left jobs in their home countries to work in countries with a higher average wage and send some money back to their families. This has been one of the major drivers of immigration within Europe.

As early as 2006 the government recognised that migrant workers were making a significant contribution to the agricultural sector. Employers reported frequent labour shortages despite heavy advertising of low-skilled work in job centres and through local adverts before the arrival of migrant workers. The employers were positive about the general attitude and work ethic of European workers, in some cases saying they had a positive effect on the work ethic of UK national colleagues. EU workers were also willing to move, and as different crops tended to be planted in different parts of the UK the workers would relocate to where additional seasonal work was needed.

With the UK's exit from the EU on the horizon it is unclear how the agricultural sector can cope with the shortage of labour that changes in migration rules might cause, combined with the removal of the CAP money which has previously gone to farms and farmers.

Case study questions

1 If the availability of labour declines and the demand for labour increases, what might have to change with agricultural jobs and production in the UK?

2 What might the impact of increased labour costs be on UK foodstuffs?

---

case study — Fracking

The world's stock of natural resources is finite and in the 1970s there was much talk of energy crises that might occur when the world's stock of fossil fuels ran out. In 1956, M. King Hubbert put forward a theory that there was a point (he called the 'peak') where maximum oil production is reached, after which it would decline and eventually run out. This is a supply-side factor, in addition to which there are demand factors in play – there have been massive increases in the demand for oil because of economic growth (in countries like China) and population growth. Both the demand and supply factors can lead to energy crises.

Hubbert predicted that peak oil would occur in the United States between 1965 and 1971. Modern-day peak oil theory suggests that peak oil production will be reached after 2020, and that reductions in the demand for oil and the search for alternative sources of energy continue to be essential (see the case study on electric cars in Chapter 17).

The demand for and the supply of natural gas in the United States was in balance in 1986, after which demand exceeded supply, the excess being met by imported natural gas from Canada. This all changed in 2006 when controversial new drilling techniques were used, which dramatically increased the output of natural gas. This technique is called hydraulic fracturing, or fracking. Natural gas extracted through fracking made up only a small percentage of all natural gas production when the technology was first available, but as the price of oil increased between 2008 and 2014 (peaking at $157/barrel in June 2008, but at around $100/barrel for most of that period) the technology became more widespread as it was worthwhile to extract the oil. It is expected to represent 30% of the world's gas production by 2040.

Fracking involves the release of oil and gas which are bound up in shale rock through the use of high-powered water sprays mixed with sand and small amounts of specialised chemicals being pumped into the rocks. The oil and gas are then pushed up into the wells. Fracking has been used extensively in the United States and has been credited with powering the economic recovery and driving down energy prices.

1 United States

Fracking is taking place across the United States from Ohio to Dakota and Texas. The production of oil in the country has increased by 90 per cent since 2008 and the production of natural gas has doubled. Since 2008 the price of gas has fallen by two-thirds. It is estimated that by 2020 shale gas and oil will add $380–690 billion to annual GDP (2–4 per cent) and will create 1.7 million permanent jobs. This will happen through growth in the energy industries – direct spending on fracking and pipelines and also indirect spending on infrastructure to support and distribute the fuels.

Coal-fired electricity generation is continuing to be changed for the use of gas (although recent announcements by President Trump might increase

▶

coal production again). Since gas is cleaner than coal in terms of CO_2 emissions, there was a 10 per cent fall in the emission of greenhouse gases in the United States between 2005 and 2015. It is estimated that by 2020 gas-generated electricity will constitute 33 per cent of total electricity production; it was 21 per cent in 2008.

Much of this is good news for the US economy. It is on its way to being energy independent and it can now be an exporter of coal. The falling cost of gas has a positive effect on manufacturing as its costs will be lower, and it is argued that this gives the United States a competitive advantage over other countries.

2 Europe

A report (Poyry Management Consulting and Cambridge Econometrics) estimated that the widespread use of fracking in the EU could produce 1 million new jobs and add £3 trillion to EU economies. It would also reduce the dependence of the EU on gas imports.

The attitude to fracking varies across the EU. The UK and Poland are very receptive to the idea, while France, Germany, Spain and Bulgaria are less keen. At present in the EU fracking is covered by the same environmental legislation that applies to full-scale oil drilling. This makes it an expensive process. The European Commission is considering the issue of fracking at the time of writing and aims to produce guidelines soon.

In the EU there is much more public opposition to fracking than in the United States. In the UK, exploratory drilling by Cuadrilla in Balcombe was halted in August 2013 because of local protests. Without exploratory investigation, it is impossible to determine how much oil and gas is contained in the shale rocks. In Poland, exploratory drilling was abandoned largely because of legislative uncertainties.

3 Pros and cons of fracking

The arguments against fracking include the following:

(a) Fracking requires huge amounts of water which needs to be transported to the site. This has environmental implications and for some countries

(the UK, for example) many argue that water shortages would preclude fracking.

(b) It is argued that fracking could contaminate the water table through use of and generation of harmful chemicals and that it could lead to carcinogenic chemicals in the soil.

(c) Fracking can lead to earth tremors. In Blackpool in the UK, there were two small earthquakes in 2011 following fracking in the vicinity. Supporters of fracking argue that the possibility of earth tremors has more to do with the construction of the wells rather than the fracking itself.

(d) Opponents argue that the race towards fracking is stopping the energy companies looking at other renewable sources of energy. One such source that environmentalists argue is being ignored is biogas, where waste is used to generate gas.

The arguments in favour include:

(a) Fracking will increase the supply of oil and gas and provide for the world's growing energy needs.

(b) In the United States fracking has led to a fall in the price of gas and this is good for industry and consumers alike. Whether this would be true in the EU is unclear as not enough is known about the extent of the reserves or the cost of extraction. In the UK the cost of extraction under the North Sea will be very high.

(c) If prices did fall, the corresponding fall in costs to firms would increase international competitiveness.

(d) There will be energy security which could extend as far as the next 100 years. The facts are not known – the International Energy Agency predicts that the United States will be the biggest oil producer from 2015 to 2030 and that its reserves will start to decline in the 2020s.

(e) Burning gas produces half of the CO_2 emissions of burning coal, so the use of a natural gas is good for the environment. CO_2 emissions in the United States have fallen faster than in the EU.

The debate over fracking is a heated one, with strong proponents on both sides, and the debate is ongoing. Even the strong arguments used in favour in the United States can be qualified, for example the one about the lower cost of gas: the price of gas is sometimes lower than the cost of extraction, which means that it is not sustainable unless natural gas is seen as a by-product of the extraction of oil. This makes the production of natural gas dependent upon the price of oil; if this were to fall, then what might happen to the production of natural gas? In Europe, the future of fracking depends upon public opinion; without exploratory studies it is impossible to know what reserves are present or what the cost of extraction might be. The guidelines being produced by the European Commission should prove interesting.

Case study questions

1 The debate on fracking was in its infancy at the time of writing. How has development continued? Has the general public accepted fracking? Have the predictions of quantities of oil and gas proved correct?

2 What impact will increased fracking have on OPEC and the price of oil?

Review and discussion questions

1 Why are industries such as electricity 'natural monopolies'? What other examples are there of natural monopolies?

2 Think of one technological advance that has been made recently. What have been the effects of that change on the economy, business and the consumer?

3 In what ways can the general and specific skills of the British workforce be improved?

4 What impact will increased use of the Internet, both for customer information and for purchasing, have on call centres?

Assignments

1 You work in the economic development unit of your local council. The unit is compiling a bid to central government in order to win some resources to improve the basic infrastructure in the locality. Your job is to identify the economic problems that exist in your local town and explain why an increase in resources would overcome the problems. Write a briefing paper to the management committee of the unit on your results.

2 You are a member of your local Chartered Institute of Personnel and Development branch and have been asked to give a talk on 'Flexibility in working practices' to a group of trainee managers from a variety of functional and industrial backgrounds. They are particularly interested in three questions:

(a) What is meant by flexibility?
(b) Why is flexibility needed?
(c) What are the implications of greater flexibility?

(Sources for this would include the second edition of this text and *People Management,* CIPD.)

Further reading

Blowfield, M., *Business and Sustainability,* Oxford University Press, 2013.

Christensen, C. M., *The Innovator's Dilemma: When New Technologies Cause Great Firms to Fail,* Harvard Business Review Press, 2016.

Worthington, I., Britton, C. and Rees, A., *Economics for Business: Blending Theory and Practice,* Financial Times/Prentice Hall, 2nd edition, 2005.

Web links and further questions are available on the website at
www.pearsoned.co.uk/worthington

8 The legal environment

Martin Morgan-Taylor

Businesses, like individuals, need to operate within a legal framework. Similarly, the legal framework must be such that it protects the freely given intentions of the parties so long as they represent legitimate commercial interests. However, these must be balanced against other factors, such as a need to protect weaker parties such as consumers. The debate concerning the adequacy of regulation was graphically illustrated in the London Grenfell Tower fire in 2017. The law aims to assist business where reasonable to create jobs and wealth, subject to this balance. This law derives from custom and practice, from the judicial decisions of the courts and from statutes enacted by governments. Like the political and economic environment with which it is intertwined, the legal environment of business is a key influence on the business organisation and an important area of study for students of business. This can be demonstrated by an examination of a number of the fundamental areas in which the law impinges on the operations of an enterprise.

Learning outcomes

Having read this chapter you should be able to:

- understand the idea of 'law' and the sources from which laws are derived
- outline the court system, including the role of the Court of Justice of the EU
- discuss the basic features of the laws of contract and agency
- analyse the reason for statutory intervention to protect the consumer and some of the principal pieces of legislation in this field

Key terms

Acceptance
Agent
Capacity
Case law
Code of practice
Consideration
Criminal law

Customs
Delegated legislation
Intention to create legal relations
Judicial precedent
Legislation
Offer

Principal
Private law
Public law
Statute law
Tort
Trust

Introduction

It is almost universally accepted that for a society to exist and function in an ordered way, a set of rules is required to regulate human behaviour. Irrespective of whether these rules are laid down in custom or practice or in statute, they constitute a means of regulating and controlling the activities of individuals and groups, and of enforcing minimum standards of conduct – even though they may be ignored or flouted on occasions. This framework of rules and the institutions through which they are formulated and enforced represent what is normally understood as the 'law', which invariably evolves over time in response to changing social, economic and political circumstances (e.g. the influence of pressure groups). As one of the constraining (and enabling) influences on business organisations, this legal environment is an important area of study for students of business, hence the tendency for courses in business-related subjects to have specialist modules or units on different aspects of business law (e.g. contract, agency, property, and so on).

The aim of this chapter is not to examine business law in detail or to provide a definitive insight into particular areas of the law as it relates to business organisations. Rather, it is to raise the reader's awareness of the legal context within which businesses function and to comment briefly on those aspects of law that regularly impinge on a firm's operations. Students wishing to examine business law in more detail should consult the many specialist texts in this field, some of which are listed at the end of this chapter.

Classification of law

Laws relating to both individuals and organisations can be classified in a number of ways: international and national, public and private, criminal and civil. In practice, there are no hard and fast rules to classification and some categories may overlap (e.g. where a person's behaviour is deemed to infringe different areas of law). Nevertheless, distinguishing laws in these terms serves as an aid to explanation and commentary, as well as helping to explain differences in liabilities and in legal remedies in England and Wales (e.g. a child under the age of 10 cannot be held criminally liable).

Public and private law

Put simply, **public law** is the law that concerns the state, whether in international agreements or disputes or in the relationship between the state and the individual. Thus public law consists of international treaties and conventions, constitutional law, administrative law and criminal law. In contrast, **private law** is law governing the relationships between individuals and comprises laws in respect of contract, tort, property, trusts and the family.

Criminal law

Criminal law relates to a legal wrong (criminal offence) – a breach of a public duty, punishable by the state on behalf of society. Decisions on whether or not to bring a prosecution in a particular instance are taken by the Crown Prosecution Service (in England and Wales) and the matter may or may not involve trial by jury, according to the seriousness of the alleged offence and the plea of the defendant(s). In some cases, the consent of both magistrates and defendants is required for a case to remain in the Magistrates' Court, although this may change in the very near future. Moreover, while the criminal process may also arise from a private prosecution, such prosecutions are rare and, in these cases, the Attorney-General (the government's senior law officer) has the right to intervene if he or she sees fit.

Tort

A **tort** is a civil wrong other than a breach of contract or a breach of trust and is a duty fixed by law on all persons (e.g. road users have a duty in law not to act negligently). The law of tort, therefore, is concerned with those situations where the conduct of one party threatens or causes harm to the interests of another party and the aim of the law is to compensate for this harm. The most common torts are negligence, nuisance, defamation and trespass.

Trusts

A **trust** is generally defined as an 'equitable obligation imposing on one or more persons a duty of dealing with property, over which they have control, for the benefit of other persons who may enforce the obligation'. This property may be in the form of money or stocks and shares or in other types of asset, particularly land, where trusts have become a very common way of permitting persons who are forbidden to own legal estates in land to enjoy the equitable benefits of ownership. Partnerships, for example, cannot hold property as legal owners, so often several partners will act as trustees for all the partners (as a partnership has no separate corporate identity it cannot own property – see Chapter 10). Similarly, minors may not hold legal estates, so their interests must be protected by a trust, administered by an individual or an institution.

---

mini case   *Verity and Spindler* v *Lloyds Bank* [1995]

Banking on advice

Banks have duties as well as rights when dealing with the day-to-day affairs of their customers. Failure to discharge these duties, in some circumstances, may be deemed negligent behaviour.

In September 1995 the High Court ruled that Lloyds Bank had been negligent in lending money to two of its customers for use on a speculative property deal which had failed to come off because of a collapse in the property market in the late 1980s. In essence, the customers had claimed that the bank owed them a duty of care in advising them on the merits of a loan to invest in property speculation and that it had been in breach of its duty when agreeing to proceed with the loan. In effect, the claimants were arguing that they had been badly advised and that this had resulted in a loss which was not only suffered but also reasonably foreseeable.

In finding for the claimants – who were suing Lloyds under the tort of negligence – the judge ruled that the bank manager was in breach of his duty of care in advising them to proceed and that the

▶

couple had relied on his advice, including claims made in the bank's promotional literature. A ruling of this kind sent shock waves through the financial community. However, Lloyds Bank counterclaimed in a second action and were awarded £104,000 against the claimants for failing to service the debt. As a result the claimants who won their case ended up owing the bank more money.

Sources of law

Laws invariably derive from a number of sources, including custom, judicial precedent, legislation, and international and supranational bodies (e.g. the EU whilst the UK remains in the EU). All of these so-called legal sources of the law can be illustrated by reference to English law, which applies in England and Wales. However, devolution means that some powers to legislate have been handed over to the Northern Ireland, Scottish and Welsh legislative bodies to create their own legislation. This means that some laws may apply to the entire UK , whilst others apply only to a devolved country such as Wales or Scotland.

Custom

Early societies developed particular forms of behaviour (or **customs**), which came to be accepted as social norms to be followed by the members of the community to which they applied. In England many of these customary rules ultimately became incorporated into a body of legal principles known as the common law. Today customs would be regarded as usage recognised by law, whether by judicial precedent (**case law**) or through statutory intervention, and hence they are largely of historical interest. Occasionally, however, they are recognised by the courts as being of local significance and may be enforced accordingly as exceptions to the general law (e.g. concerning land usage).

Judicial precedent

Much of English law is derived from **judicial precedent** (previous decisions of the courts). The present system of binding precedent, however, is of fairly recent origin, dating from the latter part of the nineteenth century, when advances in recording legal judgments and a reorganisation of the court structure facilitated its general acceptance.

In essence, judicial precedent is based on the rule that the previous decisions of a higher court must be followed by the lower courts – hence the significance of the court structure. In any judgment will be found a number of reasons, arguments, explanations and cases cited and these must all be considered carefully by judges to determine whether there are material differences in the case before the court and the earlier decision. To reach a decision, the court must find what is termed the *ratio decidendi* of the previous case. Put very simply, the *ratio* of a case is the essential steps in the legal reasoning which led the court to make that particular decision. Anything which cannot be regarded as a *rationes* is termed *obiter dicta* or 'things said by the way'. The whole of a dissenting judgment in a case is regarded as *obiter*. *Obiter dicta* are not binding but may be regarded as persuasive arguments if the facts of the case permit.

Clearly there are times when, perhaps because of the position of a court in the hierarchy, decisions are not to be regarded as binding precedent. However, if the judgment has been delivered by a jurisdiction that has a common law system (e.g. Canada, Australia) or, most importantly, by the Judicial Committee of the Privy Council, then those decisions will be regarded as being of persuasive precedent and may be used to help the court reach its own decision.

Legislation

A substantial proportion of current law – including laws governing the operations of business organisations – derives from **legislation** or **statutes law**, enacted by the monarch giving Royal Assent in Parliament. As Chapter 4 indicated, the initiative in this sphere lies effectively with the government of the day, which can virtually guarantee a bill will become law if it has a working majority in the House of Commons.

Apart from a limited number of bills proposed by backbench MPs (private members' bills), the vast majority of legislation emanates from government and takes the form of Acts of Parliament or delegated legislation. Acts of Parliament are those bills that have formally been enacted by Parliament and have received the Royal Assent and, except where overridden by EU law, they represent the supreme law of the land. In addition to creating new laws (e.g. to protect the consumer), statutes may be used to change or repeal existing laws. In some instances they may be designed to draw together all existing law (a consolidating Act) or to codify it or to grant authority to individuals or institutions to make regulations for specific purposes (an enabling Act). Under the Consumer Credit Act 1974, for instance, the Secretary of State for Trade and Industry is permitted to make regulations governing the form and content of credit agreements under delegated authority from Parliament.

As its name suggests, **delegated legislation** is law made by a body or person to which Parliament has given limited powers of law making – as illustrated by the example above. More often than not, authority will be delegated to a Minister of the Crown, but it may also be conferred on local authorities or other public undertakings, either through the use of a statutory instrument or by some other means of delegation. Since Parliament remains sovereign, such legislation is required to receive parliamentary approval and scrutiny, but time tends to prevent anything other than a cursory glance at a limited proportion of the legislation of this kind. It does, however, remain subject to judicial control, in so far as the body granted authority may be challenged in the courts for exceeding its powers (*ultra vires*).

In addition to these two principal forms of domestic legislation, developments in the law emanate from the UK's membership of the EU. After Brexit any new European legislation will not need to be incorporated into domestic law, whilst laws already incorporated will remain in place unless they are repealed following Brexit. Under the EU's main treaties – or those parts to which the British government has agreed – EU legislation becomes part of the law and takes precedence over domestic legislation, although the latter may sometimes be required to implement it. Accordingly, law that is inconsistent with EU law is repealed by implication and British citizens, like their counterparts elsewhere in the EU, become subject to the relevant EU laws (unless an 'opt-out' has been negotiated).

Whereas the provisions of the main treaties represent primary legislation, the regulations, directives and decisions emanating from the EU's institutions are secondary (or subordinate) legislation, made under the authority conferred by the Treaty of Rome (1957) as amended by subsequent treaties (e.g. the Maastricht Treaty 1992, the Amsterdam Treaty 1997, the Nice Treaty 2001 and the Lisbon Treaty 2007). As Chapter 4 indicated, regulations are of general application throughout the member states and confer individual rights and duties that must be recognised by the national courts. Their purpose is to achieve uniformity throughout the EU, as in the requirement for heavy goods vehicles to fit tachographs to control drivers' hours.

Directives, by contrast, are not directly applicable; they are addressed to member states and not individuals, although a directive may create rights enforceable by an individual citizen, as they become directly applicable if a member state fails to implement its provisions within the prescribed time limits. The aim of EU directives is to seek harmonisation or approximation between national laws rather than to achieve uniformity; hence the method of implementation is left to the discretion of the individual state, usually within a given time limit (e.g. the Companies Act of 1981 implemented the EU's fourth directive on company accounts by allowing small and medium-sized companies to reduce the amount of information provided to the Registrar of Companies).

Decisions, too, are binding, but only on the member state, organisation or individual to whom they are addressed and not on the population generally. In practice, EU decisions become effective from the date stated in the decision, which is generally the date of notification, and they are enforceable in national courts if they impose financial obligations.

The legal system: the courts

A country's legal system can be said to have two main functions: to provide an enabling mechanism within which individuals and organisations can exist and operate (e.g. companies are constituted by law); and to provide a means of resolving conflicts and of dealing with those who infringe the accepted standards of behaviour. These functions are carried out by a variety of institutions, including the government and the courts, and a detailed analysis of the legal system within a state would require consideration of the interrelationship between politics and law. Since the political system has been examined in Chapter 4, the focus here is on the courts as a central element of a country's legal system, with responsibility for interpreting the law and administering justice in democratic societies. It is worth remembering, however, that political and governmental activity takes place within a framework of law and that framework is itself a product of the political process at a variety of spatial levels.

The English legal system

Under the English legal system, a useful distinction can be made between courts on the basis of their status. The superior courts are the Supreme Court (formerly named the House of Lords), the Court of Appeal and the High Court. Law reports generally emanate from the higher courts – these cases involve a major point of law of general public interest (e.g. *R* v *R* [1991]). Inferior courts, in contrast, have limited jurisdiction and are subject to the supervisory jurisdiction of the High Court. The current hierarchy of courts is illustrated in Figure 8.1. For domestic purposes (i.e. not concerning EU legislation), the highest court is the Supreme Court, which is the final court of appeal for both civil and criminal cases. Decisions reached by the Court are binding on all other courts, though not necessarily on the Court's judges themselves.

Like the Supreme Court, the Court of Appeal has only appellate jurisdiction. In the case of the Civil Division of the Court, its decisions bind all inferior courts and it is bound by its own previous decisions and by those of the Supreme Court. The Criminal Division similarly is bound by the decisions of the Law Lords, but not by the Court of Appeal's Civil Division, nor is it bound by its own previous decisions where these were against a defendant, as exemplified in a number of celebrated cases in recent years.

The High Court is divided into three separate divisions – Chancery, Queen's Bench and Family – and has virtually unlimited original jurisdiction in civil matters, many of which are of direct relevance to business organisations. The Family court deals with such things as adoption, wardship and contested divorce cases, while the Chancery court deals with cases concerning trusts, property and taxation. Claims in contract and tort are the responsibility of the Queen's Bench division, which has two specialist courts to deal with commercial matters and with ships and aircraft. It also exercises the criminal jurisdiction of the High Court, the latter being entirely appellate in instances referred to it by the Magistrates' Courts or the Crown Court.

In criminal cases the Crown Court has exclusive original jurisdiction to try all indictable offences and can hear appeals against summary conviction or sentence from Magistrates' Courts. Broadly speaking, the latter largely deal with less serious offences

Figure 8.1   **The hierarchy of courts**

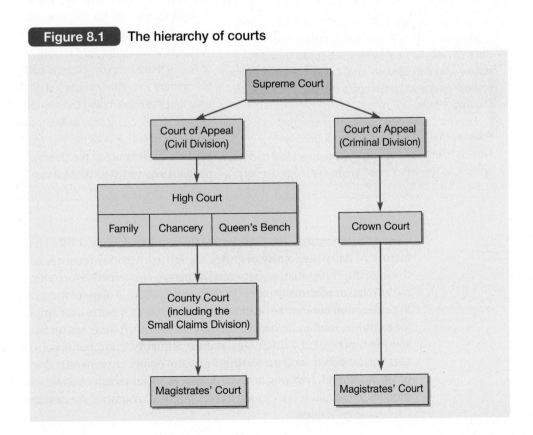

(especially motoring offences), where trial by judge and jury is not permitted – an issue still under discussion following the publication of the Runciman Report (1993). Whereas Magistrates' Courts have both criminal and civil jurisdiction – with the emphasis towards the former – the jurisdiction of the County Courts is entirely civil and derived solely from statute. Among the issues they deal with are conflicts between landlords and tenants and disputes involving small claims (e.g. concerning consumer matters) where a system of arbitration provides for a relatively inexpensive and quick method of resolving problems.

In disputes with a supranational dimension – involving EU member states, institutions, organisations, companies or individuals – ultimate jurisdiction rests with the European Court of Justice until Brexit. Under Article 220 (ex 164) of the Treaty of Rome, the court is required to ensure that in the application and interpretation of the Treaty, the law is observed. As indicated elsewhere, in carrying out this function, the Court has adopted a relatively flexible approach in order to take account of changing circumstances (see Chapter 4). Few would dispute that its judgments have had, and will continue to have, a considerable influence on the development of EU law.

mini case   Jean-Marc Bosman – a case of foul play?

Union Royale Belge des Sociétés de Football Association ASBL v Jean-Marc Bosman [1995]

An example of how EU law affects individuals and organisations in member states is provided by the case of Jean-Marc Bosman, a Belgian football player who successfully challenged the transfer fee system operated by Europe's football authorities in the mid-1990s.

Bosman, who had been under contract to the Belgian club Liège, had sought a transfer to a French team when his contract expired but had his ambitions thwarted when Liège demanded a very high transfer fee. In the judgment of the European Court of Justice, clubs could no longer demand a fee for players out of contract if the player was headed for another EU member state. According to the judges, the system allowing for a fee to be imposed violated the right enshrined in the Treaty of Rome that European citizens could go from one EU country to another in pursuit of work. They also held that the rule limiting the number of foreign players a club could field in European matches violated the principle of the free movement of workers. The impact of the Court's judgment continues down to the present day.

As a final comment, it is perhaps worth stating that while conflict remains an enduring feature of daily life, many disputes are settled without recourse to the courts, often through direct negotiation between the parties concerned. Moreover, even where negotiations fail or where one party declines to negotiate, a dispute will not necessarily result in court action but may be dealt with in other ways. Disputes over employment contracts, for example, tend to be dealt with by a specialist tribunal, set up by statute to exercise specific functions of a quasi-legal nature. Similarly, complaints concerning maladministration by public (and increasingly private) bodies are generally dealt with by a system of 'ombudsmen', covering areas as diverse as social security benefits and local authority services. Financial services such as banking and insurance are covered by the Financial Ombudsman Service.

Business organisations and the law

Business organisations have been described as transformers of inputs into output in the sense that they acquire and use resources to produce goods or services for consumption. As Table 8.1 illustrates, all aspects of this transformation process are influenced by the law.

It is important to emphasise from the outset that the law not only constrains business activity (e.g. by establishing minimum standards of health and safety at work which are enforceable by law), but also assists it (e.g. by providing a means by which a business unit can have an independent existence from its members), and in doing so helps an enterprise to achieve its commercial and other objectives. In short, the legal environment within which businesses operate is an enabling as well as a regulatory environment and one that provides a considerable degree of certainty and stability to the conduct of business both within and between democratic states.

Given the extensive influence of the law on business organisations, it is clearly impossible to examine all aspects of the legal context within which firms function. Accordingly, in the analysis below, attention is focused primarily on contract law, agency and some of the more important statutes enacted to protect the interests of the consumer, since these are areas fundamental to business operations. Laws relating to the establishment of an enterprise and to the operation of markets are discussed in Chapters 10 and 17 respectively.

Table 8.1 Law and the business organisation

Business activity	Examples of legal influences
Establishing the organisation	Company laws, partnerships, business names
Acquiring resources	Planning laws, property laws, contract, agency
Business operations	Employment laws, health and safety laws, contract, agency
Selling output for consumption	Consumer laws, contract, agency

Contract law: the essentials

All businesses enter into contracts, whether with suppliers or employees or financiers or customers, and these contracts will be important – and possibly crucial – to the firm's operations. Such contracts are essentially agreements (oral or written) between two or more persons that are legally enforceable, provided they comprise a number of essential elements. These elements are: **offer, acceptance, consideration, intention to create legal relations** and **capacity**.

Offer

An offer in law is made when a party indicates that they are willing to be bound by a clear set of terms. The person making the offer is the offeror, and the offeree is the person to whom the offer is made, who is in the position to accept it. For example, 'I will sell you 10 of this particular laptop computer, at £250 per unit, cash on delivery, with delivery next Monday at noon.' An offer may be made orally or in writing or by conduct between the parties and must be clear and unambiguous. Simply writing 'offer for sale' is not in itself enough. Furthermore, not everything that would appear to be an offer is an offer in law. In reality most exposures of goods for sale are actually not offers, but rather an invitation to treat which cannot be accepted. That is an invitation to others to negotiate, perhaps leading to an offer. For example, the display of goods in a shop window (*Fisher* v *Bell* [*1962*]), or on a shop shelf (*Pharmaceutical Society of Great Britain* v *Boots Cash Chemists Ltd* [*1952*]) and newspaper adverts (*Partridge* v *Crittenden* [*1968*]) are usually invitations. The display of goods on websites will usually be treated the same as for shop windows, as invitations. The reasons for this are that the seller may reserve the right to refuse service; there may be limited stock (unless the seller is the manufacturer), so this avoids a seller offering one van for sale and having five people accept; and adverts are often vague. Rarely an advert might be an offer, for example *Carlill* v *Carbolic Smokeball Co* [1893]. In this case the advertiser, who made an offer of a reward to anyone who used their product and caught flu, had made very clear statements which the average person would have seen as an offer. The advertiser's wording showed that they were willing to be bound to anyone who used their product, and they also manufactured the product and so could not realistically claim to run out. Tenders are offers; a request for tenders is merely an invitation for offers to be made.

Termination of an offer can happen in several ways. Clearly an offer is ended when it is accepted, but, that apart, an offer may be revoked at any time up to acceptance. Interestingly, an offer said to be open for a certain period of time can be revoked during this period, unless it has been accepted, or when some consideration is paid to make the promise to keep the offer open binding. If an offer with a set time limit has expired, then later acceptance is ineffective, and even where there is no specified time limit, the courts will imply that acceptance must be made within a reasonable time. Thus, in *Ramsgate Victoria Hotel* v *Montefiore* [1866], shares in the hotel were offered for sale. After several months the offer was 'accepted', but the court held that too much time had passed, bearing in mind that the purpose of the shares offer was to raise money.

Another way for an offer to come to an end is by the failure of a condition. Although a genuine offer is always held to be firm and certain, sometimes it may be conditional and not absolute. Thus, should A wish to buy a model car from B, B may agree but impose conditions on the deal, such as stating that A must collect at a specific time on a certain day at a particular place and must pay in cash. This is known as a 'condition precedent' and failure to complete the conditions will nullify the agreement. There is another type of condition, called a 'condition subsequent', where there is a perfectly good contract that runs until something happens. For instance, a garage may have a good contract with an oil company to buy petrol at £x per 1000 litres until the price of oil at Rotterdam reaches $x per barrel. It is only when oil reaches the stipulated price that the contract ends.

Acceptance

Just as an offer must be firm and certain, the acceptance of an offer by the person(s) to whom it was made must be unequivocal and must not contain any alterations or additions. An acceptance must be an unconditional yes to the terms of the offer. Accordingly, any attempt to alter the terms of an offer is regarded as a counter-offer and thus a rejection of the original offer, leaving the original offeror free to accept or decline the new offer.

While acceptance of an offer normally occurs either in writing or verbally, it may also be implied by conduct. In the case of *Brogden* v *Metropolitan Railways Co.* [1877], Brogden had supplied the company for many years without formalities. It was then decided to regularise the position and a draft agreement was sent to him. He inserted a new term, marked the draft 'approved', and returned it to the company where it was placed in a drawer and forgotten about, although the parties traded with each other on the terms of the draft for more than two years. Following a dispute, Brogden claimed there was no contract. The then House of Lords decided differently, saying that a contract had been created by conduct.

Silence cannot be construed as an acceptance of an offer (*Felthouse* v *Bindley* [1862]). Further, the offeror may make the method of acceptance mandatory, but only if they make this clear. Otherwise the method will be permissive (not binding), and the offeree can use any reasonable method of communication. This is usually a method that is at least equally as fast, for example replying by email to accept an offer made by voicemail.

There are two rules about the timing of an acceptance that are important. The first rule is the general rule, or the receipt rule. This means that acceptance is made at the point at which it becomes available for the recipient to read it, not when it is actually read. The Postal Rule is the exception to this rule. This states that an acceptance by hard-copy letter is communicated as soon as it has been put in the post box, or handed over at the post office counter (see *Adams* v *Lindsell* [1818]), so long as it is correctly stamped, addressed, it is reasonable to reply by post, or the offeror has permitted an acceptance by post. This rule is becoming increasingly unpopular because the offeror must wait for several days before being able to assume that their offer has not been accepted. This is why many businesses expressly exclude the Postal Rule from applying. This can be done, for example, by saying 'any acceptance must reach me by . . .'. It is almost certain that the receipt rule will apply to near-instantaneous methods of modern communication such as email. Although there is no case law on email, the House of Lords in an older case on telex stated that the general rule will usually apply to near-instantaneous methods of communication (*Brinkibon Ltd* v *Stahag Stahl GmbH* [1983]).

Consideration

Together, offer and acceptance constitute the basis of an 'agreement' or meeting of minds, provided the parties are clear as to what they are agreeing about (i.e. a *consensus ad idem* exists). However, English courts will rarely enforce a 'bare promise'. As a result, a promise must have 'consideration', or something that the courts can see has bought the promise. Consideration has been defined as some right, interest, profit or benefit accruing to one party or some forbearance, detriment, loss or responsibility given, suffered or undertaken by the other. In commercial contracts, the consideration normally takes the form of a cash payment in return for the goods or services provided (i.e. the 'price' in a contract of sale). It does not need to be the full market value, but it must be something tangible. In contracts involving barter (exchange), however, which are sometimes used in international trade, goods are often exchanged for other goods or for some other form of non-monetary consideration (e.g. information or advice).

Intention to create legal relations

Not every agreement is intended to create a legally binding relationship. For example, there is a presumption that most domestic agreements – such as the division of household chores – would not constitute a contract recognised in law. In commercial agreements, however, it is generally accepted that both parties intend to make a legally binding contract and therefore it is unnecessary to include terms to this effect. Should such a presumption be challenged, the burden of proof rests with the person who disputes the presumption.

Capacity

A contract may be valid, voidable or void and one of the factors that determines this is the contractual capacity of the respective parties to the agreement. Normally speaking, an adult may make a contract with another adult which, if entered into freely and without any defects, and which is not contrary to public policy, is binding upon them both (i.e. valid). However, the law provides protection for certain categories of persons deemed not to have full contractual capacity (e.g. minors, drunks and the mentally disordered); hence the practice by firms of excluding people under the age of 18 from offers of goods to be supplied on credit.

Concentrating on minors – those below voting age – the law prescribes that they can be bound by contracts only for 'necessaries' (e.g. food, clothing, lodging) and contracts of employment that are advantageous or beneficial, as in the case of a job which contains an element of training or education. In most other instances, contracts with minors are void or voidable and as such will be either unenforceable or capable of being repudiated by the minor.

In the case of business, legal capacity depends on the firm's legal status. Unincorporated bodies (e.g. sole traders, partnerships) do not have a distinct legal personality and hence the party to the agreement is liable for their part of the bargain. Limited companies, by contrast, have a separate legal identity from their members and hence contractual capacity rests with the company, within the limits laid down in the objects clause of its Memorandum of Association (see Chapter 10).

Other factors

To be enforceable at law a contract must be legal (i.e. not forbidden by law or contrary to public policy). Similarly, the agreement must have been reached voluntarily and result in a genuine meeting of minds. Consequently, contracts involving mistakes of fact, misrepresentation of the facts, or undue influence or duress may be void or voidable, depending on the circumstances. In insurance contracts, for instance, the insured is required to disclose all material facts to the insurer (e.g. health record, driving record), otherwise a policy may be invalidated. In this context a 'material fact' is one that would affect the mind of a prudent insurer, even though the materiality may not be appreciated by the insured.

Agency

As business activity has become more specialised and complex, firms have increasingly turned to other businesses to carry out specialist functions on their behalf, such as freight forwarding, the sale of goods, insurance broking and commercial letting. These parties (known as **agents**) are authorised by the individual or organisation hiring them (known as the **principal**) to act on their behalf, thus creating an agency relationship. As in other areas of commercial activity, special rules of law have evolved to regulate the behaviour of the parties involved in such a relationship.

In essence, the function of an agent is to act on behalf of a principal so as to effect a contract between the principal and a third party. The agent may be a 'servant' of the principal (i.e. under their control, as in the case of a sales representative) or an 'independent contractor' (i.e. their own master, as in the case of an estate agent) and will be operating with the consent of the principal, whether by contract or implication. Having established a contractual relationship between the principal and the third party, the agent generally leaves the picture and usually has no rights and duties under the contract thus made.

With regard to an agent's specific obligations under an agency agreement, these are normally expressly stated under the terms of the agreement, although some may also be implied. Traditionally, the common law of agency prescribes, however, that agents:

- *obey the lawful instruction of the principal,* otherwise they may be in breach of contract;
- *exercise due care and skill,* in order to produce a deal that is to the principal's best advantage;
- *act personally,* rather than delegate, unless expressly or implicitly authorised to do so;
- *act in good faith,* thus avoiding conflicts of interest or undisclosed profits and bribes;
- *keep proper accounts,* which separate the principal's funds from those that belong personally to the agent.

Moreover, in so far as an agent is acting under the principal's authority, the principal is bound to the third party only by acts that are within the agent's authority to make. Consequently, *ultra vires* acts affect the principal only if the latter adopts them by ratification and the agent may be liable for the breach of the implied warranty of authority to the third party.

In addition to these common law duties owed by the principal, the Commercial Agents (Council Directive) Regulations 1993 apply when an agent falls within the definition of a commercial agent (Reg. 2(1)). They apply to transactions involving the sale or purchase of goods and they bestow certain rights and obligations upon both the principal and the agent. It is clear that these duties overlap to some extent with the common law duties. Regulation 3 provides the agent's duties to their principal. A commercial agent must:

- look after the interests of their principal and act dutifully and in good faith;
- make proper efforts to negotiate and, where appropriate, conclude the transactions;
- communicate to their principal all the necessary information available to them;
- comply with reasonable instructions given by the principal.

Regulation 4 specifies the duties of the principal:

- to act dutifully and in good faith;
- to provide the commercial agent with the necessary documentation relating to the goods in question;
- to obtain necessary information for the agent (this is a higher standard, perhaps requiring searching for data, than under the common law, where all the principal needs to do is to disclose information in their possession);
- to notify the agent within a reasonable period of time if the usual volume of trade is likely to be significantly reduced;
- to inform the agent within a reasonable period of time of the principal's acceptance, refusal or non-acceptance of a commercial transaction arranged by the agent.

Law and the consumer

Older economic theories suggest that consumer protection laws are unnecessary. However, modern economists (in particular behavioural economists) have shown that these traditional assumptions are not necessarily reliable, so regulation is often required. If individuals were behaving rationally when consuming goods and services, they would arrange their consumption to maximise their satisfaction (or 'utility'), in the words of an economist. Products that because of poor quality or some other factor reduced a consumer's utility would be rejected in favour of those that proved a better alternative and this would act as an incentive to producers (and retailers) to provide the best products. In effect, market forces would ensure that the interest of the consumer was safeguarded as suppliers in a competitive market arranged their production to meet the needs and wants of rational consumers.

The 'ideal' view of how markets work is rarely borne out in practice. Apart from the fact that consumers do not always act rationally, they are usually in a weaker position compared with traders. This is because they often do not have access to the key information they require to make an informed decision when choosing a product; in some cases they may not even have a choice of products (e.g. where a monopoly exists). Similarly consumers are usually in a much weaker bargaining position compared with traders. The consumer rarely has the power to impose terms on the trader, it is usually the other way round. The consumer is often in a 'take it or leave it' situation, without a genuine choice. It is in this context that the law is seen to be an important counterbalance in a contractual relationship where the consumer usually is at a significant disadvantage with a weaker bargaining power than a business, and this can be said to provide the basis of legal intervention in this area.

Existing laws to protect consumers come from both civil and criminal law. These rights, duties and liabilities have been created or imposed by common law (especially contract and tort) or by legislation. Significantly, as the examples below illustrate, a large element of current consumer law has resulted from statutory intervention, with much of it coming from the EU by way of directives. These laws – covering areas as diverse as commercial practices, the sale of goods and services, and consumer credit and product liability – indicate a growing willingness on the part of the EU to respond to the complaints of consumers and their representative organisations and to use legislation to regulate the relationship between business organisations and their customers. Europe is keen to encourage consumers to take advantage of cross-border EU markets by harmonising consumer protection, as this boosts market access and consumer spending. To this end Europe has been adopting consumer protection directives. The Consumer Rights Act 2015 is the most recent significant consumer protection statute; it aims to consolidate or draw together many pre-existing consumer protection laws into one statute.

The Consumer Protection from Unfair Trading Regulations 2008

The Trade Descriptions Act 1968 was the mainstay of consumer protection before it was largely superseded by the Consumer Protection from Unfair Trading Regulations 2008. These Regulations implemented the Unfair Commercial Practices Directive 2005-29/EC, and extend criminal liability beyond simply misleading practices. These changes ban five categories of unfair practices: namely, a general prohibition on unfair practices, promoting unfair practices in codes of conduct, misleading actions and misleading omissions, aggressive commercial practices, and practices always deemed unfair under a 'banned list' of 31 practices. The Office of Fair Trading (OFT) (see Chapter 17), local authorities and the enforcement bodies also have powers to seek 'stop now' orders against such practices.

The Consumer Credit Acts 1974–2006

The Consumer Credit Act 1974, which became fully operational in May 1985, controls transactions between the credit industry and private individuals (including sole traders and business partnerships) up to a limit of £15,000. This statute has been updated since, especially so as to include EU directives, and it has recently been augmented by the Consumer Credit Act 2006. The Financial Conduct Authority took over regulation of consumer credit from the OFT on 1 April 2014. Under the legislation a consumer credit agreement is defined as a personal credit providing the debtor with credit up to the accepted limit. This credit may be in the form of a cash loan or some other type of financial accommodation (e.g. through the use of a credit card). The Act also covers hire purchase agreements (i.e. a contract of hire which gives the hirer the option to purchase the goods), conditional sale agreements for the sale of goods or land, and credit sale agreements, where the property passes to the buyer when the sale is effected.

The main aim of this consumer protection measure is to safeguard the public from trading malpractices where some form of credit is involved. To this end the Act provides, among other things, for a system of licensing controlled by the OFT, which must be satisfied that the person seeking a licence is a fit person and the name under which they intend to be licensed is neither misleading nor undesirable. Providing credit or acting as a credit broker without a licence is a criminal offence, as is supplying a minor with any document inviting them to borrow money or obtain goods on credit. The Consumer Credit Act 2006 created a Financial Services Ombudsman to settle disputes between consumers and their lenders. It has also created an unfair credit test that makes it easier for debtors to challenge excessive interest rates with the Ombudsman.

A further protection for the consumer comes from the requirements that the debtor be made fully aware of the nature and cost of the agreement and their rights and liabilities under it. The Act stipulates that prior to the contract being made the debtor must be supplied with certain information, including the full price of the credit agreement (i.e. the cost of the credit plus the capital sum), the annual rate of the total charge for credit expressed as a percentage (i.e. the annual percentage rate), and the amounts of payments due and to whom they are payable. In addition, the debtor must be informed of all the other terms of the agreement and of their right to cancel if this is applicable. In the case of the latter, this applies to credit agreements drawn up off business premises, and is designed to protect individuals from high-pressure doorstep sellers who offer credit as an incentive to purchase.

Performance standards in contract: description, quality and fitness obligations under the Sale of Goods Act 1979 and the Consumer Rights Act 2015

Some seller's obligations are so important that they are automatically incorporated (implied) into a contract. Some of these are implied as terms by statute, and the seller is prevented from excluding them, except under special circumstances. The law relating to statutory implied terms for the supply of goods and services changed in 2015. Since this date the Consumer Rights Act 2015 (CRA 2015) imposes certain minimum standards and obligations with respect to the sale and supply of goods, services, digital services and unfair terms where a business trades with a consumer. The intention was to draw a lot of consumer protection law together into one statute. The result is that the CRA 2015 has separated sales between a business and a consumer away from purely commercial sales.

Prior to this date these obligations were found in several statutes, including the Sale of Goods Act 1979 (SOGA 1979), the Supply of Goods and Services Act 1982 (SGSA 1982), the Unfair Contract Terms Act 1977 (UCTA 1977) and the Unfair Terms in Consumer Contracts Regulations 1999). These other statutes are still good law, but they now apply only to commercial sales. For the CRA 2015 to apply the consumer must purchase goods or services for their personal use from a party selling them in the course of business. A computer sold by an online retailer to a student, for example, is a consumer sale, while the same machine sold to a secretarial agency is not, since it has been acquired for business purposes.

Both statutes provide buyers with rights in respect of items that are faulty or that do not correspond with the description given to them, by identifying a number of implied conditions to the sale. Although consumer cases are now dealt with separately, much of the old case law remains valid, at least until the courts decide otherwise with fresh case law. The main implied conditions given by the SOGA 1979 and the CRA 2015 are:

- Sale by description/the goods to be as described (s13 SOGA 1979 and s11 CRA 2015).
- Satisfactory quality and fitness for purpose (s14 SOGA 2979 and ss9-10 CRA 2015).

Section 11 CRA 2015 broadly follows the provisions of the SOGA 1979. Goods sold by description must match the description given to them, even if the buyer has selected the goods, for example selecting an item from a shop shelf (*Grant* v *Australian Knitting Mills* [1936]). The description must describe the commercial characteristics and not be mere sales hype (*Ashington Piggeries* v *Hill* [1972]). A shirt described as 100 per cent cotton, for instance, must be just that, otherwise it fails to match the description given to it. However, describing a car as a good little runner will be sales hype and so this provision will not apply. In addition, section 11 applies to information provided by the trader about the main characteristics of the goods. Further, where the sale is not made face to face, then the trader must identify themselves, provide the total price including taxes and delivery charges, and communicate a returns policy.

The second condition relates to the quality of the goods provided. Under section 9 CRA 2015, 'The quality of goods is satisfactory if they meet the standard that a reasonable person would consider satisfactory.' This takes account of the description, price and all other relevant circumstances. These other circumstances may include whether the product is used; if so, how old; is it a brand name? A new top-of-the-range car should have no significant defects on purchase, whereas it would be unreasonable to expect the same from a used car sold said to have a defective clutch (*Bartlett* v *Sidney Marcus* [1965]). The quality expected of sale goods will normally be the same as the full-priced item, unless the description indicates otherwise.

The third implied condition requires that goods are fit for a particular purpose (i.e. capable of performing the tasks indicated by the seller). This provision from section 10 CRA 2015 applies when a use or range of uses is made known to the seller. There will be a breach if the seller, on request from the purchaser, confirms that goods are suitable for a particular purpose made known by the buyer and this proves not to be the case. Equally, if the product is unsuitable for its normal purposes, then the law would also be breached.

It is worth noting that 'satisfactory' and 'fitness for a purpose' are closely related and that a breach of one may include a breach of the other. By the same token, failure in a claim for a breach of section 9 is likely to mean that a claim for a breach of section 10 will also fail. Moreover, if, on request, a seller disclaims any knowledge of a product's suitability for a particular purpose and the consumer is willing to take a chance, any subsequent unsuitability cannot be regarded as a breach of section 14(3). The same applies if the buyer's reliance on the skill or judgement of the seller is deemed 'unreasonable'.

With respect to the sale of goods, consumers have two sets of remedies available for breach of these implied terms: namely, a short-term right to reject or a right to a repair, replacement or price reduction or refund minus money off for use of the product. There was no set time limit for the short-term right to reject before the CRA 2015 (and this remains the case for commercial sales under the SOGA 1979). The time permitted depended on the circumstances of the case, and this gave the courts an opportunity to give a fair decision on the facts. However, this was at the cost of certainty to consumers and business alike. For example, three weeks was too long to reject a car in *Bernstein* v *Pamson Motors (Golders Green) Ltd* [1987], but four months was not too long to reject a taxi in *Fiat* v *Connolly* [2007]. Section 22 CRA 2015 now imposes the certainty of a set time limit of 30 days for consumers to reject goods.

However, if this remedy is lost due to lapse of time, or the consumer chooses not to use this remedy, the consumer now has four new paired remedies. First, the right to a repair or replacement and, second, the right to a price reduction or a refund for the value of the goods minus money off for any use of the product. These are often called the 'Four Rs' and are dealt with in more detail below, in the case study section. These remedies for contracts concerning goods are found in sections 23–24 CRA 2015. These remedies come from the European Consumer Guarantees Directive (1999-44/EC) and seek to continue the move towards harmonising the cross-border sale of consumer goods. The DTI (now BIS), keen not to reduce the pre-existing levels of consumer protection, added the new remedies to those already existing. The remedies were originally added by the Sale and Supply of Goods to Consumers Regulations 2002, but this has been replaced by the CRA 2015, because the UK is obliged to implement European directives for as long as it remains part of the EU. The result is that the consumer retains the short-term right to reject the goods for non-conformity. Until this Directive the consumer had no right to require a repair or a replacement, and could sue for damages only. Note that for commercial sales of goods under the SOGA 1979 the old remedies still apply: the short-term right to reject (without a set time limit), or a right to damages. Commercial parties do not have the right to the Four Rs.

Moreover, the Directive removes the problem of goods damaged in transit. Risk previously passed to the consumer/buyer once the goods had been handed over to a third-party carrier, the result being that the purchaser would find the carrier and the seller blaming one another for the loss. Ultimately, the consumer would often go uncompensated unless they decided to sue both parties. The Directive now requires that goods must actually be received by the consumer/buyer in conformity with the contract, so risk passes later. Lastly, manufacturers must honour any guarantee that they provide, and bear the return cost for any defective goods under a manufacturer's guarantee.

These remedies apply only to consumers/buyers of goods sold in the course of a business. Section 15A of the SOGA 1979 applies to business-to-business sales where there is only a slight breach of an implied condition of description or quality. The provision seeks to prevent a business buyer from rejecting goods due to a minor technical breach, and imposes an award of damages only. As damages are based on loss, damages for a technical breach will probably be very low. As a result, businesses that find that they can get the goods cheaper elsewhere will be less tempted to try to seek to reject goods for minor breaches. This also recognises that rejection of goods is not the norm in business; normally a recalculation of the price or payment conditions takes place. Having theoretical rights is one thing, but in business one may need to trade with the other party again and it is wise to consider the impact of any decision taken.

As a final comment, the CRA 2015 has also taken over coverage of the supply of services between a trader and a consumer from the Sale and Supply of Goods and Services Act 1982. With respect to services there are implied conditions under sections 49 and 52 that a supplier acting in the course of business must carry out the service with reasonable care and skill and within a reasonable time, where a specific deadline is not stated in the contract. Reasonable care and skill tends to be seen as that which might be expected of an ordinary competent person performing the particular task, though this will, of course, depend on the particular circumstances of the case and the nature of the trade or profession.

Any attempt to deprive a consumer of the implied statutory conditions will not be binding on the consumer. Section 31 CRA 2015 covers goods and section 57 covers services. These are seen as unfair terms and are dealt with next in more detail.

The law relating to unfair contract terms in consumer contracts has also been subject to change. Again the CRA 2015 replaces the old regime which consisted of the Unfair Contract Terms Act 1977 (UCTA 1977) and the Unfair Terms in Consumer Contracts Regulations 1999. The latter had implemented the European Unfair Terms in Consumer Contracts Directive 1993 (UTCCD). This operated as a dual regime, giving the consumer the choice of law. However, this was considered to be confusing and awkward for both consumers and businesses alike and so the law was changed in 2015. The result is that the UCTA 1977 now only applies to purely commercial transactions. Consumers must use Part 2 CRA 2015, which has re-implemented the European Directive mixed with the best elements of the UCTA.

There are several reasons why the Directive did not immediately replace the UCTA to form a single law. First, the UCTA 1977 was a domestic statute which gave consumers greater protection than the Directive. Another reason was the difference in coverage: the UCTA only applies to exclusion and limitation clauses, whilst the Directive applies to any form of clause, such as those which impose an unreasonable burden on the consumer. The Directive was also a minimum harmonisation measure, meaning that member states could exceed the minimum level of protection afforded by the Directive. As a result Parliament did not want to reduce the levels of protection given in the UCTA and so they originally added the Directive's provisions to apply in addition to the UCTA. The aim of the CRA is not so much to do anything new, but rather to combine these elements of extra protection from the UCTA and re-implement the Directive to create a single statute.

The UCTA originally had the advantage in banning some unfair terms outright: those attempting to exclude or limit liability for personal injury/death or the statutory implied terms against a consumer, while all other clauses were subject to a test of reasonableness. However, no terms are automatically banned under the Directive. The CRA maintains these banned terms:

- section 31 for the sale of goods;
- section 47 for digital content;
- section 57 for services; and
- section 65 for liability in negligence for death or personal injury.

In addition, schedule 2 CRA provides the grey list of terms that 'may be regarded as unfair' (but are not automatically unfair) from the Directive. This list includes the following:

- Terms that impose a disproportionate cancellation charge on a consumer for withdrawing from a contract early.
- Terms where the business is not bound to perform its obligations.
- Where a business decides the price or subject matter of the contract after the consumer has become bound to the contract.
- Where consumers are subject to unfair penalties.

The CRA copies the test of unfairness from the Directive; a term is unfair 'if, contrary to the requirement of good faith, it causes a significant imbalance in the parties' rights and obligations under the contract, to the detriment of the consumer' (section 62(4)). This differs from the 'reasonableness' test of the UCTA. There is a large body of case law from referrals to the Court of Justice of the EU regarding interpretation of the meaning of the obligations under the Directive because this is a European Directive, and this may be generally applied to the CRA. The Directive covers a wider range of terms than the UCTA, including those which impose an unreasonable burden on consumers. In *DGFT* v *First National Bank* [2001], Lord Bingham said that: 'Fair dealing requires that the supplier should not, whether deliberately or unconsciously, take advantage of the consumer's necessity, indigence, lack of experience, unfamiliarity with the subject matter of the contract [or] weak bargaining position.' The CRA also repeats the Directive's obligation that terms must be in 'plain, intelligible language' (section 68). Where a term is vague and can have several different meanings, the interpretation that is most favourable to the consumer prevails under section 69.

Unfortunately the CRA does nothing to address the controversy concerning the Directive's exclusion of clauses dealing with the appropriateness of the price and terms that specify the main subject matter. These terms are exempt from review because they are said to be the two most obvious factors a consumer considers when buying. However, there have been cases where the price has been much higher than might reasonably be expected and the courts have been asked to review the fairness of these terms. In *Office of Fair Trading* v *Abbey National Plc* [2009] the Supreme Court controversially overruled the Court of Appeal and held that terms imposing bank charges (including those for unauthorised overdrafts) made in exchange for the services provided by the bank were exempt from review under the fairness provisions. By maintaining the same meaning, section 64 of the CRA has done nothing to change this exclusion. However, very surprisingly the courts did not refer the matter to the Court of Justice of the EU for an interpretation of the provisions. As such there is a possibility that the case might be referred, and a different decision made, at least whilst the UK is part of the EU.

The Consumer Protection Act 1987

The Consumer Protection Act 1987 came into force in March 1988 as a result of the government's obligation to implement EC Directive 85-374, which concerned product liability. In essence, the Act provides for a remedy in damages for any consumer who suffers personal injury or damage to property as a result of a defective product by imposing a 'strict' liability on the producers of defective goods (including substances, growing crops, ships, aircraft and vehicles). Naturally, the onus is on the complainant to prove that any loss was caused by the claimed defect and a claim can be made where damage to property, personal injury or death has occurred. In the case of the latter, for example, a relative or friend could pursue an action and, if American experience is anything to go by, could be awarded substantial damages if liability can be proven. As far as property is concerned, damage must be to private rather than commercial goods and property and the loss must exceed £275.

While the Act is, inter alia, intended to place liability on the producers of defective goods, this liability also extends to anyone putting a name or distinguishing mark on a product which holds that person out as being the producer (e.g. supermarkets' own-brand labels). Similarly, importers of products from outside the EU are also liable for any defects in imported goods, as may be firms involved in supplying components or parts of the process of manufacture of a product. To prevent a firm escaping its liability as a supplier claiming it is unable to identify its own suppliers, the legislation provides a remedy: any supplier unable or unwilling to identify the importing firm or previous supplier becomes liable itself for damages under the Act.

Firms seeking to avoid liability for any claim have a number of defences under section 4 of the Act. Specifically these are:

- that the defendant did not supply the product in question;
- that the product was not manufactured or supplied in the course of business;
- that the defect did not exist at the time the product was distributed;
- that where a product has a number of components, the defect is a defect of the finished product or due to compliance with any instructions issued by the manufacturer of the finished product;
- that the defect is attributable to the requirement to comply with existing laws;

- that the state of scientific and technical knowledge at the time the product was supplied was not sufficiently advanced for the defect to be recognised.

Of these, the last – the so-called development risks or 'state of the art' defence – is the most contentious, given that it applies largely to products such as new drugs and new technology where the implications of their usage may not be apparent for some years. As recent cases have shown, manufacturers faced with damages from claimants who appear to have suffered from the use of certain products often decide to settle out of court without accepting liability for their actions.

> **web link**
>
> The Competition and Markets Authority has taken over consumer protection from the Office of Fair Trading. Its website contains useful commentary on consumer protection issues, including codes of practice and the powers of the CMA. See *www.gov.uk/ topic/competition/consumer-protection*

Codes of practice

Alongside the protection provided by the law, consumers may be afforded a further measure of security when the organisation they are dealing with belongs to a trade association that is operating under a **code of practice** (e.g. the Association of British Travel Agents). In essence, codes of practice represent an attempt by trade associations to impose a measure of self-discipline on the behaviour of their members by establishing the standards of service customers should expect to receive and by encouraging acceptable business practices. In addition, such codes of conduct invariably identify how customer complaints should be handled and many offer low-cost or no-cost arbitration schemes to help settle disputes outside the more formal legal process.

Whilst codes of practice do not in themselves have the force of law, they are normally seen as a useful mechanism for regulating the relationship between business organisations and their customers and accordingly they have the support of the OFT, which often advises trade associations on their content. Businesses, too, usually find them useful, particularly if through the establishment of a system of self-regulation they are able to avoid the introduction of restrictions imposed by the law.

Synopsis

All business activities, from the establishment of the organisation through to the sale of the product to the customer, are influenced by the law. This legal environment within which businesses exist and operate evolves over time and is a key influence on firms of all sizes and in all sectors, as illustrated by an examination of some of the main laws governing the relationship between a business and its customers. The majority of consumer laws are of relatively recent origin and derive from the attempts by successive governments to provide individuals with a measure of protection against a minority of firms that behave in ways deemed to be unacceptable. Concomitantly, they also provide reputable organisations with a framework within which to carry out their business and, as such, act as an incentive to entrepreneurial activity in market-based economies.

Summary of key points

- The legal rules within which businesses exist and operate are an important part of the external environment of business organisations.

- Laws affecting businesses derive from a variety of sources, including custom, the decisions of the courts and legislation.

- Laws are sometimes made at international and supranational level (including Europe).

- Contract, agency and consumer protection are three key areas governing the day-to-day work of businesses.

- Offer, acceptance, consideration, intention to create legal relations and capacity are central elements of contract law.

- Agency relationships are a common feature of business practice.

- The relationship between businesses and their customers is governed by a variety of laws, many of which derive from statute.

- In addition to the protection provided to consumers by the law, many organisations operate under agreed codes of conduct.

case study   The sale of goods on the Internet

The sale of consumer goods on the Internet (particularly those between European member states) raises a number of legal issues. First, there is the issue of trust, without which the consumer will not buy; they will need assurance that the seller is genuine, and that they will get the goods that they have ordered. Second, there is the issue of consumer rights with respect to the goods in question: what rights exist and do they vary across Europe? Last, the issue of enforcement: what happens should anything go wrong?

Information and trust

Europe recognises the problems of doing business across the Internet or telephone and it has attempted to address the main stumbling blocks via directives which are incorporated into member states' own laws. The original Distance Selling Directive, implemented as the Consumer Protection (Distance Selling)

Regulations 2000, has been replaced by the Consumer Rights Directive (2011-83/EU). (Note that this is different from the Consumer Rights Act 2015.) The replacement Directive is a 'maximum harmonisation' measure, meaning that the provisions are binding on, and cannot be modified by, member states. Both Directives attempt to address the issues of trust in distance sale. In short, the consumer who does not buy face to face may lack important information, which they may otherwise have easy access to if they were buying face to face.

Article 6 of the Consumer Rights Directive requires inter alia for the seller to identify themselves and an address must be provided if the goods are to be paid for in advance. Moreover, a full description of the goods and the final price (inclusive of any taxes) must also be provided. The new directive bans pre-ticked boxes (e.g. for insurance), and limits card transaction charges to those of the cost actually incurred by the trader. These provisions will help to cut hidden costs.

The seller must also inform the buyer of the right of cancellation available under Article 9, where the buyer has a right to cancel the contract for 14 days starting on the day the consumer receives the goods or services (this was seven days under the Distance Selling Directive). This 'cooling-off' period is intended to place the consumer in the position as if they had seen the goods in store. Failure to inform the consumer of this right automatically extends the period to a year and 14 days. Whilst the seller can place the cost of returning goods on the buyer, the seller must refund the standard rate outgoing postage. The seller is not entitled to deduct any costs as a restocking fee. All of this places a considerable obligation on the seller; however, such data should stem many misunderstandings and so boost cross-border trade by increasing consumer faith and confidence in non-face-to-face sales.

Another concern for the consumer is fraud. The consumer who has paid by credit card will be protected by section 83 of the Consumer Credit Act 1974, under which a consumer/purchaser is not liable for the debt incurred if it has been run up by a third party not acting as the agent of the buyer. The Distance Selling Regulations extended this to debit cards, and removed the ability of the card issuer to charge the consumer for the first £50 of loss. Moreover, section 75 of the Consumer Credit Act 1974 also gives the consumer/buyer a like claim against the credit card company for any misrepresentation or breach of contract by the seller. This is extremely important in a distance-selling transaction, where the seller may disappear.

What quality and what rights?

The next issue relates to the quality that may be expected from goods bought over the Internet. Clearly, if goods have been bought from abroad, the levels of quality required in other jurisdictions may vary. It is for this reason that Europe has attempted to standardise the issue of quality and consumer remedies, with the Consumer Guarantees Directive (1999-44/EC). The Consumer Rights Act 2015 has replaced The Sale and Supply of Goods to Consumer Regulations 2002 in implementing this Directive, which not only lays down minimum quality standards but also provides a series of consumer remedies (the Four Rs) across Europe. Consumers now have a 30-day short-term right to reject goods,

or a right to a repair/replacement, or a reduction in price/refund minus an amount for any use made of the goods.

The directive requires goods to be of 'normal' quality, or fit for any purpose made known by the seller. This has been taken to be the same as our pre-existing 'satisfactory quality' and 'fitness for purpose' obligations owed under sections 9 and 10 of the CRA 2015. Moreover, the pre-existing remedy of the short-term right to reject is also retained, but it is now capped at 30 days under section 22 for goods. This right provides the buyer with a short period of time to discover whether the goods are in conformity with the contract. In practice, it is usually a matter of weeks. If that time has elapsed, or the consumer prefers, the consumer has four remedies that did not exist before, which are provided in two pairs. These are repair or replacement and price reduction or rescission. Other than the short-term right to reject, the pre-existing law only gave a right to damages, which would rarely be exercised in practice. (However, the Small Claims Court would ensure a speedy and cheap means of redress for almost all contract claims brought under £10,000.) Now there is a right to a repair or a replacement, so that the consumer is not left with an impractical action for damages over defective goods. The seller must also bear the cost of return of the goods for repair. So such costs must now be factored into any business sales plan.

If these remedies are not suitable, disproportionate or actioned within a 'reasonable period of time' then the consumer may rely on the second pair of remedies. Price reduction permits the consumer to claim back a segment of the purchase price if the goods are still useable. It is effectively a discount for defective goods. Rescission allows the consumer to reject the goods, but they do not get the full refund that they would under the short-term right to reject; here money is knocked off for 'beneficial use'. This is akin to the pre-existing treatment for breaches of durability, where goods have not lasted as long as goods of that type ought reasonably be expected to last. The level of payment would take account of the use that the consumer has (if any) been able to put the goods to and a deduction made off the return of the purchase price. However, the issue that must be addressed is the length of time that goods may be expected to last. A supplier may state the length of the guarantee period, so a £500 television set guaranteed for one year would have a life expectancy ▶

of one year. However, a consumer may expect a television set to last 10 years. Clearly, if the set went wrong after six months, the consumer would get back only £250 if the retailer's figure was used, but would receive £475 if their own figure was used. It remains to be seen how this provision will work in practice.

One problem with distance sales has been that of liability for goods that arrive damaged. The pre-existing domestic law stated that risk would pass to the buyer once the goods were handed over to a third-party carrier. This had the major problem in practice of who would actually be liable for the damage. Carriers would blame the supplier and vice versa. The consumer would be able to sue for the loss, if they were able to determine which party was responsible. In practice, consumers usually went uncompensated and such a worry has deterred many consumers from buying goods over the Internet. The CRA 2015 states that the risk remains with a commercial seller of goods to a consumer, until the goods are 'in the physical possession of the . . . consumer' (section 29 for goods). This will avoid the problem of who is actually liable and should help to boost consumer confidence.

Enforcement

Enforcement for domestic sales is relatively straightforward. Small-scale consumer claims can be dealt with expeditiously and cheaply under the Small Claims Track of the County Court. Here, claims under £10,000 for contract-based claims are brought in a special court intended to keep costs down by keeping the lawyers out of the court room, as a victorious party cannot claim for their lawyers' expenses. The judge will conduct the case in a more 'informal' manner, and will seek to discover the legal issues by questioning both parties, so no formal knowledge of the law is required. The total cost of such a case, even if it is lost, is the cost of issuing the proceedings (approximately 10 per cent of the value claimed) and the other side's 'reasonable expenses'. Expenses must be kept down, and a judge will not award value which has been deliberately run up, such as first-class rail travel and stays in five-star hotels. Such claims may now be made online via the Internet (www.moneyclaim.gov.uk outlines the procedure for MCOL, or Money Claims Online). Cases will normally be held in the defendant's court, unless the complainant is a consumer and the defendant a business.

There is now a European-wide Small Claims Court dealing with transnational European transactions valued at less than €2,000. The case will be handled by member states' existing small claims courts.

Case study questions

1 Consider the checklist of data which a distance seller must provide to a consumer purchaser. Is this putting too heavy a burden on sellers?

2 Is a consumer distance buyer any better off after the European legislation?

3 Are there any remaining issues that must be tackled to increase European cross-border consumer trade?

Review and discussion questions

1 Why are laws to protect the consumer felt to be necessary? What other means do consumers have of protecting their interests in the marketplace?

2 To what extent does the supranational structure of EU law infringe the principle of the supremacy of Parliament?

3 Do you think that tobacco companies should be made retrospectively liable for the safety of their product? Justify your answer.

4 Examine the case for and against increased government control over business practices.

Assignments

1 You are a trading standards officer in a local authority trading standards department. You have been asked to talk to a group of school sixth-form students on the Sale of Goods Act 1979. Prepare suitable PowerPoint slides outlining the following:

   (a) The main provisions of the 1979 Act.
   (b) The customer's rights in the event of a breach of the implied conditions.
   (c) The sources of help and advice available to an individual with a consumer problem.

2 Imagine you work for a Citizens' Advice Bureau. A large part of your work involves offering advice to individuals with consumer problems. Design a simple leaflet indicating some of the principal pieces of legislation in the field of consumer protection and their main provisions. Your leaflet should also give guidance on further specialist sources of help and advice.

Further reading

Canavan, R., Twigg-Flezner, C. and MacQueen, H., *The Sale of Goods,* 13th edition, Pearson Education, 2016.

Furmston, M. and Chuah, J. (eds), *Commercial and Consumer Law,* 2nd edition, Pearson Education, 2013.

Marson, J. and Ferris, K., *Business Law,* 4th edition, Oxford University Press, 2015.

web
link

Web links and further questions are available on the website at:
www.pearsoned.co.uk/worthington

9 The ethical and ecological environment

Ian Worthington

There is a growing body of opinion that businesses have a duty to fulfil objectives that stretch beyond the simple well-being of the organisation and its owners to the promotion of greater corporate social responsibility, particularly with regard to the natural environment. This chapter looks at the emergence of this perspective and analyses why and how a firm may seek to improve on its environmental performance.

Learning outcomes

Having read this chapter you should be able to:

- define the concepts of business ethics and corporate social responsibility
- discuss the emergence of corporate environmentalism as a business issue
- differentiate between the drivers of, and motivations for, green behaviour by businesses
- analyse the reasons why a firm might seek to improve on its environmental performance and what forms this could take
- illustrate how firms both affect and are affected by the natural environment

Key terms

Business ethics	Environmental management system	Public voluntary programmes
Circular economy	Environmental subsidies	Resource-based view
Competitive advantage	Environmental taxes	Shareholders
Corporate social responsibility	European Emissions Trading Scheme (ETS)	Stakeholders
Cradle-to-cradle™ (C2C)	Gold plating	Sustainable development
Eco-efficiency	Inside-out view	Tradeable (or marketable) pollution permits
Eco-label	Market niche	Unilateral commitments
Eco-Management and Audit Scheme (EMAS)	Negative externalities	Unlevel playing field
Environmental champions	Outside-in view	Voluntary approaches
	Polluter pays principle	WEEE regulations
		Win–win philosophy

Introduction

In May 1999 the largest ever survey of global public opinion took place on the expectations of businesses as we entered the twenty-first century: 25 000 people in 23 countries on 6 continents were interviewed about their perceptions of the roles and responsibilities of business organisations in the social and environmental as well as the economic spheres. This worldwide survey – known as the Millennium Poll on Corporate Social Responsibility (CSR) – confirmed what many business researchers and corporate leaders had come to recognise over the course of the previous decade or so. That is, a firm's social and environmental performance was no less important to the general public (and, therefore, customers) than its traditional roles of making profits, paying taxes and complying with the law. While there were differences in the strengths of opinions expressed in the countries surveyed, the overall message of the poll was clear: consumers believe that business organisations should behave in a socially and environmentally responsible way and should be held accountable for their actions across a range of areas, from protecting the health and safety of their employees, through avoiding unethical business practices, to protecting the natural environment. This remains a common perception.

In the analysis below, we discuss how ethical and ecological issues in business have become an increasingly important aspect of a firm's macroenvironmental context. This development can be illustrated in a number of ways. Many larger organisations now publish annual social and environmental reports, which are designed to highlight improvements in the firm's performance on a range of indicators (e.g. employee training, charitable donations, reduction in carbon emissions) to a variety of stakeholder groups (see below). To achieve these claimed improvements, a growing number of firms have appointed senior executives and managers with responsibility for directing, monitoring and auditing the social and environmental performance of the business and for communicating this both internally and externally to the various interested parties.

In the lexicon of business, concepts such as **corporate social responsibility**, social responsiveness, corporate social performance, corporate citizenship and corporate sustainability have become relatively commonplace, as have notions such as supply chain ethics, green marketing and triple bottom line accounting. Parallel developments have also taken place in the academic world as a growing number of business and management programmes now incorporate the study of **business ethics**, CSR and sustainable development into the curriculum, supported by a burgeoning literature in these fields and an expanding group of international journals focusing on the ethical and environmental aspects of business (e.g. *Journal of Business Ethics, Journal of Environmental Management, Business Strategy and the Environment*).

To provide an insight into how businesses can be affected by ethical and ecological pressures, the chapter begins with a general discussion of the notions of business ethics and CSR before moving on to a more detailed examination of the very topical issue of environmental management in business. For students wishing to investigate these subjects in more detail, we have recommended some useful sources in the 'Further reading' section at the end of the chapter. You could also consult the websites of leading multi–national corporations and bodies such as business representative organisations (e.g. Confederation of British Industry, Institute of Directors, Chambers of Commerce), environmental NGOs (e.g. Greenpeace, Friends of the Earth, Forum for the Future), advocacy groups (e.g. Business in the Community) and the various international groups/agencies whose work includes consideration of ethical and environmental issues in business (e.g. the UN, World Bank).

Ethics and business

As we saw in the previous chapter, business organisations exist and function within a framework of law emanating from various sources, including government. In many areas of life, laws essentially direct what individuals and/or organisations can or cannot do and set minimum standards of behaviour based on underlying ethical principles. Not all ethical aspects of business, however, are covered by government legislation or the common law, as in the case of selling weapons to overseas governments or paying low wages to workers producing a product in other countries. By the same token, not all laws governing individual or organisational behaviour raise what would be regarded as important ethical issues.

As Crane and Matten (2016) suggest, business ethics is basically concerned with those issues in business that are not covered by law or where there is no definite consensus on what is 'right' or 'wrong' behaviour. Accordingly, they define business ethics as 'the study of business situations, activities and decisions where issues of right and wrong are addressed', stressing quite rightly that in terms of organisational behaviour right and wrong should be seen in a moral sense, not from a financial or strategic point of view. It might make financial sense, for instance, for an organisation to exploit cheap labour or flush its waste products into a river at no cost to the business, and it might not be illegal, but is it ethical? As the Millennium Poll (Available via www.ipsos-mori.com) and other surveys have illustrated, a firm's stance on ethical issues in business is an important aspect of its external environment and one that applies to enterprises of all kinds, in all sectors and across different national jurisdictions.

While it is beyond the scope of this chapter to discuss all the potential ethical dilemmas faced by modern business organisations, it is worth noting that these have tended to intensify and broaden as business activity has become more globalised and as technological transformation has given rise to the globalisation of communications and the 24-hour instant news culture. Multinational corporations in particular are facing much closer scrutiny by different groups of stakeholders which are increasingly willing to pressurise larger businesses to behave in a more ethically and ecologically sustainable way. Allegations that some high-profile western companies are (sometimes unwittingly) exploiting child labour in the developing world or are involved in ethically questionable commercial practices (e.g. bribery, price fixing) or in environmentally damaging activities (e.g. illegal logging, oil exploration in unspoiled natural environments) inevitably attract media attention and can result in significant damage to a firm's reputation and, potentially, its bottom line. By the same token, firms recognised for having a good ethical stance may find favour with the different stakeholder interests and this could bring organisational benefits of various kinds, including increased sales, access to new customers/markets, improvements in labour recruitment and retention, lower insurance premiums and less scrutiny by governments and/or NGOs.

mini case   Illegal or unethical?

While definitions of business ethics focus on issues of right and wrong that are not covered by the law, the dividing line between behaviour that is evidently illegal and that which is unethical can sometimes be difficult to draw. Take the following cases of alleged and controversial business practices. Where would you draw the line?

1 Major banks – including UBS, Barclays, Standard Chartered, HSBC, RBS, J.P. Morgan and Lloyds – have been accused of, and sometimes fined for, a series of misdemeanours. These have included mis-selling of payment protection insurance; manipulating the key London inter-bank interest rate (LIBOR); breaches of money-laundering rules and sanctions busting; selling of sub-prime mortgages; being involved in businesses that speculate on world food prices; manipulation of exchange rates. Not all of the above-named banks have been accused of every one of these practices and some allegations are still being investigated.

2 Major international companies (e.g. Starbucks, Vodafone, Amazon, Apple, Facebook, Google) have been criticised for arranging their business affairs so as to minimise the tax paid to host governments.

3 GSK has been accused of paying bribes to win business in China. Rolls-Royce is facing similar allegations relating to past contracts in both Indonesia and China.

4 A number of major retailers – including Primark, Matalan, Marks and Spencer, H&M and New Look – have come under pressure to investigate more fully the conditions in overseas factories supplying their garments following fatal fires and factory collapses in Bangladeshi suppliers' premises. Most major retailers have now signed up to a UN-sponsored, legally binding agreement on worker safety and building regulations.

5 Some major food and drink firms have been exhorted to provide more accurate product labelling, particularly salt, sugar and calorie content, because of concerns over diabetes and obesity. Critics have accused some of the major companies in the food industry of providing unclear information and guidance to consumers.

As the above examples illustrate, there may be cases where a certain business practice may be judged to be both illegal and unethical in the moral sense of the word. Where businesses fail to provide an adequate system of corporate governance to address ethically questionable behaviour by their employees, governments are sometimes forced to intervene through the law. This is not necessarily easy, particularly if the issue is a cross-national problem (e.g. tax avoidance) requiring a coordinated approach by different national governments.

Whether 'good ethics' and 'good business' are always complementary has been the subject of considerable debate in both practitioner and academic circles and is one that is far from resolved. That said, what is clear is that the question of ethics in business and the related concept of CSR are no longer peripheral issues and have been rapidly moving up the corporate agenda in most large business organisations in recent years. If firms are to avoid the potential risks posed by a poor ethical performance (e.g. Enron) and/or exploit the anticipated opportunities offered by a positive ethical stance (e.g. The Body Shop), they need to put in place appropriate mechanisms for managing the ethical issues they face (e.g. values statements, codes of ethics, robust systems of corporate governance, accredited auditing and reporting systems). They also need to think more broadly about society's expectations of corporate behaviour and of their obligations and responsibilities beyond those to the immediate owners of the business. This notion of a firm's social responsibilities is the issue to which we now turn.

Corporate social responsibility

The idea of CSR essentially means that business organisations have responsibilities that go beyond mere profit-making and encompass voluntary activities and actions that affect people, their communities and the natural environment. The question of whether, and how far, a firm should engage in such activities if they might adversely affect profitability remains a contested arena. A central theme in this debate has been the issue of the central purpose of the business organisation and the knowledge, abilities and responsibilities of those that run profit-seeking enterprises. Under the neo-classical view of the firm, private sector businesses exist to make profits for the owners (e.g. **shareholders**) and the responsibility of the firm's managers is to act in a way that enhances the position of the providers of capital, by maximising profits and/or shareholder value. Writing in *The New York Times* in 1970, the economist Milton Friedman basically echoed this perspective when he argued that the social responsibility of a business was to increase its profits so long as it obeyed the law and operated ethically. In Friedman's opinion, a firm's directors were not only ill-equipped to make decisions on social and environmental matters but, as agents for the firm's owners (the principals), they also had a fiduciary responsibility to the shareholders, not to some broader conception of the social good. It was then up to the shareholders if they wanted to donate their wealth to charities or other **stakeholders**. Under this interpretation, allocating some of the firm's resources to the pursuit of socially responsible objectives could effectively be construed as unethical since it involves spending money that belongs to other individuals.

This conventional view of the role of business in society has been challenged on a number of grounds and to many observers of the business scene now seems outdated, narrow and arguably naive. As Chapter 1 has shown, businesses exist within and draw their resources from the broader society and therefore could be said to have a moral obligation to take account of their social and environmental performance. Added to this, shareholders are only one of the groups with which the firm interacts and consequently there are other stakeholder interests to which a business has responsibilities and obligations when carrying out its activities (see, for example, Chapter 10). Such stakeholders are both internal (e.g. employees) and external (e.g. customers) to the organisation and under the stakeholder view of the firm (see e.g. Freeman, 1984) businesses have a social responsibility to take into account the interests of all parties affected by their actions and decisions, not just the owners of the business. In contrast to the neo-classical view of the firm, the stakeholder approach stresses the necessity for managers to try to operate the business to the benefit of all stakeholder groups and to seek to gain an effective balance between the different interested parties. Using some of the firm's profits to achieve such an outcome is not necessarily detrimental to the firm's owners and indeed may ultimately help to enhance shareholder value, particularly over the longer term. Friedman might not have objected if managers used business resources to increase shareholder income in the long run.

More recent discussions of why businesses should take account of their social and environmental responsibilities have tended to focus on the strategic benefits of CSR, how acting 'responsibly' can generate advantages for the business on both the demand and the supply sides (see e.g. McWilliams *et al.*, 2006). Writers such as Porter and Kramer (2002) have argued that a firm can gain a **competitive advantage** by investing in CSR, particularly if its actions in this area become an intrinsic part of its business and corporate differentiation strategies. One important element in this debate has been the application of a **resource-based view** (RBV) of the firm in which social and environmental responsibility are portrayed as an organisational resource/capability that can lead to sustained competitive advantage. The claim is that engaging in CSR has the potential to enhance a firm's reputation with key stakeholder groups and this could give it an advantage over its rivals that is both valuable and potentially difficult to imitate. This means that it is important to assess businesses' attempts to be socially responsible critically; are they attempting to manage their reputation for profit or are they genuinely concerned with their environments and stakeholders? One arena where this might be particularly important is with regard to an organisation's environmental performance, given the growing international concerns over the impact of business activity on the natural environment. This is the subject we now investigate in more detail.

The 'environment' as a business issue: the emergence of corporate environmentalism

In Chapter 1 we portrayed goods and services as the outputs of business activity, the end result of transforming inputs into products to meet the needs and demands of individuals, organisations and governments. While such economic activity undoubtedly gives rise to significant individual and societal benefits, these desirable aspects of business come at a price; production generates 'bads' as well as 'goods', including damage to the natural environment and resource depletion. Hawken (1996) has suggested that the business community contributes to environmental degradation in three main ways: by what it takes, by what it makes and by what it wastes. This bad face of business is found at all stages of the transformation process (see e.g. Worthington, 2013) and involves environmental problems across all spatial levels from the local (e.g. litter) to the global (e.g. climate change).

Pressure on firms to accept responsibility for the negative impacts they have on the natural environment can be seen as part of the broader debate on corporate social responsibility. Worthington (2013) has argued that growing levels of corporate environmental awareness began to emerge in the closing decades of the twentieth century and can be linked to several key factors, including the publication of a number of influential books (e.g. Rachel Carson's *Silent Spring* in 1962), a series of high-profile ecological disasters (e.g. the chemical release at the Union Carbide plant in Bhopal in the 1980s), scientific discoveries (e.g. ozone depletion) and global media coverage of major environmental concerns (e.g. climate change). In helping to place the environment on both the public and political agendas, developments such as these helped to spawn a growing environmental movement and to encourage action at governmental and intergovernmental levels, both of which have had important implications for the business community and for the debate over how to reconcile the widespread demand for economic growth with the need for greater environmental protection.

As far as the latter question was concerned, what emerged from a lengthy and complex process of debate and discussion at an international level was the notion of **sustainable development**, the idea that when making choices designed to increase well-being today, countries should ensure that future generations are left no worse off than their current counterparts. In environmental terms, this implied, inter alia, the need to take steps to limit environmental damage and degradation, conserve the world's natural capital, preserve essential ecosystem functions and aim for qualitative rather than simply quantitative improvements over time. From a business point of view, this philosophical stance appeared to run counter to the traditional notion of 'business as usual', with its emphasis on year-on-year growth and unfettered access to the world's natural resources and environmental services.

The late twentieth century debate over sustainable development clearly poses an important question for the business community: how far should a firm be prepared to incorporate concern for the environment into its strategic decisions and day-to-day operations? Should environmental protection be seen as an inevitable additional cost to the business, or could it be leveraged for competitive advantage? As with CSR generally, opinions have tended to vary on this question, the latter view eventually gaining traction with business leaders of major international companies as the new millennium approached.

While it is impossible to pinpoint an exact time or event which helped to place the environment on corporate agendas, the available evidence indicates that its emergence as an important business issue has been gradual and largely incremental and has been shaped by a combination of pressures emanating from the regulatory, market and social domains of business. What these pressures have been and how and why firms have responded in different ways are the focus of the subsequent sections of this chapter.

Drivers of 'green' business

Academic researchers have long been interested in the factors that predispose businesses to engage in different forms of socially responsible behaviour (see e.g. Burke and Logsdon, 1996; McWilliams *et al.*, 2006). With regard to a firm's 'green' responses, these have been linked to four major influences: governmental action, other stakeholder pressures, economic opportunities and ethical considerations. We discuss each of these in turn.

Government action

As we saw in Chapters 4 and 5, the government is a key actor and stakeholder in a firm's external environment. Its actions and decisions can play a formative role in promoting more sustainable forms of development and in encouraging businesses to improve on their environmental performance – to address, in effect, imperfections in the market system, including the existence of **negative externalities** such as pollution (for a discussion see Worthington, 2013).

Where environmental protection is concerned, three main approaches have been used: legislation and regulation, market-based instruments and voluntary agreements.

With regard to legal instruments, this basically involves the establishment of a system of direct control over organisations and their activities via the adoption of laws and other forms of regulatory measure, including the use of directives, permits, licences and the creation of regulatory, inspection and enforcement regimes, backed by the application of sanctions in the event of non-compliance. Examples of environmental laws and regulations can be found in most, if not all, countries, and action may also be taken at an intergovernmental level, as in the case of the EU. The most visible example of this in recent years has been the EU's Waste Electrical and Electronic Equipment Directive (**WEEE regulations**), where the amount of waste electronic and electrical devices was reduced by placing responsibility for disposing of items on the manufacturers or distributors of the old and new items. So if you purchase a new television from a shop you can leave the old one and the shop is responsible for disposing of it.

While governments can and do use legislation/regulation to shape the environmental behaviour of firms, in practice instruments of this kind can vary substantially in style, content and degree of application; they are also aimed at a range of environmental problems from pollution control to resource management. Regulatory intervention can be used inter alia to outlaw or ban certain activities, apply particular standards, specify the characteristics required of certain products, determine the inputs to be used, mandate the techniques and/or technology a firm must apply, and identify its obligations regarding issues such as recycling and information disclosure. In short, they are generally imposed by a governing authority to produce outcomes that might otherwise not occur if decisions are left entirely to market forces. The evidence suggests that in this respect they have probably been the key driver of firm-level environmental behaviour (see e.g. Bansal and Roth, 2000; Etzion, 2007).

It is worth remembering that while governments are ultimately responsible for environmental laws and regulations, these are frequently shaped by different stakeholder interests, including the business community and its representative organisations. It is not uncommon for firms to lobby against proposed environmental legislation on the grounds that it will increase business costs and/or reduce international competitiveness, particularly if there are disparities in regulatory requirements between countries. Complaints that there is frequently an **unlevel playing field** or that **gold plating** of standards can occur are often used in this sphere; some businesses may even threaten to move their operations to locations (i.e. other countries) where environmental demands are less stringent, though it is unlikely that this consideration alone will be the determinant of such a strategic decision.

Turning to market-based or economic instruments, these involve the use of financial (or other) incentives or disincentives aimed at shaping business behaviour, **environmental taxes**, **environmental subsidies** and **tradeable (or marketable) pollution permits** being three major examples. In simple terms, an environmental tax or charge seeks to take account of the negative environmental impact of business activity (e.g. pollution) by imposing a cost on firms that are responsible for the problem. Action taken by a business to reduce its environmental impact is rewarded by the reduction or removal of the financial penalty. Alternatively the organisation may be granted a financial gain in the form of an environmental subsidy or other type of fiscal reward (e.g. a reduction in corporate tax).

At the heart of this approach lies the use of the price mechanism to shape the behaviour of economic actors: to correct the market for negative externalities by endorsing the **polluter pays principle**. Whereas regulation basically involves governments in deciding on the best course of action to address environmental problems, so-called green taxes and subsidies essentially leave businesses free to respond to certain stimuli in ways they themselves decide are most beneficial to the organisation, such as through investment in pollution reduction measures/technology or in changes in inputs or production or distribution methods. In this regard, taxes and subsidies can be said to work with the grain of the market and to act as a spur to innovation and investment. On the downside, they often tend to be viewed by firms as a revenue-raising exercise, can be difficult to design and implement, and can, in some cases, have an adverse effect on firm, industry and national competitiveness.

Whereas environmental taxes and subsidies work by creating a price where none previously existed or by modifying an existing price, tradeable or marketable pollution permits are an example of market creation. The government establishes, in effect, a system of tradeable pollution rights, issues quotas, allowances or permits up to an agreed level and then allows the holders of those rights to trade them like any other commodity. The trading of rights (e.g. relating to greenhouse gas emissions – sometimes known as 'carbon credits') usually takes place under prescribed rules and may be external (e.g. between different enterprises or countries) or internal (e.g. between different plants within the same firm), within a free or controlled permit market. Gunningham *et al.* (1998) have described this approach as a hybrid between direct regulations and free-market environmentalism in that governments decide on the overall quantity of pollution permissible, while market forces determine the eventual distribution of rights between participating firms or countries.

As with green taxes/subsidies, a tradeable permit system – exemplified by the **European Emissions Trading Scheme (ETS)** – has both benefits and drawbacks. On the positive side, it offers firms a degree of flexibility in their responses and acts as an inducement to reducing their emissions, not least since any unused permits can be sold to businesses which have exceeded their quota. On the negative side, the system can be extremely bureaucratic and can be difficult to implement; there are also questions over its effectiveness and its impact on poorer nations.

Alongside regulation and market-based instruments, governments also use **voluntary approaches (VAs)** in an attempt to improve the environmental performance of firms beyond existing legal requirements. The three main types of instrument employed are as follows:

- **Public voluntary programmes** – which involve commitments devised by an environment agency and in which individual firms are invited to participate, the EU's **Eco-Management and Audit Scheme (EMAS)** being a prime example.
- Negotiated agreements – which are initiatives that result from a process of bargaining between a public authority (e.g. national government) and an industry or industry sector, exemplified by the covenants that form part of the Netherlands National Environment Policy Plan.
- **Unilateral commitments** – which are environmental programmes set up by firms independently of any public authority, but which may be aimed at forestalling government regulation, hence their inclusion here. An example of this form of self-regulation is the Chemical Manufacturers' Association Responsible Care Programme.

Since this approach to environmental protection provides firms with a substantial degree of flexibility regarding how far and in what ways they respond, it tends to be popular with the business community; it also has the potential to enhance stakeholder relationships (e.g. by improving the firm's image with customers) and possibly increase participants' competitiveness.

It is also worth noting that governments also participate in reputation management through promoting themselves as involved in social and responsible practices, while sometimes pursuing alternative strategies: for example, reducing the national debts of some countries voluntarily while increasing the national debts of others by underwriting arms sales. In 2016, 18.8 million people (of a population of 27.4 million) in Yemen were in need of humanitarian assistance. The United States Agency for International Development provided $275 million of humanitarian funding, while selling Saudi Arabia (one of the main aggressors) $300 billion of military equipment over the last 10 years. As a result of deals like this, Israel is purchasing more advanced weapons systems (e.g. the latest generation of jet aircraft) to maintain its edge with the most advanced equipment.

Other stakeholder pressures

In addition to the legislative, regulatory and fiscal demands imposed by governments, firms face pressures to reduce their environmental impact from other constituencies. Customers, competitors, suppliers, creditors, investors, shareholders, employees, civil society organisations and the media can all be instrumental in inducing a green response in businesses. Consumers, for instance, may actively seek out goods with a higher level of environmental performance or may boycott products deemed to have an adverse effect on the natural environment. Other examples include pressure exerted through the supply chain and/or by major investors, shareholder activism, adverse media publicity, lobbying by environmental NGOs and withdrawal by a public authority of a licence to operate. The extent to which stakeholder pressures are likely to prove effective in shaping firm-level behaviour is normally related to their impact on an organisation's bottom line, either directly or indirectly.

Economic opportunities

Organisations may also seek to improve on their environmental performance as a means of gaining an economic and commercial benefit, with opportunities potentially available on both sides of business. Gains could be generated by:

- reducing waste and generally increasing the efficiency of factor inputs, as highlighted by the concepts of **eco-efficiency** and acronyms such as Pollution Prevention Pays (PPP) and Waste Reduction Always Pays (WRAP);
- creating revenue-raising opportunities by developing green products and processes which may allow the firm to create a **market niche** by differentiating its offering to consumers who may be willing to pay a premium price;
- enhancing the organisation's resources and capabilities, including its corporate reputation with external stakeholders and its capacity to innovate;
- managing current and future environmental (e.g. accidents) and regulatory (e.g. stricter laws) risks with their associated costs.

As with CSR generally, the claim that environmental responsibility can pay remains hotly contested (see e.g. Worthington, 2013: Chapter 6).

Ethical considerations

A firm's green behaviour can also be driven by influences emanating from within the business itself, most notably the belief by organisational decision-makers that 'it is the right thing to do'. Initiatives may come from an organisation's owners and/or senior management team or from **environmental champions** or the workforce generally. In some cases, the organisation's culture and values may be largely or wholly attuned to an ecologically responsible approach (e.g. environmental NGOs such as Greenpeace).

Why and how firms become more environmentally responsible

Whereas a discussion of the 'drivers' of corporate greening focuses on the factors that push a firm towards pro-environmental responses, examining its motivations for going in this direction raises a related, though slightly different, question: What is the underlying rationale for its behaviour?

In broad terms, the academic literature suggests three main reasons: it provides benefits or creates opportunities for the organisation; it reduces threats or risks to the enterprise; and it accords with the firm's ethical stance. In practice, of course, an organisation's actions could reflect any or all of these motivations, each of which can be expressed in several ways.

Benefit-focused or opportunity-focused explanations link a firm's responses to the various strategic advantages thought to derive from a green response. These include meeting stakeholder or societal expectations, achieving market-related benefits through product differentiation, exploiting a green market niche, making cost savings or eco-efficiencies, and enhancing the organisation's image and/or corporate reputation. To what extent these claimed advantages represent *ex ante* explanations for a firm's actions or are *ex post* rationales aimed at persuading key stakeholders that there is a sound business case for investing in proactive green behaviour is not always clear.

Risk-focused or threat-focused arguments centre around the idea that corporate environmentalism is a way of protecting the organisation from adverse stakeholder reactions and/or the consequences of a negative or limited response to external pressures for change. Reduced current and future liabilities and risk – including fines, adverse publicity, loss of business, the danger of legislative sanctions and retrospective liabilities – may all be reasons why a firm might engage in pro-environmental behaviour. While this perspective suggests a predominantly defensive rationale, it is not always easy to separate risk-based explanations from the more proactive, opportunity-related motivations, given that investments in green responses may simultaneously reduce risks and create organisational benefits.

Whereas the two above explanations suggest that organisations are motivated primarily by economic and commercial considerations, some firms may believe that they have a moral obligation to protect the natural environment and this could explain their behaviour. As discussed previously, ethical explanations reflect the view that a business has obligations to the wider society, not just to narrow stakeholder interests such as shareholders or other investors. That said, as with other forms of CSR, a firm's ethical stance could help it to gain a strategic advantage over its rivals, particularly if its actions are seen as an important aspect of doing business by powerful and influential stakeholder groups (see e.g. Porter and Kramer, 2002).

Turning to the question of what steps a firm may take to demonstrate its green credentials, these can range from relatively simple initiatives such as recycling or energy-saving measures to more complex practices and processes, including greening the supply chain, investing in new technology and developing an **environmental management system** (EMS), the latter being a multi-stage process aimed at identifying, measuring and controlling a firm's environmental impact. Some businesses may also seek external recognition for their actions and decisions, whether by engaging in a strategic alliance with an environmental NGO (e.g. McDonald's and the Environmental Defense Fund), seeking certification for their products by a recognised and reputable body (e.g. the Forest Stewardship Council), or qualifying for the display of an **eco-label**, which certifies that a given product is environmentally safe or friendly (e.g. Germany's Blue Angel, Japan's Eco-Mark, the EU's European Eco-Label).

mini case Going round in circles: Desso Carpets

Linear models of business activity – such as the systems approach presented in Chapter 1 – are essentially based on notions of 'take, make and dispose'. Inputs are acquired, a production process occurs, the product is consumed and then disposed of at the end of its life. Despite some opportunities for recycling, reclamation and reuse of materials and components, products produced in this way generate considerable levels of waste and pollution and consume large quantities of energy and raw materials, including non-renewables.

An alternative philosophy – currently exciting a degree of interest among forward-looking businesses (see below) – is the notion of the **circular economy**, a concept that focuses on waste eradication, rebuilding natural and social capital, and adopting a renewable approach. Advocates of what is sometimes called the **cradle-to-cradle™ (C2C)** stance conceive of manufacturers continuing to own their own products, the use of which they sell to customers. These products are designed in a way that

eliminates waste and involves manufacturing and distribution systems based around renewable sources of energy.

The Dutch company Desso is one of Europe's largest producers of commercial-grade carpet and carpet tiles used in a wide range of domestic and commercial situations. In 2007 the firm announced its intention of designing by 2020 a fully closed-loop system for all its products based on C2C principles. The company aims to produce products that are entirely biodegradable or are capable of being recycled to produce new goods. This will involve designing systems and processes that will allow the firm to purchase appropriate materials, use waste to provide a source of energy, reduce energy consumption, provide facilities for recycling, product take-back and composting, and completely modify the way it does business (e.g. renting rather than selling products). To achieve its ambitious aims, the firm is working in partnership with the Environmental Protection Encouragement Agency (EPEA), which has its headquarters in Hamburg.

web link

See, for example, *www.desso.com/c2c-corporate-responsibility*

On the whole, it tends to be the case that smaller firms are more limited in their responses than their larger counterparts, given that they tend to lack the knowledge, resources and capabilities needed to invest in more advanced forms of environmental behaviour. Schemes such as General Electric's (GE) Ecomagination initiative and Marks and Spencer's Plan A (see the case study) are clearly beyond the reach of smaller businesses, many of which face substantial barriers to improved environmental performance and remain to be convinced that they have a negative impact on the natural environment or that they can benefit from investment in environmental protection measures.

Another perspective: the 'outside-in' view

In examining the interaction between firms and the natural environment, much of the focus has been on the pressures exerted on business to address the negative impacts that result from their activities, what might be called an **inside-out view** from the firm to the environment. It is important to recognise, however, that the natural environment also provides critical economic functions for the business community: it is a provider of inputs (e.g. raw materials), an assimilator of waste products (e.g. pollution) and a source of amenity value for individuals and organisations (e.g. landscape). When viewed in this way (i.e. the **outside-in view**), it is clear that economic activity and organisational competitiveness, both now and in the future, are intrinsically linked with the well-being of the natural environment (see e.g. Porter and Reinhardt, 2007). In 2006, for example, the Stern Report estimated that failure to tackle climate change could result in a decline of up to 20 per cent in the size of the global economy, and a plethora of recent authoritative reports by both national and international bodies paints a picture of how environmental problems – caused in part by business activity – can impact adversely on the business community.

To repeat the assertion made in Chapter 1, the business/environment relationship flows in both directions and is complex, interactive and dynamic, varying both between places and over time. In short, organisations not only affect the natural environment, but also are affected by it and by what services it can provide. Protecting the environment may equally be a matter of self-interest, rather than simply a question of CSR or inter-generational equity and social justice.

Summary of key points

- Business ethics is concerned with issues of 'right' and 'wrong' behaviour in a business context.

- Corporate social responsibility (CSR) is the idea that organisations should be held accountable for the effects of their actions on people, their communities and the environment.

- CSR has become an important consideration for modern businesses, alongside traditional concerns with profitability and growth.

- Being socially responsible as a business does not preclude being profitable.

- Increasingly, business organisations have to take account of the views of their stakeholders on questions of social and environmental responsibility.

- One area where this has become particularly significant is with regard to the impact of business operations and decisions on the natural environment.

- The key 'drivers' of corporate environmental responsiveness are government intervention, other stakeholder pressures, economic opportunities and ethical considerations.

- Firms that implement environmental policies tend to be motivated by questions of organisational benefit or risk avoidance.

- Different businesses respond in different ways, ranging from reactive stances through to more proactive environmental approaches, which go beyond compliance with regulatory demands.

- Firms not only affect the natural environment, but also are affected by it in a variety of ways.

case study — Doing well by doing good

As consumers have become increasingly aware of environmental issues, many organisations have felt compelled to demonstrate their commitment to a greener approach by announcing a range of high-profile environmental initiatives and programmes. This case study looks at two examples: General Electric's Ecomagination initiative and Marks and Spencer's Plan A.

GE's Ecomagination initiative

Launched in 2005, GE's Ecomagination initiative is an environmentally focused business strategy aimed at producing profitable growth by providing solutions to environmental problems such as the demand for cleaner sources of energy, reduced carbon emissions and access to cleaner water. Backed by a multi-million-dollar advertising campaign, the initiative emphasised that being 'good' and being commercially successful were complementary, what has been called a **win–win philosophy**, where both the environment and the firm benefit.

To qualify for inclusion in the firm's Ecomagination portfolio, a product or service must be able to demonstrate significant and measurable improvement in operational and environmental performance or in value proposition, additional value being provided for both investors and customers. Since the initiative began, products meeting these criteria have ranged from electric vehicles and aircraft engines to energy-efficient light bulbs and water-purification technologies. Up until 2017 the company has invested $20 billion in research and development on these projects.

During the first 12 years of the initiative it is estimated that Ecomagination products and services generated $270 billion for the business, as well as reduced greenhouse gas emissions by 18 per cent. There also appears to have been a number of less tangible benefits, such as creating customer trust in GE's brands and helping the business to attract and retain high-quality employees (see e.g. Esty and Winston, 2006; Laszlo and Zhexembayeva, 2011). The company has also been able to significantly reduce its water footprint during this period and aims to achieve further reductions in environmental impact in the future as well as increasing its investment in clean technology research and development.

Marks and Spencer's 'Plan A'

M&S's Plan A was announced in early 2007 by the then chief executive Stuart Rose, who claimed that the initiative was so named because there was no Plan B. Under the new scheme the company committed itself to spending several hundred million pounds to reduce its environmental impact and to put social and environmental commitment at the heart of its commercial activities. Key aspects of the plan included reducing waste, saving energy, promoting animal welfare and trading fairly – goals which required it to consider a wide range of aspects of the business, including its logistics and retail operations, its relationship with suppliers and its sourcing policies. As the plan has been rolled out and incorporated into the fabric of the M&S brand, additional aspects have been added or developed more fully, community engagement being one example.

According to the company's reporting, M&S had saved more than £750 million through Plan A in the 10 years that it has been running, improved energy efficiency by 39 per cent, reduced waste by 28 per cent and made substantial savings in its use of glass. On the downside the company has had difficulties in meeting its targets for converting to the use of Fairtrade cotton and sustainable leather. There are also doubts as to whether it will reach its highly ambitious target of 50 million items of recycled clothing by 2020 (in the first 10 years to 2017 it had achieved 27.8 million items).

For further information on these two companies and their social and environmental initiatives go to *www.ge.com* and *www.marksandspencer.com* and follow the links.

Case study questions

1 What do you think have been the key drivers of the two initiatives mentioned in this case study?

2 Will investors in these organisations benefit from or be disadvantaged by the two schemes?

Review and discussion questions

1 To what extent are governments responsible for establishing the parameters by which organisations conduct business? Should a business be free to decide its own level of corporate responsibility?

2 How can governments influence the environmental behaviour of firms?

3 Writers have argued that the only objective of business is to make profit, within the boundaries established by government. Do you agree?

Assignments

1 As a group, select an environmental issue (e.g. business or natural feature) and write a report to the leader of a local pressure group which details an environmental impact assessment of the issue. The report should make clear reference to:

(a) a cost–benefit analysis, carried out by the group, of the salient factors;

(b) any legislation/regulation that concerns the case; and

(c) the provision of a stakeholder map that illustrates who the stakeholders are, their importance to the case and their ability to affect future decisions.

2 As a newly appointed trainee manager you have been asked to look afresh at the business, with particular reference to the implementation of an environmental management system. Your immediate superior has asked you to write a report. Accordingly, you are required to:

(a) consult the available literature and identify what you consider to be the necessary processes and procedures that would comprise an environmental management system;

(b) indicate the areas within the organisation that need to be addressed; and

(c) explain how such a policy should be implemented within the organisation.

Further reading

Bansal, P. and Roth, K., 'Why companies go green: a model of ecological responsiveness', *Academy of Management Journal,* 43 (4), 2000, pp. 717–36.

Burke, L. and Logsdon, J. M., 'How corporate social responsibility pays off', *Long Range Planning,* 29 (4), 1996, pp. 495–502.

Cairncross, F., *Green Inc: A Guide to Business and the Environment,* Earthscan Publications, 1995.

Crane, A. and Matten, D., *Business Ethics,* 4th edition, Oxford University Press, 2016.

Esty, D. C. and Winston, A. S., *Green to Gold: How Smart Companies Use Environmental Strategy to Innovate, Create Value, and Build Competitive Advantage,* Yale University Press, 2006.

Etzion, D., 'Research on organizations and the natural environment, 1992–present: a review', *Journal of Management,* 33 (4), 2007, pp. 637–64.

Frederick, W. C., Post, J. E. and Davis, K., *Business and Society: Corporate Strategy, Public Policy, Ethics,* 10th edition, McGraw-Hill, 2001.

Freeman, R. E., *Strategic Management: A Stakeholder Approach,* Prentice Hall, 1984.

Gunningham, N., Grabosky, P. N. and Sinclair, D., *Smart Regulation: Designing Environmental Policy,* Oxford University Press, 1998.

Laszlo, C. and Zhexembayeva, N. *Embedded Sustainability: The Next Big Competitive Advantage,* 2011, Greenleaf Publishing.

McWilliams, A., Siegel, D. S. and Wright, P. M., 'Corporate social responsibility: strategic implications', *Journal of Management Studies,* 43 (1), 2006, pp. 1–18.

Pearce, D. and Barbier, E., *Blueprint for a Sustainable Economy,* Earthscan Publications, 2000.

Porter, M. E. and Kramer, M. R., 'The competitive advantage of corporate philanthropy', *Harvard Business Review,* 80 (12), 2002, pp. 56–69.

Porter, M. E. and Reinhardt, F. L., 'A strategic approach to climate change', *Harvard Business Review,* 85 (10), 2007, pp. 22–6.

Sankar, A., *Environmental Management,* Oxford University Press, 2015.

Vogel, D., *The Market for Virtue: The Potential and Limits of Corporate Social Responsibility,* Brookings Institution, 2005.

Worthington, I., *Greening Business: Research, Theory & Practice,* Oxford University Press, 2013.

Worthington, I., Britton, C. and Rees, A., *Economics for Business: Blending Theory and Practice,* 2nd edition, Financial Times/Prentice Hall, 2005, Chapter 14.

Web links and further questions are available on the website at:
www.pearsoned.co.uk/worthington

Migration

In an increasingly globalised world, companies often look to international migration of labour to fill jobs if they can no longer rely on their own domestic labour markets to do this. The international migration of labour is important – although it has no overall effect on the world population, it has significant effects for individual countries. There is a difference between stocks and flows of migration.

Flows vary from year to year for many economic and political reasons and some of these are considered later in the case study. Stocks represent the historical accumulation of migration built up over the long term. In 2015 the migrant population stock was 242 million, which represented 3.3 per cent of the world population (as opposed to 2.1 per cent in 1960).[1] In 2013 the United States accounted for 20 per cent of the total; the Russian Federation was second with 5 per cent. In 2016 the war in Syria had forced large numbers of people to move out of the country. The neighbouring countries of Turkey and Jordan were home to around 2.8 million migrants; Lebanon – a country with a population of around 6 million – was a destination for 1.5 million refugees.

There are push factors and pull factors, which give rise to labour migration: push factors include poverty in the home country, natural disasters and political fear; pull factors include the possibility of employment, better standards of living and better education. A recent push factor is political unrest in the Middle East – particularly the war in Syria, but also countries which have seen unrest over the period of the Arab Spring. A pull factor is the increased opportunity and higher wages in Western Europe compared with Eastern Europe. The increase in migration from Portugal to Angola in 2013–14 can be seen as a push factor (high unemployment in Portugal) or a pull factor (high growth in Angola).

Migration can be permanent or temporary. In 2015 there were 7.2 million permanent migrants into the OECD countries and 2.3 million temporary migrants.[2] Permanent migration is dominated by family migration, where families join previous labour migrants. The rate of migration has slowed since 2007 because of the slowdown in the OECD countries.

The debate over labour migration is often heated and not based on fact, but the costs and benefits of migration need to be considered in both the sending countries and the receiving countries. It is often argued that immigrants take jobs away from people in the host country, but this is not sustained by research. In Western Europe, immigrants are often not in direct competition with the home population and take jobs at both ends of the spectrum: at the low-skill, high-risk and low-paid end, where it is difficult to fill vacancies from the home labour force; and at the high-skill, high-paid end, where home-grown skills may not be available. Research in the United States, for example, has shown that the average income of immigrants is around 20 per cent lower than that of the home workforce. Another argument often used, but again not borne out by research, is that immigration represents a drain on welfare, health and education spending in the host country. A recent report[3] found that immigrants who entered the UK since 2000 from the European Economic Area contributed 34 per cent more in taxes than they received in benefits; for immigrants from outside the EEA, the net contribution goes down to 2 per cent but it is still positive.

The migration of skilled labour is an obvious benefit to the host country, but for the sending country it represents a 'brain drain' – education, skills and knowledge are lost. This is not all negative, however, as migrants often return home, bringing with them newly acquired skills and knowledge – a 'brain gain'. The OECD estimates that between 20 and 50 per cent of migrants return to their home countries within five years. There has been a big increase in the number of foreign students, which rose by 62 per cent from 2002 to 2009 globally, with the countries benefiting the most being the United States, the UK, Australia and Canada. This brings short-term benefits in the form of extra income for fees, but this type of migration is often temporary as the students return home at the end of their studies.

One benefit of migration to the country of origin is what are called remittances – migrants sending money home to their families. These flows are expected to be $595 billion globally in 2017. The majority of this goes to the developing countries. These funds are important flows for developing countries as they are significantly bigger than official development aid, bigger than capital flows and bigger than FDI flows in some cases, and the weakening of the emerging nations will only serve to increase their importance. The biggest recipient in 2017 was India ($65bn) and the second biggest was China ($63bn). Diaspora associations (groups of émigrés from one country which link together in the host country) can also contribute to development and help relations between the host country and the country of origin. They are also instrumental in circular migration where émigrés return home. (For full figures see www.worldbank.org/en/topic/migrationremittancesdiasporaissues/brief/migration-remittances-data)

International migration is important to business – it helps fill jobs that are hard to fill or require specialised skills. In 2017 it was estimated that over 1.8 million more engineers and technically qualified people were required in the UK to fill shortages by 2025.

The UK Border Agency publishes a list of shortage occupations, which can be found here: www.gov.uk/government/collections/migration-advisory-committee-recommended-shortage-lists

At the other end of the job market, international migrants often fill the very low-skilled jobs that are difficult to fill from the UK population – fruit picking, for example. Farmers who have been largely dependent on migrant workers from Eastern Europe to carry out seasonal work - such as harvesting grown produce - are worried about the consequences of exiting the European Union. This could mean the end of relatively cheap and available labour to work on their farms.

It is clear from the above discussion that the topic of migration is a complex one, and that there are interrelationships within countries and between countries. International migration is necessary for the smooth working of markets.

Notes

1 UN, Press release, September 2012.
2 International Migration Outlook, 2012, OECD.
3 Recent Immigration to the UK, CReAM, University College London, 2013.

Part Three

FIRMS

10 Legal structures

Ian Worthington

Market-based economies comprise a rich diversity of business organisations, ranging from the very simple enterprise owned and operated by one person to the huge multinational corporation with production and distribution facilities spread across the globe. Whatever the nature of these organisations or their scale of operation, their existence is invariably subject to legal definition and this will have consequences for the functioning of the organisation. Viewing the business as a legal structure provides an insight into some of the important influences on business operations in both the private and public sectors.

Learning outcomes

Having read this chapter you should be able to:

- discuss the legal structure of UK business organisations in both the private and public sectors
- compare UK business organisations with those in other parts of Europe
- illustrate the implications of a firm's legal structure for its operations
- explain franchising, licensing and joint ventures

Key terms

Articles of Association
Black economy
Charitable Incorporated
   Organisation (CIO)
Community Interest
   Company (CIC)
Company
Company directors
Consortium
Consumer societies
Corporate governance
Executive directors
Franchising

Gearing
Gig economy
Golden share
Joint venture
Licensing
Limited Liability
   Partnerships (LLPs)
Managing director
Memorandum of
   Association
Nationalised industry
Non-executive directors
Partnership

Private limited company
Public corporation
Public limited company
   (PLC)
Public sector
   organisations
Shareholders
Social enterprises
Sole trader
Stakeholders
Unlimited personal liability
Workers' cooperatives

Introduction

Business organisations can be classified in a variety of ways, including:

- size (e.g. small, medium, large);
- type of industry (e.g. primary, secondary, tertiary);
- sector (e.g. private sector, public sector);
- legal status (e.g. sole trader, partnership, and so on).

These classifications help to distinguish one type of organisation from another and to focus attention on the implications of such differences for an individual enterprise. In this chapter we examine business organisations as legal structures and investigate the consequences of variations in legal status in some detail. Subsequent chapters in this part investigate alternative structural perspectives in order to highlight how these too have an important bearing on the environment in which businesses operate. We begin our analysis with an examination of the main forms of legal structure in the UK.

Private sector organisations in the UK

The sole trader

Many individuals aspire to owning and running their own business – being their own boss, making their own decisions. For those who decide to turn their dream into a reality, becoming a sole trader (or sole proprietor) offers the simplest and easiest method of trading.

As the name suggests, a **sole trader** is a business owned by one individual who is self-employed and who may, in some cases, employ other people on either a full-time or a part-time basis. Normally using personal funds to start the business, the sole trader decides on the type of goods or services to be produced, where the business is to be located, what capital is required, what staff (if any) to employ, what the target market should be and a host of other aspects concerned with the establishment and running of the enterprise. Where the business proves a success, all profits accrue to the owner and it is common for sole traders to reinvest a considerable proportion of these in the business and/or use them to reduce past borrowings. Should losses occur, these too are the responsibility of the sole trader, who has **unlimited personal liability** for the debts of the business (their personal wealth and property are at risk).

Despite this substantial disadvantage, sole proprietorship remains the most popular form of business organisation numerically. In the UK (and in most other countries) it is estimated that 80 per cent or more of all businesses are sole traders and in some sectors – notably personal services, retailing, building – they tend to be the dominant form of business enterprise. Part of the reason for this numerical dominance is the relative ease with which an individual can establish a business of this type. Apart from minor restrictions concerning the use of a business name – if the name of the proprietor is not used – few other legal formalities are required to set up the enterprise, other than the need to register for value-added tax (VAT) if turnover exceeds a certain sum (e.g. £85,000 in 2017) and/or to fulfil any special requirements laid down by the local authority prior to trading (e.g. some businesses require licences). Once established, the sole trader, like other forms of business, will be subject to a variety of legal requirements (e.g. contract law, consumer law, employment law) – though not the requirement to file information about the business in a public place. For some, this ability to keep the affairs of the enterprise away from public scrutiny provides a further incentive to establishing this form of business organisation – some of which may operate wholly or partly in the **black economy** (i.e. beyond the gaze of the tax authorities).

A further impetus towards sole ownership comes from the ability of the individual to exercise a considerable degree of control over his or her own destiny. Business decisions – including the day-to-day operations of the enterprise as well as long-term plans – are in the hands of the owner and many individuals evidently relish the risks and potential rewards associated with entrepreneurial activity, preferring these to the relative safety of employment in another organisation. For others less fortunate, the 'push' of unemployment rather than the 'pull' of the marketplace tends to be more of a deciding factor and one that clearly accounts for some of the growth in the number of small businesses in the UK in recent decades.

Ambitions and commitment alone, however, are not necessarily sufficient to guarantee the survival and success of the enterprise and the high mortality rate among businesses of this kind, particularly during a recession, is well known and well documented. Part of the problem may stem from developments largely outside the control of the enterprise – including bad debts, increased competition, higher interest rates, falling demand – and factors such as these affect businesses of all types and all sizes, not just sole traders. Other difficulties, such as lack of funds for expansion, poor marketing, lack of research of the marketplace and insufficient management skills, are to some extent self-induced and emanate, at least in part, from the decision to become a sole proprietor rather than some other form of business organisation. Where such constraints exist, the sole trader may be tempted to look to others to share the burdens and the risks by establishing a partnership or cooperative or limited company, or by seeking a different approach to the business venture, such as through franchising. These alternative forms of business organisation are discussed in detail below.

The partnership

The Partnership Act 1890 defines a **partnership** as 'the relation which subsists between persons carrying on a business in common with a view to profit'. Like the sole trader, this form of business organisation does not have its own distinct legal personality and hence the owners – the partners – have unlimited personal liability, both jointly and severally. This means that in the case of debts or bankruptcy of the partnership, each partner is liable in full for the whole debt and each in turn may be sued or their assets seized until the debt is satisfied. Alternatively, all the partners may be joined into the action to recover debts. The difference of a partnership to most forms of company is that the partners make profit, not the company – they pay no corporation tax; instead each partner pays their own income tax.

Since the Limited Liability Partnership Act (2000) it is possible to register a partnership where legal liability is limited to the company (partners are not personally accountable for the business's liability, unless they commit fraud or wrongful trading). Because limited liability arrangements can be achieved in a simpler way with a limited company,

limited liability partnerships (LLPs) are still uncommon except in professions such as solicitors or private medical doctors. Hence the following discussion focuses on the partnership as an unincorporated association, operating in a market where its liability is effectively unlimited.

A partnership comes into being when two or more people establish a business which they own, finance and run jointly for personal gain, irrespective of the degree of formality involved in the relationship. Such a business can range from a husband and wife running a local shop as joint owners to a very large firm of accountants or solicitors with in excess of 100 partners in offices in various locations. Under the law, most partnerships are limited to 20 or less, but some types of business, particularly in the professions, may have a dispensation from this rule (Companies Act 1985, s 716). This same Act requires businesses that are not exempt from the rule and that have more than 20 partners to register as a company. A limited company can also be a partner in a partnership since it counts as a 'legal person'.

While it is not necessary for a partnership to have a formal written agreement, most partnerships tend to be formally enacted in a Deed of Partnership or Articles, since this makes it much easier to reduce uncertainty and to ascertain intentions when there is a written document to consult. Where this is not done, the Partnership Act 1890 lays down a minimum code, which governs the relationship between partners and which provides, among other things, for all partners to share equally in the capital and profits of the business and to contribute equally towards its losses.

In practice, where a Deed or Articles exist, these will invariably reflect differences in the relative status and contribution of individual partners. Senior partners will often have contributed more financially to the partnership and not unnaturally will expect to receive a higher proportion of the profits. Other arrangements – including membership, action on dissolution of the partnership, management responsibilities and rights, and the basis for allocating salaries – will be outlined in the partnership agreement and as such will provide the legal framework within which the enterprise exists and its co-owners operate.

Unlike the sole trader, where management responsibilities devolve on a single individual, partnerships permit the sharing of responsibilities and tasks, and it is common in a partnership for individuals to specialise to some degree in particular aspects of the organisation's work – as in the case of a legal or medical or veterinary practice. The fact that more than one person is involved in the ownership of the business tends to increase the amount of finance available to the organisation, thus permitting expansion to take place without the owners losing control of the enterprise. These two factors alone tend to make a partnership an attractive proposition for some would-be entrepreneurs, while for others the rules of their professional body – which often prohibits its members from forming a company – effectively provide for the establishment of this type of organisation.

On the downside, the sharing of decisions and responsibilities may represent a problem, particularly where partners are unable to agree over the direction the partnership should take or the amount to be reinvested in the business, unless such matters are clearly specified in a formal agreement. A more intractable problem is the existence of unlimited personal liability – a factor which may inhibit some individuals from considering this form of organisation, particularly given that the actions of any one partner are invariably binding on the other members of the business. To overcome this problem, many individuals, especially in manufacturing and trading, look to the limited company as the type of organisation that can combine the benefits of joint ownership and limited personal liability – a situation not necessarily always borne out in practice. It is to this type of business organisation that the discussion now turns.

Limited companies

In law a **company** is a corporate association having a legal identity in its own right (i.e. it is distinct from the people who own it, unlike in the case of a sole trader or partnership). This means that all property and other assets owned by the company belong to the company and not to its members (owners). By the same token, the personal assets of its members (the **shareholders**) do not normally belong to the business. In the event of insolvency, therefore, an individual's liability is limited to the value of shares invested in the business but which remain unpaid. One exception to this would be where a company's owners have given a personal guarantee to cover any loans they have obtained from a bank or other institution – a requirement for many small, private limited companies. Another occurs where a company is limited by guarantee rather than by shares, with its members' liability being limited to the amount they have undertaken to contribute to the assets in the event of the company being wound up. Companies of this type are normally non-profit-making organisations – such as professional, research or trade associations – and are much less common than companies limited by shares. Hence, in what follows, we concentrate on the latter as the dominant form of business organisation in the corporate sector of business.

Companies are essentially business organisations consisting of two or more individuals who have agreed to embark on a business venture and who have decided to seek corporate status rather than to form a partnership. Such status could derive from an Act of Parliament or a Royal Charter, but is almost always nowadays achieved through 'registration', the terms of which are laid down in the various Companies Acts. Under legislation, enacted in 1985, 1989 and 2006, individuals seeking to form a company are required to file numerous documents, including a **Memorandum of Association** and **Articles of Association**, with the Registrar of Companies. If satisfied, the Registrar will issue a Certificate of Incorporation, bringing the company into existence as a legal entity. As an alternative, the participants could buy a ready-formed company 'off the shelf', by approaching a company registration agent who specialises in company formations. In the UK, advertisements for ready-made companies appear regularly in magazines such as *Exchange and Mart* and *Dalton's Weekly*. They can also be found on eBay.

 web link   Companies House can be accessed at *www.companieshouse.gov.uk*

Information on how companies are created, run and wound up is contained in the 2006 Companies Act, which essentially consolidates all previous legislation and case law into one Act of Parliament. As this Act shows, under British law a distinction is made between public and private companies. **Public limited companies (PLCs)** – not to be confused with public corporations, which in the UK are state-owned businesses (see below) – are those limited companies which satisfy the conditions for being a PLC. These conditions require the company to have:

- a minimum of one shareholder (although two or more is normal);
- at least two directors;
- a minimum (at present) of £50,000 of issued share capital;
- the right to offer its shares (and debentures) for sale to the general public;

- a certificate from the Registrar of Companies verifying that the share capital requirements have been met; and
- a memorandum which states it to be a public company.

A company that meets these conditions must include the title 'public limited company' or 'PLC' in its name and is required to make full accounts available for public inspection. Any company unable or unwilling to meet these conditions is therefore, in the eyes of the law, a 'private limited company', normally signified by the term 'Limited' or 'Ltd'.

Like the public limited company, the **private limited company** must have a minimum of one shareholder, but its shares cannot be offered to the public at large, although it can offer them to individuals through its business contacts. This restriction on the sale of shares, and hence on their ability to raise considerable sums of money on the open market, normally ensures that most private companies are either small or medium sized, and are often family businesses operating in a relatively restricted market; there are, however, some notable exceptions to this general rule (e.g. Virgin Group). In contrast, public companies – many of which began life as private companies prior to 'going public' – often have many thousands, even millions, of owners (shareholders), some of whom may be other companies, and they normally operate on a national or international scale, producing products as diverse as computers, petrochemicals, cars and banking services. Despite being outnumbered by their private counterparts, public companies dwarf private companies in terms of their capital and other assets, and their collective influence on output, investment, employment and consumption in the economy is immense.

Both public and private companies act through their **company directors**. These are individuals chosen by a company's shareholders to manage its affairs and to make the important decisions concerning the direction the company should take (e.g. investment, market development, mergers, and so on). The appointment and powers of directors are outlined in the Articles of Association (the 'internal rules' of the organisation) and so long as the directors do not exceed their powers, the shareholders do not normally have the right to intervene in the day-to-day management of the company. Where directors exceed their authority or fail to indicate clearly that they are acting as an agent for the company, they become personally liable for any contracts they make. Equally, directors become personally liable if they continue to trade when the company is insolvent and they may be dismissed by a court if it considers that an individual is unfit to be a director in view of his or her past record (Company Directors Disqualification Act 1985).

The 2006 Act sets out in detail the statutory duties of company directors, including the duty to promote the success of the organisation, to exercise reasonable care, skill and diligence, and to give appropriate consideration to issues that go beyond the balance sheet. For example, directors of UK companies now have a duty to consider the impacts of their business operations on the environment and the community generally, and quoted public companies must report on issues of social and environmental responsibility as part of an expanded review of the business (see Chapter 9).

It is usual for a board of directors to have both a chairperson and a managing director, although some companies have appointed one person to both roles. The chairperson, who is elected by the other members of the board, is usually chosen because of their knowledge and experience of the business and their skill both internally in chairing board meetings and externally in representing the best interests of the organisation. As the public face of the company, the chairperson has an important role to play in establishing and maintaining a good public image and hence many large public companies like to appoint well-known public figures to this important position (e.g. former Cabinet ministers). In this case knowledge of the business is less important than the other attributes the individual might possess, most notably public visibility and familiarity, together with a network of contacts in government and in the business world.

The **managing director**, or chief executive (often Chief Executive Officer (CEO) in the United States), fulfils a pivotal role in the organisation, by forming the link between the board and the management team of senior executives. Central to this role is the need not only to interpret board decisions, but also to ensure that they are put into effect by establishing an appropriate structure of delegated responsibility and effective systems of reporting and control. This close contact with the day-to-day operations of the company places the appointed individual in a position of considerable authority and he or she will invariably be able to make important decisions without reference to the full board. This authority is enhanced where the managing director is also the person chairing the board of directors and/or is responsible for recommending individuals to serve as executive directors (i.e. those with functional responsibilities such as production, marketing, finance).

Like the managing director, most, if not all, **executive directors** will be full-time executives of the company, responsible for running a division or functional area within the framework laid down at board level. In contrast, other directors will be **non-executive directors** and are usually part-time appointees, chosen for a variety of reasons, including their knowledge, skills, contacts, influence, independence or previous experience. Non-executive directors should not be employed by or in business with the firm. Sometimes, a company might be required to appoint such a director at the wishes of a third party, such as an investment bank or hedge fund, which has agreed to fund a large capital injection and wishes to have representation on the board. In this case, the individual tends to act in an advisory capacity – particularly on matters of finance – and helps to provide the financing institution with a means of ensuring that any board decisions are in its interests.

In the UK, the role of company directors and senior executives has come under an increasing amount of public scrutiny, culminating in a number of enquiries into issues of power and pay. In the Cadbury Report (1992), a committee, with Sir Adrian Cadbury as chairperson, called for a non-statutory code of practice, which it wanted applied to all listed public companies. Under this code the committee recommended:

- a clear division of responsibilities at the head of a company to ensure that no individual had unfettered powers of decision (the managing director and chairperson should be separate);
- a greater role for non-executive directors;
- regular board meetings;
- restrictions on the contracts of executive directors;
- full disclosure of directors' total emoluments; and
- an audit committee dominated by non-executives.

The committee's stress on the important role of non-executive directors was also a theme taken up in the Greenbury Report (1995), which investigated the controversial topic of executive salaries in the wake of a number of highly publicised pay rises for senior company directors. Greenbury's recommendations included:

- full disclosure of directors' pay packages, including pensions;
- shareholder approval for any long-term bonus scheme;
- remuneration committees consisting entirely of non-executive directors;

- greater detail in the annual report on directors' pay, pensions and perks; and
- an end to payments for failure.

Greenbury was followed by a further investigation into corporate governance by a committee under the chairmanship of ICI Chairman Ronald Hampel. The Hampel Report (1998) advocated company self-regulation and called for greater shareholder responsibility by companies and increased standards of disclosure of information; it supported Cadbury's recommendation that the role of chairperson and chief executive should normally be separated. A year later, the Turnbull Report (1999) considered the issue of **corporate governance** and information disclosure from the perspective of risk management, arguing that companies need to take steps to manage and disclose corporate risks formally.

As far as the issue of non-executive directors was concerned, this was investigated further by the Higgs Committee, which was established in 2002 and which reported the following year. The committee's report set down a code of non-binding corporate guidelines regarding the role of non-executive directors on company boards. Like the Cadbury Report, Higgs recommended that the role of chairperson and chief executive should be kept separate and that the former should be independent, though not necessarily non-executive. As for non-executive directors, Higgs recommended that at least half the board should be independent and that non-executives should play key roles in areas such as strategy, performance, risk and the appointment and remuneration of executive directors. The latter issue, in particular, has been an area of considerable controversy in the UK in recent years and seems destined to remain so for some time (see the following mini case).

mini case   Companies under pressure

Public companies have to satisfy the conflicting demands of a range of stakeholder groups (see below), not least their shareholders, who expect the organisation to operate in their interest. On the whole, individual shareholders are usually relatively quiescent, leaving the strategic and day-to-day decisions to the organisation's directors and senior executives. As an increasing number of public companies have found, however, many shareholders are becoming more actively involved in corporate decisions which they believe affect their investments and have been willing to voice their feelings at shareholders' meetings and to the media. This is particularly true of large corporate investors.

In two previous editions of this book we reported on the rise of shareholder militancy at companies such as Daimler-Benz, Marks and Spencer and Exxon Mobil, with issues ranging from poor company performance and the firm's negative impact on the natural environment to executive remuneration and the combining of the roles of chairman and chief executive. Boardroom pay has continued to be a particular bone of contention in the UK (e.g. at Tesco, Sainsbury's, Burberry), with shareholders raising questions not only about the level of total rewards but also the often less than challenging performance targets set for directors when receiving bonuses and lucrative share options. To go some way towards addressing these concerns, the UK government introduced reforms in October 2013 – under the Enterprise and Regulatory Reform Act – which will require quoted companies to provide clearer information on the pay of top executives, to give shareholders a regular vote on company remuneration policy and to set out details on the non-financial aspects of the firm's operations, including its performance on human rights, greenhouse gas emissions and gender representation at senior levels. The aim of this aspect of the legislation is to make company decisions more transparent both to the firm's owners and to its other key stakeholders; this is seen as a central aspect of good corporate governance in the UK's larger businesses.

The issue of transparency applies equally to the question of the gender composition of major companies at senior levels, particularly top executives and board members. In 2010, for example, the Financial Reporting Council proposed a corporate governance code under which the UK's largest 350 companies would be required to hold annual re-elections for board members and appoint more women to board positions, calling upon them to explain to shareholders if these two developments did not occur. The following year the Davies Committee recommended that by 2015 the UK's largest businesses should have at least 25 per cent of boardroom positions occupied by women and called for more female representation in senior positions (e.g. in executive committees), although it stopped short of imposing a quota. The Hampton Alexander Review (which replaced Davies') set a goal of one-third of FTSE 350 company's boards to be female by 2020. In a potentially crucial development in late 2013, a number of UK fund managers warned that they would vote against the chairman of any FTSE 100 company who retained an all-male board by the 2015 deadline. This has only been tested recently with the company ConvaTec in 2017, when investor Aberdeen Asset Management voted in disapproval of ConvaTec's all-male board choices. On this occasion it did not have an impact on the board, though in the future the actions of investors might prove more influential than government goals.

Cooperatives

Consumer cooperative societies

Consumer societies are basically 'self-help' organisations which have their roots in the anti-capitalist sentiment that arose in mid-nineteenth-century Britain and which gave rise to a consumer cooperative movement dedicated to the provision of cheap, unadulterated food for its members and a share in its profits. Today this movement boasts a multibillion-pound turnover, a membership numbered in millions and an empire that includes thousands of food stores, numerous factories and farms, dairies, travel agencies, opticians, funeral parlours, an insurance company, and property and development business.

Taken together, these activities ensure that the Co-operative Group remains the world's largest consumer cooperative and a powerful force in British retailing, although it has recently (October 2013) lost control of its banking arm to a number of hedge funds. Survey evidence indicates that it has been one of the UK's most trusted and ethical brand names; this may change to some degree as a result of recent developments at the Co-operative Bank.

web link   The Co-operative Group's website address is *www.co-operative.coop*

Although the cooperative societies, like companies, are registered and incorporated bodies – in this case under the Industrial and Provident Societies Act – they are quite distinct trading organisations. These societies belong to their members (i.e. invariably customers who have purchased a share in the society), who elect Area Committees to oversee trading areas. These committees have annual elections and meetings for all members and these in turn appoint members to regional boards and elect individual member directors to the Group Board. The Group Board also includes directors of corporate members who are representatives of other societies; individual stores may also have member forums. Any profits from the Group's activities are supposed to benefit the members. Originally this took the form of a cash dividend paid to members in relation to their purchases, but this was subsequently replaced either by trading stamps or by investment in areas felt to benefit the consumer (e.g. lower prices, higher-quality products, modern shops, and so on) and/or the local community (e.g. charitable donations, sponsorship). The twice-yearly cash dividend was, however, reintroduced in 2006, a move which saw a significant increase in the membership of the organisation.

The societies differ in other ways from standard companies. For a start, shares are not quoted on the stock exchange and members are restricted in the number of shares they can purchase and in the method of disposal. Not having access to cheap sources of capital on the stock market, cooperatives rely heavily on retained surpluses and on loan finance, and the latter places a heavy burden on the societies when interest rates are high. The movement's democratic principles also impinge on its operations and this has often been a bone of contention as members have complained about their increasing remoteness from decision-making centres. Some societies have responded by encouraging the development of locally elected committees to act in an advisory or consultative capacity to the society's board of directors and it looks likely that others will be forced to consider similar means of increasing member participation, which remains limited.

The movement's historical links with the British Labour Party are also worth noting and a number of parliamentary candidates are normally sponsored at general elections. These links, however, have tended to become slightly looser in recent years, although the movement still contributes to Labour Party funds and continues to lobby politicians at both national and local levels. It is also active in seeking to influence public opinion and, in this, claims to be responding to customer demands for greater social and corporate responsibility. Among its initiatives are the establishment of a customer's charter (by the Co-operative Bank) and the decision to review both its investments and the individuals and organisations it does business with, to ascertain that they are acceptable from an ethical point of view.

Workers' cooperatives

In the UK, **workers' cooperatives** are found in a wide range of industries, including manufacturing, building and construction, engineering, catering and retailing. They are particularly prevalent in printing, clothing and wholefoods, and some have been in existence for more than a century. The majority, however, are of fairly recent origin, having been part of the growth in the number of small firms which occurred in the 1980s.

As the name suggests, a workers' cooperative is a business in which the ownership and control of the assets are in the hands of the people working in it, having agreed to establish the enterprise and to share the risk for mutual benefit. Rather than form a standard partnership, the individuals involved normally register the business as a friendly society under the Industrial and Provident Societies Acts 1965–78, or seek incorporation as a private limited company under the Companies Act 1985. In the case of the former, seven members are required to form a cooperative, while the latter requires only two. In practice, a minimum of three or four members tends to be the norm and some cooperatives may have several hundred participants, frequently people who have been made redundant by their employers and who are keen to keep the business going.

The central principles of the movement – democracy, open membership, social responsibility, mutual cooperation and trust – help to differentiate the cooperative from other forms of business organisation and govern both the formation and operation of this type of enterprise. Every employee may be a member of the organisation and every member owns one share in the business, with every share carrying an equal voting right. Any surpluses are shared by democratic agreement and this is normally done on an equitable basis, reflecting, for example, the amount of time and effort an individual puts into the business. Other decisions, too, are taken jointly by the members and the emphasis tends to be on the quality of goods or services provided and on creating a favourable working environment, rather than on the pursuit of profits – although the latter cannot be ignored if the organisation is to survive. A workers' cooperative tends to focus on people and on the relationship between them, stressing the cooperative and communal traditions associated with its origins, rather than the more conflictual and competitive aspects inherent in other forms of industrial organisation.

Despite these apparent attractions, workers' cooperatives have never been as popular in the UK as in other parts of the world (e.g. France, Spain, Italy, Israel), although a substantial increase occurred in the number of cooperatives in the 1980s, largely as a result of growing unemployment, overt support across the political spectrum and the establishment of a system to encourage and promote the cooperative ideal (e.g. Co-operative Development Agencies). More recently, however, their fortunes have tended to decline, as employee shareholding and profit schemes (ESOPs) have grown in popularity. It seems unlikely that workers' cooperatives will ever form the basis of a strong third sector in the British economy, between the profit-oriented firms in the private sector and the nationalised and municipal undertakings in the public sector.

Social enterprises

Some businesses may be set up with the specific intention of helping people or the community; these are usually referred to as **social enterprises** and can take a variety of legal forms, including those identified above. Alternatively, the individuals or groups establishing a social enterprise may opt to set up a **Charitable Incorporated Organisation (CIO)** or **Community Interest Company (CIC)** in order to achieve their objectives. CIOs are the new legal form for a charitable organisation, registered by the Charity Commission as an incorporated body with particular advantages (e.g. tax exemptions) but not a company as such in the legal sense of the word. CICs, in contrast, are a special type of company in which the assets and the profits of the business are used for public good in areas such as fair trade, the environment, community support and local regeneration. While such organisations do not have the tax advantages available for CIOs, they are generally more lightly regulated and are regarded as a more flexible model for achieving public benefits.

Public sector business organisations in the UK

Public sector organisations come in a variety of forms. These include:

- central government departments (e.g. Department for Business, Innovation and Skills);
- local authorities (e.g. Lancashire County Council);
- regional bodies (e.g. the former Regional Development Agencies);
- non-departmental public bodies or quangos (e.g. the Arts Council);
- central government trading organisations (e.g. The Stationery Office);
- public corporations and nationalised industries (e.g. the BBC).

Some of these were discussed in Chapter 4, which examined the political environment, and numerous other references to the influence of government on business activity can be found throughout the book. We discuss below public sector organisations which most closely approximate businesses in the private sector, namely public corporations and municipal enterprises. An examination of the transfer of many of these public sector bodies to the private sector – usually termed 'privatisation' – can be found in Chapter 17.

Public corporations

Private sector business organisations are owned by private individuals and groups who have chosen to invest in some form of business enterprise, usually with a view to personal gain. The state can also own assets in various forms, which it uses to provide a range of goods and services felt to be of benefit to its citizens, even if this provision involves the state in a loss. Many of these services are provided directly through government departments (e.g. social security benefits) or through bodies operating under delegated authority from central government (e.g. local authorities, health authorities). Others are the responsibility of state-owned industrial and commercial undertakings, specially created for a variety of reasons and often taking the form of a **public corporation**. These state corporations or government-owned enterprises are an important part of the public sector of the economy and have contributed significantly to national output, employment and investment. Their numbers have declined substantially, however, following the wide-scale privatisation of state industries which occurred in the 1980s, a process which continued through the 1990s and beyond with the sale of corporations such as British Coal, British Rail, British Energy and Royal Mail (see Chapter 17).

Public corporations are statutory bodies, incorporated (predominantly) by special Act of Parliament and, like companies, they have a separate legal identity from the individuals who own them and run them. The statute setting up the corporation identifies the powers, duties and responsibilities of the organisation and its relationship with the government department which oversees its operations. In the past these operations have ranged from providing a variety of national and international postal services (the Post Office), to the provision of entertainment (the BBC), an energy source (British Coal) and a national rail network (British Rail). Where such provision involves the organisation in a considerable degree of direct contact with its customers, from whom it derives most of its revenue, the corporation tends to be called a **nationalised industry**. In reality, of course, the public corporation is the legal form through which the industry is both owned and run and every corporation is to some degree unique in structure as well as in functions.

As organisations largely financed as well as owned by the state, public corporations are required to be publicly accountable and hence they invariably operate under the purview of a 'sponsoring' government department, the head of which (the Secretary of State) appoints a board of management to run the organisation. This board tends to exercise a considerable degree of autonomy in day-to-day decisions and operates largely free from political interference on most matters of a routine nature. The organisation's strategic objectives, however, and important questions concerning reorganisation or investment, would have to be agreed with the sponsoring department, as would the corporation's performance targets and its external financing limits.

The link between the corporation and its supervising ministry provides the means through which Parliament can oversee the work of the organisation and permits ordinary Members of Parliament to seek information and explanation through question time, through debates and through the select committee system. Additionally, under the Competition Act 1980, nationalised industries can be subject to investigation by the Competition Commission (see Chapter 17), and this too presents opportunities for further parliamentary discussion and debate, as well as for government action. Public accountability has also, historically, been provided through the establishment of industry-specific Consumers' or Consultative Councils, which were set up to consider complaints from customers and to advise both the board and the department concerned of public attitudes to the organisation's performance and to other aspects of its operations (e.g. pricing).

It is interesting to note that mechanisms for public accountability and state regulation have been retained to some degree even where public utilities have been privatised (i.e. turned into public limited companies). Industries such as gas, electricity, water and telecommunications are watched over by regulatory bodies, which are designed to protect the interests of consumers, particularly with regard to pricing and the standard of service provided. Ofgas, for instance, which used to regulate British Gas, monitored gas supply charges to ensure that they reasonably reflected input costs, and these charges could be altered by the regulator if they were seen to be excessive. Similarly, in the case of non-gas services, such as maintenance, the legislation privatising the industry allowed prices to be raised only to a prescribed maximum, to ensure that the organisation was not able to take full advantage of its monopoly power. The regulator of the gas market is now Ofgem – see Chapter 17.

An additional source of government influence has come through its ownership of a **golden share** in a privatised state industry, which effectively gives the government a veto in certain vital areas of decision-making. This notional shareholding – which is written into the privatisation legislation – usually lasts for a number of years and can be used to protect a newly privatised business from a hostile takeover, particularly by foreign companies or individuals. Ultimately, however, the expectation is that this veto power will be relinquished and the organisation concerned will become subject to the full effects of the market. Rulings in the European courts over the last decade – against the use of golden shares by the French, German, Italian, Portuguese, Belgian, Spanish and UK governments – indicate that the demise of this mechanism may be imminent.

The existence of a golden share should not be equated with the decision by government to retain (or purchase) a significant proportion of issued shares in a privatised (or already private) business organisation, whether as an investment and/or future source of revenue, or as a means of supporting an organisation or of exerting influence in a particular industry or sector. Nor should it be confused with government schemes to attract private funds into existing state enterprises, by allowing them to achieve notional company status in order to overcome Treasury restrictions on borrowing imposed on public bodies. In the latter case, which often involves a limited share issue, the government retains full control of the organisation by owning all (or the vast majority) of the shares – as in the case of Consignia (formerly known as the Post Office). In March 2001, Consignia was incorporated as a government-owned public company. This change in legal status allowed the company more freedom to borrow and invest in the business, to make acquisitions and to enter into joint ventures and to expand internationally. The name Consignia was subsequently dropped in favour of the brand name Royal Mail. This organisation has recently been privatised, floating on the stock exchange in October 2013, with the last remaining shares held by the public sector in 2015. There have been a large number of other UK public businesses privatised over the last decade, including the public stake of the Channel Tunnel train company Eurostar and betting company Totepool.

Municipal enterprises

UK local authorities have a long history of involvement in business activity. In part this is a function of their role as central providers of public services (e.g. education, housing, roads, social services) and of their increasing involvement in supporting local economic development initiatives (see Chapter 13). But their activities have also traditionally involved the provision of a range of marketable goods and services, not required by law but provided voluntarily by a local authority and often in direct competition with the private sector (e.g. theatres, leisure services, museums). Usually such provision has taken place under the aegis of a local authority department, which appoints staff who are answerable to the council and to its committees through the department's chief officer and its elected head. Increasingly, though, local authorities have turned to other organisational arrangements – including the establishment of companies and trusts – in order to separate some of these activities from the rest of their responsibilities and to create a means through which private investment in the enterprise can occur. Under UK official definitions, some of these organisations are classified as public corporations, although municipal enterprises is arguably a more meaningful concept.

A good example of municipal enterprise is the local-authority-controlled airport, which is normally the responsibility of a number of local authorities which operate through a joint board, representing the interests of the participating district councils (e.g. Manchester International Airport). Since the Airports Act 1986, local authorities with airports have been required to create a limited company in which their joint assets are vested and which appoints a board of directors to run the enterprise. Like other limited companies, the organisation can, if appropriate, seek private capital and must publish annual accounts, including a profit and loss statement. It can also be privatised relatively easily if the local authorities involved decide to relinquish ownership (e.g. East Midlands, Stansted and Manchester Airports are part of the Manchester Airports Group).

Such developments, which have parallels in other parts of the public sector, can be seen to have had at least four benefits:

1   They have provided a degree of autonomy from local authority control that is seen to be beneficial in a competitive trading environment.
2   They have given access to market funds by the establishment of a legal structure that is not fully subject to central government restrictions on local authority borrowing.

3   They helped local authority organisations to compete more effectively under the now defunct system of compulsory competitive tendering (CCT), by removing or reducing charges for departmental overheads that are applied under the normal arrangements.

4   They have provided a vehicle for further private investment, including via a joint venture, and for ultimate privatisation of the service.

Given these benefits and the current fashion for privatisation, there is little doubt that they will become an increasing feature of municipal enterprise in the foreseeable future. That said, local authorities are restricted in their degree of ownership of companies following the passage of the 1990 Local Government and Housing Act.

Business organisations in mainland Europe

Sole traders, partnerships, cooperatives and limited companies are to be found throughout Europe and beyond, and in many cases their legal structure is similar to that of their British counterparts. Where differences occur, these are often a reflection of historical and cultural factors, which find expression in custom and practice as well as in law. Examples of some of these differences are contained in the brief discussions below, which focus on France, Germany, Denmark and Portugal. You might recognise some of the abbreviations below from items of spending that show up on your credit card or bank statements; they are where large companies are often registered in other countries.

France

Numerically, the French economy is dominated by very small businesses (i.e. fewer than 10 employees), the majority of which are sole traders. As in the UK, these are enterprises managed and operated by the owners, with a husband and wife often assuming joint responsibility for the business. Formal requirements in this type of organisation tend to be few, although individuals as well as companies engaging in a commercial business are required to register before trading officially begins. Since this process is relatively simple and there are no minimum capital requirements or significant reporting obligations, sole traderships tend to be preferred by the vast majority of individuals seeking to start a business and they are particularly prevalent in the service sector. They carry, however, unlimited personal liability for the owner, whose personal assets are at risk in the event of business failure.

Most of the remaining French business organisations are limited companies, many of which are Petites et Moyennes Entreprises (PMEs) – small and medium enterprises – employing between 10 and 250 employees. These companies come in a variety of legal forms, but two in particular have tended to predominate: the Société à Responsabilité Limitée (SARL) and the Société Anonyme (SA). A further company form, the Société Par Actions Simplifée, was created by statute in 1994 and combines the legal status of a corporation with the flexibility of a partnership.

The SARL has generally been the form preferred by smaller companies, whose owners wish to retain close control of the organisation; hence many of them are family businesses – an important feature of the private sector in France. This type of enterprise can now be established with a minimum capital of €1, cannot issue shares to the general public, has restrictions on the transfer of shares and is run by individuals appointed by the shareholders – usually the shareholders themselves and/or relatives. These various restrictions help to ensure that the owner–managers remain dominant in the organisation and the appointed head of the company will invariably be the most important decision-maker. They also provide the organisation with a defence against hostile takeover, particularly by overseas companies looking for a French subsidiary in order to avoid the special rules which apply to branches and agencies (e.g. a foreign parent company has unlimited liability for the debts of its branch or agency, since these do not have a separate legal identity).

The SA is the legal form normally chosen by larger companies seeking access to substantial amounts of capital. In the case of a privately owned company, the minimum share capital requirement is now only €1. Where capital assets are substantial, this tends to ensure that financial institutions are large shareholders in SAs and many of them have interests in a wide range of enterprises which they often manage through a holding company (see below). One advantage of this arrangement is that it provides the financial institution with a means of managing its investments and of exerting influence over companies in which it has a large minority stake. Another is that it provides a means of defending French companies from hostile takeovers and hence small and medium enterprises often seek backing from holding companies to help fend off foreign predators.

As in the UK, the legal basis of the SA provides for a clear distinction between the roles of the owners (the shareholders) and the salaried employees, and it is the former who appoint the company's board of directors. In smaller companies, the chairperson and managing director are often the same person and many smaller French companies continue to have extremely strong central control, often by the head of the owning family. In larger companies, the two roles are normally separated, with the managing director assuming responsibility for the day-to-day operations of the enterprise and forming the link between the board and the company's senior executives and managers, some of whom may have considerable delegated authority.

It is worth noting that in companies with more than 50 employees, there is a legal requirement to have elected work councils, and workers' delegates have the right to attend board meetings as observers and to be consulted on matters affecting working conditions. In companies with more than 10 employees, workers have the right to elect representatives to look after their interests and regular meetings have to take place between management and workers, over and above the obligation of employers to negotiate annually on pay and conditions. Despite these arrangements and the legal right for unions to organise on a company's premises, trade union membership – outside state-run companies – remains low and hence union influence tends to be limited.

Germany

All major forms of business organisation are to be found in Germany, but it is the limited company that is of particular interest. Some of these are of relatively recent origin, having formerly been East German state-owned enterprises which have undergone privatisation following reunification of the country.

In numerical terms it is the private limited company (Gesellschaft mit beschränkter Haftung – GmbH) that predominates and which is the form chosen by most foreign companies seeking to establish an enterprise in Germany. As in the UK, this type of organisation has to be registered with the authorities and its founding members must prepare Articles of Association for signature by a public notary. The Articles include information on the purpose of the business, the amount of capital subscribed, the members' subscriptions and obligations, and the company's name and registered address. Once the registration process is complete – usually a matter of a few days – the personal liability of the members becomes limited to the amount invested in the business. Currently, the minimum amount of subscribed share capital required for registration is €25,000, half of which must be paid by the company itself.

Large numbers of GmbHs are owned and run by German families, with the banks often playing an influential role as guarantors of part of the initial capital and as primary sources of loan finance. As in France, this pattern of ownership makes hostile takeovers less likely, as well as ensuring that the management of the enterprise remains in the hands of the owners. Significantly, the management of a proposed GmbH is subject to quality control, being required to prove that it is qualified for the task prior to trading. This requirement stands in stark contrast to arrangements in the UK, where no such guarantees are needed, other than those implicit in a bank's decisions to help finance a proposed venture on the basis of a business plan.

The procedures for establishing other types of business organisation are similar to those of the GmbH, although in the case of the public limited company (Aktiengesellschaft – AG), the current minimum amount of capital required at start-up is €50,000. Unlike British companies, the AG usually consists of two boards of directors, one of which (the supervisory board) decides on longer-term strategy, while the other (the managing board) concentrates on more immediate policy issues, often of an operational kind. Normally half the members of the supervisory board (Aufsichtrat) are elected by shareholders, while the other half are employees elected by the workforce, and it is the responsibility of the board to protect the interests of employees as well as shareholders.

Such worker representation at senior levels is an important element of the German system of business organisation and even in smaller enterprises workers have the right to establish works councils and to be consulted on social and personnel issues and on strategic decisions. Equally, all employees have a constitutional right to belong to a trade union – most of which are organised by industry rather than by craft or occupation, as is largely the case in the UK. Consequently, German companies typically negotiate with only one union, usually in an atmosphere that stresses consensus and an identity of social and economic interests, rather than conflict and confrontation.

Corporate finance is another area in which German experience differs from that in the UK, although the situation has changed to some degree in recent years. Historically, in the UK a substantial amount of company finance has been raised through the stock market and this is also the case in the United States and Japan. In Germany (and for that matter in France, Italy and Spain), the banks and a number of other special credit institutions play a dominant role, with bank loans far outstripping joint-stock financing as a source of long-term capital. Traditionally, German banks have been willing to take a longer-term view of their investment, even at the expense of short-term profits and dividends, and this has benefited German companies seeking to expand their operations. In return, the banks have tended to exert a considerable amount of influence in the boardrooms of many German companies, usually by providing a substantial number of members of a company's supervisory board, including the chairperson.

Denmark

Denmark, like France, is a country whose economy is dominated by small businesses, many of which are sole traders. As in other countries, there are very few regulations governing the establishment of this type of enterprise, other than the need to register for VAT if turnover exceeds a predetermined limit and to meet taxation and social security requirements. In keeping with practice throughout Europe and beyond, sole traders have unlimited personal liability and this imposes a considerable burden on the organisation's owner and family, who often run the business jointly. The same conditions also apply in the case of Danish partnerships – whether formal or informal – with the joint owners having full and unlimited liability for all debts accruing to the organisation.

Limited companies in Denmark also reflect practice elsewhere, being required to register under the Companies Act and having a legal existence separate from the owners and employees. Three main types of limited liability company can be distinguished:

1 The Anpartselskaber (ApS), which is a private joint-stock company, often run by a family and owned and controlled by a handful of individuals, one of whom may simultaneously occupy the roles of main owner, chairperson and managing director. Many of these companies began life as sole traders, but for reasons of taxation and liability have registered as an ApS.

2 The Aktieselskaber (A/S), which is a quoted or (more regularly) unquoted public limited company, subject essentially to the same regulations as the ApS, but having a much larger minimum capital requirement on registration. A large number of A/S companies are still small businesses, run by family members who wish to retain control of the enterprise as an increase in assets occurs.

3 The AMBA is a special kind of limited company – in essence a tax-free cooperative with its own regulations. Many of these companies have grown over the years through merger and acquisition and some of them belong to larger Danish companies and employ a substantial number of workers. They tend to be concentrated in farm-related products, but can also be found in the service sector, especially wholesaling and retailing.

Portugal

A brief look at Portuguese business organisations reveals a range of legal structures that includes sole traders, joint ventures, complementary groups, unlimited companies, limited partnerships, and public and private limited companies. In the case of the latter, capital requirements tend to be an important distinguishing feature, with the public limited company or corporation (Sociedade Anonima – SA) having a much larger minimum capital requirement than the private company (Sociedade Por Quotas or Limitada – LDA) as in other countries.

The public sector in mainland Europe

Given the number of countries involved, it is impossible to survey the whole of the public sector in the rest of Europe and beyond. Students with an interest in this area are encouraged to read further and to consult the various specialist sources of information covering the countries they wish to investigate. A number of general points, however, are worthy of note:

1   Public sector business organisations can be found in all countries and invariably exist because of the decision by the state to establish a particular organisation under state ownership and control, or to nationalise an existing private business (or industry).

2   In some countries (e.g. France, Greece, Portugal) the state has traditionally played an important role in business and still controls some key sectors of the economy.

3   State involvement in business often includes significant shareholdings in a number of large enterprises, not only by the national government but also by regional and/or local government (e.g. in Germany).

4   State intervention often occurs in organisations or industries that can be deemed 'problematic' (e.g. in Greece).

5   Privatisation of state-owned enterprises has occurred throughout Europe and in other parts of the world. In the former East Germany most of the state-owned companies have been transferred to private ownership, by turning them initially into trusts which became the vehicle for privatisation and/or joint ventures. Similarly in Portugal, the wholesale nationalisation of the economy after the 1974 Revolution has been reversed and the government is committed to a phased programme of privatisation, involving employees and small investors as well as large national and international organisations (see also Chapter 17 for a further discussion). Other European countries, too, have faced pressures to reduce the size of the public sector (e.g. Greece), particularly in response to the global financial crisis and its aftermath.

This latter point serves to re-emphasise that the business environment is subject to change over time and the fashions of today may tomorrow become things of the past. This fluctuating environment is as applicable to the public sector as it is to the private sector of the economy.

Legal structure: some implications

For businesses in the private sector, the choice of legal structure has important implications. Among the factors the aspiring entrepreneur has to take into account when deciding what form of business enterprise to establish are:

- the degree of personal liability;
- the willingness to share decision-making powers and risks;
- the costs of establishing the business;
- the legal requirements concerning the provision of public information;
- the taxation position;
- commercial needs, including access to capital; and
- business continuity.

For some, retaining personal control will be the main requirement, even at the risk of facing unlimited personal liability and reducing the opportunities for expansion. For others, the desire to limit personal liability and to provide increased capital for growth will dictate that the owner seeks corporate status, even if this necessitates sharing decision-making powers and may ultimately result in a loss of ownership and/or control of the enterprise.

This link between an organisation's legal structure and its subsequent operations can be illustrated by examining three important facets of organisational life: the organisation's objectives, its sources of finance and its stakeholders. As the analysis below illustrates, in each of these areas, significant differences occur between alternative forms of business organisation, both *within* the private sector and *between* the state and non-state sectors of the economy. In some cases, these differences can be attributed directly to the restraints (or opportunities) faced by an organisation as a result of its legal status, suggesting that the legal basis of the enterprise conditions its operations. In other cases operational considerations tend to dictate the organisation's legal form, indicating that these are as much a cause of its legal status as a result of it – a point well illustrated by the workers' cooperative and the public corporation.

Organisational objectives

All business organisations pursue a range of objectives and these may vary to some degree over time. New private sector businesses are likely to be concerned initially with survival and with establishing a position in the marketplace, with profitability and growth seen as less important in the short term. Most well-established businesses will tend to regard profits and growth as key objectives and may see them as a means towards further ends, including market domination, maximising sales revenue and/or minimising operating costs.

Organisational objectives are also conditioned by the firm's legal structure. In sole traders, partnerships and some limited companies, control of the enterprise rests in the hands of the entrepreneur(s) and hence organisational goals will tend to coincide with the personal goals of the owner(s), whatever the point in the organisation's life cycle. In public companies, however – where ownership tends to be separated from control – the goals of the owners (shareholders) may not always correspond with those of the directors and senior managers who run the organisation, particularly when the latter are pursuing personal goals to enhance their own organisational position, status and/or rewards.

The possibility of goal conflict also occurs where an individual company becomes a subsidiary of another organisation, whether by agreement or as a result of a takeover battle. This parent–subsidiary relationship may take the form of a holding company which is specially created to purchase a majority (sometimes all) of the shares in other companies, some of which may operate as holding companies themselves. Thus, while the individual subsidiaries may retain their legal and commercial identities and may operate as individual units, they will tend to be controlled by a central organisation which may exercise a considerable degree of influence over the objectives to be pursued by each of its subsidiaries. It is not inconceivable that some parts of the group may be required to make a loss on paper, particularly when there are tax advantages to be gained by the group as a whole from doing so.

Workers' cooperatives and public corporations provide further evidence of the relationship between an organisation's legal status and its primary objectives. In the case of the former, the establishment of the enterprise invariably reflects a desire on the part of its members to create an organisation which emphasises social goals (e.g. democracy, cooperation, job creation, mutual trust) rather than the pursuit of profits – hence the choice of the 'cooperative' form. Similarly, in the case of the public corporation, a decision by government to establish an entity which operates in the interests of the public at large (or 'national interest') favours the creation of a state-owned and controlled organisation, with goals laid down by politicians and generally couched in social and financial terms (e.g. return on assets, reinvestment, job creation) rather than in terms of profit maximisation.

This apparent dichotomy between the profit motive of the private sector and the broader socio-economic goals of public bodies has, however, become less clear cut over the last decade, as an increasing number of state-owned organisations have been 'prepared' for privatisation and successive governments have sought to bring private money into public projects by creating public/private partnerships. Equally, in other parts of the public sector – including the health service and local government – increasing stress is being laid on 'best value' and on operating within budgets – concepts that are familiar to businesses in the private sector. While it is not inconceivable that a change in government could reverse this trend, current evidence suggests that a shift in cultural attitudes has occurred and public bodies can no longer rely on unconditional government support for their activities. If this is the case, further convergence is likely to occur between state and privately owned bodies, with the former moving towards the latter rather than vice versa.

Finance

Business organisations finance their activities in a variety of ways and from a range of sources. Methods include reinvesting profits, borrowing, trade credit and issuing shares and debentures. Sources include the banks and other financial institutions, individual investors and governments, as well as contributions from the organisation's original owners. A detailed discussion of business finance can be found in Chapter 11.

In the context of this chapter it is appropriate to make a number of observations about the topic as it relates generally to the business environment:

1   All organisations tend to fund their activities from both internal (e.g. owner's capital, reinvested profits) and external sources (e.g. bank borrowing, sale of shares).
2   Financing may be short term, medium term or longer term, and the methods and sources of funding chosen will reflect the time period concerned (e.g. bank borrowing on overdraft tends to be short term and generally needed for immediate use).
3   Funds raised from external sources inevitably involve the organisation in certain obligations (e.g. repayment of loans with interest, personal guarantees, paying dividends) and these will act as a constraint on the organisation at some future date.
4   The relationship between owner's capital and borrowed funds – usually described as an organisation's **gearing** – can influence a firm's activities and prospects in a variety of ways (e.g. high-geared firms with a large element of borrowed funds will be adversely affected if interest rates are high).
5   Generally speaking, as organisations become larger, many more external sources and methods of funding become available and utilising these can have implications for the structure, ownership and conduct of the organisation.

This latter point is perhaps best illustrated by comparing sole traders and partnerships with limited companies. In the case of the former, as unincorporated entities neither the sole trader nor the partnership can issue shares (or debentures) and hence their access to large amounts of external capital is restricted by law. Companies have no such restrictions – other than those which help to differentiate a private company from a public one – and consequently they are able to raise larger amounts by inviting individuals (and organisations) to subscribe for shares. Where a company is publicly quoted on the stock market, the amounts raised in this way can be very large indeed and the resultant organisation may have millions of owners who change on a regular basis as shares are traded on the second-hand market.

Organisations that decide to acquire corporate status in order to raise funds for expansion (or for some other purposes) become owned by their shareholders, who may be the original owners or may be individual and institutional investors holding equity predominantly as an investment and with little, if any, long-term commitment to the organisation they own. As indicated above, in the latter case, a separation tends to occur between the roles of owner (shareholder) and controller (director) and this can lead to the possibility of conflicting aims and objectives or differences in opinion over priorities within the enterprise – a problem discussed in more detail below under 'Stakeholders'.

A further illustration of the relationship between an organisation's legal structure and its ability to raise finance is provided by the public corporation. In this case, as a public body accountable to Parliament and the public via government, the public corporation is normally required to operate within a financial context largely controlled by the government and this will be conditioned by the government's overall fiscal policy, including its attitude to the size of the public deficit. One aspect of this context in the UK in recent decades has been the establishment of external financing limits (EFLs) for each nationalised industry, arrived at by negotiation between the government and the board running the public corporation, and used as a means of restraining monetary growth and hence the size of the public debt. Unfortunately this has also tended to prevent the more financially sound corporations, such as British Telecom before privatisation, from borrowing externally on a scale necessary to develop their business – a restriction that tends to disappear when the corporation becomes a fully fledged public company, either through privatisation or by some other means.

Stakeholders

All organisations have **stakeholders**; these are individuals and/or groups who are affected by or affect the performance of the organisation in which they have an interest. There is no set list of an organisation's stakeholders; they are determined by the context of this individual business, but typically they would include employees, managers, creditors, suppliers, shareholders (if appropriate) and society at large. As Table 10.1 illustrates, an organisation's stakeholders have a variety of interests which range from the pursuit of private gain to the more nebulous idea of achieving public benefit. Sometimes these interests will clash, for example when managers seek to improve the organisation's cash flow by refusing to pay suppliers' bills on time. On other occasions, the interests of different stakeholders may coincide, as when managers plan for growth in the organisation and in doing so provide greater job security for employees and enhanced dividends for investors.

Table 10.1 Organisational stakeholders and their interests

Types of stakeholder	Possible principal interests
Employees	Wage levels; working conditions; job security; personal development
Managers	Job security; status; personal power; organisational profitability; growth of the organisation
Shareholders	Market value of the investment; dividends; security of investment; liquidity of investment
Creditors	Security of loan; interest on loan; liquidity of investment
Suppliers	Security of contract; regular payment; growth of organisation; market development
Society	Safe products; environmental sensitivity; equal opportunities; avoidance of discrimination

The legal structure of an organisation has an impact not only on the type of stakeholders involved, but also to a large degree on how their interests are represented. In sole traders, partnerships and smaller private companies, the coincidence of ownership and control limits the number of potential clashes of interest, given that objectives are set by and decisions taken by the firm's owner–manager(s). In larger companies, and, in particular, public limited companies, the division between ownership and control means that the controllers have the responsibility of representing the interests of the organisation's shareholders and creditors and, as suggested above, their priorities and goals may not always correspond.

A similar situation occurs in public sector organisations, where the interest of taxpayers (or ratepayers) is represented both by government and by those individuals chosen by government to run the organisation. In this case, it is worth recalling that the broader strategic objectives of the enterprise and the big decisions concerning policy, finance and investment tend to be taken by politicians, operating with advice from their officials (e.g. civil servants, local government officers) and within the context of the government's overall economic and social policies. The organisation's board of management and its senior executives and managers are mainly responsible for the day-to-day operations of the business, although the board and the person chairing it would normally play a key role in shaping overall objectives and decisions, through regular discussions with government and its officials.

One important way in which public sector organisations differ from their private sector counterparts is in the sanctions available to particular groups of stakeholders who feel that the organisation is not representing their best interests. Shareholders in a company could withdraw financial support for a firm whose directors consistently disregard their interests or take decisions which threaten the security and/or value of their investment, and the possibility of such a reaction normally guarantees that the board pays due attention to the needs of this important group of stakeholders. The taxpayer and ratepayer have no equivalent sanction and in the short term must rely heavily on the government and its agencies or, if possible, their power as consumers to represent their interest vis-à-vis the organisation. Longer term, of course, the public has the sanction of the ballot box, although it seems highly unlikely that the performance of state enterprises would be a key factor in determining the outcome of general or local elections.

The relative absence of market sanctions facing state-owned organisations has meant that the public has had to rely on a range of formal institutions (e.g. parliamentary scrutiny committees, consumer consultative bodies, the audit authorities) and on the media to protect its interest in areas such as funding, pricing and quality of service provided. As these organisations are returned to the private sector, the expectation is that the sanctions imposed by the free market will once again operate and shareholders in privatised utilities will be protected like any other group of shareholders in a privately owned enterprise. To what extent this will occur in practice is open to question, while the newly privatised public corporations face little, if any, competition. Government, it seems, prefers to hedge its bets on this question, at least in the short term – hence the establishment of regulators with powers of investigation into performance and some degree of control over pricing.

Franchising, licensing and joint ventures

To complete this review of the legal structure of business organisations, it is useful to consider three developments which have a legal aspect: franchising, licensing and joint ventures. All three may be seen as a means of carrying out a business venture in a way that reduces some of the risks normally faced by the entrepreneur.

Franchising

Franchising, which has grown significantly in recent years, is an arrangement where one party (the franchiser) sells the right to another party (the franchisee) to market its product or service, in effect to use its business model. In terms of their legal status the parties involved could be any of the forms described above, but in practice it is usually the case that the franchiser is a company while the franchisee tends to be a sole trader or partnership. Both parties in law have a separate legal identity, but the nature of the contract between them makes their relationship interdependent and this has important implications for the operation of the franchise.

Franchise arrangements come in a variety of forms. Probably the best known is the 'business format franchise' (or 'trade name franchise') under which the franchiser agrees to allow the franchisee to sell the product or service with the help of a franchise package which contains all the elements needed to set up and run a business at a profit. These would typically include the brand name, any associated supplies, promotional material and other forms of support and assistance. In return the franchisee usually pays an initial sum or fee for the use of the service and its various elements, remits royalties based on sales and/or profits, agrees to make a contribution for consultancy, training and promotion, and undertakes to maintain standards. Subway, Kentucky Fried Chicken, Burger King and Dynarod are examples of this type of franchise.

Other forms include manufacturer/retailer franchises (e.g. car dealers), manufacturer/wholesaler franchises (e.g. Coca-Cola, Pepsi) and wholesaler/retailer franchises (e.g. Spar and Mace). It is estimated by the industry's trade body – the British Franchise Association – that, in retailing alone, franchising accounts for more than 20 per cent of sales in the UK. One indication of its growing significance is the spread of franchising into further and higher education, with universities and other colleges of higher education franchising some of their courses to local further education colleges, which in turn may franchise some of their courses to schools and/or sixth-form colleges. Another indicator is the decision by many clearing banks and firms of accountants to establish franchise sections to help and advise individuals who want to open a franchise or who have already done so and are seeking further guidance.

 web link   The British Franchise Association's main website is *www.thebfa.org*

Undoubtedly the mutual benefits to be derived from a franchise arrangement help to explain its popularity as a way of doing business in both domestic and external markets and it has proved an attractive vehicle for some companies seeking rapid overseas expansion, without undertaking substantial direct investments – although this is sometimes necessary to support the operation (e.g. McDonald's had to invest in a plant to make hamburger buns in the UK). Equally, many would-be entrepreneurs find the security of a franchise more attractive than other methods of starting a business, especially as there is some evidence to suggest that franchises have better survival rates than the more conventional forms of independent enterprise (e.g. sole traders).

Licensing

Licensing is another form of non-equity agreement under which a firm in one country (the licensor) authorises a firm in another country (the licensee) to use its intellectual property (e.g. patents, copyrights, trade names, know-how) in return for certain considerations, usually royalty payments. Licences may be granted to individuals, independent companies, subsidiaries of a multinational company or to government agencies, and the rights granted may be exclusive or non-exclusive.

Companies invariably enter into licensing agreements to gain certain advantages. These might include:

- reducing competition by sharing technology;
- seeking overseas profits without direct foreign investment;
- protecting an asset from potential 'pirates';
- avoiding restrictions on foreign investment or imports imposed by other countries;
- recouping some research and development costs; and
- gaining a share of an overseas market.

Needless to say, most organisations granting licences tend to be based in the advanced industrial economies and are frequently multinationals, which regard their trademarks and technologies as an integral part of their asset base. One problem of transferring the use of such assets to another firm is that the owner loses a degree of control over the asset, including the quality of production, and this may affect the product's image and sales elsewhere. Another is the possibility of the licensee dominating the market after the agreement ends, even to the extent of excluding the licensor from the marketplace by aggressive competition or the development of an alternative product.

Joint ventures

The term **joint venture** tends to be used in two ways: to describe a contractual agreement involving two or more parties; or to describe a jointly owned and independently incorporated business venture involving more than one organisation that has been established in order to carry out a specific project or to achieve a continuing business relationship. It is the latter usage that is mainly applied here.

Joint ventures – which are popular with international companies – can take a variety of legal forms and almost every conceivable type of partnership may exist, ranging from two companies joining together in the same domestic market (e.g. Sainsbury's and British Home Stores set up the SavaCentre chain) to joint private/public sector ventures between participants from different countries. Sometimes numerous organisations may be involved and these may be based in one country or in several. Where this occurs, the term **consortium** is often used, as in the case of TransManche Link (TML), the international joint venture that built the Channel Tunnel. Both joint ventures and consortia are also discussed briefly in Chapter 11 as aspects of size structure.

The gig economy

The **gig economy** refers to a market characterised by short-term contracts or extensive use of freelance work, where a normal business would employ people to provide services such as delivering food. These businesses now provide platforms which put people together: one party who would like a service, and another who would be willing to provide it. Such companies are enabled by widespread technology adoption in the form of websites and mobile phone applications (apps).

The gig economy is a part of two wider phenomena. First, the rise of the digital economy as a means of trade. Early Web-based businesses such as eBay provided platforms for people and buy and sell to each other, with eBay taking a percentage of the value of the transaction (usually 10 per cent). Other websites allowed people to rent their one or two parking spaces outside their home, making use of their unused assets. The digital economy has expanded considerably, with websites such as Airbnb serving as a platform for people to offer their spare rooms for short stays rather than customers renting often more expensive rooms in hotels. Uber works in much the same way, with cars offering rides instead of conventional taxis. The government has realised that people are engaged with this sort of commerce and that it should have tax implications (since the income from these sorts of transactions is taxable). The Digital Economy Act 2017 allows people to make up to £1,000 through these sorts of transactions before they pay tax. This is important because otherwise these people would have to register as self-employed.

The second trend involved with the gig economy is the casualisation of labour. Workers involved with these businesses are legally classed as subcontractors, not employees, and as such they do not have employment rights such as insurance, sickness or annual leave, or other benefits. These people are often left financially insecure because they do not know how much they might earn each week or month. The business makes money and pays costs on each transaction, but takes none of the risk (instead pushing it onto workers). Companies who utilise gig workers continue to assert that they are not responsible for their workers, despite recent court rulings which state otherwise. Casualisation is discussed further in Chapter 7.

mini case Cross-national joint ventures

Joint ventures (JVs) between firms in different countries have become increasingly popular in recent years and are felt to provide many potential benefits. Participants frequently cite the exploitation of synergies, reduced costs and risks, access to markets and resources, and knowledge sharing as some of the main advantages in setting up this form of partnership arrangement. As the following examples illustrate, JVs range across all industries, sectors and countries, including a growing trend towards collaborations between businesses in the emerging economies:

1 Volkswagen has a JV with China's state-owned FAW Group to produce VW and Audi vehicles. It also has another JV with China's SAIC Motor Group. The latter in turn has a partnership with General Motors.
2 Microsoft has formed a JV with Shanghai-based BesTV to develop games and related services, foreign games consoles having previously been banned in China because of concerns over their content.

3 Spanish cooperative Maier (part of the Mondragon Corporation) has linked up with India's UM Group to supply decorative plastic units and parts for the automotive sector.
4 India's Sterlite Technologies has established a JV with Brazil's Conduspar to build a plant in Brazil to produce optical fibre cables for the Latin American market. Sterlite has a similar collaboration with China's TCGI to produce optical fibres.

While JVs can potentially deliver considerable commercial and strategic benefits – including access to fast-growing markets – they are not without their difficulties. National laws and regulations, for example, may impose restrictions on what a foreign business can do or on how it operates, a point illustrated by Walmart's decision (October 2013) to end its retailing JV with India's Bharti because of strict foreign investment rules which prevented it from selling directly to customers.

As with licensing and franchising, JVs have increased in popularity in the last 30 to 35 years and have been one of the ways in which international companies have sought to develop an overseas market, particularly in the face of import restrictions, or heavy research and development costs. Multinational car companies have been active in this field – as evidenced by past links between General Motors and Toyota, Ford and Mazda – and these arrangements look likely to continue as markets become more global. For western companies wishing to exploit the gradual privatisation of the former planned economies of Eastern Europe, JVs with indigenous producers are likely to prove a safer bet than direct inward investment, particularly given the degree of economic and political uncertainty. They are also likely to prove more politically acceptable in states seeking to establish their economic independence and identity after almost 50 years of regional domination.

Synopsis

Market-based economies throughout Europe and beyond have a range of business organisations with broadly similar legal structures. These legal structures help to determine not only the ownership and control of the enterprise but also other aspects of its operations, including its objectives, its access to finance and its external relationships and obligations. Viewing businesses as legal entities provides a useful insight into a number of the external influences which impinge upon their daily existence and highlights some of the consequences faced by organisations that transfer from public (i.e. state) to private ownership. It also sheds light on other important developments in entrepreneurial activity, including franchising, licensing and joint ventures.

Summary of key points

- Business organisations have a legal structure.

- The three most common forms of business in the private sector are sole traders, partnerships and limited companies.

- Whereas the owners of the first two types of business organisation face unlimited personal liability, in companies the legal separation of the firm from its owners affords the latter limited personal liability.

- Companies are normally run by directors who are appointed to represent the interest of the owners (the shareholders). In public companies this separation of ownership and control is a key distinguishing feature.

- Other forms of business organisation exist in the public sector (e.g. the public corporation) and the 'third sector' (e.g. the cooperative).

- Government-owned businesses are increasingly adopting private sector forms of organisation to provide for greater flexibility and freedom of action.

- The legal status of the organisation has implications for the objectives of the enterprise, how it is financed and its stakeholder relationships.

case study   Uber

Uber is a good example of a company which has used organisational structures to its advantage. The company has dramatically disrupted the taxi market in large numbers of cities across the world, varying its product offering but keeping to a simple model of using the 'gig economy' or 'sharing economy' depending on your perspective.

Uber was founded by Garrett Camp and Travis Kalanick, along with two programmers. The company launched in San Francisco in 2011. The company quickly changed from one offering its own cars and services to one which allowed other people to drive for the company with very basic checks. This meant that through a mobile app people could either request a ride, or register as a driver and receive ride requests from people wanting them. Crucially, the people who were drivers were not employed by Uber, but were legally self-employed and had a business contract with the company to abide by terms of service - in a similar way to those using the service for rides. This meant that Uber did not have to provide them with any benefits or pay insurance for them. Drivers did not have any fixed hours and could work as much or as little as they wanted. The model depended on Uber taking a share of the value of each transaction, and in some cases tips that are given by customers through the app as well. Uber is also able to change ride prices rapidly based on demand – when demand for rides is dramatically greater than the service can provide, Uber implements 'surge pricing' which is up to four times the normal rate. The market then effectively deals with demand by either lowering it (people will wait until demand at the new price decreases) or shifting it to alternatives (people take other forms of transport, including conventional taxis).

Uber argues that its business model is more efficient and effective than taxi companies which have to abide by regulation (and bear the cost that regulation brings) and find it hard to restructure if demand changes. Critics argue that this system is unfair on drivers, who earn money for Uber while having none of the protection of employees. Finally,

where Uber services are less regulated than taxi firms, there have been cases where drivers have been accused of crimes against passengers – and Uber accused of not taking these crimes seriously.

Case study questions

1 Given the choice, would you rather work for a company with employment rights and responsibilities, or work as a self-employed contractor with limited security? What are the advantages and disadvantages of this position?

2 What advantages are there to regulated services and formal organisations?

3 Uber has recently launched Uber Eats – a food delivery service provided by cyclists on the same non-contractual basis as its drivers. What other types of service and companies can you think of?

Review and discussion questions

1 Numerically, the sole proprietorship is the most popular form of business organisation throughout Europe. How would you account for this?

2 To what extent is corporate status an asset to a business organisation? Does it have any disadvantages?

3 Examine the implications of privatising a public sector business organisation.

4 Discuss how the legal status of a business affects its objectives, its methods of finance and its stakeholders.

5 How would you explain the rise in the popularity of franchising in recent years?

Assignments

1 You have recently been made redundant and decide to set up your own small business, possibly with a friend. Assuming that you have £25,000 to invest in your new venture, draft a business plan which is to be presented to your bank manager in the hope of gaining financial support. Your plan should include a clear rationale for the legal form you wish your business to take, your chosen product(s) or service(s), evidence of market research, an indication of anticipated competition and supporting financial information.

2 You work in a local authority business advice centre. One of your clients wishes to start a business in some aspect of catering. Advise your client on the advantages and disadvantages of the various legal forms the proposed enterprise could take.

Further reading

Campbell, D. J. and Craig, T., *Organizations and the Business Environment,* Butterworth–Heinemann, 2005.

Morrison, J., *The Global Business Environment,* 4th edition, Palgrave, 2016.

Palmer, A. J. and Hartley, R., *The Business Environment,* 7th edition, McGraw-Hill, 2011.

Worthington, I., Britton, C. and Rees, A., *Economics for Business: Blending Theory and Practice,* 2nd edition, Financial Times/Prentice Hall, 2005.

Web links and further questions are available on the website at:

www.pearsoned.co.uk/worthington

11 Size structure of firms

Chris Britton

Businesses range in size from the single proprietor at one extreme to the large multinational which employs thousands of people over several countries at the other. The structures of these businesses will be very different and the problems they face will vary as a result of the differences in size. The size structure of business will depend on many factors, which range from choice (the sole proprietor may choose to remain small) to external factors that are beyond the control of the firm.

Learning outcomes

Having read this chapter you should be able to:

- outline the size structure of UK industry
- provide reasons for why organisations grow in size
- demonstrate the way in which organisations grow and the methods of finance
- explain the limitations to growth
- survey the level of merger activity in the UK and the EU
- demonstrate the role and importance of the small-firm sector
- discuss the idea of networking between firms

Key terms

Capital market	Flexible firm	Networking
Concentration	Gearing	Profit
Conglomerate merger	Horizontal merger	Small firm
Debentures	Industrial concentration	Stock exchange
Diseconomies of scale	Internal growth	Subcontracting
Diversification	Joint venture	Takeover
Dividends	Merger	Vertical integration
Enterprise	Money market	Virtual organisation
Equity	Multinational corporations	
Establishment	(MNC)	
External growth		

Introduction

Evidence suggests that national concentration levels have increased over time due to mergers and takeovers but that global concentration levels are lower than national ones. Such an increase in the size of business organisations gives rise to worries about the concentration of power in the hands of a few producers and potential abuses of this power. If the companies are multinationals, they may be beyond the control even of national governments. More recently the trend towards greater **concentration** has been reversed and there seems to be a movement towards employment in smaller units. This chapter will look at the size structure of British industry and the reasons for such a structure, with some international comparisons. It will consider the role of small and large firms in the economy. It will also examine the reasons for growth, the ways in which organisations grow, the financing of growth and the limits to growth. Consideration will be given to the relatively more recent trend towards cooperation in production, rather than competition, through activities such as joint ventures and networking.

The size structure of UK industry

When looking at the size of firms it is important to define the terms used in official data. The firm, or **enterprise**, is the organisation as a whole, and it might be composed of several units or **establishments**. Small firms like the corner shop will mostly be enterprises with only one establishment. Large firms like Sainsbury's will have many establishments as they have branches in most towns.

There are many different ways to measure the size of firms. Common measures used are turnover, the value of output, the capital employed or the level of employment. Such measurement is beset by problems, not least the difficulty of defining the small firm, as we will see later in this chapter. The three measures mentioned above might give conflicting pictures, as an industry that is becoming increasingly mechanised will probably have rising levels of average capital employed and output but falling average levels of employment. Table 11.1 shows the 'top 10' companies in the world in 2017 by turnover; it also shows the number of employees. This demonstrates that different measures of the size

Table 11.1 The 10 largest companies in the world by turnover, 2017

Company	Turnover ($ million)	Country	Employees
Walmart	482 130	USA	2 300 000
State Grid	329 601	China	927 839
China National Petroleum	299 271	China	1 589 508
Sinopec Group	294 344	China	810 538
Royal Dutch Shell	272 156	Netherlands/UK	90 000
Exxon Mobil	246 204	USA	75 000
Volkswagen	236 600	Germany	610 076
Toyota Motor	236 593	Japan	348 877
Apple	233 715	USA	110 000
BP	255 982	UK	79 800

Source: Fortune Global 500, 2017.

Table 11.2 Size structure of UK industry by employment, 2016

Employment size group	Number of organisations	% of total
0–4	1 985 220	77.7
5–9	292 260	11.4
10–19	148 815	5.8
20–49	78 635	3.1
50–99	25 485	1.0
100–249	14 405	0.6
249+	9 690	0.4
Total	2 554 510	

Source: UKBAD01 – Enterprise/local units by employment size band 2016 data (ONS).

of a firm will give different rankings. Some of these names will be familiar to you while others will be less so. State Grid, for example, is China's state-owned energy producer and distributor, and Sinopec Group is a Chinese petrochemical company.

The most common measure of size used is the level of employment. Table 11.2 shows the size structure of units in all industries by the number of employees in the UK in 2016. The table shows that smaller firms predominate in terms of numbers, with 98 per cent of firms employing fewer than 50 employees. In terms of employment, however, the small number of large firms represents about a third to a half of all employment, depending on the industry. The pattern of size structure varies across industries and over time. In the last 30 years there seems to have been an increase in the importance of small firms and a decline in the importance of large firms in their contribution to employment. In 1980, establishments with fewer than 200 employees accounted for 31.9 per cent of total employment and establishments with more than 500 employees accounted for 49.8 per cent.

Many of the large companies listed in Table 11.1 operate in more than one country and are therefore multinationals. As indicated in Chapter 3, **multinational corporations** strictly defined are enterprises operating in a number of countries and having production or service facilities outside the country of their origin. Multinationals pose particular problems for governments and economies because of their size.

Organisational growth

The reasons for organisational growth

Firms grow in size for many reasons. Growth could be an explicit objective of management or could be necessary for the successful operation of the firm:

- Growth could be a managerial objective if it brings benefits to management such as greater security and higher remuneration.
- It could be that the market in which the business operates is expanding and growth is necessary to maintain market share. This is especially the case as markets become more international.
- Growth enables the organisation to reap the benefits of economies of scale (see Chapter 15).

- Growth enables firms to diversify into other markets, which means that risk can be spread further.
- Industries that are capital intensive will of necessity be composed of large firms.
- In the area of product development it is possible that the necessary research and development could be carried out by large companies only.
- Growth could be pursued as a defensive strategy, as a reaction to the activities of competitors.

The European Commission puts forward the following motives for merger and acquisition activities: a search for efficiency gains through new combinations of material and immaterial assets; a drive to increase market shares and market power; a desire to safeguard access to important inputs; a search for access to new technologies and know-how; a drive to gain access to new customer groups or new geographic markets; and a desire for **diversification**. The OECD recognises that there are efficiencies involved in growth and it classifies these into 'static' and 'dynamic' efficiencies. Static efficiencies are one-off improvements such as economies of scale in production. Dynamic efficiencies are those that enable improvements in cost, quality, service or new product development on an ongoing basis. In considering the benefits of a takeover or merger, for example, it may be that the dynamic efficiencies will eventually overtake the initially bigger static efficiencies. Examples of dynamic efficiencies include:

- economies of scale and scope in R&D;
- better risk spreading, especially for R&D;
- increased financial resources for R&D;
- better intellectual property rights protection.

In industrial economics, firm size is seen as a function of growth. It is suggested that although there is no limit on the size of a firm, there are limits on the rate of expansion. Growth rates are seen by different theorists to depend on different things, including the availability of finance, the level of consumer demand and the limitations of management. These theories, however, are primarily concerned with large firms and their development. Small firms are seen as potentially large firms that failed to grow for some reason or other. One interesting theory of growth is the stages model, where the firm is seen as passing through various stages in its development from small sole proprietor/partnership to the decision to expand into a large organisation. This again is a 'grow or fail' theory, which does not apply well to industries that are dominated by successful small firms, as we will see later in the chapter.

Methods of growth

Firms grow in size internally as part of normal business operation or externally through takeover and merger.

Internal growth

Growth is a natural process for many firms that start small, capture a segment of the market and then continue to expand either by producing more of the same goods or by extending their product lines. The advantage of **internal growth** over external growth is that the company grows within the existing structure of management; there are none of the problems of bringing together two different management systems. There might also be economies of scale from building a bigger plant that might not be available when companies merge and plant size does not change. Set against these, internal growth has certain disadvantages and this is why most of the growth in the size of organisations has occurred through external growth.

External growth

Growth by acquisition is called **external growth** and occurs through **takeover** or **merger**. A merger is the voluntary coming together of two companies with the agreement of the management of both companies, the result of which is the creation of a new legal identity. A takeover is where one company makes an offer to the shareholders of another. If the management of the threatened company resists, it is called a hostile takeover, but if the price offered to shareholders is high enough, they will accept. Takeover bids can be and have been successfully fought off by the management of the second firm. A holding company is a new company that is formed to acquire assets in other companies. The acquired companies retain their independent identities but are directed by the holding company.

External growth can be seen to have a number of advantages:

1   It is fast, so that productive capacity can be increased very quickly.
2   The acquiring firm has access to an established management team and system.
3   If the shares of the acquiring company have sufficiently high values relative to the acquired firm, there might be no need for additional cash to be raised.
4   The purchase of existing assets could be cheaper than building new productive capacity.

But set against these is the fact that the process might not be an easy one; it is a difficult job to merge two companies smoothly and successfully and there are likely to be many teething problems. Research by PricewaterhouseCoopers found that top executives regarded half of the takeovers in which they had been involved as failures. The main reasons for failure were lack of planning and managerial problems.

Although the definitions of merger and takeover are clear enough, it is often difficult to tell them apart in practice and they are usually put together in official publications under the heading of acquisitions. In order to understand fully the motivation for mergers and takeovers it is important to recognise that there are different types of mergers.

Horizontal mergers

A **horizontal merger** is where a combination between firms at the same stage in a production process takes place, for example between two car manufacturers or between two brewers. The vast majority of mergers that take place are of this type and many of our largest companies have been formed through horizontal merger. Examples include mergers between banks and building societies. The main motives for this type of merger are as follows:

●   To benefit from economies of scale. Horizontal mergers allow the merged firms a greater level of specialisation and the benefits of other economies of scale (see Chapter 15).

- Greater market share. When firms come together there will be a reduction in competition in the market and the resulting firm will automatically have a much larger share of the market.
- Rationalisation of output. If the level of demand for a good is shrinking, merger between the producers could be necessary in order to rationalise output.
- Reaction to competitors. In markets where mergers are taking place, companies may feel that they have to do the same in order to maintain their market position.

A fairly recent example of a horizontal merger is that between American AB InBev and SABMiller in 2015, which created the biggest brewer in the world; 30 per cent of all beer in the world is made by this one company.

Vertical mergers

A vertical merger involves firms at different stages of the same production process. It is vertical since it runs along the production process from extraction of raw materials to distribution. An example would be a merger between a car manufacturer and a metal-pressing company. **Vertical integration** can take place 'backwards' towards the beginning of the production process or 'forwards' towards the end of it and it can occur for several reasons:

1 In the case of backwards integration, to control the supplies of raw materials with respect to their quantity and quality. This brings greater security to the acquiring firm.
2 To restrict supplies of the raw materials to competitors.
3 In the case of forwards integration, to control the quality of the outlets for the finished product. Manufacturers finance the majority of advertising and they might well feel that a forwards merger would enable them to ensure that the good was being sold in the most appropriate setting.
4 In both cases, economies of scale are possible if different parts of the production process are brought together.
5 Again, vertical mergers can be carried out as a reaction to the activities of competitors.

The proposed and talked about takeover of Time Warner by AT&T in 2016 is an example of a vertical merger, where a communications group now owns a company which produces content for it to deliver.

Conglomerate mergers

These mergers are neither vertical nor horizontal but involve a merger between firms involved in producing different goods. The takeover of Boston Dynamics, a manufacturer of robots, by Google in 2013 is an example of a **conglomerate merger**. The main motivation for this type of merger is diversification. It reduces the risk involved in producing for only one market and allows the firm to spread risk further. It can also provide the firm with another option if the original market declines in size. There has been much speculation over Google's motive in taking over Boston Dynamics, its ninth such acquisition in 2013, so there is a clear indication that Google is diversifying into new territory.

As far as the economy is concerned, the main gains of mergers are in increased efficiency resulting from economies of scale and also the increased scope for research and development. A common view is that merger and takeover activity serves the purpose of rationalising business. The weak businesses go and the strong survive. Even when a takeover is carried out for the purpose of asset stripping, this will be the case.

mini case   The story of a failed merger

In 2012 a merger was proposed and agreed between two large soft drinks producers in the UK, A. G. Barr, which produces Irn-Bru and Orangina, and Britvic, which produces Tango and Robinsons. The merger would produce a new company called Barr Britvic Soft Drinks, 37 per cent owned by shareholders of A. G. Barr and 63 per cent owned by shareholders of Britvic. This is an example of a horizontal merger, both companies producing similar products, and as such benefits would accrue to both companies. It was argued that the merger would:

- enhance the market position of each company – A. G. Barr has a strong presence in Scotland and Britvic has a strong pub presence, so they complemented each other;
- achieve synergies for both companies – the merger would give rise to £40 million in cost savings through rationalisation of production and the subsequent loss of up to 500 jobs;
- increase shareholder value.

Despite these strong arguments, some commentators suggested that the proposed merger was a defensive one, as the soft drinks market in the UK had suffered as a result of the bad weather in the summer of 2012 and Britvic had experienced an embarrassing recall of its Fruit Shoot brand because of problems with the bottle tops, an exercise which cost the company

£25 million. Early in 2013 the merger was referred for investigation to the Competition Commission, which cleared it in June 2013. It ruled that the proposed merger would not adversely affect competition in the market or affect prices to the consumer. By the time the Competition Commission had ruled, Britvic had managed to regroup, recruit a new CEO and recover from the Fruit Shoot recall. Britvic rejected the revised offer from A. G. Barr. The merger was off. The negotiations had cost A. G. Barr £5 million and Britvic £9.6 million.

What has happened to these companies since then? The market for soft drinks did well in 2013, largely due to very hot weather in the UK in the summer. Both companies posted positive sales and profits growth for the second half of 2013. A. G. Barr has managed to expand into England and Wales successfully without the help of Britvic, and has opened new production capacity in Milton Keynes. Britvic has managed to expand into the United States and Europe and had India in its sights for 2014. It has managed to obtain synergies without merger through the proposed closure of two factories in 2014 and the loss of 300–400 jobs.

It seems that the two companies have gained the benefits resulting from merger without having to go ahead with it, and this is at least partly due to market conditions.

Growth by merger and takeover

Growth through merger and takeover first appeared in the United States more than 100 years ago and merger activity tends to come in waves (see the discussion later in this chapter). Six periods of heightened merger activity have been identified in the United States:

- The period 1880 to 1905 – this coincided with the proliferation of the joint-stock company and the international establishment of stock exchanges. This period was characterised by mergers of a horizontal nature.

- The 1920s – at this time the mergers were largely vertical in nature, as manufacturers took control of both suppliers and distributors.
- The 1960s – mergers in this period were mainly about diversification and the establishment of conglomerates.
- The post-1980 period – this wave of activity took place in a period of recession and was largely about cost-cutting and rationalisation.
- The late 1990s – companies in mature industries attempted to become global operators. The pace of this surge of activity slowed for a period after 11 September 2001, but by 2004 the boom in activity had restarted.
- The 2000s – from 2004 to 2007 the boom continued until the credit crunch in the United States caused a sharp fall in merger activity, including a 36 per cent decline in the first half of 2008. Since then the level of activity has remained fairly constant.

The first two periods of heightened merger activity in the United States had little effect in Europe; however, there were waves of activity in Europe which coincided with the later periods. The first wave of merger activity in Europe came in the 1960s after obstacles to trade were removed by the establishment of the European Economic Community (EEC) in 1957. The second wave of mergers came in the 1980s in the run-up to the establishment of the Single European Market in 1992. Since then the cycles in merger and acquisition activity in the United States have been mirrored in Europe. The frequency of mergers and acquisitions tends to run in cycles: when economies are doing well, they are more common. In the year 2007 the number and value of mergers was at a worldwide peak, between 2009 and 2013 it was in a trough, and by 2015 it had achieved another peak again, nearing that of 2007.

Finance for growth

Internal sources

As part of its operation the firm will generate income in the form of **profit**. Part of this profit will be distributed in the form of **dividends** to shareholders; the rest can be used for reinvestment and to finance growth. Although this is seen as a relatively easy and cheap source of finance, it does carry an opportunity cost and therefore should be judged on its rate of return like any other source of finance. Table 11.3 is provided for illustrative purposes and shows that internal funds were the largest single source of finance for UK industry during the 1990s. It also shows that the totals available and the pattern of sources vary a great deal from year to year. (These data are no longer compiled by the Office for National Statistics.)

External sources

As the size and availability of retained earnings will be limited, most firms will also have to seek other sources of finance for expansion. There are many external sources of finance and a typical firm's capital structure will comprise a combination of these. The sources are as follows.

Table 11.3 Sources of funds for industry, 1990, 1994 and 1997 (£ million)

Source	1990	1994	1997
Internal funds	33 838	61 406	56 363
Banks and other short-term borrowing	19 911	−4841	6630
Loans and mortgages	9120	4557	4384
Ordinary shares	1880	8495	19 616
Debentures and preference shares	6367	1008	10 640
Other capital issues	7485	5067	10 526
Other overseas investment	11 233	−1400	25 938
Other	1444	3766	953
Total	91 278	78 056	135 050

Source: Financial Statistics, January 1993, 1996 and 1999. Crown copyright 1999. Reproduced by permission of the Controller of HMSO and of the Office for National Statistics, UK.

Banks

Banks provide short- and medium-term finance to companies in the form of loans or overdrafts. The relative cost of these depends upon how the firm wishes to use the funds. Loans carry a lower rate of interest but the interest is paid on the whole amount, while the interest on overdrafts is paid only on the amount drawn. British banks have been criticised for failing to provide longer-term finance for business, as banks do in other countries.

Capital market

The **capital market** is the place where stocks and shares are traded and is therefore a key provider of long-term finance to firms. The main institution in the capital market is the **stock exchange**. The capital market is made up of two parts: the primary part, which involves the buying and selling of new stocks and shares; and the secondary part, which involves the buying and selling of existing stocks and shares. It is therefore the primary part of the market that is the source of finance for firms. The secondary part of the market is also important in this process, however, as individuals and organisations are more likely to buy stocks and shares with the knowledge that there is a ready market on which they can be traded at a later date.

The main institutions that buy stocks and shares are the insurance companies, hedge funds, pension funds, investment trusts, unit trusts and other large financial institutions such as building societies.

A new issue of shares takes place when an existing company needs extra finance or when a company becomes a public limited company.

Types of stocks and shares

1 *Preference shares.* These are shares in a company that carry a fixed dividend. Holders have preference over other shareholders in the payment of dividends and on the liquidation of the firm. Preference shares usually carry no voting rights, so holders have little influence over how the company is run.

2 *Ordinary shares.* Ordinary shares are called the **equity** of the company. They do not usually carry a fixed dividend; the company declares a dividend, depending upon its performance in that year. This means that in good years ordinary shareholders could receive high dividends, while in bad years possibly none at all. Ordinary shares are therefore more risky than preference shares, and in recognition of this

they usually carry voting rights, so that holders can exercise some influence over how the company is run.

3   *Debentures.* **Debentures** or loan stock are bonds that are given in exchange for a loan to the company. The company agrees to repay the borrowed amount at some date in the future and to make annual payments of interest in the meantime. Interest on debentures is paid before payment of any dividends and the interest is allowable against tax. A debenture holder is a creditor of the company, a shareholder is an owner of the company.

New issue of shares

A company will go to an issuing house or investment bank, which will advise it on the type and number of shares to issue, the price at which they should be offered and other matters. The bank will often carry out the issue of shares on behalf of the firm. A new issue of shares is not a big source of finance for growth as it is fairly expensive; retained earnings are more convenient and cheaper. Also the amount of information that is required from companies that issue shares to the general public can act as a disincentive.

It is worth noting that in recent years in the UK the stock market has had two main equity markets, the main market and the Alternative Investment Market (AIM), the former dealing in the shares of large and well-established companies, the latter providing an opportunity for growing smaller companies to raise capital and to have their shares traded in a market without the considerable expense of a full market listing.

Money market

The **money markets** provide short-term finance for companies, often for as brief a period as overnight.

Government and other institutions

The government is a source of finance for firms. Through its regional policy it gives tax allowances, loans, grants and training allowances to firms in certain parts of the country (see Chapter 13). It has many schemes for helping business, particularly small businesses. This will be covered more fully later in this chapter.

Other sources

Other sources include trade credit and hire purchase (i.e. receiving assets now and paying later). This is only a small source of finance for companies. UK businesses also draw a fairly high proportion of their funding from overseas. This includes finance from many different sources, including individuals, governments, financial institutions overseas and companies.

Firms will typically go for a mixture of different types of finance. The exact combination will depend upon many factors, including their relative costs, their availability and the desired capital structure of the firm. A firm's desired capital structure will largely depend upon the type of market in which it operates. The different types of finance are classified under the two headings of debt and equity. Debt refers to all types of capital on which payments have to be made each year regardless of how the firm has performed;

this would include loans and preference shares. Equity refers to ordinary shares where the payment of a dividend depends upon the performance of the firm. As a source of finance, debt is generally cheaper but it is also riskier since in bad years the firm will have to meet the interest payments. The ratio of debt to equity is called the **gearing** of the company. Debt is not well suited to firms in industries where profits fluctuate and such firms will have lower gearing than those in more stable markets.

Limits to growth

Several factors tend to act as a limit to organisational growth:

● To finance growth, excessive borrowing might have taken place and the firm may have trouble meeting debt repayments; therefore there is increased risk of bankruptcy.
● A serious constraint to growth might be the abilities of management. As organisations grow in size they may experience **diseconomies of scale**, which are mainly to do with managerial problems, including communication and control.
● If the size of the market for the product is stagnant or declining it may be both unnecessary and impossible for the firm to grow.
● Government policies, too, can have an important impact on growth. Every government has policies on competition which seek to limit anti-competitive practices and which normally regulate merger activity (see Chapter 17).

Merger activity in the UK

There are two common ways of measuring the level of merger activity – by the number of transactions or by the total value of the transactions. Figure 11.1 shows the level of merger activity in the UK according to the number of companies acquired there by UK companies. It can be seen that there was a sharp rise in merger activity around 2006–8.

Figure 11.1 UK merger activity by number, 2006–16

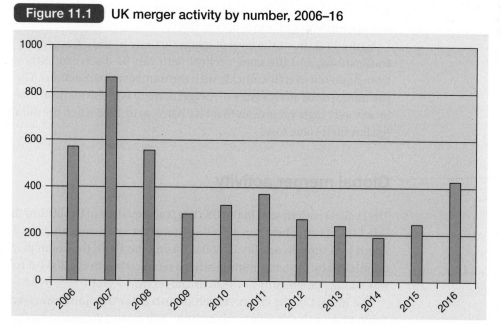

Source: www.ons.gov.uk

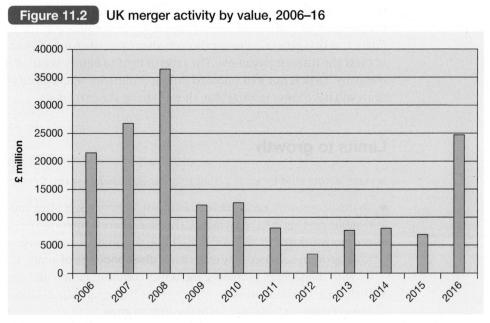

Figure 11.2   UK merger activity by value, 2006–16

Source: www.ons.gov.uk

The cyclical pattern drops to a low in 2014. This indicates that there is a link between merger and takeover activity, and the economy.

The rise around the year 2007 was due partly to an improvement in the state of the economy, which made finance for takeover bids more freely available. The fall throughout the following years was due partly to the recession and partly to the problems that some companies subsequently experienced by overstretching themselves. The subsequent rise in the level of merger activity was due to the restructuring that took place in many diverse industries, such as the financial services sector and the public utilities. Since 2008 – the start of the credit crunch – both the number of transactions and their value fell, up until a large bounce back in 2016.

Figure 11.2 shows the level of merger activity in the UK according to the value of the transactions, and the same cyclical path can be discerned, although the peaks and troughs do not exactly coincide with the number of transactions. The use of the value of the transactions as a measure of merger activity is problematic in that it will be distorted by any very high-value deals that take place, as in 2008 when the number of transactions fell but their value rose.

Global merger activity

The cyclical pattern seen in the UK data is also evident in the EU and the world as a whole (see Table 11.4). There was a decline in merger and acquisitions in the early 2000s followed by a surge in activity in 2004. During the 1990s the boom in merger activity was dominated by the telecommunications sector, while in the 2004–8 recovery the activity was taking place mainly in the financial services sector.

The impact of the credit crunch on merger and acquisition activity can be seen in Table 11.4, with a dramatic fall in 2009. The market recovered somewhat after that but

Table 11.4 Cross-border mergers and acquisitions to and from OECD countries, 1999–2012 ($ billion)

Year	Outwards	Inwards
1999	801	775
2000	1166	1136
2001	606	585
2002	376	410
2003	321	338
2004	422	444
2005	673	635
2006	847	818
2007	1028	1033
2008	1644	1060
2009	912	650
2010	1052	737
2011	1284	916
2012	982*	578*

*Estimated.
Source: Adapted from Figures D.10.1. and D.10.2. from OECD (2010), Measuring Globalisation: OECD Economic Globalisation Indicators 2010, OECD Publishing. http://dx.doi.org/10.1787/9789264084360-en

fell back again in 2012. Global merger and acquisition activity was at its lowest for eight years in 2013 and in the EU it was at its lowest for three years and there were fewer 'mega-deals' (over $10 million) in 2013. The number of deals globally was 37 257 in 2013 and the total value of those deals was $2.3 trillion. Globally, the biggest market for mergers is the United States, followed by Asia-Pacific, with the EU in third place. General political and economic uncertainty and low growth rates in the EU have contributed to this – the markets are still cautious.

Small firms

There are serious problems in the analysis of the small-firm sector, including the lack of data over a long period of time and the problem of defining exactly what is a **small firm**. *The Bolton Report,* published in 1971, was the report of a committee set up to look into the role of small firms in the UK economy. It used various definitions for statistical purposes, depending upon the industry being considered, on the grounds that what is small in one industry might be large in another. Table 11.5 shows the size distribution of firms based on their turnover for a selection of industries for 2012.

It is clear from Table 11.5 that the definition of 'big' will vary with the industry. In *The Bolton Report* the definition used for small firms in manufacturing was 'less than 200 employees', while in construction it was 'less than 25 employees'. In some industries turnover limits were chosen, while in others a mixture of employment and turnover was used. Although this is confusing and makes comparison between industries and countries difficult, it was accepted that there could not be a single definition that would apply to all sectors. The European Commission in 2005 introduced a new measure based on employment and turnover to improve consistency between member states and to

Table 11.5 Size of companies by turnover across different industries, 2012 (%)

Industry	Turnover size (000s)		
	<£250	£250–500	>£500
Agriculture, forestry and fishing	80	11	9
Mining and quarrying and public utilities	53	13	34
Manufacturing	57	13	30
Construction	70	13	17
Wholesaling	47	14	39
Retailing	63	19	18
Financial services and insurance	72	11	17
Business services	71	11	18

Source: Adapted from Table B5.1, *UK Business Activity by Size and Location,* National Statistics, 2012.

Table 11.6 The EU SME definition

Enterprise category	Headcount	Annual turnover	Annual balance sheet total
Micro	0–9	<€2 million	<€2 million
Small	0–49 (includes micro)	<€10 million	<€10 million
Medium	50–249	<€50 million	<€43 million
Large	250+	>€50 million	>€43 million

Source: Evaluation of the user guide to the SME Definition, 2014, http://ec.europa.eu/docsroom/documents/5766/attachments/1/translations/en/renditions/pdf

facilitate the aid offered to SMEs in the EU. This definition is shown in Table 11.6 and uses employment size and annual turnover *or* annual balance sheet total in its definition.

Applying this definition to Table 11.2, it can be seen that 89.1 per cent of enterprises in the UK are micro businesses, 98 per cent are small, 1.6 per cent are medium sized and 0.4 per cent are large. Although there are some national differences (the southernmost countries have relatively more micro businesses than the northern countries), the pattern of size structure is similar in the EU as a whole: 92.1 per cent of all enterprises are micro businesses, 6.6 per cent are small, 1.1 per cent are medium sized and 0.2 per cent are large. Using these definitions it is estimated that 99.8 per cent of all enterprises in the EU27 were SMEs and that they provided around 86.8 million jobs.

No matter how small firms are defined, they will suffer from similar problems, which are very different from those faced by larger companies.

Trends in the small-firm sector

The percentage share of small establishments in total manufacturing employment in the UK was in decline for the 1930s up to the early 1970s, when its importance increased dramatically. In recent years the percentage has stayed around 40 per cent. Table 11.2 showed that for UK industry small firms are very important in terms of the number of businesses, accounting for 98 per cent of total firms. Even though they were less important in terms of employment, they still accounted for more than a third of total employment. Figure 11.3 shows the share of employment in SMEs by sector; as can be seen, there is a great deal of variation between sectors.

Figure 11.3 Share of employment of SMEs (%), UK, 2016

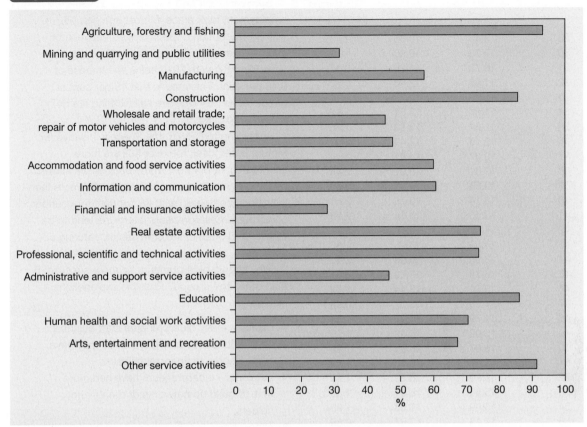

Source: 'Business Population Estimates, 2016', Department for Business, innovation and Skills.

mini case   'Olderpreneurs' and small firms

The recent rise in the number of over 50 year olds starting their own businesses in the UK has given rise to the new term 'olderpreneurs'. Table 11.7 shows that there has been a gradual increase in the level of self-employment in the UK over time, with a more rapid increase after 2008, the start of the economic downturn. According to the Office for National Statistics, 85 per cent of the increase in self-employment since 2008 has been in those over the age of 50 years.

Table 11.7 shows the age profile of all self-employed people in 2001 and 2015 and it can be seen that the overall growth varies by age group. There has been a growth in the 18–24 age group and the over 50s. The other two age groups have declined in importance.

Table 11.7 The age profile of the self-employed (shown as a percentage of the total), 2001 and 2015

Age group	% 2001 rate	% 2015 rate	Percentage point change
18	1.91	2.60	0.70
19	2.47	3.67	1.20
20	3.22	4.49	1.28
21	3.32	5.50	2.18
22	3.79	6.36	2.56
23	4.42	7.41	2.98
24	5.18	8.24	3.06
25	5.80	8.55	2.76
26	6.76	8.92	2.16
27	7.25	9.55	2.30
28	8.07	10.27	2.20

▶

Age group	% 2001 rate	% 2015 rate	Percentage point change
29	8.43	10.86	2.43
30	9.79	10.90	1.11
31	10.73	11.20	0.47
32	11.36	12.06	0.70
33	11.60	12.73	1.14
34	11.84	13.51	1.67
35	12.04	13.83	1.80
36	12.49	14.49	2.00
37	12.37	14.81	2.44
38	12.61	15.07	2.46
39	12.53	16.03	3.50
40	13.14	15.75	2.61
41	13.46	15.64	2.18
42	14.07	15.17	1.11
43	14.09	15.95	1.86
44	13.98	16.08	2.10
45	13.72	15.89	2.17
46	13.81	15.44	1.63
47	14.39	15.37	0.98
48	14.79	15.97	1.18
49	15.02	16.52	1.50
50	15.07	16.99	1.92
51	15.07	16.60	1.52
52	15.20	16.70	1.50
53	15.53	16.91	1.38
54	16.00	17.93	1.93
55	17.19	17.87	0.68
56	18.15	17.80	−0.35
57	18.54	17.95	−0.58
58	18.87	18.85	−0.02
59	19.70	20.31	0.60
60	22.01	21.00	−1.01
61	22.52	22.37	−0.14
62	23.75	24.16	0.41
63	25.00	28.26	3.26
64	28.98	31.61	2.63
65	31.17	33.98	2.81
66	33.52	36.06	2.54
67	35.94	37.00	1.07
70+	39.68	49.13	9.46

ONS: Trends in Self-Employment in the UK: 2001 to 2015.

Between 2001 and 2015 growth in self-employment took place in most age groups, with the exception of people aged between 56 and 61. There is a significant expansion in ages 63 to 67, with 70+ seeing an increase of 9.46 per cent. This means that 49 per cent of people aged 70+ who are still working are doing so self-employed.

According to PRIME (the Prince's Initiative for Mature Enterprise), the over 50s are more successful: 70 per cent of the businesses started by people over the age of 50 survive for more than five years, compared with 28 per cent for younger age groups. Olderpreneurs' start-ups tend to be smaller and often in the craft sector, catering or services.

Why should olderpreneurs be more successful than other age groups? Possible explanations include:

- capital – many olderpreneurs start business after redundancy or retirement so they have some degree of financial fallback;
- networks – olderpreneurs have had more time to build up networks of clients and helpers;
- experience – learning through mistakes;
- good knowledge of the sector – competitive advantage.

Their number is likely to increase with lower pensions, increased health and higher retirement ages.

Reasons for the growth in the small-firm sector

There has clearly been a resurgence in the importance of the small-firm sector, which appears to have been more pronounced in the UK than in other countries. Why? Some causal factors are as follows:

1   *The changing pattern of industry.* Chapter 12 will show that there has been a change in the industrial structure of the UK away from manufacturing and towards services.

Since many services are dominated by small firms, there will be a corresponding change in average firm size. However, this does not provide the full explanation as there has been a growth in the share of small firms even in the manufacturing sector. And it does not explain the international differences since there have been similar changes in industrial structure in other countries.

2 *Changes in consumer spending habits.* A move from mass-produced goods to more specialised products puts small firms at an advantage as they can react more quickly to changes in demand and shorter product life cycles.

3 *Flexible specialisation and the growth of subcontracting.* A debate that started in the late 1980s centres round the idea of the **flexible firm**. As a result of the recession of the early 1980s there was a drive by firms to reduce their costs in order to remain competitive. One way of reducing overhead costs was to move to a flexible firm structure whereby the firm's activities are divided into core and peripheral activities. The core activities, which are central to the activities of the firm, would be kept 'in-house' and carried out by full-time permanent workers. The peripheral activities would be carried out by temporary workers or would be subcontracted. The firm has then reduced its overheads and can react to peaks in demand by increasing the amount of temporary labour it uses or increasing the amount of **subcontracting**. This might also have had the effect of increasing the relative importance of the small-firm sector, although, as the case study on Serco in Chapter 12 will show, outsourcing does not happen only to small firms.

4 *Reorganisation and job reduction.* There has been an increase in the phenomenon of downsizing by organisations in an attempt to reduce costs – 90 per cent of large companies have reorganised and cut jobs since 1985.

5 *Government policy.* After *The Bolton Report* there was much greater interest in the role of the small firm in the regeneration of the economy and in the provision of jobs. But most of the initiatives designed to help the small firm came after the start of the resurgence of the small-firm sector in the early 1970s.

6 *The growth in self-employment.* A part of the growth in the small-firm sector has been due to the growth in the number of self-employed. The self-employed accounted for 9.8 per cent of the workforce in 1984, then 12 per cent in 2000 and 14.9 per cent in 2016 (see Table 11.8). This represents a 35 per cent increase in the number of those self-employed over this period, much of it since 2008, the beginning of the economic downturn (see mini case study on 'olderpreneurs').

The level of self-employment is likely to be related to the level of unemployment, so that as unemployment increased after 2008, there was an increase in the level of self-employment. Again, however, it does not provide the full explanation as business births were growing in the late 1960s when unemployment was falling.

7 *Technological change.* Changes in technology, particularly information technology and the miniaturisation of components, have made it possible for small firms to benefit to a similar extent to large firms. This has had the effect of reducing the importance of economies of scale and enabling small firms to compete more effectively with large ones. The use of 3D printers could potentially benefit small firms at the expense of other businesses.

8 *Competitive forces.* As far as the international differences are concerned, *The Bolton Report* found that industry in the UK was biased towards large size in comparison with other countries. So what may have happened as a result of competitive forces is that the balance of industry in the UK has moved towards the norm of other countries.

Table 11.8 Percentage of workforce self-employed, 2000–16 (UK)

Year	Self-employment share
2000	12.0
2001	11.9
2002	11.9
2003	12.2
2004	12.7
2005	12.5
2006	12.8
2007	13.1
2008	13.1
2009	13.1
2010	13.6
2011	13.5
2012	14.2
2013	14.0
2014	15.0
2015	14.5
2016	14.9

The role of the small-firm sector

The growing importance of the small-firm sector implies that small firms do have a valuable role in the economy apart from being mere providers of employment. The areas in which the small firm has advantages over large firms are those where there are the following:

1 *Clearly defined small markets.* It is not worthwhile for large firms to enter such markets since there are no economies of scale and no scope for mass production.
2 *Specialist, quality, non-standardised products.* Again it would not be worth a large firm entering such a market as the benefits of large-scale production cannot be reaped.
3 *Geographically localised markets.* For example, the small corner shop.
4 *Development of new ideas.* It is often argued that the small firm is the 'seedbed' of ideas and that, because of greater motivation and commitment on the part of the owner of the small firm, it is conducive to invention and innovation.

Aid to the small-firm sector

The thinking on small firms has changed over time. Initially they were viewed favourably, but after the Second World War the dominant thinking was that large-scale production could take advantage of large economies of scale and that costs would be lower and production more efficient. It was not until more recently that the interest in the small-firm sector increased again. The main reasons for the renewed interest are seen in the results of empirical studies which have shown that the role of the small firm is greater than previously thought in areas such as innovation, the balance of payments and employment.

The main argument for giving support to the small-firm sector is that it has a valuable role to play in the economy. In the 1980s and 1990s, for example, small firms were seen as a mechanism for reducing the very high levels of unemployment. Between 1983 and 1993 the small-firm sector created 2.5 million jobs. The basic premise for support is that small firms are at a disadvantage with respect to large businesses in areas such as raising capital, research and development, and risk bearing. The 2007 EU Observatory Survey of SMEs in Europe found that there were three main problems facing small firms:

- The burden of regulation – reported as acting as a constraint by 36 per cent of SMEs within Europe. It is estimated that large firms spend €1 per employee on regulatory compliance compared with €10 for SMEs. The Small Business Act for Europe (2008) has put in place measures to reduce the regulatory burden for SMEs.
- Access to finance – including cash flow problems resulting from late or non-payment of bills. In the UK all public limited companies are required by law to state in their annual reports the average length of time it takes to pay their bills. The Federation of Small Business in the UK publishes a 'name and shame' list of slow payers.
- Access to new markets – between 1996 and 2010 it has been estimated that 58 per cent of the UK's productivity growth came from exporting firms. Only 13 per cent of European SMEs export outside of the EU single market.

Government policy

Within the UK, national policy for small firms has increasingly become a vital component of governmental attempts to create a competitive economy capable of achieving sustainable economic growth. To this end policy initiatives in recent years have become more focused and have tended to adopt a multi-agency approach, aimed at improving the environment in which small businesses emerge and grow, and at fostering enterprise and innovation. Key developments over the last decade or so have included:

- Business Link – a national network of 'one-stop shops' to provide information and support to small firms – this was disbanded in 2011.
- Local Enterprise Partnerships – partnerships between local authorities and businesses to decide on priorities for regional development and investment.
- The Knowledge Transfer Partnerships – these are part-government-funded measures to link UK higher education establishments and businesses.
- The SMART Awards – designed to promote technological development and innovation.
- The Red Tape Challenge – a scheme which aims to identify areas where regulations can be simplified and reduced.
- Greatbusiness – a joint private/public partnership which brings together links on growing, financing and exporting for small business.
- Mentorsme – an online gateway which brings together mentors with small companies needing mentoring.
- Funding for Lending Scheme – a government scheme which provides banks and building societies with £17.6 billion at low rates of interest for lending to businesses and households.
- Other state-backed SME lending and equity schemes, including Start-Up Loans, the Enterprise Finance Guarantee, UK Export Finance and Angel Coinvestment Funds.

There have also been a number of legislative and fiscal changes aimed at reducing the burdens on small businesses (e.g. levels of corporation tax). Some of the more recent developments have included the launch of the University for Industry (now a charitable trust), the Business Enterprise Fund (a social enterprise) and the H2020 initiative of the EU. The latter, introduced in 2013, aims to provide a single online portal for all EU financial instruments for SMEs. There have also been attempts to reduce the flow and improve the quality of regulation affecting smaller businesses and an action plan to make the UK the foremost location for starting and growing a business.

In November 2013 the UK government announced a major campaign to help small firms. The measures included the initial funding for the Business Bank (£1 billion to dispose of to business starting in 2014), a new Mentoring Challenge Fund with £1 million of funding, a fund of £10 million to the Biotechnology and Biological Sciences Research Council to help synthetic biological start-ups, and a Growth Accelerator Scheme, which provides coaching to small businesses with high growth potential. In addition to these, in January 2014, other measures were announced which included a doubling of the Small Business Rate Relief, the introduction of growth vouchers to help small firms with the cost of hiring and marketing, and the Red Tape Challenge.

> **web link** *www.greatbusiness.gov.uk*

Networking between firms

While competition between firms remains the norm in a market economy, cooperation between businesses can, and does, also sometimes occur. This cooperation can take many forms: for example, subcontracting, networking (both formal and informal) and joint ventures. Such cooperation can be (and is) used by large as well as small and medium-sized enterprises. For large companies it is a way to grow and diversify without risk. For smaller firms it allows them to stay small but at the same time to benefit from some of the advantages of large-scale production such as specialisation.

Subcontracting

There has been an increase in the amount of subcontracting, where firms do not carry out the whole of the production process themselves but subcontract some of their activities to other firms. This represents a rejection of vertical integration and it is related to the notion of the flexible firm mentioned earlier. Subcontracting goes some way to explaining the phenomenal growth rate in 'business services' that occurred in the 1980s. It is increasingly common for businesses to subcontract specialist work in areas such as human resource management to outside consultancies. 'Partnering' between companies and consultancies is becoming more common, where the consultancy is retained on a semi-permanent basis to give advice on a whole range of human resource matters, from recruitment to planning for succession. This will obviously boost the small-firm sector. There has also been an increase in 'partnership sourcing' as large firms are developing long-term relationships between themselves and their suppliers. This phenomenon brings benefits to the large firms in the form of reducing stock levels and associated costs and facilitating just-in-time production methods. It also brings benefits to small firms, many of which are the suppliers, in the form of greater security.

Networking

Networking refers to the relationships that exist between organisations and the people within those organisations. These relationships can be of different types, both formal and informal, and there is increasing recognition of the importance of these relationships, especially to small firms (e.g. they may be based on the exchange of goods and services, like the relationship between a firm and its supplier or client). Subcontracting is an example of this kind of network, but there are other links not based on exchange, such as the relationship between a firm and the bank manager or other advisers. There are also informal links between the entrepreneur and family and friends, and between entrepreneurs in different organisations. There might also be cooperative links between firms. This can be seen in the market for executive recruitment where there has been a growth in the links between consultancies, particularly for international work. The creation of the Single European Market and the increased internationalisation of business left the smaller consultancies in a weak position relative to the large international recruitment firms, such as Korn Ferry International, which have branches in most European countries.

The smaller consultancies have reacted by forming networks. There are basically two types of network:

1   Where firms are members of a network but where the network has a different name from the individual firms and the firms operate under their own name (i.e. the network has an identity of its own). The members are independent firms that cooperate in carrying out their business. There are 16 such groups in Europe, including EMA Partners International and Amrop.
2   Where firms are part of a network of independent firms but where the network does not have a separate identity and the firms operate under their own names. There are 10 such groups in Europe.

> **web link**
>
> For information on companies mentioned see *www.kornferry.com*; *www.ema-partners.com*; and *www.amrop.com*

The firm is seen as existing within a spider's web of relationships, as Figure 11.4 shows. It is possible for two firms to be linked in a variety of ways: in one market they may be competitors, in the next cooperators, customers in another and suppliers in another.

Networking has taken on greater significance because of changes that are taking place in the economy, which include the reversal of the trend towards higher **industrial concentration**, the adoption of Japanese methods of production, the decline of 'mass markets' and technological change that requires greater specialisation than previously. All of these changes favour the formation of networks.

The role of strategic alliances between firms has been recognised, especially in the small-firm sector where expansion through other means is often impossible and in the process of internationalisation.

The virtual organisation

The **virtual organisation** is a network-based structure built on partnerships where a small core operating company outsources most of its processes. It is a network of small companies specialising in various aspects of production. The organisation can be very big in

Figure 11.4   A typical network

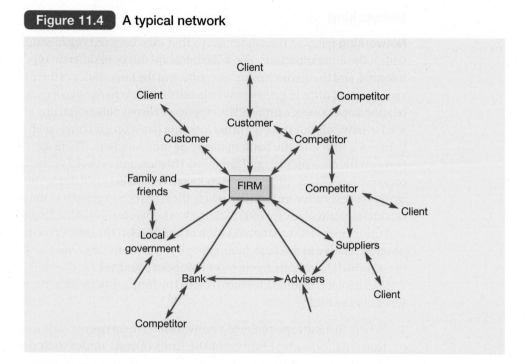

trading terms but very small in the numbers of permanent staff. The process is typically mediated by information technology.

The main benefit of the virtual structure is that it helps organisations to deal with uncertainty. When virtual organisations are managed properly they can simultaneously increase efficiency, flexibility and responsiveness to changes in market conditions. The organisation is reaping the benefits of specialisation without having to develop those specialisms itself. Therefore overhead costs are minimised, as are training costs and support costs. Information technology assumes many of the coordinating and managing roles that managers and committees carry out in large organisations. Information technology enables communication and the sharing of information across geographical boundaries. It is often the case, however, that the creation of a virtual organisation is driven solely by cost considerations rather than strategic considerations, in which case the benefits might not be realised. There will be a loss of control over outsourced activities and it may actually cost more to manage such activities. The organisation can become locked into contracts and specific relationships so that flexibility is reduced. There may be a lack of commitment of key resources (i.e. contractors) to the company and the loss of a contractor will be very serious.

There is some evidence that the incidence of virtual organisations is on the increase, facilitated by developments in information technology. It is a matter of 'wait and see' if this will become the dominant organisational structure in the future.

Joint ventures

As indicated earlier in this chapter, **joint ventures** are a good way for firms to diversify and enter other countries' markets. Joint ventures benefit both parties as each can diversify with the benefit of the experience of the other, and the level of risk is minimised. Again, there are examples in the area of executive recruitment. The International Search Group, for instance, was set up as a joint venture between five companies in France, the UK, Austria, Germany and Italy in order to offer a European service to its customers.

Consortia

In some industries cooperative behaviour has come about for particular reasons. In process plant contracting, for example, the projects are often too large for single firms and so they form consortia in order to bid for the contract. The consortium will include contractors, suppliers and bankers who together will have the expertise and the resources to carry out the project.

Multinationals

At the opposite end of the scale from the very small business are companies which have the capability to produce goods or services in more than one country but where control usually resides in a central location. Multinationals are often well-known household names, as the examples below illustrate:

- UK multinationals – BP, GlaxoSmithKline.
- European multinationals – Nestlé, Volkswagen.
- US multinationals – General Motors, IBM.

These multinationals are huge organisations and their market values often exceed the GNP of many of the countries in which they operate. They are estimated to account for a quarter of the world's output.

The growth in the multinationals is due to the relaxation of exchange controls, making it easier to move money between countries, and the improvements in communication, which make it possible to run a worldwide business from one country. See Chapter 3 for a full discussion of the operation of multinational enterprises.

For information on the companies mentioned on this page see: *www.bp.com*; *www.gsk.com*; *www.nestle.com*; *www.vw.com*; *www.gm.com*; and *www.ibm.com*

Synopsis

This chapter has looked at the size structure of industry in the UK and Europe as a whole. It examined the motives for and the methods of growth, as well as the sources of finance for such growth. The role of the small firm was considered, including the growth in self-employment. Although many industries are dominated by huge companies, the trend seems to be moving away from growth towards a process of disintegration for a variety of reasons. As a result of this trend there has been an upsurge in the small-firm sector and an increase in the level of cooperative behaviour between firms.

Summary of key points

- The size structure of firms varies greatly within industries, within a country and between countries.

- Firms can grow internally through organic growth or externally through merger and takeover.

- There are many motivations for growth, including increased market share, the reaping of economies of scale, the diversification of risk.

- Growth can be financed internally through reinvested profits or externally through banks, the capital market and the money market.

- There are limits to organisational growth, such as diseconomies of scale.

- The level of merger activity in the UK and in Europe follows a cyclical pattern and is related to economic conditions.

- The small-firm sector is an important source of output and employment, and this importance has increased over time.

- Many factors have influenced the growth of the small-firm sector, including the changing pattern of industries, changes in demand, technological change, the trend towards increased subcontracting and government policy.

- At the other end of the size spectrum, multinational corporations have a massive impact on world output and employment through their activities.

case study   Gazprom, the Russian giant

Gazprom was created in 1989 as a result of the privatisation of the Russian Ministry of Gas, and the Russian government still owns 50.232 per cent of the company. The company is the biggest extractor of natural gas in the world and it is one of the world's largest companies. Gazprom supplies natural gas to Russia and the rest of the world – in 2012 it accounted for 14 per cent of the world output and 74 per cent of Russian output of natural gas. It owns the largest gas transmission network in the world – 168 000 km of pipeline – and exports gas to more than 30 countries. It extracts natural gas from very difficult terrains, most of it coming from the Yamal Peninsula, which lies east of Moscow in North-West Siberia, a permanently frozen area.

The sheer size of Gazprom protected it; it has a monopoly in domestic gas production and on gas exports. The price of gas worldwide was high and as a result profits flowed back into Russia. The situation, however, is changing. Gazprom has been badly affected by the following:

1 Economic downturn in Europe, which has had a negative impact on the demand for gas. Europe is a very important market for Gazprom: 25 per cent of the gas bought in Europe in 2012 came from Gazprom.
2 The exploitation of shale gas (see case study in Chapter 7) through fracking, which has increased the supply of natural gas from other countries and made them more self-sufficient in gas.

3 The price of Gazprom's gas, which compares unfavourably with the price of shale gas.

4 Negative reputational effects – in 2009 Gazprom cut off the supply of gas to Ukraine for two weeks, making people nervous and distrustful. This happened again following the Russian annexation of Crimea in 2014.

Gazprom reported that its net income had fallen by more than 80 per cent in 2017, citing a stronger rouble and foreign exchange fluctuations as causes for this decline (Russian workers are paid in roubles, making the cost of production higher). Many business commentators say that Gazprom is too big (e.g. it has subsidiaries in banking, media, agriculture and other industries) and needs to be broken up. This is unlikely to happen.

One problem Gazprom faces is that it has to keep two groups of people happy: on the one hand it has shareholders who are expecting returns on their investment; and on the other it has the government. Russian President Vladimir Putin has made Gazprom a 'national champion', which gives it two objectives – making profits and advancing Russian national interests. These sometimes come into conflict: for example, gas is sold inside Russia at lower than the price set outside through the use of subsidies. This advances Russian national interests but at the expense of lower profitability. The controlling interest of the government makes Gazprom susceptible to political meddling; in fact, Putin oversees all major energy deals in Russia and many claim that it is used as a tool of Russian foreign policy.

So what is the future for Gazprom? Increased production of shale gas will push the price of gas downwards and means that other countries do not have to buy from Gazprom. Putin has been negotiating for several years with China, which is the world's biggest user of energy, to supply it with gas. They have not managed to agree on a price so far, but if they did it would reduce the dependence of Gazprom on Europe. A six-year-long anti-trust investigation by the EU into some of the activities of Gazprom is showing signs of concluding, with a draft agreement being reached in 2017. Gazprom has allegedly blocked supplies of gas in Central and Eastern Europe and been overcharging its customers by linking the price of gas to oil. Depending upon the outcome of this investigation, Gazprom could face a €10 billion fine. There are also problems with bilateral agreements made with six EU members regarding the construction of gas pipelines; the agreements do not comply with EU rules. Within Russia itself Gazprom is facing increased competition from two other gas producers: Novatek, established in 1994, and Rosneft, established in 1993.

Many argue that the way forward involves splitting up the business into parts – the pipeline business from the gas production – but as this case study shows, the situation is a complex one where market forces are not the most important factor.

Case study questions

1 Why does the nature of the product, natural gas, make this an industry that is likely to be dominated by large companies?

2 What impact is fracking (see Chapter 7) likely to have on this market and this company?

Review and discussion questions

1 How might a global financial crisis impact on merger and acquisition behaviour?

2 Can you see any dangers in the creation of super-utilities (large, diversified organisations which supply a range of utilities – gas, electricity and water)?

3 What advantages does networking bring to small firms and the economy as a whole?

4 How has the balance between large and small firms in manufacturing changed in the last 10 years? Do you expect these trends to continue?

Assignments

1 You are an information officer at your local business advice centre and you have been given the job of designing and writing a leaflet aimed at the proprietors of small firms, outlining the government aid that is available to small businesses. Your brief is to keep the leaflet short and readable but with maximum information. (Information on government aid will be available at your local library or business advice centre.)

2 As part of 'Business Week' you have been asked to give a short talk on the size structure of UK industry to local sixth-formers doing Business Studies A-level. Prepare your talk by choosing two industries, describing and giving reasons for the typical size structure of the firms in those industries.

Further reading

Griffiths, A. and Wall, S., *Applied Economics,* 12th edition, Financial Times Press, 2011.

Web links and further questions are available on the website at:

www.pearsoned.co.uk/worthington

12 Industrial structure

Chris Britton

Within any economy, there will be a whole range of industries producing a variety of products for a variety of users. The particular combination of industries within a country is called the industrial structure of that country. There will be international differences in industrial structures because of differences in the many factors that affect the determination of industrial structure.

Learning outcomes

Having read this chapter you should be able to:

- explain the concept of industrial structure and illustrate how it is measured
- outline the industrial structure of the UK and the EU as a whole
- analyse the reasons for particular industrial structures and the factors that influence industrial structure
- illustrate how and why the industrial structure of the UK and the EU has changed over time

Key terms

Crowding out
Deindustrialisation
Entrepreneurship
Industrial structure
Life cycle model

Manufacturing sector
Primary sector
Productivity
Reshoring
Secondary sector

Skill shortages
Standard Industrial
 Classification (SIC)
Tertiary sector

Introduction

A country can produce many different and diverse types of goods and services, ranging from the production of cars to the delivery of legal services to farming. The mix of these and the combination of industries that exists to produce them is called the **industrial structure** of a country. There are likely to be large differences in industrial structure between countries for many reasons. This chapter will look at the industrial structure of the EU as a trading bloc and the UK in particular. There is a need for the industrial structure of a country to be measured in some way so that changes over time can be identified and international comparisons made. This chapter will look at the definitions of industries, the problems with such definitions and the official classification of industry used by the government in the UK. It will also identify the changes in industrial structure and the causes of these changes.

The structure of industry

The process of production

In Chapter 7 the three factors of production – labour, land and capital – were considered. Textbooks often add a fourth factor of production to this list, called 'entrepreneurship'. **Entrepreneurship** is the process of bringing together the other factors in order to produce goods and services. A firm produces goods and services because they are demanded and because a profit can be earned by selling them. Figure 12.1 shows a much simplified profit and loss account for a car manufacturer. The items on the expenditure side represent the payments to the factors of production. Wages are payments to labour, raw materials and an element of overheads would be the payments to capital, and the payment for land would be included in overheads. The payment to the entrepreneur is in the form of profit.

What has happened in this process is that the factors of production have been combined to make finished cars and in the process value has been added to the initial value of the raw materials.

Figure 12.1   A simplified profit and loss account

Revenues	£m	Expenditures	£m
Sales of cars	30.0	Raw materials	7.5
		Wages and salaries	10.0
		Overheads (rent, rates lighting, etc.)	2.5
			20.0
		Profit	10.0
	30.0		30.0

Figure 12.2 A simplified production process

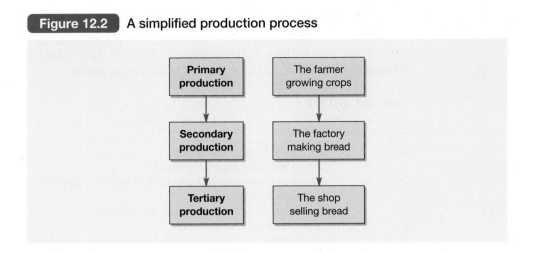

The car manufacturer can be thought of as being in the centre of a process of production which links together raw materials at one end with the consumers at the other end. The raw materials are extracted and processed and then the finished goods are sold. In economic terminology, the extraction of raw materials is called *primary production*, the manufacture of cars is called *secondary production* and the distribution of the finished cars is called *tertiary production* (see Figure 12.2). Although this simple path from primary production through to tertiary production is the case for many industries, it is likely to be much more complicated in practice.

The discussion at present is confined to a single firm, but it can be moved to the *industry level.* The industries that deal with natural resources, such as farming and mining, comprise the **primary sector**. Industries which process these natural resources comprise the **secondary sector**, which will include manufacturing, construction and energy suppliers. The service industries make up the **tertiary sector**. There are great difficulties involved in such a classification of industry, as we will see later, but consideration will now be given to the official classification of industry in the UK.

The Standard Industrial Classification

The **Standard Industrial Classification (SIC)** of economic activity is the official classification of industries in the UK into different sectors. It was introduced in 1948 and has been updated and changed on occasions to take account of the development of new products and industries for producing those products. It was changed in 1980, mainly in order to bring the UK classification in line with the activity classification used by the Statistical Office of the European Communities (Eurostat), which is called Nomenclature générale des activités économiques dans les Communautés européennes (NACE).

web
link

Data on industrial structure in the UK is available from *www.statistics.gov.uk*
For the EU from *http://ec.europa.eu/eurostat*

The 1980 SIC is shown in Table 12.1. The 1980 classification had 10 *divisions* (denoted by a single digit). Each of these was divided into *classes* (two digits), which in turn were divided into *groups* (three digits) and *activity headings* (four digits). In total there were 10 divisions, 60 classes, 222 groups and 334 activity headings.

Table 12.1 SIC (80)

Division	Industry
0	Agriculture, forestry and fishing
1	Energy and water supply industries
2	Extraction of minerals and ores other than fuels; manufacture of metals, mineral products and chemicals
3	Metal goods, engineering and vehicle industries
4	Other manufacturing industries
5	Construction
6	Distribution, hotels and catering; repairs
7	Transport and communication
8	Banking, finance, insurance, business services and leasing
9	Other services

The term 'production industries' refers to divisions 1 to 4 of the above classification; the term 'manufacturing industries' refers to divisions 2 to 4. The SIC does not comply exactly with the broad classification of industry used in the last section. The primary sector of the economy is found in division 0 and parts of divisions 1 and 2; the secondary sector in parts of divisions 1 and 2 and all of divisions 3 to 5; the tertiary sector would be divisions 6 to 9.

The SIC is changed periodically to reflect changes taking place in industry, most notably in 1990, 2003 and 2008 (see below). In 1990 the EC approved a new statistical classification of economic activities in the EU (NACE Rev. 1). This meant that the UK had to introduce a new SIC in 1992. The standardisation of industrial classification across Europe makes inter-state comparisons easier. The SIC (92) which replaced SIC (80) was based on NACE Rev. 1. It had 17 sections instead of the 10 divisions of SIC (80); each of these sections was denoted by a letter from A to Q. The sections were divided into subsections which were denoted by the addition of another letter. The subsections were then broken down into two-digit divisions and again into groups (three digits), into classes (four digits) and into subclasses (five digits).

In January 2003 the EU made a minor revision of NACE Rev. 1, which was known as NACE Rev. 1.1. As a result, the UK government had to introduce a new SIC (2003). On 1 January 2008 a major revision of the SIC was introduced in the UK, SIC (2007), the broad outline of which is given in Appendix 12.1 at the end of this chapter. There are now 21 sections (A to U), 88 divisions (2 digit), 272 groups (3 digit), 615 classes (4 digit) and 191 subclasses (5 digit). An example is given in Table 12.2. Some sections are

Table 12.2 SIC (2007)

Section C	Manufacturing (Divisions 10 through 33)
Division 13	Manufacture of textiles
Group 13.1	Manufacture of other textiles
Class 13.93	Manufacture of carpets and rugs
Subclass 13.93/1	Manufacture of woven or tufted carpets and rugs

sub-divided more than others, Section A (Agriculture, forestry and fishing), for example, has only 3 divisions while Section C (manufacturing) has 24. The level of detail depends upon the diversity of production included within the section.

The new SIC brings the UK in line with the EU (NACE Rev. 2) and the United Nation's International Standard Industrial Classification of all economic activities (ISIC Rev. 4). The main differences between SIC (2007) and SIC (2003) are in the number of sections and the distribution of industries between the sections. For example, Section K in SIC (2003) is now distributed across three sections (L, M and N). There is a much more detailed breakdown of the services sector, which illustrates the increased importance of this sector in the economy.

Problems in classifying industries

The classification of industry is problematic. Firms could be grouped together according to similarities in what they produce, but some firms produce a range of goods for quite different markets. Firms could be grouped together according to what they 'do', so that if their production processes are similar they could be considered as part of the same industry. The service industries are particularly problematic as they have traditionally been defined by the function they perform, but developments in technology have led to these functions overlapping and therefore becoming more difficult to distinguish: for example, publishing and printing. All of this leads to industries that are seemingly very diverse being grouped together in the SIC. Although the SIC does not succeed in overcoming all of these problems, it does provide an accepted classification of industry which can be used for many purposes. The information collected provides a basis for comparing the structure of industry within a country over time and between countries.

Measuring industrial structure

The structure of industry in a country is not static and it changes over time for a variety of reasons. For example:

- The development of new products means that new industries come into existence (e.g. the inventions and innovations in the field of electronic games).
- New patterns of demand mean that some industries will be declining while others become increasingly important.
- Changes in society will be reflected in industrial structure. For example, according to the census in 1851, 22 per cent of the UK workforce was engaged in agriculture, forestry and fishing, while in 2012 the figure was 1.2 per cent. This obviously reflects the movement away from an agriculturally based society to an industrial society.

Industrial structure is usually measured by the level of employment or output of the various sectors of the economy, and changes in industrial structure over time can be observed by looking at the changes in the employment and output levels in different industries. These will usually (but not always) paint the same picture; a sector in decline will have falling employment and output.

Industrial structure in the EU

Figure 12.3 shows the industrial structure of the EU as a whole measured by employment in 1979, 2005 (EU27) and 2012 (EU27). This figure illustrates that there has been a change in industrial structure during this time period; some of this is due to differences between the older EU countries and some of the newer members of the EU. During the period there has been a steady fall in the level of employment in agriculture and manufacturing and a rise in employment in the service sector. In 2012, 5 per cent of the working population of the EU27 was employed in agriculture, 25 per cent in industry and 70 per cent in the service sector. This trend away from employment in the primary and secondary sectors towards the service sector is evident in other advanced industrial economies.

Table 12.3 shows that while there are some differences in industrial structure between countries, the tertiary sector in all cases is predominant in employment terms (except for India).

Within the EU, the UK has a smaller agricultural sector in terms of employment than other EU countries (and the EU average) and also has the biggest service sector. Table 12.3 also shows that the newer members of the EU have had an impact on the average, many of which have big agricultural sectors; the two biggest are shown in the table – Poland and Romania. There are exceptions to this pattern – Portugal has a big agricultural sector and Slovenia has a structure much more in line with EU27 members. Four other countries are shown for comparison, including the fast-developing economies of China and India, which have very different patterns of industrial structure.

Industrial structure can also be gauged by looking at output figures. Here the same pattern is evident – the importance of the primary and secondary sectors of the main industrial countries has declined (reasons for this will be considered later in this chapter). Table 12.4 shows the contribution of the output of the three sectors to GDP for the same countries as in Table 12.3.

Figure 12.3 Percentage shares of employment in the three main sectors of the EU, 1979, 2005 and 2012

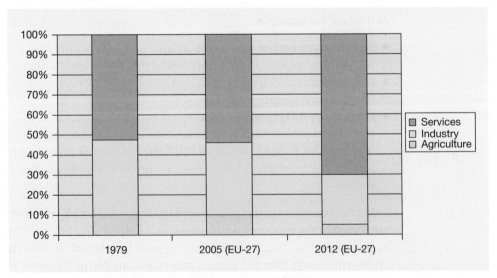

Source: Adapted from Eurostat, 2008, 2013 © European Union, 1995–2014.

Table 12.3 Percentage employed in different sectors of selected countries, estimates as of 2017

	Agriculture	Industry	Services
UK	1.3	15.2	83.5
Germany	1.4	24.2	74.3
Slovenia	3.7	31.7	64.6
France	2.4	18.3	79.3
World	11.5	34.4	43.4
Ireland	5.0	11.0	84.0
Portugal	8.6	23.9	67.5
Poland	11.5	30.4	57.6
Romania	28.3	28.9	42.8
Japan	2.9	26.2	70.9
USA	0.7	20.3	79.1
China	28.3	29.3	42.4
India	47.0	22.0	31.0

Source: Adapted from *The World Fact Book, www.cia.gov*

Table 12.4 Contribution towards GDP for different sectors of selected countries, 2012 (%)

	Agriculture	Industry	Services
UK	0.6	19.2	80.2
Germany	0.6	30.3	69.1
Slovenia	2.3	33.6	64.1
France	1.7	19.4	78.8
World	6.4	30.3	62.6
Ireland	1.0	41.3	57.6
Portugal	2.4	21.9	75.9
Poland	2.7	38.5	58.9
Romania	3.3	35.4	61.3
Japan	1.2	27.7	71.1
USA	1.1	19.4	79.5
China	8.6	39.8	51.6
India	16.5	29.8	45.4

Source: Adapted from *The World Fact Book, www.cia.gov*

Using output to assess industrial structure makes China and India look more similar to the others. In the EU there are three main reasons for the restructuring of manufacturing that has taken place over the past 50 years: first, deregulation, which has led to greater internal competition; second, greater competition, both internally and externally from third-party countries, especially the less developed, low-wage countries; and third, the expansion of the Single European Market and the resulting increases in competition brought about by increased market size. There is a great variety of ways in which companies have reacted to these changes, but the *Panorama of EU Industry* has identified several 'typical' responses, some of which will have contradictory effects. These include the following:

- Increased investment for the prime purpose of increasing productivity. This has led to an increase in the level of unemployment in the EU as machinery has replaced relatively expensive labour in the production process.

- A tendency towards greater concentration in industry both vertically and horizontally through merger and acquisition, in order to benefit from economies of scale and to be in a position to benefit from the increased competition (see Chapter 11).
- Greater specialisation in production. Many companies in quite diverse industries (window frames, chemicals, clothing and textiles) have decided to reduce product lines and concentrate on particular market segments.
- Greater flexibility in the production process. This has been achieved by greater automation in production processes, the externalisation of certain activities, subcontracting and increased use of part-time and temporary workers.

mini case   The end of manufacturing?

Some commentators are calling 3D printing or additive manufacturing the new industrial revolution. If people can reproduce products at home using a 3D printer, is this the end of manufacturing as we know it?

The 3D printer is not new – the first one was developed in the United States in 1986 – but it has become big news in recent years. These printers have uses in lots of different areas, ranging from medicine, through orthopaedic implants (e.g. a titanium jaw bone was successfully implanted in 2012), to food, where food items like ravioli can be produced. They have also been used in business for many years – the car industry, for example, has been printing 3D prototypes for a long time. What is new is the more widespread availability and the affordability of 3D printers – it is possible that there will be one in every home in the not too distant future.

The implications for business are huge:

1 *Manufacturing.* Once there is a 3D printer in every house, will there be any need for manufacturers? Surely customers could just print their own products? Such a scenario is unlikely as most products are produced to high tolerances out of specific materials. It is not possible for parts of a washing machine to be printed at home and be capable of working to the correct specification. The main niche for 3D printers, at least to begin with, is in small-scale, one-off, customised production.

2 *Stockholding.* Instead of companies holding large supplies of stock or parts, they (or the 3D company) could hold the designs for the parts and have them printed up as they need them. There will be less waste and the cost of keeping and storing inventories will therefore be drastically reduced. This will have an impact on warehousing companies.

3 *Logistics.* Similarly, if stock or parts do not have to be delivered between companies, the cost of transportation will be reduced, as too will the level of emissions, so there will be an environmental impact. The firms operating in logistics will be affected. UPS is already testing 3D printing in its stores in the United States. Customers will be able to bring in their designs and have them printed up in 3D plastic.

4 *Industrial structure.* **Reshoring** refers to the repatriation of jobs once lost to the low-wage countries like China. Both rising wages in these countries and technological change make it economical to bring production home. A recent report found little large-scale reshoring in the UK, but some isolated examples. Hornby brought back from China to the UK 60 per cent of the production of its model paint brand Humbrol in 2012. It is possible that 3D printers reduce the competitive advantage that low-wage countries have.

5 *Labour markets.* The mini case study on robotisation has already discussed the likely impact on the labour force in the UK. The skills needed for the future of 3D printing will be in high-tech design roles.

It would seem that the advantage of 3D printers over traditional forms of manufacturing is for one-off specialised production where the investment needed in machinery would be prohibitive or where storage costs of inventories are high. In industries where customisation is important, 3D printers come into their own. There are benefits to 3D printing – the reduction of waste, products can be made as light as possible, less long-distance travel and hence fewer emissions, and the individual customisation of products. There are, however, some questions that will need to be answered.

One important one is the question of intellectual property – who owns the patents and copyright on the products? It is possible that reverse engineering can take place, where a product can be stripped back to its component parts and made up from scratch using a 3D printer. There is also the possibility that dangerous or illegal products can be made. The first 3D gun was made in the United States in 2013. These questions will need to be answered as it is clear from this mini case that 3D printers are here to stay and will have a large impact on the way business operates.

Industrial structure in the UK

The UK does not fare well in international comparisons, as the trend is the same as in the EU, but the decline in the **manufacturing sector** has been more pronounced in the UK. It is also true that while there has been a relative decline in the output of manufacturing in all countries, it is only in the case of the UK that there has been an absolute decline.

Figure 12.4 shows a graph of employment in manufacturing in four countries over the period 1974 to 2012. It is clear from this graph that the decline in employment in

Figure 12.4 Index of employment in manufacturing industry in selected countries (1995 = 100)

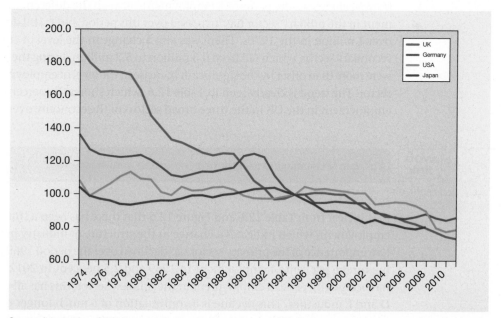

Source: Adapted from STAN Database for Structural Analysis from OECD.StatExtracts *http://stats.oecd.org/* (20 May 2014).

manufacturing has been much greater in the UK than the others. The UK started from a much higher base in 1974 and in 2011 had the lowest level of employment in manufacturing.

Table 12.5 gives an indication of the change in industrial structure in the UK between 1997 and 2017. It is important to realise that when different years are compared the figures will be affected by the state of the economy in each of those years, but nevertheless the comparison will give an indication of changes in the relative importance of the three sectors of the economy. The change in the SIC that occurred during this period would have had a minimal effect on the figures and has been corrected as far as possible.

Table 12.5 Total numbers in employment, 1997, 2007 and 2017 (UK)

Section	1997 (000s)	2007 (000s)	2017 (000s)
A/B/D/E	775	739	918
Total primary	**775**	**852**	**918**
C	4 370	3 216	2 901
F	1 891	2 527	2 336
Total secondary	**6 261**	**5 743**	**5 237**
G/H	5 335	5 686	5 692
I	1 275	1 324	1 747
J/K	1 907	2 320	2 523
L–N	2 727	3 436	4 267
O–T	7 848	9 751	11 250
Total tertiary	**19 092**	**22 517**	**25 479**
Total employment	**26 128**	**29 112**	**31 634**

Source: Adapted from EMP13, *www.ons.gov.uk*

There was an increase in the level of total employment during this period and a substantial change in the pattern of employment between the different industries. Employment in the primary sector has increased over this period, but is still down from highs of over 1 million in the 1970s. There was also a change in the level of employment in the secondary sector, which fell from 6.3 million to 5.2 million during the period. These falls were more than offset by the significant increase in the level of employment in the tertiary sector. The trend is clearly seen in Table 12.6, which shows the percentage share of total employment in the UK in the three broad sectors of the economy over a period of time.

 web link For data on employment/output by sector see *www.oecd.org*

It is clear from Table 12.6 and Figure 12.5 that there has been a shift in the pattern of employment, which indicates a change in the structure of industry in the UK. The relative importance of the primary sector has declined over the period 1969 to 2012, accounting for 3.6 per cent of employment in 1969 and 2.5 per cent in 2012. Since 2007 there has been an increase in employment in the primary sector, this has all come from section D and E industries. This decline is a continuation of a much longer trend of decline in the primary sector. There has also been a dramatic fall in the relative importance of the

Table 12.6 Percentage share of total employment of primary, secondary and tertiary sectors (UK), selected years, 1969–2012 (data no longer collected)

Year	Sector		
	Primary	Secondary	Tertiary
1969	3.6	46.8	49.3
1973	3.5	42.1	54.3
1979	3.1	38.2	58.7
1984	3.8	31.1	65.1
1989	2.4	28.5	68.9
1993	2.1	25.0	72.9
1999	1.6	22.5	76.0
2000	1.7	22.1	76.2
2001	1.5	19.5	79.0
2002	1.4	18.6	80.0
2003	1.4	18.5	80.1
2004	1.4	18.3	80.3
2005	1.4	18.2	80.3
2006	1.4	17.9	80.7
2007	1.4	17.8	80.8
2008	1.5	17.5	80.9
2009	1.8	17.2	81.0
2010	2.4	16.1	81.5
2011	2.6	15.9	81.5
2012	2.5	15.6	82.0

Source: Adapted from *www.statistics.gov.uk*

secondary sector in providing employment, which fell from 46.8 per cent to 15.6 per cent of employment during the period. Again this table shows that the relative importance of the service sector has increased.

Figure 12.5 Percentage share of total employment in the secondary and tertiary sectors of the UK economy

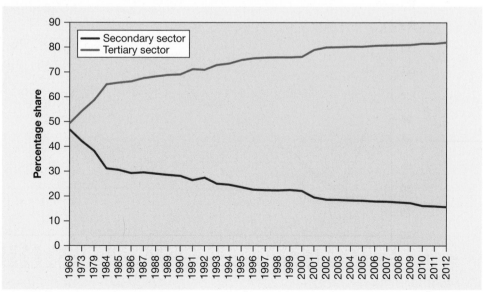

Source: Adapted from *www.statistics.gov.uk*

Before consideration is given to the reasons for these changes, the other key indicator of changes in industrial structure will be considered – the level of output. These figures show a similar pattern to those on employment. There has been a fall in the relative importance of the secondary sector and an increase in the importance of the tertiary sector. There was an increase in the importance of the oil and natural gas industries in the late 1970s and early 1980s because of the production of North Sea oil and gas; this trend, however, has now been reversed. The broad classification used in Table 12.7 hides the fact that there are differences within the sectors, where some industries grow while others decline in importance.

Table 12.7 Economic output by industry 1990–2015 (£ billion, non-inflation adjusted)

Industry	1990	1995	2000	2005	2010	2015
Agriculture, forestry and fishing	8	11	8	8	10	11
Mining and extractives	13	11	24	27	30	17
Manufacturing	107	132	142	138	141	162
Construction	42	42	57	82	81	102
Services	420	536	715	960	1120	1328

Source: Industries in the UK, House of Commons Library, 2016 – table.

The changes in relative sizes of the different sectors of the economy in the UK mirror those of other countries. It is only in the UK, however, that there have been periods of decline in the output of manufacturing industries, as Figure 12.6 shows. This decline in manufacturing is regarded by many as relatively unimportant; it is seen as a natural

Figure 12.6   Output of manufacturing industry in the UK, 1979–2012 (2011 = 100)

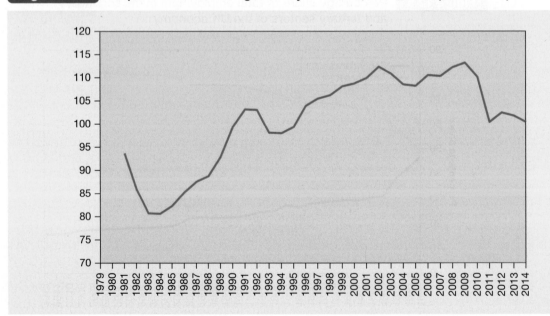

Source: Adapted from Table IOP5, Output of Production Industries, ONS.

process of change which started with the Industrial Revolution and the movement from the land to service-based economic activities. To some extent this natural growth argument is supported by Tables 12.3 and 12.4. Countries at an earlier stage of development tend to have higher employment in agricultural sectors.

This change in industrial structure is a trend that is evident in other countries. It might also be the case that some of the growth in the service sector is illusory. For example, if firms are externalising services that they once carried out themselves, there is actually not an increase in the amount of work done but a change in where it is done. It is not surprising that employment levels in manufacturing should fall, given the expansion of services and increases in productivity. What is more disturbing is that the absolute value of output in manufacturing has fallen and while similar patterns can be observed in other countries, the UK does not fare very well in international comparisons.

Causes of changes in industrial structure

There are several explanations put forward for the changes that take place in industrial structure. Broadly speaking these can be classified into demand and supply factors.

Demand factors

Changing patterns of demand will cause changes in the structure of industry. Demand will change as a result of changes in tastes and fashions, changes in the structure of the population and changes in the levels of income. As income increases there is normally an increase in total spending on goods and services, but there will be differences between types of goods. There will be relatively large increases in expenditure on goods with high income elasticities of demand and relatively small increases or even falls in demand for other goods. Goods with low income elasticities are necessities such as food, fuel, clothing and footwear. Luxury items have high income elasticities of demand; these would include things like durable goods, alcohol and services such as tourism and leisure activities. Naturally what constitutes a necessity and luxury would change over the years. Figures 12.7 and 12.8 show the trend in expenditure on selected goods and services over a period of time in the UK.

Figure 12.7 shows that the expenditure on food, alcohol and tobacco has remained fairly constant over time, as expected. The expenditure on durable goods is much more affected by movements in the trade cycle and the level of income – there was a drop in spending following the credit crunch of 2008. Figure 12.8 reinforces the findings above that services are like durables in that their demand is closely linked to the level of income – the pattern of expenditure is very similar to that for durables. It should also be remembered that suppliers have an impact upon the level of demand for products as they can manipulate demand through advertising and other forms of promotion.

The differential effects of rising income on demand for goods and services would in part explain the growth in the size of the service sector over the years. The change in industrial structure can then be seen as a natural process of change. During the Industrial Revolution there was a movement from agriculture to industry, in the same way as there is now a movement from manufacturing towards services. Changes in demand, however, cannot explain all of this change. Growth in the service sector does not necessarily

Figure 12.7 Expenditure on selected goods in the UK, 1997–2012

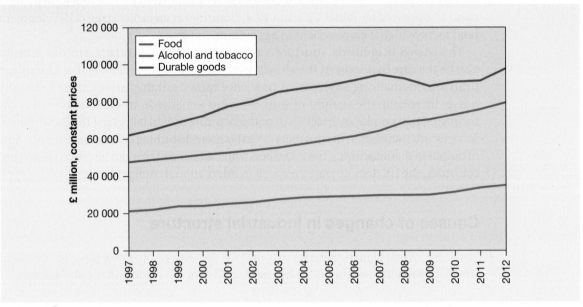

Source: Consumer trends 2013, ONS.

mean that there should be a decline in the size of the manufacturing sector when there are high levels of unemployment in the economy. Labour can be drawn from the unemployed rather than from manufacturing industry. During the time period under consideration there have been periods of high unemployment. It is also the case that the

Figure 12.8 Expenditure on services in the UK, 1997–2012

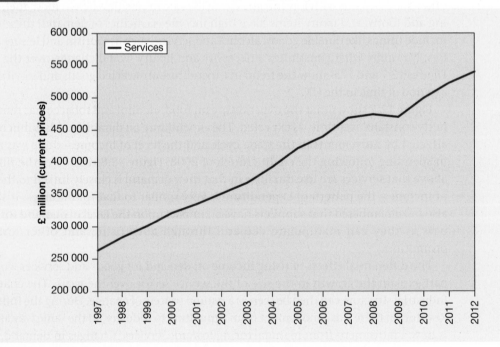

Source: Consumer trends 2013, ONS.

import of manufactured goods has not fallen, so it is not that demand has fallen for those goods but that we are buying them from abroad.

Supply factors

Changes in industrial structure can also be triggered by changes in supply conditions. The oil crisis of the 1970s is a good example of this. As a result of the massive increase in oil prices, there was a concerted campaign to reduce the consumption of oil and a search for other forms of energy. Technological change gives rise to new products and/or new processes of production. Different industries will vary in the scope for technological change and for increases in productivity (this is considered more fully later in this chapter).

Demand and supply forces are interlinked so it is often difficult to separate their effects as new products will generate new demands or could be developed to meet new demands.

Added to these internal factors is the fact that the UK is part of an international economy and competition from abroad will have an impact on the structure of industry through both demand and supply factors.

mini case   The life cycle model

A common way of looking at a product and the organisation that produces it is through the use of the **life cycle model**, where the position of the product in its life cycle will have implications for such things as the marketing of that product. The life cycle model can be applied equally to a market, an industry or even an industrial sector, where the position in its life cycle will have implications for industrial structure, market structure (see Chapter 15) and the strategic choices that will confront the organisation in that industry.

The four phases in a life cycle – development, growth, maturity and decline – are shown in Figure 12.9.

The first phase is the development, birth or entry phase of the life cycle when the industry is in its infancy and growth is still very low. The growth phase is where there is rapid growth in sales and profitability. Firms are likely to have larger market shares and there will be lower costs due to economies of scale and the experience effects. The maturity phase, where growth has stabilised, is the most common state of the majority of industries and it could last a very long time.

The decline phase is where the growth rate starts to fall for many possible reasons, for example technological change which has made the

industry obsolete, or changing patterns of demand by consumers, to mention two. There is likely to be cost-cutting and the market can be 'niched', possibly looking to overseas markets.

Various points can be made about this life cycle. First, a product or an industry may not go through all of these stages; for example, an industry may not make it past the development stage for a variety of reasons, as in the case of the disc cameras which never found popularity with the public. Second, the length of each of the stages of the life cycle is not uniform and is likely to vary a great deal between industries – this can be seen by applying the model to the agricultural sector, where the growth phase lasted for several hundreds of years. Third, it is possible to miss the decline phase altogether, through diversification and innovation, in which case the growth path runs along the dashed line in the figure and the organisation has embarked upon another life cycle. The implications of the stage in the life cycle for various factors are summarised in Table 12.8.

It is important to note that the behaviour of organisations will affect the shape of the life cycle of the product and the industry. Porter (1979) looks at the strategic possibilities confronting a firm at various stages in its life, depending upon its

Figure 12.9   A life cycle

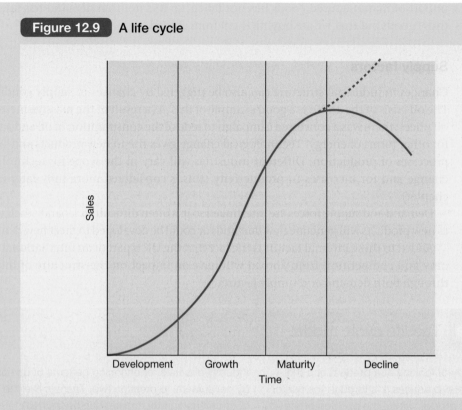

position in the market – a leader or a follower. One important factor is that a product might be at a different stage in its life cycle at different geographical locations, so an industry that is saturated in the west might be able to extend its life by expanding into other countries.

Table 12.8 Implications of the different stages of the life cycle

Stage	Development	Growth	Maturity	Decline
Market growth	Low	Very rapid	Slowing or constant	Negative
Degree of competition	Low because there are few firms in the industry	Increasing as new firms enter	High Market stabilising	Declining Tendency towards oligopoly or monopoly
Marketing activities	Market research Promotion of new product	Promotion Increasing market share	Maintaining or increasing market share Product differentiation	Depends on strategy
R&D expenditure	High on new products and processes	Mainly on processes	Fairly low	Depends on strategy
Costs	High	Slower rate of increase (economies of scale)	Cost-cutting	Depends on strategy
Profits	Low or zero	Growing fairly rapidly	Margin of profit squeezed by competition	Falling

Deindustrialisation

The decline in the importance of manufacturing has been termed '**deindustrialisation**' by many economists. The following causes are put forward for deindustrialisation.

'Crowding out'

The argument here is that the growth in the size of the public sector has been at the expense of the private sector. The resources that could have been used to expand the private sector have instead been used in the public sector, so that the public sector has been **crowding out** the private sector (see also Chapter 17). This was a popular argument used in the 1980s to call for reductions in public spending. With higher levels of unemployment the argument loses its validity because it is not just a matter of using resources in the private or public sector – they are lying idle. As a result the 'crowding-out' argument is less popular now. It is also argued that the higher rates of interest that might accompany higher spending on the public sector discourage private spending. Again, there is little concrete evidence that lower investment results from higher rates of interest. It could be that investment falls because of lower returns on that investment, and the returns on capital employed have been lower in the UK than in other countries.

Productivity

In terms of **productivity** the UK has not performed as well as other countries. Low productivity has implications for international competitiveness. It can be offset by lower wages in order to stop costs from rising, which might be passed on in the form of higher prices or through exchange rates so that prices remain competitive internationally. There are a number of ways of measuring productivity. The productivity of labour can be measured by output per person employed or by output per hour worked. Neither of these is a perfect measure because they will both be affected by the amount of capital employed and the productivity of this capital, but as there are great problems involved in measuring the productivity of capital this problem will be ignored for the time being. Table 12.9 shows output per person employed in selected countries in 2015. Table 12.10 shows output per hour worked.

Table 12.9 Output per person employed, selected countries, 2015 (EU28 = 100)

France	116.2	EU28	100
Germany	105.9	Euro area	107.2
UK	101.2		

Source: Adapted from Labour Productivity per Person Employed, Eurostat, 2015 © European Union, 1995–2015.

Table 12.10 Output per hour worked, % change from 2010 to 2016

France	8.1	EU28	5.8
Germany	5.7	Euro area	5.7
UK	0.9		

Source: Adapted from Labour Productivity per Person Employed, Eurostat, 2013 © European Union, 1995–2014.

These figures show that the UK has not performed well compared with the other countries listed.

It appears that there is a widening 'productivity gap' between the UK and some other countries; the UK change from 2010 to 2016 is actually the lowest of all EU member countries. Why is this the case? Two main reasons put forward for the UK's poor performance are as follows:

- The quality of the inputs used. There are two main inputs into the production process – labour and capital. Improving the quantity and quality of both of these will have an impact on productivity levels. As discussed in this chapter, the UK compares badly on both of these counts.
- How these inputs are used. This is measured by 'total factor productivity', which measures the efficiency of both labour and capital. Recent figures are not available for total factor productivity, but figures for 1999 showed that the UK did rather better on this measure of productivity.

The gains in productivity made by the UK from the mid-1990s to the late 2000s have reversed; it seems that employment growth in the UK has been powered by lower wages rather than increased productivity. As the UK economy starts to grow again, it might be expected that productivity will also pick up.

International competition

Because of competition from both the developed world and the developing world, where wage rates are lower than the UK rates, the UK has lost markets. At home much demand for goods and services is met by imports. Internationally the UK has lost markets too, as the level of its exports has fallen. There is evidence of this from the UK balance of payments. For example, in the mid-1980s the UK started to import more manufactured goods than it exported for the first time since the Industrial Revolution, and there was a widening deficit on the balance of payments in manufactured goods. At times high exchange rates have not helped the situation and have contributed to the decline. It is often argued that the UK competes badly in both price and quality.

Specialisation

The UK tends to specialise in sectors that do not have great export potential; its percentage shares in sectors such as electrical equipment, computers and transport equipment are less than the EU averages. The energy sector is of great importance to the UK economy.

Research and development

In the UK the proportion of spending on research and development has not changed very much over recent decades. This is not the case for other countries. It is also true that in the UK a much greater percentage of R&D is financed by government rather than private industry (see Chapter 7).

The educational system

The UK educational system is said to be biased towards the arts and pure sciences rather than applied scientific, engineering and business-type subjects. In the UK, 30 per cent of engineers have a professional qualification, while in Germany the figure is 70 per cent. And 5 per cent of UK retail workers have received training similar to an apprenticeship; in Germany, the corresponding figure is 75 per cent. As far as international trade is concerned, the UK also lags behind other European countries in its language training.

Level and type of investment

The level of investment in the UK is low. This means that the stock of capital may be too low and that it will be relatively 'old' (see Chapter 7).

Non-price factors

Non-price factors include quality, design and after-sales service. The UK has been late compared with other countries to take up total quality management. These techniques were started in the west but then taken up and honed by the Japanese and are now being used worldwide. Quality management schemes can be successful only if other conditions are right, such as a well-trained and qualified and highly motivated workforce.

Skills shortages in manufacturing

Even in times of high unemployment, there are still **skill shortages**. In a survey carried out by the Confederation of British Industry in 2015, 65 per cent of companies said they expected to need more employees with higher skills, and 55 per cent of companies said that they were concerned about having enough people with the right skills available to fill their jobs.

The financial system

It is often argued that the UK banks are less supportive of business than banks in other countries. In the UK, banks tend to offer only short-term to medium-term finance for industry; the only long-term finance would be in the form of mortgages. In other countries banks are large providers of long-term finance to industry through the purchase of stocks and shares.

Lack of qualified managers

It is frequently claimed that manufacturing has not recruited the best-qualified candidates for management, although management training can overcome this to some extent.

North Sea oil

The existence of North Sea oil has had a mixed effect on the UK. On the one hand, it has led to an inflow of cash, which has helped the balance of payments, but on the other it has also served to keep the exchange rate of the pound higher than it would have been in its absence. A higher exchange rate has the effect of making UK goods more expensive abroad and foreign goods cheaper in the UK. Thus there is a corresponding deterioration in the balance of payments. A strong currency makes the UK less competitive in international markets, and as the biggest part of what we export is industrial goods, this sector will be most affected.

Government policy

During the 1980s the UK government repeated the argument that the decline in manufacturing was not important. It was seen as the working of the market mechanism and would be replaced by services. The government therefore took a relaxed view of the decline. In the early 1980s the adherence to a strict monetarist policy of high interest rates and cutbacks in government expenditure contributed to the decline in manufacturing. More recently, the importance of manufacturing in the process of wealth and job creation has been recognised, and policies to encourage manufacturing have been implemented.

Synopsis

Industrial structure refers to the relative sizes of the different industries in the economy. Firms are grouped together into industries and industries are grouped together into sectors in some way, although this is often difficult to do. The government has an official Standard Industrial Classification, which has been changed to bring it in line with the EU classification.

The size of industries and sectors of the economy is measured by looking at the level of employment or the level of output. In the UK, the primary sector is small and declining, although there was an increase in its importance in the 1980s due to the discovery and extraction of North Sea oil and gas. The secondary sector has also been declining in importance, in terms of both employment and output. The biggest sector of the economy at present is the tertiary sector. This pattern is similar to what is happening in other industrialised countries, although the detail varies slightly between countries. The industrial structure of a country and the way it changes depend upon many factors, most of which have been considered in this chapter.

Summary of key points

- Each country has a particular mix of primary, secondary and tertiary sectors which make up its industrial structure.

- Over the last 100 years there has been a shift in industrial structure in all countries, first from agriculture to manufacturing and then from manufacturing to services.

- This shift has taken place in terms of both employment and output.

- Changes in demand are one of the major causes of changes in industrial structure, as evidenced by the case study.

- Supply factors such as technological change are also important in the process of change.

- The decline in manufacturing has been termed deindustrialisation and this process has been particularly pronounced in the UK.

- Reasons put forward for this include 'crowding out', productivity, investment, research and development, the educational system and the high value of the pound.

Appendix 12.1 The Standard Industrial Classification (SIC), 2007

Division	Industry
Section A	Agriculture, forestry and fishing
Section B	Mining and quarrying
Section C	Manufacturing
Section D	Electricity, gas, steam and air-conditioning supply
Section E	Water supply, waste management and remediation activities
Section F	Construction
Section G	Wholesale and retail trade; repair of motor vehicles and motor cycles
Section H	Transportation and storage
Section I	Accommodation and food service activities
Section J	Information and communication
Section K	Financial and insurance activities
Section L	Real estate
Section M	Professional, scientific and technical activities
Section N	Administrative support service activities
Section O	Public administration and defence; compulsory social security
Section P	Education
Section Q	Human health and social work activities
Section R	Arts, entertainment and recreation
Section S	Other service activities
Section T	Activities of households as employers
Section U	Activities of extraterritorial organisations and bodies

The rise of the public service companies: the case of Serco

The process of outsourcing from the public sector to the private sector began in the UK in the 1970s and has continued apace since then, changing the face of industry. As far as the SIC is concerned, there is a movement of activities from divisions O, P and Q into divisions M and N. It is estimated that the UK outsourcing market stood at £207 billion in 2012 (which represents about 8 per cent of GDP) and it employed 10 per cent of the workforce. It is a sizeable industry and a recent report by the National Audit Office (NAO) talked about these outsourcing contractors as being 'too big to fail'.

First Research put the United States and Europe as the biggest market for outsourcing. Some of the companies involved in outsourcing include Atos (France) – health and technology; Adecco (Switzerland) – human resource management; Veolia Environmental (France) – waste services; G4S (UK) – security services; Capita (UK) – business professional service; Accenture (Ireland/United States) – IT business consulting; Serco (UK) – facilities support services. In the UK there are the 'big four': Atos (£11.5 billion per year) and G4S (£7.6 billion per year) are the biggest in terms of revenue, then Capita (£4.9 billion), followed by Serco (£3 billion).

What differentiates Serco from the others is the diversity of its offering: it operates in many different sectors, from hospitals to job centres and army bases. Among other activities it partly operated the electronic tagging of prisoners (with G4S); runs school inspections for OFSTED and also the Northern Rail and Merseyside train networks; manages NHS services in Suffolk and some immigration removal centres; operates the bike scheme in London; and has responsibility for the maintenance of Greenwich Mean Time. This means that key services in the UK depend upon the operation of Serco and the other outsourcers, hence the idea that they are too big to fail. The Ministry of Defence now advertises for defence contracts online through www.contracts.mod.uk. In the event of failure some of these companies would have to be bailed out in the same way as the banking sector in 2008. Security for the London 2012 Olympics was contracted to G4S, but the company suffered a failure of organisation and the

UK government had to bring in the army to act as security at some venues.

Why has there been such an increase in outsourcing? The benefits claimed for outsourcing are an improvement in value for money through a reduction in costs and an improvement in the quality of the service. The way in which this happens is through the use of a specialist who can bring economies of scale and expertise to the production process – there is access to skills that may not be present in-house. The involvement of the private sector could inject an element of market forces into the provision of the service – through the use of commercial incentives. The NAO has recently pointed out that these benefits rely on three things: the existence of competitive markets, a sound incentive system and good transparent accountability (NAO report, 2013). Its assessment was as follows:

Effective competition – there were a large number of mergers and takeovers in this industry in 2013. Kier Group (a UK construction and property development group) took over May Gurney (a support services business) in July. In April, Amey plc (an infrastructure support service provider) took over Enterprise (a maintenance contractor). These are just two examples, but they are typical in that the company doing the takeover was moving into new markets. These companies are positioning themselves for further rounds of outsourcing. It is also true that when a company is taken over, the acquiring company acquires its contracts too. All of this could lead to a reduction in the level of competition in the market. In addition, the whole process means that as the end of the contract is nearing, the incumbent has a natural advantage over other companies bidding for the jobs. So again, maybe less competition?

The existence of sound incentives – transactions cost economics sees the decision to outsource as depending upon the relative costs of doing something in-house or outsourcing it [Williamson, 1981; for a discussion of transactions cost economics, see also Worthington et al., 2005]. One of the costs of outsourcing is the cost of writing the contract – specifying the terms of the contract, the incentives and the mechanisms for enforcing the contract. It is very important to get this right but it is also a difficult thing to do, as both the incentives and the punishments have to be appropriate to ensure the desired outcomes.

Good accountability – the contracts have to be monitored to ensure that the outsourcer is acting properly, and the cost of monitoring is another transactions cost. In order that monitoring can take place, good, transparent accountability is needed. This is difficult because often balance sheets do not provide enough detailed information to allow monitoring to take place. Companies do not like to release too much information that could be used by their competitors to secure competitive advantage. Serco's contracts are subject to 'commercial confidentiality' and as it is a private company it does not have to respond to Freedom of Information requests. Even the Public Accounts Committee, whose job it is to look at these contracts, cannot obtain all of the information it requires.

Although outsourcing is here to stay, there are some problems. There were discrepancies with the electronic tagging of prisoners in 2012, when it was alleged that the two companies responsible (Serco and G4S) were being paid for tagging when the prisoners were back in prison or even dead. Serco has agreed to repay £68.5 million to the UK government and G4S has been referred to the Serious Fraud Office for investigation. Both companies have lost the contracts, which have now been taken over by Capita. A cross-government review found that there were weaknesses with the way the contracts had been written. Meanwhile, controversy over the out-of-hours GP service in Cornwall has resulted in Serco having to finish the contract 17 months early, at the end of May 2015. Serco issued a profits warning late in 2013 and at the end of that year was engaged in a process of corporate renewal to ensure that public contracts would continue to be awarded.

It is clear that outsourcing from the public sector to the private sector will continue in the UK (and other countries) and that the size of the public sector will diminish. It is also clear that these companies are so entwined with the economy that it would be difficult to do without them. Even if Serco were not awarded any new contracts, some of the contracts it already has will run for another 20 years. So although there are some problems with the specifying and the monitoring of contracts, this is a change in industrial structure that is here to stay.

Case study questions

1 What impact are the changes described in this case study likely to have on the workforce of the UK? (Approximately 90 per cent of the workforce of Serco is said to be former public sector employees.)

2 What would happen in the UK economy if one of these companies did fail? What would the government have to do? (Hint: look back to the collapse of Connaught in 2010 and Carillion in 2018.)

---

web links

www.bifm.org.uk (British Institute of Facilities Management)
www.fm-world.co.uk (British Institute of Facilities Management online magazine)
www.ifma.org (International Facility Management Association)

Review and discussion questions

1 Select industries in various stages of their life cycles. How closely do the observed characteristics of these industries correspond with the expected characteristics summarised in Table 12.8?

2 On what basis could you judge whether manufacturing was more important to an economy than services?

3 What would be the effect on the industrial structure of a country of the widespread use of 'fracking'?

4 What is the difference between an industry and a market?

5 What policies can governments introduce to increase productivity?

Assignments

1 You are the research assistant for an MP who is to participate in a debate on the importance of the manufacturing sector to the economy. You have been asked to produce a list of the arguments that are likely to be used by both sides in the debate: that is, reasons why the decline does matter and the set of counter-arguments. Provide a suitable list.

2 You work for an organisation that provides European intelligence to local businesses and the media. Your line manager has to give a presentation at an international conference on the likely effects that enlargement of the EU will have on industrial structure and has asked you to research the topic. You are required to:

(a) collect the necessary information on the industrial structures of the potential new entrants;
(b) assess the impact that the accession of these countries would have on the industrial structure of the EU;
(c) assess the likely impact of membership on the industrial structures of the countries themselves.

Further reading

Allen, R. C., *The British Industrial Revolution,* Cambridge University Press, 2009.

Anderson, C., *Makers: The New Industrial Revolution,* Random House, 2013.

Griffiths, A. and Wall, S., *Applied Economics,* 12th edition, Financial Times/Prentice Hall, 2011.

National Audit Office report 'The Role of Major Contractors in the Delivery of Public Services', November 2013.

Porter, M., 'The structure within industries and companies' performance', *Review of Economics and Statistics,* 61 (2), pp. 214–27, 1979.

Williamson, O. E., 'The economics of organisation: the transactions cost approach', *American Journal of Sociology,* 87, pp. 548–77, 1981.

Worthington, I., Britton, C. and Rees, A., *Economics for Business: Blending Theory and Practice,* 2nd edition, Financial Times/Prentice Hall, 2005.

web link

Web links and further questions are available on the website at:
www.pearsoned.co.uk/worthington

13 Government and business

Ian Worthington

In any society multiple interactions exist between government and business and these occur at a variety of spatial levels and in a wide range of contexts. One such interaction stems from the government's attempts to alleviate the problems of regional and/or local economic decay and decline, and these tend to be the focus of governmental policies at local, regional, national and even supranational level. While such measures are formulated and administered by government agencies, business organisations in market economies often exercise considerable influence on government decisions. This influence can be enhanced if the views of the business community are expressed through powerful and persuasive representative organisations.

Learning outcomes

Having read this chapter you should be able to:

- explain the rationale for government involvement in the economy
- demonstrate the nature and scope of UK government regional policy
- identify government policy initiatives at sub-regional level, including the role of local government in economic development
- characterise the role of business as an influence on government

Key terms

Assisted Area
British Business Bank
Business angels
Business Link
Chambers of Commerce
City Action Teams
City Challenge
City Grant
Combined authority
Community initiatives
Confederation of British Industry
English Partnerships
Enterprise Grants
Enterprise Zones

European Structural Funds
Externalities
Free market
General power of competence (GPC)
Growing Places Fund
Industrial policies
Inner-city Task Forces
Invisible hand
Local Enterprise Agencies
Local Enterprise Partnership (LEP)
Market failure
Merit goods
Negotiated environment

Public goods
Region
Regional chambers
Regional Development Agencies
Regional government offices
Regional Growth Fund
Regional Selective Assistance
Single Regeneration Budget
Trade associations
Urban Development Corporations
Urban Regeneration Companies

Introduction

Capitalist societies are organised on the basis that free markets are capable of organising activity better than a small group of people in charge of every part of an economy. A **free market** is the principle that anyone is able to produce and sell anything that they want to anyone else. The person looking to buy something will make their own decisions based on a number of factors, including the cost and quality of the product, and in this way providers of goods and services compete to win customers and to make profit on their sales. Adam Smith (the man pictured on the current £20 note) described the mechanism of the free market as an **invisible hand**, guiding how supply and demand organise activity in markets. The concept of markets is discussed in detail in Chapter 14.

All democratic market-based economies accept the need for government involvement in the day-to-day workings of the economy. The critical question, therefore, is not whether a role for government should exist, but what that role should be and where the boundaries should be drawn between private and public (i.e. collective) action. Governments of a 'socialist' (or 'left wing') persuasion normally favour a substantial role for the state as both producer and regulator, whereas non-socialist (more capitalist or 'right wing') administrations tend to prefer limited state influence that is directed towards improving the operation of the free market. Either way, the actions of the state in the economy can be influential at both the macro and the micro levels and this has important implications for the conduct of business in the non-state sector.

In examining the role of government in the macroeconomy, Chapter 5 emphasised how changes in fiscal and monetary policy could be used to influence aggregate levels of income, output and employment in the economy and how attempts to regulate the overall level of economic activity were related to a government's macroeconomic policy objectives. In this and a number of subsequent chapters (especially Chapter 17) the focus is on the ways in which government actions impinge upon the operations of firms and markets and the rationale underlying the decisions by the state to intervene at the micro level. Such interventions may take place at the request of the business community or despite its opposition, but it is rare for them to occur without business expressing an opinion which it expects government to take into consideration. This role of business as an important influence on government policy is examined in the concluding section of this chapter.

Government and business: an overview

In considering reasons for government intervention in the economy, economists have traditionally pointed to the problem of **market failure**. This is the notion that if left entirely to their own devices, markets can operate in a way that is not always economically or socially desirable. To this extent interventionist policies can be portrayed as an attempt by governments of all political complexions to deal with the problems inherent in the operation of free markets.

The key areas of 'market failure' are well known. Primary concerns include the following:

1 The unwillingness of markets to produce goods and services which are either unprofitable or which it is not practical to provide through private means (i.e. **public goods** such as defence, social services, and so on).

2 The likely under-provision of certain goods and services felt to be of general benefit to the community (e.g. **merit goods** such as education and libraries).

3 The failure to take into account the external costs and benefits of production or consumption (i.e. **externalities** such as pollution and congestion).

4 The danger of monopoly power if businesses can be freely bought and sold.

5 The under-utilisation of economic resources (e.g. unemployment resulting from demand deficiency, new technology or structural or frictional problems).

6 The tendency for output to be determined and distributed on the ability to pay rather than on the basis of need or equity.

Historically, government responses to these problems have taken a number of forms, including public ownership, legislation and administrative or fiscal regulation, and examples of all these approaches can be found to a greater or lesser extent in all countries. In recent years, however, under the influence of economists of the 'new right', governments have begun to take steps to disengage the state from some of its activities (e.g. public ownership) and have increasingly turned to market solutions to problems emanating primarily from the operation of the market system itself (e.g. schemes to charge for the use of roads which are heavily congested).

While all forms of government intervention in the economy invariably have direct or indirect consequences for businesses, it is possible to distinguish certain policies designed specifically to influence the industrial and commercial environment – sometimes described as '**industrial policies**' (see below for a discussion of the Coalition's industrial strategy). In the UK and elsewhere, these have typically included:

- attempts at direct industrial intervention (e.g. the establishment of the National Enterprise Board);
- privatisation policies;
- strategies aimed at promoting long-term economic growth;
- policies relating to competition and monopoly control;
- policies designed to influence industrial location and to encourage economic regeneration at different spatial levels.

Though it cannot be claimed that such measures amount to a single and coherent policy for business, nevertheless they indicate that successive governments accept they have an important role to play in shaping the environment in which private businesses function. Competition and privatisation policy – discussed in detail in Chapter 17 – tend to focus on the operation of markets and on the benefits which derive from private provision under a competitive market structure. Government spatial policies – the main subject matter of this chapter – are primarily concerned with addressing the problems of regional disparities in income, employment and output, and the associated problem of localised economic decline as businesses fail or decide to relocate their premises.

Regional policy

Regions

A **region** is a geographical area which possesses certain characteristics (e.g. political, economic, physical) which give it a measure of unity that allows boundaries to be drawn round it, thus differentiating it from surrounding areas. Outside of London the standard planning regions in the UK have traditionally been the North, North-West, Yorkshire and the Humber, East Midlands, West Midlands, South-West, East Anglia, South-East, Wales, Scotland and Northern Ireland, with each of these further divided into sub-regions based on administrative counties and on designated metropolitan areas. These planning regions and sub-regions have traditionally formed the units of classification for a wide range of official government statistics (see Chapter 18).

A regional focus to economic planning and development in the UK is perhaps best seen in the period between 1997 and 2010. Following the establishment of **regional government offices** in England in 1994 under the previous administration, the incoming Labour government set up a system of **Regional Development Agencies** (RDAs) to coordinate initiatives on economic development in the regions, to devise regional economic strategies and to administer the allocation of structural funding from the EU. In addition, outside of London – which was to establish its own directly elected assembly – **regional chambers** (or 'assemblies') were introduced and given responsibility for a number of strategic functions including housing and spatial planning. These voluntary bodies comprised a range of stakeholder interests drawn from local government, employer and employer bodies, the health service and a range of other social and environmental groups. Subsequent attempts to turn some assemblies into directly elected bodies found little sympathy with the public, who seemed to see them as largely irrelevant and rather faceless structures.

With a change of administration in 2010, this machinery of regional government has been effectively dismantled. The regional government offices have been closed, the RDAs have been abolished and the regional chambers (excluding London) have been phased out, the associated responsibilities and funding streams being reallocated to other agencies (including central government) or, in some cases, discontinued altogether. The approach championed by the coalition government emphasised 'localism' and the establishment of multi-stakeholder partnerships between local authorities and the business community aimed at promoting local economic development and growth. To support its community-based philosophy, the government set up a **Regional Growth Fund** aimed at promoting private enterprise in regions badly hit by public spending cuts because of their over-reliance on public sector employment. Since many of the affected areas tended to be large cities, the distinction between regional support, urban policy and local economic development had become increasingly blurred.

The basis of regional policy

Many countries have a recognisable regional policy of one kind or another. Such policies are generally designed to identify and demarcate those geographical areas which are experiencing substantial economic and/or social problems and which are felt to require government assistance. Using a range of socio-economic indicators – such as unemployment levels, population density, economic activity rates, income – governments tend to distinguish those regions which depart significantly from the national average and designate these regions **Assisted Areas**. These areas then become the focus of government assistance and tend to be given priority in the provision of financial aid for capital projects and for measures designed to increase employment and growth, aid coming in a variety of forms, including assistance from international and supranational sources, as in the case of EU regional policy (see below).

UK regional policy

The origins of UK regional policy can be traced back to the 1930s when the government first began to provide help to a number of depressed areas in the form of low-interest loans, subsidised rents and the establishment of government trading estates. By the closing decades of the twentieth century the system had evolved into one in which the government designated three types of Assisted Area that became eligible for regional aid. These were:

1 Development areas (DAs).
2 Intermediate areas (IAs).
3 Northern Ireland – which received special regional help owing to the problems it was experiencing in attracting investment in industrial and commercial projects.

The areas qualifying for government regional assistance under this scheme underwent some revision in 1993. Subsequently, following new European Commission rules on regional aid in March 1998, all EU member states were required to further revise their Assisted Areas maps by 1 January 2000 in preparation for the enlargement of the EU. The UK's initial response – which was submitted to the Commission in July 1999 – was rejected and the proposed regional aid map had to be adjusted following consultation with the various interested parties. The revised proposals for a new Assisted Areas map for the UK were published on 10 April 2000.

> **web link**
>
> Information on the new Assisted Areas arrangements is available via the Europa website.

Under this scheme, regional aid was available in those areas covered by existing EU law (e.g. Amsterdam Treaty Articles 87[3]a and 87[3]c). These areas, designated Tiers 1 and 2, remained in force until the end of 2006, subject to adjustments to reflect any significant socio-economic changes which occurred during the period. Where any additions were made to the agreed regional aid map, these had to be offset by exclusions in other areas to maintain the overall population ceiling.

The UK government also designated a new Tier 3, which extended outside Tiers 1 and 2, and where the emphasis was on aid to small and medium-sized enterprises in the form of enterprise grants. This decision was designed to complement other measures to encourage smaller businesses, including the establishment of the Small Business Service (SBS) and the creation of the Enterprise Fund.

Within the designated areas, **Regional Selective Assistance** (RSA) was the main form of discretionary grant aid. This was administered by the RDAs and designed to secure employment opportunities and increase regional competitiveness and prosperity. In order to qualify, businesses had to be investing in fixed capital items, with minimum fixed costs over £500,000, and had to demonstrate that a project met a number of predetermined criteria, including creating/safeguarding jobs and contributing positive benefits to both the regional and the national economy. Grants were available to firms of all sizes in Tier 1 and Tier 2 Assisted Areas, with the regional aid guidelines allowing higher maximum grant levels in areas designated Tier 1 (e.g. Cornwall).

In Tier 2 and 3 areas, **Enterprise Grants** were also available to SMEs investing in fixed capital items. The maximum fixed costs had to be no more than £500,000 and the grant ceiling was 15 per cent of those costs, up to a maximum grant of £75,000. The grant was specifically, though not exclusively, targeted at high-growth businesses seeking to max-imise value-added projects with demonstrable quality outputs and aimed to support projects in these areas that would not otherwise have gone ahead without grant aid.

In April 2004, Regional Selective Assistance and Regional Enterprise Grants in England were replaced by Selective Finance for Investment in England (SFIE), a discretionary grant (or occasionally a loan), with a minimum threshold of £10,000 that was aimed at sup-porting new investment projects which led to long-term improvements in productivity, skills and employment in the Assisted Areas. Support under the scheme – which was initially administered by the RDAs – was made available to businesses of all sizes located in (or planning to locate in) an Assisted Area and which could meet certain criteria (e.g. employment benefits). Assistance was also available to SMEs investing in Tier 3 areas, with further support provided through agencies such as English Partnerships, the RDAs and the Learning and Skills Council, as well as through the Regional Venture Capital Funds and the long-standing Small Firms Loan Guarantee Scheme.

Following a revision in the European Commission's guidelines on regional aid, a new Assisted Areas map for the UK came into effect for the period 2007–13. Under this scheme, 4 per cent of the UK population remained eligible for regional aid up to agreed levels under Article 87(3)(a) and a further 19.3 per cent under Article 87(3)(c), with the whole of Northern Ireland a designated Assisted Area. As in the previous period, the main form of discretionary grant aid in England was SFIE; for Wales and Scotland, the equivalent schemes were via RSA.

Regional aid within the European Union

In addition to any funding provided by the national government, businesses in the mem-ber states of the EU can benefit from grant aid under agreed European programmes that have been designed to tackle national and regional disparities within the EU. The major-ity of this aid is provided from **European Structural Funds**, which are used to assist those areas that compare unfavourably with the EU's average levels of prosperity. The EU's four structural instruments have traditionally been:

1 The European Regional Development Fund (ERDF).
2 The European Social Fund (ESF).
3 The European Agricultural Guidance and Guarantee Fund (EAGGF).
4 The Financial Instrument for Fisheries Guidance (FIFG).

For the period 2000–6 it has been estimated that around €195 billion were spent by these four sources of funding, with a further €18 billion provided through the Cohesion Fund (see Table 13.1). There was an additional allocation for new member states from 2004.

Under the new Structural Fund Regulations which came into effect on 1 January 2000, the EU identified three priorities or 'objectives' for grant aid:

- Objective 1 – promoting the development and structural adjustment of regions whose development is lagging behind.
- Objective 2 – supporting the economic and social conversion of industrial, rural, urban and fisheries areas facing structural difficulties.
- Objective 3 – supporting the adaptation and modernisation of policies, systems of education, training and employment.

Table 13.1 European Structural Funds, 2000–6

Fund	Main focus
ERDF	Designed to redress the main regional imbalances within the EU through the development and structural adjustment of regions whose development is lagging behind. Funding supports investment in sites and facilities for business, infrastructure, local economic development initiatives, environmental protection and improvement, tourism and cultural projects, etc.
ESF	Aimed primarily at improving employment opportunities and reducing social exclusion by promoting employability and equal opportunities and by investing in human resources, particularly through education and training initiatives
EAGGF	Designed to support rural development and encourage rural restructuring and diversification in order to promote economic prosperity and social inclusion, while protecting and maintaining the environment and rural heritage
FIFG	Aims to contribute to achieving a sustainable balance between fishery resources and their exploitation. Funds projects to modernise the structure of the fisheries sector and related industries and to encourage diversification of the workforce and the industry into other sectors

Table 13.2 Objective areas and funding, 2000–6

Main funding instruments	EU Objective areas	Main aims of funding	Main focus of funding	Eligible areas within EU
ERDF/ESF/ EAGGF/FIFG	Objective 1	To support development in the less prosperous regions of the EU so as to narrow the gap between development levels in the various regions	Funding for take-off of economic activities by supporting projects concerning infrastructure, human resources, and aid for production sectors	Regions where GDP per head is at or below 75 per cent of EU average (e.g. Saxony, Western Greece, Galicia, Sicily, Algarve, West Wales and the Valleys, Merseyside, South Yorkshire, Cornwall and the Isles of Scilly)
ERDF/ESF	Objective 2	To revitalise areas facing structural difficulties whether industrial, rural, urban, or dependent on fishery	Funding for economic and social conversion	Eligible areas must meet specified criteria related to structural decline. Covers 18 per cent of EU population
ESF	Objective 3	To support national efforts to modernise policies and systems of education, training and employment	Funding aimed at combating unemployment and developing human resources	All areas have Objective 3 status outside Objective 1 regions

In the period 2000–6 it has been estimated that Objective 1 areas covered around 22 per cent of the EU population and probably commanded around 70 per cent of the designated funding, with 11.5 per cent going to Objective 2 areas and 12.3 per cent to support Objective 3 in areas not accorded Objective 1 status. The main aims and focus of funding in the three areas are shown in Table 13.2.

Alongside the three key objectives, the EU also designated a number of **community initiatives**, which focused on finding common solutions to specific problems and which accounted for around 5 per cent of spending from the European Structural Funds over the same period. Interreg III, for example, focused on cross-border, transnational and international cooperation and was funded under the ERDF. Urban II sought to promote sustainable development in the troubled urban districts of the EU through the design and implementation of innovative models of development for economic and social regeneration, again funded under the ERDF. Leader+ promoted rural development through local initiatives using funds from the EAGGF.

Smaller amounts of funding were also provided under schemes to promote innovative actions and for the adjustment of fisheries structures outside the Objective regions, with the former designed to encourage the testing of new ideas and practices that might not be funded under the traditional programmes of the European Structural Funds.

With the enlargement of the EU in May 2004, the issue of further reform of EU regional policy (also known as Cohesion Policy) became increasingly important and a variety of schemes was put forward by member states, culminating in new arrangements for the period 2007–13. Under this scheme, the EU budgeted for €308 billion of expenditure under the Structural and Cohesion Funds, which were designed to pursue its three main redesignated objectives: convergence; regional competitiveness and employment; European territorial cooperation.

Funding, which subsequently amounted to €347 billion (i.e. about one-third of the total EU budget), was made available through three main sources: the ERDF, the ESF and the Cohesion Fund, the latter being aimed at countries whose per capita GDP was below 90 per cent of the EU average. The source and allocation of funding in relation to the three objectives of regional policy was as follows:

- Convergence objective – funded through the ERDF, ESF and Cohesion Fund. Almost 82 per cent of the total resources allocated.
- Regional competitiveness and employment objective – financed through the ERDF and ESF and accounting for 16 per cent of total allocated resources.
- European territorial cooperation objective – financed through the ERDF and around 2.5 per cent of total allocated funding.

In the latest six-year cycle of regional or cohesion policy covering the period 2014–20, further reform has taken place aimed at bringing funding allocations (referred to as an 'investment policy') further in line with the EU's Europe 2020 goals. Portrayed as a strategy to promote 'smart, sustainable and inclusive growth', Europe 2020 has set ambitious targets in areas such as employment, innovation, education, poverty and climate change, and the funding regime has been adjusted accordingly. The current agreed plan is to spend around €367 billion (equivalent to €325 billion at 2011 prices), which is to be targeted at key priorities and growth sectors, including support for SMEs. This funding will be made available to regions, cities and economies generally and will be drawn from five main sources of what is now called the European Structural and Investment Funds (ESI): the ERDF, the ESF, the Cohesion Fund, the European Agricultural Fund for Rural Development and the European Maritime and Fisheries Fund. At the time of writing, several calls are open for ESI funding bids (these calls can be seen at www.gov.uk/european-structural-investment-funds). It is not yet clear how schemes like this are going to be replaced (or not replaced) following the Brexit transition period, likely at the end of the EU budget cycle in 2020.

mini case   The EU and state aid

Within the EU, state aid is defined as an advantage in any form whatsoever conferred on a selective basis to undertakings (e.g. businesses) by national public authorities (e.g. a national government). Under the Treaty on the Functioning of the European Union (TFEU), intervention by the state or via state resources – for example, grants, loans, tax reliefs – is generally banned if it has distorted or threatens to distort competition within the internal market. Countries seeking to support their businesses or industrial sectors through the use of rescue or restructuring aid are required to notify the European Commission and to seek approval; however, some categories of aid are exempt from this requirement (e.g. schemes to support smaller businesses or to protect the environment), as is EU regional aid generally.

Three UK cases of state aid recently referred to the EC are:

- A decision by the UK government to compensate the Post Office Ltd for providing Services of General Economic Interest (e.g. keeping post offices open where they are not profitable).
- Support provided by the UK government to partially fund wind farms on remote islands. Tax relief for manufacturers of 'high-end television' (e.g. television programmes of European cultural interest).

If these are deemed to have had the effect of distorting competition (e.g. by artificially keeping afloat a company that would otherwise have exited the market), the recipients concerned could be required to reimburse their governments.

UK urban policy

The urban 'problem'

The progressive decline and decay of urban areas – with the associated unemployment among the low-paid, unskilled and ethnic members of the population – first came to prominence in the 1960s and gave rise to an Urban Programme, aimed predominantly at funding capital projects and education schemes in deprived inner-city locations. Implicit in this programme was the view that the urban 'problem' was largely one of physical decline coupled with failings on the part of individuals, which could be corrected by selective government intervention, designed to improve the prospects and environment faced by local citizens. This largely 'pathological' perspective was ultimately exposed by both academic research and community projects undertaken in the 1970s, with the result that the government came to see the problem as one of economic and social change, and its impact on the local environment. This 'structuralist' view suggested that policy should be directed towards economic development through partnership between the centre, the localities and the private sector, with the emphasis on schemes to overcome structural weaknesses. Riots in several large UK cities in the 1980s served to emphasise that the problem was particularly acute in those inner-city core areas that had suffered a significant loss of industry and population over a number of years.

The focus of policy implementation: 1970s–2000

Whereas regional policy is managed centrally through a single government department, urban policy has traditionally operated through a variety of agencies, including local authorities, voluntary organisations, quangos and a number of independent bodies set up by central government. The relative importance of these agencies in implementing government policy has changed significantly over time.

The initial focus of policy implementation under the Urban Programme was the local authorities, which acted as a channel for central government funds into projects designed to regenerate economic activity (e.g. by providing premises), to improve the physical environment (e.g. by clearing land or renovating buildings) and to meet social needs (e.g. by providing community facilities for deprived groups). This role was further enhanced by the Inner Urban Areas Act 1978, which conferred wide powers on certain designated local authorities to assist industry wherever a need was felt to exist and where government help was seen to be appropriate. Central to the government's strategy was its attempt to regenerate inner-city areas through capital investment and through environmental improvement, some of which was to be funded from the private sector. To encourage private sector investment, local authorities in the designated areas were allowed to declare industrial and commercial improvement areas and to give financial assistance to companies which located in such areas.

With the election of the Conservative government in 1979, a number of new initiatives were introduced, which indicated a move towards an even more spatially selective policy for urban areas. These initiatives – which included Enterprise Zones, Urban Development Corporations, freeports and City Action Teams (see below) – frequently by-passed local authorities or reduced their powers over the allocation of resources and/or land use, and were seen by many commentators as a vote of no confidence in local government's ability to stimulate urban regeneration. At the heart of the new approach lay an attempt by central government to turn inner-city areas into investment opportunities for the private sector by clearing dereliction and improving infrastructure. The basic idea, as the *Financial Times* (30 October 1990) pointed out, was to reduce downside risk to a level where private investors would see enough potential to develop in cities rather than take softer profits elsewhere.

In March 1988, the government launched its 'Action for Cities' initiative, which covered a range of programmes administered by different government departments designed to promote industrial and commercial investment and hence create employment in the inner-city areas. Programmes under this initiative were coordinated by a special unit located at the Department of the Environment and local coordination occurred through City Action Teams. After 1994, in an attempt to achieve greater coordination in policy and to introduce competition for resources, the government began to amalgamate a wide range of inner-city programmes under the **Single Regeneration Budget** (SRB), with the funds initially being administered by the newly integrated regional government offices, which brought together the existing regional offices of a number of major government departments (e.g. Environment, Trade and Industry, Transport, Employment). It also established a new development agency (**English Partnerships**) that was to draw its public funding from the SRB. From April 1999 English Partnerships' regional functions and the SRB Challenge Fund became the responsibility of the newly established RDAs. The latter had been set up to take the lead in delivering more effective and integrated regeneration programmes, which promote sustainable economic, social and physical regeneration within the regions. They were seen as a key actor in developing and delivering partnership-based regeneration strategies at subnational level, a responsibility that has now passed to Local Enterprise Agencies (see below).

Selected urban policy instruments

The Urban Programme

The Urban Programme was designed to help combat the economic, social and environmental problems of urban areas and was the main mechanism for allocating funds to those inner-city areas facing the greatest need. Of the 57 designated local authority areas which fell into this category, 9 were 'partnership authorities', where the government formed a close partnership with local authority agencies to tackle the problem of urban decay (e.g. Hackney, Liverpool, Manchester, Salford). The remaining 48 'programme authorities' (including Barnsley, Bolton, Sandwell, Wrekin) had no such partnership, but were eligible for government assistance for projects which contributed to the economic development of the inner area. In both cases, requests for funds had to be submitted from or via the local authorities, which assessed the application and paid the grant for projects receiving official approval.

With the advent of the SRB, the Urban Programme was gradually phased out and all cities, towns and rural areas were brought within the remit of government regeneration policy. Since the new regime was designed to be competitive, towns and cities within an area were effectively required to compete for funding against each other.

Urban Development Corporations (UDCs)

Urban Development Corporations were independent development agencies, established by central government to oversee inner-city development within designated areas. The first two such areas were London Docklands and Merseyside, which gained UDCs in 1980. Subsequently, UDCs were established in Trafford Park (Manchester), the Black Country (Birmingham and surrounding districts), Teesside, Tyne and Wear, Cardiff Bay, Central Manchester, Leeds, Sheffield and Bristol. These 10 agencies – whose powers of development within their designated areas superseded those of the local authorities in their area – ceased operations in 1998.

Using funds mainly provided by central government and employing around 500 permanent staff in total, the UDCs had the following objectives:

1 To bring land and buildings into effective use.
2 To encourage the development of industry and commerce.
3 To ensure housing and other social facilities were available in order to encourage people to live and work in the designated area.

To achieve these aims, corporations were given wide powers to acquire, reclaim, assemble, develop, sell or lease land and to provide the necessary infrastructure; they also had powers to build houses for rent or sale and to renovate and reuse existing buildings. In short, they were the development control authorities for their areas.

A fundamental aspect of the UDC's role as an agency for urban regeneration was its ability to act as a catalyst for encouraging private sector investment. Using public money to bring about environmental improvement and infrastructural development, corporations sought to attract private investors by removing some of the abnormal costs of development such as land clearance and servicing. This 'pump-priming' role cost the taxpayer over £500 million in the early 1990s, with the lion's share of the funds going to the London Docklands Development Corporation (LDDC), whose fortunes were considerably affected by the collapse in property prices in the late 1980s and early 1990s.

Enterprise Zones (EZs)

Like UDCs, **Enterprise Zones** were established in the early 1980s, with the first batch of 11 EZs being designated in 1981 with a planned lifespan of 10 years. By the late 1980s the number of EZs had risen to 27, though the number fluctuated over time as some of the original EZs (e.g. Corby) were wound up and new ones announced in the wake of the closure of a large number of pits in the UK coal industry.

EZs were essentially small areas of territory within a locality where the government was seeking to encourage industrial and commercial activity by the removal of certain tax burdens and other impediments to enterprise (e.g. bureaucratic procedures). Among the principal benefits for firms located or locating in an EZ were:

- exemption from rates on industrial and commercial property;
- allowances of 100 per cent for corporation and income tax purposes on all capital expenditure related to industrial and commercial development;
- a greatly simplified planning regime.

In addition, businesses normally faced fewer requests from public bodies for statistical information and were often exempt from other administrative procedures.

Whether EZs were successful in attracting enterprise and in creating significant numbers of jobs in inner-urban areas is open to dispute. Some evidence exists to suggest that the net job-creation effect proved relatively small and that many of the 'new' jobs were simply relocations by local businesses moving to take advantage of the benefits offered to firms within an EZ. However, according to an evaluation of EZs in the later 1990s, it was estimated that the experiment helped to create over 50 000 net new jobs at a cost in the region of £1,700 per year, per job.

The recent reincarnation of Enterprise Zones is discussed below.

City Action Teams (CATs)

City Action Teams were designed to bring together government departments, local authorities, local community groups, voluntary organisations and businesses working in inner-city areas. As well as providing information and advice to any business working in or moving to an inner-city area, a CAT could help with funding for schemes which safeguarded or created jobs, improved the environment, provided training places or encouraged enterprise and the growth of business. It also funded feasibility studies and assisted with consultancy fees for local projects. With a change in emphasis of government regeneration policy, funding for CATs steadily fell and was a mere £1 million by 1995–6. Like UDCs, CATs have been phased out.

City Challenge

City Challenge was designed to concentrate resources on key areas in the 1990s. Under the initiative, local authorities in partnership with the private sector, local organisations and the local community were asked to draw up detailed plans for solving the problems of their area and special government funds were allocated to acceptable projects. The first 11 partnerships completed their five-year programmes to bring self-sustaining economic regeneration in deprived areas by March 1997. Nineteen Round 2 partnerships finished their programmes the following year.

City Grant

City Grant was the descendant of the Urban Development Grant – an idea copied from the United States after the Toxteth and Brixton riots in the early 1980s. The aim of the grant was to support private sector capital projects which benefited local areas (e.g. bringing derelict land and buildings into use) by bridging any adverse gap between the estimated costs of a project and its expected market value, thus allowing a developer to make a reasonable profit on the venture. Large-scale projects that give rise to new jobs or housing and which improved the environment were the main focus of the grant aid, and priority was given to schemes within City Challenge areas before those from the 57 local authorities that were part of the old Urban Programme.

Inner-city Task Forces

Inner-city Task Forces were composed of small teams of civil servants from various government departments and people on secondment from the private sector who worked directly with local authorities and local businesses to stimulate economic development in inner-city areas. Their role was to coordinate and monitor the whole range of government initiatives within the designated area. The Task Force programme ceased on 31 March 1998.

Developments in urban policy: 1997–2010

With the change of government in 1997, urban policy in the UK took on a more targeted and focused approach, with funding increasingly being directed towards a range of economic, social and environmental initiatives. Key developments included the following:

- The New Deal for Communities programme – designed to combat social exclusion through focused and intensive neighbourhood renewal projects in the most deprived neighbourhoods. This scheme has now ceased.
- SRB Challenge Rounds 5 and 6 – which included a more regional focus and an increased emphasis on partnership capacity building, the majority of new resources being concentrated in the most deprived areas.
- Housing estate regeneration – through Housing Action Trusts and Estate Action.
- Coalfields initiatives – especially the Coalfields Regeneration Trust and the Enterprise Fund.
- Initiatives to tackle problems such as education, drugs, health and crime.

In 1998, the government established an Urban Task Force chaired by Lord Rogers to examine the causes of urban decline and to recommend solutions to bring people back into towns and cities. In its report in June 1999 the Task Force made 105 recommendations, including the establishment of **Urban Regeneration Companies** (URCs) to lead and coordinate redevelopment and new investment in declining areas. This suggestion was subsequently endorsed in a White Paper on Urban Renaissance published in 2000 which also underlined the need to create local strategic partnerships in order to develop a coordinated approach to strategy formulation and implementation.

To emphasise the increased importance being attached to tackling urban issues and problems, the government established a Cabinet Committee on Urban Affairs and an Urban Policy Unit within the Department of the Environment, Transport and the Regions. It also announced a review of the work of English Partnerships, the discontinuation of the national rounds of the SRB (after Round 6) and an Urban Summit to discuss the whole area of urban regeneration policy. This meeting, which took place in late 2002, examined the idea of developing 'sustainable communities', a concept which was subsequently taken up in a White Paper published in February 2003 ('Our Towns and Cities: The Future'). The basic idea was to revitalise the UK's towns and cities through local schemes of urban regeneration which would involve a range of stakeholders including the private sector and would require substantial coordination of existing and future government programmes and a high degree of cooperation both within and between different tiers of government. In keeping with this philosophy, the government set up a review of subnational economic development and regeneration which reported in July 2007. To achieve its aims of strengthening economic performance at regional, city and local level, the government announced its intention to enhance the role of local government in promoting economic development and neighbourhood renewal and highlighted its wish to further devolve power and resources to the regional and local level. It also announced a number of other reforms at subnational level, including changes to the role of the Learning and Skills Council and a streamlining of the regional tier outside London.

Urban and industrial policy developments in the UK since 2010

Reference has already been made to the difficulty of separating analytically a number of governmental policy domains; initiatives aimed at promoting growth in UK cities, for example, can have social and economic implications that affect individuals, businesses, local authorities and communities at local, city and regional levels. In this section we examine how the coalition government's policies and strategies for urban areas – especially large cities – and for industrial regeneration generally have centred on a number of overlapping initiatives designed to promote sustainable economic growth and development.

The overall direction of government policy under the Coalition was set out in its 'Plan for Growth' strategy published at the time of the 2011 Budget. This strategy has the declared aim of providing a route to sustainable long-term economic growth that would be more evenly spread across the country and across industries and centres on achieving four major ambitions:

- to create the most competitive tax system in the G20;
- to make the UK one of the best places in Europe to start, finance and grow a business;
- to encourage investment and exports as a means of achieving a more balanced economy;
- to create a flexible and more educated workforce.

In pursuit of these goals, the government put forward what it described as an 'industrial strategy' comprising a variety of initiatives and programmes, the key elements of which included the establishment of a Business Bank, government support for emerging technologies, public/private partnerships designed to develop strategies for particular sectors of the economy, increased investment in skills, and reform of public procurement, including supply chain initiatives. Underlying this strategy was the idea that the government should use both policy and its financial resources to leverage private sector funding and investment, an interventionist approach which did not appeal to some elements of the Conservative Party.

As the strategy has emerged and taken shape, a number of measures have been put in place. Important elements have included the following initiatives.

The Business Bank

The institution has been established in order to address the long-standing problem of a lack of credit for smaller businesses. Under the scheme the government has injected more than £1 billion to expand existing funding streams and to create new ways of unlocking finance for SMEs. It has also taken over the management of billions of pounds of existing commitments.

The bank's role is not to lend directly to businesses but to use a combination of government funding and government-backed guarantees to encourage more private sector lending and investment in smaller firms by existing banks and other financial institutions. The scheme – which has the support of both the British Chambers of Commerce and the Federation of Small Businesses – was initially run from the Department for Business, Innovation and Skills. Once the government had received state aid clearance from the European Commission in 2014, the bank became a government-owned institution operating under the title of the **British Business Bank** plc.

City Deals

The underlying philosophy of City Deals is that powers of economic development should be moved from the centre to large cities and their surrounding areas, the place where the vast majority of UK citizens live. In the December 2011 White Paper 'Unlocking Growth in Cities', the government announced that there was to be a move away from a one-size-fits-all approach towards individual, tailored deals which would take account of local opportunities and challenges. To access government funding (including via the Regional Growth Fund), an applicant city is required to work with central government on proposals to strengthen local economic growth and create private sector investment and employment. In return for being granted new powers to act, city leaders are required to demonstrate that they have put in place robust systems of governance, decision-making and accountability.

Enterprise Zones

Like their predecessors, EZs are specific geographical areas, which offer a range of incentives for firms to set up and expand. Within a designated zone, firms can benefit from reduced planning restrictions, various tax breaks and enhanced capital allowances, superfast broadband, and targeted support aimed at specific industries. They can also gain from government funding used to improve local infrastructure (e.g. through road improvements and land clearance) and can compete for capital grants under the Regional Growth Fund initiative.

By April 2017, 48 EZs had been created within different **Local Enterprise Partnership (LEP)** areas. LEPs – another key element of the government's strategy – are discussed in the next section.

The Growing Places Fund (GPF)

The **Growing Places Fund** is designed to promote economic growth in EZs and LEP areas by pump-priming the development of local funds which address infrastructure constraints and deliver employment and housing. Projects being supported under the GPF include site clearance, broadband and transport infrastructure schemes, flood defence systems and building refurbishment.

The Northern Powerhouse

Some areas have been the focus of renewed interest in regional policy. For example, the 2010–15 coalition and 2015–17 Conservative governments supported a 'Northern Powerhouse' plan to rapidly increase investment in infrastructure, science and innovation, and arts spending in the north of England (Manchester, Liverpool, Leeds, Sheffield, Hull and Newcastle). This has included devolution of power to some areas like Manchester, where, under these arrangements, Manchester would be given money and allowed to decide how to spend it with minimal central government involvement. After Theresa May became Prime Minister in 2016 this project has been significantly softened in favour of national-level projects.

Local government and business in the UK

The basis of local economic development

As a major service provider, consumer, employer and landowner, local government has always played an important role in the economy and its influence on business activity at local level remains considerable. Large local authorities annually spend hundreds of millions of pounds, employ tens of thousands of workers and support many thousands of additional jobs through the placement of contracts with local businesses. Further employment is also created through the 'multiplier effect', as local authority employees spend their income in the local economy and local citizens consume local authority services such as transport and leisure.

Not content with local economic conditions, many local authorities have actively intervened in the local economy by establishing economic development programmes which are designed to alleviate the familiar problems of unemployment, industrial decline and environmental decay. These programmes – often coordinated through an economic development unit within the local authority – normally comprise a range of initiatives designed to create or safeguard local jobs by supporting local businesses and encouraging enterprise in a variety of ways (see below). While the origins of such initiatives can be traced back to the nineteenth century, the majority of measures have been introduced in the last three to four decades and represent a move from a reactive to a proactive role by local authorities in local economic development.

The basis for such local authority intervention is partly legal and partly political. Under the law, local authorities in the UK have, until recently, only been able to engage in activities for which they have statutory authority, whether granted by public statute (i.e. applying to all authorities) or by private Act (i.e. applying to a specific authority). These statutes have not only imposed specific duties on local authorities to provide certain services (e.g. education, special housing, care in the community) but also often granted them both general and permissive powers which allow them to engage in different forms of development activity such as the purchase and sale of land and other assets, the granting of financial assistance to industry, and the provision of promotional and advisory services. It is worth noting that the 1989 Local Government and Housing Act introduced, for the first time, a clear statutory basis for local authorities' economic development activities. Under subsequent legislation (i.e. The Local Government Act 2000) local authorities in England and Wales have a duty to prepare 'community strategies' which improve the economic, social and environmental well-being of their area and its inhabitants and contribute to the achievement of sustainable development in the UK.

The Coalition's stated aim of devolving more decision-making powers from the centre to individuals, communities and councils – as outlined in the discussions above – has resulted in a significant change in the law that could affect local authority involvement in economic development in the coming years. Under the Localism Act (2011), local authorities have been granted a **general power of competence (GPC)**, which gives them the power to do anything that individuals of full legal capacity can currently do for the benefit of the authority, the area or its citizens, in effect changing the emphasis from doing what the law says they can do, to doing anything an individual can do which is not prohibited by law. Engaging in a wider range of trading activities and setting up local authority-owned businesses are two areas that could result from this important change in the legal basis of local authority responsibility.

In carrying out local economic development activities, local councils have traditionally drawn their funds from local, national and supranational sources, though not all authorities qualify for all three. By far the largest contribution has normally come from locally generated income, which includes the council tax, local authority reserves and revenue derived from charging for local authority services. Central funding includes the government's block grant to support local authority services, income from other centrally funded programmes (e.g. environment) and from the various initiatives which are part of the government's regional and urban policy. In the case of the latter, these have usually been available to authorities within the assisted areas and/or the Urban Programme areas, though some funds have been channelled through other agencies (e.g. the Scottish and Welsh Development Agencies).

Supranational support from the EU has come mainly from the ERDF and has been used in the assisted and Urban Programme areas to fund infrastructural projects (e.g. Tyne and Wear Metro, Liverpool Ring Road). Other sources have included the ESF (e.g. for training), the European Coal and Steel Community (e.g. for support for declining steel and coal areas), the European Investment Bank (e.g. low-interest loans for infrastructural investment) and a number of other funding streams. More often than not, these funds have been directed at those areas identified by the national government as areas of greatest need – hence the decision by the UK government in the 1980s to extend the number of authorities covered by its Urban Programme, thus qualifying those added to the list for EU financial aid (see discussion above). As with other funds from non-local sources, EU funding has increasingly required the provision of match funding and the establishment of cross-community partnerships before funds can be accessed for economic development purposes.

Types of intervention

Local authority aid to industry and commerce takes a wide variety of forms, but three areas in particular are worth noting: help with land and buildings; financial assistance; and the provision of information, advice and other support services. These were three of the major priorities identified by local authorities in a survey carried out in the late 1980s by the chartered accountants Deloitte Haskins & Sells.

As far as land and buildings are concerned, local councils, as planning authorities, land-owners and site developers, clearly have an important role to play in industrial development, and despite some attempts by central government to reduce their influence, their involvement in the local property market has remained significant over time. Among the key activities undertaken by local government in this area have been the following:

1 The identification of land available for industrial use (e.g. local authority registers of vacant land and land use), including services connected with attracting inward investment.
2 The provision of local-authority-owned land for industrial and commercial development.
3 The supply of on-site infrastructure (e.g. roads, drainage).
4 Land reclamation and site assembly.
5 Environmental improvement (including derelict land).
6 Advice and help to private sector developers.

In addition, local authorities have often been involved in the provision and/or conversion of premises for business use (including starter units, workshops and small factories) and have encouraged the development of a number of science parks, usually working in conjunction with private companies and institutions of higher education.

Financial assistance has also been important in encouraging business activity, with local authorities sometimes providing grants to firms seeking to move to new premises or to expand and/or convert existing buildings, particularly if additional jobs are likely to be created. Funds – mainly in the form of grants or loans – have also been made available to firms wishing to purchase new equipment or to establish certain types of enterprise (e.g. cooperatives) or to meet some of the costs of creating jobs for the unemployed or to cover rental charges. Added to this, some councils established Enterprise Boards, which were essentially trading companies concerned with the provision of long-term development capital for investment in local businesses and property. Using funds from local sources, the boards invested in local companies – usually by taking an equity stake – and managed their portfolio of investments through a specially created company which was independent of the local authority. Through such investments the boards sought to attract additional funds from financial institutions such as pension funds, thus creating a financial leverage which was designed to multiply the impact of the support from the public sector.

To complement these direct forms of intervention, all local authorities have sought to encourage local economic development through their promotional and advisory activities which are aimed at both existing and would-be entrepreneurs. Many councils, for example, produce publicity material, booklets, leaflets, information packs and other types of promotional literature, extolling the advantages of their area for tourism or for industrial and commercial use. This can be one of the factors encouraging investment, including direct inward investment by multinational companies, particularly if it is supported by financial and/or other incentives offered by the local authority (e.g. the Toyota development at Burnaston near Derby) or under regional or urban assistance programmes (e.g. the Nissan plant near Sunderland). State aid of this kind is, of course, subject to EU rules, as the mini case points out.

Similarly, as active providers of information to businesses on matters such as vacant premises and sites, local labour market conditions, housing availability and sources of finance, local councils deliberately promote their respective areas and many make use of trade fairs or trade delegations to ensure that the 'message' is not restricted to a domestic audience but also reaches potential overseas investors. For the most part, these activities tend to be coordinated through the economic development unit or some other agency operating under the purview of an authority's chief executive officer. Significantly, however, an increasing number of authorities have established specialist marketing departments in an effort to 'sell' their area to organisations and individuals who are likely to contribute to the regeneration of the local economy through investment in capital assets and through job creation.

Partnerships between local authorities

In order to carry out their responsibilities under delegated authority, local councils sometimes enter into collaborative arrangements with other bodies in the public sector. One area where this has occurred over recent decades has been the issue of public procurement, exemplified by the establishment in 1981 of the Eastern Shires Purchasing Organisation (ESPO), which has become one of the UK's largest public sector procurement organisations. Serving a variety of public and third-sector bodies in the east of England – including local councils, NHS agencies, charities and education establishments – ESPO uses its purchasing power to obtain purchasing economies of scale, which it passes on as savings to its customers. Similar not-for-profit organisations have also been set up in other regions of the country, some of which have subsequently joined with ESPO to form a central buying consortium with considerable purchasing power and influence.

Where economic development and regeneration are concerned, local councils in England (outside Greater London) can now establish a **combined authority** under the Local Democracy, Economic Development and Construction Act (2009). As a voluntary but legally recognised entity, a combined authority involves the pooling of local authority responsibilities and powers by two or more councils in areas such as transport, infrastructure development and economic policy in order to promote local economic growth and job creation across coterminous geographical boundaries – although there are also motives for achieving cost savings. At the time of writing nine combined authorities exist, seven of which have directly elected mayors who are ultimately responsible for coordinating spending for local development.

Partnership with the private sector: the emergence of the Local Enterprise Partnership

While local authorities acting either alone or with other public sector bodies can be an important agency for local economic development, their support for local businesses often involves some form of partnership with the private sector. Such partnerships – including the establishment of **Local Enterprise Agencies** (LEAs) and, more recently, LEPs – have been regarded as a vital element in effective economic regeneration in the SME sector at both local and regional level.

Local Enterprise Agencies (known as Enterprise Trusts in Scotland) date back to the early 1970s, but their main period of growth began a decade later, with the number of agencies reaching around 300 by the end of the 1980s. Using funds provided by industry and commerce and by central and local government, LEAs have acted essentially as business development organisations assisting both new and existing enterprises. Their core activity has been to provide information and business counselling (often referred to as 'signposting') which points individuals wishing to start a business to sources of help or assists those already running a business with specific problems. In addition most LEAs have provided a number of other services, including business training, workspace, help with the preparation of business plans, provision of ad hoc services (e.g. solicitors), advice on marketing, taxation, personnel matters and help in locating premises. In recent years LEAs have worked increasingly in partnership with other support organisations, particularly through the now defunct **Business Link** network and the Learning and Skills Council. There is also a National Federation of Enterprise Agencies (NFEA), which represents LEA views in government circles, and an umbrella organisation known as Business in the Community (BITC), which promotes community-based partnerships between local businesses, government and local groups aimed at regenerating local economies.

Unlike Enterprise Boards which were essentially interventionist bodies established by Labour local authorities, Enterprise Agencies have operated as independent organisations that are either private sector initiatives or more regularly a partnership between the public and private sectors, with a board that is private sector led. Increasingly, LEAs have tended to work together to provide a more effective service to small businesses, as exemplified by the formation of the Local Investment Networking Company (LINC) in 1987. LINC – which was run jointly by a number of LEAs located throughout the UK and sponsored by several large companies including BP and Lloyds Bank – was established to help small businesses seeking funding and additional managerial input to find suitable investors. The aim of the organisation was to help both small start-up and growing firms whose financial requirements tended to fall into an 'equity gap' (below £250,000), which was often difficult to bridge through conventional sources. It did this by bringing together private investors willing to invest in new or expanding small businesses and companies looking for such investment and/or additional management skills to aid their development. LINC was replaced in 1999 by the National Business Angels Network – a network of informal investors (**business angels**) willing to invest time and money in supporting cash-starved entrepreneurs.

The latest manifestation of the public–private partnership approach to local economic development and regeneration is the LEP. Set up to replace the RDAs, an LEP is a partnership between local business and civic leaders aimed at determining local strategies and priorities and taking decisions to drive economic growth and job creation within its area. As part of the government's stated policy of shifting power to local communities, LEPs are expected to play key roles in areas such as transport and infrastructure development, supporting high growth business (e.g. via the establishment of new growth hubs), employment and regulatory issues and strategic housing delivery. To support their activities, LEPs can apply for funding from the Local and Regional Growth Funds and from European Structural and Investment Funds such as the ERDF and ESF. They are also being encouraged to cooperate in areas of common interest (e.g. with neighbouring LEPs or where important industrial clusters exist) and to share knowledge and ideas by joining the Local Enterprise Partnership Network, which is facilitated by the British Chambers of Commerce.

web link For further information on LEPs and on the LEP network see, for example, *www.lepnetwork.net*

Business as an influence on government

Both individually and collectively, business organisations in a market economy are an important influence on government decision-making. They are an essential part of what has been termed the **negotiated environment** in which individuals and groups bargain with each other and with governments over the form and content of regulation of the environment that political decision-makers may be seeking to impose.

At an individual level, it tends to be large companies – and in particular multinational corporations – that are in the strongest position to influence government thinking, by dint of their economic and political power, and some of them have direct contacts with government ministers and officials for a variety of reasons (e.g. large defence contractors supply equipment to the Ministry of Defence). In addition, many large businesses use professional lobbyists, or create their own specialist units, whose role is to liaise directly with government agencies and to represent the interest of the organisation at national, supranational and international levels (e.g. in Brussels, Washington), using the kind of techniques described in Chapter 4. While such activities do not ensure that governments will abandon or amend their proposals or will pursue policies favourable to a particular company's position, they normally guarantee that the views of the organisation are considered alongside those of the other vested interests. Added weight tends to be given to these views when they are supported by all the leading firms in an industry (e.g. the tobacco lobby's fight against a complete ban on tobacco advertising).

The voice of business is also heard in political circles through various voluntary representative organisations such as Chambers of Commerce, employers' associations, trade associations and the **Confederation of British Industry** (CBI). **Chambers of Commerce** largely represent the views and interests of small businesses at local level, but also have a national organisation that lobbies in Whitehall and Brussels. **Trade associations** – which are sometimes combined with employers' associations – are usually organised on an industry basis (e.g. the Society of Motor Manufacturers and Traders) and handle consultations with appropriate government agencies, as well as providing information and advice to members about legislation and administration pertinent to the industry concerned.

mini case　A taxing issue

Campaigning employer organisations such as the CBI are active across a wide spectrum of economic and business issues. Current preoccupations include the growth of SMEs, trading relationships, access to finance, rebalancing the UK economy, maximising the potential of green businesses and business taxation. Influencing government policy and/or legislation in each of these areas is a major aspect of the CBI's regular work.

Where the issue of business taxation is concerned, the CBI has been keen to dispel the view that tax evasion – particularly by larger companies – is widespread and to try to draw a clear distinction between evasion and what it calls tax planning and management, activities it regards as both sensible and acceptable. As well as pointing to the large contribution that UK businesses make to the public finances, the organisation is calling for tax reform, including a reduction in the rate of corporation tax, which it claims is higher in the UK than in most of its competitor countries. The core of the CBI's argument is that the UK government should make the country's tax regime the most competitive in the G20 in order to promote growth and attract inward investment. Given increasing competition and globalisation, it claims that a competitive level of corporation tax will inevitably become an important factor in shaping future investment decisions by highly mobile businesses looking to gain an advantage over their rivals.

For further information on the CBI's view on taxation see 'Tax and British Business: Making the Case' (2013), available via its website.

The Confederation of British Industry

The CBI is the UK's premier business lobbying and campaigning organisation, representing the interests of more than 200 000 firms of all sizes and from all sectors, including many of the country's best-known organisations. Through its council, board, director-general and system of national and regional committees – and with permanent offices in Brussels, Washington, Beijing and New Delhi – the organisation promotes the interests of the business community in discussions with governments and with national and international organisations, as well as seeking to shape public opinion. Much of its influence stems from its regular contacts with politicians, the media and leading academics and from the encouragement it gives to businesses to take a proactive approach to government legislation and policy. Additionally, through its authoritative economic surveys, forecasts and research reports, the CBI has become an important part of the debate on government economic policy generally, as well as a central influence on legislation affecting the interests of its members, particularly in the area of regulatory control on business activity. Its website (*www.cbi.org.uk*) is a rich source of information on the organisation's current campaigns and areas of focus (see also the mini case immediately above).

While it is impossible to say with any degree of certainty how influential industry bodies such as the CBI are in shaping government policy and legislation, there is little doubt that the views of leading industrialists and their representative organisations and associations have received increased attention, particularly under past Conservative administrations. Regular pronouncements by senior government ministers frequently refer to the fact that a particular policy or piece of legislation has been framed 'with industry in mind' and there are clear signs that governments of all persuasions regularly pay heed to industry's opinions and preferences. It is not without just cause that the CBI claims that it has 'unparalleled access to decision-makers in Whitehall, Westminster and Brussels' and that it is often consulted informally before new proposals are published for full public debate.

Synopsis

State involvement in business activity takes many forms and can be seen as an attempt by government to tackle the problems caused by the operation of the free market. One such problem – regional imbalance – is normally the focus of a government's regional policy that seeks to correct economic disparities through spatially selective forms of assistance. Similarly, the adverse consequences associated with urbanisation and localised economic decay and decline have generally given rise to a range of government initiatives, often in partnership with the private sector, and involving different forms of state intervention at local, national and supranational levels.

Local government, too, has been active in this sphere and has used a variety of means to encourage local economic development and to support the local business community, both as agent for central government and as sponsor in its own right. Many of its activities have involved direct collaboration with businesses and with the voluntary organisations that represent them, and the private sector has remained a key influence on government policy at all spatial levels. Given the increasing emphasis on free-market activity, the voice of business is destined to remain a key input into the process of economic decision-making in the UK and elsewhere for the foreseeable future.

Summary of key points

- Government involvement in the workings of market-based economies is often rationalised on the grounds of 'market failure'.

- Market failure is the notion that if left entirely to their own devices, markets do not always deliver economically or socially desirable outcomes.

- Different forms of government intervention occur, some of which are designed specifically to influence the industrial and commercial environment and can be loosely called 'industrial policies'.

- Regional policy seeks to reduce disparities in the economic and social performance of different areas of a country, predominantly through different systems of grant aid for business and for other projects.

- Funds for such projects may be available from local, national, international and/or supranational agencies.

- Urban policy is targeted at problems in urban areas, including unemployment, social exclusion, physical decline and environmental degradation.

- Over the years governments have experimented with a range of policies and schemes to regenerate urban locations.

- Local authorities are normally involved in the implementation of the various centrally devised schemes and also support local businesses through their own programmes of local economic development as well as through their various roles in the local community.

- Increasingly, many of the current schemes require the establishment of multi-sector partnerships involving government, business and other agencies.

- Business involvement in the development of local communities can bring certain commercial benefits.

- Businesses can also gain influence in the policy sphere through their actions and through their representative organisations.

case study · Public sector procurement – the Royal Navy

The public sector is not only a producer and provider of services, but also a vast pool of organisations which are customers to many businesses in the UK and elsewhere. Most parts of the public sector are subject to strict European rules on competition which act to prevent any EU country's government awarding contracts for works over €5,000,000 or supplies or services over €130,000 to businesses in their own nations for political reasons. Remember that one of the principles of the EU was that of a common market in which people and companies could compete and capital can move freely. For contracts over these thresholds there must be a tendering process, where the public sector organisation offers the work contract to bids from interested companies around the world; the cheapest bidder might not get the contract – but price will certainly enter into considerations.

One recent example of this is the recent procurement of four fleet resupply ships (the Tide class) which were procured by open tender. The company that won the £453 million contract was Daewoo, a company previously known for selling cars in the UK. The first of the ships is now in service with the Royal Fleet Auxiliary, with three more on the way.

There are some exemptions to these procurement laws, which include ships intended to be armed and used in combat. The two new Royal Navy aircraft carriers and six new 'Type 45' destroyers are good examples, each programme costing more than £5 billion for each class of ships. With these contracts the government could choose who to award the contracts to, and a great deal of the production work was carried out in the UK by British workers – a politically and economically popular decision, but possibly not the most cost-effective one.

Case study questions

1 What other products and services are governments buyers and providers of?

2 How easy would it be to set up organisations to compete with existing large providers of these services?

Review and discussion questions

1 Why should a government committed to the free market intervene in the working of the economy?

2 Explain the connection between 'market failure' and the need for some form of government regional policy.

3 Why are some local authorities more interventionist than others?

4 Why have cross-sector partnerships to tackle social and economic problems become so fashionable in recent years?

Assignments

1 You are employed in the publicity and promotion unit of a local authority. Part of your work involves promoting the area as a suitable location for industrial and commercial activity. Your task is to produce a leaflet – for distribution to potential clients – indicating the advantages of locating within the area and the forms of assistance available.

2 You are the chairperson of the local Chamber of Commerce. The local authority has written to you concerning its plans to pedestrianise the town (or city) centre and asking for the reaction of local businesses. Your task is to produce a short report, for the next meeting of the Chamber, outlining the benefits and disadvantages to the local business community of such a scheme and indicating how the Chamber could make its views known in political circles.

Further reading

Ball, R. M., *Local Authorities and Regional Policy in the UK*, Sage, 2013.

Griffiths, A. and Wall, S. (eds), *Applied Economics: An Introductory Course*, 12th edition, Financial Times/Prentice Hall, 2011.

Ho, S. Y., *Evaluating British Urban Policy: Ideology, Conflict and Compromise*, Ashgate, 2003.

Hornby, W., Gammie, R. and Wall, S., *Business Economics*, 2nd edition, Financial Times/Prentice Hall, 2001.

Imrie, R. and Raco, M. (eds), *Urban Renaissance? New Labour Community and Urban Policy*, Policy Press, 2003.

Mulhearn, C., Vane, H. R. and Eden, J., *Economics for Business*, Palgrave, 2001, Chapter 7.

Turner, M. A., Wial, H. and Wolman, H., *Urban and Regional Policy and Its Effects*, Vol. 1, Brookings Institution Press, 2009.

Worthington, I., Britton, C. and Rees, A., *Economics for Business: Blending Theory and Practice*, 2nd edition, Financial Times/Prentice Hall, 2005, Chapter 11.

web link

Web links and further questions are available on the website at:
www.pearsoned.co.uk/worthington

A lot of bottle

Many organisations have ambitions to grow and to increase their market share, turnover and profitability. For very large businesses operating on an international scale, merger or acquisition is a popular way of achieving such objectives and can result in the creation of a huge company with a truly global reach. In the discussion below we report on one major example, InBev's acquisition of Anheuser-Busch in 2008, and on subsequent major developments in the global market for beer.

Prior to the takeover deal, the Belgium-based InBev was one of the world's leading brewers of beer, with around 13 per cent of the world market. While the roots of the business go back to the fourteenth century, InBev itself came into being in 2004 following a merger between Belgium's Interbrew and the Brazilian brewer AmBev. With key global brands such as Skol, Brahma Chopp, Stella Artois, Becks, Leffe, Staropramen and Hoegaarden, the company had a portfolio of products that could appeal to different markets across the globe. Annual group sales in 2006–7 were around 40 billion pints and its turnover was estimated to be around €14 billion.

InBev's main rival at the time was the London-based SABMiller, a merger of South African breweries and Miller, which created a business with key brands such as Snow and Miller Lite that helped to give the company a similar market share and annual sales to those of InBev. The latter's other main competitors were Anheuser-Busch and Heineken, each with a market share of just under 9 per cent and key brands such as Bud Light (AB), Budweiser (AB) and Heineken. Like InBev and SABMiller, these two companies were also businesses that had grown from previous mergers/acquisitions as the world's leading brewers sought to dominate the growing global market, especially in the developing countries in the Far East and South America.

While there was some opposition by the Anheuser-Busch board to the InBev takeover, the deal went through in the second half of 2008, resulting in the creation of a huge global company named Anheuser-Busch InBev, which was expected to sell around 65 billion pints of beer a year, about a fifth of the total world market. Apart from the obvious opportunities to make significant cost savings and economies of scale from combining the two businesses, the new company has brought together some of the major global brands sold to beer drinkers throughout the world and created an organisation that seems destined to become one of the world's top consumer goods companies, alongside such famous names as PepsiCo and Procter and Gamble.

As predicted in the previous edition of this book, the AB–InBev merger has helped to spark off a number of other deals as the major brewing companies continue to fight to gain a greater foothold in the emerging markets in Africa, China and Latin America. In 2010, Heineken bought the Mexican brewer Femsa Cerveza, the makers of Sol, for almost $8 billion and followed this up with the purchase of Asia Pacific Breweries (APB) in 2012 after a battle with the Thai brewer ThaiBev. APB had been a joint venture since 1931 between Heineken and the Singapore conglomerate Fraser and Neave. The latter's shareholders finally agreed to sell their stake to Heineken in September and the deal subsequently received regulatory approval in Singapore and New Zealand. In other developments, SABMiller snapped up Fosters in 2011 for $7.5 billion and the following year opened up a multi-million-dollar brewery in Nigeria in order to capitalise on the rapidly growing African market. Carlsberg, the world's fourth largest brewer, announced plans in 2012 to expand in Asia via a joint venture with Singha Corporation, designed at marketing and selling its beers in Thailand, to go alongside its existing presence in China and India.

From a strategic point of view, these moves are not difficult to rationalise. As people in the emerging markets have become richer, they have provided the global brewers with an opportunity to shift their focus from the declining markets in North America and Europe towards markets that are expected to yield substantial levels of growth and profitability.

Heineken, for example, estimates that growth rates in the Asia-Pacific region alone will be around 8 per cent per annum until 2021, with China achieving rates of 12 per cent during this period; AB InBev expects to generate around 6 per cent of group profits from China by 2021, compared with just 1 per cent in 2011.

While all the emerging markets appear to provide golden opportunities, China in particular looks likely to prove the biggest cash cow for the major brewers given the remarkable growth in the popularity of beer over the last two decades or so. In 1991, average per capita beer consumption in the country was about 12 pints; in 2011 this had grown to 63 pints. By 2021 the figure is expected to rise to 93 pints. That said, this is still a long way short of levels currently being experienced in some countries in Europe, with the Czech Republic leading the way with an annual consumption of around 250 pints per person. Whether this is an enviable distinction is, of course, a matter of opinion.

Part Four

MARKETS

14 The market system

Chris Britton

As part of their normal production activity, businesses are involved in buying (inputs – such as labour and raw materials) and selling (outputs – the finished product). Buying and selling take place in markets and although there are many different types of market, the basic analysis remains the same.

Learning outcomes

Having read this chapter you should be able to:

- explain the working of the market system
- apply the theory to the real world
- demonstrate the importance of key concepts such as elasticity to business
- discuss the wider economic effects of changes in market forces

Key terms

Buyers' market
Complements
Cross-price elasticity
Demand
Demand curve
Effective demand
Effective supply
Elasticity
Elasticity of demand
Elasticity of supply
Equilibrium price

Equilibrium quantity
Excess demand
Excess supply
Factor market
Free market
Income elasticity
Inelastic
Inferior goods
Law of demand
Law of supply
Market

Market system
Normal goods
Price ceiling
Price controls
Price elasticity
Price floor
Product market
Sellers' market
Substitutes
Supply
Supply curve

Introduction

As indicated in Chapter 5, the **market system** is an economy in which all of the basic economic choices are made through the market. The **market** is a place where buyers and sellers of a product are brought together. The nature and location of the market depend on the product. For example, within your local town there is likely to be a vegetable market where you would go to buy vegetables. Here, buyers and sellers meet face to face in the same location, but this is not always the case. The market for used cars might be the local newspaper classified section; the sale of stocks and shares passes through a broker so that the buyer never meets the seller. There are many different types of market, involving different buyers and sellers. Firms sell the goods and services they produce to households on the **product markets**, while in the **factor markets** firms are buying resources such as labour and raw materials. The discussion in this chapter will concentrate on the product markets, but much of the analysis could also be applied to the factor markets.

A free-market system is one in which the basic economic choices are made through the market, without any intervention by the government. In reality, markets are not completely free; governments intervene in markets for many reasons and in many different ways (see Chapter 17), but in this chapter such intervention will be ignored.

The market mechanism

In every market there will be a buyer and a seller, and somehow they have to be brought together so that a sale can take place. The market mechanism is the way in which this takes place in a market economy. In the product market, the buyer is the household and the seller is the firm. In economic language, the household **demands** the good or service and the firm **supplies** the good or service. Each of these will be considered separately first and then brought together.

Demand

The quantity demanded refers to the quantity of a good or service that households are willing and able to purchase at a particular price. This definition shows that it is **effective demand** that is important; although many people would like to own a Rolls-Royce, they could not afford it and so their demand is not effective on the market. The demand for a good or service depends on a number of factors, the most important of which are:

- the price of the good;
- the prices of other goods;
- disposable income;
- tastes.

To begin with, the relationship between quantity demanded and price will be looked at, assuming that the other factors above remain the same. This assumption will be relaxed in the subsequent analysis.

Table 14.1 The demand for 'Real Brew' draught beer (prices for illustration only)

Price (£ per pint)	Quantity demanded (000s of pints/week)
0.90	83
1.00	70
1.10	58
1.20	48
1.30	40
1.40	35
1.50	32

Table 14.1 shows what happens to the quantity demanded of beer as the price per pint goes up. Note that demand is measured over some period of time. The information is then presented in a graphical form in Figure 14.1; the line joining the various combinations of price and quantity demanded is called a **demand curve**. The demand curve shows that if all of the other factors that influence demand are constant, then, as price goes up, quantity demanded goes down. This is commonly referred to as the **law of demand**. What happens when price rises is that some individuals will cut down their consumption of beer and others may switch to other types of beer. There are some goods where this relationship might not hold: for example, in the stock market where a rise in share prices might lead to the expectation of further price rises and therefore an increase in demand on the part of those wishing to make a capital gain. However, these exceptions are rare and it is therefore safe to assume that the law of demand holds.

If the price of beer changes, there is a movement along the demand curve. For example, if the price of beer goes up from 90p a pint to £1.00 a pint, the quantity demanded goes down from 83 000 pints per week to 70 000 pints per week. In drawing the demand curve, the assumption was made that other factors affecting demand are constant. If this assumption is relaxed, what happens to the demand curve?

Figure 14.1 A demand curve for 'Real Brew' draught beer

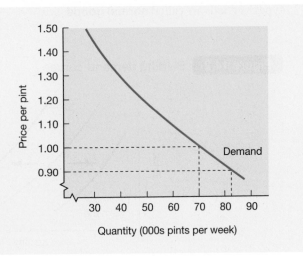

Price of other goods

The quantity of beer consumed will be affected by the prices of other goods. These other goods are likely to be **substitutes** or **complements**. A substitute for beer may be lager, and if the price of lager goes down, some individuals may switch from beer to lager; thus the demand for beer goes down. What happens to the demand curve is that, at all price levels, the demand for beer is now lower. Thus the demand curve shifts to the left, indicating that at £1.00 per pint only 60 000 pints of beer are demanded per week. If the price of a substitute goes up, there will be an increase in the demand for beer. The demand curve moves to the right. These movements are shown in Figure 14.2. The closer the goods are as substitutes and the greater the change in the price of the substitute, the greater will be the shift in the demand curve.

A complementary good is one that tends to be consumed with another good. For beer, it is possible that individuals eat crisps or smoke cigarettes at the same time as drinking beer. The relationship is the opposite of that for substitutes. If the price of a complement goes up, individuals might be less likely to drink beer, and demand will fall. The demand curve moves to the left. If the price of a complement goes down, the demand for beer will rise. Again, the closer the goods are as complements, and the greater the price change of that complement, the greater will be the shift in the demand curve.

Disposable income

Changes in disposable income will clearly affect demand. If the economy moves into recession, then retail sales and the housing market might suffer. As incomes increase once the economy recovers, then such sectors will pick up again. Higher incomes will lead to increased consumption of most goods. If your income is boosted, how will this affect your consumption? You might buy more textbooks, and probably spend more money on leisure activities and clothes. Most students might also drink an extra pint of beer per week. Thus, an increase in disposable income will lead to an increase in demand for these goods, indicated by a rightward shift in the demand curve. As incomes fall the demand for these goods will fall, indicated by a leftward shift in the demand curve. These types of goods are called **normal goods**.

Figure 14.2   Shifting demand curves

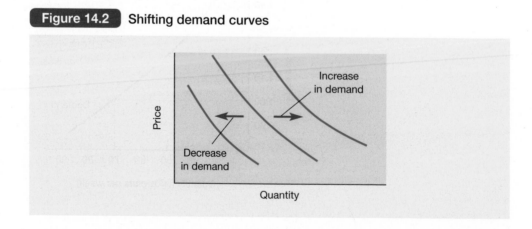

There are goods, however, that experience a fall in demand as a result of income increases. These goods are called **inferior goods**. A good example is rough toilet paper; as individuals become richer, they are likely to substitute more expensive soft toilet paper, and thus the demand for rough toilet paper will fall.

Tastes

Taste includes attitudes and preferences of consumers, and will be affected by such things as fashion, and advertising campaigns by producers or by governments. For example, a successful advertising campaign by the government pointing out the effects of smoking would cause tastes to change and demand for cigarettes to fall.

The demand curve, then, is downward sloping, indicating that as the price of the good rises the quantity demanded by households falls, shown by a *movement along the demand curve*. Changes in the other determining factors lead to *movements of the demand curve*.

Supply

The other side of the market is the supply side. In the market for goods and services it is the firm that is the supplier. The quantity supplied of a good is defined as the quantity that firms are willing and able to supply to the market at a particular price. Again, notice the wording of the definition is such that it only includes **effective supply** and, as with demand, it is measured over a specific time period.

The quantity supplied to the market depends on a number of factors, the most important of which are:

- the price of the good;
- the prices of other goods;
- the prices of the resources used to produce the good;
- technology;
- expectations;
- number of suppliers.

In the same way as for demand, all factors other than price will be assumed to be constant and the relationship between quantity supplied and price will be considered first.

Table 14.2 provides some information on price and quantity supplied of beer. The same information is represented graphically in Figure 14.3; the line joining the points

Table 14.2 The supply of 'Real Brew' draught beer

Price (£ per pint)	Quantity supplied (000s of units/week)
0.90	0
1.00	35
1.10	43
1.20	48
1.30	55
1.40	60
1.50	68

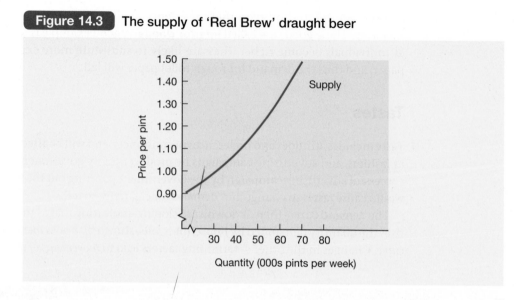

Figure 14.3 The supply of 'Real Brew' draught beer

together is called the **supply curve**. The upward-sloping curve illustrates the **law of supply**. This states that, as the price of a good rises, the quantity that firms are willing to supply also rises. This is because if costs are constant as we have assumed, then higher prices must mean higher profits to the firm.

Note that there is no supply at a price below 90p per pint; this is the minimum price required by the producer to produce the beer. If the price per pint changes, there is a movement along the supply curve in the same way as for demand. If any of the other factors listed above change, there will be a movement of the supply curve.

Other prices

The supply of one good can be influenced by the price of another. For example, if the brewery in which Real Brew beer is brewed is also producing lager, then an increase in the price of lager (with the price of beer remaining the same) will encourage the firm to produce less beer and more lager, as lager is now more profitable to produce. The supply curve for beer would shift to the left, indicating that, at every possible price, less is now supplied than before. If the price of lager fell, the supply of beer would increase. This is shown by a rightward shift of the supply curve. The size of the shift would depend upon the degree to which the goods could be substituted for each other in production, and the size of the price change. These shifts are illustrated in Figure 14.4.

Goods can also be complements in their production process; for example, beef and leather hides. An increase in the price of beef would increase not only the supply of beef but also the supply of hides. There would be a corresponding shift in the supply curve for hides.

The prices of the resources used in the production of the good

If any of the costs of production (wages, rent, rate of interest, and so on) increased, then the profitability of that good at each price would fall and there would be a tendency for

Figure 14.4 Shifting supply curves

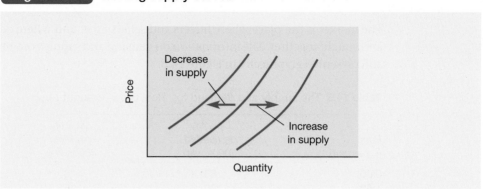

supply to be reduced. The supply curve would move to the left. If costs of production fell there would be an increase in supply and a rightward movement of the supply curve. The extent of the shift depends upon the size of the price change, the significance of that factor in production, and the degree to which the factor could be substituted for another factor.

Technology

As illustrated in Chapter 7, technical development in all aspects of production has led to great improvements in output per worker. Such improvements generally result in either more being produced with the same resources, or the same being produced with fewer. In most cases it would also lead to a substitution of one factor of production for another. For example, car production becomes less labour intensive as robotic techniques take over. Even such a product as traditional British beer has benefited from significant technical improvements in production. The effect of such advances would result in increased supply at each price level and hence a movement of the supply curve to the right.

Business expectations

Expectations play a crucial role in the decision-making of firms. Good expectations of the future would encourage firms to invest in new plant and machinery, which would increase their productive potential. Chancellors of the Exchequer are occasionally accused of trying to 'talk the economy up': that is, they may paint a rosy picture of the current and future state of the economy in the hope that this will enhance business expectations, and help pull the economy out of recession. If business does become increasingly confident, or perhaps more inclined to take risks, then this would shift the supply curve to the right. The reverse would shift it to the left.

The number of suppliers

As the number of suppliers in a market increases, the supply will rise; the supply curve shifts to the right. If suppliers leave the market, supply will fall and the supply curve moves to the left.

Price determination

The market is the place where buyers and sellers meet and where demand and supply are brought together. The information on demand and supply is combined in Table 14.3 and presented graphically in Figure 14.5.

Table 14.3 The supply and demand for 'Real Brew' draught beer

Price (£ per pint)	Quantity demanded (000s/wk)	Quantity supplied (000s/wk)
0.90	83	0
1.00	70	35
1.10	58	43
1.20	48	48
1.30	40	55
1.40	35	60
1.50	32	68

The equilibrium price

At a price of £1.20, the quantity demanded is the same as the quantity supplied at 48 000 pints per week. At this price the amount that consumers wish to buy is the same as the amount that producers wish to sell. This price is called the **equilibrium price** and the quantity being bought and sold is called the **equilibrium quantity**. The point of equilibrium can be seen on the figure at the point where the demand and supply curves cross.

At price levels above £1.20 the quantity that producers wish to supply is greater than the quantity consumers wish to buy. There is **excess supply** and the market is a **buyers' market**. At prices less than £1.20 consumers wish to buy more than producers wish to supply. There is **excess demand** and the market is a **sellers' market**.

In competitive markets, situations of excess demand or supply should not exist for long as forces are put into motion to move the market towards equilibrium. For example,

Figure 14.5 The market for 'Real Brew' draught beer

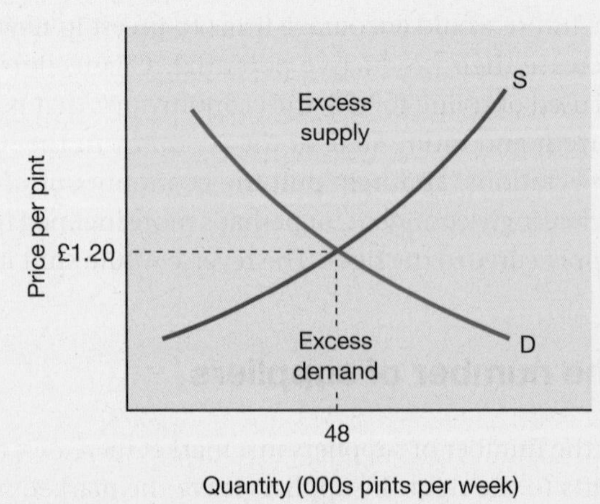

if the price level is £1.30 per pint, there is excess supply and producers will be forced to reduce the price in order to sell their beer. Consumers may be aware that they are in a buyers' market and offer lower prices, which firms might accept. For one or both of these reasons, there will be a tendency for prices to be pushed back towards the equilibrium price. The opposite occurs at prices below equilibrium and price is pushed upwards towards equilibrium.

Shifts in demand and supply

So long as the demand and supply curves in any market remain stationary, the equilibrium price should be maintained. However, there are numerous factors that could shift either or both of these curves. If this were to happen, then the old equilibrium would be destroyed and the market should work to a new equilibrium. How does this happen?

In Figure 14.6 the original equilibrium price for Real Brew draught beer is P_1. Assume that the demand curve moves from D_1 to D_2. This increase in demand could be due to a variety of factors already mentioned. For example, the price of a rival drink may have increased; disposable income could have risen; or sales may have benefited from a successful advertising campaign. In any event, at the old equilibrium price there now exists an excess of demand over supply of Q_1Q_3. It is likely that price will be bid upwards in order to ration the shortage in supply. As price rises, demand is choked off and supply exhausted. Eventually, there is a movement to a new equilibrium of P_2. At this new price both supply and demand at Q_2 are higher than they were at the previous equilibrium. If, alternatively, the demand curve had shifted to the left, then the process would have been reversed and the new equilibrium would have been at a level of demand and supply less than Q_1, with a price below P_1. Illustrate this process diagrammatically for yourself.

In Figure 14.7 there is a shift in the supply curve from S_1 to S_2. Refer back in this chapter to envisage specific reasons for such a shift. At the original equilibrium price of P_1 there would now be an excess supply over demand of Q_1Q_3. Price would therefore fall in a free market. As it does, demand will be encouraged and supply diminished. Eventually there

Figure 14.6 A shift in the demand curve

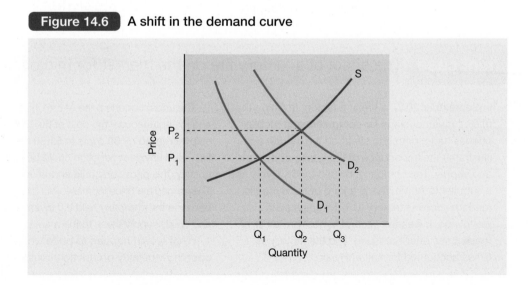

Figure 14.7 A shift in the supply curve

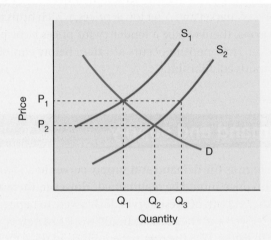

will be a new equilibrium at P_2 with a higher quantity demanded and supplied than at the previous equilibrium. If the supply curve had instead shifted to the left, then market forces would have resulted in a lower quantity supplied and demanded than before. Once again, illustrate this diagrammatically for yourself.

The analysis so far has been relatively straightforward; it has been assumed that either the demand or the supply curve moves alone. However, it is likely that in any given time period both curves could move in any direction and perhaps even more than once.

Given the many factors that may shift both the demand and the supply curves, it is easy to imagine that markets can be in a constant state of flux. Just as the market is moving towards a new equilibrium, some other factor may change, necessitating an adjustment in an opposite direction. Given that such adjustment is not immediate, and that market conditions are constantly changing, it may be the case that equilibrium is never actually attained. It is even possible that the very process of market adjustment can be destabilising. The constant movement of price implied by the analysis may also be detrimental to business. The firm might prefer to keep price constant in the face of minor changes in demand and supply.

mini case · The effect of a factory fire on the market for microchips

In September 2013, a fire at a factory in China that makes memory chips for computers and mobile phones had a dramatic effect on the market and illustrates the importance of the forces of demand and supply. The company, owned by SK Hynix and a supplier to Apple, made a third of the dynamic random access memory (DRAM) chips sold worldwide. It was the second largest producer of these chips after Samsung, and the factory in China accounted for half of Hynix's output.

The impact on the price of the chips was dramatic and instantaneous – the cost of the DDR3 2-gigabit chip increased by 30 cents to $1.90 the day after the fire – and unless production could be increased fairly quickly, this price rise could endure for some time. The immediate price increase was moderated because the company held big inventories of the chip and could supply these to the market.

What would happen to price would depend upon how quickly production could return to normal. Some limited production started in the company the week after the fire, but it was not known how long it would take to resume production at normal levels. Hynix responded in the short term by switching production out of other products into the production of DDR3 chips. As a direct result of the fire Hynix missed its analyst's estimates of profits for the last quarter of 2013.

This case can be illustrated using a demand and supply diagram. In Figure 14.8, the demand curve is shown as fairly inelastic; this is because worldwide demand for mobile phones and computers is high and growing and the fact that for many these products are now necessities. Three supply curves are shown:

1 S4/9 is the supply curve on the day of the fire (price of a chip $1.60).
2 S5/9 is the supply curve the day after the fire (price of a chip $1.90).
3 S4/10 is the supply curve on 4 October 2013 (price of a chip $2.34).

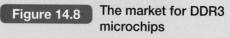

Figure 14.8 The market for DDR3 microchips

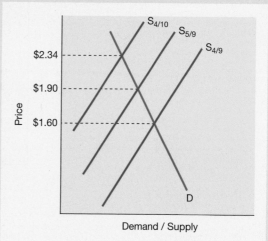

The price increase would, of course, have a knock-on effect on the price of mobile phones and computers, and this case illustrates well the effects of demand and supply on the price of products and interdependence between markets worldwide.

Price controls

Governments occasionally take the view that a particular equilibrium price is politically, socially or economically unacceptable. In such circumstances, one course of action is the imposition of **price controls**. This involves the institutional setting of prices at either above or below the true market equilibrium. For example, if it was felt that the equilibrium price of a good was too high, then the government might try to impose a lower price on the market. This would now be the maximum acceptable price or **price ceiling**. Price may not rise above this ceiling. Alternatively, the equilibrium price could be seen as too low. In this case, a higher price, or **price floor** is imposed, below which price should not fall.

Figure 14.9 illustrates the market for a basic foodstuff. Imagine that it is wartime and the disruption has shifted the supply curve to the left. This could be largely due to a movement of resources away from the production of this good and towards munitions. The free market price at P_1 is seen to be unacceptably high relative to the pre-war price, and the decision is made to impose a price ceiling of P_2. It is hoped that such a ceiling will alleviate the problems of consumers who could not afford the free-market price. The problem now is that at the price ceiling only Q_3 units will be supplied, whereas demand is for Q_2. The volume of output Q_3Q_2 therefore represents an excess of demand over supply. Many customers are frustrated in their desire to purchase that good. To help bring order to the situation, a system of rationing might be introduced. This could allocate the

Figure 14.9 Imposition of a price ceiling

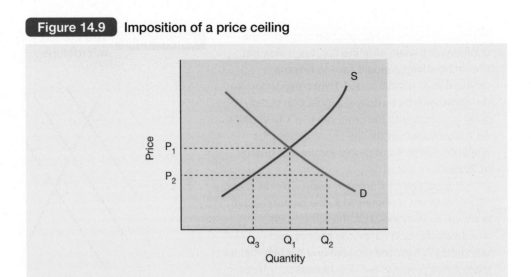

limited output between the many customers in a more orderly fashion than 'first come, first served'. For example, one unit could be allocated per person and priority could be given to the old and the sick. This does not solve the problem of excess demand. It is commonly found in such situations that illegal trading starts to emerge at a price above the ceiling. To obtain the good, many would be willing to pay a higher price. This is commonly referred to as black market trading.

Figure 14.10 illustrates the market for a specific type of labour. The downward-sloping demand curve indicates that, at lower wages, employers will wish to take on additional workers. The supply curve shows how more people will offer themselves for work as wage rates increase. At the intersection of the curves, the market is in equilibrium. Imagine that this equilibrium wage is seen to be too low, and the authorities seek to impose a minimum wage of W_2. Employers are not permitted to pay any less than this amount. It is hoped that the policy will improve the welfare of workers by raising their living standards to some acceptable level.

Figure 14.10 Imposition of a price floor

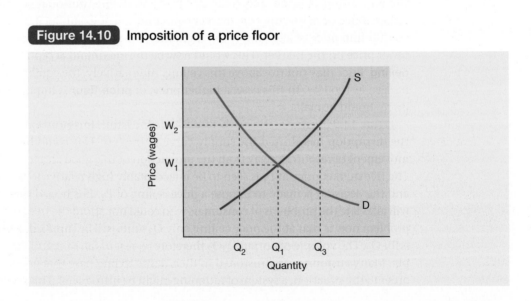

At this minimum wage, employment becomes more attractive, and Q_3 persons seek employment. However, employers only wish to take on Q_2 workers. There is now a situation of excess supply. Only Q_2 find work; the remainder Q_2Q_3 are unsuccessful. The policy has actually reduced the level of employment from Q_1 to Q_2. In such a situation, there will be a temptation to flout the legislation. For example, unscrupulous employers observing the ranks of unemployed would realise that many would willingly work at less than the minimum wage.

The above examples illustrate the problems that arise once price is imposed away from its equilibrium. Further examples of such price controls would include the guaranteed minimum prices to farmers within the Common Agricultural Policy (CAP) of the EU, and various post-war attempts to control the cost of rented accommodation at a price affordable to the low paid. The former has been associated with overproduction and the need to control the mountains of excess supply, while the latter tended to result in landlords taking their properties off the rental market in order to seek more profitable returns. The success of such policies requires careful control and monitoring. In many circumstances, it might be better to consider alternative ways of achieving the policy goals.

mini case   The price of toilet rolls in Venezuela

In 2013 there were shortages of many goods in Venezuela, including basic foodstuffs such as milk, cooking oil and sugar and the one that has really hit the news – toilet rolls. In a free market, shortages are dealt with by rising prices, but this disadvantages the poor and goes against the policies of the Venezuelan government. This situation is illustrated in Figure 14.9; there is excess demand for toilet rolls. The solution to this problem adopted in Venezuela was to ration toilet rolls – there were queues outside supermarkets and customers were restricted to 12 rolls per visit. An Android app was even produced called Abasteceme (supply me), which alerts customers to the whereabouts of supplies of the shortage products.

There is much debate about the causes of the shortages, so what is at the bottom of the problem? Opponents of the government blamed the volatile nature of the economic policy-making of the Chavez government, including regular devaluations of the currency and routine takeover of private companies, which make for high levels of uncertainty for business. It is argued that price controls are a disincentive for local producers to produce. In other words, it is a supply issue.

The government blamed an international conspiracy against its policies. It is a fact that income distribution in Venezuela was much more equal than in other countries in South America, but the problem was that national income was not growing. This, together with the shortages, meant that the population did not feel any better off. In September 2013, the scarcity index stood at 21 per cent according to the Venezuela Central Bank, which meant that 21 out of 100 goods were not available or in short supply. It was widely reported that the National Statistics Office of Venezuela attributed the shortage of toilet rolls to the fact that Venezuelans were eating three meals a day and hence the demand for toilet rolls was higher. In other words, it is a demand issue.

Whether the shortage of toilet rolls was due to demand or supply factors is up for debate, but the fact remains that there was a shortage. The population of Venezuela is 28.5 million and consumers use 125 million toilet rolls per month, thus there is a shortfall of 40 million rolls per month. The government has done two things to try to alleviate this: it has increased the import of toilet rolls to meet the demand and in September 2013 it took Manpa (the company that supplies 40 per cent of toilet rolls in Venezuela) into public ownership. It hopes that this will prevent hoarding on the part of the company and help meet the excess demand.

Elasticity of demand

It has been shown that as long as other factors affecting demand remain constant, a decrease in price would be expected to increase the quantity demanded by consumers. This knowledge is obviously important to business, in that it implies that sales will expand as the good becomes more price competitive. It does not, however, say anything about the degree to which sales might increase. As prices change, will demand change by a large or a small amount? At the end of the day, will the extra sales bring in more or less total revenue? In short, a measure is needed of the responsiveness of demand to price changes. In the same way, the responsiveness of quantity demanded to other factors like income or other prices can also be measured. It is also important to be aware of the responsiveness of supply to changes in prices. All of these are measured by the concept of **elasticity**.

Price elasticity of demand

Figure 14.11 illustrates two different-shaped demand curves and shows the effect of a price increase from 40p to 60p in each case. On the left-hand figure, the increase in price causes demand to fall from 25 to 20 units. Total revenue received by the producer (i.e. price multiplied by the number of units sold) changes from £10.00 (40p × 25 units) to £12.00 (60p × 20 units). As illustrated, the area A represents the gain in revenue as a result of the price change, while B shows the loss of revenue. In this case there is a clear net gain. The reason for this is that the significance of the price rise is greater than the fall in demand. Compare this with the right-hand figure. The same price rise now causes total revenue to fall from £20.00 (40p × 50 units) to £6.00 (60p × 10 units). The loss of revenue, area B_1, is clearly greater than the gain in revenue, area A_1. There is a net loss of revenue.

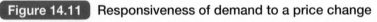

Figure 14.11   Responsiveness of demand to a price change

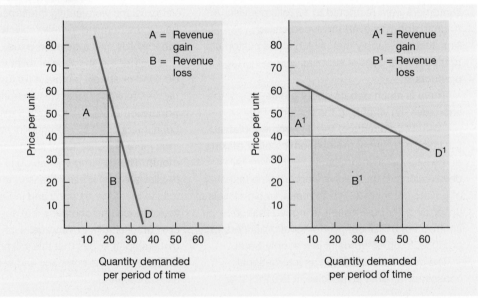

This is a situation where the decrease in demand is of greater significance than the increase in price.

The traditional way of measuring the responsiveness of demand to a change in price is via the concept of **price elasticity**, the formula being:

$$\text{Price elasticity of demand (Ep)} = \frac{\text{Percentage change in quantity demanded}}{\text{Percentage change in price}}$$

$$\text{Ep} = \frac{\% \text{ change QD}}{\% \text{ change P}}$$

The significance of this formula lies in whether the value of price elasticity is greater or less than 1. If it is greater, then the percentage change in quantity demanded is greater than the percentage change in price. Demand is referred to as being relatively elastic, or responsive to price changes. If, however, the percentage change in quantity demanded is less than the percentage change in price, then price elasticity will be less than 1. Demand is now referred to as being relatively **inelastic**, and demand is not very responsive to price changes.

The higher or lower the value of price elasticity, the greater or lesser the responsiveness of demand to the price change. Table 14.4 demonstrates the connection between price elasticity and total revenue. It will be observed that if price elasticity is greater than 1, then there is a negative relationship between price changes and total revenue. For example, an increase in price results in a decrease in total revenue, whereas if elasticity is less than 1, then there is a positive relationship.

Table 14.4 Elasticity and total revenue

Elasticity	Price change	Change in total revenue
Elastic	Upward	Downward
	Downward	Upward
Inelastic	Upward	Upward
	Downward	Downward

Calculating elasticity

From the information portrayed in Figure 14.11, in the left-hand figure price rose from 40p to 60p and demand fell from 25 to 20 units. Thus:

$$\text{Ep} = \frac{\% \text{ change QD}}{\% \text{ change P}} = \frac{5/25 \times 100}{20/40 \times 100} = \frac{20\%}{50\%} = 0.4$$

This shows that demand is inelastic. One problem with this measurement is that if you measured elasticity when price fell from 60p to 40p the answer would be different:

$$\text{Ep} = \frac{\% \text{ change QD}}{\% \text{ change P}} = \frac{5/25 \times 100}{20/60 \times 100} = \frac{20\%}{33.3\%} = 0.60$$

The reason for this variation is that the percentage change in each case is being measured from a different base. When price rises from 20p to 40p, this is a 50 per cent rise. Yet when it falls from 60p to 40p this is only a 33.3 per cent fall. The value of elasticity therefore varies. To avoid this ambiguity, elasticity is measured as the percentage change from the average value of price and quantity before and after the change, that is:

$$\% \text{ change} = \frac{\text{Change in value} \times 100}{\text{Average value}}$$

The value of elasticity for the price increase and decrease must now be identical:

$$Ep = \frac{\% \text{ change QD}}{\% \text{ change P}} = \frac{5/22.5 \times 100}{20/50 \times 100} = \frac{22.2\%}{40\%} = 0.55$$

The determinants of elasticity

There are a number of factors that determine how responsive quantity demanded is to price changes. First, the nature of the good and how it is viewed by consumers. A good that is a necessity will have a low value of elasticity, as an increase in price will not have a very big impact on the quantity consumed. Goods like cigarettes will have inelastic demand because they are habit forming. The tastes of consumers will be important: whether they view a television, for example, as a necessity or a luxury will determine the value of elasticity. Another factor is whether substitutes are available for the good or not. If there is no substitute for a particular good and the household wishes to continue to consume it, an increase in price will have little effect on the level of demand. Other factors include the importance of the good in the household's total expenditure. The smaller the proportion of the household's budget spent on a particular good, the smaller will be the effect on demand of any change in price.

Income elasticity of demand

Income elasticity of demand is a measure of the responsiveness of quantity demanded to changes in income. It can be negative in the case of inferior goods, where an increase in income leads to a fall in the demand for a good, or positive in the case of a normal good, where an increase in income leads to an increase in demand. There is also a difference between luxuries and necessities. Luxuries will have positive income elasticities with values over 1. This means that an increase in income will cause an increase in demand for that good and that a 1 per cent increase in income will cause a more than 1 per cent increase in demand.

A necessity will also have a positive income elasticity, but its value will lie somewhere between 0 and 1, showing that an increase in income of 1 per cent causes an increase in demand by less than 1 per cent.

Income elasticity is calculated in a similar way to price elasticity except that it is income which is changing rather than the price of the good:

$$\text{Income elasticity} = \frac{\% \text{ change in quantity demanded}}{\% \text{ change in income}}$$

The effect of changes in income on the overall level of expenditure depends upon the type of the good being considered, as Table 14.5 shows.

Table 14.5 Income elasticity and total expenditure

Type of good	Income elasticity	Change in total expenditure brought about by an increase in income of 1%
Inferior	Negative	Downward
Normal	Positive	Upward
Luxury	Positive and above 1	Upward by more than 1%
Necessity	Positive between 0 and 1	Upward by less than 1%

Cross-price elasticity of demand

Cross-price elasticity of demand is a measure of how the demand for one good is affected by changes in the prices of other goods. It is calculated with the formula:

$$\text{Cross-price elasticity} = \frac{\text{\% change in quantity demanded of good X}}{\text{\% change in the price of good Y}}$$

Like income elasticity it can be positive or negative, depending this time upon the nature of the relationship between the goods. If the goods are substitutes for one another, as the price of Y goes up, the quantity demanded of X will also rise, as consumers substitute the relatively cheaper good (e.g. margarine for butter). Therefore cross-price elasticity will be positive. If the goods are complements, as the price of Y rises, the demand for X will fall and cross-price elasticity will be a negative value. The size will depend upon how closely the goods are related, either as substitutes or complements.

Elasticity of supply

The concept of elasticity can be applied to supply as well as to demand, and is a measurement of how responsive quantity supplied is to changes in the price of a good. Figure 14.12 illustrates two differently shaped supply curves and the effect of the same price change in each case.

Elasticity of supply is measured with the following formula:

$$\text{Elasticity of supply} = \frac{\text{\% change in quantity supplied}}{\text{\% change in price}}$$

The higher the numerical value, the more responsive is supply to changes in price.

The main determinants of the elasticity of supply for a good are the nature of the production process and the time-scale in question. It may well be easier to increase the supply of manufactured goods than agricultural goods, given the nature of the production processes involved. Even agricultural goods can be increased in supply, given time to replant stock, so supply is more responsive to price changes in the longer time period.

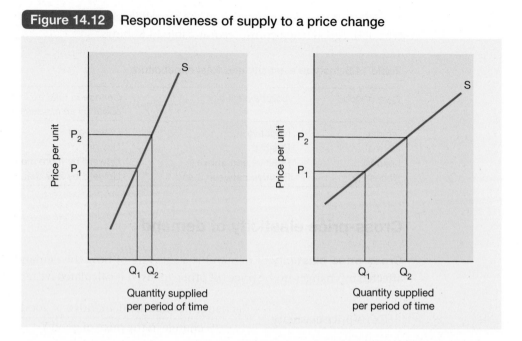

Figure 14.12 Responsiveness of supply to a price change

The importance of the market to business

All firms operate in markets, whether they are localised, national or international. Although firms might be able to influence the market conditions that face them, they need a knowledge of their own markets and how markets fit together in the market economy. Firms often have a range of products and they need to be aware of the differing conditions in each of their markets. They need a knowledge of the shape and position of the demand curve they face, including the following aspects:

- the nature of the good they produce;
- the way in which it is viewed by consumers;
- the factors that affect the demand for their good;
- any changes likely in the future which will affect the market;
- any likely government intervention in the market.

Only through this information can the firm hope to retain markets, expand existing markets and move into new ones.

An understanding is also needed of the concept of **elasticity of demand**. Knowing how the demand for its product responds to changes in its price will help the firm in its pricing policy. Measures of income elasticity help the firm in forecasting the effects of changes in income on the demand for its products. Economic growth will affect markets with high income elasticities much more than markets with low income elasticities. This knowledge will also help the firm in developing its marketing strategy. For example, goods with low income elasticities could be marketed as 'economical', thus hopefully increasing the market share.

If the firm wishes to be successful in existing markets and to expand into new markets, as well as detailed knowledge of demand conditions, it also needs to know about its own supply curve and production process and the supply curves of other firms.

Although the economy in which the firm operates is not a totally free-market economy (see Chapter 5), the firm needs to know and understand the importance of market forces which form the basis of our economic system.

Changes in market forces can have dramatic effects not only on the affected market, but also on other related markets and the wider economy. Changes in one market will affect all other markets to a greater or lesser degree.

Synopsis

In this chapter, the market has been examined in some detail. The determinants of demand and supply have been considered and the effects on the market of changes in any of these factors have been shown. The concept of elasticity has also been examined and calculated and the importance of all these issues to business has been demonstrated.

Summary of key points

- In a free market both the quantity being traded and the price of a product are determined by the forces of demand and supply.

- The demand for a good or service depends upon a number of factors, including price, the price of other goods, the income of consumers, tastes, and so on.

- The supply of a good or service also depends upon a range of influences, including price, the costs of production, technology and the number of suppliers.

- Changes in demand and supply cause changes in the price of the product and the quantity being traded.

- Where demand and supply are equal, the market is said to be in equilibrium.

- Where this occurs, equilibrium price and quantity result.

- Intervention in the market mechanism can take the form of minimum or maximum prices, taxation or subsidy.

- Elasticity is a measure of the responsiveness of demand or supply to various factors, including price, income and the price of other goods.

- It is important for businesses to be aware of the demand and supply characteristics of the good or service they are producing.

case study The housing market in the UK

One market where the operation of the market mechanism can easily be seen is in the market for houses. In the UK in July 2017 the average price for a house or flat was £226,185, up 5.1 per cent on the year before (see Figure 14.13). House prices rose steadily through the 1990s and then rapidly through the 2000s when banks and building societies were lending to individuals with poor credit ratings up to 125 per cent of the value of the property, often without requiring any deposit. Banks were not sufficiently concerned with lending the money as the property (which could be repossessed if needed) had a value on track to catch up with the value of the loan. This created the 'housing bubble', which burst in 2007 and took nearly 10 years to recover. Many people ended up in negative equity during this period, where the value of the house was less than the value of the mortgage loan. This was not confined to the UK – the same thing happened in many other countries, including the United States.

Like all products, the price of houses depends upon demand and supply factors.

Supply factors

The supply of housing is inelastic; it is very difficult to increase the stock of houses quickly. House building in the UK has been low historically, and the housing charity Shelter estimates that England needs 250 000 new homes to be built each year to meet the demand, compared with around 127 000 which are currently being built yearly. There is an increasing trend of 'letting to buy', where people buy a new property but rent out their old one instead of releasing it to the market, which means that the supply of houses to buy is further restricted. In 2017

Figure 14.13 Average house price in the UK, first quarter 2000–2017

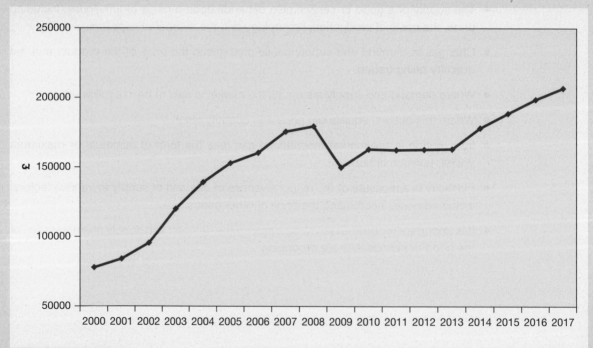

Source: Halifax Price Index

around 1 in 10 people owned (or jointly owned) a second home, primarily as a source of rental income.

Demand factors

In the UK there is a comparatively high propensity for owner occupation – 62.9 per cent of households were either buying or owned their home outright in the 2015–16 period. This is higher than other countries; in Germany, for example, it is 52 per cent and in Switzerland it is only 43.4 per cent. This means that in the UK, demand is high. As most houses are bought through mortgages or loans, both the availability and the cost of these loans will be important.

As mentioned above, before the crash of 2007, banks and building societies were lending too much to the wrong people with little or no security. After the crash, the banks and building societies became much more cautious about their lending, mortgages of 100 per cent or more disappeared and house buyers were required to put down a sizeable deposit. This made buying houses difficult or even impossible for many and therefore had an impact on demand. Landlords of multiple homes who used them for renting had both the capital for a deposit and income to pay a mortgage – the buy-to-let sector grew a great deal between 2009 and 2015, where the buy-to-let share of all new mortgages rose from 10 to 20 per cent. The cost of borrowing depends upon the rate of interest, and this has been low in much of the world since the crash of 2007. In the UK, the Bank of England has said that the rate of interest will not be changed until the level of unemployment reaches 7 per cent and even then might stay low. Towards the end of 2017 the base rate of interest increased for the first time since 2007, to 0.5 per cent. This means that both the cost of borrowing and the cost of repayment are low at present.

Income levels are expected to have a positive effect upon the demand for houses: as income increases, the demand for houses will increase. Since the crash, bank and building society lending has reverted to how it used to be. The old rule they used in determining who to lend to was the ratio of three times salary: if your income was £30,000 per year, you would be awarded a mortgage of £90,000. This rule, and the typical requirement to put down a deposit, ensured that people had the ability to repay their loans. These new rules would again make buying a house difficult for many. In 2017 most banks lent 4.75 times a borrower's annual income as long as he or she had a deposit, so someone earning £25,000 could borrow £118,750.

Another important demand factor is 'other prices', which in this market means rents, and these are at record highs according to the Land Registry. The cost of rent can often be higher than the cost of repaying a mortgage, in which case it would be better for people to buy; the costs are lower and there will be an asset at the end of the repayment period. This is again tempered by the availability of houses and the availability and affordability of finance. The lack of these forces more people into the rental market and therefore will push up rents. Population size impacts upon demand, and this would include the level of immigration, the incidence of second homes, the increase in the number households because of things like divorce and the buy-to-let market. There are regional differences in the increases in house prices in the UK: house prices in East England and the Midlands are growing faster than the UK average (7.4 per cent compared with 4.7 per cent) while the London market is experiencing below-average growth after years of rapid value increases (currently 3 per cent). Many of the purchasers of property in London are still non-residents, so the market is international.

This brief analysis shows how the forces of demand and supply impact upon the price of houses, and that these forces have myriad effects. In addition to market forces, the housing market is a very political one and not immune to influence by the government. In the UK, the government has introduced two schemes which have had an effect on the housing market. The first, called Funding for Lending, was introduced in July 2012 and gave banks and building societies access to low-cost finance provided they lent it to small and medium-sized businesses or individuals. In December 2013 the Governor of the Bank of England announced that the scheme would be refocused on business from January 2014, as much of the finance had gone to individuals in the form of mortgages. Another scheme, called Help to Buy, was introduced in April 2013 and gave help to buyers of new properties. Both of these were introduced to get the housing market moving and help the economy, but some fear it may fuel another housing bubble.

▶

From April 2014, banks and building societies have had to apply much tougher affordability checks on those to whom they lend money, to ensure that repayments can still be made if the rate of interest goes up. New orders in the construction industry decreased by 12.6 per cent in the second quarter of 2017; much of this change has been predicted to have been in response to the UK triggering Article 50 to leave the EU.

Case study questions

1 What has happened to house prices since this case study was written? You should think about both demand and supply factors to answer this question.

2 The average price of houses in parts of the North-East remained about the same, below inflation. What factors might have made this happen?

 web link www.nationwide.co.uk/hpi/; www.lloydsbankinggroup.com/media1/economic_insight/halifax_house_price_index_page.asp

Review and discussion questions

1 The mini case study on Venezuela discusses two opposing views of how the shortage of toilet rolls has arisen – because of excess demand or because of reduced supply. Show both of these on demand and supply diagrams. What possible solutions are there in each case?

2 Considering the market for CDs, show the effects of the following changes using demand and supply diagrams:

   (a) an increase in the number of people owning CD players;
   (b) a fall in the cost of producing CDs;
   (c) an increase in the number of people downloading music to mobile devices.

3 Have the changes you predicted in your answers to question 2 actually happened in the real world? If not, why not?

Assignments

1 Your company produces heavy products that are transported by road and recent increases in the price of fuel have had to be passed on to the consumer. Investigate possible solutions for the company. (You should use demand and supply diagrams to illustrate your answer.)

2 You work in the marketing department of a company that produces light bulbs. The company is considering increasing the price of its light bulbs by 20 per cent.

At present a 100-watt light bulb costs 80p. The only information available is a study carried out in the previous year on the sensitivity of sales to price, the results of which are shown below.

Price	Sales (million)
80p	5800
100p	4000

Write a report for your manager on the likely effects of the proposed price increase, explaining the concept of elasticity of demand and the factors that are likely to affect it for this product.

Further reading

Begg, D., Fischer, S. and Dornbusch, R., *Economics,* 10th edition, McGraw-Hill, 2011.

Griffiths, A. and Wall, S., *Applied Economics: An Introductory Course,* 12th edition, Financial Times/Prentice Hall, 2011.

Lipsey, R. and Chrystal, A., *Economics,* 12th edition, Oxford University Press, 2011.

Worthington, I., Britton, C. and Rees, A., *Economics for Business: Blending Theory and Practice,* 2nd edition, Financial Times/Prentice Hall, 2005.

web link

Web links and further questions are available on the website at:
www.pearsoned.co.uk/Worthington

15 Market structure

Chris Britton

All businesses operate in a market that will be peculiar to that industry. Each market will have its own particular characteristics which depend upon many factors, and although it is not possible to have a model that describes every market, there are some economic models that provide some guidance to the kinds of characteristics and behaviour that will be found in individual markets.

Learning outcomes

Having read this chapter you should be able to:

- explain the market structures of perfect competition, monopoly, oligopoly and monopolistic competition and indicate their implications for the behaviour of firms

- demonstrate the applicability of these predictions to the real world

- apply Porter's five-forces model to an analysis of the structure of industries

- understand the measurement of competition by concentration ratios

- survey differences in industrial concentration between industries, countries and over time

- indicate what determines market structure and what determines the behaviour of firms

Key terms

Abnormal profits	Interdependence	Perfect mobility
Average cost of production	Market structure	Price competition
Barriers to entry	Minimum efficient scale	Price discrimination
Barriers to exit	Monopolistic competition	Price leadership
Cartel	Monopoly	Price maker
Collusion	Monopsony	Price taker
Concentration ratio	Natural monopoly	Price war
Contestable market	Non-price competition	Sticky prices
Differentiation	Normal profits	Structure–conduct–
Economies of scale	Oligopoly	performance model
Five-forces model	Perfect competition	Transaction cost
Homogeneous products	Perfect knowledge	economics

Introduction

In economics the behaviour and the performance of firms in an industry are thought to depend upon some basic structural characteristics. This view is exemplified by the **structure–conduct–performance model**, where structure determines conduct, which in turn determines performance. The basic elements included under these headings are given in Table 15.1.

The structure–conduct–performance model provides a good framework for classifying and analysing an industry. A simple example of the process can be seen in the soap powder industry. Here the market is dominated by two large producers, Unilever and Procter & Gamble. This apparent lack of competition gives rise to certain behavioural characteristics, such as the massive amount of advertising, the existence of many brand names and fairly uniform prices. This process will be considered in more detail later in the chapter, but the example serves to indicate the relationship between the structure of the market and the behaviour and ultimately the performance of firms in an industry.

web link — For more information on these companies see *www.unilever.com* and *www.pg.com*

Market structure refers to the amount of competition that exists in a market between producers. The degree of competition can be thought of as lying along a continuum with very competitive markets at one end and markets in which no competition exists at all at the other end. This chapter looks at the two extremes (perfect competition and monopoly) and the market structures that exist between. The theory predicts the effects of market structure on behaviour and performance in those markets. However, as with the working of the market mechanism, the real world is often different from the theory and therefore this chapter will look at real markets and the relevance of the theory to the real world. The structure–conduct–performance model is open to criticism since it says little about what determines structure in the first place. It also tends to view the firm as passive in the face of market structure, accepting the implications for conduct and performance, rather than actively trying to change and mould market structure. Michael Porter's **five-forces model** will be used to broaden out the analysis.

Table 15.1 Structure–conduct–performance model

Structural factors
  Amount of actual competition: (a) seller concentration and (b) buyer concentration
  Existence of potential competition
  Cost conditions
  Demand conditions
  Existence of barriers to entry
Conduct factors
  Pricing policy
  Amount of advertising
  Merger behaviour
  Product differentiation
Performance factors
  Profitability
  Technological innovation

Market structure is important not only because of the implications it has for conduct and performance, but also because it has an impact upon the strategic possibilities that face the organisation, its ability to act strategically and the likely effects of such strategic behaviour (see Chapter 18).

In addition, this chapter will examine how the level of competition is measured in a market, how the level of competition varies between industries and countries, and how and why this has changed over time.

Market structures – in theory and practice

As mentioned above, market structures can be thought of as lying along a continuum with perfect competition at one end and monopoly at the other (see Figure 15.1). Both of these market structures are unrealistic representations of the real world, but are useful as benchmarks in assessing the degree of competition in a market. Between these two extremes lie other market structures, which are more realistic. Two will be described: oligopoly and monopolistic competition.

Perfect competition

This is the most competitive market structure. A number of conditions need to be fulfilled before **perfect competition** is said to exist. These conditions are as follows:

1 There are so many buyers and sellers in the market that no *one* of them can influence price through its activities.
2 The good being sold in the market is a **homogeneous product** (i.e. all units of the good are identical).
3 **Perfect knowledge** exists in the market. This means that producers have perfect knowledge of prices and costs of other producers and that consumers know the prices charged by all firms.
4 There exists **perfect mobility** of both the factors of production and consumers. This means that people, machines and land can be used for any purpose, and that consumers are free to purchase the good from any of the producers.
5 There are no **barriers to entry** or **barriers to exit** in the industry. There is nothing to prevent a new firm setting up production in the industry.

Figure 15.1   Market structures

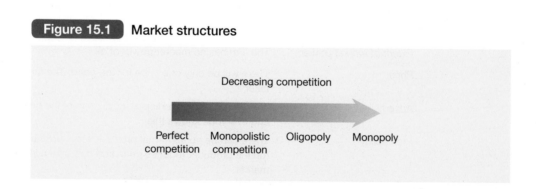

Naturally, this is a highly theoretical model and these conditions are unlikely to be all met in reality, but if they were, and the theory was followed through, the conclusion is that there would be only one price in the market for the good being sold. For example, if one firm is charging a higher price for the good than other firms, everyone in the market will know (because of perfect knowledge), and because the good is homogeneous and because of perfect mobility on the part of consumers, consumers will simply purchase the good from another firm. The firm that was charging a higher price would be forced to reduce the price of the good in order to sell it, or face mounting stocks of the good. There is therefore only one price for the good and this will be determined by market demand and supply – that is, total demand and total supply, no one consumer or producer having enough market power to influence the price. Accordingly, the firm is said to be a **price taker**.

Price determination in perfect competition

Firms need to cover the costs of production and to earn a certain level of profits in order to stay in business. This minimum level of profits is called **normal profit**, and profit over and above this level is called **abnormal profit**. If the firm is trying to maximise its profits it will decide what level of output to produce by setting the cost of producing the last unit of the good equal to the revenue gained from selling the last unit: in economic terminology, where marginal cost equals marginal revenue. Included in cost would be elements of wages, rent, rates, interest, raw materials and normal profits. If these costs are not being covered, the firm will be making a loss.

As there is only one price in perfect competition, the revenue derived from selling the last unit must be equal to its price. Therefore, the price of the good depends on the level of marginal cost.

In the short run, individual firms can earn abnormal profits, but these are not sustainable in the longer term. If one firm is earning abnormal profits, given the assumption of perfect knowledge, everyone will know and, since freedom of entry exists, other firms will enter the market in order to earn abnormal profits. This means that there is an increase in market supply and price will fall back to a level where abnormal profits have been competed away. Similarly, when losses are being made, freedom of exit means that supply will be reduced and price will rise again until normal profits have been regained.

The implications of perfect competition for market behaviour and performance are summarised in Table 15.2. Perfect competition involves very restrictive assumptions,

Table 15.2 Implications of perfect competition for conduct and performance of firms in an industry

Extent of market power	The firm has no market power at all
Price	There will be only one price for the good. The firm will be a 'price taker'
Advertising	There will be no advertising, as all units of the good are the same and everyone knows this
Profitability	There can be no abnormal profits, except possibly in the very short run if a producer reduces price and captures a larger share of the market

which will rarely be fulfilled in the real world. The usefulness of the model lies in its role as an *ideal market* in which competition is at a maximum, rather than in its applicability to the real world.

An example of perfect competition?

The nearest example to perfect competition is probably the fruit and vegetable market in the centre of a large town. The goods will be fairly homogeneous, with perhaps slight variation in the quality. Knowledge will be almost perfect with respect to prices charged, as consumers could quickly walk around the market and ascertain the price of tomatoes, for example. Mobility of consumers is also high because the sellers are located in the same place. Thus, the conditions for perfect competition nearly hold. The prediction is that there will be only one price for a particular good. Again this prediction is nearly fulfilled; the price of tomatoes tends to be rather similar across such a market, and when one trader reduces the price towards the end of the day, others tend to follow suit.

Another market that is said to be close to perfect competition is the stock exchange, although with the increasing use of computers this is less likely to be true in the future.

Monopoly

Monopoly lies at the opposite end of the spectrum to competition. In its purest form a monopolistic market is one in which there is no competition at all; there is a single producer supplying the whole market. The monopolist has considerable market power and can determine price or quantity sold, but not both, because he or she cannot control demand. The power of the monopolist depends on the availability of substitutes, and on the existence and height of barriers to entry. If there are no close substitutes for the good being produced, or if there are high barriers to entry, the power of the monopolist will be high and abnormal profits can be earned in the long run.

A monopolist could also be a group of producers acting together to control supply to the market: for example, a **cartel** such as OPEC (Organization of Petroleum Exporting Countries).

 web link   For information on OPEC see *www.opec.org*

In monopolistic markets the producer might be able to charge different prices for the same good: for example, on an airliner it is quite likely that there will be passengers sitting in the same class of seat having paid very different prices, depending upon where and when the tickets were bought. Essentially they are paying different prices for the same service, and the producer is said to be exercising **price discrimination**. Why is this possible? There are certain conditions that must hold for this type of price discrimination to occur. First, the market must be monopolistic and the producer must be able to control supply. Second, there must be groups of consumers with different demand conditions. For example, the demand for train travel by the commuter who works in London will be more inelastic than the demand of a student going to London for the day, who could use alternative forms of transport or even not go. This means that the willingness to pay among consumers will vary. The final condition necessary is that it must be possible to separate these groups in some way. For example, telephone companies are able to separate markets by time so that it is cheaper to phone after a certain time; British Rail used to separate groups by age for certain of its railcards.

The monopolist will maximise its profits by charging different prices in different markets. Price discrimination is often thought of as a bad thing as the monopolist is exploiting the consumer by charging different prices for the same good. But there are some advantages, in that it makes for better use of resources if cheap tickets are offered to fill an airliner that otherwise would have flown half-full. It can also lead to a more equitable solution in that higher-income users pay a higher price than lower-income users. The main problems with the notion of price discrimination is not that it is always a bad thing, but that it is the monopolist who has the power to decide who is charged what price.

Again the effects of monopoly on the behaviour and performance of the firm can be predicted (see Table 15.3). Like perfect competition, this is a highly theoretical model and is mainly used as a comparison with perfect competition to show the effects of the lack of competition.

Table 15.3 Implications of monopoly for conduct and performance of firms in an industry

Extent of market power	The firm has absolute market power
Price	There will only be one price for the good, except in the case of price discrimination. The firm is a **price maker**
Advertising	There will be no need for advertising, as there is only one firm producing the good
Profitability	Abnormal profits can exist in the long run as there is no competition that might erode them away

A comparison of perfect competition and monopoly

- It would be expected that price would be higher under monopoly than under perfect competition because of the absence of competition in the monopolistic market. It is argued, for example, that the large telephone companies (including BT) are overcharging the consumer. The benefits of the considerable technological advances that have been made in this area have not been passed on fully to the consumer. This can be sustained only by virtue of the monopolistic power of the companies. But to counter this, it could be argued that a monopolist is in a better position to reap the benefits of economies of scale, therefore it is possible that price might be lower.
- There might be less choice under monopoly since firms do not have to update their products continually in order to stay in business. But it is also possible to think of examples where monopolies provide greater choice (e.g. in the case of radio stations), where under perfect competition all radio stations would cater for the biggest market, which would be for pop music. A monopolist, however, would be able to cover all tastes with a variety of stations.
- There is less incentive to innovate under monopoly, since the monopolist is subject to less competition. But, equally, a monopolist might have more incentive to innovate as it can reap the benefits in terms of higher profits. It may also have more resources to devote to innovation.

As we can see, there is not a clear set of arguments implying that perfect competition is better than monopoly, and, as we will see in Chapter 17, this is taken into account in UK competition policy.

An example of monopoly

Although it is easy to think of examples of industries where the dominant firm has a great deal of monopoly power, there is no such thing as a pure monopoly, as substitutes exist for most goods. For example, British Rail used to have monopoly power in the market for rail travel, but there are many alternative forms of travel. This point highlights the difficulties of defining markets and industries discussed in Chapter 10. The nearest examples of monopolies are the old public utilities, such as gas, electricity, water, and so on, which have been privatised.

The government, in determining whether monopoly power exists in a market, has a working definition of what constitutes a monopoly: it is when 25 per cent of the market is accounted for by one firm or firms acting together. This would form grounds for investigation by the Competition and Markets Authority. The process of UK competition policy is discussed in more detail in Chapter 17. The sources of monopoly power are the existence of barriers to entry and exit and the availability of substitutes (these will be discussed later in this chapter).

For information on the operation of the Competition and Markets Authority see *www.gov.uk/government/organisations/competition-and-markets-authority*

Oligopoly

In both perfect competition and monopoly firms make independent decisions. In the case of monopoly there are no other firms in the industry to consider; in the case of perfect competition the firm has no power to affect the market at all. So for different reasons they act as though they have no rivals. This is not true in the case of oligopoly. **Oligopoly** is where a small number of producers supply a market in which the product is differentiated in some way (see Table 15.4). The characteristics of oligopoly are as follows:

Table 15.4 Implications of oligopoly for conduct and performance of firms in an industry

Extent of market power	A great deal of market power
Price	A stable price level. Prices set by price leadership or collusion
Advertising	Much advertising and branding. Non-price competition is common
Profitability	Abnormal profits can exist; their extent depends on the strength of competitors

- A great deal of **interdependence** between the firms; each firm has to consider the likely actions of other firms when making its decisions.
- A lack of **price competition** in the market; firms are reluctant to increase their prices in case their competitors do not and they might lose market share. Firms are also

reluctant to reduce their prices, in case other firms do the same and a price war results that reduces prices but leaves market share unchanged and so everyone is left worse off.

- This lack of price competition means that different forms of **non-price competition** take place, such as branding or advertising. Oligopolists will sell their products not by reducing the price but through heavy advertising, brand names or special offers. In the UK, Tesco was one of the first companies to have a reward scheme whereby customers accrue points on their grocery shopping and use them to get money off their next shop, increase their value when buying other products such as visits to theme parks or buying magazine subscriptions. Now many others have similar schemes.

The way in which price is determined in an oligopolistic market is through either **price leadership** or some sort of **collusion**. Price leadership is where one firm takes the lead in setting prices and the others follow suit. The price leader is not necessarily the firm with the lowest cost, as it depends upon the power of the firm. So price could be set at a higher level than in a competitive market. Collusion is an explicit or implicit agreement between firms on price, which serves to reduce the amount of competition between firms. Collusion is illegal in most countries as it is seen as a form of restrictive practice, but this does not mean that collusion does not take place. A cartel is a form of collusion where firms come together to exercise joint market power. Cartels are outlawed in most states, but the most famous of all is OPEC, which has had a dramatic effect on the oil industry over the last 30 years. Collusive agreements, as well as possibly being harmful to the consumer, tend to be unstable as there is great temptation on the part of individual firms/countries to cheat. What is clear in the case of oligopoly is that once price is set, there is a reluctance to change it. Therefore price competition is replaced by non-price competition of the sort mentioned above.

The most often quoted examples of oligopoly are the markets for tobacco and soap powder, both of which are dominated by a very small number of producers and exhibit the predicted characteristics. There is little price competition and price is fairly uniform in both markets. Compared with monopoly and perfect competition, oligopoly is a much more realistic market structure, with many markets exhibiting the characteristics stated above. Table 15.5 gives a few examples.

Table 15.5 The top firms' share of the market in the UK (percentages)

Industry	Percentages
Instant coffee brands	85**
Dishwashing product manufacturer	77**
Lager brands	57*****
Cordial and squash brands	48**
Condom brands	82*
Bottled water brands	51*****

Note: *Top firm in the industry. **Top two firms. *****Top five firms.
Source: Mintel Report, 2016.

For information and reports on specific industries see *www.mintel.co.uk* and *www.keynote.co.uk*

Monopolistic competition

Monopolistic competition exists when all of the conditions for perfect competition are met except for the existence of a homogeneous good, so that each firm has a monopoly over its own good but there is a great deal of competition in the market from other suppliers producing very similar products. In **monopolistic competition** the good is slightly differentiated in some way, either by advertising and branding or by local production. There does not have to be a technical difference between the two goods, which could be identical in composition, but there must be an 'economic difference' – that is, a difference in the way the goods are perceived by consumers. There is also some degree of consumer loyalty, so that if one firm reduces price, consumers might not necessarily move to that firm if they believe that the difference between the brands justifies the higher price. Abnormal profits can exist in the short run but cannot persist since new firms are free to enter the industry and compete away abnormal profit (see Table 15.6).

Table 15.6 Implications of monopolistic competition for conduct and performance of firms in an industry

Extent of market power	The firm has little market power
Price	There will be small differences in price
Advertising	There will be heavy advertising and branding
Profitability	Small abnormal profits can exist in the short run but will be competed away in the longer run

An example of monopolistic competition

There are many examples of this type of industry: for example, the paint industry, where AkzoNobel is the only producer of Dulux, but there are many other types of paint on the market.

How accurate is the theory?

The implications of the theory of market structures for the behaviour and performance of firms are summarised in Table 15.7.

Table 15.7 Implications of theory for behaviour of firms

	Market power	*Price*	*Advertising*	*Profitability*
Perfect competition	None	One price	None	Only normal profits
Monopoly	Absolute	Price discrimination possible	None	Abnormal profits
Oligopoly	High	One price	High	Abnormal profits
Monopolistic competition	Little	Small differences in price	High	Only normal profits in long run

As argued above, both perfect competition and pure monopoly tend to be based on assumptions that are somewhat unrealistic and should be regarded as 'ideal types' of market structure, in the sense that they establish the boundaries within which true markets exist and operate, and against which they can be analysed. In contrast, oligopoly and monopolistic competition are much nearer to the types of market structure that can be found in the real world, and economic theory does appear to explain and predict behaviour in these markets to a certain extent. In oligopolistic markets, for example, prices tend to be **sticky prices** and much of the competition between firms occurs in non-price ways, particularly branding, advertising and sales promotion (see Table 15.8). Occasionally, however, **price wars** do occur – as in the petrol market in the 1980s and more recently between the four biggest supermarkets in the UK.

Table 15.8 shows the top advertisers in the UK ranked for 2016. The names in the list are familiar and largely expected from the predictions: for example, Procter & Gamble and Unilever account for around 90 per cent of the market for washing powder. A less familiar name is Reckitt Benckiser, which acquired Boots in 2007. It is interesting to note that many well-known brands do not appear in the top 10 – Apple lies at number 39 and Coca-Cola at number 46. In total, advertising spending in the UK hit a record £21.4 billion in 2016.

Table 15.8 Top advertisers in the UK, 2016

Rank	Advertiser
1	Procter & Gamble
2	British Sky Broadcasting
3	BT Group
4	Reckitt Benckiser
5	Virgin Media
6	Unilever
7	Amazon
8	Vodafone
9	McDonalds
10	Lidl

 web link For information on advertising see *www.adassoc.org.uk*

It is much more difficult to judge how accurate the behavioural implications are. Lack of data is one problem, as is the fact that only one structural characteristic has been considered here – the level of competition between producers. The other structural factors listed in Table 15.1 will also have an effect, such as the level of demand, the degree of competition between the buyers and the degree of potential competition. Profitability, price and advertising, for instance, will be affected by the level of demand in the market.

Porter's five-forces model

Porter's model says that the structure of an industry and the ability of firms in that industry to act strategically depend upon the relative strengths of five forces: current competition, potential competition, the threat of substitute products, the power of buyers and the power of suppliers. Each of these five forces will be examined in turn. The case study at the end of this chapter uses this model to analyse the tobacco industry.

Current competition

Current competition has already been considered under the heading of market structure, but the important point to remember is that by acting strategically firms can change the structure of the industry. Firms in a highly competitive market might be unhappy with the lack of power they have over various factors such as pricing and may, through their strategic actions, try to change the situation. If they are successful there will be a change in the level of current competition and therefore in market structure.

Potential competition (or threat of new entry)

It has been shown that market structure or current competition affects the behaviour of firms in an industry. However, looking at the number of firms in an industry does not provide the whole picture. It is possible that firms in an oligopolistic market might act in a way consistent with perfect competition because of the threat of potential competition. This threat can affect the behaviour of firms even if it does not happen. The degree of potential competition depends upon the existence and height of barriers to entry and exit.

Barriers to entry

Barriers to entry are any barriers which prevent or inhibit the entry of firms into the industry. There are several sources of barriers to entry.

Some industries are in a **natural monopoly**, where the production process is such that competition would be wasteful. The old public utilities are good examples of these, as it would be very wasteful for there to be two national grid systems in the electricity industry.

Some production processes are subject to **economies of scale**. As firms grow in size, or as the scale of production increases, certain economies occur that serve to reduce the **average cost of production**. The scale of production can be increased in many ways, for example by increasing the capacity of the existing plant, by increasing the number of plants or by increasing the product range. Figure 15.2 shows how the average *cost* of production changes as the *scale* of production changes.

Figure 15.2   A firm's average cost curve

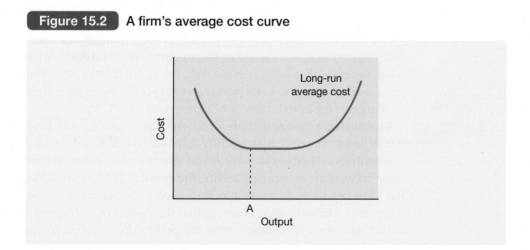

The downward-sloping part of the curve shows falling average cost or economies of scale. The upward-sloping part shows rising average cost or diseconomies of scale. Economies of scale reduce average cost and therefore benefit the producer and also the consumer if they are passed on in lower prices.

The sources of economies of scale are usually classified under three headings: technical; marketing; and financial.

- *Technical economies* come from increased specialisation and indivisibilities. The larger the scale of production, the more the production process can be broken down into its component parts and the greater the gain from specialisation. There are certain indivisibilities involved in production, which only large firms can benefit from. For example, a small firm cannot have half a production line as that is meaningless, but might not be big enough to use a whole production line. Another type of indivisibility is involved in the notion of fixed costs. Fixed costs like the cost of rates or the fees of an accountant, for example, remain the same irrespective of the level of production. Therefore the greater the level of production, the lower will be the average cost of items as it is being spread over a larger output.
- *Marketing economies* come from spreading marketing costs over a larger output, so that average costs will be lower. The company can also take advantage of bulk buying, and will probably have a specialised department devoted to marketing.
- *Financial* economies come from the fact that larger companies find it easier and often cheaper to borrow capital.

Added to these is *risk diversification,* which is possible with larger companies as they may well have interests in other industries. All of these economies of scale give rise to falling average cost and therefore explain the downward-sloping part of the cost curve in Figure 15.2. Economies of scale are a very effective barrier to entry. If the incumbent firm in an industry has lower average cost as a result of economies of scale, it will be hard for a newcomer to compete effectively at a smaller scale of production. Gas, electricity and water are examples of this. The production processes of these goods are subject to economies of scale and it is therefore difficult for others to come into the market in competition with established firms. This is why such industries are called 'natural monopolies'.

Barriers to entry can be legal ones, as in the case of patents and franchises, which serve to restrict competition and prevent new firms from entering an industry. Advertising and branding can also be barriers, in that industries where brand names are well established are difficult to enter without massive expenditure on advertising. Some industries require a high initial capital investment to enter, for example dry cleaning, where the machinery is very expensive. Switching costs can also be regarded as a barrier to entry. If the consumer has to bear a cost in switching from one good to another, that might be enough to deter the consumer from doing so and therefore serve as a barrier to entry. The recent practice of the building societies and banks of offering low fixed-rate mortgages with penalties for early withdrawal can be seen as an example of the introduction of switching costs into the market.

A **contestable market** is one in which there are no barriers to entry or exit. This means that all firms (even potential entrants) have access to the same technology and there are therefore no cost barriers to entry. It also means that there are no sunk or unrecoverable costs that would prevent a firm leaving the industry. It follows that it is possible to ensure that firms behave in a competitive way, even if the market structure they operate in is imperfectly competitive, by ensuring that the market is contestable. What is regulating market behaviour, then, is not *actual* competition but *potential* competition.

mini case   Open Skies and contestability

The 'Open Skies' agreement between the United States and the EU, which was introduced in 2008, is a policy that was designed to make markets more contestable. It eased restrictions on air travel between the United States and the EU so that any airline could fly to US destinations and not necessarily from its home nation, as was previously the case. British Airways could now fly from Paris to New York, whereas previously it could only fly from London Heathrow to New York. Similarly, any US airline could do the same for European destinations. The second phase of this agreement was put into place in 2010.

This policy was not designed to break up existing companies or to introduce more competition into the market directly. It makes the market more contestable – it opens up the market for the possibility of competition. The stated aims are to increase free-market competition, allow price to be determined by the market, allow fair and equal opportunity to compete, cooperative marketing arrangements and the provision of a mechanism for dispute resolution. The agreement has led to structural changes in the market. For example, as a direct result of this deal:

- British Airways launched a new airline called OpenSkies, which flew between Paris and Newark, New York. It has since been renamed Elysair.
- In December 2012 Delta Airlines purchased a 49 per cent stake in Virgin Atlantic in order to launch a joint venture in January 2014 – this led to daily flights between Seattle and London.

Theory predicts that more competition will lead to lower prices. Unfortunately this agreement came into force at a time of rapidly rising oil prices so this was unlikely to happen – Virgin Atlantic declared that prices could not be any lower. Whether this will happen or not will have to be seen. EU airlines also argue that the agreement is unbalanced: US airlines can fly between EU destinations (from Paris to London, for example) but EU airlines cannot do the same within the United States. In addition to this, US carriers are allowed to buy up their EU rivals but foreign ownership of US airlines is not allowed. The second stage of the agreement, which came into place in 2010, has done nothing to dispel this view as there was still no indication that European carriers would be allowed to carry inter-US routes and there was no further progress on ownership, only a 'commitment to engage in a process towards reforming airline ownership'. This, then, is not true contestability.

Barriers to exit

Exit barriers are those that prevent or deter exit from an industry; they are mainly related to the cost of leaving the industry. The cost of exit depends upon how industry specific the assets of the firm are. If we take physical assets as an example, a printing press is highly specific to the printing industry and could not be used for anything other than printing. There will be a second-hand market for printing presses, but the press would probably have to be sold at a loss, therefore incurring a high cost. A van, however, would be different, as it is still a physical asset but one that would not be specific to a particular industry, therefore the loss involved in selling would be less. Generally speaking, the more industry specific an asset is, the lower will be the second-hand value and the higher the cost of exit. An intangible asset such as knowledge of the market or expenditure on research and development cannot be resold and must be left in the market, and therefore is a sunk cost – a non-recoverable cost.

Barriers to entry and exit can be 'innocent' or can be deliberately erected. Economies of scale can be regarded as innocent barriers to entry since they are inherent in the production process. Advertising and branding can be thought of as deliberately erected barriers to entry since they increase the expense of any firm entering the market. Similarly, the introduction of penalty clauses on mortgages is a deliberately erected barrier since it incurs switching costs for the consumer.

Where innocent barriers to entry or exit are low, potential competition will be high and firms within such a market are faced with the choice of accepting the situation or deliberately erecting some barriers. This is an example of strategic behaviour on the part of firms; whether it is attempted or not depends on the likelihood of success and the relative costs and benefits. It is another area where game theory is used to formulate strategic possibilities.

The threat of substitute products

The threat from substitute products largely depends upon the nature of the good being traded in the market and the extent of product **differentiation**. It has a clear impact upon market structure, because if there are no substitutes for a good the producer of that good will face little competition and have a great deal of market power. However, as we saw earlier, even industries that appear to be pure monopolies (the former British Rail, for instance) can face competition from substitutes since there are other ways to travel. Much of the expenditure by firms to differentiate their products is designed to reduce the threat from substitute products.

The power of buyers

So far this chapter has concentrated on the competition between producers in a market, but the amount of competition between buyers will also have an impact on an industry. Markets will range from those where there are many buyers, as in the case of retailing, through markets where there are a small number of buyers, as in the case of car and parts manufacturers, to markets where there is only one buyer. This latter type of market is called a **monopsony**, and it is the buyer who has a great deal of market power rather than the seller. An example of this is the coal industry, where the majority of output goes to the electricity producers. Increasingly in retailing the giant retailers are exerting a great deal of power over the manufacturers. Many large retailers are involved by manufacturers very early on in the design process for new products; as a result they can secure exclusives that are not available in other shops.

The level of buyer power could be measured in the same way as seller power (see later in this chapter), but no data are collected centrally on the level of buyer concentration. It is clear, however, that there are many markets in which powerful buyers can and do exert a great deal of control over suppliers, and this power is an important source of marketing economies of scale. It is possible to put together the level of competition between producers and consumers in order to predict behaviour. For example, a market that consists of a single buyer and a single seller will have quite different characteristics from a market that has many buyers and sellers. The existence of strong buyers might have beneficial effects on the market as they could offset the power of strong producers or it could lead to higher seller concentration as sellers come together to counteract the power of the buyer.

In markets where there are strong sellers and weak buyers the producers' power can be offset by, for example, consumer advice centres or regulatory bodies, as in the case of the former public utilities.

A distinction can be made between existing and potential customers. Existing customers are particularly significant to firms in industries where repeat orders are important or where goods are supplied on a regular basis, as in grocery retailing. It is no surprise that the large grocery retailers are using loyalty cards to increase the loyalty of existing customers. The power of existing customers is much lower where the firm supplies goods on a one-off basis, although the firm cannot disregard existing customers as this will affect its reputation and the ability to attract potential customers. Potential customers might be new to the market or can be buying from an existing competitor at present.

The power of suppliers

The power of suppliers over the firm is likely to be extremely important in certain markets, depending upon the nature of the product being supplied. For example, is the product highly specialised? Is the same or similar product available from elsewhere? How important is the product in the production process? The importance of good and reliable supplies has assumed greater significance since firms have started to adopt just-in-time production methods. Reducing stock levels to reduce costs can be effective only if firms can depend upon their suppliers; hence there has been the development of partnership sourcing as firms nurture long-term relationships with their suppliers.

Another important factor here is whether or not the firm itself can produce the components it needs in the production process. If it can, the power of suppliers is greatly reduced. The decision as to whether to produce or to buy from a supplier is the subject of an interesting area of economics called **transaction cost economics**.

Porter's five-forces model provides a good structure for looking at market structures. The case study at the end of the chapter uses the framework to analyse the market for cigarettes in the UK, while the mini case study on Prosecco uses Porter's model to identify which of the forces are important.

---

mini case   The success story of Prosecco

Wine sales in the UK have averaged a growth rate of around 3 per cent per annum since 2008. Sales were badly affected by the economic downturn – there was a fall in the sales of wine of 4 per cent in 2009, but there were big differences between market segments. The sales of still wine and Champagne both fell in 2009 by 3.8 per cent and 22 per cent respectively, while sales of non-Champagne sparkling wine rose by 11.3 per cent in 2009. As Figure 15.3 shows, annual sales of sparkling wine overtook Champagne in 2011, and the trend is forecast to continue into the foreseeable future. According to Mintel, sales of Champagne in the UK were forecast to fall to £609 million by 2017, while sales of other sparkling wine are forecast to rise to £835 million.

In the non-Champagne sparkling wine market, Cava accounts for half of the market and Prosecco around one-third, but sales of Prosecco have been growing fast. The Cooperative's own-brand Prosecco won a *Which?* best value award in 2013 and as a result the sales of this wine rose by 875 per cent over the Christmas 2013 period. Similar success can be seen from other wine sellers:

▶

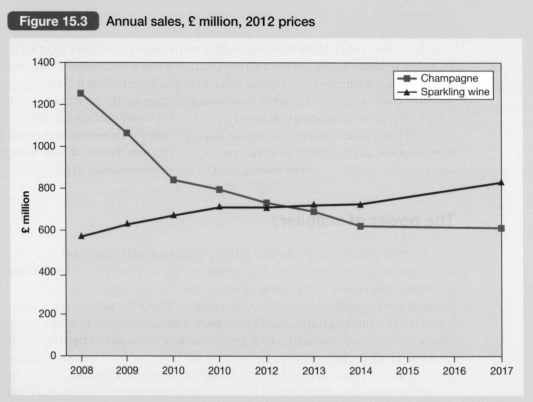

Figure 15.3   Annual sales, £ million, 2012 prices

Source: Adapted from Figures 29 and 30, Mintel Report, Still, Sparkling and Fortified Wine, 2013.

Sainsbury's own-brand Prosecco increased its sales by 41 per cent in volume between 18 and 31 December 2013, its Prosecco magnums rising in sales by 291 per cent; Prosecco was the fourth most popular wine at Majestic in 2013 and sales rose by 39 per cent in the summer of 2013. Majestic Wine attributed at least part of a rise in profits for the second half of 2013 to sales of Prosecco.

Why has it been so successful? Clearly there is a price difference between Champagne and sparkling wine and in times of economic downturn, price will be very important. In addition to this there has been clever promotion – while Champagne is the drink of celebration and special occasions, Prosecco has been marketed and accepted as the drink of every day. The sales figures above show that Prosecco is seen as a drink for summer days as well as at Christmas time. In addition, Prosecco is scoring well on flavour – it is much lighter than Champagne and often lower in alcohol, and this makes it popular among its demographic, which (according to Mintel) is female and aged between 18 and 35 years old. One limitation to this growth is that, under EU law, only wines produced in the Prosecco region of Italy (north of Venice), which includes Conegliano and Valdobbiadene, can use the name Prosecco, which limits the output. This means it might not be able to continue to grow at the present rate, but there are other sparkling wines waiting to fill any gaps in the market – English sparkling wines and wines from other parts of the world, including Chile and Australia.

From this brief analysis, it can be seen that, of Porter's five forces, the most important one is buyer behaviour – the impact of economic downturn on demand and the characteristics of buyers. In addition, producers have cleverly marketed the wine as an everyday drink (current competition), although there may be limitations to the growth of the market (suppliers).

Measuring the degree of actual competition in the market

In industrial economics the level of competition in a market is measured by the **concentration ratio**. This measures the percentage of value added, total output or employment that is produced by a stated number of the largest firms in the industry. The common numbers are three or five. The five-firm concentration ratio measures the percentage of employment or output accounted for by the five largest firms in the industry.

Table 15.9 shows the five-firm concentration ratios for a selection of industries in 2004 as measured by output. These data are no longer collected or collated by the UK government, but given the nature of these industries, concentration levels are likely to be very similar.

Table 15.9 Five-firm concentration ratios for selected industries in the UK, 2004

Industry	Output (%)
Sugar and sugar by-products	99
Tobacco	99
Iron and steel	61
Pharmaceutical products	57
Rubber products	45
Leather goods	30
Footwear	25
Legal service	9
Other business services	5

Source: Adapted from Appendix 1, 'Concentration ratios for businesses by industry in 2004', Sanjiv Mahajan, *Economic Trends,* ONS, October 2006.

Although Table 15.9 shows only a small selection of industries, it does illustrate that there is a wide variation in the degree of concentration across industries. Only two services industries are listed because there is a general lack of data on the service sector. Generally, services are less concentrated than manufacturing industries because of the nature of the production process and the fact there is less scope for economies of scale. The differences between the market shares of sugar and tobacco in Tables 15.5 and 15.9 are due to the fact that the large producers also produce the own-brand labels.

While it is relatively easy to compare the level of concentration in particular industries over time, it is more difficult to make any conclusion about the 'average' level of concentration (see mini case on concentration in the previous edition of this text). Table 15.10 gives an illustration of the percentage share of total employment and sales of the largest 100 private firms in the UK between 1979 and 1992. Although these are not concentration ratios as such, the data do provide an indication of how concentration has changed over time in aggregate. The change in the Standard Industrial Classification during this period has only a small impact on the figures. Note how the level of 'average' concentration decreased slightly during the first part of the period, reversing the trend of the first half of this century where industrial concentration increased. The reason for the decrease is largely the process of privatisation and the growth in the small-firm sector during the 1970s and 1980s. In the later part of the period concentration started to rise again, mainly due to the industrial restructuring taking place and the increased level of merger activity identified in Chapter 11. As the UK government ceased publication of these figures in 1992 it is difficult to assess what has happened to concentration more recently.

Table 15.10 The 100 largest private enterprise groups

Year	Percentage share of total Employment	Sales
SIC(68)		
1979	12	18
SIC(80)		
1980	13	15
1981	13	16
1982	12	15
1983	12	16
1984	15	19
1985	9.5	14
1986	9.7	15.4
1987	10.8	17.1
1988	9.8	17.6
1989	12.1	21.6
1990	14.6	23.6
1991	14.9	21.2
1992	16.9	24.9

Source: *Census of Production,* various. Crown copyright. Reproduced by permission of the Controller of HMSO and of the Office for National Statistics, UK.

Making comparisons between different countries tends to be difficult because of this problem of 'averaging' concentration and because of national differences in the way in which data are collected and reported. Moreover, official EU publications on industry have changed the way in which they report data, so comparisons over time are problematical. Despite the difficulties in comparing concentration ratios, the general view of industrial economists is that concentration is greater in the UK than in other member states.

Reasons for high concentration

Many industries in the UK are highly concentrated and it is believed that the UK has higher concentration ratios than other large industrial countries. Why are there different market structures between industries?

Referring back to Figure 15.2, the point at which the curve becomes horizontal (A in the figure) is called the **minimum efficient scale** (MES) of production. It is the point at which all economies of scale have been reaped by the firm, and the point at which firms that wish to maximise their efficiency must operate.

The higher the MES relative to the total output of the industry, the fewer will be the number of firms operating in an industry and therefore the higher will be the level of concentration. For example, if the MES in an industry is half of the industry output, the industry could support only two firms, as smaller firms could not achieve low enough costs to compete with the large firms.

As the MES of production continues to increase, average costs eventually start to rise. This is due to diseconomies of scale, which are mostly attributed to managerial inefficiencies. These are the difficulties faced by management in controlling, coordinating and communicating in a large organisation.

Firms in every industry will face differing average cost curves and therefore market structures will be different. In services, for example, because of the nature of the product, the scope for economies of scale is small and, accordingly, the MES is small relative to the size of the total market and the industries tend to be unconcentrated. The level of concentration in manufacturing tends to be much higher because of the nature of the production process and the scope for economies of scale.

The size of the MES is not the only explanation of why there are different market structures. If it was, one might expect that the same industry would have similar levels of concentration in different countries, but this is not the case, as indicated above. The strength of the five forces will differ greatly between industries and will therefore give many different structures. Obviously government policy can influence the type of market structure, and this will differ between countries. It is also true that the significance of barriers to entry varies between countries. Empirical results from Germany and the UK show that in both countries barriers to entry are high, but that in the UK advertising is the most important barrier, while in Germany it is economies of scale.

Synopsis

In this chapter, four different market structures were considered that embraced the whole spectrum of competition: perfect competition, monopoly, oligopoly and monopolistic competition. Each of these market structures gives predictions about the behaviour of firms in those markets. Generally, the more realistic of these market structures predict well what happens in the real world. This analysis was then incorporated into Porter's five-forces model, which includes further factors largely ignored by traditional economic theory. Nevertheless, these factors are particularly important in certain industries, like the power of the giant retailers as buyers and the importance of potential customers to industries where the level of repeat business is high.

The amount of competition in a market is measured using concentration ratios and evidence on concentration was examined both within the UK and between countries as far as that was possible.

Summary of key points

- There are four different market structures identified by business economists. These are (arranged with the most competitive first): perfect competition, monopolistic competition, oligopoly and monopoly.

- Perfect competition is a market structure which is very competitive and where the producers are 'price takers'.

- Pure monopoly is a market structure with a single producer that is a 'price maker'.

- Monopolistic competition is a market structure where there is a great deal of competition but where the product is slightly differentiated, so producers have a little market power.

- Oligopoly is a market structure where there are a small number of large producers, interdependent in their decision-making. This is a common market structure.

- The determinants of market structure include the existence and height of barriers to entry and exit and the existence of economies of scale.

- Knowledge of market structure gives some indication of likely behaviour of firms with respect to factors such as pricing and advertising.

---

case study

A Porter's five-forces analysis of the cigarette industry in the UK

Porter's five-forces model will be used to analyse the cigarette industry in the UK. Cigarette smoking has fallen since 1974, as Figure 15.4 shows, being 12 per cent of men and 11 per cent of women in 2016.

Figure 15.5 shows the age profile of smokers in the UK in 2016.

The UK government has specific objectives in place with respect to smoking – that is, to have a tobacco-free generation by 2025. Although the percentage of smokers has fallen, it is still higher in some parts of the UK than others, as

Table 15.11 shows. This is because of tax and price increases.

The incidence of smoking in other countries is much higher than in the UK: the top three in 2015 were Kiribati (52.2 per cent), Nauru (47.5 per cent) and Greece (42.4 per cent).

Current competition

The cigarette market is an oligopoly both globally and in the UK. Worldwide, four firms account for 50 per cent of the market – Philip Morris International,

---

Figure 15.4   Percentage of men and women smokers over 16 in the UK

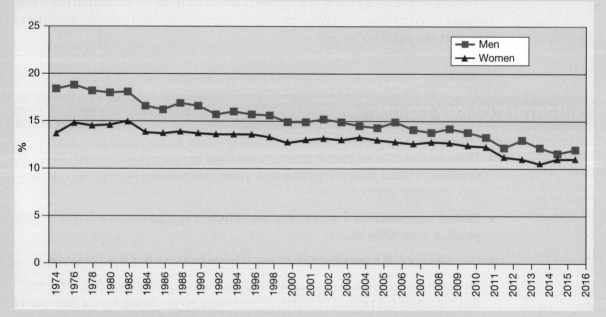

Source: Adult smoking habits in the UK, ONS.

Figure 15.5   Percentage of adult population who are smokers by age, UK

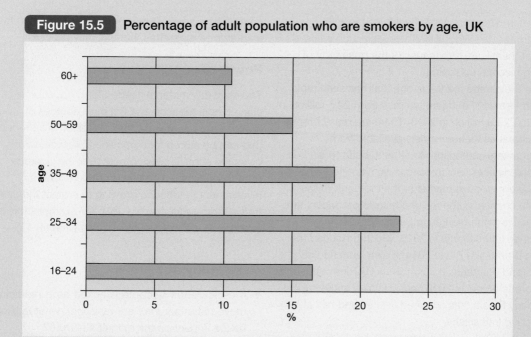

Source: Adult smoking habits in the UK, ONS.

Table 15.11 Average weekly spending on cigarettes

England	£2.90
Wales	£3.00
Scotland	£4.90
Northern Ireland	£6.60

Source: ONS: *Family spending in the UK: financial year ending March 2016.*

British American Tobacco (BAT), Imperial Tobacco and Japan Tobacco International (JTI). In the UK, Imperial Brands (formerly Imperial Tobacco) accounts for 45 per cent of the market, JTI 39 per cent and BAT 8 per cent.

The traditional tools available to firms to increase their market share, such as pricing and promotion, are severely curtailed in this industry by legislation. A large proportion (80 per cent) of the price of a packet of cigarettes is taxation and many countries have bans in place on smoking in public spaces. The extent of advertising that companies can do has been reduced by the government. Plain cigarette packaging has been introduced by the UK government after a series of delays.

Power of buyers

As Figure 15.4 shows, the rate of smoking in the UK has fallen over the last 50 years. This is mainly due to greater awareness of the health effects of smoking, government campaigns to reduce smoking and increased taxation. In 2013, the price of a packet was around £8–10 for 20 and the tax component of that was around £6.20–8.00. The demand for cigarettes is inelastic because they are habit forming and difficult to give up. This explains why, although the incidence of smoking has fallen, revenue to the tobacco companies has gone up. It would be expected that the economic downturn would have had a negative impact on the market for cigarettes in the UK as households tightened their belts; the inelastic nature of demand, however, would tend to negate this.

The availability of substitutes

Substitutes for cigarettes include hand-rolled tobacco, which is cheaper than ready-rolled. There is some evidence in the UK that substitution has taken place – since 1990 there has been an increase in hand-rolled tobacco, and in 2016 the market for hand-rolled tobacco was worth £2.2bn.

A newer substitute is the electronic cigarette or e-cigarette. These enable smokers to consume nicotine but without the more harmful chemicals like carbon monoxide or tar. These were patented in 2003; by 2013 more than 1 million people in the UK were using them, and by 2016 this figure had increased to

2.6 million. There are some health issues with e-cigarettes: the World Health Organization advised against them in 2013 because of the possibility of getting nicotine poisoning.

The e-cigarette market is one that has seen rapid growth – sales of e-cigarettes rose from £2.5 million in 2012 to £23.9 million in 2013. There are many brands of e-cigarettes that are widely available from supermarkets and online. Another substitute is e-shisha devices, which contain no nicotine. Although this is a competitive market at the moment, this is likely to change as the major cigarette producers are very active in the market. Imperial Brands bought Dragonite International in 2013 (which produced the Ruyan brand) and Blu in 2014; it also launched its own brand (Puritane) in 2014; while BAT introduced its e-cigarette (Vype) in 2013 and JTI has a stake in US company Ploom, has acquired E-Lites and has also diversified into shisha.

Potential competition

This industry is one with a small number of large producers globally and with high barriers to entry. It is also a declining market, so the level of potential

competition is low. This is not true at present in the market for e-cigarettes, but this may change.

Power of suppliers

The main raw material needed for production of cigarettes is tobacco and the main sources of tobacco are Brazil and China. Tobacco is a product that can be stored for a considerable time, which gives the suppliers less power over the cigarette producers. Some cigarette producers have an involvement in tobacco growing to protect themselves further from seller power – BAT, for example; this is an example of vertical integration (see Chapter 11).

Case study questions

1 If e-cigarettes become licensed as a medicine (a move manufacturers are resisting), what is likely to be the impact on the market structure?

2 Given that cigarette smoking is a declining market which is predicted to continue to decline, use the life cycle model (in Chapter 12) to show how e-cigarettes can rejuvenate the market.

web link For information on smoking and e-cigarettes, see *www.ash.org.uk*, *www.ecita.org.uk* and Smoking Cessation and E-Cigarettes – UK – January 2017, a report from Mintel.

Review and discussion questions

1 Use Porter's five-forces model to analyse two industries of your choice. Try to choose industries which have contrasting market structures.

2 What economies of scale are likely to exist in retailing?

3 Think of examples of a market which is very competitive and a market which is not very competitive. Does the behaviour of the firms in these markets comply with the predictions in Table 15.7?

4 Why are goods such as washing powders and coffee advertised more heavily than goods like matches or bread?

Assignments

1 You are working in the strategic planning department of a large recorded music producer and have been asked to write a briefing document for a board meeting on the structure of the industry. Use either the structure–conduct–performance model or Porter's five-forces model as a framework for this briefing. (Sources of information: Competition and Markets Authority reports, the previous editions of this book, media and local libraries, Mintel and Key Note.)

2 You are working in the local consumer advice centre, which each week produces an information sheet giving the prices of a typical 'basket of goods' in local shops. Choose 10 branded items (Nescafé, for example) to constitute your basket of goods and survey three types of retail outlet: a small corner shop, a mini-market on a local main road and a large supermarket. Design the information sheet and present the information you have gathered in the form of a table. Include a list of bullet points that might explain any differences in price.

Further reading

Begg, D., Fischer, S. and Dornbusch, R., *Economics,* 10th edition, McGraw-Hill, 2011.

Griffiths, A. and Wall, S., *Applied Economics: An Introductory Course,* 12th edition, Financial Times/ Prentice Hall, 2012.

Worthington, I., Britton, C. and Rees, A., *Economics for Business: Blending Theory and Practice,* 2nd edition, Financial Times/Prentice Hall, 2005.

web link

Web links and further questions are available on the website at:
www.pearsoned.co.uk/worthington

16 International markets and trade

Chris Britton

The importance of international markets will vary between firms and industries, but most businesses do not operate solely within national boundaries. Businesses which operate in the export market will obviously need an understanding of international markets, but even the sole proprietor producing for a small local market may well use imported raw materials in the production process and so will be affected by changes that take place internationally.

Learning outcomes

Having read this chapter you should be able to:

● explain why international trade takes place

● examine the international organisations that serve to promote free trade

● outline the balance-of-payments position in the UK

● describe the working of the foreign exchange markets

Key terms

Article 50	European Economic Area	J-curve effect
Balance of payments	European Monetary	Protectionism
Balance of trade	System	Qualitative control
Capital account	Exchange control	Quota
Common agricultural policy	Exchange rate	Single market
Common external tariff	Exchange rate mechanism	Specialisation
Common market	Financial account	Speculation
Current account	Fixed exchange rate	Subsidy
Current balance	Floating exchange rate	Surplus
Customs union	Free trade	Tariff
Deficit	Import control	Visible trade
Devalue	Invisible trade	

Introduction

International markets are important to most firms; even if they do not produce for the export market they may well be dependent upon raw materials which are imported and they will almost definitely be affected by movements in the exchange rate. The UK, like all other advanced industrial countries, is highly dependent upon international markets and that dependence has grown over the years. What makes international trade different from trade within a country is that the trade is taking place across national borders. Thus, a system for international payments is needed. It is essential for students of business to have an understanding of international markets, exchange rates and the balance of payments.

International trade – why it takes place

Trade between countries takes place because resources are unevenly distributed throughout the world and the mobility of the factors of production is limited. Consequently some countries are better at producing certain goods than others. Some countries could not actually produce a particular good: for example, the UK cannot produce minerals that are not indigenous or fruit that can only be grown in tropical weather conditions. If there is a demand for these goods in the UK, there are a number of possibilities: the British could do without these goods; or an attempt could be made to grow them (in the case of the fruit) despite the climatic conditions; or the UK could buy the goods from other countries that can produce them. In other words, it can trade for them.

It is easy to see that if country A can produce video cameras more cheaply than country B and B can produce wheat more cheaply than A, **specialisation** should occur, so A should produce video cameras and B should produce wheat and they should trade with one another. Complete specialisation is, however, unlikely, for strategic reasons. It is also true that even if country A can produce both goods more cheaply than country B, there is scope for benefits from trade. As this may not be so easy to imagine, Table 16.1 gives a numerical example. Country A can produce 100 video cameras or 100 units of wheat using 100 workers. Country B can produce 20 video cameras or 40 units of wheat with the same number of workers. Country A can therefore produce both goods at lower cost than country B. To show that even in this situation trade will benefit the world, assume that both countries produce both goods and that they each devote half of their workforce to each good.

Table 16.1 Production of video cameras and wheat

	Number of units that 100 workers can produce	
	Video cameras	Wheat
Country A	100	100
Country B	20	40

The total output of video cameras is 60 units and of wheat is 70 units. Country A is 5 times more efficient at producing video cameras than country B, but only 2.5 times more efficient than B in producing wheat (see Table 16.2). It would therefore benefit both countries if production was rearranged. If B specialised completely in wheat and A produced 35 units of wheat and 65 video cameras, world output would be as indicated in Table 16.3.

Table 16.2 Production of video cameras and wheat

	Video cameras	*Wheat*
Country A	50	50
Country B	10	20
	—	—
	60	70

Table 16.3 World output of video cameras and wheat

	Video cameras	*Wheat*
Country A	65	35
Country B	0	40
	—	—
	65	75

Source: Adapted from Financial Indicators – Stocks: Private Sector Debt, http://stats.oecd.org/index.aspx?queryid=34814. OECD. StatExtracts http://stats.oecd.org/

In short, world output has been increased and everyone is better off provided that trade takes place. This simplified example illustrates the basic argument for **free trade**. Free trade brings the advantages of higher world output and higher standards of living. Countries will produce the goods in which they have a cost advantage and trade with other countries for other goods. So countries can buy goods at lower prices than they could be produced for at home. Where economies of scale are present, the savings as a result of specialisation can be immense.

Theoretically, free trade brings most benefit; however, there are often restrictions to such trade and it is unlikely that complete specialisation will take place. Most countries would regard being totally dependent on another country for a particular good as a risky proposition.

Restrictions to international trade

There are a number of things that governments do to restrict international trade. These restrictions include:

- **quotas**: physical limitations on the import of certain goods into a country, sometimes by mutual agreement (e.g. voluntary export restraints);
- **tariffs**: taxes placed on imported goods;
- **exchange controls**: limits to the amount of a currency that can be bought, which will limit the import of goods;
- **subsidies**: payments made to domestic producers to reduce their costs and therefore make them more competitive on world markets;
- **qualitative controls**: controls on the quality of goods rather than on quantity or price.

All of these serve to restrict international trade and therefore reduce specialisation on a world level. They invite retaliation and could lead to inefficiencies. **Import controls** have a wide effect on industry. In January 2014 China announced a tariff of 57 per cent on polysilicon imports from the United States (this is used in the production of photovoltaic cells for solar panels). This move would have an important effect on the industry in the United States and its workforce, jobs would be lost, companies would close and there would be a knock-on effect on allied industries. But there are powerful arguments used in support of import controls. For example, they can be used to protect industries, whether these industries are 'infant' industries or strategic industries. The main reason for the imposition of tariffs by China is believed to be retaliatory, as a case was filed against the Chinese solar panel industry with the US International Trade Commission in 2011 by SolarWorld, which claimed that China was 'dumping' its solar panels in the United States. Import controls can also be used to improve the balance-of-payments position in the case where a deficit exists. This sort of blocking of international trade is called **protectionism**.

The UK is a member of a number of international organisations that serve to promote free trade and control the restrictions to free trade, such as the World Trade Organization (see Chapter 5 and the mini case below).

---

mini case	The cotton dispute

In January 2014, Brazil was given permission by the World Trade Organization (WTO) to impose import tariffs on around 100 US items, including cotton products (100 per cent tariff), cars with small engines (50 per cent) and methanol (36 per cent). The WTO took the unusual step of allowing 'cross retaliation' so that Brazil could take action against US copyrights and patents. This is an escalation of the long-running trade dispute between Brazil and the United States on cotton.

In 2002 Brazil lodged a complaint with the WTO against US government actions in the cotton industry. There were two issues: the first was the level of subsidies paid to cotton producers in the United States; the second was the export guarantee scheme operated by the US government which made exporting cotton from the United States both cheaper and easier. Brazil argued that both of these practices were anti-competitive and adversely affected other cotton-producing countries. In 2004 the WTO ruled in Brazil's favour – the US cotton subsidies were declared illegal. The WTO estimated that, in the absence of subsidies, the price of cotton would have risen, benefiting cotton farmers in developing nations, and that cotton production in the United States would have been 15 per cent lower. The

United States is the world's largest exporter of cotton and the industry supports around 200 000 jobs in the United States.

The issue rumbled on until 2009 when the US government promised to revise its cotton subsidies and to pay an annual fee to Brazil's cotton industry; this was an agreement between the two nations. Between 2010 and September 2013 the United States paid $147 million per annum to the Brazilian Cotton Institute in monthly instalments. These payments stopped in September 2013, when the last Farm Act expired. Under the new Farm Bill 2014, cotton is not a product which is subsidised by the US government. However, the government does offer subsidy for insurance for US cotton farmers if they achieve lower than expected revenue.

More recently there have been disagreements between China and other countries with regard to Chinese steel and steel products. It appears that the Chinese steel industry is being supported by its government to outcompete its international rivals. In March 2018 the United States responded by saying it will impose tariffs on all steel imports. Countries across the world have said that they are ready to retaliate against the US measures.

---

web link	For information on the work of the WTO see *www.wto.org*

The establishment and growth of the European Union

The EU was established in 1958 by the Treaty of Rome. The six original members, namely France, West Germany, Italy, the Netherlands, Belgium and Luxembourg, were joined in 1973 by the UK, Ireland and Denmark. Greece joined in 1981, followed by Spain and Portugal in 1986 and Austria, Finland and Sweden on 1 January 1995. In 2004, 10 further countries joined the EU, mainly from Eastern Europe: Czech Republic, Cyprus, Estonia, Hungary, Latvia, Lithuania, Malta, Poland, Slovakia and Slovenia. In January 2007 Romania and Bulgaria were admitted. In July 2013 Croatia joined, and all these countries, along with the former East Germany, currently constitute the 28 member states of the EU. Other countries that are waiting to join are Albania, Iceland, Macedonia, Montenegro, Serbia and Turkey. Iceland suspended discussions in 2013. In addition to these member states Canada agreed a free trade deal with the EU in 2017 which allows 98 per cent of goods to be traded without tariffs.

As a result of the enlargement of the EU, a new constitution was put forward which included changes in voting rights, the size of the EU Commission and maintaining national sovereignty. The new constitution had to be ratified by all member states of the EU. The new constitution was shelved in 2005 after 'no' votes in referendums held in France and the Netherlands. In 2007 a new reform treaty was agreed by EU leaders – the Lisbon Treaty – and was put in place in 2009 (see Chapter 4). Included in the new treaty was an exit clause for countries wanting to leave the EU.

> **web link**
>
> For information on the European Commission see *http://europa.eu*
> For European statistics see *http://ec.europa.eu/eurostat*

The primary aim of the Treaty of Rome was to create a **common market** in which member states were encouraged to trade freely and to bring their economies closer together, ultimately culminating in the creation of a **single market** within the Union. To bring this about, a protected free trade area or **customs union** was established, which involved the removal of tariff barriers between member states and the institution of a **common external tariff** (CET) on goods from outside the Union. Institutional structures (see Chapter 4) and Union policies – most notably the **Common Agricultural Policy** (CAP) – also contributed to this end and to the creation of a trading bloc of immense proportions. Within this bloc, member states were expected to gain numerous advantages, including increased trade and investment, huge economies of scale and improvements in productivity and cost reductions. To support the goal of increased trade and cooperation between community members, a **European Monetary System** was established in 1979 in which a majority of member states undertook to fix their exchange rates within agreed limits (see below).

A significant step towards the creation of a single market – capable of competing effectively with the United States and Japan – was taken in 1986 when the then 12 community members signed the Single European Act. This Act established 31 December 1992 as the target date for the creation of a single European market: an area (comprising the 12 EU countries) without internal frontiers, in which the free movement of goods, services, people and capital was to be ensured within the provisions contained in the Treaty. Among the measures for making the single market a reality were agreements on the following issues:

- the removal or reduction in obstacles to cross-border travel and trade (e.g. customs checks);
- the harmonisation or approximation of technical and safety standards on a large number of products;

- closer approximation of excise duties and other fiscal barriers (e.g. VAT);
- the removal of legal obstacles to trade (e.g. discriminatory purchasing policies);
- the mutual recognition of qualifications.

Further steps in the development of the Union came with the decision to establish a **European Economic Area** (EEA) – which permits members of the European Free Trade Area (EFTA) to benefit from many of the single-market measures – and, in particular, the Treaty on European Union, agreed by the 12 member states in December 1991 at Maastricht. Apart from the institutional changes mentioned in Chapter 4, the Maastricht Treaty contained provisions for:

- increased economic and monetary union between member states;
- a single currency;
- a social charter to protect workers' rights;
- a common foreign and security policy;
- community citizenship.

These various measures were scheduled to be introduced over a number of years, although in some cases – most notably the UK – specially negotiated 'opt-out' clauses meant that some provisions were not implemented simultaneously by all member states (e.g. the single currency, the social charter).

European monetary union (EMU) was finally achieved on 1 January 1999 with the creation of the eurozone. Eleven members of the EU were included – the UK, Denmark and Sweden chose not to participate, while Greece failed the convergence criteria for membership but joined in 2001. Six more countries have joined – Slovenia (2007), Malta and Cyprus (2008), Slovakia (2009), Estonia (2011) and Latvia (2014), taking the total up to 18 (EU18). The eurozone is effectively a single economic zone since it operates with a single currency – the euro (see the text later in this chapter) and members have given up sovereignty over monetary policy, which is now determined by the European Central Bank. National sovereignty over fiscal policy has been retained, so there can be some differences in tax rates and government spending, but this is to operate in a framework of 'harmonisation'. The creation of the eurozone enables increased specialisation across the whole of Europe and bigger economies of scale. It embraces more than 330 million people and is responsible for one-fifth of the world's output and as such comes a close second to the United States as an economic superpower.

'Brexit' and Euroscepticism

One of the core principles of the EU is that of 'ever closer union', the idea that the countries involved are working together to become closer aligned, and while the ends are not set out it might be towards a single European state. Some have spoken out against the idea of a 'United States of Europe' where currently the EU has made substantial progress towards a single currency and universal laws. The idea of working towards so close an alignment is controversial, and there is scepticism (or doubt) from some parties in most EU countries about the idea of this integration. This has been particularly strong in the UK in recent years.

The UK chose not to join the eurozone and the single currency until a referendum had been held. In 1997 the Chancellor of the Exchequer set out five economic tests of whether the UK should join or not. By 2008, the debate over membership of the euro in the UK had disappeared from the political agenda in view of the more pressing problems encountered by the EU during the year over the new constitution and the global financial crisis (see case study at the end of this chapter). By 2013 any talk of a referendum in the UK was about the UK leaving the EU rather than joining the eurozone. The arguments put forward for and against leaving the EU are similar to the arguments put forward for and against joining the eurozone. The arguments for leaving included freedom for business from EU regulation, to save money on membership costs, control over borders and that other countries like Norway and Switzerland do well outside the EU. Arguments against leaving included that the UK will become marginalised, that the EU is the UK's biggest trading partner and markets will be lost, and that multinational companies locate in the UK *because* it is a member of the EU and these will leave.

In 2016 the Prime Minister, David Cameron, announced that he was calling a referendum in which the British people would be asked if they wanted to remain in the EU or leave. On 23 June 2016, 51.9 per cent of voters opted to leave; the next day David Cameron announced his resignation. Theresa May, the next Prime Minister, formally triggered the process of leaving the EU in March 2017 by triggering **Article 50** of the Lisbon Treaty, which allows member states a way to exit the EU two years after starting the process. At the time of writing it is not really clear what this means, as there are different degrees of membership of the EU. It may be that the government will negotiate to stay within the EU customs union to preserve free trade, though some have argued that we should leave in order to trade with other nations around the world. There are lots of EU institutions that the UK might choose to remain a part of, if both the UK and EU agree to continue to cooperate (e.g. around medical and aviation regulation). It has been the case in some states with a negotiated position (e.g. Norway) that they have had to comply with EU regulations as a condition of free trade whilst having no say in what the regulations are because these countries are outside of the EU.

The balance of payments

The **balance of payments** is a record of a country's international trade with other countries over a period of time, usually a year. It records the flows of money rather than goods, so that an import will be recorded as a negative amount since the money is flowing out of the country to pay for the good, and an export is recorded as a positive amount. Money flows into and out of a country for two basic reasons: first, in exchange for goods and services (current transactions); and second, for investment purposes (capital transactions). In the UK these two flows are recorded separately in the UK balance-of-payments accounts, which are produced by the government. Since 1992, when customs posts were abolished, balance-of-payment figures have been collected through Intrastat and are based on VAT returns.

 For information on the balance of payments in the UK see *www.statistics.gov.uk*
For information on international trade see *www.oecd.org* and *www.wto.org*

Current transactions

In the UK the **current account** records the flows of money received and paid out in exchange for goods and services. It is sub-divided into **visible trade** (the import and export of goods) and **invisible trade** (the import and export of services). Invisible trade includes:

1   Services such as banking, insurance, tourism.
2   Interest, profits and dividends.
3   Transfers, which include grants to developing countries, payments to international bodies like the EU and private transfers such as gifts.

The balance of these flows on visible trade is called the **balance of trade** and the balance on the current account overall is called the **current balance**. It is to one of these balances that journalists and politicians are usually referring when they talk about the balance of payments. Table 16.4 shows the balance of payments for the UK in 2016. It can be seen that the balance of trade was –£113,567 million, the invisible balance was +£94,818 million and the current balance was –£113,567 million. More will be said later about the history of the balance of payments in the UK.

Table 16.4 UK balance of payments, 2016 (£m)

Current account	
Trade in goods and services	
Trade in goods (visible balance)	−135 495
Trade in services (invisible balance)	94 818
Total trade	**−40 677**
Primary income	
Compensation of employees	−360
Investment income	−49 128
Other primary income	−896
Total primary income	**−50 384**
Secondary income	
Central government	−20 072
Other sectors	−2 434
Total secondary income	**−22 506**
Current balance	**−113 567**
Capital balance	**−1 693**

Source: Adapted from UK Economic Accounts: Balance of Payments – Current Account, and Ompendium: Capital Account – www.ONS.gov.uk

Capital transactions

As well as these current transactions there are flows of money for investment purposes. These include funds from both the public and private sectors and long-term and short-term monetary movements.

Long-term capital transactions include the following:

- Overseas investment in the UK (e.g. purchase of shares, acquisition of real assets, purchase of government securities by non-residents).
- UK private investment overseas, where UK residents buy shares, acquire real assets, and so on, in overseas countries. The capital account does not include interest, dividends or profits but only flows of money for investment purposes. A capital transaction can give rise to a current flow in the future. If a non-resident bought shares in a UK company, the initial amount would appear on the capital account. The resulting flow of dividends paid in the future would be recorded as a flow on the invisible account.
- Official long-term capital (i.e. loans from the UK government to other governments).

Short-term transactions include the following:

- Trade credit – as goods are often not paid for as they are received the physical export or import of goods is not matched with an inflow or outflow of money. In order that the balance of payments balances, these amounts would be included here as trade credit.
- Foreign currency borrowing and lending abroad by UK banks.
- Exchange reserves held by other countries and other organisations in sterling.
- Other external banking and money market liabilities in sterling.

These capital transactions are recorded in the UK balance of payments as changes from the previous year; they are not a record of all the transactions that have taken place over time. If money is flowing into the UK for investment purposes, there is an increase in the UK liabilities and these are shown as positive amounts on the balance of payments. If money is flowing out of the country, there is an increase in the UK assets and these are shown as negative amounts in the balance of payments.

The UK balance of payments comprises three sections:

- The current account, as before.
- The **capital account**, which records capital transfers and transfers of non-financial assets into and out of the UK. The balance on this account was –£1,378 million in 2016.
- The **financial account**, which gives the balance of trade in financial assets. This section of the balance of payments is itself sub-divided between direct investment, portfolio investment, other investments and reserve assets. The balance on the financial account for 2016 was –£116,902 million.

Speculative flows of currencies would appear in the financial account of the balance of payments. Portfolio investment is the purchasing of shares in companies while direct investment is the setting up of subsidiaries. Reserve assets shows the change in official reserves – an increase in official reserves is shown as a negative amount and a decrease is shown as a positive amount.

The balance of payments overall should balance as negative flows will be balanced by positive flows. As this is often hard to understand, two examples will be given.

Example 1

If a UK resident buys foreign goods, there will be a negative entry in the current account equal to the value of those goods. That individual has to pay for those goods in foreign currency and could do this by using money from a foreign currency bank account if he or she has one, or by borrowing the foreign currency from a bank in that country. Either way, there is an increase in the amount of liabilities and the same amount would be shown as a positive amount in the capital account.

Example 2

If a foreign investor purchased shares in a UK company, there would be a positive amount recorded in the capital account. The investor might pay for these shares by using sterling from a sterling bank account and so there would be an equal negative amount shown in the capital account.

The balance of payments should therefore always balance but invariably fails to do so, owing to errors and omissions in the recording process, and so a balancing item is included to ensure that it does. As can be seen from Tables 16.4 and 16.5, the balancing item can be very large, and this calls into question the accuracy of the figures.

Table 16.5 UK balance of payments, selected years 1998–2016 (£m)

	1998	2000	2002	2004	2006	2008	2010	2012	2015	2016
Visible balance	−21 813	−32 976	−46 675	−57 944	−77 555	−92 877	−98 514	−108 698	−118 626	−135 495
Invisible balance	17 841	8 882	29 060	32 262	26 830	67 809	49 948	48 856	86 256	94 818
Current account	−3 972	−24 094	−17 615	−25 682	−50 725	−25 068	−48 566	−59 842	−98 145	−113 567
Capital account	516	1 527	868	2 073	853	3 393	3 704	3 788	−1 978	−1 693
Financial account	2 219	24 944	10 272	27 028	44 800	18 121	40 996	53 50	90 892	105 844
Balancing item	1 237	−2 377	6 475	−3 419	5 072	3 554	3 866	2 204	9 231	9 416

Source: Adapted from *Balance of payments, various years*, www.ons.gov.uk

Equilibrium in the balance of payments

If the balance of payments always balances, how can there be a deficit on the balance of payments? The answer is that the media and politicians are referring to the current balance or the balance of trade rather than the overall balance-of-payments position. A balance-of-payments surplus on the current account is where the value of exports exceeds the value of imports. A deficit is where the value of imports exceeds the value of exports. As explained above, if there is a surplus on the current account, this will be matched by an outflow in the capital account, for example a reduction in the size of sterling bank balances, or an increase in official reserves. The opposite is true for a deficit.

This implies that there cannot be a balance-of-payments problem; however, persistent surpluses or deficits on the current account are considered to be problematic. A persistent deficit has to be financed in some way, either through borrowing, to increase the external liabilities, or by selling more assets. A deficit will also lead to pressure on the exchange rate, as will be shown later. A continued surplus is also a problem, since one country's surplus must mean that other countries are experiencing a deficit, and they will be faced with the problem of financing the deficit. Political pressure will be brought to bear, and there is the possibility of the introduction of tariffs or other import controls in order to reduce a deficit.

Methods of correcting balance-of-payments deficits

Since **surplus** is not regarded as being such a problem as a **deficit**, this section will concentrate on actions needed to overcome a deficit, although the actions would be reversed for a surplus. When there is a current account deficit, the outflow of funds is greater than the inflow of funds from international trade. The authorities need to increase exports and/or reduce imports. Thus:

1   A fall in the exchange rate will have the double effect of making exports cheaper abroad and imports dearer at home, thus encouraging exports and discouraging imports. This will be explained fully later.
2   To increase exports, UK companies that produce for the export market could be subsidised. This would have the effect of reducing the price of UK goods abroad, making them more competitive.
3   Import controls could be imposed to restrict the level of imports coming into the country.
4   A rise in the rate of interest would make the UK more attractive to investors and therefore increase capital flows into the UK and help offset the current account deficit.

The history of the balance of payments in the UK

Table 16.5 gives a summary of the balance of payments in the UK between 1994 and 2016. The table shows that the current account was in deficit for the whole period. The weaknesses on the current account pre-date this and are somewhat hidden in the overall figures. The current account deficits started in 1987, the visible balance has been in deficit since 1983 (and still is) and within this the non-oil balance has been in deficit since 1982. This did not show in the overall current account figures until 1987 because of the offsetting effect of invisibles and oil. The UK's underlying weaknesses on the current account come from several sources:

1   Exports have risen but imports have risen faster. In the UK there is a high propensity to import goods.
2   The collapse of oil prices during the 1990s reduced the value of the UK's oil exports.
3   The recession of the early 1980s left the UK manufacturing base in an extremely weak position. This meant that it was difficult to produce enough goods for export or even to meet domestic demand, so the balance of payments was hit from both directions. The changes in the structure of industry in the UK described in Chapter 12 have implications for the balance of payments, as services are less exportable than goods.
4   The economy is unbalanced in favour of consumption spending (which sucks in imports) and investment spending by companies (which boost exports).
5   The high value of the pound up to 2008 hit the UK's export market.
6   Poor competitiveness – productivity rates in the UK are low (see Chapter 12).
7   Since 2008, the global credit crunch and the disarray in the eurozone, our biggest market, have affected the UK balance of payments badly.

Figure 16.1 shows the breakdown of the current account between visibles and invisibles and it is clear that good performance on invisibles has partly offset poor performance in visibles.

Figure 16.1   Components of the current account, UK, 1991–2012

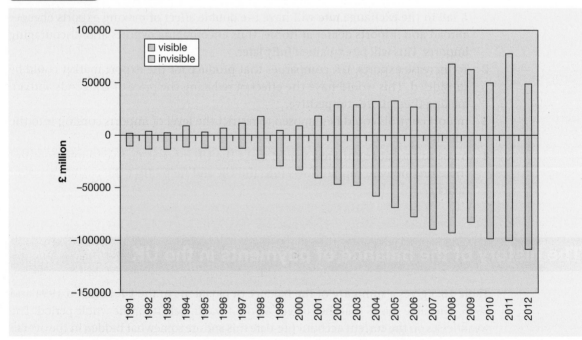

The current account of the balance of payments

Figures on the balance of payments are produced every month by the government in the UK and are often seized upon by commentators as indications of either an improvement in the UK's economic performance or a deterioration, depending upon the details of the figures. There are a number of reasons why their observation is incorrect. First, balance-of-payments figures are notoriously unreliable and are often revised by very large amounts. Between September and December 2013, for example, the current account deficit for the second quarter of 2013 was revised from £13.0 billion to £6.2 billion. Second – and this applies to all short-term economic indicators – there are very short-term changes in economic variables which are not translated into long-term trends. So the balance of payments can vary quite dramatically each month due to short-term factors which are evened out over the course of the year. In addition, the balance of payments, like other indicators, often does not behave as expected.

Figure 16.2 shows the UK current balance for the period 1970 to 2012. Two points can immediately be made about the behaviour of the balance of payments. First, the data move in a cyclical way and are therefore affected by the trade cycle. Second, the balance of payments generally improves in times of recession (e.g. the early 1980s, early 1990s and early 2000s) and worsens in times of boom. The reasons for this are two-fold: in a recession the level of imports falls as income falls; and the level of exports is unlikely to fall unless other countries are experiencing the same level of economic downturn. The balance of payments therefore improves. Usually the balance of payments improves enough in a recession to push it into surplus, although this pattern seems to have been broken. In the early 1990s and late 2000s, the balance of payments improved but remained in the red.

The unpredictability of the balance of payments is very evident in the figures for the 2000s. In 2006 the balance of payments worsened, despite the

Figure 16.2 UK current balance, 1970–2012 (£ million)

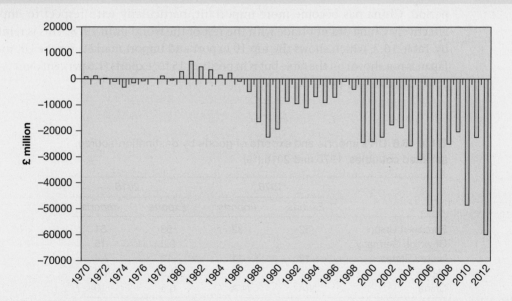

Source: Adapted from balance of payments, various years, *www.ons.gov.uk*

lower growth rate in the UK, which would have been expected to improve the balance of payments. The fall in the value of the pound since 2008 should have improved the balance of payments, but it did not. One possible explanation for the apparently contrary behaviour of the balance of payments is the J-curve effect (see Figure 16.7, page 408). It could be that the worsening in the balance of payments in the late 2000s was caused by the high value of the pound prior to 2008 because of the time lags involved. Similarly, the effects of the lower value of the pound have not been seen yet.

The deficit on the balance of payments in the UK in the third quarter of 2013 was £20.7 billion, the largest quarterly figure since 1989. The rebalancing of the balance of payments between consumption and investment has not happened. The UK wants improvements which are based on increasing exports, but although the growth in the service sector has been 1.3 per cent since the peak of 2008, production output is still 12 per cent lower. Low productivity rates in the UK have not helped the balance of payments (see Chapter 12) and neither has the eurozone crisis as Europe is the biggest export market for the UK.

The multitude of factors impacting upon the balance of payments and the difficulties involved in accurate data collection make the balance-of-payments figures unreliable and difficult to predict. The use of one month's figures by commentators to prove either that recovery is under way or that a recession is imminent is unsound.

Patterns of trade

Over time, patterns of trade change, for many reasons. Table 16.6 shows UK patterns of trade by destination/source for 1970 and 2016. The most obvious change is that trade with the EU has become much more important over the last 40 years – in 2016, 51 per cent of UK imports came from the EU and 53 per cent of exports went to the EU. Despite this, the United States remains important to the UK. Although it is not shown in the table, there has been a decline in UK trade with other OECD countries over the whole period. China has become more important, particularly with respect to imports – effectively China did not trade with the rest of the world until 1978. This is reinforced by Table 16.7, which shows the top 10 export and import markets for the UK in 2016. Japan is not shown on the table but is in position 15 for exports (1.6 per cent) and position 13 for imports (2.1 per cent).

Table 16.6 UK's imports and exports of goods by destination/source, selected countries, 1970 and 2016 (%)

	1970		2016	
	Exports	Imports	Exports	Imports
European Union	32	32	53	51
Of which Germany			9.3	15
United States	12	11	13	7.4
Japan	2	2	1.5	1.7
China	N/A	N/A	6.5	10

Source: Adapted from Table 12, UK trade June 2016, www.ons.gov.uk, Annual Abstract of Statistics, 1971, ONS.

Table 16.7 UK's top 10 export markets and import sources, 2016

Export market	Percentage of total exports	Import source	Percentage of total imports
1 USA	18.86	1 Germany	12.87
2 Germany	9.30	2 USA	11.36
3 France	6.41	3 The Netherlands	7.26
4 The Netherlands	5.88	4 China	7.24
5 Ireland	5.05	5 France	6.44
6 Switzerland	3.97	6 Spain	4.80
7 Italy	3.28	7 Belgium	4.49
8 China	3.18	8 Italy	3.87
9 Belgium	3.00	9 Ireland	3.56
10 Japan	2.77	10 Norway	2.55

Source: Adapted from Table 14, UK Trade June 2016, *www.ons.gov.uk*

Tables 16.8 and 16.9 show the types of goods imported to and exported from the UK.

Table 16.8 Pattern of trade by type of good (£ million)

	Imports		Exports	
	1998	2016	1998	2016
Total exports	163 997	302 067	186 481	437 562
A Products of agriculture, forestry & fishing	1 479	3 062	5 340	9 921
B Mining & quarrying	7 398	14 653	6 054	20 734
C Manufactured products	149 747	270 983	170 000	397 945
D Electricity, gas, steam & air-conditioning	3	103	353	761
E Water supply, sewerage & waste management	909	4 211	1 042	2 700
J Information & communication services	2 977	3 492	2 244	2 632
M Professional, scientific & technical services	44	79	17	5
R Arts, entertainment & recreation	1 440	5 484	1 431	2 863
S Other services	0	0	0	1

Source: Adapted from UK Trade Goods By Activity, 2017, *www.ons.gov.uk*

Table 16.9 UK's top five commodities exported and imported (by %), 2016

Exported	Percentage of total exports	Imported	Percentage of total imports
1 Motor vehicles and trailers	13.3	1 Motor vehicles and trailers	12.6
2 Other transport equipment	10.8	2 Computer, electronic and optical products	11.0
3 Machinery and equipment	8.9	3 Other transport equipment	7.3
4 Pharmaceutical products	8.6	4 Machinery and equipment	6.9
5 Chemicals and chemical products	8.3	5 Pharmaceutical products	6.6

Source: Adapted from UK Trade Goods By Activity, 2017, *www.ons.gov.uk*

The difference between UK import and export growth can be seen in Table 16.8, where the total imports grew by 84 per cent over the period, compared with 134 per cent growth in exports. The UK is importing proportionately more now than it did in 1998. Manufacturing is clearly the most important category of good as far as the balance of payments is concerned. Manufacturing has retained its importance for inward and outward trade, accounting for 89 per cent of exports and 90.9 per cent in 2016. As far as imports are concerned, the percentage has increased a great deal over the last 20 years. The UK is now a net importer of manufactured goods. In 2016 the value of imported manufactured goods was £270,983 million, whereas the value of exported manufactured goods was £397,945 million.

Exchange rates

The **exchange rate** of a currency is the price of that currency in terms of other currencies. If each country has its own currency and international trade is to take place, an exchange of currencies needs to occur. When a UK resident buys goods from France, these must be paid for in euros. The individual will probably purchase euros from a bank in exchange for sterling in order to carry out the transaction. There must therefore be an exchange rate between sterling and euros. Likewise, there will be exchange rates between sterling and all other currencies.

Basically, there are two types of exchange rate: the **floating exchange rate** and the **fixed exchange rate**. There are also hybrid exchange rate systems, which combine the characteristics of the two main types.

The floating exchange rate

A floating exchange rate is one that is determined within a free market, where there is no government intervention and the exchange rate is free to fluctuate according to market conditions. The exchange rate is determined by the demand for and the supply of the currency in question.

As far as sterling is concerned, the demand for the currency comes from exports – that is, overseas residents buying pounds either to buy British goods and services or for investment purposes. The supply of pounds comes from imports – that is, UK residents who are buying foreign currencies to purchase goods and services or for investment purposes and who are therefore at the same time supplying pounds to the market.

The market for sterling can then be drawn using simple demand and supply diagrams. In Figure 16.3, the price axis shows the price of £1 in terms of US dollars and the quantity axis shows the quantity of pounds being bought and sold. The equilibrium exchange rate is determined by the intersection of demand and supply at £1 = $2. As this is a totally free market, if any of the conditions in the market change, the exchange rate will also change.

The demand for and supply of sterling, and therefore the exchange rate, is affected by:

1 Changes in the balance of payments.
2 Changes in investment flows.
3 Speculation in the foreign exchange markets.

Figure 16.3   **The determination of the exchange rate of £ for $**

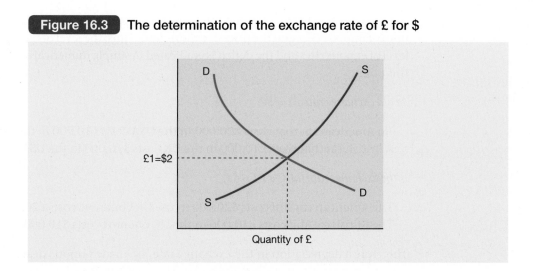

Quantity of £

Changes in the balance of payments

Figure 16.4 shows the effect on the exchange rate of changes in the balance of payments. The original demand curve is DD and the original supply curve is SS. At the equilibrium exchange rate of £1 = $2 the demand for pounds is equal to the supply of pounds. In other words, if the demand for pounds comes from exports and the supply of pounds comes from imports, imports and exports are equal and the balance of payments is in equilibrium. Now it is assumed that a balance-of-payments deficit appears, caused by the level of imports rising while the level of exports stays the same. If exports remain the same, there will be no change in the demand curve for pounds. As imports rise, there will be a rise in the supply of pounds to the market; the supply curve moves to the right to S^1S^1. At the old exchange rate of £1 = $2, there is now excess supply of pounds, and as this is a free market there will be downward pressure on the value of the pound until equilibrium is re-established at the new lower exchange rate of £1 = $1. At this exchange rate the demand for pounds is again equal to the increased supply of pounds and the balance between imports and exports is re-established.

Figure 16.4   **The effect of changes in the balance of payments on the exchange rate**

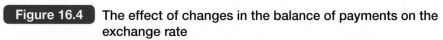
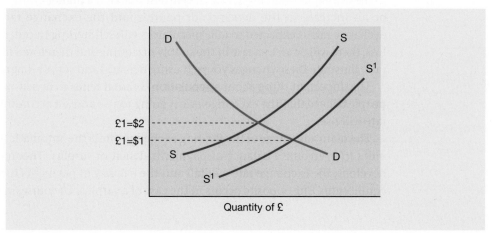

Quantity of £

How does this happen? When the value of the pound falls, two things happen: the price of imports rises and the price of exports falls. Thus, the level of imports falls and the level of exports rises and the deficit is eradicated. A simple numerical example illustrates this point:

At old exchange rate £1 = $2:

> An American car that costs $20,000 in the USA costs £10,000 in the UK.
> A British car that costs £10,000 in the UK costs $20,000 in the USA.

If the exchange rate falls to £1 = $1:

> The American car still costs $20,000 in the USA but now costs £20,000 in the UK.
> The British car still costs £10,000 in the UK but now costs $10,000 in the USA.

Therefore a depreciation in the exchange rate has made imports dearer (the American car) and exports cheaper (the British car). Thus, a fall in the value of the pound helps to re-establish equilibrium in the balance of payments.

In the case of a surplus on the balance of payments, the exchange rate will rise, making exports more expensive and imports cheaper, thereby re-establishing equilibrium in the balance of payments. You should test your understanding of the working of the foreign exchange markets by working through what happens if a surplus develops.

A fall in the value of the pound in a free market is called a 'depreciation' in the value of the pound; a rise in its value is called an 'appreciation'.

Changes in investment flows

In Figure 16.5, the original equilibrium exchange rate is £1 = $2. If there is an increase in the level of investment in the UK from overseas, there will be an increase in the demand for pounds. The demand curve moves to the right (to D^1D^1), and the exchange rate rises to £1 = $2.5.

The effect of speculation

If the exchange rate of sterling is expected to rise, speculators will buy sterling in order to make a capital gain by selling the currency later at a higher exchange rate. There will be an increase in the demand for pounds and the exchange rate will rise. If the exchange rate is expected to fall, speculators will sell sterling in order to avoid a capital loss, there will be an increase in the supply of sterling and therefore a fall in the exchange rate. Illustrate these changes yourself using demand and supply diagrams.

The important thing about **speculation** is that it tends to be self-fulfilling. If enough people believe that the exchange rate is going to rise and act accordingly, the exchange rate will rise.

The main advantage of the floating exchange rate is the automatic mechanism it provides to overcome a balance-of-payments deficit or surplus. Theoretically, if a deficit develops, the exchange rate will fall and the balance of payments is brought back into equilibrium. The opposite occurs in the case of a surplus. Of course, in reality it does not

Figure 16.5 The effect of changes in the investment flows on the exchange rate

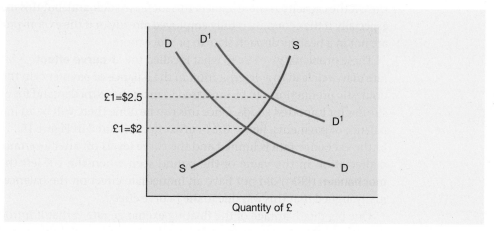

work as smoothly or as quickly as the theory suggests. A depreciation is supposed to work as demonstrated in Figure 16.6.

There are, however, a number of problems that may occur to prevent this self-correcting mechanism working properly. First, if in the UK the goods that are imported are necessities that cannot be produced at home, then even if their price goes up as a result of a depreciation, they will continue to be demanded. Thus, not only will the balance of payments deficit not be automatically rectified, but also another economic problem will result – that of inflation. The UK will continue to buy the imported goods at the new

Figure 16.6 The effect of depreciation

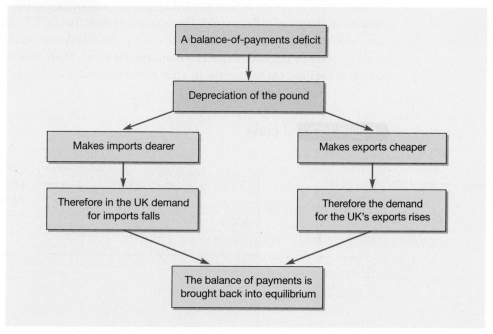

higher price. A second problem occurs on the other side of the equation. It is assumed above that, as the price of exports falls, more exports are sold. This presupposes that in the UK the capacity is there to meet this increased demand, but this may not be the case, especially if the economy is fully employed already or if the export-producing industries are not in a healthy enough state to produce more.

These problems give rise to what is called the '**J-curve effect**'. A fall in the exchange rate may well lead to a deterioration in the balance of payments in the short term, until domestic production can be increased to meet the extra demand for exports and as substitutes for imported goods. Once this can be done there will be an improvement in the balance of payments, hence the J-curve effect pictured in Figure 16.7. The effect of a fall in the exchange rate is limited and the curve levels off after a certain time period. The depreciation in the value of the pound seen when the UK left the **exchange rate mechanism** (ERM) did not have an immediate effect on the balance of payments and many argued that this was due to the J-curve effect.

One big disadvantage of the floating exchange rate is that it introduces uncertainty into the market, and for firms that operate internationally, this is another variable that needs to be considered when planning. Moreover, since the possibility of speculation exists with the floating exchange rate, this can be destabilising and unsettling to markets, something which businesses do not welcome.

The fixed exchange rate

The fixed exchange rate is one that is fixed and maintained by the government. An exchange rate can be fixed in terms of other currencies, gold or a basket of other currencies. In order to maintain a fixed exchange rate the government has actively to intervene in the market, either buying or selling currencies.

Figure 16.8 shows the action needed by the UK authorities in the case of downward pressure on the value of the pound. The exchange rate is fixed at £1 = $2, and the government wants to maintain that rate. If a balance-of-payments deficit develops, brought about by an increase in imports, exports remaining the same, there will be excess supply of pounds at the fixed exchange rate. In a free market the value of the pound would fall until

Figure 16.7   J-curve

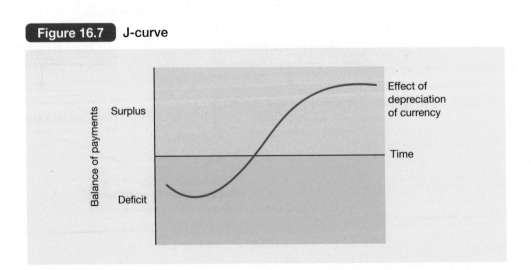

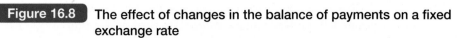

Figure 16.8   The effect of changes in the balance of payments on a fixed exchange rate

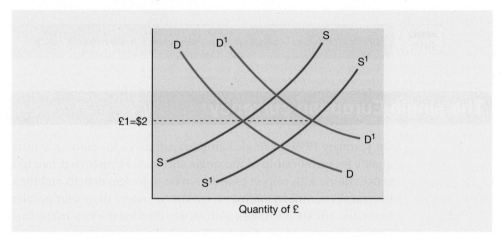

the excess supply had disappeared. However, this is not a free market, and the government must buy up the excess supply of pounds in order to maintain the exchange rate at £1 = $2. Thus, the demand curve moves to the right and the exchange rate has been maintained at the same level. Alternatively, if there is excess demand for pounds, the government has to supply pounds to the market in order to maintain the fixed exchange rate.

A prime advantage of a fixed exchange rate is that there is less uncertainty in the market; everyone knows what the exchange rate will be in a year's time, and long-term planning is made easier. It also reduces the likelihood of speculation in the foreign exchange markets. One serious disadvantage, however, is that there is no longer an automatic mechanism for rectifying any balance-of-payments problems as there is in the case of the floating exchange rate, and this means that government intervention is necessary not just to support the exchange rate, but also to overcome any balance-of-payments problems. Added to this, a fixed exchange rate is not sustainable in the case of persistent deficits or surpluses. In the event of a surplus, the government must supply pounds to the market and if the surplus persists then eventually the government will exhaust its reserves and might well have to revalue the pound (i.e. increase the exchange rate of the pound). In the case of a persistent deficit, the size of the government's reserves will be increasing over time and the government may have to **devalue** the pound to correct the problem.

There are, then, advantages and disadvantages to both types of exchange rate and there have been hybrid exchange rate systems which serve to combine the advantages of both systems. In such an exchange rate system the exchange rate is basically fixed but is allowed to fluctuate by a small amount either side of the central value. The ERM of the EU was an example of this. When the UK entered the ERM, the exchange rate was fixed against other member currencies but allowed to vary by 6 per cent either side of the central value before action was needed.

Over the years the UK has had a variety of types of exchange rate. Before the First World War and for some time between the wars, the exchange rate was fixed in terms of gold – the gold standard. From the Second World War until 1972, the UK was part of the Bretton Woods system of fixed exchange rates, where the pound was fixed in terms of dollars. Then from 1972 to 1990, there was a floating exchange rate. In 1990, however, the UK joined the ERM, which was again a fixed exchange rate. In September 1992, the pound left the ERM and was allowed to float once more.

web link

For information on exchange rates see *www.bankofengland.co.uk*

The single European currency

On 1 January 1999 the single European currency – the euro – was introduced. In order to qualify for membership of the single currency, EU members had to fulfil strict convergence criteria with respect to inflation rates, budget deficits and the rates of interest. In the end all countries qualified except Greece, where there were problems with high inflation rates. The UK, Denmark and Sweden decided not to join the single currency, while Greece, Slovenia, Malta, Cyprus, Slovakia, Estonia and Latvia have since joined. Each of the currencies of the 18 members is fixed to the euro at a specified rate, but each is a sub-unit of the euro rather than a separate currency.

Even though the UK has not joined the single currency, many businesses in the UK have already adapted to its existence. Many large companies use the euro for accounting purposes – Marks and Spencer stores are fully equipped to accept the euro. Even without entry, preparation is necessary for practical reasons, since many large companies have started to invoice and pay bills in euros – computer systems will have to be adapted to allow for this. There will also be a cost involved in the UK as banks are charging fairly high commission for converting euros, particularly for small users. Preparation is also a strategic issue for business. First, EMU will result in greater competition, as price differences will be more obvious to consumers. The cost of converting currencies serves to increase the costs of UK businesses and make them less competitive. Second, EMU will probably result in more mergers and acquisitions across Europe and this will have dramatic effects on the structures of industries.

In the UK the debate over the single European currency continues, although this issue has been pushed into the background by other problems. The pro single-currency camp claims that the UK will be further marginalised in Europe if it does not join in the single currency. As already noted, these arguments are similar to the ones over whether the UK should leave the EU or not. It also argues that there are great benefits to membership – a reduction in transaction costs like the cost of currency exchange, a reduction in the uncertainty caused by changing exchange rates, lower interest rates and the continuance of London as a financial centre in currencies. The anti single-currency camp argues just as vociferously that all of this would be at the expense of the loss of sovereignty – the UK would be unable to change its exchange rate in order to boost the competitiveness of UK goods. The performance of the euro since its birth has been variable. Figure 16.9 shows the value of the euro against sterling since January 1999 when €1 was worth 70p. In June 2017, €1 was worth 87p in the UK.

The euro found itself in great danger of falling apart in 2012–13. The European Central Bank acted to prevent this happening. As a result of the eurozone crisis (see case study at the end of the chapter) there are ongoing discussions towards banking union in the eurozone.

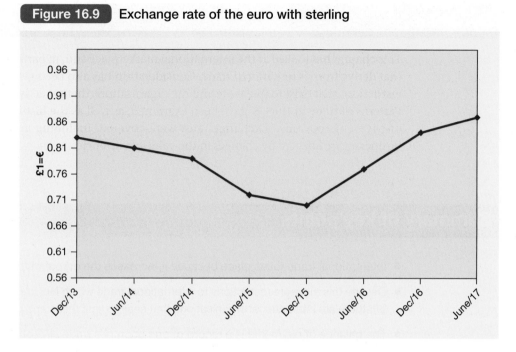

Figure 16.9 Exchange rate of the euro with sterling

Exchange rates and business

Reference has already been made to the fact that changes in exchange rates can affect businesses in several ways. These would include:

- making it easier or harder to export (as prices change);
- making it easier or harder for foreign competitors to penetrate the domestic market (again through the price effect);
- causing uncertainty in both trading and investment terms;
- adding to or reducing the cost of imported raw materials and component parts.

In addition, if a falling exchange rate causes inflationary pressures within the economy, this could add to a firm's production costs (e.g. through higher wage bills) and could encourage the government to introduce counter-inflationary policies, which might subsequently depress demand in the home market.

For businesses regularly involved in currency dealing and/or multinational activities, changing currency values can also bring other gains or losses. In the first quarter of 2014 Toyota's profits jumped 70 per cent (despite selling fewer cars), mainly due to gains made from changes in the exchange rate of the yen. Clearly the introduction of a single European currency will reduce such gains or losses, at least in the eurozone.

Synopsis

This chapter has looked at the international marketplace and, in particular, the benefits that derive from international trade. Consideration has also been given to some of the restrictions that exist to free trade and the organisations that are active in promoting it. Patterns of trade in the UK have been examined, as well as the history of the balance-of-payments position. Exchange rates were covered, including an analysis of how businesses are affected by changes in the value of currencies.

Summary of key points

- International trade takes place because it increases the output of the whole world.

- Despite this there are restrictions to international trade which include tariffs and quotas, but there are international organisations that seek to limit these and promote free trade.

- The balance of payments is a record of one country's trade with other countries.

- A balance-of-payments deficit is a situation where imports are greater than exports; a balance-of-payments surplus is the opposite, where exports are greater than imports.

- The exchange rate is the price of one currency in terms of another.

- A floating exchange rate is determined by the free market; a fixed exchange rate is determined by the government or some other authority.

- The euro is a single currency introduced into circulation in January 2002 by the members of the eurozone.

case study   Eurozone crisis

Crisis hit the eurozone after the collapse of Lehman Brothers in 2008 and the start of the credit crunch, as Figure 16.10 shows.

In 2009, all EU economies (except Poland) ran into difficulties; even Germany recorded negative growth in GDP. By 2010 there was some recovery in most EU countries, but not in Ireland, Greece or Spain. This continued through 2011 but changed again in 2012 when several EU countries exhibited negative growth, including France, Belgium and Italy. By 2013 things looked better, except in the case of Spain, Portugal, Italy and Greece. As these four countries were

members of the single European currency, this caused major problems for the eurozone – hence the term 'the eurozone crisis'.

At the beginning of 2013 many commentators saw the exit of Greece from the eurozone as inevitable and even the possibility of the failure of the single European currency was being contemplated. By the end of 2013 the situation looked very different. There had been no new bailouts in 2013 and Ireland exited its €85 billion EU–IMF bailout in December 2013. It looked as though the eurozone had weathered the storm.

Figure 16.10 Real GDP growth in the eurozone (% change)

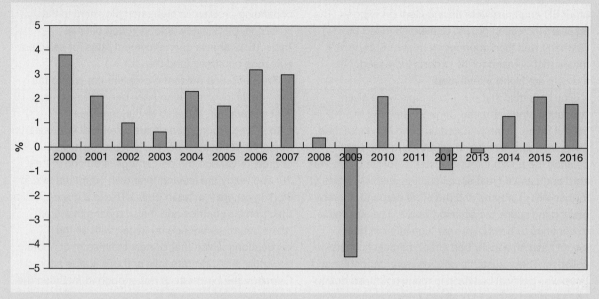

Source: Eurostat.

What caused the eurozone crisis? The main cause was indebtedness from the private as well as the public sector. Table 16.10 shows total public debt as a percentage of GDP for selected years between 2008 and 2015. Although the UK is not part of the eurozone, it is included for comparison.

Table 16.10 Government debt as a percentage of GDP, selected years

	2008	2010	2012	2015
France	81.5	96.8	110.4	120.3
Germany	68.1	84.5	87.0	78.0
Greece	117.5	127.1	164.5	181.6
Ireland	47.4	67.6	129.3	89.4
Italy	113.0	124.9	136.2	157.3
Portugal	82.8	104.1	137.1	149.2
Spain	47.2	66.6	92.5	116.8
UK	63.4	89.1	107.0	112.6

Source: Adapted from oecd.org

This table shows that as the credit crunch hit, the size of the government debt went up. There are two reasons for this: first, in times of economic downturn tax revenues will fall; and second, as unemployment rises, government spending in the form of benefits goes up. This makes it more difficult for governments to balance the books and hence there will be an increase in government borrowing. The government is not the only source of debt – private individuals and companies borrow to finance their expenditure, and Table 16.11 shows private debt as a percentage of GDP for the same countries in 2016.

Table 16.11 Private sector debt as a percentage of GDP, 2016

	2016
France	234.0
Germany	147.7
Greece	138.3
Ireland	406.7
Italy	172.6
Portugal	269.7
Spain	207.4
UK	219.7

Source: Adapted from oecd.org

From these tables it can be seen that private debt is more of a problem than public debt for most countries, and this problem remains even though growth rates in the EU are improving. This private borrowing was good for Germany as it meant that other EU countries were buying German exports. The resultant increased growth rate experienced by Germany was then good for the rest of Europe as it meant that demand for its exports increased. The markets are highly interrelated.

The countries that ran into trouble were given bailouts by the European Central Bank and the IMF, a bailout being a loan with certain conditions attached. These conditions required countries to attempt to balance the books through austerity policies. This was hard and carries great social cost as austerity leads to further falls in income and therefore demand, thereby making the economic situation worse. The alternative – to continue to borrow (at very high interest rates) – would have an equally bad effect, namely financial collapse. These austerity policies were unpopular and there was political backlash in many countries during 2011 and 2012. The EU called 17 crisis summits in the two years up to February 2012 in an attempt to save the euro. It seems that it was successful – no country left the eurozone in this period, and there were no bank failures and no new bailouts in 2013. Ireland had come out of its bailout at the end of 2013 and Portugal in mid-2014. Rather than the end of the eurozone, 2014 saw the extension of the eurozone as Latvia joined in January.

Is the eurozone crisis over? The immediate crisis seems to be over, but some national problems remain. Commentators have likened the situation to a life-threatening illness turning into a long-term chronic condition. The problem of indebtedness continues, particularly in the private sector, and is a double-edged sword as private borrowing feeds spending which feeds economic growth. Another continuing problem is high unemployment in the eurozone, particularly among young people. Table 16.12 shows unemployment rates for selected eurozone countries (and the UK).

These figures present a problem not just to the individuals involved, who have been labelled as a 'lost generation', but also to the countries themselves. Young people are often well educated (in Spain 40 per cent of people in their 20s have a degree; in Greece the percentage is 30 and in Italy 20) and many are leaving their own countries to find work in others – a 'brain drain'. This is a great loss for their home countries and it also means that their home countries are ageing faster, with all the implications which that brings. In times of economic downturn the birth rate falls and this is true now – in Germany the birth rate is not enough to maintain the population size.

It seems that although the immediate eurozone crisis has been averted, problems remain in Europe – by 2015 Greece had fallen to a CC credit rating, at the time of writing it has increased back to B– (towards the end of 2016 the UK lost its AAA rating as a consequence of Brexit). Banking union in the eurozone is seen as the way forward – to promote stability and to make bailouts a thing of the past. There are three pillars to banking union:

- single supervisory mechanism – a common banking supervisor who has the power to monitor banks in the EU and intervene if necessary (the European Central Bank);

Table 16.12 Unemployment rates in the eurozone, November 2016, 2017

	Unemployment as a % of workforce(2017)	Youth unemployment as a% of 16–24 age group (2016)
Eurozone	7.5	18.7
France	9.7	24.6
Germany	3.6	7.0
Greece	21.0	47.4
Ireland	6.1	17.2
Italy	11.1	37.8
Portugal	8.6	27.9
Spain	16.7	44.5
UK	4.2	13.0

Source: OECD, 2016; Eurostat, 2017.

- single resolution mechanism – with the power to help or close ailing banks, the funding to come from a levy on all eurozone banks;
- common deposit guarantee – all depositors will have their deposits guaranteed up to the value of €100,000.

Discussions continue on banking union.

Case study questions

1 How did the European Central Bank support the euro?

2 What are the implications of high youth unemployment for a country?

Review and discussion questions

1 For a business considering expansion into Europe, what methods of expansion are available?

2 Using demand and supply diagrams, show the effect on the market for foreign exchange of the following:

   (a) a decreased level of imports;
   (b) a fall in the rate of interest; and
   (c) the development of a balance-of-payments surplus.

3 What is the likely effect on a system of fixed exchange rates of continued speculation in one of the member currencies?

4 Explain why businesses generally prefer fixed rather than floating rates of exchange.

5 How might the US government help its cotton industry without resorting to trade sanctions?

Assignments

1 You work in a local chamber of commerce and have been asked to make a presentation to its members on the arguments for and against the UK leaving the EU. The audience is likely to be mixed in its attitude towards the EU. Prepare the presentation, anticipating and answering any possible questions the audience might have.

2 You work for a trade union in the hosiery industry, which strongly supports the use of import restrictions to protect its workers from competition from countries where wage rates are much lower. You have been asked to take part in a debate on the issue by the local Conservative MP, who is a champion of the free market. Present a set of arguments that will counter any points that your opponent is likely to make.

Further reading

Buckley, P., *International Business Strategy*, Routledge, 2015.

Daniels, J. D., *International Business: Environments and Operations*, 13th edition, Pearson Education, 2011.

Griffiths, A. and Wall, S., *Applied Economics*, 12th edition, Financial Times/Prentice Hall, 2011.

Worthington, I., Britton, C. and Rees, A., *Business Economics: Blending Theory and Practice*, 2nd edition, Financial Times/Prentice Hall, 2005.

web link

Web links and further questions are available on the website at:
www.pearsoned.co.uk/worthington

17 Governments and markets

Ian Worthington

The central role played by government in the operation of the economy and its markets has been a recurrent theme of this book. Paradoxically, many of the government's interventionist policies have been designed to remove existing barriers to the operations of free markets and to promote greater competition and choice. In some cases, the government's strategy has been to disengage the state from some of its involvement in the economy – as in the case of 'privatisation'. In other cases, policy changes and legislation have been deemed the appropriate course of action – as in the government's approach to competition policy and to the operation of the labour market.

Learning outcomes

Having read this chapter you should be able to:

- outline the rationale underlying the government's approach to markets
- analyse and evaluate UK privatisation policy and give examples of privatisation in other countries
- explain the changing nature of UK competition policy, including the legislative and institutional framework within which it operates
- identify government initiatives in the labour market and, in particular, its approach to employment and trade union power

Key terms

Competition Act 1998	Enterprise and Regulatory Reform Act 2013	New Deal
Competition and Markets Authority	Keynesianism	Office of Fair Trading
Competition Commission	Labour market	Privatisation
Competition policy	Labour market flexibility	Training and Enterprise Councils
Director General of Fair Trading	Learning and Skills Council	Work Programme
Economic efficiency	Monetarism	

Introduction

A belief in the virtue of competition and in the need to develop competitive markets remains a central tenet of government economic policy in capitalist states. At the heart of this belief lies the widely accepted view that competition provides the best means of improving **economic efficiency** and of encouraging wealth creation. Proponents of this view argue that competition:

- ensures an efficient allocation of resources between competing uses, through the operation of the price system;
- puts pressure on firms to perform as efficiently as possible;
- provides a mechanism for flexible adjustment to change, whether in consumption or in the conditions of supply;
- protects consumers from potential exploitation by producers, by offering alternative sources of purchase.

It follows that an absence or lack of competition in either the factor or product markets is seen as detrimental to the well-being of the economy as a whole and that governments have a responsibility for ensuring wherever possible that markets operate freely, with a minimum of state interference.

Much of the philosophical basis for this perspective can be traced to **monetarism**, where the monetarists tended to dominate official thinking in the UK and elsewhere for much of the last two decades of the twentieth century. Broadly speaking, monetarists argue that levels of output and employment in the economy are supply determined, in contrast to the view of **Keynesianism** which emphasises the importance of demand in shaping economic activity. Accordingly, supply-side policies seek to improve the output responsiveness of the economy, by focusing on the workings of markets and in particular on removing the obstacles that prevent markets from functioning efficiently.

The influence of the supply-side approach to economic management can be seen in a number of key areas, and in particular in the UK government's policy of privatisation and in the reforms in the labour market in the 1980s. Concerns over competition and potential abuses of market power also figure prominently in governmental approaches to monopolies and mergers. These three aspects of government intervention in markets – privatisation, competition policy and labour market reforms – are considered separately below and illustrate how state involvement can be a key influence in the environment of individual business organisations on both the input and the output side.

Privatisation policy in the UK

On privatisation

In its broadest sense, **privatisation** involves the transfer of assets or different forms of economic activity from the public sector to the private sector. In the UK such transfers began to occur after the election of a Conservative government in 1979 and gathered pace through much of the next two decades with the sale of major state-owned assets, including the public utilities (see below). Private sector involvement in activities that were normally the preserve of government also occurred through the introduction of the Private Finance Initiative (PFI), which has been used to fund the building of hospitals, schools and roads. In 2013 the UK coalition government sold off the majority of Royal Mail to private investors and in 2015 it divested the final 13 per cent of the company. The Coalition also sold the betting agency Tote (in 2011) and divested itself of Northern Rock (2012).

The term 'privatisation' has been applied to a range of activities that involves a measure of state disengagement from economic activity. As the above discussion illustrates, typically these have included:

- the sale of government-owned assets, especially nationalised industries (e.g. British Telecom, British Gas) or industries in which the government had a substantial share-holding (e.g. BP);
- the contracting out of services normally provided by the public sector (e.g. school meals, hospital cleaning);
- the deregulation or liberalisation of activities over which the state had previously placed some restriction (e.g. the deregulation of bus routes or postal services);
- the injection of private capital into areas traditionally financed by the public sector, including various Private Financing Initiatives;
- the sale of local-authority-owned property to private citizens or organisations (e.g. council houses, school playing fields);
- the privatisation of government agencies (e.g. Her Majesty's Inspectors for Education).

Of these, the sale of state assets – especially the public corporations and nationalised industries – has been the main plank of UK privatisation policy and the one that has captured the most public and media attention. For this reason, we focus on this aspect of the privatisation programme.

The scope of government asset sales in its heyday period between 1979 and 1996 is indicated in Table 17.1. In the first phase, between 1979 and 1983, these tended to generate relatively small sums of money compared with what was realised in later years and generally involved the sale of government shares in companies such as British Aerospace, Britoil, BP, ICL and Ferranti. Between 1983 and 1988, the government disposed of a number of its largest industrial and commercial undertakings, including British Telecom, British Gas and British Airways, along with Rolls-Royce and Jaguar.

Table 17.1 Major asset sales, 1979–1996

Amersham International	British Telecom	National Grid
Associated British Ports	Britoil	Railtrack
British Aerospace	Cable & Wireless	Rolls-Royce
British Airports Authority	Electricity industry	Rover Group
British Airways	Enterprise Oil	Royal Ordnance
British Coal	Fairey Aviation	Sealink (British Rail)
British Energy	Ferranti	Short Brothers
British Gas	Forestry Commission	Unipart (Rover)
British Petroleum	Istel (Rover)	Water authorities
British Rail Hotels	Jaguar (British Leyland)	Wytch Farm onshore oil (British Gas)
British Steel	National Bus Company	
British Sugar Corporation	National Enterprise Board Holding	

These were followed by the sale of British Steel, the Rover Group, the National Bus Company and, more significantly, by the regional water authorities and the electricity industry in the late 1980s and early 1990s. Subsequent sell-offs included British Coal, Railtrack, the flotation of the National Grid, the privatisation of the nuclear industry and the National Air Traffic Services (NATS). It is worth noting that Railtrack, having gone through a period of administration, has subsequently been turned into a not-for-profit organisation called Network Rail.

In disposing of national assets governments have used a number of different methods, including selling shares to a single buyer, usually another company (e.g. the sale of Rover), selling shares to the company's management and workers (e.g. the management buyout of the National Freight Corporation), and selling shares on the open market for purchase by individuals and institutions (e.g. the stock market flotation of British Telecom). In some cases the process took place in several stages, as a proportion of shares was released on to the market over several years (e.g. BP); in other cases a one-off sale occurred, with investors invited to subscribe for the whole of the equity (e.g. British Steel). As the recent sale of Royal Mail has demonstrated, fixing a price at which to dispose of state assets is often controversial, with critics arguing that those advising the government on the privatisation process (i.e. the investment banks) may have set the recommended price too low and hence may have cost the taxpayer billions of pounds in lost revenues. Similar criticisms have also been aimed at other asset sales in the past (particularly the major utilities) and at many of the PFIs where taxpayer liabilities are spread over several decades and can be very substantial indeed.

Somewhat paradoxically, the onset of the global financial crisis has forced some governments to intervene to protect their financial institutions. Frequently this has meant the nationalisation or part-nationalisation of those bodies, including banks such as the Royal Bank of Scotland (RBS). While this suggests a reversal of the privatisation process, in reality it should be seen as a particular response aimed at addressing a specific problem, not a general trend. All the evidence from across Europe and beyond indicates that the disposal of state assets is seen by policy-makers as a key weapon in addressing the problem of burgeoning public sector deficits and in bringing about a phased restructuring of national economies.

Rationale

The roots of UK privatisation policy lie in the attempt by the Conservative government, then under the leadership of Margaret Thatcher (1979–90), to tackle the perceived deficiencies in the supply side of the UK economy. Central to the government's philosophy was the belief that the free market was a superior method of allocating economic resources and that large-scale state involvement in business activity hampered economic progress. 'Rolling back the frontiers of the state' – by reducing the size of the public sector – was consequently seen as a key component in improving the country's economic performance at both national and international level.

The government's case for privatisation centred on the claim that the sale of state-owned businesses would improve their efficiency and general performance, and would give rise to increased competition that would broaden consumer choice. Under state control, it was argued that businesses had no incentive to strive for efficiency or to respond to consumer preferences, since many of them lacked any direct competition and all of them could turn to the government for financial support, if revenue was insufficient to meet operating costs. In contrast, firms that were exposed to the 'test' of the market would have to satisfy both the consumer and the financial markets if they were to survive or to avoid takeover by more efficient and competitive organisations.

Allied to this argument was the proposition that privatisation would improve the performance of an organisation's management and workers. Freed from the need to meet objectives laid down by government, management could concentrate on commercial goals such as profitability, improved productivity and cost reduction, and on encouraging greater flexibility and technical innovation within the organisation. Implicit in these claims was the acceptance that a considerable degree of restructuring would need to occur within each privatised company and that this was likely to act as an incentive to the workforce to improve its performance. Additional encouragement was expected to derive from the use of employee share-ownership schemes, under which current employees within a newly privatised company were offered a proportion of the equity, thus giving them a vested interest in the organisation's fortunes.

The sale of shares to employees and to the public generally was also presented as a benefit of privatisation in that it helped to encourage wider share ownership and to create a 'share-owning democracy', with increased sympathies towards capitalist modes of production (and possibly the Conservative Party). Selling state assets also served to reduce the size of the public sector borrowing requirement (PSBR) – since revenue from sales was counted as negative public expenditure – thereby helping to reduce the government's debt burden and taking some of the pressure off interest rates, as well as releasing funds for use by the private sector.

Criticisms of privatisation

Opponents of privatisation have likened the process to 'selling the family silver' – disposing of important national assets for short-term financial gains. Under privatisation, these assets, once owned by the general public, have passed into the hands of those individuals and organisations able and willing to buy shares, including overseas buyers who could ultimately gain control of important parts of British industry, unless prevented from doing so by government action (e.g. through a 'golden share'). To add to this criticism, some observers claimed that valuable assets, bought over many years by public funds, were sold off too cheaply to private investors who have reaped the benefit at the expense of the general public. Only industries that were not attractive to the stock market have tended to remain in public ownership and this has meant that the taxpayer has had to pay the bill to support their continued existence.

Further criticisms have included the loss of future government revenue from the sale of profitable state-owned businesses and the problem of ensuring that commercial goals are not allowed to displace completely the broader economic goals once pursued by nationalised industries (e.g. the possible closure of unprofitable rural telephone boxes or railway lines under privatisation). The fear has been that once freed from government regulation, privatised companies will tend to replace the loss-making 'public service' element of their former activities with products or services that offer the greatest levels of profit. While this will benefit some consumers, the cost is likely to be borne by other buyers who have limited market power and, in some cases, no alternative product to turn to.

This problem of lack of choice has been particularly acute where the privatisation of a state monopoly has given rise to a private monopoly, as initially was the case with many of the privatised utilities. Despite the establishment of 'regulators' to oversee the operations of some of the newly privatised concerns (see Table 17.2) and to act as a kind of proxy for true competition, some opponents still feel that the interests of consumers are not fully protected under the current arrangements. They also feel that exploitation through higher prices or other abuses of market power remains possible, a point underlined by the recent controversy over rising energy prices in the UK. Evidence from investigations by the former Monopolies and Mergers Commission (see below) and from the regulatory authorities suggests that this view is not without foundation. This evidence has also conveniently been used by the Treasury in recent years as a justification for levying windfall taxes on the profits of the privatised utilities as a means of boosting Exchequer revenues.

Table 17.2 Key regulatory bodies for selected privatised utilities

Name	Date established	Main activities
Office of Tele-communications (Oftel)	1984	Regulated BT – especially line rentals, inland calls, overseas calls; provided conditions for new entrants and regulated the equipment market. Its duties have now passed to Ofcom (see below)
Office of Water Services (Ofwat)	1989	Regulates domestic and non-domestic supply by water and sewerage companies. Regulates price increases to customers and monitors service quality and company performance
Office of Gas and Electricity Markets (Ofgem)	2000	Regulates the gas and electricity industries in England, Scotland and Wales with the aim of promoting energy security and enhancing customer choice and value via competition and controlling monopolies. Replaced Ofgas and Offer
Office of Communications (Ofcom)	2003	The regulatory and competition authority for the UK communications industries with responsibilities for television, radio, telecommunications and wireless communications services. In 2011 acquired responsibility for postal services from Postcomm

web link

Regulatory body websites include *www.ofcom.org.uk*, *www.ofwat.gov.uk*, *www.ofgem.gov.uk*

Privatisation overseas

Before offering an assessment of privatisation in the UK, it is worth remembering that most other states have embarked on similar experiments in economic liberalisation, irrespective of their size, ideology or level of economic development. At the end of the 1980s it was estimated that worldwide sales of state assets to the private sector exceeded $25 billion or about £14,000 million, and this figure has continued to grow with the ongoing privatisation process in Eastern Europe and elsewhere. According to *The Economist* (23 November 1996), in the period 1985–95 the combined revenues from privatisation in France, Germany, Italy, the Netherlands and Spain alone were in excess of $70 billion, with France having the lion's share of $34 billion. For the same period the

UK's receipts were estimated at $85 billion, making it the most significant privatisation programme within the OECD.

The following examples of overseas privatisation give some idea of the wide range of state assets from different sectors of the economy that have been sold by governments of different political complexions over the last two to three decades:

- In Portugal major privatisations between 1989 and 1997 included banks, insurance companies, public utilities and businesses producing cement, oil, paper products, tobacco and beer. In recent years the Portuguese government has come under pressure from EU leaders to embark on a further programme of state sell-offs as a condition of receiving financial assistance in the wake of the global financial crisis, with organisations involved including an airports owner (ANA), an energy supplier (Energias de Portugal) and the electricity grid operator (REN).
- The third EU bailout of Greece in 2015 was dependent on Greece selling off many state assets such as marinas and airports – totalling $50bn over the life of the repayment of the loans. Some German law makers originally proposed that as a part of the conditions of the loan, Greece would have to sell off some of its islands to private owners and ancient archaeological sites, though these measures never came to pass.
- In the Netherlands privatisations have included the national airline (KLM) and the water, gas and electricity utilities. Interestingly, in October 2013 the government halted its privatisation programme and cancelled plans for the partial sale of two state-owned energy companies.
- In Brazil parts of the country's rail, road and port networks have been sold off and two airports were privatised in November 2013 as the country prepared for hosting the World Cup in 2014; in Jamaica privatisation has included the National Commercial Bank and the Caribbean Cement Company.
- In France privatisations have ranged from chemicals and oil to insurance, banking, public utilities, vehicles and parts of the motorway network; in some cases the state has, however, retained a share of privatised businesses.
- In India the government has divested a significant proportion of public sector enterprises with sales including businesses involved with steel, zinc and petrochemicals; some airports have also been sold.
- In China the government has proceeded cautiously with privatisation, starting with the sale of the smaller state-owned enterprises to private owners and more recently the partial privatisation of some larger listed companies. Further privatisation has recently been mooted as a possible way of funding future growth.

Arguably the most dramatic and exciting experiments in privatisation have taken place in Eastern Europe, particularly among the so-called transition economies, which have moved from a planned economic system towards private enterprise. Following German reunification, for instance, the federal government appointed a special privatisation agency (Treuhand) to oversee and assist in the large-scale privatisation of former East German state industries and firms, and other governments (including those in Hungary, the Czech Republic and Poland) have embarked on similar programmes of rolling privatisation and have undertaken legal and institutional changes to speed up the process. While progress has varied in the different states and has generally been influenced by questions of economic and political stability (e.g. in the Russian Federation), the large-scale sell-off of public assets by the former communist states has continued to gather pace. Current evidence suggests that the transition in these countries has proved to be a more painful experience

mini case   Government to the rescue

While privatisation has gripped the imaginations of governments of all persuasions for the last two to three decades, there often comes a time in economic history when circumstances dictate that a particular economic orthodoxy has to be temporarily (if not permanently) abandoned. Arguably one of the best examples of this was the decision by the US government to take the two American mortgage giants Fanny Mae and Freddie Mac into temporary public ownership.

At the time the two companies concerned accounted for about 50 per cent of all US home loans and had played an active role in buying up mortgages from lenders, parcelling them up and then selling them on to financial institutions across the globe. With the onset of the credit crisis in 2007–8, Fanny Mae and Freddie Mac were faced with multi-billion-dollar losses as homeowners defaulted and house prices tumbled. While the two US institutions were far from being the only businesses facing severe financial problems, their importance to the US housing market meant that their precarious position

threatened not just the property market in the United States but also the wider global financial system (see e.g. 'International business in action: The global financial crisis' in the previous edition of this book).

In an effort to reassure the financial markets, the US government decided that the two government-sponsored enterprises should become government-owned businesses on a temporary basis – what in the United States is known as 'conservatorship' – and run by the Federal Housing Finance Agency and underwritten by public money. In the event this seems to have proved a good decision. With the gradual recovery in the US economy and housing market and with gains from tax changes and legal settlement, the two firms had managed to repay (to the US Treasury) most of the cost of the bailout by late 2013. The US government's interests in the two banks were planned to be sold off to private owners once the firms became profitable again. To this day the government still holds its bailout interest in the banks – now making a good return on the dividends from its shares.

than that encountered in states already possessing a market-based economic system (see e.g. the article by Nick Potts in the Further reading section at the end of the chapter).

Assessment

Measured against some of the UK government's stated objectives, privatisation appears to have been successful, and has involved a transfer of ownership of a significant percentage of GDP from the public to the private sector. Apart from the fact that many other national governments have sought to emulate the UK's approach to asset sales, the privatisation programme has been cited as an important component of the improvement in the supply side of the economy after 1979. It has also been a critical element in promoting the free-market approach, which has come to dominate governmental thinking in the UK and elsewhere for over three decades. All of this has evidently been achieved with the support of the British public (although some opinion polls have indicated a decline in the popularity of privatisation). In 1979, for instance, only 7 per cent of adults owned shares in public companies. By the early 1990s this figure had risen to 25 per cent, or 11 million shareholders, many of whom had bought shares for the first time in the 1980s with the sale of the big public utilities.

This significant growth in the number of ordinary shareholders can be explained in a number of ways. For a start, most stock market flotations were accompanied by extensive and costly advertising campaigns which helped to raise public awareness and to attract investors (e.g. British Gas's 'Tell Sid' campaign). Added to this, investors in public utilities were often offered special incentives to buy shares in businesses they dealt with on a regular basis (e.g. cheaper telephone bills) or in which some of them worked and therefore had a vested interest. Perhaps most importantly, and with the benefit of hindsight, some privatisation stock was manifestly sold at substantially lower prices than the market would bear, thus guaranteeing quick profits for people who bought and then sold immediately as prices rose. In the circumstances it is not surprising that many flotations were hugely oversubscribed – a fact which led to claims that some privatisation stock (including Royal Mail) had been considerably undervalued. Lloyds sale halted.

Many shareholders who invested for longer-term capital gains also benefited from underpricing of share issues and in some cases received free additional shares and other benefits (including annual dividends) by holding onto their investment. An analysis by Gary Cook (1992) of the share performance of privatised companies shows that some of the earlier privatisations have produced spectacular long-term gains, though some privatised company shares performed less well. Cable & Wireless shares, for example, were issued at an average price of 56p in the early 1980s and were trading at 588p by August 1991. Similarly, BT's initial issue price of 130p in 1984–5 had risen to 391p by the same date, a three-fold increase despite the stock market crash in 1987. The flotation of Royal Mail may very well show similar results over the next decade if the initial market response is anything to go by.

Whatever the reason for the growth in share ownership, it is clear that privatisation, along with the sale of council houses, helped the Conservative government of the day to claim that it encouraged the growth of a 'property-owning democracy' in which an increasing number of citizens held a stake in the success of the economy and therefore in the performance of the private sector. That said, it is still the case that the majority of shares in public companies are held by individuals in better-paid professional and managerial occupations and that overall the percentage of *all* UK shares owned by individuals has fallen dramatically over the last three to four decades. In contrast, the holdings of institutional investors (such as hedge funds, insurance companies and pension funds) and overseas buyers (e.g. Chinese government agencies) have risen rapidly – a fact that not only gives them significant influence over the future of many public companies, but also suggests that the claim of wider share ownership has to be treated with a degree of caution.

Notwithstanding this latter point, the government's relative success in selling state assets also helped it initially to achieve another one of its objectives – that of reducing the size of the public deficit. From the early 1980s onwards, public expenditure as a percentage of GDP fell substantially – partly as a result of the revenues from the privatisation programme – and by the latter part of the decade the government had a budget surplus (or public sector debt repayment) as revenue exceeded spending. Once again, however, this apparent benefit needs to be seen in context. For a start, much of the improvement in public finances during this period was a result of the government's restraint on public spending, rather than the effects of privatisation, though the receipts clearly helped the government to balance its books. Added to this, by the early 1990s, as the recession took hold, public spending rapidly began to outstrip the amounts raised in revenue, causing a dramatic growth in the size of government borrowing, despite a decade of privatisation receipts. Understandably, some critics have asked whether the sale of valuable state assets was in vain and distracted the incumbent government from addressing some of the underlying structural weaknesses in the British economy.

With regard to privatisation as a spur to greater organisational efficiency and performance, this is an area in which assessment is particularly problematical. Part of the difficulty arises from the fact that direct comparisons between state and privatised companies are often impossible, since some goods and services have not normally been provided by both the public and private sectors simultaneously (e.g. railways). Even where such provision occurs (e.g. the health service), the public sector usually has to pursue a number of non-commercial objectives laid down by politicians and this makes direct comparisons somewhat unfair, particularly if profitability alone is taken as a measure of performance.

One way of approaching some of these problems is to attempt a comparison between the performance of an organisation before privatisation and its performance after it has become part of the private sector – using measures such as relative profitability, productivity or levels of service. Yet, once again, significant methodological difficulties exist which call into question the validity of many of the conclusions. Industries such as British Gas and British Telecom have always been profitable and profits have tended to grow since privatisation, but this could as easily reflect the benefits of monopoly price rises as improvements in efficiency resulting from a change in ownership. Conversely, the decline in the fortunes of the once publicly owned steel industry could be interpreted as a decline in efficiency and/or performance under privatisation, when in fact a combination of overcapacity in the world steel industry and the impact of the recession have clearly been the main culprits.

Comparisons of productivity can also be misleading and usually fail to take into account the substantial 'economic' costs of privatisation (e.g. large-scale redundancies). Many state industries were substantially restructured prior to flotation in order to attract investors, and the resulting job losses – invariably at the taxpayer's expense – helped many newly privatised businesses to claim substantial productivity gains in their first few years of trading. Perhaps ironically, the greatest improvements in productivity in the period 1984–91 often occurred within industries nationalised at the time – such as British Coal and British Rail – whose massive redundancy programmes helped them to outpace the productivity gains of manufacturing industry by anything up to three times, according to Treasury figures. In such circumstances, it would be easy – though probably unreasonable – to conclude that while being privatised was good for productivity, it was not as good as not being privatised!

Further complications arise when one compares the performance of privatised companies which have remained monopolies with the performance of those which have consistently operated under competitive market conditions. Writing during the heyday of privatisation (*The Guardian,* 3 March 1993), Victor Keegan argued that the fortunes of companies such as British Steel, Rolls-Royce and Rover had been seriously affected by the sort of violent cyclical disturbances which had previously driven them into the public sector and that this had significantly influenced their attractiveness to private investors. In comparison, businesses that had faced little effective competition in some areas of the market (e.g. Cable & Wireless, British Airways) and those facing none (e.g. the water companies, British Gas) had invariably performed well for their shareholders, though the price of this success had frequently been paid by customers (in the form of inflated charges) and workers (in the form of redundancy).

Keegan's conclusion, that it is competition rather than ownership which acts as a spur to increased efficiency, is one that is widely held and underlies some of the recent attempts by government and by the regulatory bodies to identify ways of reducing the monopoly power of the privatised public utilities. The proposition is that under a more competitive market structure the commercial pressures of the marketplace force management to seek ways of improving organisational efficiency and performance, for fear of the consequences if management fails to meet the needs of the consumer and the investor. If left to their own devices, the large utilities are unlikely to put themselves to such 'tests' voluntarily, and this approach would presumably find favour with shareholders who have a vested interest in maximising revenue. Paradoxically, in order to improve the position of the consumer, the government may be forced to intervene more aggressively and imaginatively in the marketplace to promote greater competition among producers and increased choice for the consumer. Such intervention could easily be justified under current competition policy.

Competition policy

Whereas privatisation has focused on the balance between public and private provision within the overall economy, UK government **competition policy** has largely been concerned with regulating market behaviour and in particular with controlling potential abuses of market power by firms acting singly or in concert in specific markets. To achieve these aims, successive British governments have relied mainly on legislation, as well as on a measure of self-regulation and persuasion, and have generally taken a more liberal view of market structures than that taken in the United States, where monopolies have been deemed illegal for over a century. This legislative framework to regulate market activity, and the institutional arrangements established to support it, are considered below.

> **web link**
>
> There are lots of useful websites relating to UK competition policy. A good starting point is the archive for the Office of Fair Trading (OFT): see *www.oft.gov.uk*. You could also try the archives of the Competition Commission at *www.competition-commission. org.uk*, and the Competition and Markets Authority (CMA) at *www.gov.uk/government/ organisations/competition-and-markets-authority*

The evolving legislative framework

Official attempts to control market behaviour through statutory means date back to the late 1940s with the passage of the Monopolies and Restrictive Practices Act 1948. This Act, which established the Monopolies Commission (later the Monopolies and Mergers Commission), empowered it to investigate industries in which any single firm (a unitary monopoly), or a group of firms acting together, could restrict competition by controlling at least one-third of the market. Following such an investigation, the Commission would publish a report which was either factual or advisory and it was then the responsibility of the relevant government department to decide what course of action, if any, to take to remove practices regarded as contrary to the public interest. In the event, the majority of the Commission's recommendations tended to be ignored, though it did have some success in highlighting the extent of monopoly power in the UK in the early post-war period.

In 1956 investigations into unitary monopolies were separated from those into restrictive practices operated by a group of firms, with the enactment of the Restrictive Trade Practices Act. This Act, which outlawed the widespread custom of manufacturers jointly enforcing the retail prices at which their products could be sold, also required firms to register any form of restrictive agreement that they were operating (e.g. concerning prices, sales, production) with the Registrar of Restrictive Practices. It was the latter's responsibility to bring such agreements before the Restrictive Practices Court and they were automatically deemed 'against the public interest', unless they could be justified in one of a number of ways (e.g. benefiting consumers, employment, exports). Further extensions to the Act in 1968 (to cover 'information agreements') and in 1973 (to cover services) were ultimately consolidated in the Restrictive Trade Practices Act 1976. This new Act vested the responsibility for bringing restrictive practices before the court in the recently established Director General of Fair Trading (see below).

A further extension of legislative control came with the passage of the Monopolies and Mergers Act 1965. The Act allowed the Monopolies Commission to investigate actual or proposed mergers or acquisitions which looked likely to enhance monopoly power and which involved, at that time, the takeover of assets in excess of £5 million. The aim of this Act was to provide a means of regulating activities which threatened to be contrary to the public interest, by permitting the government to decide which mergers and acquisitions should be prohibited and which should be allowed to proceed and, if necessary, under what terms. Additional steps in this direction were taken with the passage of the Fair Trading Act 1973 and the Competition Act 1980, the main provisions of which are summarised below:

1   A scale monopoly exists where at least 25 per cent of a market is controlled by a single buyer or seller; this can be applied to sales at local as well as national level and can include monopolies resulting from nationalisation.
2   Investigations can occur when two related companies (e.g. a parent and a subsidiary) control 25 per cent of a market or when separate companies operate to restrict competition even without a formal agreement (e.g. tacit collusion).
3   Mergers involving gross worldwide assets of more than £70 million or a market share of over 25 per cent can be investigated.
4   Responsibility for overseeing consumer affairs, and competition policy generally, lies with the **Director General of Fair Trading** (DGFT), operating from the Office of Fair Trading. The DGFT has the power to make monopoly references to the renamed Monopolies and Mergers Commission (MMC) and to advise the relevant government minister on whether merger proposals should be investigated by the MMC.

In the latter context, it is worth observing that while there was no legal obligation on companies to inform the OFT of their merger plans, the Companies Act 1989 introduced a formal procedure enabling them to pre-notify the DGFT of merger proposals, in the expectation that such pre-notification would enhance the prospects for rapid clearance in cases which were deemed straightforward.

While the question of market share remains an important influence on official attitudes to proposed mergers or takeovers, there is no doubt that in recent years increasing attention has focused on anti-competitive practices and under the Competition Act 1980 such practices by individuals or firms – as opposed to whole markets – could be referred to the MMC for investigation. In addition, the Act allowed the Commission to scrutinise the work of certain public sector agencies and to consider the efficiency and costs of the service they provided and any possible abuses of monopoly power, and similar references could also be made in the case of public utilities which had been privatised (e.g. under the Telecommunication Act 1984, the Gas Act 1986, the Water Industry Act 1991).

Additional statutory control has also come in the form of EU legislation governing activities which have cross-border implications. Article 81 (formerly Article 85) of the

Treaty of Rome prohibited agreements between enterprises which result in a restriction or distortion in competition within the EU (e.g. price fixing, market sharing). Article 82 (formerly Article 86) prohibited a dominant firm, or group of firms, from using their market power to exploit consumers, while further Articles prohibited the provision of government subsidies if they distorted, or threatened to distort, competition between industries or individual firms. Following the implementation of the Lisbon Treaty in December 2009, Articles 81 and 82 were renumbered Articles 101 and 102 respectively under the Treaty on the Functioning of the European Union, or TFEU.

Moreover, under Regulation 4064/89, which came into force in September 1990, concentrations or mergers that had a 'Community dimension' became the subject of exclusive jurisdiction by the European Commission. Broadly speaking, this meant that mergers involving firms with a combined worldwide turnover of more than €5 billion became subject to Commission control, provided that the EU turnover of each of at least two companies involved exceeded €250 million and the companies concerned did not have more than two-thirds of their EU turnover within one and the same member state. Mergers that did not qualify under the regulation remained, of course, subject to national competition law. Merger regulation 4064/89 has since been replaced by ECMR 139/2004, which gives the Commission the right to intervene where a merger would 'significantly impede effective competition' in the market or a substantial part of it, particularly as a result of the creation or strengthening of a dominant position.

At national level, too, the competition law regime has continued to evolve down to the present day. Under the **Competition Act 1998** – which came into force on 1 March 2000 – two basic prohibitions were introduced:

1 A prohibition on anti-competitive agreements, based closely on Article 85 of the Treaty of Rome (subsequently Article 81).
2 A prohibition of abuse of dominant position in a market, based on Article 86 (subsequently Article 82).

These prohibitions, which replaced a number of other pieces of legislation (e.g. the Restrictive Trade Practices Act 1976; the Resale Prices Act 1976; the majority of the Competition Act 1980), were designed to be enforced primarily by the DGFT, together with the utility regulators, which were given concurrent powers in their own sphere of operations. Companies breaching either or both of the prohibitions would be liable to fines and could be required to pay compensation to third parties affected by their anti-competitive behaviour.

mini case   Accusations of price fixing

Governments in market-based economies normally argue that markets work best when there is competition between businesses and that this benefits consumers in a variety of ways, including increased choice and more competitive prices. For a market to work effectively and in the interests of consumers, firms involved in the supply side of the market (e.g. producers and retailers) need to work independently and should not collude or share information with their rivals in any way that could distort competition. Cartels, price fixing and other anti-competitive practices are usually outlawed by governments, but this does not guarantee that such practices do not exist in some markets.

To illustrate the 'problem' of anti-competitive behaviour, we can highlight a number of cases in the UK and elsewhere where there have been allegations of 'price fixing' by suppliers/retailers. Of course, not all allegations are subsequently upheld.

- Major supermarkets were accused of price fixing of dairy products and were fined more than £100 million after admitting they acted together on the pricing of milk, butter and cheese. British Airways and Virgin Atlantic admitted colluding to fix fuel surcharges for passengers on the transatlantic route and large fines were imposed.
- In 2008, the OFT accused the tobacco groups Imperial and Gallagher of collaborating with some major retailers (including major supermarkets) on the prices of cigarettes and rolling tobacco.
- The OFT has also investigated more than 100 British construction companies that were alleged to have fixed bids when tendering for major contracts such as schools, hospitals and private sector developments.

- In May 2013 the London offices of oil giants BP and Shell were raided by European regulators after allegations that they had colluded to rig oil prices for over a decade.
- US courts ruled (in July 2013) that Apple had conspired with book publishers to raise e-book prices in violation of US antitrust laws.

A central feature of all these cases is the claim that the alleged collaboration between the companies involved worked to the disadvantage of consumers (whether individuals, other businesses or public sector bodies such as local authorities). In short, price fixing – whatever form it takes – tends to make products/services more expensive than they would be under truly competitive market conditions. Under UK law, firms that are found to engage in such practices can be fined up to 10 per cent of their UK turnover, although this rarely happens, particularly as some of the accused tend to admit a degree of liability in exchange for a reduced fine. Similar arrangements exist in other countries.

With the passage of the Enterprise Act in 2002, further significant changes were introduced, including the addition of strong deterrents for individuals involved in breaches of competition law, the modernisation of the monopoly and merger rules, and the restructuring and extension of the powers of the competition authorities (see below). Whereas the Fair Trading Act emphasised the notion of the 'public interest' in examining anti-competitive practices, the new legislation applies the test of a 'substantial lessening of competition' when the competition authorities are called upon to assess an existing or planned merger. To be deemed a 'relevant merger situation', one of two thresholds has to be met: the value of UK turnover of the enterprise acquired/to be acquired exceeds £70 million (the turnover test); or the share of goods/services in the UK or a large part of the UK that is/will be held by the merged enterprise is at least 25 per cent (the share of supply test).

In a further development in 2004, the European Commission adopted a regulation that gave the national competition authorities and courts additional responsibilities for the application of what was at the time Articles 81 and 82 (see above). In essence, the OFT and the sectoral regulators were vested with the power to enforce EC competition rules and, as a consequence, the Competition Act 1998 was amended to bring it in line with the new European system. This growing harmonisation of EU law has been a dominant theme in this area of legislative control in recent decades, though it is unclear as to how closely tied UK and EU markets will remain following the outcome of the referendum on the UK's membership of the EU in 2016.

The institutional framework

The formulation and implementation of UK competition policy has traditionally involved a variety of agencies, including the former Department of Trade and Industry (DTI), the **Office of Fair Trading** (OFT), the Monopolies and Mergers Commission (MMC) and the Mergers Panel. Of these, the MMC (subsequently the Competition Commission) and the OFT deserve special attention.

From its foundation in 1948 until its replacement in 1999, the MMC remained a statutory body, independent of government both in the conduct of its inquiries and in its conclusions, which were published in report form. Funded by the DTI, the MMC had a full-time chairperson and around 35 other part-time members, three of whom were deputy chairpersons and all of whom were appointed by the Secretary of State for Trade and Industry. Such appointments normally lasted for three years at the outset and included individuals drawn from business, the professions, the trade unions and the universities. To support the work of the appointed members, the MMC had a staff of about 80 officials, two-thirds of whom it employed directly, with the remainder being on loan from government departments (especially the DTI) and increasingly from the private sector.

It is important to note that the MMC had no legal power to initiate its own investigations; instead, references – requests for it to carry out particular inquiries – came either from the Secretary of State for Trade and Industry or from the Director General of Fair Trading, or from the appropriate regulator in the case of privatised industries and the broadcasting media. Where a possible merger reference was concerned, the initial evaluation of a proposal was made by a panel of civil servants (the Mergers Panel) who considered whether the merger should be referred to the MMC for further consideration. The decision then rested with the Secretary of State, who took advice from the DGFT before deciding whether the proposal should be investigated or should be allowed to proceed.

Under the legislation, references to the MMC could be made on a number of grounds; these included not only monopoly and merger references, but also references concerned with the performance of public sector bodies and privatised industries and with anti-competitive practices by individual firms (i.e. competition references). In addition, the MMC was empowered to consider general references (involving practices in industry), restrictive labour practices and references under the Broadcasting Act 1990, as well as questions of proposed newspaper mergers, where special provisions apply.

On receipt of a reference, the MMC's chairperson appointed a small group of members to carry out the relevant inquiry and to report on whether the company (or companies) concerned was operating – or could be expected to operate – against the public interest. Supported by a team of officials, and in some cases including members appointed to specialist panels (e.g. newspaper, telecommunications, water and electricity), the investigating group gathered a wide range of written and oral evidence from both the party (parties) concerned and from others likely to have an interest in the outcome of the inquiry. In reaching its conclusions, which tended to take several months or more, the group had to take into account the 'public interest', as defined under section 84 of the Fair Trading Act 1973, which stressed the importance of competition, the protection of consumer interests and the need to consider issues related to employment, trade and the overall industrial structure. While in most references, issues relating to competition were the primary concern, the MMC was able to take wider public interest issues into account and could rule in favour of a proposal on these grounds, even if the measure appeared anti-competitive.

The culmination of the MMC's inquiry was its report which, in most cases, was submitted to the Secretary of State for consideration and was normally laid before Parliament, where it often formed the basis of a debate or parliamentary questions.

In the case of monopoly references judged to be against the public interest, the Secretary of State – with the advice of the DGFT – decided on an appropriate course of action, which could involve an order to prevent or remedy the particular adverse effects identified by the MMC. In the case of merger references, a similar procedure occurred in the event of an adverse judgment by the MMC. The Secretary of State, however, was not bound to accept the MMC's recommendations, nor was he or she able to overrule the conclusion that a merger does not operate, or may be expected not to operate, against the public interest.

At all stages of this multi-stage process, a considerable degree of lobbying occurred by the various interested parties, in an attempt to influence either the outcome of the investigations or the subsequent course of action decided upon. Moreover, considerable pressure tended to occur, even before a decision was taken as to whether or not to make a reference to the MMC. As a number of actual cases have shown, lobbying *against* a reference can represent a key step in justifying a proposed merger. By the same token, lobbying *for* a reference has tended to become an important weapon used by companies wishing to resist an unwelcome takeover, particularly where matters of public interest appear paramount.

Following the passage of the Competition Act 1998, the MMC was replaced (on 1 April 1999) by the **Competition Commission**, an independent public body whose role primarily was to examine mergers and market situations referred to it by another authority, usually the Office of Fair Trading. It had no powers to conduct inquiries on its own initiative. Under the Enterprise Act 2002, the Commission was given the responsibility for making decisions on competition questions and for making and implementing decisions on appropriate remedies. It also investigated references on the regulated sectors of the economy, including the privatised public utilities, the broadcasting and media businesses and the financial services sector. In 2013 the Competition Commission was merged with the Office of Fair Trading; the new combined agency is called the **Competition and Markets Authority**.

The Office of Fair Trading was initially a non-ministerial government department headed until recently by a Director General, who was appointed by the Secretary of State for Trade and Industry. Under the Fair Trading Act 1973, the DGFT was given the responsibility of overseeing consumer affairs as well as competition policy, and this included administering various pieces of consumer legislation, such as the Consumer Credit Act 1974 and the Estate Agents Act 1979. In carrying out his or her responsibilities in both these areas, the Director General was supported by a team of administrative, legal, economic and accountancy staff and had a Mergers Secretariat to coordinate the OFT's work in this field.

With regard to competition policy, the OFT's duties were originally governed primarily by the Fair Trading Act and the Competition Act 1980; in addition, under the Restrictive Trade Practices Act 1976, the Director General had responsibility for bringing cases of restrictive practices before the Restrictive Practices Court. With the passage of the Competition Act 1998, the new prohibition regime has been applied and enforced by the DGFT, and the OFT was given additional resources to root out cartels and restrictive behaviour. The legislation gave the Director General considerable powers to investigate if he or she had a reasonable suspicion that either of the prohibitions was being infringed. Under certain circumstances the DGFT could also grant exemptions from the scope of the two prohibitions and could be called upon to defend its decisions before the Competition Commission.

Following the Enterprise Act 2002, the OFT became a corporate body headed by a board which replaced the role of the DGFT. Under the legislation, the OFT was given a leading role in promoting competition and consumer interests and was the main source of reference for mergers referred to the Competition Commission. According to the OFT website, the organization's mission was to make markets work well for consumers by promoting competition across all sectors. Its Annual Plan – required under the 2002 Act – is a useful source of reference on the work of the OFT and on its key objectives.

The **Enterprise and Regulatory Reform Act 2013** established the Competition and Markets Authority (CMA) by merging the Competition Commission and the OFT. This simplified the institutional framework for regulating competition and consumer protection. The CMA's role is to be responsible for promoting effective competition in markets across the whole economy for the benefit of consumers and it is expected to provide better coordination with other consumer-focused organisations, including local authority Trading Standards, the Citizen Advice Service and the new National Trading Standards Board. It has been established as a non-ministerial department, with a chief executive officer and board directly accountable to Parliament.

Some illustrative cases of competition policy

Since it was established in 1948, the MMC/Competition Commission has produced hundreds of reports, covering a wide range of issues and affecting firms of different sizes in a variety of markets. At the outset most of its inquiries concerned monopolies – reflecting its initial role as the Monopolies Commission. In more recent times, its work has embraced not only mergers, which have tended to be its major preoccupation, but also nationalised industries and the work of the privatised large utilities. The functions of the Competition Commission transferred to the Competition and Markets Authority (CMA) in 2014.

The examples below provide a good insight into the Commission's role in competition policy and its relationship with the OFT. Students wishing to investigate a particular case in more detail should consult the appropriate report, a full list of which can be obtained from the Commission's library in London or via its website archive (see www.competition-commission.org.uk for information on this). The CMA website can be found at www.gov.uk/government/organisations/competition-and-markets-authority.

British Gas, 1992

This involved two parallel references to the Commission by both the President of the Board of Trade (under the terms of the Fair Trading Act) and the Director General of Gas Supply (under the Gas Act 1986). The first asked the Commission to investigate the supply of gas through pipes to both tariff and non-tariff customers, the second to investigate the supply of gas conveyance and gas storage facilities. According to the OFT, very little competition existed in the gas industry, since 17 million domestic household customers had no alternative source of supply and BG's control over storage and transmission facilities inhibited true competition in the industrial market where, theoretically, industrial customers could buy from other suppliers. In the Commission's report published in August 1993, the MMC called for BG to lose its monopoly of supply to domestic households by no later than 2002 and for the privatised utility to be split into two separately owned companies.

Midland Bank, 1992

This concerned two bids for the Midland Bank, made by Lloyds Bank and the Hong Kong and Shanghai Banking Corporation (now HSBC), and illustrates the question of split jurisdiction between the UK and the EU. Lloyds' bid fell within the UK's jurisdiction and was referred to the MMC as raising potential competition issues – a course of action that caused Lloyds to abandon its proposed merger. In contrast, the HSBC bid was deemed to be of wider concern and was referred to the competition authorities in Brussels. Following clearance by the EU, HSBC proceeded with its bid and this was accepted by Midland's shareholders.

Morrison's takeover of Safeway, 2003

In March 2003 the Competition Commission was asked to look at the proposed acquisition of the supermarket chain Safeway by four other rival supermarket groups: Asda, William Morrison, Sainsbury's and Tesco. The key concern was whether the proposed acquisition would lead to a lessening of competition that would adversely affect the consumer. After a lengthy investigation of the likely competitive impact, if any, if the proposed mergers went ahead, the Commission recommended that Asda, Sainsbury's and Tesco be prohibited from acquiring the whole or any part of Safeway, while Morrison's bid could go ahead subject to the company divesting some Safeway stores in certain localities.

Supermarkets inquiry, 2006–8

A two-year inquiry by the Competition Commission into the major UK supermarkets basically concluded that consumers were getting a 'good deal' from the big four supermarket chains. The investigation found evidence that the major grocery retailers at times exercised considerable power in their relationship with suppliers, but this issue was beyond the Commission's responsibilities, which are essentially to protect the interest of consumers. The Commission did, however, propose an enhanced code of practice to govern retailer/supplier relationships, which would be overseen by an independent ombudsman or woman.

Ryanair 2013

In August 2013 the low-cost carrier Ryanair was ordered by the Competition Commission to reduce its minority shareholding in Aer Lingus from almost 30 per cent to 5 per cent in order to protect competition on UK–Ireland routes. It also faced other obligations, including the requirement not to acquire further shares in its competitor airline. The Competition Commission's investigations followed a referral by the OFT in June 2012 and came on the back of a decision by the European Commission in February 2013 to block Ryanair's latest attempt to gain control of Aer Lingus. Ryanair called the decision unjust and indicated its intention of launching an appeal, despite having lost a previous appeal on the EC's ruling earlier in the year.

European equivalent – the European Commission and Google 2017

In June 2017 the EC announced that it was fining Google a record €2.4 billion (£2.1 billion) after a seven-year investigation into how the company influenced Internet shopping. The EC found that when searching for products Google would promote links to its own outlets and those who paid for promotion without clearly labelling that they were any different to its normal search services. Margrethe Vestager, the European Commissioner, said that 'what Google has done is illegal under EU antitrust rules. It denied other companies the chance to compete on the merits and to innovate. And most importantly, it denied European consumers a genuine choice of services and the full benefits of innovation.'

Government and the labour market

Government involvement in the **labour market** has taken a variety of forms and its influence on market conditions can be direct or indirect and can operate at different spatial levels. Many of the government initiatives mentioned in Chapter 13 seek to affect employment prospects in the regions or in local economies and thus clearly have labour market implications – largely aiming to create jobs and employment. Similarly, in its general management of the economy through fiscal and monetary means (see Chapter 5), the government will influence the overall demand for labour, which is derived from the demand for the products that labour produces. Some of that demand, of course, will come from the government itself, as a central provider of goods and services and hence a key employer of labour, and its attitude to pay settlements will affect wage levels throughout the public sector (where the government directly sets the wage). This, in turn, can spill over to the wage bargaining process in the private sector and on occasions may even involve the use of statutory or voluntary restrictions on wage rises that invariably interfere with the operations of the free market (e.g. incomes policies).

While all of these areas would need to be considered in any detailed analysis of labour market policies, in the brief discussion below we look at government initiatives to improve employment prospects and training opportunities for the unemployed, and at the government's efforts to curb the power of the trade unions. Both of these approaches are particularly pertinent to the discussion on how government has sought to improve the efficiency of markets as part of its supply-side approach to economic management – using, in this case, a combination of policy and legislation to achieve its objectives.

Curbing trade union power

As a major force in the labour market, representing the interests of millions of workers, trade unions have been seen as an obstacle to the operation of market forces and as a cause of high wage costs and low labour productivity in the UK. For almost 20 years after 1979, Conservative governments sought to curb the influence of the trade unions through legislative means, in the belief that more **labour market flexibility** would develop and that this would benefit businesses seeking to respond to competition and change. To assist further in this direction, the government – with the general support of industry – abolished the Wages Councils (which were set up to protect the interests of the lower-paid) and originally refused to participate in the Social Chapter of the Maastricht Treaty (which included a provision for works' councils and the principle of equal pay for male and female workers for equal work).

The government's step-by-step approach to reducing the influence of trade unions is demonstrated by the following legislative measures, enacted in the period 1980–2016.

The Employment Act 1980

This Act gave employers legal remedies against secondary picketing and most other types of secondary action. It also provided for all new 'closed shops' to be approved by four-fifths of the workforce and for public funds to be made available to encourage unions to hold postal ballots.

The Employment Act 1982

This Act further tightened the law on closed shops and outlawed union-labour-only contracts. Employers were given legal remedies against 'political' strikes and trade unions were made liable for damages, if they instigated unlawful industrial action (e.g. 'secondary' action).

The Trade Union Act 1984

This Act sought to strengthen internal union democracy. Unions were required to hold a secret ballot every 10 years if they wished to keep a political fund and union executives had to submit themselves for re-election by secret ballot every 5 years. In addition, pre-strike ballots were required if unions wished to retain their immunity from civil action for damages in the event of a strike.

The Employment Act 1988

This Act strengthened the rights of individual union members. Unions were banned from disciplining members who refused to support strike action; all senior union officials had to be elected by secret ballot; workers were permitted to apply for court orders instructing unions to repudiate industrial action organised without a secret ballot. Moreover, strikes in defence of the closed shop lost all legal protection.

The Employment Act 1990

This Act made unions legally liable for 'wildcat' strikes called by shop stewards without a proper ballot. Pre-entry closed shops were banned and so individuals could not be refused a job for not belonging to a trade union prior to appointment.

Trade Union and Labour Relations (Consolidation) Act 1992

This Act consolidated previous legislation in the field of labour relations.

The Trade Union Reform and Employment Rights Act 1993

This Act essentially had two main purposes: first, to impose further restrictions on trade unions and trade union activity; second, to enact certain employment rights as a consequence of EU directives and case law. Under section 13, for example, employers are permitted to provide inducements to employees to opt out of collective bargaining or to leave a union, while section 17 introduces a requirement for industrial action ballots to be conducted fully by postal voting.

The Trade Union Act 2016

This Act made it harder for trade unions to obtain a legal mandate for action by requiring 50 per cent turnout of voters, as well as all of those voting for action to represent at least 40 per cent of those eligible to vote. This really means that non-voters count as votes against action. Second, the mandate for a strike is now time limited to 6 months (or 9 months with employer agreement), and unions have to give 14 days' notice. Employers have more time to plan for strikes, which means that strikes have to take place for longer periods with more disruption if they are to be effective.

While there is no doubt that such legislation has altered the balance of power between employee and employer and has significantly weakened the power of the trade unions, this has been only one influence, and arguably not the most important. Apart from the fact that union membership has fallen significantly over recent decades, weakening their financial position and making them less able to sustain union action, the unions have at times had to operate in a market that has been severely affected by changes in the economic cycle. Gone are the days when governments aspired to full employment and were willing to use fiscal and monetary means to achieve this objective. In a climate of less than full employment (a policy of having a 'pool of unemployed labour' was deliberate under some governments that followed the economic teachings of Milton Friedman), the influence of organised labour in the economy has inevitably been reduced and has been replaced, to some degree, by the pursuit of individual self-interest. One example of this has been the rise of the appraisal for negotiating pay on an individual level.

With the election of a Labour government in 1997 (a party originally created by trade unions in 1900) came a kind of rehabilitation of the trade unions and an attempt by government to enshrine certain employment rights in law. Following the Employment Rights Act of 1996, other significant pieces of legislation have included the Employment Rights (Dispute Reduction) Act 1998, the National Minimum Wage Act 1998, the Working Time Regulations 1998, the Human Rights Act 1998, the Employment Relations Act 1999, the Employment Act 2002, the Employment Relations Act 2004, Work and Families Act 2006, the Employment Equality (Age) Regulations 2006 and the Disability Discrimination Act 2005.

The increase in workers' rights associated with much of the above legislation has arguably gone into reverse to some extent with the election of the coalition government in 2010. As part of its 'Plan for Growth' announced at the time of the 2011 budget, the newly elected administration called for the creation of a labour market that was more flexible, efficient and fair. Alongside substantial reforms to the welfare system aimed at encouraging employment and discouraging welfare claimants, the government made a number of changes to employment law. These have included increasing the time an employee needs to work before he or she can make a claim for unfair dismissal; the introduction of employment tribunal fees for claimants; a reduction in the redundancy notification period; scrapping of the compulsory retirement age; the removal of legal aid for most employment tribunal cases. The Coalition's effort to impose fees on employees taking their employers to tribunal was reversed in 2017. In a case bought by UNISON, the Supreme Court ruled that this was illegal, 'making it unaffordable' for people to exercise their rights.

Employment policies

Employment policies are targeted specifically at the unemployed and over recent decades have included a wide range of measures aimed at assisting individuals to prepare themselves for employment and to gain a job. Many of the schemes have been designed to give a limited amount of work experience and/or to improve vocational training, with increasing emphasis being given to the problem of skills shortages in the economy and to matching the needs of labour with the requirements of firms. Additionally, as the following examples illustrate, governments have sought to promote the idea of 'self-help' among the unemployed and to encourage the growth of self-employment, in the hope that an expanding small-firms sector will generate a large number of jobs, to replace those lost in medium- and larger-sized enterprises.

- *Restart* – introduced in 1986 and requiring anyone drawing unemployment benefit for over six months to see a specialist counsellor to try to identify possible routes back into employment.
- *Youth Training (YT)* – replaced the Youth Training Scheme in 1990. Under this scheme any person under 18 who was unemployed was guaranteed a YT place (with some exceptions, e.g. students). It was used to combine training and education and to allow individuals to acquire nationally recognised qualifications (e.g. NVQs).
- *Employment Training (ET)* – introduced in 1988 for long-term unemployed people and others with specific needs, including those returning to the labour market. It aimed to provide training in order to help individuals to acquire the skills needed to get jobs and vocational qualifications (or credits towards them).
- *Employment Action (EA)* – introduced in 1991 and designed to help the unemployed to maintain their skills and find employment. It provided opportunities for individuals to undertake community work and offered structured job-search support.
- *Training for Work (TfW)* – started in 1993 to replace ET and EA, combining the characteristics of both programmes.
- *Work Trials* – designed to give long-term unemployed people a chance to prove themselves to employers by working on a trial basis while receiving benefit.

The change in government in 1997 saw the introduction of the **New Deal**, a flagship scheme designed to get individuals claiming unemployment benefits off welfare and into work. Targeted initially at 18–24 year olds, the scheme was subsequently extended to other categories of person (e.g. those over 25 and those over 50, lone parents, the disabled and partners). Funded initially from a windfall tax levied on the privatised utility companies, the New Deal was an attempt to reduce reliance on state benefits and to make work more attractive to groups often excluded from the labour force. Like other measures, including working families' tax credits and efforts to increase the numbers going into further and higher education, it was part of an attempt by the Labour government to improve the supply side of the economy.

With the subsequent change in government in 2010, the New Deal and its successor the Flexible New Deal were replaced (in summer 2011) by the Coalition's **Work Programme**. Essentially a payments-by-results, welfare-to-work project, the project is aimed at getting the long-term unemployed back to work by outsourcing the task to organisations in the public, private and voluntary sectors. Together with the introduction of the system of universal credits, many see the initiative as part of the administration's welfare reform programme with its underlying message that individuals are better off in employment rather than claiming welfare benefits.

Local schemes

Historically, local schemes have taken a variety of forms, including interest-free loans for individuals wishing to set up a local business (e.g. Sir Thomas Whyte Charity in Leicester), local training awards to stimulate interest among local employers or individuals (e.g. Bedfordshire TEC), programmes for groups with specific training needs such as women returners (e.g. Calderdale and Kirklees TEC) and partnerships with local companies to part-fund new training initiatives (e.g. Birmingham TEC's Skills Investment Programme). As a final comment it is important to note that the government's national training programme was initially run by a system of local **Training and Enterprise Councils** (TECs), which was responsible for providing training schemes for the unemployed and school-leavers and for administering various business enterprise schemes. Funded by central government and run by a board of directors drawn predominantly from industry, the TECs (known as Local Enterprise Councils in Scotland) had control of the training funds for existing training programmes and were given the wider role of encouraging training and enterprise in the economy, including supporting initiatives aimed at promoting local economic development. To this end the TECs were expected to work closely with local employers in both the public and private sector and to improve the quality and effectiveness of training in their locality, by identifying priorities and needs within the local community. TECs were replaced by the **Learning and Skills Council** (LSC) in April 2001, which became responsible for all post-16 education and training, excluding higher education, and which operated through a network of local LSCs to deliver national priorities at a local level.

In March 2010, the LSC was superseded by two other organisations, the Skills Funding Agency (SFA) and the Young People's Learning Agency, with the latter's responsibilities quickly passing in April 2012 to the Education Funding Agency which focuses on the education of those of school age. The SFA is a partner organisation with the Department of Business, Innovation and Skills and is responsible for funding and promoting adult further education and training in England, including traineeships and apprenticeships. Its remit is delivered by the placing of contracts with colleges, private training organisations and employers willing to provide the necessary opportunities and services to those no longer in full-time compulsory education.

Synopsis

In market-based economies, governments exercise considerable influence over the structure and functioning of markets, not only through their economic activities but also through their legislative and policy preferences. Privatisation policy seeks to reduce the role of the state in the workings of the economy through the sale of government-owned assets, in the belief that this will improve the operation of the free market. Competition policy tends to focus on the use of legal and institutional changes to curb the growth of monopoly power and to regulate market behaviour in a manner felt to be conducive to the public interest.

In both these areas the focus of government attention is essentially on the supply side of the economy and this parallels its approach to the operation of the labour market. Through a variety of legislative and administrative changes, the government has sought to create a more 'flexible' market for labour through the introduction of initiatives on training and employment and through its attempts to curb the power of the trade unions through statutory means.

Summary of key points

- Competitive markets are thought to provide major advantages, particularly with regard to enhancing wealth creation, economic efficiency and consumer choice.

- Governments, through policy and legislation, can promote increased competition within the economy and its markets.

- Privatisation has become a global phenomenon and reflects the belief in official circles that competitive, private markets are a superior method of allocating economic resources.

- Privatisation in practice has both advantages and disadvantages.

- Competition policy is basically concerned with regulating market behaviour and with controlling potential abuses of market power.

- Governments in the UK and elsewhere use legislation and regulation to promote competition and have established institutional arrangements to implement and over-see their chosen policies.

- Through its membership of the EU, the UK is influenced by competition laws that have been adopted at Community level.

- Other forms of government intervention in markets include steps taken to improve the workings of the labour market and, in particular, to promote greater labour market flexibility.

- Key approaches in this area in the UK have included legislation to curb the power of the trade unions and the use of targeted employment policies designed to boost employment opportunities and generally improve the supply side of the economy.

case study   Who leads who?

At the start of July 2017 Volvo announced that by 2019 it would stop introducing new car models that would be powered by petrol and diesel engines. Instead it would be introducing new hybrid (a car with an electric engine as well as a petrol or diesel engine) or wholly electric engines with a view to stopping the production of petrol and diesel only models by 2025. VW, BMW and Renault-Nissan have all announced plans for similar projects to introduce electric vehicles and work towards phasing out oil-based fuels. In September 2017 Jaguar Land Rover was the latest to pledge the move to electric, with all models to be at least hybrid by 2020.

There are indications from the market that this is a positive move; hybrid cars are already prevalent on UK roads, representing more than 250 000 cars. The number of wholly electric cars in the UK will reach more than 100 000 by 2018. Tesla was formed as a car company which would produce only electric cars. Over the five years from the end of 2012 to the end of 2017 Tesla's share price has increased by more than 1000 per cent to become the most valuable car company in the United States. In the first three days of the new 'Tesla Model 3' being announced in 2016, the company received in excess of 250 000 worldwide pre-orders. All indicators suggest that the electric and hybrid car sectors are growing rapidly.

In late July 2017 (the same month as Volvo's announcement) the UK government followed the Netherlands, Norway, India, Germany and France in announcing that it was going to ban new petrol and diesel cars from the roads by 2040 (the Scottish government has said it will aim for 2032). After this date existing cars would be allowed to remain, but newly registered cars must be 'emission free', meaning they cannot have a petrol or diesel motor – such as a hybrid.

All of this should be good news for the environment, but the government also earns fuel duty (tax on petrol and diesel), which was worth £27.6bn in 2015–16, three times the amount collected on tobacco duty. In addition, the government is offering to subsidise £4,500 of the price of an electric car. If drivers continue to switch to electric vehicles the government may have to look at ways to replace that lost revenue.

The question amongst all of this is: who is driving the change? Is it car companies scaling up technologies and choosing to switch to electric – such as Volvo? Is it consumers choosing the vehicles, which pushes the manufacturers to produce more of them? Is it the government legislating to ban polluting alternatives to new, clean electric cars? Or is it following pressure from environmental groups and voters? In reality it is probably a mix of all of these different factors.

case study   'What a fine mess you've got me into'

If governmental and intergovernmental competition policies are to achieve their objectives, careful consideration needs to be given to creating an effective competition regime or architecture. In addition to devising laws and regulations outlining what are (or are not) acceptable business practices, policy-makers need to establish an institutional framework capable of investigating alleged legal transgressions and abuses of market power; gathering (or, in some cases, seizing) information and

data from the various parties involved; reaching an evidence-based judgement on the merits of the allegation(s); suggesting a remedy; imposing, where appropriate, a fine or other form of penalty on the transgressing organisation(s); and publicising the results of the investigation for the benefit of the different stakeholder interests. As this chapter has demonstrated, incremental changes in competition law and its supporting institutional framework have become relatively commonplace as the competitive ▶

landscape has evolved and become increasingly complex both within and across state boundaries.

In this case study we look at two examples of action taken by the competition authorities against global businesses deemed to have been involved – whether accidently or deliberately – in unacceptable business practices said to have a negative effect on consumers and/or other organisations.

Microsoft

In March 2013 Microsoft was fined €561 million by the European Commission when it broke a binding commitment to give users a choice of web browser when they first logged into Windows. The fine – which covered the period between May 2011 and July 2012 – applied to a problem thought to have affected around 15 million users, Microsoft having made a five-year commitment in 2009 to offer users a choice of browsers other than the pre-installed Internet Explorer, which dominated the market at the time.

According to the company, the error had arisen because its programmers had forgotten to include a single line of code that would have automatically triggered a browser choice programme on an updated version of Windows 7. When Microsoft realised the error, it contacted the EC's competition authorities to admit that it had failed to follow a directive to create a level playing field where browser choice was concerned. For cooperating with the competition authorities, Microsoft faced a reduced fine; under EU rules, it could have been required to pay as much as 10 per cent of its revenues for 2012, which would have amounted to almost €6 billion.

The banking sector

In the five years between 2008 and the end of 2012 it has been estimated that 10 major US and European banks were fined or required to pay compensation of between £100 billion and £130 billion for a range of scandals including rigging Libor, mis-selling payment protection insurance, money laundering and backing highly risky sub-prime mortgages. A report in *The Guardian* on 5 December 2013 gave the following breakdown of the amounts thought to be involved:

Bank of America	£40 billion
Barclays	£3 billion
Citi	£10 billion
Goldman Sachs	£1.8 billion
HSBC	£5 billion
JP Morgan Chase	£33 billion
Lloyds Banking Group	£8 billion
Royal Bank of Scotland	£4.5 billion
Santander	£3 billion
UBS	£23 billion

In total, by 2017 US and European regulatory bodies had brought prosecutions against several global banks which have resulted in $9 billion in fines and settlements for colluding to fix key interest rate benchmarks. As with the previous case, the fact that some of the banks affected had admitted their part in a cartel arrangement or brought it to the attention of the competition authorities meant they faced a reduced penalty or escaped the fine altogether.

Case study questions

1 Why is a cartel thought to be disadvantageous for consumers?

2 When an organisation is fined for some form of anti-competitive behaviour, who do you think is likely to pay the penalty for the transgression?

Review and discussion questions

1 Explain the paradox that government needs to intervene in the economy to allow markets to work more freely. What forms does this intervention take?

2 Why is privatisation felt to be a spur to greater efficiency in the major utilities? How would you measure such efficiency 'gains'?

3 In what ways might a government's policy on privatisation be related to its policy on competition?

4 What is meant by 'labour market flexibility' and why is it thought to be important?

Assignments

1 Draft a press release on behalf of the government explaining why it favoured turning Railtrack into a not-for-profit company. Indicate in your statement why the option to renationalise the company was rejected.

2 You are employed by a firm of professional lobbyists which has been commissioned by a group representing European consumer interests to lobby the European Commission over the labelling of food products (e.g. contents, origin, environmental aspects). Produce a report outlining the benefits of more informative labelling on food products within the EU.

Further reading

Cook, G. C., *Privatisation in the 1980s and 1990s,* Hidcote Press, 1992.

Crane, D. A. and Hovenkamp, H., *The Making of Competition Policy: Legal and Economic Sources,* Oxford University Press, 2013.

Crouch, C., *The Strange Non-Death of Neoliberalism,* Polity Press, 2011.

Griffiths, A. and Wall, S. (eds), *Applied Economics,* 12th edition, Financial Times/Prentice Hall, 2011.

Parker, D., 'The UK's privatisation experiment: the passage of time permits a sober assessment', CESIFO Working Paper No. 1126, 2004, available in electronic form from *www.cesifo.de*

Potts, N., 'Privatisation: a false hope', *International Journal of Public Sector Management,* 12 (5), pp. 388–409, 1999.

Roland, G., *Privatization: Successes and Failures,* Columbia University Press, 2013.

Worthington, I., Britton, C. and Rees, A., *Economics for Business: Blending Theory and Practice,* 2nd edition, Financial Times/Prentice Hall, 2005.

web link

Web links and further questions are available on the website at:
www.pearsoned.co.uk/worthington

Working with the grain of the market

In economics the term 'market' basically means a situation where buyers and sellers come together to effect an exchange. Some markets have a physical manifestation (e.g. a local farmers' market), others do not (e.g. ebay). The essential point is that a market is an arrangement where a transaction takes place; this can occur at any spatial level from local to national through to international and global, and under differing structural conditions (e.g. oligopoly, monopoly, monopsony, etc.).

As Chapter 15 has shown, the issue of market structure – and in particular the degree of competitiveness existing within a given market – has important implications not only for the behaviour of suppliers but also for consumers concerned with questions of price and choice of products available for purchase. In general, economists (and most politicians) believe that markets dominated by either one or a few major firms can operate to the disadvantage of consumers compared with those where greater competition between suppliers is the norm. Government attempts to improve a market's competitiveness, whether through policy or legislation, are one manifestation of this view.

To illustrate how even global markets can become dominated by just a handful of major suppliers which possess immense market power, we look at the global grain trade, which was the subject of a special report published in *The Guardian* on 2 June 2011. According to the report's author, four major transnational companies dominate this globally strategic market, accounting for an estimated 75–90 per cent of the supply of the raw materials going into the global food system. The four firms – ADM, Bunge, Cargill and Dreyfus (known as the ABCD group) – have major interests across the whole supply chain from the provision of seeds and fertilisers, through the processing of different food and animal crops, to the trading of oil, flour, grains, sugar, bioenergy, fats and food additives. The products derived from their activities go into many of the foods grown and consumed globally – particularly in the developed economies – and major customers include McDonald's, Unilever and Walkers Snack Foods. Their supply has had important implications for the natural environment in countries such as Argentina and Brazil, with the latter losing millions of acres of rainforest as land is cleared for crop production. Other concerns currently making the headlines include the impact of some of these products and their derivatives on human health, with diabetes and obesity being linked by some observers to high consumption of fatty foods.

The report also points to a further issue of importance to the operation of this market, namely that three of the four global giants have developed strategic alliances and joint ventures with huge seed and agrochemical companies – including Monsanto, DuPont, Bayer and Syngenta – which dominate the supply of agricultural inputs into the global food chain and have been active in the field of genetically modified technologies. As the discussion in Chapter 10 has indicated, collaborations of this kind can be an important means of entering a new market or of gaining access to different parts of the supply chain, thereby helping to extend a firm's reach and influence in the marketplace. When the product being supplied is a necessity such as food, being a key player on a global scale clearly has the potential to be very lucrative to the organisations involved and to their shareholders.

While a major part of *The Guardian* report focuses on the dominant position of the four major players in the global food chain, it also raises a further issue of contemporary interest to observers of the business environment: the question of tax avoidance (see, for instance, Chapter 9). The claim is that while the ABCD group have made multi-billion-dollar earnings through their activities in Argentina, they have effectively exported their profits from the country by setting up offices in tax havens, thus reducing their corporate tax liabilities. While there is no suggestion that this arrangement is in any way illegal, critics have pointed to the question of its social and economic impact on the host nation and to the wider notion of corporate social responsibility. In this context, the current discussions in the G20 over how to close the tax loopholes that allow multinational corporations to 'game' national tax systems may prove significant. Present indications are that gaining cross-national consensus on this issue will prove difficult, not least because of fierce opposition from vested interests.

Part Five

CONCLUSION

18 Strategy and the changing environment

18 Strategy and the changing environment

David Orton and Ian Worthington

Business organisations operate within a changing and often uncertain environment. To ensure that corporate resources are used effectively in pursuit of organisational objectives, firms ideally need to examine the external influences upon them and, where possible, to anticipate the nature and extent of environmental change. The study and practice of strategic management and decision-making have provided a number of useful approaches in this area and generated a variety of techniques for analysing the business environment. These techniques rely on the generation of data and information, much of which is in the public domain. Accessing this information has become significantly easier with improvements in computer technology and in collecting and collating material from both national and international sources.

Learning outcomes

Having read this chapter you should be able to:

- demonstrate the need to monitor the changing business environment
- explain broad approaches to environmental analysis
- analyse a range of qualitative and quantitative techniques used by business organisations as an aid to decision-making
- access a variety of national and international sources of information and data useful to both students and practitioners of business

Key terms

Brainstorming
Cross-impact matrix
Delphi method
Environmental analysis
Environmental scanning

LoNGPEST/LoNGPESTLE analysis
PESTLE analysis
Porter's five-forces model
Scenario planning

Strategic fit
Strategic management
SWOT (or TOWS) analysis
Trend extrapolation
Trend–impact analysis

Introduction

The purpose of strategy is to provide the future direction and objectives of the organisation and to identify and gather the resources necessary to achieve these objectives. A simplified and popular perspective of strategy views it as a series of chronological phases: strategic analysis, identification and selection of strategic choices and, finally, implementation. For many managers this begins with a consideration of the following questions:

- Where are we now?
- What is the situation we face?
- Where do we wish to be?
- Which factors in our environment may pose challenges or opportunities for us in the future?

Managers need to be keenly aware of their organisation's internal environment (where its strengths and weaknesses may lie), and also be able to diagnose their external environment. It can be argued that the successful strategies are those that best match the organisation's resources to the pressures and forces of the environment. In short, the organisation is seeking a **strategic fit** between the internal and external environments.

Kenneth Andrews, a Harvard professor acclaimed as one of the earliest and foremost thinkers in corporate strategy, believed that strategy could be prescribed and should adopt the structure shown in Figure 18.1 in its development and application within an organisation. This structure emphasises the importance of assessing environmental conditions and trends as a necessary first stage in the generation of organisational strategies. The external environment is examined with the objective of identifying opportunities and risks (commonly termed threats). At the same time, the organisation should also identify its strengths and weaknesses, which result from analysing its

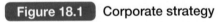

Figure 18.1 Corporate strategy

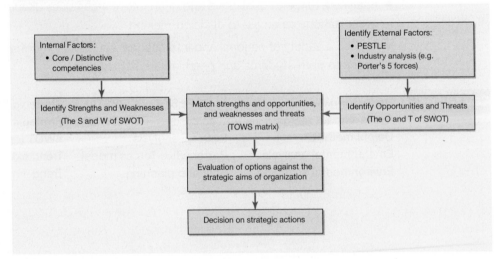

internal resources. The organisation may then bring together these two forms of analysis, external and internal, and seek to identify an optimal 'fit' or 'best match' between the two. This process led to the development of the popular SWOT tool, which we will explore later in this chapter.

The need to monitor environmental change

Every organisation, from the smallest sole trader to the largest multinational firm, whether public or private sector, ought ideally to monitor its environment continually in order to identify potential changes or the development of long-term trends that could affect the enterprise. For some organisations, the environment is likely to be relatively stable during the mid-term, as in the case of civil service departments, the emergency services and heavy manufacturing. That said, there will always exist the possibility of environmental shocks that can destabilise the status quo, such as acts of terrorism, financial scandals, environmental disasters and, more recently, the effects of the global financial crisis.

In other organisations and industries, the environment may prove to be far more turbulent. The retail sector, especially the fast-moving consumer goods (FMCG) sector and consumer electronics, experiences continual innovation in product development that both shapes and reflects changing consumer demand patterns as well as increasing competition through the bewildering proliferation of product choices and condensing of product life cycles. The markets for mobile phones and portable MP3 players are just two such examples, and, of course, technological developments and technology transfer now permit the boundaries of these previously distinct markets to become blurred.

The nature of the environment, or at least the way it may be perceived by each organisation in terms of stability versus dynamism, may then reflect the actions and efforts of organisations with regard to engaging in external analysis.

For organisations that perceive their environment as turbulent, the impetus for thorough and formal external analysis may be high and efforts towards such analysis might be afforded a prominent role in formulating strategies. This, however, is sometimes not sufficient. Some organisations may see their environment as so chaotic and complex that they simply do not know where to start or what to consider. With an absence of direction and clarity, organisations may inadvertently enter into a phase of soporific stupor or inertia. Alternatively, for many organisations, undertaking external analysis may seem too resource intensive, in terms of money, time and people, and hence may not be an attractive proposition. The act of external analysis per se will not confer a competitive advantage for the organisation and therefore it can sometimes become difficult to justify the initial resource commitment when the returns or rewards for doing so may be unknown or uncertain.

Equally, for organisations that may perceive their environment as relatively stable, the act of continual monitoring may seem inappropriate or even illogical. If the organisation believes that the external environment in the future is likely to share the same or broadly similar characteristics as the environment it has operated within in the past, then there is little incentive to engage in external analysis.

This attitude can be likened to the simple parable of the 'boiled frog syndrome'. A frog that is placed into a pot of boiling water will immediately jump out. If the frog is placed into a tepid pot of water, it will sit there contentedly. If that pot is then slowly heated up, the frog will continue to stay in the water, until it becomes too late. The frog is unable to identify incremental changes in its environment, given that its internal apparatus is geared towards sensing sudden changes instead.

An example of this 'boiled frog syndrome' can be seen with the American giant car manufacturer General Motors (GM). In 1998, GM bought the Hummer brand name, and the off-road vehicle became an icon for GM during the early part of the millennium as it was favoured by the celebrity and Hollywood set, including high-publicity owners such as David Beckham and Governor of California and former movie star Arnold Schwarzenegger. With rising fuel prices and concern over its impact on the natural environment, the vehicle subsequently became increasingly unpopular and sales of the Hummer SUV fell dramatically. As a result, GM eventually decided to sell the brand, with China the likeliest destination. In February 2010, the company announced its intention of closing the Hummer plant after a deal to sell it to a Chinese manufacturer collapsed. The last Hummer rolled off the production line in May of that year, much to the delight of environmentalists.

Analysing the environment is therefore important for all organisations. To do nothing is at best foolish and at worst potentially disastrous.

Analysing the business environment: broad approaches

Environmental analysis is the process of scanning the environment to identify changes or trends that have the potential to generate opportunities and threats to the organisation's current or future intended strategies. The form and means by which this **environmental scanning** may be operationalised within an organisation will vary from firm to firm and can be undertaken informally or using quite sophisticated analytical tools and techniques that may require significant employment of an organisation's resources.

Informal scanning may take the form of getting information about, and from, the organisation's customers, suppliers, rivals, consultants and pressure groups. Such information from customers could, for instance, be gathered through questionnaires, sample interviewing or from feedback from the organisation's own sales and customer service staff. In retail, it is not uncommon for shop staff within a town or shopping centre to visit local rival stores and shops to get information about the prices being charged and promotional activities of competitors. All such informal activities, while relatively low cost to implement and generally lacking structure, should not be undervalued. While neither elaborate nor sophisticated, for smaller organisations especially, such informal techniques can provide necessary local market information.

An example of such informal scanning is where a local independent music store sends out a staff member from its small team at the beginning of each week to check up on the prices the large music chain retailers within the town are charging for popular CD albums. This ensures that the small independent record shop is able to price its products competitively and react quickly to any price changes or promotional activities by its competitors.

Many larger organisations, however, may prefer a more systematic and formal m
for scanning and analysing the environment. In broad terms, these more deliberate
approaches to environmental analysis tend to focus on the firm's societal and task
environments.

As discussed in Chapter 1, the societal and general environment (often termed the
'macroenvironment') is typically analysed through the lens of **PESTLE** analysis, which
focuses attention on political, economic, socio-cultural, technological, legal and environmental and/or ethical issues. A further development of this approach is the concept
of **LoNGPEST/LoNGPESTLE analysis**, which formally incorporates the spatial dimension into any analysis of an organisation's external environment. The basic argument
is that any examination of the macroenvironmental influences on the firm needs to
recognise that these can operate at all spatial levels: local (Lo), national (N), global (G).
Hence the acronym LoNGPEST(LE). To take one example, a local business may be subject to political changes in its immediate vicinity (e.g. new by-laws on trading) and/or
at the national level (e.g. changes to employment regulations) and/or at the global level
(e.g. new agreed global standards on greenhouse gas emissions). The same approach
can be adopted for all the other influences in an organisation's general environment.

At this point for the organisation a distinction can be drawn between environmental
scanning and environmental analysis. The process of scanning is the identification of
trends and changes, while analysis is the consideration of which trends and environmental changes will, or are likely to, impact on the organisation in terms of presenting new
challenges and also opportunities. For example, a period of relatively high or rising interest rates may be of general concern, but it is how increases in interest rates may directly
affect a firm's borrowing capacity, expansion or plans for further investment that is really
of relevance to the organisation.

mini case — Multinational inward investment: a PESTLE analysis

In highly competitive markets businesses must
be constantly alert to the challenges they face
and ideally should attempt to gain some form
of advantage over their main rivals. For some
organisations this might mean investing in
production and/or service facilities in other
countries, either as a means of reducing costs
(e.g. by exploiting cheaper sources of labour) or as
a strategy for boosting demand (e.g. by developing
new markets). Given that many industries could
be described as 'footloose' (i.e. relatively free to
locate anywhere), one key question facing
organisational decision-makers is where to invest:
what are the relative merits of one country over
another? One way of beginning to answer this
question is to undertake a PESTLE analysis in

order to provide useful information about the broad
macroenvironmental context against which the
final decision has to be taken.

To illustrate how this might occur, the
hypothetical example in this mini case looks at
how a major car manufacturer considering
investing in a new greenfield facility in Eastern
Europe might identify some of the key influences
on the locational decision. Given that there is no
definitive way in which to undertake an analysis of
this kind, the approach adopted here is to highlight
some of the key questions that are likely to be
considered by those charged with the final
decision on where to invest. For convenience these
questions are presented in tabular form
(Table 18.1). You should note that the allocation

of questions to categories can be a matter of personal choice (e.g. is a government tax law political or legal or economic?); the important point is that the questions are asked, not which category they go in.

As Table 18.1 illustrates, a PESTLE analysis can provide a valuable insight into some of the potential risks and uncertainties of a locational decision and can encourage corporate decision-makers to examine future as well as current circumstances in each of the alternative locations. By adding weightings to reflect the relative importance of the different factors to the final decision and building in some allowance for the perceived degree of risk, the analysis can become more sophisticated and hence a more useful tool that can be used by the organisation.

While it is likely that an approach of this kind will often be used negatively (i.e. to rule out certain locations), the fact that a particular country looks a less favourable location than the alternatives does not necessarily mean it will not be chosen. It could be, for example, that other factors weigh heavily on the final choice of location and that the PESTLE analysis has more influence on the level and nature of the investment undertaken (e.g. a joint venture might be seen as preferable to a direct commitment of funds) rather than where it occurs.

Table 18.1 Locating a car plant: a PESTLE approach

Political	*Economic*
● How stable is the government now and in the future?	● Is there a favourable economic framework within which to engage in business?
● Is the political regime favourable to foreign investment?	● Is the economy likely to remain stable over the longer term?
● Is membership of the EU planned and likely in the near future?	● Is there a favourable business infrastructure?
Social	*Technological*
● How will the structure of the population impact upon the demand for the product and/or the supply of labour?	● What is the current state of technological advance?
● Are economic conditions likely to provide increased market opportunities?	● Is technology transfer feasible?
● What skills currently exist within the labour force?	● Will the current (or future) infrastructure help or hinder the investment process?
● Are the welfare and educational systems supportive of the planned investment?	● What facilities exist for technological training?
Legal	*Ethical*
● Is the current legal framework likely to support or hinder business operations?	● Are the ethical standards in a chosen location likely to affect the operations of the business favourably or unfavourably and/or the company's image?
● Do the current (or planned) employment laws provide an advantage or disadvantage to the business?	● How will the organisation be affected by current (or planned) environmental standards and regulations?
● Do the current tax laws favour the organisation?	

Organisations can also analyse their task or competitive environment (frequently termed the microenvironment). Analysis of this kind focuses attention on external factors that are most proximal to the organisation, typically residing at the industry level. A number of models and frameworks have been designed that explore how industry-level factors influence organisational performance, with the best known being Harvard professor Michael **Porter's five-forces model**, discussed in detail in Chapter 15. You will recall that Porter argued that average industry profitability and therefore organisational performance was predominantly determined by five key industry characteristics:

- the intensity of incumbent rivalry;
- the threat of new entrants;
- the threat of substitutes;
- the power of buyers;
- the power of suppliers.

In very broad terms, the greater the power of each of these forces, the lower the profitability for competing organisations within the industry. The influence or power of each force will vary from industry to industry and therefore explains why some industries (e.g. pharmaceuticals) are inherently more profitable than others (e.g. airlines). An important additional component of Porter's work was his application of 'barriers to entry'. While the concept of barriers to entry was not new, Porter used it to demonstrate how their existence would determine the extent to which the stability of average profitability could be maintained. With barriers to entry high, the threat of new entrants would remain low, while low barriers to entry would encourage new firms to enter the industry and increase the level of rivalry and therefore reduce profitability. These barriers to entry have already been described in the chapter on market structure, but what is of relevance here is to recognise that an organisation's external analysis should not just be restricted to consideration of the five forces, but needs to incorporate environmental factors that might influence the height of these barriers to entry.

An example of this was in the United States during October 2001. During that month there had been a series of terrorist attacks using the US postal system to deliver letters containing anthrax spores to American citizens. The government, assuming the worst and unaware of the potential scale of the threat, wished to procure treatments for exposure to anthrax for up to 12 million people. Treatment against anthrax was a patented drug called ciprofloxacin, which was sold under the brand name Cipro by the German pharmaceutical firm Bayer. The US government had significant concerns as to Bayer's ability to supply such large volumes of Cipro in an extremely short period of time and at a relatively high cost. Congress indicated its intention to disregard Bayer's patent and buy ciprofloxacin cheaper elsewhere. After a series of talks between US officials and Bayer, the pharmaceutical firm eventually maintained its patent but had to agree to a reduction in the contracted price from $1.83 to less than $1 a tablet.

The five-forces framework remains perhaps the most influential method for analysing an industry and understanding a firm's performance. Underpinning the framework is an acceptance that value and, ultimately, profit are distributed between these five forces, and the extent to which the firm can capture an increasing share of the profit is determined by its ability to reduce the power of these forces. Inherent within the framework is the notion that relationships between the five forces are competitive, with all organisations competing in what may be considered a 'zero-sum' game.

While the five-forces framework therefore provides a useful means of exploring industry characteristics, it has not been beyond criticism. Brandenburger and Nalebuff, for example, in 1995 introduced their 'value net' framework. In many ways it is similar to Porter's five forces, in that it also identifies competitors, suppliers and customers as key industry characteristics, but it introduced a further component, that of 'complementors'. For Brandenburger and Nalebuff, competing firms could also at times be complementors

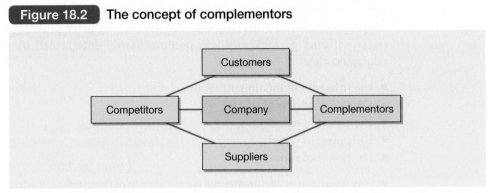

Figure 18.2   The concept of complementors

Source: Adapted from Brandenburger, A. and Nalebuff, B. (1995) 'The right game: use game theory to shape strategy', *Harvard Business Review,* July–August, pp. 57–71.

and in so doing could further add value (and, ultimately, profitability) to the industry (Figure 18.2). They argued that a complementor existed if customers were to value an organisation's product more when they had another organisation's product. This has led to a popular view that the five-forces framework should be extended to incorporate a sixth force, that of complementors. In short, in undertaking external analysis an organisation will need to consider both competition and cooperation, which have become known by the portmanteau term 'co-opetition'.

Techniques

Organisations may employ a range of techniques to assist them in analysing the external environment. Some of these techniques use statistical measures, such as the various forms of trend extrapolation and cross-impact matrices, while others, such as Delphi methods and scenario planning, use qualitative or narrative assessments. Some techniques for external analysis seek to predict likely future states or identify relationships between external variables, while others strive to illuminate possible future states. Furthermore, each tool presented below often focuses on different future time frames.

The value of the techniques will vary from organisation to organisation, and there is no hierarchy in terms of their quality. Each technique that will be explored within this chapter has both strengths and limitations. These methods of external analysis should not be considered as surrogates for each other, but rather on whether the merits of a particular technique or techniques can help illuminate understanding of the external environment and aid the organisation in its identification of environmental opportunities and threats. The various techniques presented here also have differing resource requirements in terms of cost, labour and time, and therefore the organisation needs to find a balance between its desire for understanding and gaining insight into the environment and its willingness to commit resources to achieve such understanding. There is also the danger of paralysis – achieved through analysis. The organisation can never gain a complete appreciation of all external issues, and nor should it attempt to. Analysis by itself has value only once it is acted upon by the organisation in terms of designing new strategies either to take advantage of opportunities or to mitigate environmental threats. A well-thought-through and considered strategy is desirable, but one that is well thought through, considered and implemented before those of the organisation's rivals is preferable.

> If you would like more details of the various techniques referred to in this section (e.g. SWOT, the cross-impact matrix, the Delphi technique), try typing these terms into a search engine.

Trend extrapolation

As its name suggests, **trend extrapolation** is essentially a technique for predicting the future based on an analysis of the past. Implicit in this is the assumption that, in the short run at least, most factors tend to remain fairly constant and critical changes in the key variables are unlikely to occur. Accordingly, extending present trends into the future is seen as a useful means of anticipating forthcoming events and tends to be one of the techniques most frequently used by business organisations seeking a relatively simple and inexpensive means of forecasting.

At its simplest level, trend analysis tends to be used to predict changes over time (e.g. in the likely demand for a product), a process which can sometimes prove relatively accurate where there are sufficient historical data to allow seasonal and cyclical fluctuations to be taken into consideration. The analysis can also be refined to examine an observed relationship between one factor (e.g. sales) and another (e.g. levels of disposable income) and can even be extended to the simultaneous consideration of several variables felt to influence the subject under consideration (e.g. by using multiple regression techniques). Techniques also exist to investigate causal or explanatory factors that link two or more time series (e.g. statistical modelling techniques) and to consider the likely impact on forecasted trends of a range of factors, identified by analysts as likely both to occur and to have an effect on the predicted outcome. The latter technique is generally known as **trend–impact analysis** and is sometimes used by large companies in conjunction with other methods of forecasting, including the Delphi approach and opinion canvassing (see below).

The fundamental drawback in the use of trend analysis as a forecasting tool is that there is no guarantee that the trends identified from historic patterns will continue in the future; sudden discontinuities – such as the UK's decision to leave the ERM in the 1990s – can invalidate or undermine the existing assumptions on which a trend was predicted. In a majority of cases, trends are based on a series of patterns or relationships among a wide range of variables, a change in any one of which can drastically alter the future course of events. These variables are not always easy to identify and the interactions between them are not necessarily fully understood. Attempts to link a simple cause with a simple effect run the danger of underestimating the complexities of the business environment.

Scenario planning

Scenario planning is about undertaking a disciplined method for imagining and examining possible futures. It is not an attempt to predict the future and indeed it would be typical for an organisation to generate between two and four generically different possible futures as an outcome of the scenario planning process. This technique often focuses on 'best case' and 'worst case' scenarios, although Royal Dutch Shell – the company most renowned for the use of scenario planning as a core component of its environmental analysis activities for more than 30 years – has in its recent scenarios often expressed a preference for one particular scenario case (see the case study at the end of this chapter).

Scenario planning as a strategic tool can be traced back to the Rand Corporation in the early 1960s, and is often associated with the work of one of its employees, physicist and mathematician Herman Kahn. At the time of his research, the Cold War between the United States and the Soviet Union was at its peak. In 1962, the Cuban Missile Crisis brought the two Cold War superpowers perhaps within only a matter of days of nuclear war, when US Air Force reconnaissance aircraft took aerial photographs of Soviet installations of nuclear bases on the island of Cuba, which would provide a direct nuclear threat to American soil.

Herman Kahn, in conjunction with the Rand Corporation, in 1962 presented his text entitled 'On thermonuclear war', which argued against common views at the time that 'mutually assured destruction' would happen in a nuclear war. Instead, Kahn presented the view that, as with any other form of warfare, a nuclear war could be ultimately winnable and his text identified a range of scenarios by which this might be possible.

In business organisations, scenario planning seeks to consider the possible effects of, and interactions between, various external environmental forces on the future and to test the resiliency of specific strategies that the organisation may be considering, in such a scenario. Typically, scenario planning is most relevant to large organisations, as it is a resource-intensive technique and is most commonly found in industries considered to have highly dynamic, complex and uncertain environments and/or those industries that require heavy forward investment (e.g. energy companies).

The process of scenario planning normally begins with the organisation considering which key environmental trends to consider, and over what time period. Royal Dutch Shell has historically published scenarios on a three- to four-year cycle, projecting 20 to 25 years ahead. Its most recent scenarios consider the possible nature of global energy markets in the mid- to late twenty-first century. General consensus, however, suggests that scenarios should ideally be looking at least 10 years ahead. Once the key trends have been identified, organisational focus then moves to considering what external forces or developments are likely to have the greatest ability to shape the future, which could include such factors as regulatory policy and corporate social responsibility.

mini case Bucking the trend

In April 2013, the bargain clothing retailer Primark – which is owned by Associated British Foods – announced a 24 per cent increase in sales and a 56 per cent rise in operating profits, figures that ran counter to the general gloom being felt by most high-street big brands. Unlike its rivals, which were moving towards multi-channel sales, smartphone apps and click-and-collect services, Primark's preferred strategy was to focus on the high street rather than the Internet, opening new and bigger stores and investing in floor space in the form of upgrades and expansions. In the six months prior to its announcement, the company had opened 15 new stores (6 in Spain, 4 in the UK, 2 in Germany, 2 in Austria and 1 in the Netherlands) and was about to make its first foray into the French market by the end of the year. It was also looking at other potential sites across all regions of the UK to add to its portfolio of more than 250 stores.

It is interesting to note that while retailers such as Tesco, B&Q and Debenhams have all predicted that future stores are likely to become smaller as shoppers turn to online retailing, Primark is heading in the opposite direction, increasing the size of its high-street outlets. The company believes that many shoppers still like to experience purchasing their fashion items on the spot, rather than engaging in virtual browsing. Emulating its competitors' strategy, at least for the moment, does not appear to be on the agenda.

> **web link**
>
> Information on Primark is available at *www.primark.com*; its parent company's web address is *www.abf.co.uk*

Expert opinion: the Delphi method

To predict future developments or to build likely scenarios, some organisations turn to experts, an increasing number of whom work as consultants. These experts often operate as a group to produce an analysis which is presented to management in the form of a report or which emanates from a discursive technique known as **brainstorming**. Alternatively, the organisation may prefer to canvass the views of an anonymous panel of experts, using a technique known as the **Delphi method**, which was originally developed by the Rank Corporation in the United States to forecast likely military events.

In essence, the Delphi approach involves eliciting opinions from a group of experts who operate individually, and anonymously, unaware of the other members of the group. Each expert is asked to respond to an initial set of questions and the answers are clarified and tabulated by a neutral investigator, who uses them to generate a more refined set of questions that is then put to the experts. Following their replies, further revisions may occur and the respondents may be asked again to provide another set of predictions that takes into account the information provided in the earlier replies. This process may continue for several rounds until a measure of convergence occurs between the views of the panel and a form of consensus is reached on likely future developments.

As a technique the Delphi method tends to be expensive and time consuming and there is no guarantee that a clear view will emerge. It can, however, be used to investigate any aspect of a firm's environment and to identify not only the effects of predicted changes but also their causes, and this information may be incorporated into other forms of environmental analysis of both a qualitative and quantitative kind.

Cross-impact matrices

The **cross-impact matrix** provides a more complex means of assessing and forecasting environmental change than some of the other methods previously described. Under this approach, analysts identify a set of events that is forecast to occur within a given time period, and specify not only the expected timing of each event but also its probability of occurrence. Arranging these events in anticipated chronological order in rows

Figure 18.3   A simple cross-impact matrix

Probability and timing	Event 1	Event 2	Event 3	Event 4	Event 5
Event 1 (probability/ timing)					
Event 2 (probability/ timing)					
Event 3 (probability/ timing)					
Event 4 (probability/ timing)					
Event 5 (probability/ timing)					

and columns of a matrix (see Figure 18.3) permits attention to be focused on the interaction between the events and, in particular, on the extent to which one may influence the timing or likely occurrence of another.

As a means of predicting likely interactions between anticipated future developments, cross-impact analysis serves at least two significant purposes. First, it can be used to check the consistency of the various forecasts which go into it – such as the prediction of events and their relationships – given that inconsistencies will become apparent from an analysis of the results. Second, it provides a means of identifying events and trends that will have the greatest impact on subsequent developments, whether they be in individual segments of the environment or across a range of segments, as in the case of interactions between economic, technological, social and political factors.

SWOT or TOWS analysis

It is widely accepted that corporate performance is influenced by a combination of internal and external factors. These factors can be characterised as the organisation's internal 'strengths' and 'weaknesses' and its external 'opportunities' and 'threats'. Systematically analysing these factors as an aid to strategic decision-making represents a form of situational analysis known commonly by the acronym **SWOT (or TOWS)**.

The starting point for a SWOT analysis is usually a review of the organisation's internal strengths and weaknesses, which may be undertaken by management or by external consultants brought in to provide a more objective view. The identified factors may then be given scores to indicate their importance, with the more significant issues receiving a larger score. This process is then repeated for the firm's external opportunities and threats in order to highlight those external factors that are likely to occur and are expected to have an impact

Figure 18.4 A SWOT matrix

EXTERNAL ASPECTS \ INTERNAL ASPECTS	Strengths (S) List major organisational strengths (e.g. quality products)	Weaknesses (W) List major organisational weaknesses (e.g. poor distribution)
Opportunities (O) List major organisational opportunities (e.g. new markets)	SO strategies	WO strategies
Threats (T) List major organisational threats (e.g. competition)	ST strategies	WT strategies

on the organisation's future position. The resultant SWOT grid can then be used to focus attention on the key environmental influences faced by the organisation and to consider how far current strategy is relevant to the changes taking place in the business environment.

It is worth pointing out that the analysis of opportunities and threats cannot be absolute, since what might at first appear to be an opportunity may not be so when viewed against the organisation's resources or its culture or the expectations of its stakeholders. Moreover, the true value of the SWOT approach lies not in the listing of influences but in their contribution to the formulation of appropriate organisation strategies. One means of focusing attention on the latter is to produce a SWOT (TOWS) matrix, which matches the firm's opportunities and threats against its internal strengths and weaknesses (see Figure 18.4). The result is four sets of possible strategic alternatives – termed SO, ST, WO and WT strategies – which range from the positive exploitation of strengths in order to take advantage of opportunities to the essentially defensive strategy of minimising weaknesses and avoiding anticipated threats.

Limitations to environmental analysis

The techniques described above represent some of the ways in which organisations can examine the changing business environment in an attempt to understand what changes are likely to occur, how these may affect the organisation and what responses would be appropriate in the circumstances. In short, the value of such analysis lies not only in the information provided but also in the process of gathering and evaluating it and in applying it to the task of **strategic management**.

Despite its potential value as a tool of decision-making, environmental analysis is not without its limitations and these need to be taken into account. For a start, analysing the business environment is not a precise science and does not eliminate uncertainty for an organisation, caused, for instance, by unanticipated events which do not follow the normal pattern. Nor should it be regarded by managers as a means of foretelling the future, allowing them to avoid their responsibilities as strategic planners and decision-makers by blaming problems on a deficiency in the application of a particular technique or on inaccuracies in the data provided.

Added to this, environmental analysis of itself is by no means a guarantee of organisational effectiveness, and can sometimes complicate the decision-making process by providing information that calls into question the intuitive feeling of experienced managers. The danger is that the analysis may become an end in itself and may obscure information and data coming from other sources, rather than being used in conjunction with them. As a consequence, its value in strategic thinking and strategic decision-making may not be exploited to its full potential and this may represent a lost opportunity to the organisation, as well as an inefficient and ineffective use of resources.

Sources of information

by Nathan Rush

Researching the business environment can be a daunting task, given the extensive amount of information and statistical data available. To help in this direction the final section of this chapter outlines some of the key national and international information sources which are readily accessible to both students and businesses. While the list is by no means exhaustive, it gives a good indication of the wide range of assistance available to researchers and of the different formats in which information is published by government and non-government sources for different purposes. There has been a decided move away from publishing statistical data in print, although the print format is not yet completely redundant. The Internet is an invaluable resource and is now usually the starting point for anyone needing business information.

Statistical sources

Statistical information is an important component of business research and students need to be aware of what is available, particularly as some data turn up in the most unexpected places. Key guides in locating statistical information are:

1   *National Statistics – the official UK statistics site,* a portal to UK officially produced statistics. The Office for National Statistics is the UK national statistics institute responsible for collating and disseminating government statistics. Most information is available online as downloadable datasets (*www.ons.gov.uk*). Data are disseminated in publications (discussed below) and can be browsed in the Publications

Hub (*www.statistics.gov.uk*); this can be an easier way to access the vast amount of data produced by, and for, the UK government.

2 The *World Directory of Business Information Sources,* published by Euromonitor, now in its second edition. A two-volume set listing 22 000 providers of business information across a range of industries in 82 countries, this is a useful guide for hard-to-find, obscure business data.

3 Business information on the Internet, a gateway maintained by Karen Blakeman, including links to websites covering most aspects of business (see *www.rba.co.uk/sources/index.htm*).

Some of the main statistical sources are discussed below:

1 *Annual Abstract of Statistics.* Published by the ONS, this is an authoritative source of official statistics arranged under various headings, which include population, production, energy, transport, trade and public services. Figures usually cover a 10-year period and are presented in tabulated form. There is a detailed alphabetical index at the end. It is available to download at no charge from the National Statistics website (*www.statistics.gov.uk*).

2 *Datastream.* A finance and economics online database, produced by Thomson Reuters. Accounts for public companies around the world, as well as share prices and stock market indices, are available. The economics databases cover a vast range of current and historical international economic series, including money supply, inflation and interest rates, for 150 countries. Data are taken from many statistical sources, including the OECD and UK government, central banks and unofficial statistical sources.

3 *United Nations Economic Commission for Europe (UNECE).* Another source of European economic data can be found on the UNECE website (*www.unece.org/stats/stats_h.html*). Data on national accounts, labour figures, gender and transport statistics can be accessed for individual countries and compared with other European, North American or central Asian countries.

4 *Economic Review.* Since January 2012 the *Economic & Labour Market Review* has divided to become the *Economic Review* and *Labour Market Statistics*. Both are monthly releases by the ONS and a key guide to the current economic indicators (e.g. prices, unemployment, trade interest rates and exchange rates) and labour market data.

5 *The Economist Intelligence Unit.* Reviewing the business environment for selected countries, the EIU produces Country Reports for around 195 countries. Demographic data, risk analysis, political, regulatory and economic indicators, forecasts and analysis are given. More in-depth analysis is provided on a subscription basis. This is a useful online resource for PEST/PESTLE analysis (see *www.eiu.com*).

6 *Employment and Social Developments in Europe.* Combining the Social Situation Report and the Employment in Europe report, this publication contains an excellent overview of employment issues in Europe. Published annually online by the European Commission (see *http://ec.europa.eu/social/home.jsp*).

7 *Europa World Year Book.* A Routledge publication available in print and online. An annual publication covering political and economic information in more than 250 countries, not just European countries as the title suggests (see *www.europaworld.com/pub*).

8 *Europe in Figures: Eurostat Yearbook.* A comprehensive and useful introduction to statistical data on the EU and its member states. The yearbook is also a useful alternative if you are overwhelmed by the Eurostat website. Background data and more than 500 statistical tables, graphs and maps are presented. Areas covered include the economy, education, the labour market, industry and services, international trade, transport and the environment. The yearbook is available online only and is free to download from the Eurostat website (*http://ec.europa.eu/eurostat*) where the most up-to-date statistical tables can also be found.

9 *Family Spending.* The Living Costs and Food Survey (LCF) is conducted annually by the ONS. Primarily collecting information on expenditure of goods and services for private households, the survey also captures data about the income of household members. It also collects specialist food data, which are used and sponsored by the Department for Environment, Food and Rural Affairs (DEFRA). The results of the survey form the ONS annual publication 'Family Spending', available online (*www.ons.gov.uk*). The LCF is primarily used to provide information for the Retail Price Index. Historically in 2008 the Expenditure and Food Survey became part of the Integrated Household Survey (IHS), which itself was renamed as the Living Costs and Food Survey. Much of the General Household Survey was integrated into the IHS after its cessation in January 2012.

10 *Annual Survey of Hours and Earnings.* Replacing the *New Earnings* Survey in 2004, the ASHE presents detailed data in tables on earnings and hours paid for employees within industries, occupations and regions. It is free to download from the ONS website (*www.statistics.gov.uk*).

11 *United Kingdom National Accounts.* Also known as the 'Blue Book', this annual ONS publication contains data on domestic and national output, income and expenditure, and includes a sector-by-sector analysis. Figures often cover 10 years or more and an alphabetical index is provided. Best accessed through the Publications Hub if the whole publication is to be viewed (see *www.statistics.gov.uk*).

12 *OECD Economic Outlook.* A bi-annual assessment of economic trends, policies and prospects in OECD and non-member countries, the Outlook includes articles as well as figures, tables, charts and short-term projections, and looks at developments on a country-by-country basis. Available for subscribers to download or alternatively free to read online.

13 *OECD Economic Surveys.* Surveys are presented as country reviews containing comprehensive analysis of developments in the subject country, along with individual chapters covering key economic challenges being faced and recommendations for dealing with the challenges. The member country reviews are updated every 18 months, while non-member reviews are done on an ad hoc basis. Available for subscribers to download or alternatively free to read online.

14 *Regional Trends.* An annual ONS publication providing a wide range of information on social, demographic and economic aspects of the UK's standard planning regions, together with some data on the sub-regions and on the EU. The guide includes a subject index.

15 *Social Trends.* Another annual ONS publication, in this case looking at different aspects of British society, including population, education, environment, housing, leisure and transport. It provides a more detailed analysis of data produced for the Annual Abstract of Statistics and includes a large number of charts and

diagrams. Information often spans a 15–20-year period and an alphabetical subject index is included.

16 *United Kingdom Balance of Payments.* Known as the 'Pink Book'. It is a comprehensive guide to the UK's external trade performance and contains a wide range of statistics covering a 10-year period. Available on the ONS website (see *www.ons.gov.uk*).

17 *United Nations Statistical Yearbook.* Written in both English and French, the Yearbook is a detailed international comparative analysis of UN member countries. Data cover a wide variety of topics, including international finance, transport and communications, population, trade and wages, and a World Statistical Summary is provided at the beginning. Particularly helpful if finding the statistics section of the UN website overwhelming. More useful to look at historical trends and data rather than the latest statistics. Available to purchase in print, chapters are also available to view online (see *http://unstats.un.org/unsd/syb/default.htm*).

18 *World Economic Outlook.* Usually published twice a year by the International Monetary Fund (IMF); the focus is on the analysis and projections of global economic developments in the short and medium term. It also considers current world economic policy issues. It is available in print and also as a free download from the IMF website (*www.imf.org*), where other useful statistics can be found, including the World Economic Outlook interactive database.

Other useful statistical sources

1 Most government departments publish statistics on their own websites. Of particular interest are the following:

   (a) *Department for Business, Innovation and Skills.* This is the government department to peruse for statistics on a wide variety of information, including SME statistics, UK competitiveness indicators, construction and energy statistics, and regional data, such as economic performance indicators. The Statistics tab gives access to these data (see *www.gov.uk/government/organisations/department-for-business-innovation-skills*).

   (b) *HM Treasury.* HM Treasury has control over public spending, setting the direction of the UK's economic policy. It is the government's economic and finance department and a good source of statistics on the UK economy, freely accessible from its website (see *www.gov.uk/government/organisations/hm-treasury*).

2 *Eurostat.* The Statistical Office of the European Communities (Eurostat) is responsible for producing data for the EU. There are numerous links to information on areas including general and regional statistics, demography, economic development and trade statistics. All are available to view on the Eurostat website (*http://ec.europa.eu/eurostat*).

3 *UK Data Archive.* The UK Data Archive (University of Essex) is a specialist national resource containing the largest collection of accessible data in the social sciences and humanities in the UK. Most universities are members of the UK Access Management Federation (UKAMF), meaning students and staff gain free access to the data after completing a short registration form; other users must register. Some data, including UK census and international databanks, can be used only by HE/FE authenticated users (see *www.data-archive.ac.uk*).

4   *Bank of England.* For the very latest information on UK interest rates and inflation the Bank of England website is invaluable (*www.bankofengland.co.uk*). Other financial data are available as well as full text publications on surveys and working papers.

5   Sources of further information. By selecting a gateway site, you will often find links to just the information you need much more quickly than by simply using Google. For example:

(a) *Useful UK Statistics sites from the University of Glasgow Library.* A very thorough summary (see *www.gla.ac.uk/services/library/collections/mapsofficialpublications andstatisticsunit/statisticscollection/internetsitesforstatistics*).

(b) *RBA Information Resources.* A gateway maintained by Karen Blakeman, including links to websites covering most aspects of business (see *www.rba.co.uk/sources/ index.htm*).

Information sources

Information on the different aspects of the business environment can be found in a variety of sources, including books, newspapers and periodicals. These often provide a wealth of contemporary data and commentary which can be located relatively easily in most cases, using specialist databases designed to assist the researcher. While an increasing amount of information is available on the Internet, the fastest and most reliable way of finding what you want tends to be to use newspapers and magazines, which are often available electronically.

In the last few years more and more abstracting databases have moved over to the Web and now also offer the full text of articles, thereby reducing the amount of time it takes to research a topic. ProQuest (see below) can be used to trace information, but there are other alternatives (e.g. LexisLibrary). It is even possible to customise your business databases to cover the most popular titles in a particular library. But remember, the situation tends to change on a regular basis, so you need to keep up to date. Some key sources in this area are discussed below:

1   *RDS Business Suite.* Covers worldwide trade and business news, sourcing information from journals, national and international newspapers, and industry newsletters. Useful when searching for broad profiling information about companies or industries. It is available as an online subscription database.

2   *Ebsco.* Has a range of business databases, including the Business Source range that offers full text articles and abstracts in the areas of business, economics and management.

3   *Emerald.* An Internet version of all the journals published by MCB University Press; includes some keys titles like the *European Journal of Marketing.* Also includes abstracts from many other journals in the Emerald reviews section.

4   *FT.com.* Online subscription database combining a rolling archive of the *Financial Times* and *Europe Intelligence Wire.* Especially good for European financial and economic news, it is a good starting point when researching current events.

5   *ProQuest.* Has a series of databases useful for business students. Particularly noteworthy is ABI/Inform Global. ProQuest databases are noted for the quality of their abstracting and information retrieval.

Other useful sources

1 *Bank of England Quarterly Bulletin.* An assessment of economic developments in the UK and the rest of the world. It includes articles and speeches, together with general commentary on the economy, and is available from the Bank of England website (www.bankofengland.co.uk).

2 *Bank reviews.* Quarterly publications by some of the leading clearing banks and often available free on request.

3 *CBI Business Surveys.* The CBI states that its quarterly surveys are the longest-running UK private sector qualitative business tendency surveys, the first being in 1958. The surveys are a comprehensive look at industrial trends, service sector, financial services, distributive trades and investment intentions. They provide a useful insight into business prospects and an indicator of future changes. They are available in full on a subscription basis, but the key findings are available on the CBI website (see *www.cbi.org.uk/business-issues/economic-intelligence*).

4 *Company Annual Reports.* An annual report is a description of a company's activities and financial performance for a particular period of time, usually the previous calendar year. Libraries used to hold vast collections of print annual reports, but since the Companies Act 2006 allows for the provision of an electronic rather than printed report, accessing them online has become the norm. For those conducting historical research, The Guildhall Library, City of London (see *www.cityoflondon.gov.uk/things-to-do/visiting-the-city/archives-and-city-history/guildhall-library/Pages/default.aspx*) holds a range of historical business sources, including annual reports of companies listed on the London Stock Exchange 1880–1965. For current annual reports there are various options. First, the company's own website should be consulted; second, various databases such as Mergent Online and Proquest's ABI/Inform Global contain annual reports to browse; finally, online directories compile annual reports for perusal in one accessible place. Three such services are recommended:

(a) *AnnualReports.com* offers free access to companies listed on UK and US stock exchanges. Companies are searchable by exchange, industry sector or company name. Though you are unlikely to find some of the more obscure, unlisted companies, this is still a useful resource (*www.annualreports.com*).

(b) *Financial Times Company Content Hub.* The Company Content Hub is an interactive tool from FT.com that allows you to search for UK and global companies by country, sector, exchange or company name. Where available, an archive of annual reports is offered along with interim reports. Older annual reports can sometimes be difficult to find on company websites, making this feature particularly useful (*http://markets.ft.com/research/Markets/Company-Content*). Basic information is also given about the company as well as the major shareholders, details of directors and forecasts.

(c) *The Annual Reports Service.* Companies listed on the London Stock Exchange are presented in an alphabetical list or by industry. Compiled by PrecisionIR, who will deliver small numbers by post or forward electronic reports to a supplied email (www.orderannualreports.com).

5 *Wright Investors' Service.* This site includes information on 31 000 companies in more than 50 countries. The information provided is just a 'snapshot' but is current and

is usually sufficient to form the basis of a company profile (see *www.wisi.com/ramainnew.htm*). The site includes *Corporate Information,* a subscription service with full reports on the listed companies, giving further details on industry sectors, economic data, and country- and regional-specific searches.

6 *Accountancy firms.* Many accountancy and audit firms produce their own reports and research, much of which is freely available from their websites. These can be written from a UK or global perspective covering the state of industry and any likely changes that may impact upon that industry. Three firms that produce particularly good reports and research are Ernst & Young (*www.ey.com*), PricewaterhouseCoopers (*www.pwc.com*) and Deloitte (*www.deloitte.com*). The reports are often categorised on their websites as industries, insights or issues.

7 *Newspaper Index.* A very useful website (*www.newspaperindex.com*) giving online access to newspapers from around the world. The main international quality newspapers are available here, as well as the Sunday papers. Where an English translated website is available, this is indicated.

8 *Income Data Services.* A regular series of studies and reports on pay and other labour market issues (e.g. teamworking, child care, redundancy), containing valuable up-to-date information and some statistical analysis. Available on the Internet via *www.incomesdata.co.uk*

9 *Key British Enterprises.* A multi-volume compendium from Dun & Bradstreet giving details of the UK's top 50 000 companies. Companies are listed alphabetically and are also indexed by trade, product and geographical location. Available in print and online (see *www.dnb.co.uk*).

10 *Kompass (United Kingdom).* A multi-volume directory with details on companies including products and services, industrial trade names and employee numbers. The Kompass website (*www.kompass.com*) allows a product or company search in 66 countries worldwide. Basic information is free.

11 *Haymarket Media.* Haymarket Media produces a range of magazines on various aspects of the business environment, for example *Marketing* and *PR Week*. They are an accessible source of facts and articles presented in a journalistic style. Details available on the Internet via *www.haymarket.com/home.aspx*

12 *Market research.* Market research reports cover market factors, trends, market share, the supply structure and consumer characteristics, and frequently include forecasts of future prospects. Sometimes dismissed by non-marketing students, these are very useful sources of information placing companies in their market context. Sometimes available freely online, most current market research is accessible only on a subscription basis. Major UK suppliers of market research include Mintel and Key Note; there are also providers of international market research including Euromonitor's Passport database.

13 *Retail Price Index – Headline Rate.* A site maintained by the Office for National Statistics giving a table with the RPI (headline rate), month by month, for the last 20 years. Available at *www.ons.gov.uk/economy/inflationandpriceindices*

14 *The Economist.* A standard reference source published weekly and examining economic and political events throughout the world. It is an invaluable publication for business students and regularly contains features on specific business-related topics. It has a useful update on basic economic indicators. Available on the Internet via *www.economist.com*

15 *WARC Advertising and Marketing Knowledge.* The World Advertising Research Center's Advertising and Marketing Knowledge database is a vast collection of case studies and articles from authoritative sources. It covers all areas of advertising, marketing and media activity. Available at *www.warc.com*

16 *Who Owns Whom.* An annual publication which identifies parent companies and their subsidiaries. It is a useful source of information for examining the pattern of corporate ownership in the UK. There is no size criteria for entry; however, companies and organisations are included only if ownership is greater than 51 per cent by other companies or organisations. Companion volumes are also available covering other parts of the world.

A final comment

When researching a business topic you are particularly recommended to use library catalogue sites, especially the British Library catalogue (*www.bl.uk*) and COPAC (*http://copac.ac.uk*), which is the combined catalogue of major British academic libraries. WorldCat (*www.worldcat.org*) is an integration of more than 10 000 library catalogues from across the world, so could be useful when searching for more obscure international business information. You might also want to check references on Internet bookshop sites such as Blackwell's (*http://bookshop.blackwell.co.uk*) or Amazon (*www.amazon.co.uk*). For older material AbeBooks (*www.abebooks.co.uk*) is useful as it specialises in older, out-of-print books.

Synopsis

As the chapter has demonstrated, there is a need for business organisations to monitor the environment in which they exist and operate and, where possible, to anticipate changes that are likely to affect the enterprise. Rather than being an optional extra, environmental analysis and scanning should be seen as an intrinsic part of strategic management and should ideally provide data and information that are used to guide the decision-making process. Many of these data and much of the information already exist in published form and/or can be easily gathered from both literary and electronic sources on a national and international basis. Analysing them is also possible, using a range of techniques which has been developed by businesses and academics over a considerable number of years.

Summary of key points

- A firm's business environment changes over time.

- Firms need to consider and anticipate potential changes in their general and operational environments in order to take advantage of opportunities and/or minimise possible threats.

- Environmental analysis should be seen as a key part of the strategic management process; ideally it should form part of the basis on which corporate decisions are taken.

- Such analysis can occur at both a societal level (e.g. through PESTLE analysis) and at a task level (e.g. through industry-based approaches) and can involve the use of a wide variety of established techniques.

- Key techniques include trend extrapolation, scenario planning, the Delphi approach, cross-impact matrices and SWOT analysis.

- In researching the business environment, students and practitioners can utilise a wide range of information sources, many of which are relatively inexpensive and readily accessible.

- Accessing this information has been made considerably easier with improvements in information technology, especially the Internet

case study

Scenario planning at Shell

Royal Dutch Shell has utilised scenario planning as an integral part of its range of techniques for undertaking external analysis since the early 1970s. Its first scenarios were developed in 1972 and were narrow in scope, concentrating on forecasts for economic growth and the impacts of a discontinuity or shortage of supply of oil on prices. Until this point, both economic growth and oil supply had shown high levels of consistent and predictable growth, and Royal Dutch Shell was interested in exploring a 'what if' scenario should oil supply become destabilised. This scenario became realised in October 1974, following the Yom Kippur War and subsequent Arab oil embargo on supply of oil to the United States and supporting governments of the state of Israel.

The realisation of Shell's first scenarios acted as a powerful argument for the continued investment in scenario planning, and Shell has continued to produce scenarios, typically on a three-year cycle, to the present day.

Initially, Shell's scenarios tended to focus narrowly on economic perspectives of oil demand and supply over a relatively short time horizon (three–five years). The scenarios were presented as 'in-house' publications only, having been produced by the organisation's own strategic analysts. As Shell's experience, willingness to invest increasing resources and scenario planning skills matured, the scenarios gradually became more complex and broader in scope, incorporating both geo-political and geo-societal trends. The decade of the 1980s was characterised by Shell as being driven by what it termed 'transition', trends that would see the end of the Cold War, the beginning of the collapse of the former Soviet bloc and increasing market liberalisation. The 1990s would be one of continuing liberalisation, underpinned by powerful forces for globalisation and technological innovation. So pervasive and dominant were these trends considered to be that Shell coined the expression 'TINA' (There Is No Alternative) to describe them.

In 2005, Shell introduced three new scenarios that were looking ahead to 2025. These scenarios questioned for the first time the assumptions of its 'TINA' trends. The scenarios published – named 'Open Doors', 'Low Trust Globalisation' and 'Flags' – suggested that there might be a break on globalisation and market liberalisation. Shell drew upon the events of 9/11 and the financial scandal of Enron as examples of geo-political crises of security and trust. These environmental shocks could foreshadow a period of slowing international trade, as governments became more protective in their policies towards their own domestic industries and, specifically, energy resources. Additionally, there would be increased pressure on all organisations to be far more transparent and accountable towards society in all their business activities and disclosure of performance.

In early 2008, Shell published further scenarios, which looked at plausible future developments in global energy markets up to 2050. In the foreword of its published report, Shell's Chief Executive, Jeroen van der Veer stated:

'Never before has humanity faced such a challenging outlook for energy and the planet. This can be summed up in five words: "more energy, less carbon dioxide." '

The company identified three key trends that were likely to alter the energy landscape significantly. It termed these its 'three hard truths':

- There will be a surge in energy demand (global requirements are predicted to double by 2050), especially resulting from the growth in economic activity from both China and India.
- Traditional energy sources are struggling to keep up with demand.
- Current and future projected uses of energy will continue to raise carbon dioxide emissions and other greenhouse gases, with adverse effects on the environment.

Given the above trends – which when compared can be seen to create obvious tensions – Shell characterised the possible future energy landscape as 'TANIA' (There Are No Ideal Answers).

From these trends, two scenarios were developed, one entitled 'Scramble', the other 'Blueprints'.

In the scenario of 'Scramble', Shell suggested that events will continue to outpace action. For the next decade, people from all walks of life will join the debate about energy and climate change, but for governments, security of energy supply and fears of losing economic ground will shape decision-making and policy. The primary focus will be on meeting the needs of global demand and there will be little in the way of consideration of investing in more efficient

means of providing energy until traditional sources become critically depleted. In a 'Scramble' future, focus on addressing greenhouse gas emissions would receive scant attention much before around 2020, by when an increasing frequency of climate shocks would force governments to respond belatedly to the needs of the natural environment. Even then, Shell believed that such responses would be localised, with both governments and firms taking individual action, with little framework for a coordinated, considered global response. Although by 2050 greenhouse gas emissions would have been reduced, it argued that the efforts may be seen as too little, too late.

In 'Blueprints', groups of seemingly disconnected people (e.g. politicians, environmentalists, venture capitalists, farmers and businesses) all begin to recognise the profitable potential of finding solutions to the challenges of economic development, energy security and environmental pollution at the same time. These seemingly disparate groups would begin to collaborate together in localised and regionalised areas, motivated by recognising the need to take action before it was forced upon them by circumstance.

These actions would receive public support, which then would transfer into public pressure on governments for change. Buildings would become more energy efficient, and government efforts to reduce greenhouse gas emissions and improve air quality would occur. Participating governments would use a range of individualised, local initiatives and policy investments, from tax breaks to subsidies, mandates, and investment and support for new 'cleaner' technologies. While governments would begin to take a holistic view of the challenges posed, multinational firms could find international investment decisions and strategies difficult to implement given the patchwork of government initiatives. These firms would therefore begin to pressure local, national and international authorities to harmonise approaches towards energy consumption, supply and environmental management.

With harmonisation would come widespread adoption of good efficiency practices. Trading schemes for carbon dioxide emissions' rights would begin to cover a critical mass of industry sectors in a critical mass of countries and transport would become 'greener' through growth in vehicle engine hybrids and, later, fully electric vehicles.

In its latest iteration (2013) of what it calls its 'new lens scenarios', Shell has proposed two further visions of future worlds which it terms 'Mountains' and 'Oceans'. These are based on the expectation that demand for critical resources such as water, energy and food – referred to as the 'Stress Nexus' – will rise by 40–50 per cent as the global population heads towards 9 billion by mid-century and poverty declines. 'Mountains' is essentially a world in which those at the top generally work to create a stable environment in ways which ensure the maintenance of the status quo. Rigid power structures and institutions will tend to hamper economic development, but enable established sectors to gain an advantage by unlocking resources that require significant capital and new technology. Under this view of the future, there is a strong role for government and for the introduction of policy measures that will help to create more compact cities and transform the global transport network. The expectation is that natural gas resources will become the largest global energy source by the 2030s and that policy will drive the introduction of carbon capture and storage technology, thereby supporting a cleaner energy system.

'Oceans' by way of contrast is a world which is both more prosperous and volatile, one in which competing economic and political interests are accommodated intermittently. As those at the top recognise that their future success depends on compromise, reform of existing economic and financial structures is likely to occur and this will increase aspirations for further reform by empowered constituencies. Given the wider distribution of power, the expectation is that governments will take longer to agree major decisions and that consequently market forces rather than policy will shape the development of the energy system. Liquid fuel and coal will continue to hold a key role in the energy mix until solar becomes the world's largest energy source by the 2070s.

Case study questions

1 In what ways might scenario planning be useful to a firm?

2 Why is scenario planning not more widely used in business?

> **web link**
>
> The Shell website at www.shell.com contains a wealth of information on the company's involvement with scenario planning.

Review and discussion questions

1 Discuss the costs and benefits to businesses of the introduction of a system for monitoring and analysing the changing external environment in which they operate.

2 To what extent do you agree with the proposition that only large firms should or can make use of the various techniques of environmental analysis?

3 Using a firm or organisation of your choice, attempt a 'SWOT' analysis. For example, can you apply such an analysis to the organisation in which you work or study?

4 Using the information sources discussed in the text, and any others with which you are familiar, provide a comparative analysis of consumer markets in at least eight leading European countries (including Eastern Europe).

Assignments

1 You work for a medium-sized private company in the UK fashion industry (it can be on either the production or the retailing side). As a personal assistant to the managing director, your brief is to provide help and advice on various aspects of the firm's operations. You have recently become concerned about the lack of a system for monitoring changes in the business environment and have agreed to produce a report on the issue for the board of directors. In producing this report, you are required to identify both the costs and the benefits to the business of implementing a system of environmental scanning.

2 As a librarian in a college (or university) library, with responsibility for help and advice to students on business studies courses, you are frequently asked for guidance on how to access information and data on a particular company. Choosing any well-known company you wish, produce a diagrammatic representation (e.g. flow chart) of the steps you would advise students to undertake to get the information they require. At each step, indicate what type of information is available and how and from where it can be obtained.

Further reading

Brandenburger, A. and Nalebuff, B., 'The right game: use game theory to shape strategy', *Harvard Business Review,* July–August, pp. 57–71, 1995.

Cooke, S. and Slack, N., *Making Management Decisions,* 2nd edition, Prentice Hall, 1991.

Fahey, L. and Narayanan, V. K., *Macroenvironmental Analysis for Strategic Management,* West Publishing, 1986.

Finlay, P. N., *Strategic Management: An Introduction to Business and Corporate Strategy,* Financial Times/Prentice Hall, 2000.

Grant, R. M., *Contemporary Strategy Analysis,* 8th edition, Wiley, 2010.

Gupta, U. and Clarke, R., 'Theory and applications of the Delphi Technique: a bibliography (1975–1994)', *Technological Forecasting and Social Change,* 53, pp. 185–211, 1996.

Johnson, G., Scholes, K. and Whittington, R., *Exploring Corporate Strategy,* 9th edition, Financial Times/Prentice Hall, 2011.

Proctor, T., 'Strategic marketing management for health management: cross impact matrix and TOWS', *Journal of Management in Medicine,* 14 (1), pp. 47–56, 2000.

Ringland, G., *Scenario Planning: Managing for the Future,* 2nd edition, Wiley, 2006.

Rowe, G. and Wright, G., 'The Delphi Technique as a forecasting tool: issues and analysis', *International Journal of Forecasting,* 15, pp. 353–75, 1999.

The Economist, 'There will be blood', 23 February 2008.

Wheelen, T. L. and Hunger, J. D., *Strategic Management and Business Policy,* 13th edition, Pearson Education, 2012.

Worthington, I., Britton, C. and Rees, A., *Business Economics: Blending Theory and Practice,* 2nd edition, Financial Times/Prentice Hall, esp. Chapter 15, 2005.

Web links and further questions are available on the website at:
www.pearsoned.co.uk/worthington

Abnormal profit: profit over and above normal profit.

Accelerator effect: increases in investment spending as a result of changes in output or sales.

Acceptance: under contract law, acceptance is the notion of legally agreeing to an offer that is made.

ACORN: an acronym for A Classification Of Residential Neighbourhoods, a method of segmenting consumer markets.

Age structure: the proportions of a population in different age bands.

Ageing population: the increase in the average age of a population.

Agent: a person or organisation who is authorised by another person or organisation to act on behalf of the latter.

Aggregate monetary demand: the total demand for goods and services in the economy.

Article 50: This term refers to Article 50 of the Lisbon Treaty (signed in 2007). Article 50 states that 'Any Member State may decide to withdraw from the Union in accordance with its own constitutional requirements.' Article 50 was triggered by British Prime Minister, Theresa May, on 29 March 2017 by notifying the European Union of the country's intention to withdraw.

Articles of Association: a document regulating the internal administration of a company including the rights of shareholders, the qualifications required of directors, rules relating to company rules, etc.

Assisted Areas: areas qualifying for state aid under government regional policy.

Authoritarian: the disposition to settle disputes through the enforcement of rules, regulations and orders by an established authority.

Average cost of production: total costs per unit of output.

Backbench MPs: ordinary Members of Parliament who do not occupy a role in government or on the Opposition front bench.

Balance of payments: a record of the transactions between one country and the other countries with which it trades.

Balance of trade: the balance of the import and export of goods.

Barriers to entry: any barriers which prevent or inhibit the entry of firms into an industry or market.

Barriers to exit: any barriers which prevent or inhibit the exit of firms out of an industry or market.

Birth rate: usually measured by the number of live births per thousand of the population in a given year.

Black economy: unofficial economic activity beyond the gaze of the tax authorities.

Brainstorming: is normally taken to mean a discursive activity designed to generate ideas and solutions to problems.

British Business Bank: a state-owned bank established to address the problem of obtaining credit for smaller businesses.

Bureaucracy: an organisational form associated with hierarchy and a system of rules and procedures.

Bureaucrats: in government those who are official and permanent advisers to elected decision-makers (e.g. civil servants).

Business angels: informal investors in business organisations, especially smaller enterprises.

Business (or industrial) cluster: a geographic concentration of interconnected companies and associated businesses and institutions.

Business culture: the underlying attitudes and values of business organisations which affect their decisions and operations.

Business ethics: concerned with issues of 'right' and 'wrong' behaviour in a business context.

Business Link: an agency which provides advice and information to UK small businesses.

Business-to-business (B2B) commerce: the full spectrum of e-commerce that can occur between two business organisations, including supply management, procurement and purchasing, sale activities, payments, and service and support.

Business-to-consumer (B2C) commerce: the full spectrum of e-commerce business models, in which businesses sell to consumers.

Buyers' market: a market where there is excess supply of the product. This affords the buyer greater market power.

Buy-side marketplace: a marketplace where one organisation does all the buying.

Cabinet: in UK central government the core decision-making body comprising the Prime Minister and the other senior ministers responsible for formulating government policy and overseeing its implementation.

Capacity: under contract law, capacity is the notion that a party to an offer is legally able to enter into a binding contract.

Capital: human-made assets that are capable of producing goods and services.

Capital account: a record of the international flows of money for investment purposes.

Capital market: the market for longer-term loanable funds.

Capital market flows: flows of money from private investors wishing to include foreign assets in their portfolios.

Capitalist economy: a politico-economic system based upon private property and the pursuit of private profit through entrepreneurial activity.

Cartel: a collection of firms acting together as one producer to exercise market power.

Case law: law established by previous judicial decisions (i.e. judicial precedent).

Central bank: a country's state or national bank, usually responsible for exercising control over the country's monetary system.

Centrally planned economy: an economy in which the state makes the major decisions over resource allocation.

Chambers of Commerce: bodies representing the interests of smaller firms in a particular locality.

Charitable Incorporated Organisation (CIO): a legal structure which allows smaller charitable organisations to register with the Charities Commission without registering as a company (as a larger charity might do). This eliminates the requirements for charities to appoint directors and have £5,000 of income.

Checks and balances: in a democratic system the existence of social, economic and political arrangements that act as a constraint on the power of government.

Circular economy: an economy that, by design or intention, is restorative and eliminates waste.

Circular flow of income: a simplified model of the economy, which portrays economic activity as a flow of income and expenditures passing between households and firms in a circular motion.

City Action Teams: teams of individuals drawn from government, voluntary organisations, local community groups and businesses to tackle problems in inner-city areas.

City Challenge: a scheme designed to concentrate resources in areas experiencing urban problems by establishing cross-sector partnerships to bid for project funding.

City Grant: a system of grant aid that was designed to support private sector capital projects in urban areas.

Civil servants: permanent officials appointed to advise government ministers and to implement government decisions. Also called bureaucrats.

Classical theories of organisation: theories of organisation which essentially focus on organisations as formal structures established to achieve certain objectives under the direction of management.

Coalition government: a government formed by representatives of two or more parties either by choice or following an election in which no single party wins a majority of the seats being contested.

Code of practice: a code of conduct, usually drawn up voluntarily with the aid of a professional or trade association, which members of the trade or profession are expected to follow.

Collusion: cooperation between independent firms to modify their behaviour.

Combined authority: where local authorities pool powers and responsibilities to address local issues.

Common Agricultural Policy: a policy set up by the European Union to help the agricultural sector in Europe.

Common external tariff: a tariff payable on goods entering the European Union from non-member countries.

Common market: a group of countries acting as one in terms of trade – there are no barriers to trade between members and a common external tariff for non-members.

Community Incorporated Organisation: a special type of company whose assets and profits are used for the public good.

Community initiatives: policy initiatives within the European Union to address specific problems such as rural development.

Community Interest Company: a new legal form of a charitable organisation.

Company: a corporate body recognised by law as having a legal identity separate from that of its members (i.e. shareholders).

Company directors: individuals appointed or elected by a company's shareholders to run the company and to represent their interest.

Competition Act 1998: a major piece of UK competition policy designed to bring UK law in line with EU law on issues of anti-competitive agreements and abuse of dominant market position.

Competition and Markets Authority: the new competition body in the UK that has replaced the Competition Commission.

Competition Commission: a public body which replaced the UK Monopolies and Mergers Commission with responsibilities in the field of competition policy.

Competition policy: government policy aimed at promoting competition in the marketplace by regulating market behaviour and controlling potential abuses of market power by firms acting singly or in concert.

Competitive advantage: the sources of superior performance by an organisation.

Complements: products which are related to each other such that as the price of one goes up, the demand for the other goes down (e.g. CD players and CDs).

Computer-aided design (CAD): the use of computers in the design of products and processes.

Concentration: a measure of the level of competition in an industry or market. Concentration can be measured by sales or employment.

Concentration ratio: a ratio which calculates the percentage of the total market accounted for by the largest firms.

Confederation of British Industry: a body formed to promote the interests of British industry and to represent its views in government circles in an attempt to influence government decisions.

Conglomerate merger: a merger or takeover between firms in different, unrelated industries.

Consideration: under contract law, some right, interest, profit or benefit accruing to one party or some forbearance, detriment, loss or responsibility given, suffered or undertaken by the other.

Consortium: an association or syndicate of business organisations normally established in order to undertake a major enterprise by polling resources and/or expertise.

Constitution: in the political sense it usually refers to a written statement or document identifying where formal political power resides in a country and the relationships between political institutions.

Consumer Price Index: the latest UK measure of inflation.

Consumer societies: a form of 'self-help' organisation set up to serve its members.

Consumer sovereignty: the notion that the pattern of supply and hence the allocation of resources in the economy is dictated by the demands of consumers.

Contestable market: a market where there are no barriers to entry or exit.

Contingency approach: in organisational theory the idea that organisational design and management should adapt to the situation confronting an organisation.

Corporate governance: the structures and processes within an organisation by which control and decision-making are exercised in accordance with the law and the aims of the organisation's primary stakeholders (e.g. the shareholders).

Corporate image: essentially how an organisation is seen by its customers and other interested parties.

Corporate social responsibility: the idea that an organisation should be responsible for the effect its actions might have on the broader society.

Cost–benefit analysis: a technique which seeks to evaluate the social costs and benefits of an investment project as an aid to decision-making.

Council: in local government, the central elected decision-making body.

Council of Ministers: the EU's ultimate decision-making body, also referred to as The Council of the European Union.

Cradle-to-cradle^{TM} **(C2C):** an approach to business that seeks to eliminate waste and create completely safe and healthy products by adopting eco-effective ways of working.

Credit rating agency: an organisation that rates the creditworthiness of both companies and countries.

Criminal law: the branch of law that relates to a legal wrong, a breach of public duty punishable by the state on behalf of society.

Cross-impact matrix: a technique for evaluating and assessing environmental change based on an identification of events thought likely to occur, including an indication of their sequencing and probability of occurrence.

Cross-price elasticity: the responsiveness of quantity demanded of one product to changes in the price of other products.

Cross-subsidisation: where profits from one market can be used to keep prices down in another market – common in multinationals.

Crowding out: the thesis that the use of funds by government for public expenditure denies the private sector access to those funds for entrepreneurial activity.

Cultural diversity: normally associated with countries which have a mixture of citizens of different racial and ethnic origins.

Culture: a complex set of values, norms, beliefs, attitudes, customs, systems and artefacts handed down from generation to generation.

Current account: a record of the international flows of money in exchange for goods and services.

Current balance: the balance of payments on the current account.

Customs: particular forms of behaviour that have come to be accepted as social norms within a specific community.

Customs union: a union of countries that constitutes a single customs territory (see 'Common market').

Cyclical unemployment: unemployment which results from downswings in the trade cycle.

Death rate: usually measured as the number of deaths per thousand of the population in a given year.

Debentures: long-term bonds or loans to the company on which it pays interest.

Decisions: within the European Union, a decision that is binding on those states, companies or individuals to whom it is addressed.

Deficit: a situation where imports are greater than exports, so that there is an outflow of money from a country.

Deindustrialisation: a decline in the importance of manufacturing industry in the economy.

Delegated legislation: law made by a person or body to which Parliament has given limited powers of law making.

Delphi method: a technique of environmental analysis involving several iterations by expert observers of the business environment. Also called expert opinion.

Demand: the quantity of a product that buyers are willing and able to buy at every conceivable price level.

Demand chain management (DCM): the management of the organisation's activities related to its customers, distribution channels and markets.

Demand curve: a graph that shows the relationship between the price of a product and the quantity demanded of that product.

Democracy: literally government by the people. In practice democracy refers to the idea of elected government, based upon universal suffrage and regular, free and fair elections.

Demographic time bomb: the shortage of young people entering the labour force as a result of low birth rates 16 years earlier.

Demography: the study of populations.

Dependent population: those non-working members of a population (e.g. pensioners, the young) who depend on the working population for various forms of support.

Derived demand: a demand for a product that is not required for its own sake but because it is used to produce another product.

Devalue: a deliberate reduction in the exchange rate of a currency.

Differentiation: making a product different in the minds of consumers – these differences may be real or imagined.

Digital products (services): products that are transformed to information that can be expressed digitally. Music, computer software and movies are examples of products that can be digitised and delivered electronically to buyers.

Direct controls: government policies designed to tackle specific economic problems such as the control of imports or wage inflation.

Direct (or pure) democracy: where government decisions are based upon the expressed preference of the people, usually through a referendum.

Direct taxation: taxes imposed on income and wealth.

Directives: EU decisions which lay down compulsory objectives but which leave it to member states to translate them into national legislation.

Director General of Fair Trading: in the UK the person responsible for overseeing consumer affairs and competition policy on behalf of the government.

Directorates-General: major administrative and executive structures within the European Union to administer and oversee EU policy.

Diseconomies of scale: increases in average costs of production, which occur when an organisation grows in size (or scale). These mainly stem from the problems of managing large organisations.

Diversification: extending production into unrelated areas through development of new products or entry into unrelated markets.

Dividends: the distribution of part of a company's profit to its shareholders.

Divisional structure: an organisational form involving the splitting up of an organisation into a number of self-contained units or divisions, each of which operates as a profit centre.

Downsizing: a reduction in the size of the firm, normally through redundancy and/or delayering.

Eco-efficiency: a principle based on increasing productivity while decreasing both resource use and pollution.

Eco-label: a system of labelling products so as to identify those that have a reduced impact on the environment.

Eco-Management and Audit Scheme (EMAS): a voluntary EU standard indicating a participating firm's level of environmental management.

Economic efficiency: efficiency in the use and allocation of resources.

Economic growth: a country's increase in national income (national output) over time.

Economic scarcity: a situation in which there are insufficient resources to satisfy all the actual and potential demands for those resources.

Economics: a social science concerned primarily with the production, distribution and consumption of goods and services under conditions of relative economic scarcity.

Economies of scale: reductions in average costs of production which occur when an organisation grows in size (or scale). These can stem from a variety of sources, including technical, marketing and financial.

Educated workforce: a workforce that has the necessary level of education and training for a modern economy.

Effective demand: demand for a product backed up by the willingness and ability to pay for that product.

Effective supply: supply that firms are able and willing to make available to a market.

Elasticity: a measurement of the responsiveness of one variable (e.g. demand, supply) to a change in another variable (e.g. price, income).

Elasticity of demand: the responsiveness of quantity demanded of a product to changes in its price.

Elasticity of supply: the responsiveness of quantity supplied of a product to changes in its price.

Electoral system: a system for electing a country's or area's governing authority.

Electronic business (e-business): the exchange of products, services or information, whether paid or unpaid, across electronic networks, at any stage within the value system (including the supply chain, the value chain and the distribution chain). The term embraces activities such as servicing customers and collaboration with partners.

Electronic commerce (e-commerce): e-commerce covers a narrower sphere of activities than e-business, and refers in particular to the process of electronic transactions involved in the exchange of products, services and information between a buyer and seller.

Electronic customer relationship management (eCRM): software and management practices designed to serve the customer from order through delivery and after-sales service.

Electronic data interchange (EDI): the computer-to-computer exchange of structured data, sent in a form that allows for automatic processing with no manual intervention. This is usually carried out over specialist EDI networks.

Electronic enterprise (e-enterprise): An organisation that uses the Internet and/or the Web to execute some, or all, of its main business processes.

Electronic funds transfer (EFT): the process of exchanging account information electronically over private communications networks.

Electronic markets (e-markets): the business centre, where business transactions take place, is a network-based location, and not a physical location. This is sometimes referred to as the marketspace. The buyers, sellers and intermediaries are all situated at different locations. The electronic market handles all the necessary transactions, including the transfer of payments.

Electronic point of sale (EPOS): the application of electronic technology at the point of sale.

Emerging economies: those developing economies that often have increasing levels of income and have considerable potential for future growth.

English Partnerships: a government development agency involved in reclaiming industrial sites for economic purposes.

Enterprise: the business unit or organisation as a whole.

Enterprise and Regulatory Reform Act 2013: a piece of UK government legislation basically aimed at promoting private enterprise and competitive markets via various reforms.

Enterprise Grants: government grants designed to promote entrepreneurial activity.

Enterprise Zones: an experiment introduced by the UK government in the early 1980s to promote industrial and commercial activity within designated localities. Recently reintroduced.

Entrepreneurship: often added as a fourth factor of production, it is the act of bringing together land, labour and capital in the production of goods and services.

Environmental analysis: consideration of which environmental trends and changes might impact upon the organisation in the future.

Environmental champions: individuals in an organisation who actively promote sound environmental principles and approaches.

Environmental change: the predisposition of the business environment to undergo change rather than to remain static.

Environmental management system: a formalised set of procedures designed to guide an organisation on how to control its impact on the natural environment.

Environmental scanning: the identification of trends and changes in an organisation's environment.

Environmental subsidies: financial rewards used by a government to promote good environmental practices in organisations.

Environmental taxes: fiscal penalties used by a government to penalise firms which have a negative impact on the natural environment.

Equilibrium price: the price at which demand and supply are equal. It is the market clearing price.

Equilibrium quantity: The point at which supply satisfies demand. For example, there is demand for 100 units of a product and 100 units are produced. If 101 units were produced there would be an excess of demand and more competition between suppliers to sell their product – prices would decline. If 90 units were produced there would be unmet demand, and prices would increase as people tried to secure one of the 90 units, knowing there are not enough for everyone.

Equity: the ordinary share capital of the company.

Establishment: parts or branches of an enterprise. Large enterprises such as supermarkets are likely to have a number of branches or establishments.

European Central Bank (ECB): The EU's central bank, based in Frankfurt, responsible for the euro and for monetary policy within the eurozone.

European Commission: the EU's major bureaucratic arm responsible for implementing EU decisions, for proposing policies and legislation and for acting as guardian of the Treaties.

European Council: annual meetings of the President of the European Commission and the heads of government/state and foreign ministers of EU member states.

European Court of Justice: the major judicial body within the European Union responsible for interpreting EU law.

European Economic Area: an organisation that consists of members of the European Union and members of the European Free Trade Association.

European Emissions Trading Scheme (ETS): a scheme where countries are permitted certain levels of pollution, with that level falling over time. Countries can then trade these allowances with other nations, typically for money. In some countries this has been devolved to companies responsible for high levels of pollution – so that they own the costs of pollution and potential rewards if they significantly reduce it.

European Monetary System: a system of fixed exchange rates for members of the European Union.

European Parliament: the EU's elected decision-making body.

European Structural Funds: various financial support mechanisms within the European Union to address structural problems within disadvantaged EU regions.

Excess demand: where market price is below equilibrium price and as a result demand exceeds supply.

Excess supply: where market price is above equilibrium price and as a result supply exceeds demand.

Exchange control: a limit on the quantity of currency that can be purchased.

Exchange rate: the price at which one currency exchanges for another currency.

Exchange rate mechanism: a system of fixed exchange rates.

Executive directors: company directors with responsibility for a division or functional area within an organisation.

Export subsidy: a payment made to the producers of goods and services for export.

External environment: the external context within which an organisation exists and operates.

External growth: growth in firm size that takes place through merger or takeover.

Externalities: the spill-over effects of economic activity that are over and above the private costs and benefits that occur.

Extranet: a Web-based network that connects an organisation's network to the networks of its business partners, selected customers, or suppliers.

Factor market: the market where factors of production are bought and sold.

Factor of production: a resource used in the production of goods and services in an economy – land, labour, capital and entrepreneurship.

Factory gate prices: literally, the price of goods leaving an organisation that can be used as an indication of possible future inflationary pressures in the economy.

Family life cycle: the stages through which families can pass as they mature over time.

Federal system of government: a system of government in which decision-making authority is split between a central (i.e. federal) government and government at subnational level.

Financial account: a record of the international flows from trade in financial assets.

Financial intermediaries: individuals or institutions that help to link borrowers to lenders in the financial system.

First-mover advantage: in the context of e-business, an assumption that the deployment of the Internet would increase switching costs and create strong network effects, which would provide first movers with competitive advantages and robust profitability.

First-past-the-post system: a system of elections in which the winner in a given constituency is the person with a simple majority of the vote cast. Also called a plurality system.

Fiscal policy: government policy concerned with the taxing and spending decisions of government.

Five-forces model: an economic model used to characterise industries and markets. It says that these are formed by five forces acting upon them: current competition, potential competition, the power of buyers, the power of sellers and the power of suppliers.

Fixed capital: the investment in fixed physical assets within a firm – buildings, plant and machinery are examples.

Fixed exchange rate: where the exchange rate is determined by the government or some other authority.

Flexible firm: a firm that is organised in such a way that it distinguishes between core and peripheral activities as a cost-saving measure.

Floating exchange rate: where the exchange rate is determined by the free market.

Foreign direct investment (FDI): the establishment of production facilities in overseas countries.

Formal structures: the intended or official structure within an organisation that represents the way it is intended to function.

Fracking: the process of releasing oil and gas deposits in shale rock.

Franchising: an agreement between two parties in which the one permits the other to market something in its possession according to an agreed format and under certain contractual conditions.

Free market: a market without restrictions on its operations.

Free-market economy: an economic system in which resource allocation is determined by market forces.

Free trade: trade without barriers.

Free trade area: where members of an area abolish barriers to trade with other members, but maintain their own barriers against non-members.

Full employment: when all or virtually all the labour force in a country is employed in paid work.

Functional organisation: an organisational form based on the grouping of individuals by common purpose or function.

Functional specialisation: where individuals within an organisation specialise in particular tasks associated with a specific function such as marketing or production.

G7 nations: the group of seven leading industrial nations, namely the United States, Japan, UK, France, Germany, Canada, Italy. The G8 incorporates Russia.

G20 nations: a group of 20 nations whose governments and central bank governors meet to discuss issues of international concern, such as economic stability. The G20 is made up of 19 countries and the European Union.

Gearing: the proportional relationship between a firm's debt capital and its equity capital.

General (or contextual) environment: the broad external context in which an organisation exists and operates. It comprises the PESTLE factors.

General power of competence (GPC): a new power given to UK local authorities, which gives them the right to do anything that an individual can do which is not prohibited by law.

Genetically modified (GM) foods: food products which have undergone some element of genetic modification.

Geo-demographic segmentation: segmentation of a market on the basis of geographical and demographic variables.

Geographically immobile: the inability to move between geographical locations.

Gig economy: a term used to encapsulate less formal forms of work, small jobs, self-employment and casual contracts. Examples include people setting up short-term lets on spare rooms or delivery workers being paid per day or per delivery. These people are usually self-employed and are very uncertain about their income, but they might have more discretion about when they work.

Globalisation: the internationalisation of products and markets.

Gold plating: the tendency by an organisation or government to go beyond what is required by law or regulation.

Golden share: a special retained shareholding by government when privatising a state-owned organisation that permits the government to exercise some control over future developments.

Government: the structures and processes within a given territory by which laws are made and put into effect.

Government departments: large, state bureaucratic agencies that play a key role in shaping and implementing government policy within their sphere of competence.

Government spending: spending by government on public goods and services. Also called public spending or public expenditure.

Gross domestic product: the value of total economic activity within an economy over a particular period of time.

Gross investment: the total amount of capital goods purchased by firms.

Growing Places Fund: a fund established by the UK government to promote economic growth in certain designated areas.

Headline inflation: the rate of inflation in the UK, including the effect of mortgage interest payments. Known as RPI.

Hierarchy of needs: Maslow's notion that human needs form a kind of hierarchy of importance.

Holding company: a company set up to maintain or gain control of one or more other companies by holding a majority of shares of these subsidiaries.

Homogeneous product: products that are regarded by consumers as identical to each other and therefore perfect substitutes.

Horizontal merger: a merger or takeover between competitor firms at the same stage of the production process.

House of Commons: the lower house of the UK Parliament with major responsibility for discussing and deciding on laws proposed by the government.

House of Lords: the upper house of the UK Parliament, currently with limited powers.

Human relations approach: an approach to the study of organisation and management that emphasises the importance of social and psychological factors in the workplace.

Human resource management: the management of people within an organisation, including the processes of selection, recruitment, performance evaluation, rewards and compensation, and training and development.

Hyperglobalisation: where the world market is seen as a borderless global marketplace consisting of powerful multinational corporations and powerless nation states.

Immediate (or operational) environment: the more immediate external influences on an organisation from its customers, competitors, suppliers and other stakeholder groups.

Immobility of labour: the inability of labour to move between geographical locations, jobs or occupations.

Import control: a control placed on the import of goods and services into a country. This could be in the form of a quota, a tariff or exchange controls.

Import penetration: a measurement of the degree of importation relative to home demand.

Income elasticity: the responsiveness of quantity demanded to changes in household income.

Income flows: flows of income or expenditure in the economy between its constituent parts as a result of economic activity.

Indirect taxation: taxation imposed on consumption or spending.

Industrial concentration: the proportion of an industry which is dominated by large firms.

Industrial policies: loosely speaking, any government policy designed to improve the performance of a country's industries.

Industrial structure: the combination of industries and sectors in an economy.

Inelastic: Meaning that as something changes, demand remains the same – this could refer to a number of factors, including price (where price changes, demand remains the same) or income (where income changes, demand remains the same). Across product classes this might be seen quite commonly – for example, toothpaste: as you earn more, or the price falls, you are unlikely to buy more of it.

Inferior goods: goods where, as income rises, demand falls.

Inflation: an increase in the general level of prices within the economy that results in a fall in the value of money (i.e. in the purchasing power of a given nominal sum of money).

Information technology: the use of computer systems for storing, retrieving and communicating information.

Infrastructure: services considered to be essential to a developed economy, such as power and transport systems.

Injection: in the circular flow of income model, the major increase in spending over and above consumption which increases the level of income in the economy (e.g. export spending, investment spending, government spending).

Inner-city Task Forces: small teams of civil servants and others established to promote economic development in inner-city urban locations.

Innovation: the use of new ideas, methods or approaches.

Inputs: the resources that flow into the production process in order to produce outputs.

Inside-out view: looking at how the firm impacts on the environment.

Intention to create legal relations: under contract law, the notion of an intent to enter into a contract that is recognised in law as being legally binding.

Interdependence: the idea of the interconnectedness of firm behaviour in an oligopoly market.

Interest rates: the price(s) of borrowed money.

Internal growth: a term describing growth which is internally driven through gradual accumulation of profits and scaling up of operations. Sometimes known as 'organic growth'. This is the alternative to 'external growth'.

Internationalisation: increased links between countries with respect to trade and the movement of resources.

International trade: the exchange of goods, services and capital between countries.

Internet: a global network of computer networks that use a common protocol (TCP/IP) for communication.

Intranet: a network within a single organisation that enables access to company information using Internet technology such as web browsers and email.

Investment: spending by firms on capital goods – physical productive assets.

Investment appraisal: the analysis of the costs and benefits of possible new investment projects with a view to deciding on the desirability of committing resources to them.

Invisible hand: A term coined by Adam Smith (1723–90) to mean the means of automatic correction that takes place within a perfect free market. As prices go up, demand falls; as companies compete on price and quality, people decide how much they are willing to pay for things.

Invisible trade: the import and export of services.

J-curve effect: a curve that describes the effect of a devaluation of a currency on the balance of payments over time.

Joint venture: a jointly owned and independently incorporated business venture involving more than one organisation.

Judicial precedent: see 'Case law'.

Judiciary: the legal institutions within a country responsible for enacting and interpreting the law.

Keynesianism: broadly speaking, the view that economic activity is predominantly shaped by demand.

Knowledge management infrastructure: an infrastructure that provides an organisation with a framework for making knowledge available where it is required internally.

Labour: human resources.

Labour market: the market(s) in which wage levels are theoretically determined by the supply and demand for labour.

Labour market flexibility: the degree to which individuals in the labour market are able to respond to changing market demands.

Land: natural resources; resources that are not human-made, including the soil, air, seas, minerals, etc.

Law of demand: as the price of a product rises, the quantity demanded will normally fall.

Law of supply: as the price of a product rises, the quantity supplied will normally rise.

Leakage: in the circular flow of income model, the activities which potentially cause a reduction in spending on domestically produced products and hence on income flows in the economy (e.g. taxation, import spending, saving).

Learning and Skills Council: a body responsible for funding and planning education and training for over-16 year olds in England. Abolished in 2010 and replaced with the Skills Funding Agency and the Young People's Learning Agency in 2010.

Learning curve effect: the idea that performance can be improved as a result of experience in carrying out a procedure or action.

Legislation: laws made by the elected decision-makers. Also called statute law and (in the UK) Acts of Parliament.

Legislature: a country's law-making body.

Licensing: a form of non-equity agreement in which one party (e.g. a firm) grants another party or parties (e.g. another firm) the right to use its intellectual property (e.g. patent, trade name) in return for certain considerations (e.g. royalty payments).

Life cycle analysis: a technique for assessing the environmental impact of a product throughout its life cycle. Sometimes called 'cradle-to-grave' analysis.

Life cycle model: a model of the changes in sales and profitability of a product over time. There are four phases: development, growth, maturity and decline.

Lifestyle: the way in which people live and spend their money.

Limited Liability Partnerships (LLPs): these are partnerships with limits to liability to their partners. Partnerships do not declare profit; instead any income remaining after costs are deducted is classed as the personal income of partners. Usually this means that partners are personally liable (they could be sued for their personal wealth and belongings) but in an LLP the liability is limited to the goods and funds of the partnership.

Lobbying groups: groups of individuals actively seeking to influence decision-makers.

Local Enterprise Agencies: companies limited by guarantee, typically set up as partnerships between the private sector and local authorities, to deliver business support services to clients.

Local Enterprise Partnership (LEP): a partnership between local businesses and civic leaders aimed at promoting local economic development and regeneration.

LoNGPEST/LoNGPESTLE analysis: an approach to PEST(LE) analysis (see below) that includes a spatial dimension.

Macroeconomic analysis: economic analysis concerned with interactions within the economy as a whole.

Macroeconomic environment: the broad economic influences that are part of the external environment within which firms exist and operate.

Management: the structures and processes involved in directing an organisation towards the achievement of its objectives.

Managing director: the chief administrative or executive officer within a company who is responsible for ensuring that board decisions are put into effect and who forms the key link between the board of directors and the management team of senior executives.

Manifesto: a document setting out a political party's views and policy preferences when seeking election to government.

Manufacturing sector: the sector of the economy that produces manufactured products.

Market: a place where buyers and sellers are brought together.

Market failure: the notion that free markets sometimes deliver solutions which are not always socially or economically desirable.

Market mechanism: the interaction of demand and supply.

Market niche: a gap in a market which can be exploited by a firm by satisfying a need that is not currently being met.

Market segmentation: breaking down a market into different segments on the basis of particular variables.

Market structure: the amount of competition that exists between producers in a market.

Market system: an economic system based on the operation of free markets.

Marketing: essentially those processes involved in finding out what customers want and supplying them with the product in a way that is profitable to the organisation.

Marketing concept: the idea that organisations should seek to satisfy consumer wants by adopting a customer-focused orientation.

Marketing mix: the set of controllable variables which a firm can use to try to influence the consumer's response.

Marketspace: the digital equivalent of a physical-world marketplace.

Mass customisation: the ability to provide tailored products or services for individual customers or a group of similar customers, but retaining the economies of scope and the capacity of mass marketing or production.

Matrix structure: an organisational form based on both functional specialisation and structures built round products, projects or programmes.

Memorandum of Association: a document setting out the name of a company, its legal status, the address of its registered office, its objective, the amount of nominal share capital and a number of other aspects of the firm's operations.

MEPs: directly elected Members of the European Parliament.

Merger: the voluntary combination of two or more separate companies into one.

Merit goods: goods/services which the government feels to be of general benefit to the community and which are therefore often funded by the state (e.g. education).

Microeconomic analysis: economic analysis that focuses on economic decisions by both individuals and firms.

Minimum efficient scale: the level of production where all economies of scale have been reached by the firm.

Minimum wage: the specification of a minimum level for wage rates.

Ministers: individuals who occupy senior decision-making roles in government.

Monetarism: broadly speaking, the view that the level of output and employment in the economy are supply determined.

Monetary aggregates: the different measures used to calculate the money stock.

Monetary policies: government policies concerned with the availability and/or price of credit within the economy.

Money market: the market for short-term funds.

Money stock: the quantity of money in existence in an economy as determined by which monetary aggregates are included in the calculation.

Monopolistic competition: a market structure where there are a large number of sellers producing a differentiated product.

Monopoly: a market structure where there is one dominant producer.

Monopsony: a market where there is a single buyer.

MOSAIC: a tool to assist with market segmentation designed by Experian.

MPs: Members of Parliament, elected representatives in UK national elections.

Multinational corporations (MNCs): enterprises that operate in a number of countries and which have production or service capabilities outside the country of origin.

Multiplier effect: a measure of the effect on total national income of some component change in aggregate monetary demand.

National debt: the accumulated debt from borrowings by past and present governments.

Nationalised industry: a state-owned and controlled industry.

Natural monopoly: an industry where production conditions (e.g. large economies of scale) mean that the least wasteful market structure is monopoly.

Natural population change: the difference between the birth rate and the death rate in a given population over a specific period of time.

Natural resources: resources that are not human-made (see 'Land' above).

Negademand: where the use of less resources produces negative demand for particular commodities.

Negative externalities: adverse spill-over effects from business activity (e.g. pollution).

Negotiated environment: the idea that the policy-making environment in a democratic country is characterised by a bargaining process involving individuals, groups and government in shaping decisions.

Net investment: the level of investment after replacement investment has been taken out – it represents net additions to the capital stock.

Net migration: the number of people coming into the country to live and work, minus the number of people who leave. UK net migration figures currently include students coming into the country to study.

Networking: the relationships that exist between organisations and the people within those organisations.

New Deal: a UK government programme aimed at tackling the problem of social exclusion.

Non-executive directors: directors in a company (usually part-time) without functional responsibility.

Non-price competition: the use of non-price factors to sell a product (e.g. advertising, branding or special offers).

Non-renewable resources: resources that cannot be replenished after use, such as oil and coal.

Normal goods: goods where, as income rises, demand falls.

Normal profit: the minimum profit required by the entrepreneur to stay in production.

NVQs: National Vocational Qualifications.

Occupational immobility: the inability of workers to move between different occupations.

Occupational structure: the proportions of the workforce in different occupational groups.

Offer: under contract law a declaration by the offeror that they intend to be legally bound by the terms stated in an offer if it is accepted by the offeree.

Office of Fair Trading: a non-ministerial government department formerly responsible for consumer affairs in the UK.

Oligopoly: a market structure where there are a small number of large producers and a great deal of interdependence of decision-making.

One-to-one marketing: a unique dialogue that occurs directly between an organisation and individual customers.

Open system: a system in interaction with the external environment.

Opportunity cost: the real cost of a decision expressed in terms of the value of the alternative courses of action which have been sacrificed.

Ordinary shares: or 'equity' are shares in a company that do not carry a fixed dividend. Dividends paid depend upon the performance of the company.

Organisation chart: a diagram that seeks to portray the responsibilities and relationships within an organisation or part of an organisation.

Outputs: the goods or services or other results that derive from the production process.

Outside-in view: looking at how the environment impacts on the firm.

Parliament: in the UK the supreme law-making body.

Parliamentary system of government: a system of government based on election to a parliament from whom the senior members of the political executive are chosen.

Participation rate: the proportion of the population that works.

Partnership: an unincorporated form of business organisation comprising two or more individuals working together for mutual benefit.

People: human resources or labour.

Perfect competition: a market structure in which there are many buyers and sellers all producing an identical product and where the degree of competition is very high.

Perfect knowledge: where all actors in a market have complete knowledge of everything in the market.

Perfect mobility: a situation where there are no barriers to movement – it can be applied to firms, consumers and workers.

PESTLE analysis: analysis of the business environment which focuses on the political, economic, social, technological, legal and ethical influences on the firm.

Plebiscites: see 'Referendums'.

Political accountability: the idea that elected politicians are ultimately accountable for their actions and decisions to the people who elected them.

Political executive: the key elected decision-making part of government responsible for the formulation and implementation of government policy and legislation.

Political parties: voluntary groups of like-minded individuals who organise themselves to contest elections and to seek formal political office.

Politics: the processes that help to determine how conflicts are contained, modified, postponed or settled.

Polluter pays principle: the idea that the responsibility for resolving environmental problems rests with the person causing them.

Porter's five-forces model: see 'Five-forces model'.

Preference shares: shares in a company that carry a fixed dividend.

Presidential system of government: a system of government in which the head of government or chief executive is elected separately by the people and is not normally part of the elected legislature.

Pressure groups: voluntary groups of like-minded people who join together in order to seek to influence government decision-makers. See also 'Lobbying groups'.

Price ceiling: a maximum price above which the price of the product is not allowed to rise.

Price competition: the use of changing prices to sell products.

Price controls: a control exercised over price which prevents the working of the market mechanism.

Price discrimination: the charging of different prices to different users for the same product.

Price elasticity: the responsiveness of quantity demanded of a product to changes in its price.

Price floor: a minimum price below which the price of the product is not allowed to fall.

Price leadership: where one firm in an industry takes the lead in setting prices and other firms follow.

Price maker: a producer that has enough market power to influence price.

Price taker: a producer that has no power over price, as in perfect competition.

Price war: a situation where a reduction in price by one company is followed by reductions in price by other companies.

Primary reference groups: groups that have a direct and face-to-face influence on a person's attitudes and behaviour.

Primary sector: the part of an economy that deals with the extraction of raw materials, including agriculture and mining.

Prime Minister: the head of government and of the majority party in the UK Parliament.

Principal: under agency law, a person or organisation hiring an agent to act on their behalf.

Private law: law governing the relationship between individuals.

Private limited company: an incorporated business organisation restricted by its Articles of Association from any invitation to the general public to subscribe for its shares or debentures.

Private sector: that part of an economy where businesses are owned and controlled by private individuals or groups.

Privatisation: the process of transferring the ownership of state assets to the private sector.

Process innovation: the development of new approaches in the production process.

Product innovation: the development of new products.

Product market: the market where products are bought and sold.

Productivity: the relationship between input and output, for example labour productivity measures output per worker.

Professional lobbyist: a person or organisation paid to lobby on behalf of another person or organisation.

Profit: the payment or reward to the entrepreneur for bringing together the other factors of production.

Profit centre: a section or area of an organisation to which revenue can be traced and costs attributed so that profits (or losses) can be ascribed to that area.

Project team: a temporary form of organisational structure set up to carry out a particular task.

Proportional representation: a form of voting system in which the final result of a ballot more closely approximates the number of votes cast for a candidate or candidates than under a first-past-the-post system of voting.

Protectionism: Countries which seek to restrict access to their markets can be said to be 'protectionist'. This enables a country to maintain demand from domestic businesses. Protectionist policies include state subsidy of national interests and erecting trade barriers such as tariffs on imported goods. Often protectionist countries still seek to export their goods abroad to gain income.

Psychographic segmentation: market segmentation on the basis of variables such as social class and lifestyles.

Public corporation: a state-owned and controlled organisation set up to run a publicly owned enterprise.

Public goods: goods that must be supplied communally because they cannot be withheld from one individual without withholding them from all (e.g. national defence). Public law: laws relating to the relationship between individuals and the state.

Public limited company (PLC): an incorporated form of business organisation which can invite the general public to subscribe for its shares and debentures.

Public sector: that part of an economy under the control of the government and its agencies.

Public sector net borrowing: the extent to which a government's annual expenditure on public goods and services exceeds its revenue from taxation and other sources of income.

Public sector organisations: organisations in the state sector of the economy.

Public voluntary programmes: programmes designed by an environment agency in which firms are invited to participate.

Qualified majority vote (qmv): a voting system in which the outcome of a vote is determined by a previously agreed proportion of votes cast by the majority of voters.

Qualitative control: controls on the quality of goods in international trade rather than quantity or price.

Quality of people: the quality of labour in a country, which is largely determined by the level of education and training.

Quantitative easing (QE): a policy in which a country's central bank essentially creates money electronically by purchasing assets held by other organisations.

Quota: a physical limitation on the level of imports.

Real cost: see 'Opportunity cost'.

Real flows: flows of good and services and resources in the economy as a result of economic activity.

Real interest rates: the true cost of borrowing allowing for inflation.

Real national income: the value of the national income having allowed for price inflation.

Recession: a downturn in economic activity, currently defined in the UK as two successive quarters of negative economic growth.

Recommendations and Opinions: EU statements which have no binding force but merely state the view of the institution which issues them.

Re-engineering: radical redesign of business processes.

Reference groups: groups that influence a person's attitudes and behaviour.

Referendums: an example of direct democracy in which individuals are able to cast their vote for or against a proposal with the expectation that the majority view will prevail. Also called plebiscites.

Region: a geographical area possessing certain characteristics which help to differentiate it from surrounding areas, thus permitting boundaries to be drawn around it.

Regional chambers: bodies set up in the English regions to represent the various regional interests.

Regional Development Agencies: agencies established in the UK regions for designing and delivering integrated programmes of regional regeneration.

Regional government offices: the regionally based offices of central UK government departments.

Regional Growth Fund: a UK government funding initiative to promote private enterprise in regions badly affected by public spending cuts.

Regional Selective Assistance: a discretionary form of government assistance to businesses under UK regional policy.

Regional trade agreements (RTAs): trade agreements between countries within a given regional area.

Regionalism: essentially the move towards regional trade agreements (e.g. NAFTA) in an age of globalisation.

Regulations: EU decisions that apply directly to all member states and are legally binding without recourse to national parliaments.

Renewable resources: resources that can be replenished after use, such as fishing stocks and solar power.

Replacement investment: spending on capital goods that replace old and worn out capital goods.

Representative system of government: government chosen to represent the people through a system of democratic election.

Research and development (R&D): the introduction of and the development of new ideas.

Reshoring: the repatriation of jobs once lost to low-wage countries.

Resource-based view: an approach to strategy that emphasises firm processes and suggests that superior firm performance is related to the accumulation of valuable resources and capabilities.

Resources: scarce inputs into the production process used to produce goods and services.

Retail Price Index (RPI): a weighted index of a 'basket of consumer goods and services' used in the UK to calculate the rate of inflation.

Revaluation: a deliberate increase in the exchange rate of a currency.

Scenario planning: a technique of environmental analysis based on imagined future developments in the business environment.

Scientific management: an approach to organisation and management which essentially believes that scientific methods can be used to improve performance in the workplace.

Secondary reference groups: groups that tend to have a more indirect influence on a person's attitudes and behaviour.

Secondary sector: the part of an economy that includes industries which process raw materials, such as manufacturing and construction.

Secretary of State: in the UK government, the political head of a major government department.

Self-regulation: where the state allows organisations (e.g. businesses) to regulate themselves in certain areas (e.g. environmental performance).

Sellers' market: a market where there is excess demand for the product. This affords the seller greater market power.

Sell-side marketplace: a marketplace where one organisation does all the selling.

Separation of powers: where the three major functions of government are held by separate authorities.

Sex distribution of population: the balance of men and women in a population.

Shareholders: the owners (or members) of a limited company.

Single market: a common market (see above). Often applied to the European Union.

Single Regeneration Budget: a scheme to bring together a number of programmes from different government departments aimed at simplifying and streamlining the assistance available for local regeneration.

Skill shortages: shortages that exist in certain skills (e.g. IT skills) and which at times can coexist with unemployment.

Small firm: a firm that is small in terms of the number of people it employs or its turnover.

Smart cards: physical cards that contain a memory chip that can be inserted into a smartcard reader before items can be purchased.

Social capital: capital that is owned by the community such as hospitals and schools.

Social class: a system of grouping together people with a similar social status, based on variables such as income, education and occupation.

Social enterprises: businesses specifically set up to help people or the community.

Social mobility: the ability to move between different strata in society, for example different social classes.

Sole trader: an unincorporated form of business organisation owned by one individual. Also called a sole proprietorship.

Sovereignty: in a general sense, the power to influence events and decisions.

Specialisation: the tendency for countries to specialise in producing goods where they have a comparative advantage.

Speculation: the buying and selling of currencies in order to make a capital gain on any movements in exchange rates.

Stakeholders: anyone with an interest in an organisation and who is affected by and can affect its performance.

Standard Industrial Classification (SIC): the official classification of industries in the UK, it is based on the European classification – Nomenclature générale des activités économiquees dans les Communautés européennes (NACE).

State bank: see 'Central bank'.

Statute law: see 'Legislation'.

Sticky prices: describes the phenomenon of rigid prices commonly found in oligopolistic markets.

Stock: the capital of a business entity.

Stock exchange: a market for second-hand securities.

Strategic alliance: a collaborative agreement between firms to achieve a common aim.

Strategic fit: the notion of achieving a match or fit between the organisation's internal and external environments in pursuit of its objectives.

Strategic management: the management of the organisation as a whole through strategic analysis, choice and implementation.

Structural unemployment: unemployment caused by a decline in a particular industry as a result of a long-term change in demand or technological conditions.

Structure–conduct–performance model: an economic model used to characterise industries and markets. It says that the structure of the market determines conduct which in turn determines performance.

Subcontracting: the outsourcing of part of the production process to another firm.

Sub-culture: groups of individuals within the broader culture who have shared value systems based on common experiences, origins and/or situations.

Subsidy: in the export field, government financial support for businesses involved in exporting.

Substitutes: products that are related to each other such that as the price of one goes up, the demand for the other goes up (e.g. different brands of petrol).

Sub-systems: the component parts of a system.

Supply: the quantity of a product that sellers are willing and able to sell at every conceivable price level.

Supply chain management (SCM): the management of the organisation's activities related to its suppliers, and supply channels.

Supply curve: a graph that shows the relationship between the price of and the quantity supplied of a product.

Supreme Court: the ultimate judicial authority in interpreting the law under a written constitution.

Surplus: a situation where the value of exports is greater than the value of imports, so that there is an inflow of money into a country.

Sustainable development: an approach to economic growth and development which takes account of the social and environmental consequences.

SWOT (or TOWS) analysis: a technique for analysing a firm's internal strengths and weaknesses and its external opportunities and threats.

Systems approach: an approach to organisational analysis which portrays organisations as socio-technical systems interacting with their external environment.

Takeover: the acquisition of one company by another.

Tariff: a tax imposed on imported products.

Technological change: changes in the technology used in production – automation and computerisation are examples.

Technological unemployment: unemployment resulting from the replacement of labour by technology (e.g. robotics).

Technology: the sum of knowledge of the means and methods of producing goods and services.

Tertiary sector: the part of the economy devoted to the production of services.

The Council of the European Union: see 'Council of Ministers'.

Theory X and Theory Y: the idea that management sees individuals in the workplace as either inherently lazy or committed to the organisation and seeking responsibility.

Theory Z: an approach to management that gives individuals a positive orientation towards an organisation as a result being of provided with a number of discernible benefits.

Third way: broadly speaking, the notion of new progressivism in politics based on the traditions of social democracy as applied to the modern world.

Top-down approaches: the tendency for decisions to be determined by those in formal positions of authority.

Tort: a civil wrong other than a breach of contract or a breach of trust; a duty fixed by law on all persons.

Trade associations: bodies formed to protect and assist members in the same industry.

Trade union: organisations of workers that are designed to counteract and protect their members from the power of the employer.

Tradeable (or marketable) pollution permits: notional rights created by a government (or governments) which permit pollution up to a predetermined level and which are tradeable.

Training and Enterprise Councils: a system set up by the UK government to run its national training programme, subsequently replaced by the Learning and Skills Council.

Transaction cost economics: a branch of economics that looks at the make or buy decision based on the relative costs of transactions.

Transfer pricing: internal pricing used in large organisations to transfer products (e.g. raw materials) between divisions.

Transformation system: a system by which inputs are converted into outputs.

Transformationalism: the idea that globalisation brings about changes both in the power of countries and companies and in national characteristics and culture.

Transnational corporation: an international organisation that does not have a national base.

Trend extrapolation: a technique for predicting the future based on an analysis of the past.

Trend–impact analysis: a technique of environmental analysis designed to examine the likely impact on forecasted trends of a range of variables.

Trust: an equitable obligation imposing on one or more persons a duty of dealing with property, over which they have no control, for the benefit of other persons who may enforce the obligation.

Trusted Control Protocol/Internet Protocol (TCP/ IP): the standard for passing of data packets on the Internet.

Underlying rate of inflation: the rate of inflation excluding the effect of mortgage interest payments. In the UK known as RPIX.

Unilateral commitments: environmental initiatives set up by an organisation independently of any public authority.

Unitary system of government: a system of government in which sovereign power is vested in a single central authority.

Unlevel playing field: an environment in which organisations compete on unequal terms (e.g. because of different legal obligations in different countries).

Unlimited personal liability: in unincorporated business organisations the legal liability of the owner of the business for all the debts of the business.

Urban Development Corporations: independent government development agencies set up to oversee inner-city regeneration in designated areas.

Urban Regeneration Companies: specialist organisations set up in declining urban areas to lead and coordinate redevelopment and new investment.

VALS: an acronym for Values And Lifestyles, a form of psychographic segmentation developed by SRI International.

Value system: an interconnection of processes and activities within and among organisations that create benefits for intermediaries and end consumers.

Vertical merger: a merger or takeover between firms at different stages of the production process.

Virtual organisation: broadly speaking, a loose web of freelance individuals or businesses who organise themselves to produce a specific consumer product. Also an organisation where the core operating company outsources most of its processes to a network of other companies.

Visible trade: the import and export of goods.

Voluntary approaches: approaches to environmental protection in which organisations have a degree of voluntary response.

Voluntary (or third) sector: that part of the economy where economic activity is carried out by not-for-profit and non-governmental organisations such as charities and voluntary bodies.

Wage rate: earnings per hour or per standard working week excluding overtime payments.

Wages: the payment made to people for their labour services.

Wages/prices inflationary spiral: a situation in which wage increases fuel inflation which in turn fuels further wage demands, causing further inflation, and so on.

WEEE regulations: Waste Electrical and Electronic Equipment Directive or European Community Directive 2012/19/EU. These regulations move the burden of safe disposal of products to the original manufacturer or supplier of the goods. Products must be made for disassembly at the end of their useful lives, and recyclable where possible, and when buying a new product the retailer should offer to take the old one for safe disposal.

Win–win philosophy: the view that an action has benefits for both the organisation and the natural environment. Also called the 'double dividend'.

Withdrawal: see 'Leakage'.

Work Programme: a government programme aimed at getting the unemployed back into work.

Workers' cooperatives: businesses owned and controlled by the people who work in them and who cooperate for mutual benefit.

Workforce: the number of people able and eligible to work and offering themselves for work.

Working capital: the investment in a firm in capital used on a day-to-day basis such as raw materials; often called circulating capital.

Working week: the number of hours spent in work per week.

Index